W9-CEV-401

EDUCATING EXCEPTIONAL CHILDREN 79/80

ANNUAL EDITIONS

the dushkin publishing group, inc.
Sluice Dock, Guilford, Ct. 06437

BRIAR CLIFF COLLEGE
LIBRARY
SIOUX CITY, IOWA

Volumes in the Annual Editions Series

- Abnormal Psychology
- ● Aging
- ● American Government
- ● American History Pre-Civil War
- ● American History Post-Civil War
- ● Anthropology
- Astronomy
- ● Biology
- ● Business
- Comparative Government
- ● Criminal Justice
- Death and Dying
- ● Deviance
- ● Early Childhood Education
- Earth Science
- ● Economics
- ● Educating Exceptional Children
- ● Education
- Educational Psychology
- Energy
- ● Environment
- Ethnic Studies
- Foreign Policy
- Geography
- Geology
- ● Health
- ● Human Development
- ● Human Sexuality
- ● Macroeconomics
- ● Management
- ● Marketing
- ● Marriage and Family
- ● Microeconomics
- ● Personality and Adjustment
- Philosophy
- Political Science
- ● Psychology
- Religion
- ● Social Problems
- ● Social Psychology
- ● Sociology
- ● Urban Society
- Western Civilization
- Women's Studies
- World History

● *Indicates currently available*

© 1979 by the Dushkin Publishing Group, Inc. Annual Editions is a Trade Mark of the Dushkin Publishing Group, Inc.

Copyright © 1979 by the Dushkin Publishing Group, Inc., Guilford, Connecticut 06437

All rights reserved. No part of this book may be reproduced, stored, or transmitted by any means—mechanical, electronic or otherwise—without written permission from the publisher.

First Edition

Manufactured by George Banta Company, Menasha, Wisconsin, 54952

5 4 3 2 1

LC
3951
.E3

5436181

EDITORIAL ADVISORY BOARD

Dr. Betty Boller
College of Education and Social Services
University of Vermont

Dr. William Jones
Department of Special Education
Bloomsburg State College

Professor Donalene Andreotti
Department of Psychology
El Camino College

Professor Carol S. Kushnor
Department of Education
Averett College

Professor Roberta Lubinsky
Division of Educational Studies
S.U.N.Y. College at Geneseo

Dr. Mack McCoulsky
Department of Education
Angelo State University

Dr. Ann Netick, Acting Chairperson
Department of Special Education
University of Louisville

Dr. Robert Nickelsburg
Department of Special Education
Youngstown State University

Dr. Alice Suroski
Department of Special Education
University of Northern Iowa

Professor Ruth Walker
Department of Education
Greenville College

Dr. Ken J. Weber, Chairman
Department of Special Education
University of Toronto

Professor Constance Tarczan
Educational Consultant

Susan Friedman
Editorial Consultant

AND STAFF

Rick Connelly, Publisher
Celeste Borg, Editor
Addie Kawula, Acquisitions Editor
Brenda Filley, Production Supervisor
Cheryl Kinne, Permissions Coordinator
Charles Vitelli, Designer
Jeremy Brenner, Graphics Coordinator
Retia Cutbill, Design Assistant
Bertha Kinne, Typsetting Coordinator

CONTENTS

1

Legislative Concerns: Special Education and the Law

2

Professional Concerns: Development, Classification and Parental Involvement

3

The Gifted Child

4

The Mentally Retarded Child

5

The Learning Disabled Child

6

The Emotionally Troubled Child

7

The Physically and Sensorially Handicapped Child

TOPIC GUIDE

Because articles from popular sources are rarely as specialized as journal textbook articles, many of those appearing in *Annual Editions: Educating Exceptional Children 79/80* encompass a number of academic topics. In the first column of this guide, topic areas are specified according to the concepts most likely to be identified in introductory Educating Exceptional Children textbooks. The second column lists those articles in *Educating Exceptional Children* providing primary emphasis to each topic. The third column lists those articles providing secondary emphasis to each topic.

Topic Area	Treated as a Central Issue in:	Treated as a Secondary Issue in:
Disability & Discrimination	1. It's a New Day for Disabled People 2. A Primer on Due Process 9. The Past and Future Impact of Court Decisions 10. Mainstreaming 14. Handicapism	3. The End of the Quiet Revolution 5. Public Law 194-142 8. The Educational Least Restrictive Alternative 16. Labeling 54. Some Thoughts on the Education of Blind People
Education rights	1. It's a New Day for Disabled People 2. A Primer on Due Process 3. The End of the Quiet Revolution 5. Public Law 194-142 6. 10 Steps to Special Ed 7. The Who, Where and What of IEP's 8. The Educational Least Restrictive Alternative 9. The Past and Future Impact of Court Decisions 10. Mainstreaming 14. Handicapism 57. The Severely, Profoundly Handicapped 59. Administering Education for the Severely Handicapped	
Due process	2. A Primer on Due Process 5. Public Law 194-142 6. 10 Steps to Special Ed 8. The Educational Least Restrictive Alternative 9. The Past and Future Impact of Court Decisions 10. Mainstreaming 59. Administering Education for the Severely Handicapped	3. The End of the Quiet Revolution 8. The Educational Least Restrictive Alternative 14. Handicapism 22. The Gifted Child
Classification labeling	3. The End of the Quiet Revolution 4. Definitions of Handicapping Conditions 15. Classification Options 16. Labeling 24. Identifying and Nurturing the Intellectually Gifted 37. Learning Disabilities, Part One 39. The LD Tightrope 43. "Learned Disabled" or "Slow Learner" 45. Childhood Autism 57. The Severely, Profoundly Handicapped 59. Administering Education for the Severely Handicapped	1. It's a New Day for Disabled People 6. 10 Steps to Special Ed 20. Perspective on Parental Involvement 22. The Gifted Child 27. What Is Mental Retardation? 40. Learning Disabilities: A Puzzlement
IEP's & Individualized teaching	3. The End of the Quiet Revolution 5. Public Law 194-142 7. The Who, Where and What of IEP's 9. The Past and Future Impact of Court Decisions 10. Mainstreaming 12. Integrating Children with Handicaps 59. Administering Education for the Severely Handicapped	6. 10 Steps to Special Ed 38. Learning Disabilities, Part Two 45. Childhood Autism
Mainstreaming	8. The Educational Least Restrictive Alternative 10. Mainstreaming 12. Integrating Children with Handicaps 32. Mainstreaming for the Secondary Educable Mentally Retarded 51. Can Schools Speak the Language of the Deaf? 52. There's a Deaf Child in My Class 56. Mainstreaming Handicapped Students	9. The Past and Future Impact of Court Decisions 16. Labeling 31. The Child with Down's Syndrome
Funding & Costs	9. The Past and Future Impact of Court Decisions 10. Mainstreaming	16. Labeling 56. Mainstreaming Handicapped Students 59. Administering Education for the Severely Handicapped
Detecting developmental lags	11. Watching for Developmental Lags and Disabilities 53. Speech Problems	
Early childhood education	12. Integrating Children with Handicaps 42. The Silent Crippler	
Referrals to specialists	13. How to Prepare the Child for the Psychologist 53. Speech Problems	17. The Donnellan-Walsh Syndrome 21. A Place for Noah 40. Learning Disabilities: A Puzzlement
Professional & Parental involvement	17. The Donnellan-Walsh Syndrome 18. Let Us All Stop Blaming the Parents 19. Communicating with Parents 20. Perspective on Parental Involvement 21. A Place for Noah 23. The Gifted Child: Common Sense and Uncommon Children 25. Let's Go Slow on Acceleration 38. Learning Disabilities, Part Two	45. Childhood Autism 52. There's a Deaf Child in My Class

Topic Area	Treated as a Central Issue in:	Treated as a Secondary Issue in:
Giftedness	22. The Gifted Child 23. The Gifted Child: Common Sense and Uncommon Children 24. Identifying and Nurturing the Intellectually Gifted 26. Reflections of Gifted Learners	
Acceleration	24. Identifying and Nurturing the Intellectually Gifted 25. Let's Go Slow on Acceleration	23. The Gifted Child: Common Sense and Uncommon Children 26. Reflections of Gifted Learners
Mental Retardation	27. What Is Mental Retardation? 28. We Can Do More to Prevent the Tragedy of Retarded Children 29. The Dignity of Risk 30. First Steps for the Retarded 31. The Child with Down's Syndrome 32. Mainstreaming for the Secondary Educable Mentally Retarded	37. Learning Disabilities, Part One 43. "Learning Disabled" or "Slow Learner"
Down's Syndrome	29. The Dignity of Risk 31. The Child with Down's Syndrome	27. What Is Mental Retardation? 28. We Can Do More to Prevent the Tragedy of Retarded Children
The Severely Retarded	30. First Steps for the Retarded 33. The Profoundly Retarded 57. The Severely, Profoundly Handicapped	
Learning Disabilities	34. Myths and Realities in Learning Disabilities 35. The Tenth Myth 36. LD and the Problem of Scientific Definitions 37. Learning Disabilities, Part One 38. Learning Disabilities, Part Two 39. The LD Tightrope 40. Learning Disabilities: A Puzzlement 41. Learning Disabilities and the Professional Educator 42. The Silent Crippler 43. "Learning Disabled" or "Slow Learner"	

Topic Area	Treated as a Central Issue in:	Treated as a Secondary Issue in:
Dyslexia		37. Learning Disabilities, Part One
Receptive Language Disability	42. The Silent Crippler	
Emotional Disabilities	44. Troubled Children 45. Childhood Autism 46. Their Fingers Do the Talking	
Autism	44. Troubled Children 45. Childhood Autism 46. Their Fingers Do the Talking	17. The Donnellan-Walsh Syndrome
Schizophrenia	44. Troubled Children	
Hyperkinesis	44. Troubled Children 47. Why Can't Bobby Sit Still? 48. Battle Lines in the Ritalin War 49. Helping the Hyperkinetic Child	
Sign Language	46. Their Fingers Do the Talking	51. Can Schools Speak the Language of the Deaf? 52. There's a Deaf Child in My Class
Deafness & Speech problems	51. Can Schools Speak the Language of the Deaf? 53. Speech Problems	
Blindness	54. Some Thoughts on the Education of Blind Children 55. Data Concerning the Partially Sighted and the Functionally Blind	
Severe & Multiple handicaps	57. The Severely, Profoundly Handicapped 58. Current Directions in Education of the Severely/Multiply Handicapped 59. Administering Education for the Severely Handicapped	

Preface

Today when we speak of those who educate our exceptional children we no longer speak of a small core of educational specialists, for a new federal law has substantially broadened our reference. This law mandates that all handicapped children be provided a free and appropriate education within the least restrictive environment. For many of the handicapped, that means placement into standard classes to be taught alongside their peers by educators often not previously trained to teach exceptional children. This enhanced responsibility for our educational system provides a substantial challenge for all of us.

Obviously a law alone cannot succeed in educating all children, including the handicapped and gifted, to their fullest potential. Such success can come only through a totally cooperative effort on the part of school boards, administrators, parents, and teachers. It is these groups which must provide the facilities and equipment, create the atmosphere for properly tailored programs, and openly and honestly communicate with the needs of each pupil.

The greatest challenge of all will rest with the individual teacher. Within the classroom, on a day-to-day basis, it will be his/her responsibility to provide for the special educational needs of the students, to facilitate daily interaction among peers, and to communicate regularly with parents and others regarding each child's development. To do this well will require not only special training in the many new skills necessary to educate exceptional children but also an understanding of the issues and controversies within the field of special education.

It is the purpose of *Annual Editions: Educating Exceptional Children 79/80* to provide students and professional educators with convenient access to current articles addressing the wide-range of social and professional issues and concerns within special education today. The articles selected for inclusion were chosen from among hundreds written in the last few years. Within this collection you'll find articles examining the historical foundations of special education, past and present laws, classification, labeling, parental involvement, the gifted and talented, mental retardation, learning disabilities, emotional disorders, and physical handicaps.

It is assumed that the material contained in *Educating Exceptional Children 79/80* will be used in conjunction with other sources of information—a textbook, supplemental materials exploring individual areas in a greater depth, or other foundational materials. Thus, these articles chosen for inclusion can serve as springboards to discussion, debate, and further exploration.

We think *Annual Editions: Educating Exceptional Children 79/80* is one of the most useful, up-to-date books available, but we would like to know what you think. Your comments on this volume are important. With your help we can develop subsequent volumes which will continue to meet your needs. Please fill out the reader response form on the last page of this book and return it to us. Any anthology can be improved. This one will be—annually.

Rick Connelly,
Publisher

EQUAL JUSTICE UNDER LAW

1 Legislative Concerns: Special Education and the Law

The 1970s have been watershed years for handicapped individuals, their parents, teachers, and all of those in various fields that pertain to special education. At both federal and state levels, dramatically far-reaching—and, some would say, very long overdue—legislation has been passed and legal decisions handed down that affect, with real immediacy, the lives of all students in special education. What are some of these pieces of legislation and these laws that will insure "least restrictive" opportunities for education, due process for the handicapped, and "free, appropriate public education"?

Under Title V of the Rehabilitation Act of 1973, the handicapped cannot be discriminated against by any recipient of U.S. tax dollars. PL 93-380 guarantees children due process in educational placement. PL 94-142, perhaps the most sweeping piece of legislation, is a culmination of earlier legislation as it provides special education and stringent standards for deciding what that special education shall consist of to *all* handicapped children and youth who need it, the mentally retarded, hard of hearing, deaf, orthopedically impaired, other health impaired, speech impaired, visually handicapped, seriously emotionally disturbed, or children with specific learning disabilities who by reason thereof require special education and related services.

The articles in this section of *Educating Exceptional Children* provide an overview of the important legislation, its past trends and its implications for the future. The last articles in this section are devoted to clarifying and describing the provisions of legislation that are important to educators. They will answer the special educator's need to know how to identify and place handicapped children under PL 94-142, how to undertake the individualized education provision of the law, how to interpret and implement the "least restrictive alternative" provision, and how to evaluate the policy of "mainstreaming."

The articles in this section are designed to provide the special educator with basic tools for understanding the significant new legislation that affects the life of every public school child, handicapped or normal, and every public school teacher and administrator. The articles here raise questions, too. How the nation's educators will answer those questions is the subject of later sections of this book.

Looking Ahead: Challenge Questions

What is the most serious problem for administrators and taxpayers in implementing the programs called for by PL 94-142?

What is mainstreaming? Who benefits from it?

What are the goals of mainstreaming?

What principles of special education law have recent court decisions established? How will these decisions affect the handicapped population in the future?

IT'S A NEW DAY FOR DISABLED PEOPLE

In administering its 300-plus programs, HEW begins the enforcement of a wide-ranging law to protect the rights of more than 36 million handicapped individuals living in the United States

First grader Chris Powers was the only youngster left behind when his class went to the zoo. He was the only one asked to step aside when the class picture was taken. He was also the only pupil forbidden to eat with his classmates in the school cafeteria. In each instance, the principal felt that the emotional outbursts Chris is subject to would upset other children. Chris is an autistic child.

When George C. Jackson, a psychologist and professor at Howard University in Washington, D.C., was recuperating from surgery, the hospital staff insisted that he stay in his room rather than walk down the hall to visit with other patients in the solarium. The operation had nothing to do with the restriction. Dr. Jackson is blind.

"They thought I might fall over something in the hallway," he recalls, "but they never offered to guide me through that hallway obstacle course a time or two."

Thomas Maske, disabled as a teenager by polio, knows most of the world's airline routes by heart, as his job with an agricultural supply firm in Wheeling, Illinois, requires almost constant foreign travel. Nonetheless, some airlines, citing safety factors, have refused to accept Mr. Maske as a passenger unless he flies with a companion. Other airlines have stored—and sometimes damaged—his wheelchair in aircraft luggage compartments after refusing his request to store it in the passenger cabin. Mr. Maske has threatened to go to court on both counts. He now flies alone and carries a special Federal Aviation Administration permit for passenger cabin storage of his wheelchair.

Barbara A. Hoffman, a clinical psychologist with a successful private practice in Houston, Texas, works primarily with brain-damaged children but is seldom invited to share her expertise with other psychologists at professional meetings. She has cerebral palsy. Conference planners assume, falsely, that she also has a speech impairment, a condition often associated with the disease. "I have learned not to waste my time showing my genuine interest in community projects," Dr. Hoffman says, "because the doors are closed to handicapped persons."

John Lancaster, a 1967 Notre Dame graduate, went to Viet Nam as a Marine Corps second lieutenant. Wounded in action, he came home paralyzed from the waist down. Despite his disability, he returned to college and earned a law degree. Looking back, he says that was the easy part. Finding a job was harder.

"I looked pretty good on paper," Mr. Lancaster says, "but when I showed up for an interview in a wheelchair, that was usually the end of it. I applied to more than 40 companies and government agencies before I finally landed a job."

Today Mr. Lancaster is director of Barrier-Free Design for Paralyzed Veterans of America.

The irony attending each example—each instance—of discrimination against a disabled person lies in the indisputable fact that no one is invulnerable to disease and injury that can shut out sight or hearing or terminate physical mobility or any of life's other basic functions. Yet disability continues to confer second-class citizenship. The more than 36 million handicapped people in the country not only must live with their disability, they must constantly suffer the usually subtle but sometimes flagrant public biases against them.

Solely because of their disability, handicapped people have been consistently denied opportunities in education, employment, health care, social services, and nearly all other aspects of daily life. Consciously or not, able-bodied people tend to see an individual's disability rather than look beyond it at a person's ability, training, and experience.

Betty Davidson, a biochemist at Massachusetts General Hospital in Boston, possibly speaks for the majority of the nation's handicapped people. Says Dr. Davidson, who has a congenital deformity, "Growing up disabled in America is like trying to swim the English Channel. It's a struggle all the way. And that is wrong for our country and our time."

What is wrong for our country and our time will be changed over the next few years. Congress has provided a "bill of rights" for disabled people that is now becoming fully effective. That "bill of rights" is Title V of the Rehabilitation Act of 1973 (Public Law 93-112). In effect, Title V says: Handicapped people must not be discriminated against in any aspect of our national life that is *supported in full or in part by U.S. tax dollars.*

Title V has four sections which cover all types of activities involving federal funds.

- Section 501 requires that federal agencies have affirmative action programs to hire and promote qualified handicapped persons.
- Section 502 authorizes the Architectural and Transportation Barriers Compliance Board, which is charged with enforcing a 1968 law requiring that all buildings con-

Prepared by the HEW Task Force on Public Awareness and the Disabled.

Reprinted from *American Education*, Vol. 13, No. 10, December 1977.

structed in whole or part with federal funds—as well as buildings owned or leased by federal agencies—have ramps, elevators, or other barrier-free access for persons who are blind, deaf, in wheelchairs, or otherwise disabled.

□ Section 503 requires that all business firms, universities, foundations, and other institutions holding contracts with the U.S. government have affirmative action programs to hire and promote qualified handicapped persons.

□ Section 504 prohibits discrimination against qualified disabled persons—as employees, students, and receivers of health care and other services—in all public and private institutions receiving federal assistance.

Section 504 applies to all federally funded institutions and activities, including those assisted under programs of the Department of Health, Education, and Welfare (HEW). Because most school districts, colleges, universities, hospitals, nursing homes, welfare and rehabilitation centers, and similar institutions, whether public or private, receive federal support, they must comply with section 504's antidiscrimination provisions.

Nelda Barnes, a teacher in Spartanburg, South Carolina, is one of the first of the disabled individuals who exercised their due process rights under section 504. Last summer Mrs. Barnes enrolled in two courses at a small private college near her home. She needed the courses to maintain her state teacher certification. After enrolling, she learned that the subjects were being taught by lecture, which she was unable to follow because she is deaf. She asked the college to provide a sign-language interpreter, a request the college refused for the reason of additional cost. Claiming violation of her section 504 rights, Mrs. Barnes sued the college in U.S. District Court and won. She was able to take her case to court because the college, though private, receives federal assistance.

Although President Nixon signed the Rehabilitation Act in 1973, the provisions of section 504 have not been widely known or understood. Last April, HEW Secretary Joseph A. Califano, Jr., signed the regulation spelling out section 504 requirements under all HEW-administered programs. The regulation became effective on June 3, 1977.

With more than 300 programs to help the nation improve and expand its services in health, education, welfare, and related areas, HEW was the logical place to begin full implementation of section 504 protections. By presidential order, HEW was given the lead to develop a general standard for other federal agencies to use in formulating their own section 504 regulations in areas like public housing and transportation. The standards follow the HEW regulation. Failure to comply with the section 504 regulation by any institution receiving federal assistance could lead to withdrawal of this aid.

Employment Rights

HEW's section 504 regulation says that handicapped persons must be considered for jobs and promotions on the basis of ability, training, and experience. Their disability is not a factor unless it prevents acceptable job performance. For example, disabled people cannot be required to take a physical examination before a job is offered. After a job is offered, they can be required to get a medical checkup if it is also required of other employees. This is an important safeguard. Many employers in the past required physical examinations for handicapped job applicants, then turned them down because they couldn't pass.

Clyde Y. Kramer, a professor of statistics at Virginia Polytechnic Institute and State University, was among many World War II veterans who could have used this protection a quarter century ago. As a teenage soldier, he sustained a severe leg injury in the allied advance into Germany. After several years in and out of veterans hospitals, he went to college on crutches and earned a doctorate in statistics.

"My handicap in no way hinders my ability to perform as a statistician," Dr. Kramer says, and his career bears him out. "But when I started out, many companies found me unemployable because I couldn't pass their physical exam."

Once hired, handicapped persons covered by HEW's section 504 regulation have the same rights as nonhandicapped employees to promotions, job assignments, sick leave, vacations, training programs, and other fringe benefits. Moreover, employers are required to take reasonable steps to accommodate a worker's disability. For instance, an employer may need to provide a reader for a blind employee who handles paperwork, an interpreter for a deaf worker who uses a telephone, or adequate workspace and access to it for an employee in a wheelchair.

Before Secretary Califano signed the section 504 regulation, U.S. Attorney General Griffin B. Bell ruled that alcoholics and drug addicts are handicapped individuals. Consequently, they have the same job and other rights under HEW's section 504 regulation as persons with physical or mental disabilities. This does *not* mean that a school system must—or should—hire a bus driver who may become intoxicated on the job. It does *not* mean that a hospital is required to hire a drug addict for a job that may require access to drugs in its pharmacy.

With regard to persons addicted to alcohol or drugs, the HEW regulation has a built-in protection for employers: *If the disability causes inadequate job performance,* the person is not qualified for the job.

Education Rights

From preschool through graduate school, section 504 protects the right of handicapped students to the same educational opportunities available to nonhandicapped pupils in any school, college, and adult basic or vocational training program that gets federal assistance. In the elementary and secondary grades, section 504 requires that education for handicapped children be *free* and *appropriate.* These are two important "musts" to end discrimination.

Many cities formerly segregated disabled children in special schools, bright children with physical disabilities thus being taught with pupils who were mentally retarded or emotionally disturbed. Because students were expected to learn together, the pace was geared to the slowest learners. And there were few "frills."

In her biochemistry laboratory at Massachusetts General Hospital, Dr. Davidson recalls her segregated elementary school. "We had no music, art, physical activities, crafts, or contact with other children," she says. "Our goals and hopes were set by our limited enclosed world."

She regrets her lost opportunities to play and learn with abled-bodied children, and they with her. She feels children should get to know one another as individuals and to accept disability wherever it occurs.

Section 504 requires that states and local school districts receiving federal assistance pay all education costs for handicapped children in the learning setting best suited to their needs. As determined by school officials in consultation with parents or guardians, this setting may be a regular public-school classroom where handicapped and nonhandicapped pupils learn together. It may be a special-education class in the public school. It may be a residential school. Or it may be a hospital if a child is receiving long-term medical care.

Whatever the learning environment—or the nature or severity of a child's handicap—the most appropriate education must be provided at public expense. Parents will no longer have to bear the financial burden of privately educating their handicapped child, though they can choose to send the child to private school at their own expense. What's more, free and appropriate education must be available no later than school year 1978-79.

In addition to section 504, disabled children and young people, 3-21, have more specific education guarantees under the Education for All Handicapped Children Act of 1975 (Public Law 94-142). This law says that every state receiving federal assistance for special education must find and begin educating every disabled child and young person, 6-17, living in the state. This must be done by September 1, 1978, and at public expense. By the same date, the state must also find and begin educating all disabled children, 3-5, if state law and court decisions permit. Disabled youth, 18-21, must be in an appropriate education program by September 1, 1980, if state law and court decisions permit.

The Education for All Handicapped Children Act establishes priorities: first, to disabled children receiving no public education; second, to children in each disability group who are currently receiving an inadequate education. The legislation also calls for an individualized education program to accommodate each child's disability and learning needs. (For details of the provisions of the Education for All Handicapped Children Act, see *American Education,* July 1976.)

At the postsecondary levels—college, vocational and technical education—section 504 requires that handicapped students be judged for admission and advancement on the basis of their ability and performance. Disability doesn't count. A college or professional school, for example, may not base admissions decisions on preadmission tests that inaccurately measure academic achievement and ability because the applicant is blind, deaf, or otherwise disabled. Nor may a college or professional school inquire about any disability an applicant may have until after an offer of admission—unless the school is trying to overcome the effects of prior limited enrollment of handicapped students and the applicant is willing to volunteer the information.

James Marsters earned a degree in dentistry without these safeguards some 25 years ago. It wasn't easy. Deaf from birth, he was denied admission to a number of dental schools because of his disability. Then, along with 1,400 other applicants, he took the aptitude test for admission to New York University's College of Dentistry. Academically, he came out near the top and was eligible for admission.

An admissions officer exclaimed in dismay, "But we've never had a deaf student!" James Marsters replied, "Just give me a chance."

For many years now, Dr. Marsters has been practicing in Pasadena, California, and has taught orthodontia at the University of Southern California.

Judith Ann Pachciarz, on the other hand, has had her dream of becoming a physician thwarted because she is deaf. Repeatedly denied admission to medical schools, she finally took another road, earning a doctorate in microbiology, and now teaches that subject at the University of Kentucky.

Colleges are not required under section 504 to lower academic standards or degree requirements for disabled students. Depending on a student's disability, however, they may have to extend the time needed to earn a degree. They may also have to provide reference materials in Braille or on audiocassettes, and other learning aids not available from other sources. Moreover, they may be called upon to modify teaching methods, which in some cases can be as simple as asking a professor to talk to the class instead of to the blackboard so that a deaf student can lip-read.

Health Care and Social Service Rights

Hospitals are the largest group of health-care providers affected by section 504. They must give handicapped persons an opportunity to receive all medical services and medically related courses of instruction available to the general public. Among other things, hospitals receiving federal assistance must provide an emergency-room interpreter or make other provisions to communicate with deaf patients. They must treat patients with a physical injury or illness, even though these patients are under the influence of alcohol or drugs. However, hospitals are not required to give rehabilitative treatment for patients' alcoholism or drug addiction.

Hospitals must admit disabled persons to such public service instruction as natural childbirth and anti-smoking. Handicapped persons must also be permitted to participate in vocational rehabilitation, senior citizen, and other social welfare programs on an equal basis with nonhandicapped persons, provided, again, that federal funds assist the activity.

A vocational rehabilitation center director may know from experience, for instance, that it can take longer and cost more to train a blind person for paid employment than it does to train a partially sighted person. In the past, that director could have refused to accept a blind person for training, giving any one of a number of reasons which, though plausible on the surface, cloaked what was possibly the real reason that the training center's job-placement rate would be adversely affected. Section 504 prohibits this kind of discrimination.

Physical Access to Buildings

For the disabled person in a wheelchair, the logistics of daily life assume the complexity of a game of chess: Strategy must be planned several moves ahead before the first move is made. Specifically, questions must be answered about building access—to school, place of employment, or shopping center—that never occur to abled-bodied persons. Are parking spaces reserved for handicapped people near the entrance? Do sidewalks have curb cuts to accommodate wheelchairs? Do entrances have ramps if there are steps? Are elevators and interior doorways wide enough? Are water fountains and public telephones low enough? Are there grab rails in restrooms?

Blind persons must ask similar questions. Are corridors obstacle-free? Are directional signs and room numbers marked in Braille? A decade ago, these questions when applied to most buildings in the United States had a single answer: No. There was no barrier-free access for disabled people.

One of the first congressional actions to end this type of discrimination against handicapped people was the Architectural Barriers Act of 1968. It said that handicapped individuals must have access to and use of all buildings and facilities constructed leased, altered with federal funds, or for federal use. The law was observed in some buildings, but not in most. Then in 1973, Congress added section 502 to Title V of the Rehabilitation Act authorizing the Architectural and Transportation Barriers Compliance Board to enforce the 1968 legislation.

In the same vein, HEW's section 504 regulation enforces the barrier-free provisions of the 1968 law in buildings housing HEW-supported programs. The regulation requires that all construction and alteration by HEW recipients begun after June 3, 1977—the regulation's effective date—be barrier free. Existing facilities need to be altered only if other means are not available to make a recipient's program accessible to handicapped persons. Other means to provide program accessibility could be simply moving a college, health care, or social service program from an inaccessible to a a barrier-free building. If structural changes in existing buildings are needed, they must be completed by June 2, 1980.

A New Day

As federal law, Title V will be enforced under affirmative action programs to increase employment and promotion of handicapped persons in federal agencies and in firms working under U.S. government contracts. It will also be enforced in school districts, colleges, hospitals, and other institutions receiving federal assistance.

WHO IS HANDICAPPED?

Under the HEW section 504 regulation, HEW identifies a handicapped person as anyone with any type of physical or mental disability that substantially impairs or restricts one or more such major life activities as walking, seeing, hearing, speaking, working, or learning. Handicapping conditions include but are not limited to:

Cancer	Muscular dystrophy
Cerebral palsy	Othopedic, speech, or visual impairment
Deafness or hearing impairment	Such perceptual handicaps as
Diabetes	Dyslexia
Emotional illness	Minimal brain dysfunction
Epilepsy	Developmental aphasia
Heart disease	
Mental retardation	
Multiple sclerosis	

The U.S. Attorney General has ruled that alcoholism and drug addiction are physical or mental impairments that are handicapping conditions if they limit one or more of life's major activities.

Title V is expected to reach beyond its legal authority, changing public attitudes toward disabled persons in much the same way that the civil rights acts of the 1960s changed public attitudes toward racial minorities and Title IX of the Education Amendments of 1972 changed public attitudes toward women.

A lasting change in public attitudes would be the most meaningful "bill of rights" for handicapped individuals. George Jackson at Howard University points out that corporate executives, government officials, and college and hospital administrators tend to move up or out every few years.

"We sensitize management to the needs and abilities of handicapped people," Dr. Jackson says, "then there's a big turnover at the top and we have to start over. A fair shake for disabled people needs to be built into the system."

Title V mandates changes insofar as the system receives federal support, and in this way it is like a sunrise, beginning a new day for disabled people. The implications are many. For autistic children like Chris Powers, the new day means special learning programs in regular classrooms with a chance to go to the zoo. For disabled veterans like John Lancaster and Clyde Kramer, it means career opportunities based solely on their ability and education. For determined teachers like Nelda Barnes, it means essential learning aids provided at college expense.

Growing up disabled in America no longer need be like trying to swim the English Channel. And that's right for our country and our time.

FOR MORE INFORMATION

For more information, write to Handicapped, Department of Health, Education, and Welfare, Washington, DC 20201.

A Primer on Due Process: Education Decisions for Handicapped Children

ALAN ABESON
NANCY BOLICK
JAYNE HASS

Extensive litigation and legislation have resulted in mandates that state and local education agencies guarantee due process protection to handicapped children in all matters pertaining to their identification, evaluation and educational placement. This article presents excerpts from a new CEC publication which contains an approach to meeting those requirements. The background of due process, sequential procedures required, structure and operation of hearings, the surrogate parent and sample forms are all included in the full publication.

ALAN ABESON *is Assistant Director of State and Local Governmental Relations, The Council for Exceptional Children, Reston, Virginia;* NANCY BOLICK *is Information Associate, and* JAYNE HASS *is Research Associate, Special Education Administrative Policy Manuals Project, The Council for Exceptional Children, Reston, Virginia.* *The work performed herein was done pursuant to a grant from the Bureau of Education for the Handicapped, US Office of Education, Department of Health, Education and Welfare. The opinions expressed herein, however, do not necessarily reflect the position or policy of the US Office of Education, and no official endorsement by the US Office of Education should be inferred.*

Children's rights cannot be secured until some particular institution has recognized them and assumed responsibility for enforcing them. In the past, adult institutions have not performed this function partly . . . because it was thought children had few rights to secure. Unfortunately, the institutions designed specifically for children also have failed to accomplish this aim, largely because they were established to safeguard interests, not to enforce rights, on the assumption that the former could be done without the latter. (Rodham, 1973, p. 506)

Exclusion and the Right to an Education

With the conflict between safeguarding interests and assuring individual rights as a backdrop, the rights of children in many areas of American life are being examined and clarified, often through judicial intervention. Nowhere is this examination more intense than in public education. In this decade, questions of "rights" for public school students have been raised in relation to freedom of expression, personal rights such as hair length and dress regulations, marriage and pregnancy, police intervention, corporal punishment, discipline, and confidentiality of records. While all of these have an impact on handicapped children, none is more pervasive than the right to due process which governs decisions regarding identification, evaluation, and educational placement.

Much litigation has been concerned with handicapped children seeking affirmation of their right to an education and the protection of due process of law. This wave of litigation is evidence of the way in which public schools in the past often ignored appropriate legal processes in denying these children their rights. The public schools often based such action upon law which was interpreted to give them the right to deny the opportunity of a public education to some children, either on a short term or permanent basis.

Today, it is a matter of public policy that the purpose of the public school is to provide every child with the opportunity for a free, public, and appropriate education. This policy makes it clear that to solve the problems a child is having in school by excluding him is not to solve the problems of the child, but of the school. It is unreasonable for the public schools to expel a child because of a behavioral problem (more popularly known as a discipline problem), an inability to learn, or any handicapping condition. Regardless of the types of exclusion that have been used and regardless of where they have occurred, the common denominator is that such practices have usually occurred with little or no regard for due process of law.

Placement in the Least Restrictive Alternative Educational Setting

Beyond the situation with excluded children is the requirement that handicapped children be placed for educational purposes in the least restrictive alternative setting. Public Law 93-380, the Education Amendment of 1974, focused specifically on this programing thrust by requiring that a state, in order to retain its eligibility to receive federal funds for the education of the handicapped, must develop a plan to be approved by the US Commissioner of Education, that will contain:

> (B) procedures to insure that, to the maximum extent appropriate, handicapped children, including children in public or private institutions or other care facilities, are educated with children who are not handicapped, and that special classes, separate schooling, or other removal of handicapped children from the regular education environment occurs only when the nature or severity of the handicap is such that education in regular classes with the use of supplementary aids and services cannot be achieved satisfactorily. (Public Law 93-380, Title VIB, Sec. 612(d)(13B))

"A Primer on Due Process: Education Decisions for Handicapped Children," by Alan Abeson, Nancy Bolick and Jayne Hass, *Exceptional Children,* Vol. 42, No. 2, October 1975. Copyright 1975 The Council for Exceptional Children. Reprinted with permission of The Council for Exceptional Children.

The relationship between due process and placement in the least restrictive alternative educational setting is extremely close. Due process establishes the procedures that require the schools to consider all program alternatives and to select that setting which is least restrictive. The basis of this entire concept is the existence of a variety of options or program settings that can be used to provide education to handicapped children depending on their individual needs.

Public Law 93-380 mandates the closeness by also requiring the states in their plans to:

(13) provide procedures for insuring that handicapped children and their parents or guardians are guaranteed procedural safeguards in decisions regarding identification, evaluation and educational placement of handicapped children including, but not limited to (A) (i) prior notice to parents or guardians of the child when the local or State educational agency proposes to change the educational placement of the child, (ii) an opportunity for the parents or guardians to obtain an impartial due process hearing, examine all relevant records with respect to the classification or educational placement of the child, and obtain an independent educational evaluation of the child, (iii) procedures to protect the rights of the child when the parents or guardians are not known, unavailable, or the child is a ward of the State including the assignment of an individual (not to be an employee of the State or local educational agency involved in the education or care of children) to act as a surrogate for the parents or guardians, and (iv) provision to insure that the decisions rendered in the impartial due process hearing required by this paragraph shall be binding on all parties subject only to appropriate administrative or judicial appeal. (Public Law 93-380, Title VIB, Sec. 612(d)(13A))

Due Process Procedures, Sequence

Providing a child with an appropriate education is of equal interest and importance to the child, the family, and the schools. To insure that education, it is imperative that, when initial educational evaluation and placement decisions or changes in existing placement are being considered, due process protections must be provided to the child, the family, and the schools. All of these parties will benefit from adherence to well developed educational practices and the elements of due process. When appropriate decisions about a child's education are made in a forthright manner, these parties will be in harmony and the challenges inherent in due process need not be involved. Under other less positive circumstances, however, conflict will emerge and require resolution. Hearings conducted by impartial officers serving as designees of the chief state school officer will be convened, not to place blame or determine right or wrong, but to achieve resolution of the conflict and define an appropriate education program for the child. While the procedures presented may appear complex and perhaps circuitous, it must be emphasized that none of the alternative routes to challenge need be used if all parties agree on

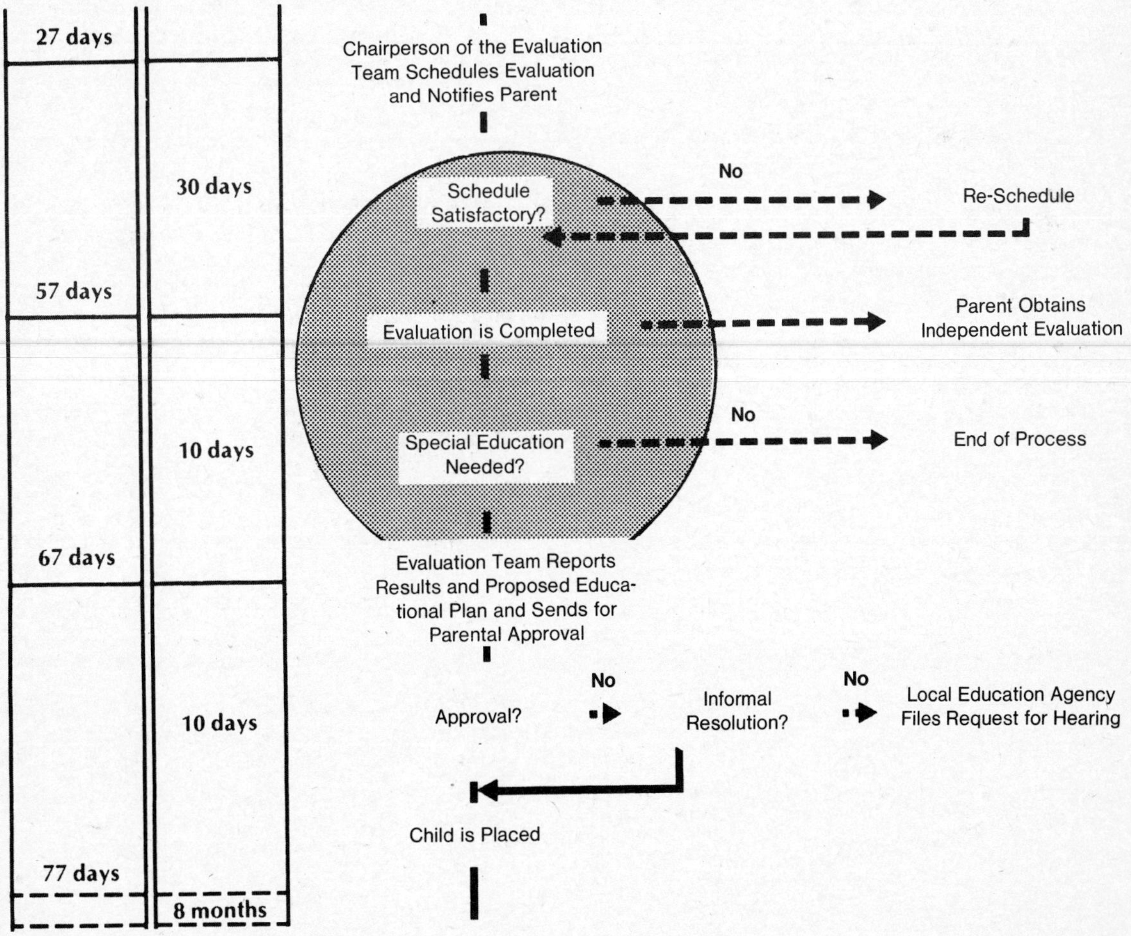

the educational needs of the child and the appropriateness of the program proposed by the schools.

A review of judicial orders, existing state and federal legislation, and the work of legal analysts suggests that the following procedures must be provided in order to meet minimum due process standards in identification, evaluation, and educational placement of handicapped children:

1. Written notification before evaluation. In addition, parents always have the right to an interpreter/translator if their primary language is not English.
2. Written notification before change in educational placement.
3. Periodic review of educational placement.
4. Opportunity for an impartial hearing including the right to:
   Receive timely and specific notice of such hearing.
   Review all records.
   Obtain an independent evaluation.
   Be represented by counsel.
   Cross examine.
   Bring witnesses.
   Present evidence.
   Receive a complete and accurate record of proceedings.
   Appeal the decision.
5. Assignment of a surrogate parent for children when:
   The child's parent or guardian is not known.
   The child's parents are unavailable.
   The child is a ward of the state.

Typically, these procedures should be initiated when there is reason to believe that a preschool or school age child is in need of special education services and the child becomes a candidate for individual evaluation procedures including informal assessment or observation and formal testing. Then written permission must be obtained by the local education agency from the parents before the process can begin. This shall also apply when periodic reevaluation is planned.

Prior to the performance of an evaluation the parent shall be provided with both written and oral notices of intent to conduct an evaluation. The written notice shall be in the primary language of the home and in English and will be delivered to the parent during a conference or mailed by certified mail. Oral interpretation shall always be given in the primary language of the home. If the primary language of the home is other than English and a member of the household requests that English also be used, then a second oral interpretation shall be given in English. When necessary, arrangements shall be made to effectuate communication with hearing and visually handicapped parents.

The proposed procedures include a provision that no later than 8 calendar months after a child's educational status has been changed and during each calendar year thereafter, so long as the child continues to receive special services, the local education agency should conduct a review of the child's program to evaluate its effectiveness in meeting the educational needs of the child. At least 5 days prior to each review, the parent should be notified in writing, in the primary language of the home and in English, and orally in the primary language of the home, that the review is scheduled. The notice should also indicate the following information:

1. The date, time, and place of the review.
2. An invitation to the parents to participate in the review.
3. A description of the procedures to be used in the review.
4. A statement that the parents will receive the findings and recommendations of the review team within 10 days after completion of the review.
5. A reiteration of the procedures and rights first encountered at the initial evaluation.

Hearing Procedures and Officers

Public policymakers, whether legislators or judges at both the state and federal level, have made clear that decisions about identifying, evaluating, and placing exceptional children in education programs must be governed by due process safeguards. Implicit in that requirement is that whenever a decision is contested to the point that a hearing is to be convened, the hearing must be conducted in an impartial manner by an impartial hearing officer or a neutral review panel.

Specifying criteria which can be used for the selection of effective hearing officers in all settings is an impossible task. There are, however, a few general rules which can be made. Individuals selected should:

1. Not be involved in the decisions already made about a child regarding identification, evaluation, placement, or review.
2. Possess special knowledge, acquired through training and/or experience, about the nature and needs of exceptional children. An awareness and understanding of the types and quality of programs that are available at any time for exceptional children is essential.
3. Be sufficiently open minded so that they will not be predisposed toward any decisions that they must make or review. However, they must also be capable of making decisions.
4. Possess the ability to objectively, sensitively, and directly solicit and evaluate both oral and written information that needs to be considered in relation to decision making.
5. Have sufficient strength to effectively structure and operate hearings in conformity with standard requirements and limits and to encourage the participation of the principal parties and their representatives.
6. Be sufficiently free of other obligations to provide sufficient priority to their hearing officer responsibilities. They must be able to meet the required timelines for conducting hearings and reporting written decisions.
7. Be aware that the role of the hearing officer is unique and relatively new, requiring constant evaluation of the processes, their own behavior, and the behavior of all the principals involved for purposes of continuously trying to improve the effectiveness of the hearing process.

The Parent Surrogate

The specific due process procedures of Public Law 93-380 secure a child's right, through representation by his parents or guardian, to the opportunity for full participation in the total educational identification, evaluation, and placement process. The assumption is that the parents or guardians will be available and willing to participate in this decision making process, fully accepting the responsibility of representing the child's best interests.

There are, however, children who lack this kind of personal representation, protective legal doctrines notwithstanding. They are the children whose parents or guardians are unknown or unavailable, or children who are wards of the state. The rights of these children are not safeguarded if they are without an advocate to act for them. Recognizing this, Public Law 93-380 provides for the appointment of a "parent surrogate," i.e., an individual appointed to safeguard a child's rights in the specific instance of educational decision making-identification, evaluation and placement.

The task of locating individuals to act as surrogates could be done by a state level standing board or advisory committee established to advise and work with the state as it delivers services to handicapped children. Members of this type of board are concerned with quality education and generally include parents, teachers, professionals involved with the education and treatment of children with special needs, and other community members who are interested in the education of handicapped children. Such a group has channels of communication open to local professional organizations concerned with the handicapped (Association for Retarded Citizens for example) and to individuals such as parents of handicapped and nonhandicapped children, pediatricians, or attorneys sensitive to the needs of children. These are individuals who may be considered for selection as surrogates. It is recommended that any pool of surrogates not include state or local education employees. Because of their employment, they may be unable to act as impartially as desired. A surrogate must have the child's best interests constantly in mind, and if he is employed by a local or state system concerned with handicapped children, he is placed in the position of serving two masters.

Once the state board has identified persons it feels would be effective surrogates, it will send their names to the state education agency, which has the responsibility of assigning a surrogate to a specific child. Individuals should be located in all parts of the state so that every child will have easy access to his/her surrogate. The state agency should develop a training program, devise a system of compensation, determine the rules and regulations governing the employment of a surrogate, and develop plans to disseminate information about the program.

Implications for Public Education Agencies

It is important for public educators to understand that implementing due process may produce many positive benefits. The availability of due process procedures, particularly hearings, provides the parent with the opportunity for holding the professional accountable, a desire of many professionals. In this context, the procedures of due process that require parent-school communication create the opportunity for school personnel to be open and honest with the ultimate consumers of their services. These requirements will also enable educators to adopt an additional procedure that has long been a goal—the provision of individually designed education programs. Individual plans provide the basis for intelligent assessment of a child's progress in relation to the objectives initially established. The concept of periodic review, also a requirement of total due process protection, conforms with good educational programing as well.

Finally, educators must be aware that adherence to due process procedures will in no way reduce their professional responsibility or authority. It can provide them with the leverage to do that which must be their goal—to act openly and in the best interests of the children they serve.

Reference

Rodham, H. Children under the law. *Harvard Education Review*, 1973, *43*, 487–514.

A Primer on Due Process contains an appendix with forms designed to implement the procedures described above. 57 pages. Available from Publications Sales, CEC, 1920 Association Dr., Reston VA 22091, $4.95. Stock no. 104.

The End of the Quiet Revolution: The Education for All Handicapped Children Act of 1975

Editorial Comment: The Education for All Handicapped Children Act of 1975, Public Law (P. L.) 94-142, is not revolutionary in terms of what it requires nor is it revolutionary in terms of a role for the federal government. As the article that follows will show, P. L. 94-142 represents the standards that have over the past eight years been laid down by the courts, legislatures, and other policy bodies of our country. Further, it represents a continued evolution of the federal role in the education of children who have handicaps. For example, much of what is required in P. L. 94-142 was set forth in P. L. 93-380, the Education Amendments of 1974.

Most importantly, P. L. 94-142 reflects the dream of special educators and others concerned about the education of children with handicaps for it has been the hope of our field that we as special educators would one day be able to assure every child who has a handicap an opportunity for an education, that we would be free to advocate for appropriate educational services for these children, that we would be unfettered by inappropriate administrative constraints, and that we would not always have to temper critical decisions about children's lives by the inadequacy of public resources. In this sense, P. L. 94-142 becomes the national vehicle whereby the promises of state and local policy that we have heard for so long, and the dreams that we in the profession have hoped for, for so long, may become a reality.

P. L. 94-142, however, may become nothing more than another hollow promise. How many times have we in special education been impressed by state laws or court decisions only to find later that their full intent was never achieved? P. L. 94-142 will only work if we and others make it work by using the procedures set forth in the law. To do this we must all learn what P. L. 94-142 requires, what it does not require, what our responsibilities are, what the responsibilities of others are, and what the procedures of the Act offer to those who would like to see it fully implemented.

The following article is only part of the continuing effort by CEC to help all of us better understand P. L. 94-142 and our role in its implementation. This article will not tell you all that you need to know but rather give you a sense of background in where this law came from. Articles in future issues and in other CEC publications and products will try to unfold the complete story.

We urge you to invest in learning the law and its meaning accurately. It is the knowledge of this public policy that will be the arsenal to use with advocates and to deal with detractors. We must not be swayed by rhetoric but must look at what is actually required. CEC and its federations through their political action network will be working to help you to understand the law. Find out what your federation and network are doing and if you have further questions or concerns, feel free to contact us and we will try to provide answers or direct you to those who might be able to help.

FREDERICK J. WEINTRAUB
Assistant Executive Director, Governmental Relations
The Council for Exceptional Children

"The End of the Quiet Revolution: The Education for All Handicapped Children Act of 1975," by Alan Abeson and Jeffrey Zettel, *Exceptional Children,* October 1977. Copyright 1977 The Council for Exceptional Children. Reprinted with permission of The Council for Exceptional Children.

ALAN ABESON
JEFFREY ZETTEL

ALAN ABESON *is Assistant Executive Director, Evaluation, Planning, and Development; and* JEFFREY ZETTEL *is a Specialist for Policy Implementation, Governmental Relations, The Council for Exceptional Children.*

ON the opening day of school in September 1978, a quiet revolution[1] will end. The end will not come silently, easily, nor dispassionately. The officers and soldiers who led and fought the revolution will not fade away for they recognize that the passing of this revolution may merely be signalling the beginning of the next. Accompanying this end, however, will be celebration—celebration for children who are handicapped and who, since the beginning of public education in the United States, have been the victims of discrimination that often prevented them from receiving an education. On that day in 1978, it will be a violation of federal law for any public education agency to deny to a handicapped child in need of a special education an appropriate program. As stated by the National Advisory Committee on the Education of the Handicapped (1976), "In law and as national policy, education is today recognized as the handicapped person's right" (p. 143).

The beginning of the end of the final phase of the revolution to achieve public policy affirming the right to an education for every child with a handicap was on November 29, 1975, when President Gerald Ford signed into law Public Law (P. L.) 94-142, the Education for All Handicapped Children Act of 1975, which becomes fully effective in September 1978. This law, which concluded the policy revolution begun in 1970, was built heavily on the policy victories that were won since that time in the Nation's courts and state legislatures. Additionally, the Act is based upon principles of sound educational practice that, although applicable to all children including the handicapped, were often pioneered and articulated by special educators.

Since the enactment of P. L. 94-142, it has been a central theme of discussion for virtually every element of the education community in the United States. The discussions have centered around strengths and perceived weaknesses of the Act and the implications for professionals and for parents. The settings of these discussions have extended from the Congress, the United States Office of Education, state legislatures, and state departments of education to local school boards and local education agencies.

Too frequently, however, the topic not discussed is implementation. It is implementation that begins for some children in October 1977 but that must be extended to all school age youngsters in September 1978. Too frequently as well, discussions of P. L. 94-142 have been based on misinformation or misinterpretation. Too often during these debates, the history is forgotten, administration reigns supreme, and the danger of this law becoming a comprehensive set of empty promises looms large. As will be discussed more fully later, the thrusts that lie ahead, while not revolutionary in the establishment of policy, may be in establishing appropriate practice.

In large measure, the burden for overseeing the effective implementation of this Act rests at least in part with special educators, many of whom are the veterans of the battles just concluded. Teachers, administrators, psychologists, therapists, and parents, for example, are all members of the implementation community. So too are all other members of the education community who may not be aware nor think of themselves as having responsibilities for children who have handicaps. One effect of the Act will be to bring about a closer alignment of all educators—a goal that is desirable so all children can receive an appropriate education. It is in the spirit of signalling the end of the quiet revolution, moving forward with implementation, and relating the recent history to the major policies contained in the Education for All Handicapped Children Act of 1975 that this article has been written.

Public Policy and the Education of Children

Educational public policy is established at the Federal, state, intermediate, and local governmental levels by boards, legislatures, courts, and administrative bodies that often have responsibilities both within and outside educational settings. The purpose of these policies is to provide the basis for the total operation of the American education system. These policies, when totally considered, serve as the elasticity that permits variations between the federal, state, intermediate, and local education agencies yet maintains some commonality of purpose, procedure, and function.

P. L. 94-142, as a statute passed by the US Congress, represents one expression of public policy regarding the education of children who have handicaps. Similar policy is represented by statutes that are passed by state legislatures. Other expressions of public policy can be found in rules and regulations,

[1] In one of the early articles written about the litigation and education of the handicapped, the movement was titled "The Quiet Revolution" (Dimond, 1973).

guidelines, and bylaws that are developed at both the state and federal levels to provide instruction and guidance to state and local education agencies, respectively, in their carrying out of each agency's statutes.

Occasionally, the intent, form, or substance of statutory or regulatory policies are challenged either substantively or for purposes of clarification. These issues are often dealt with in rulings by attorneys general who are most active at the state governmental level. A second and more well known setting for resolve is the Nation's judicial system where case law is created. It was in a federal district court in Philadelphia in 1971 where the Pennsylvania Association for Retarded Children, now known as the Pennsylvania Association for Retarded Citizens, in a lawsuit against the Commonwealth of Pennsylvania, first raised the cornerstone of the quiet revolution—the right of every mentally retarded child of school age to receive a public education.

The significance of public policy in relation to the education of children requires emphasis. In reality, virtually every decision made in a public school setting is controlled by policy. For example, policy leads to definition of those children who are eligible to participate in programs; it defines the services to be provided; it leads to specification of the nature and quantity of personnel to be made available for the delivery of services to eligible children; and finally, it provides for the availability of resources such as dollars, space, and time to allow the above responsibilities to be implemented. Public policy also serves to provide for the stability, consistency, and continuity of program operations over time and throughout individual agencies. During the quiet revolution, the placement practices used in individual school buildings within local school districts were often described in court as arbitrary and capricious because their standards and procedures differed drastically from building to building. In part, such conditions occurred because little or no districtwide policies were available and in force to guide the behavior of the individual building teachers and administrators. Clearly, the presence of policy that is modern, written, and familiar to the entire educational community is in the best interests of all those employed or served by the public schools.

A Recent History of the Inadequacy of Educating Children Who Have Handicaps

> With minor exceptions, mankind's attitudes toward its handicapped population can be characterized by overwhelming prejudice. [The handicapped are systematically isolated from] the mainstream of society. From ancient to modern times, the physically, mentally or emotionally disabled have been alternatively viewed by the majority as dangers to be destroyed, as nuisances to be driven out, or as burdens to be confined . . . . (T)reatment resulting from a tradition of isolation has been invariably unequal and has operated to prejudice the interests of the handicapped as a minority group. (*Lori Case v. State of California*, 1973, p. 2a)

The manifestations of these attitudes occurred in schools in a variety of ways including the exclusion of children who have handicaps, incorrect or inappropriate classification, labeling or placement, and the provision of inappropriate education programs, as well as arbitrary and capricious educational decision making. While this listing is not exhaustive, it is illustrative of the major practices in use prior to the initiation of the quiet revolution. To a large degree, the Congress designed P. L. 94-142 to respond at least in part to these illegal and inappropriate practices.

Exclusion, Postponement, and the Right to An Education

The Congress of the United States in the statement of findings and purposes that are a part of P. L. 94-142 (1975), indicated that "one million of the handicapped children in the United States are excluded entirely from the public school system and will not go through the educational process, with their peers" (Sec. 3, b, 4). Related is an analysis of 1970 census data done by the Children's Defense Fund (1974) who concluded that "out of school children share a common characteristic of differentness by virtue of race, income, physical, mental or emotional 'handicap' and age" (p. 4).

While this factual picture could lead to conclusions of condemnation against the educators who perpetuated this injustice, it must be acknowledged that in many jurisdictions, existing policy permitted—even sanctioned—the exclusion of children with handicaps from public school attendance. State compulsory school attendance statutes, for example, frequently permitted such steps when a local superintendent of schools, with or without notice to the state, determined (in an unspecified manner) that a child could not profit from an education or had learned all that he or she was capable of learning. If a child with a handicap was in need of transportation to get to a program or a program was needed but not readily available, then denial of service was considered in some jurisdictions to be legitimate.

Beginning in 1970 and continuing today, the legality of denying a public education to a child with a handicap by exclusion, postponement, or by any other means has been successfully challenged in both state and federal judicial systems. The rationale for such litigation has been primarily derived from the equal protection clause of the Fourteenth Amendment of the United States Constitution, which guarantees equal protection of the law to all the people. In other words, where a state has undertaken to provide a benefit to the people, such as public education, these benefits must be provided to all of the people unless the state can demonstrate a compelling reason for doing otherwise. The language most often used to express this concept in education was the 1954 *Brown v. Board of Education* Supreme Court decision that proclaimed:

> In these days it is doubtful that any child may reasonably be expected to succeed in life if he is denied the opportunity for an education. Such an opportunity, where the state has undertaken to provide it, is a right which must be made available to all on equal terms. (74S. Ct. 686, 98L. Ed. 873)

Two of the most heralded and precedent setting right to education lawsuits occurred in the early 1970's in Pennsylvania and the District of Columbia. It was in fact these cases that initiated the quiet revolution. In January 1971, the Pennsylvania Association for Retarded Children (PARC) brought a class action suit against the Commonwealth of Pennsylvania in Federal District Court for the alleged failure of the state to provide all of its school age children who were retarded with access to a free public education. The court supervised agreement which resolved that phase of the suit decreed the state could not apply any policy that would postpone, terminate, or deny children who were mentally retarded access to a publicly supported education. Further, it stated that all retarded children in the State of Pennsylvania between the ages of 6 and 21 were to be provided with a publicly supported education by September 1972 (*Pennsylvania Association for Retarded Children v. Commonwealth of Pennsylvania*, Consent Agreement, 1972).

Following the *PARC* decision, a second, similar federal decree was achieved in 1972. In *Mills v. Board of Education of the District of Columbia* (1972), the parents and guardians of seven District of Columbia children brought a class action suit on behalf of all out of school handicapped children. The outcome of the *Mills* decision was a court order providing that all school age children, regardless of the severity of their handicap, were entitled to an appropriate free public education.

In both the *PARC* and *Mills* cases, allegations were made regarding the manner in which identification, evaluation and placement activities, and decisions were rendered regarding the education of children who have handicaps. Consequently, both the *PARC* consent agreement and the *Mills* decree required specific due process procedures to be established. Also litigated in these cases was the issue of where children with handicaps should be placed in relation to nonhandicapped children for receipt of their education. Both of these policy areas will be examined later in this article.

Following the precedents established by these two cases, the right to education principle became further solidified through the passage of a number of state statutes and regulations, thus adding to the impetus and policy breadth of the revolution. By 1972 it was reported that nearly 70% of the states had adopted mandatory legislation requiring the education of all children who have handicaps as defined in each state's policies (Abeson, 1972; p. 63). By 1975 all but two state legislatures had adopted some form of mandatory law calling for the education of at least the majority of its handicapped children (US Congress, Senate, 1975). Today all but one state has enacted such legislation. Further, the Education Amendments of 1974; P. L. 93-380, required that, in order for states to participate in the financial assistance available under the Act, they were to establish a goal of providing full educational opportunities to all children with handicaps.

Incorrect or Inappropriate Classification or Labeling

A major component of the quiet revolution, the labeling and classification dilemma also became the subject of litigation. It must be recognized, however, that Dunn in 1968 published an historic article that described the issue and brought it to the attention of the field. For purposes of litigation, however, substantial evidence was gathered which supported the claim that schools too often assigned labels, subjected children to individual psychological assessments, and altered their educational status without the appropriate supporting data and often without parental knowledge.

The classification of children with handicaps by categorical labels was shown to produce major problems (Abeson, Bolick, & Hass, 1975, p. 5). Among the adverse effects of inappropriate labeling are:

- Labeled children are often victimized by stigma associated with the label. This may be manifested by isolation from usual school opportunities and taunting and rejection by both children and school personnel. In the latter instance, it may be overt or unconscious.
- Assigning labels to children often suggests

to those working with them that the children's behavior should conform to stereotyped behavioral expectations associated with the labels. This often contributes to a self fulfilling prophecy in that a child, once labeled, is expected to conform with the stereotyped behavior associated with the label and ultimately does so. When a child is labeled and placement is made on the basis of that label, there is often no opportunity to escape from either the label or the placement.

- Children who are labeled and placed in educational programs on the basis of that label may often not need special education programs. This is obviously true for children who are incorrectly labeled, but it also applies to children with certain handicaps, often of a physical nature. The fact that a child is physically handicapped does not mean that a special education is required.

Other researchers questioned the alleged preponderance of minority group children found in special education classes. Studies conducted by the California State Department of Education, for example, discovered that while Spanish surnamed children comprised only 13% of their total school population, they accounted for more than 26% of the students in their classes for the educable mentally retarded (Weintraub, 1972, p.4). Mercer (1970), examining the process of special educational placement in Riverside, California, found three times more Mexican Americans and two and a half times more Black Americans in those programs than would be expected from their percentage in the general population.

In January 1970, *Diana v. State Board of Education* was filed in the District Court of Northern California. The suit, brought on behalf of nine Mexican American students ages 8 through 13, alleged that the students had been improperly placed in classes for the mentally retarded on the basis of inaccurate tests. Coming from homes where Spanish was the predominant or only spoken language, the plaintiffs argued they had been placed in classes for the educable mentally retarded on the results of an IQ score obtained from either a Stanford-Binet or Wechsler intelligence test. When the nine were retested in Spanish, however, seven scored higher than the IQ cutoff for placement in classes for the educable mentally retarded.

On the basis of this data, the plaintiffs argued that the tests relied primarily on a verbal aptitude in English and ignored their learning abilities in Spanish and that the tests were standardized on White, native born Americans and related in subject matter solely to the dominant White, middle class culture (Ross, DeYoung, & Cohen, 1971, p. 7).

A similar landmark decision regarding the testing and classification of students was filed in late 1971 on behalf of six Black, elementary students attending the San Francisco Unified School District. The plaintiffs in *Larry P. v. Riles* (1972) alleged they had been inappropriately classified as educable mentally retarded on the basis of a testing procedure that failed to recognize their unfamiliarity with the White middle class culture and that ignored learning experiences they might have had in their homes.

In resolving these suits, various agreements were established requiring the use of the following types of practices:

- Children were to be tested in their primary language. Interpreters were to be used when a bilingual examiner was not available.
- Mexican American, Black American, and Chinese American children already in classes for the mentally retarded were to be retested and evaluated.
- The state was to undertake immediate efforts to develop and standardize an appropriate IQ test.

As with right to education, these cases and the growing literature led to the concept of nondiscriminatory evaluation. This concept was also added to state law in many states particularly in the form of requiring school districts to consider multiple data and sources for consideration by teams of professionals prior to making classification and placement decisions. In addition, mandates appeared requiring that parents of children suspected of being handicapped be provided with notice and the opportunity to approve or reject evaluation of their child. These principles were also articulated in P. L. 93-380. Specifically required of the states was that they were to adopt procedures to insure that testing materials and procedures used for classification and placement of handicapped children were to be selected and administered so as not to be racially or culturally discriminatory.

Provision of Inappropriate Education Programs

While the quiet revolution at times seemed to be focusing on major rights issues, attention was also focused upon more than simple access to the public schools. The evidence that emerged in the process of documenting the effects of classification and their resulting placements seemed to suggest that many assignments were made as a function of administrative convenience rather than an awareness of the individual needs of children. Consequently, the goal of access was modified and expanded to include the concept of access to appropriate programs.

This concern was reflected in the judicial orders that emerged from both the right to education and classification litigation. Similarly, the emerging statutes qualifying the nature of the education to be provided to children with handicaps was abundant with the words "suitable" and "appropriate" and the phrases "specialized instruction," "appropriate to the child's capacity," and "designed to develop the maximum potential of every handicapped person."

These qualifiers were further translated principally in state statute and regulation into requirements for the development of some type of individually designed and delivered program. A notable example comes from Illinois, which adopted a regulation (State of Illinois, 1974, p. 6) requiring that educational plans be developed that include specific objectives to be attained by each child.

Such directives were clearly related to the use of multiple professionals in the evaluation process. Without such a procedure and goal, much of the valuable individual information acquired about each child was lost and never considered in relation to the unique needs of individual children. Further, it became apparent as the revolution progressed that the spectre of accountability was also going to be applied to the education of handicapped children.

A major aspect of the suitability or appropriateness measure of a handicapped child's program, which was further addressed in the litigation, was where children with handicaps should be placed for educational purposes in relation to their nonhandicapped contemporaries. The conceptual basis for considering this issue came largely from Reynolds (1962) who portrayed the existence of a continuum of placements for children with handicaps ranging from the least restrictive (i.e., being placed in a regular classroom setting with considerable opportunity to interact with nonhandicapped children) to the most restrictive setting (i.e., a special school or a nonpublic school placement, such as a private institution, that would provide little if any contact with nonhandicapped individuals). It is well recognized, however, that the implementation of this continuum was never intended nor should be interpreted to mean that all handicapped children should be placed in regular classrooms. What is intended is that individual children, possessing individual needs, will be placed on the basis of these needs in the least restrictive setting.

As of 1974 only six states were required by law and 11 by regulation to adhere to the principle of least restrictive placement (Bolick, 1974). However, by October 1975, the National Education Association reported that 22 or half of their state affiliates reported having statutory or regulatory language requiring that children with handicaps were to be placed in regular classes at least some of the time.

Perhaps one of the clearest and most comprehensive statutory definitions of least restrictive environment as it applies to children with handicaps can be found in the following 1972 Tennessee state statute, which was essentially echoed in P. L. 94-142:

> To the maximum extent practicable, handicapped children shall be educated along with children who do not have handicaps and shall attend regular classes . . . . Special classes, separate schooling or other removal of handicapped children from the regular educational environment, shall occur only when, and to the extent that the nature or severity of the handicap is such that education in regular classes, even with the use of supplementary aids and services, cannot be accomplished satisfactorily (Tennessee Code Annotated, Sec. 23, Chap. 839, 1972).

Inappropriate Educational Decision Making

As has been briefly mentioned, the quiet revolution also was concerned with the manner in which education decisions were being made about children with handicaps in the public schools. The litigation revealed students were frequently misplaced and misclassified not only as a result of inappropriate evaluation instruments and procedures, but also because of inappropriate decision making occuring often in local schools. Traditionally, school administrators were able to decide whether a child with behavioral problems, a child restricted to a wheelchair, or a child who was especially difficult to teach could come to school and, if so, where that child was to be placed. Often these decisions were made unilaterally, without data, without legal basis, and without parental involvement or notice.

When these practices were brought to the attention of the court in Pennsylvania, the court ruled first, prior to consideration of the right to education question, that such practices must cease. To remedy the situation, the court first established the right of all children who are mentally retarded to the protection of procedural due process (in accordance with the 5th and 14th Amendments). This was contained in the 1972 *PARC* consent agreement which decreed that no child who is mentally retarded or thought to be mentally retarded can be assigned initially or reassigned to either a regular or special educational status or excluded from a public education without a prior recorded hearing before a special hearing officer.

Second, the court approved as part of the agreement a 23 step process to meet the due process mandate. Some of the requirements included:

- Providing written notice to parents or guardians of the proposed action.
- Provision in that notice of the specific reasons for the proposed action and the legal authority upon which such actions can occur.
- Provision of information about the parents' or guardians' right to contest the proposed action at a full hearing before the state secretary of education or his designate.
- Provision of information about the purpose and procedures of the hearing, including parents' or guardians' right to counsel, cross examination, presentation of independent evidence, and a written transcript of the hearing.
- Indication that the burden of proof regarding the placement recommendation lies with the school district.
- Right to obtain an independent evaluation of the child, at public expense if necessary (Weintraub & Abeson, 1974, p. 528).

A similar set of requirements was contained in the *Mills* order. In addition to the litigation, due process requirements also became assimilated into state and federal public policy. A 1974 survey conducted by the State-Federal Information Clearinghouse for Exceptional Children revealed that 12 states were required by statute to provide such procedures and 13 were similarly required by regulation (Bolick, 1974). The constitutional responsibility of each state to provide its residents with due process procedures was further affirmed by P. L. 93-380, in which Congress ordered assurances from the states that proper due process procedural safeguards would be adhered to in all decisions regarding the identification, evaluation, and placement of children with handicaps.

The Education for All Handicapped Children Act of 1975, P. L. 94-142

By April 1975, when the Subcommittee on Select Education and the Subcommittee on the Handicapped began a series of legislative hearings in both Washington, D.C., and elsewhere across the country to extend and amend the Education of the Handicapped Amendments of 1974 (Public Law 93-380), the quiet revolution to win for every handicapped child an appropriate education had reached something of a crescendo. Over half of the states by that time had either been through or were in the process of going through litigation. Increasingly, parents of handicapped children and professionals were forming statewide coalitions to file and maintain lawsuits, to advance state and local policy, and to implement newly won policy directives.

Despite this momentum, however, these congressional committees learned:

- Over 1.75 million children with handicaps in the United States were being excluded entirely from receiving a public education solely on the basis of their handicap.
- Over half of the estimated 8 million handicapped children in this country were not receiving the appropriate educational services they needed and/or were entitled to.
- Many other children with handicaps were still being placed in inappropriate educational settings because their handicaps were undetected or because of a violation of their individual rights.

It became clear that, although federal and state judicial and legislative actions had brought about progress since 1970 toward providing appropriate educational services for children with handicaps, there remained a need for greater effort. The Congress decided this effort should take the form of legislation that would later be referred to as the "Bill of Rights for Handicapped Children." Approved by an 83 to 10 vote of the Senate on June 18, 1975, and a subsequent 375 to 44 affirmation of the House of Representatives on July 29, President Gerald Ford signed this historic bill on November 29, 1975. P. L. 94-142, the Education for All Handicapped Children Act, had become law, and thus the quiet revolution to achieve the basic educational rights of all children with handicaps began to conclude.

Descriptions of this comprehensive law can take many forms. One approach is to consider it from the basic perspective of the history of circumstances described earlier. While this treatment may be effective in the context of this article, it must be clear at the outset that the Act also included extensive management and finance aspects that will be addressed here in only a limited fashion.

Right to Education

The intent of the Congress to insure that this Act will provide for the education of all children with handicaps is reflected in its statement of purpose:

> It is the purpose of this Act to assure that all handicapped children have available to them, within the time periods specified, a free appropriate public education which emphasizes special education and related services designed to meet their unique needs. (Public Law 94-142, 1975, Sec. 3, c)

The time periods specified are that beginning

in September 1978 all handicapped children aged 3 to 18 shall receive a free appropriate public education. The law further orders that by September 1, 1980, such an education shall be available to all handicapped children aged 3 to 21 (except in instances where the education of the 3 to 5 and 18 to 21 age ranges would be inconsistent with state law or practice or any court decree).

Inclusion of this right in P. L. 94-142 makes abundantly clear that it is as the National Advisory Committee stated, national policy. After the dates specified occur, there simply will not be any grounds for depriving a handicapped child who, because of that handicap, possesses unique learning needs requiring special education. No longer will it be permissible for school persons to exclude or postpone the education of such handicapped children on the grounds that they cannot learn, their handicap is too severe, programs do not exist, or for any other reason.

This civil rights principle can also be clearly expressed in educational terms that were in fact recognized by the Nation's courts and legislators during the period prior to P. L. 94-142. First, it means that no child is uneducable or stated in another way, all children can learn. Closely related to this statement is that education cannot be defined traditionally but rather must be considered as a continuous process by which individuals learn to cope and function within their environment, regardless of their environment. It was this definition that emerged from *PARC*, specifically from testimony presented by Dr. Ignacy Goldberg. Translated to curriculum planning, it means that to provide mobility training for blind children, adaptive physical education for physically handicapped children, or instruction in bodily functioning for some mentally retarded children is no different than teaching driver education, physical education, or health and hygiene to nonhandicapped children.

The right to education also means that children with handicaps are eligible for participation in all programs and activities provided or sponsored by the schools as all other children are eligible. The presence of a handicap no longer can mean automatic ineligibility for music, athletics, cheerleading, or other extracurricular activities. By the same standard, children with handicaps may no longer be considered for noninclusion in all course offerings, most notably vocational education. Similarly, if the presence of a handicap and related special learning needs leads to the provision of special education, it does not render the child ineligible for other special services.

Included within the mandate of the right to education for all children with handicaps are those children who possess learning needs that require program delivery in public or private day or residential settings that operate on a tuition basis. In the past, some or all of these costs were, because of various state statutory approaches, partially or totally a family responsibility. Trudeau and Nye (1973) indicated that policies for partial or total tuition reimbursement for children in this situation existed in 40 states. Frequently, families were simply unable to bear these costs.

To rectify this situation, the Congress in P. L. 94-142 requires that every handicapped child be provided a free appropriate public education at no additional expense to that child's parents or guardians. Furthermore, when it is determined that the child's appropriate education should be provided in a tuition based school program, the cost for receiving such services, including tuition, transportation, and room and board where necessary, must also not be automatically assigned to the parents. Misunderstanding of this mandate must not occur. Placement in tuition based programs at public cost does not occur as a function of parental option. It is only when it has been determined either through public school recommendation or as the result of due process that a tuition based setting is required to provide a child with an appropriate education that the parents shall not be required to bear the cost.

Right to Nondiscriminatory Evaluation

P. L. 94-142 addresses the well documented and researched problem of discriminatory evaluation activities as did its predecessor, P. L. 93-380. The policy directives contained in P. L. 94-142 are straightforward and clear in their intent to remedy these negative practices that have had impact not only upon minority group children but also upon some handicapped children.

Essentially, the Act requires that the testing and evaluation materials and procedures that are used for the purposes of evaluation of children with handicaps, will be selected and administered so as not to be culturally discriminatory. Further, the law specifies that such materials and procedures are to be provided in the child's native language or mode of communication. Finally, no single procedure or test can be the sole criterion for determining the appropriate educational program for a child. This last requirement clearly builds upon the maxim that standardized procedures including tests are not in themselves evil but, rather, become so if inappropriately used.

After passage of P. L. 93-380, the Bureau of Education for the Handicapped (1974) issued "advisories," which are interpretative statements designed to assist in understanding and implementing the Act. Throughout the area of nondiscriminatory evaluation in which, although a well recognized problem, few easy solutions exist, the advisories recommended to education agencies:

> A procedure also should be included in terms of a move toward the development of diagnostic-prescriptive techniques to be utilized when for reasons of language differences of deficiencies, non-adaptive behavior, or extreme cultural differences a child cannot be evaluated by the instrumentation of tests. Such procedures should insure that no assessment will be attempted when a child is unable to respond to the tasks or behavior required by a test because of linguistic or cultural differences unless culturally and linguistically appropriate measures are administered by qualified persons. In those cases in which appropriate measures and/or qualified persons are not available, diagnostic-prescriptive educational programs should be used until the child has acquired sufficient familiarity with the language and culture of the school for more formal assessment. These evaluation procedures should also assure that persons interpreting assessment information and making educational decisions are qualified to administer the various measures and qualified to take cultural differences into account in interpreting the meaning of multiple sets of data from both the home and the school. (p. 29)

Inclusion in P. L. 94-142 of the "mode of communication" requirement is an important addition to the nondiscriminatory policy requirements. While the culturally and linguistically discriminating attributes have been recognized, no attention has been directed to the problems of children with handicaps who, because of the manifestation of their handicap, are in evaluation activities, particularly testing, and thus are also victims of discrimination. At issue is the point that the activities evaluate what is intended to be evaluated. Illustrative of these problems are children who possess motor difficulties in their arms and hands and are unable to adequately carry out various performance tasks that are common to many types of standardized tests not intended to measure motor functioning. Because a youngster can not stack or rearrange the blocks does not mean the child does not know what is required nor how to do it. Consequently, evaluators under P. L. 94-142 must consider the child's mode of communication.

Right to an Appropriate Education

To deal with the past problems of inappropriate educational services being provided to children who have handicaps, the Congress included as a major component of P. L. 94-142 a requirement that each child be provided with a written individualized education program known as the IEP. The IEP required for each handicapped child is the central building block to understanding and effectively complying with the Act. In order to understand the IEP, it is important that the following progression, as described by Weintraub (1977), be understood.

> Handicapped children are defined by the Act as children who are "mentally retarded, hard of hearing, deaf, orthopedically impaired, other health impaired, speech impaired, visually handicapped, seriously emotionally disturbed, or children with specific learning disabilities who by reason thereof require special education and related services" [Sec. 4 (a)(1)]. This definition establishes a two-pronged criteria for determining child eligibility under the Act. The first criteria is whether the child has one or more of the disabilities listed in the definition. The second is whether the child requires special education and related services. Not all children who have a disability require special education, many can and should attend school without any program modification.
>
> Special education is defined in P. L. 94-142 as "... specially designed instruction, at no cost to parents or guardians, to meet the unique needs of a handicapped child, including classroom instruction, instruction in physical education, home instruction, and instruction in hospitals and institutions" [Sec. 4 (16)]
>
> The key phrases in the above definition of special education that impinge upon the IEP are "specially designed instruction ... to meet the unique needs of a handicapped child." Again, by definition, then, special education is special and only involves that instruction which is specially designed and directed to meet the unique needs of a handicapped child. Thus, for many children special education will not be the totality of their education. Furthermore, this definition clearly implies that special proceeds from the basic goals and expected outcomes of general education. Thus, for example, intervention with a child does not occur because he is mentally retarded but because he has a unique educational need that requires specially designed instruction.
>
> Equally important to understand is the concept of related services which are defined in the Act as: "transportation, and such developmental, corrective, and other supportive services (including speech pathology and audiology, psychological services, physical and occupational therapy, recreation, and medical and counseling services, except that such medical services shall be for diagnostic and evaluation purposes only) as may be required to assist a handicapped child to benefit from special education, and includes the early identification and assessment of handicapping conditions in children" [Sec. 4(a)(17)].
>
> The key phrase here is "as required to assist the handicapped child to benefit from special education." This leads to a clear progression: a child is handicapped because he or she requires special education and related services; special education

> is the specially designed instruction to meet the child's unique needs; and related services are those additional services necessary in order for the child to benefit from special educational instruction.
>
> The term "individualized education program" itself conveys important concepts that need to be specified. First, "individualized" means that the IEP must be addressed to the educational needs of a single child rather than a class or group of children. Second, "education" means that the IEP is limited to those elements of the child's education that are more specifically special education and related services as defined by the Act. Third, "program" means that the IEP is a statement of what will actually be provided to the child, as distinct from a plan which provides guidelines from which a program must subsequently be developed. (p. 27)

Finally, a specific definition describing the components of an IEP is included within the Act:

> A written statement for each handicapped child developed in any meeting by a representative of the local educational agency or an intermediate educational unit who shall be qualified to provide, or supervise the provision of, specially designed instruction to meet the unique needs of handicapped children, the teacher, the parents or guardians of such child, and, whenever appropriate, such child, which statement shall include (A) a statement of the present levels of educational performance of such child, (B) a statement of annual goals, including short-term instructional objectives, (C) a statement of the specific educational services to be provided to such child, and the extent to which such child will be able to participate in regular educational programs, (D) the projected date for initiation and anticipated duration of such services, and appropriate objective criteria and evaluation procedures and schedules for determining, on at least an annual basis, whether instructional objectives are being achieved. (Public Law 94-142, 1975, Sec. 4,a, 19)

The IEP requirement of P. L. 94-142 has received much attention in terms of its potential for achieving the goal of the Act—appropriately educating every handicapped child. Inclusion of the teacher, for example, in the development of the IEP is designed to insure that realistic teacher concerns and needs will be considered as part of the IEP development process. It is appropriate that teachers have a major voice in program planning since they have major responsibility for program provision. Similarly, parent participation is designed to insure that the extensive amounts of information parents possess about their children and their judgments as to the education program needed will be considered. Establishment of jointly determined expectations for individual children that are known to all involved and interested in the form of goals and objectives is highly regarded because with such specificity comes a clear basis for assessing a child's progress so that inappropriate programs do not continue and necessary program changes will occur.

The importance of the total IEP provision cannot be overemphasized, nor can it be misinterpreted. It should be emphasized that the IEP is an agreement between all parties and that, while it is not a contract, it is clearly a statement setting forth what will be provided to the child. School systems, however, are legally responsible for provision of the "specific educational services" set forth in the IEP. Related then is that the IEP is a management device, not an instructional plan specifying daily teacher-child activities. Finally, the IEP serves to define for each handicapped child in need of special education services what is appropriate for that child.

No discussion of appropriate education for children who have handicaps is complete without consideration of the least restrictive placement principle. As noted, the statutory definition of the IEP itself requires consideration of "the extent to which such child will be able to participate in regular educational programs." In addition, each state must establish

> procedures to insure that, to the maximum extent appropriate, handicapped children, including children in public and private institutions or other care facilities, are educated with children who are not handicapped and that special classes, separate schooling, or the removal of handicapped children from the regular education environment occurs only when the nature or severity of the handicap is such that education in regular classes with the use of supplementary aids and services cannot be achieved satisfactorily. (Public Law 94-142, 1975, Sec. 612, 5,B)

Implementation of this portion of the appropriate requirement has been interpreted by some to mean that all handicapped children, regardless of the severity of their handicap, are to be placed in regular classroom programs. To others, these mandates mean that all handicapped children are to be placed in self contained special education classes. Neither of these is correct. What must exist is school system capacity to provide programs that are appropriate for individual children in the least restrictive alternative setting. Conceptualizing the requirement in this manner indicates that, although placement decisions must be indicated in the child's IEP, it must follow determination of the child's learning needs and programs. Available placement options no longer can dictate placement decisions for individual children.

Right to Due Process of Law

During the revolution, the manner in which

identification, evaluation, and placement decisions were made about children with handicaps were reviewed virtually throughout the country. To solve these problems, the courts ordered adherence to procedural due process. It was this solution that was also selected by the Congress as part of P. L. 94-142. Like most of the elements of this law, due process has received wide attention and discussion. It is included in the Act to insure that all of the rights created by the Act are in fact made available to children who have handicaps, their families, and the public schools. One way of expressing this intent is to suggest that the presence of due process is designed to allow for equal consideration of the interests of all who are involved in the education of a handicapped child—the child, the family, the schools.

The specific elements of due process the Congress included in the law are as follows:

1. Written notification before evaluation. In addition, the right to an interpreter/translator if the family's native language is not English (unless it is clearly not feasible to do so).
2. Written notification when initiating or refusing to initiate a change in educational placement.
3. Opportunity to present complaints regarding the identification, evaluation, placement, or the provision of a free appropriate education.
4. Opportunity to obtain an independent educational evaluation of the child.
5. Access to all relevant records.
6. Opportunity for an impartial due process hearing including the right to:
   a. Receive timely and specific notice of the hearing.
   b. Be accompanied and advised by counsel and by individuals with special knowledge or training with respect to the problems of children with handicaps.
   c. Confront, cross examine, and compel the attendance of witnesses.
   d. Present evidence:
      (1) Written or electronic verbatim record of the hearing.
      (2) Written findings of fact and decisions.
7. The right to appeal the findings and decisions of the hearing.

The procedural safeguards section of the Act includes two provisions that are of special importance. First is the requirement that, for children whose parents or guardian "are unknown, unavailable or the child is a ward of the state" and who are being considered for service under this Act, procedures must be established to assign an individual "who shall not be an employee of the State educational agency, local educational agency, or intermediate educational unit involved in the education or care of the child to act as a surrogate for the parents or guardian" (Public Law 94-142, 1975, Sec. 615, 6, 1, B). Without this requirement children without parents or guardians would essentially be deprived of access to their rights of due process.

Until P. L. 94-142 was enacted, the circumstances under which due process could be invoked was limited to identification, evaluation, and placement. Under this Act, however, the Congress has extended the due process opportunity by providing "an opportunity to present complaints with respect to any matter relating to the identification, evaluation, or educational placement of the child, or the provision of a free appropriate public education to such child" (Sec. 615, b, 1, E). What is intended is to provide, as indicated earlier, a mechanism for review and rectification of inappropriate practice.

Many school systems operating under well established and understood due process systems have found that it can provide an effective means of guiding communications with the families of children with handicaps. It sets out a series of procedures for communication that allow all interested parties to be informed as to the educational status of a handicapped child. In the vast majority of situations, the communication is what has been missing and is what is sought. When, however, there is disagreement as to the status or what is in the appropriate interest of the child, the more extensive procedures can be used. School personnel as well as parents can use these procedures to insure that what is required—the appropriate education of the child—is achieved.

The Future

Throughout this article, reference has been made to the end of the quiet revolution. Beginning in 1970 and continuing until the opening of school in September 1978, the quiet revolution effectively established in policy the educational rights of all handicapped children. With the conclusion of this revolution or at least one aspect of it, the efforts of all educators and particularly those in special education who have long worked to establish these rights must shift to achieve implementation of these rights. P. L. 94-142 is the national policy—it is specific as to what is to occur and it appropriates some funds to assist state, intermediate, and local education agencies in carrying out their state mandated responsibilities of providing for the education of all the children residing within each state. Clearly that mandate now applies equally to children who have handicaps.

Reference to individual state responsibilities for the education of its resident children is appropriate. For too long in many states, their own mandatory requirements for educating children with handicaps were insufficiently implemented. In part, P. L. 94-142 can provide the leverage for the states to carry out their own mandates and provide for the education of all handicapped children. P. L. 94-142 in fact is designed to effectively join local, state, and federal resources to achieve the full service goal.

Of crucial importance in undertaking the implementation task is for all elements of the education community to correctly understand the Act and the reasons for its creation. Misinterpretation and misinformation is a critical danger. Citizen voters, legislators, school board members, administrators, teachers, support personnel, and parents of children with handicaps must be aware of what the law does say, not what someone thinks it says. What will happen inside the schoolhouse door will largely depend upon members of this population who have had little or no exposure or knowledge about children with handicaps. Above all, the entire school community needs to become sensitized to the fact that handicapped children are first children, and second children with special learning needs. In large measure, the responsibility for conveying correct information rests with those who know—special educators.

The difficulties of implementation for even those children who are well recognized as having handicaps and possessing unique learning needs is only a portion of the future. Special attention must be directed to insure that an unknown number of such children in special circumstances also receive the benefits of the Act. Included are American Indian handicapped children who are located on or near Indian reservations across the country as well as in usual educational communities; abused and neglected children who because of their mistreatment become handicapped children possessing unique learning needs requiring special education; and a long neglected population of handicapped children that are in the Nation's foster care and juvenile corrections programs. Not to be forgotten as well are children with handicaps who, although identified, are inappropriately served in institutions and those who reside in the acutely educationally difficult inner city or sparsely populated areas.

When all is said and done and historians examine the quiet revolution, they may well determine that, while P. L. 94-142 is the premier educational policy attainment for the handicapped, the most notable overall policy for this group is Section 504 of the Vocational Rehabilitation Act of 1973 (Public Law 93-112). This small section of law prescribes that:

> no otherwise qualified handicapped individual in the United States . . . which solely by reason of handicap be excluded in the participation in, be denied the benefit of, or be subjected to discrimination under any program or activity receiving Federal financial assistance.

While this law requires that virtually the total society must provide handicapped persons with equal rights, it is of special importance in the implementation of P. L. 94-142. The regulations that accompany Section 504 contain a portion devoted totally to preschool, elementary, secondary, and postsecondary education. These regulations, which to a large degree conform to many of the P. L. 94-142 requirements, will enhance the implementation process because virtually every education agency receives federal financial assistance. To be in violation of P. L. 94-142, in most situations, also will mean a violation of Section 504, which in its finality can mean the withholding of all federal funds. This is particularly true in relation to the basic educational rights of children who have handicaps. Section 504 in concert with P. L. 94-142 will be the substance of implementation. How well that effort occurs will determine if there will be need for another revolution, and if so, the magnitude of its volume.

References

Abeson, A. Movement and momentum: Government and the education of handicapped children. Exceptional Children, 1972, 39, 63-66.

Abeson, A., Bolick, N., & Hass, J. *A primer on due process: Education decisions for handicapped children.* Reston VA: The Council For Exceptional Children, 1975.

Bolick, N. (Ed.). *Digest of state and federal laws: Education of handicapped children* (3rd ed.). Reston VA: The Council For Exceptional Children, 1974.

Brown v. Board of Education. 1954, 347 U.S. 483, 74 S.Ct. 686, 98L.Ed.873.

Bureau of Education for the Handicapped, US Department of Health, Education, and Welfare, Office of Education. *State plan amendment for fiscal year 1975 under part B, Education of the Handicapped Act, as amended by Section 614 of P. L. 93-380: Basic content areas required by the act and suggested guidelines and principles for inclusion under each area.* Washington DC: Author, 1974 (draft).

Children's Defense Fund. *Children out of school in America.* Cambridge MA: Author, 1974.

Dimond, P. The constitutional right to education: The quiet revolution. *The Hastings Law Journal,* 1973, *24,* 1087-1127.

Diana v. State Board of Education. Civil Action No.

C-70 37 R.F.P. (N.D. Cal., Jan. 7, 1970 and June 18, 1973).

Dunn, L. M. Special education for the mildly retarded—Is much of it justifiable? *Exceptional Children*, 1968, *35*, 5-22.

Larry P. v. Riles, Civil Action No. 6-71-2270 343F. Supp. 1036 (N.D. Cal., 1972).

Lori Case v. State of California, Civil No. 13127, Court of Appeals, Fourth Dist. Calif., filed Dec. 14, 1973.

Mercer, J. The ecology of mental retardation. In *The proceedings of the first annual spring conference on the institute for the study of mental retardation*, Ann Arbor, Michigan, 1970.

Mills v. Board of Education of the District of Columbia, 348F. Supp. 866 (D.D.C., 1972).

National Advisory Committee on the Education of the Handicapped. *The unfinished revolution: Education of the handicapped*. Washington DC: GPO, 1976.

National Education Association. Schools must face serious problems posed by integrating handicapped, NEA president says. (NEA Press Release). Washington DC: Author, October 10, 1975.

Pennsylvania Association for Retarded Children v. Commonwealth of Pennsylvania, F. Supp. 279 (E.D. Pa. 1972, Order, Injunction and Consent Agreement).

Public Law 93-112, *Vocational Rehabilitation Act of 1973*, Section 504, July 26, 1973.

Public Law 93-380, *Education Amendments of 1974*, August 21, 1974.

Public Law 94-142, *Education for All Handicapped Children Act*, November 29, 1975.

Reynolds, M. C. A framework for considering some issues in special education. *Exceptional Children*, 1962, *28*, 367-370.

Ross, S. L., Jr., DeYoung, H. G., and Cohen, J. S. Confrontation: Special education placement and the law. *Exceptional Children*, 1971, *38*, 5-12.

State of Illinois. *Rules and regulations to govern the administration and operation of special education*, Article X, 1974.

Tennessee Code Annotated, Sec. 1, 8A, 23, Chap. 839, 1972.

Trudeau, E., & Nye, R. *The provision of special educational services in nonpublic facilities*. Arlington VA: The Council For Exceptional Children, 1973.

US Congress, Senate, *Education for All Handicapped Children Act*, S.6., 94th Congress, 1st Session, June 2, 1975, Report No. 94-168.

Weintraub, F. Recent influences of the law regarding the identification and educational placement of children. *Focus on Exceptional Children* 1972, *4*, 1-10.

Weintraub, F. Understanding the individualized education program (IEP). *Amicus*, March 1977, 23-27.

Weintraub, F., & Abeson, A., New educational policies for the handicapped: The quiet revolution. *Phi Delta Kappan*, 1974, *55*, 528.

Definitions of Handicapping Conditions

Handicapped children are identified in the Education for All Handicapped Children Act (PL 94-142) as being: "mentally retarded, hard of hearing, deaf, speech-impaired, visually handicapped, seriously emotionally disturbed, orthopedically impaired or other health impaired." Also included are children "having specific learning disabilities who because of those impairments need special education and related services."

The following definitions can be located in Section 124a.4 of the proposed regulations published December 30, 1976 in the *Federal Register.*

The *mentally retarded* child possesses a "significantly subaverage general intellectual functioning" which exists "concurrently with deficits in adaptive behavior" and is manifested during the developmental period, adversely affecting the child's educational performance.

Seriously emotionally disturbed children are defined as exhibiting one or more of the following characteristics over a long period of time and to a marked degree: 1) an inability to learn which cannot be explained by intellectual, sensory, or health factors; 2) an inability to build or maintain satisfactory interpersonal relationships with peers and teachers; 3) inappropriate types of behavior or feelings under normal circumstances; 4) a general pervasive mood of unhappiness or depression; or 5) a tendency to develop physical symptoms or fears associated with personal or school problems.

The term includes children who are schizophrenic or autistic. Children who are socially maladjusted but not emotionally disturbed are not included in this category.

Other health impaired children are those with "limited strength, vitality or alertness due to chronic or acute health problems such as a heart condition, tuberculosis, rheumatic fever, nephritis, asthma, sickle cell anemia, hemophilia, epilepsey, lead poisoning, leukemia, or diabetes."

A *hard of hearing* child possesses a "permanent or fluctuating" hearing impairment which "adversely affects" his educational performance but "is not included under the definition of deaf."

A *deaf* child has a "hearing impairment which is so severe that the child's hearing is non-functional for the purposes of educational performance."

A *visually handicapped* child possesses an "impairment which, after correction, adversely affects a child's educational performance." This category includes both partially sighted and blind children.

An *orthopedically impaired* child possesses a severe orthopedic impairment which adversely affects his educational performance. The term includes "impairments caused by congenital anomaly, (e.g., clubfoot, absence of some member, etc.) impairments caused by disease (e.g., poliomyelitis, bone tuberculosis, etc.) and impairments from other causes (e.g., fractures or burns which cause contractures, amputation, cerebral palsy, etc.).

The *speech impaired* child has a "communication disorder, such as stuttering, impaired articulation, a language impairment, or a voice impairment" which adversely affects the educational performance.

From *Federal Register,* December 30, 1976. Reprinted by permission.

Public Law 94-142 and Section 504: What They Say about Rights and Protections

JOSEPH BALLARD

JEFFREY ZETTEL

JOSEPH BALLARD *is Assistant Director for Policy Implementation, and* JEFFREY ZETTEL *is a Specialist for Policy Implementation, Governmental Relations Unit, The Council for Exceptional Children.*

This is the second article in *Exceptional Children* during the current volume year that deals with Public Law (P. L.) 94-142, the Education for All Handicapped Children Act. The primary objective of this series is to provide the reader with a background as well as a substantial understanding of this monumental and most complex piece of federal legislation as it relates to the education of all handicapped children. The October issue of *Exceptional Children* contained the feature article "The End of the Quiet Revolution: The Education for All Handicapped Children Act of 1975."

The purpose of that article was to provide a historical perspective of state and federal litigation and legislation that both directly and indirectly influenced the conception of P. L. 94-142. What follows in this and subsequent articles will be an in-depth analysis of the specific language and principal intent of the law. For the sake of clarity, as well as brevity, the vehicle for the majority of the ensuing discussions will be in the form of a question and answer format. Finally, it should be noted that frequent reference will be made to Section 504 of the Vocational Rehabilitation Act of 1973 with the expectation that the parallels and similarities between the two laws in regard to their potential impact on the education of handicapped children will be apparent.*

Basic Thrust, Objectives, and Target Populations

What is P. L. 94-142?

P. L. 94-142, the Education for All Handicapped Children Act, is legislation passed by the United States Congress and signed into law by President Gerald R. Ford on November 29, 1975. The "94" indicates that this law was passed by the 94th Congress. The "142" indicates that this law was the 142nd law passed by that session of the Congress to be signed into law by the President.

**Editor's note: See A/E p. 2, article #1 for further discussion.*

What are the purposes of P. L. 94-142?

P. L. 94-142 can be said to have four major purposes:

- Guarantee the availability of special education programing to handicapped children and youth who require it.
- Assure fairness and appropriateness in decision making with regard to providing special education to handicapped children and youth.
- Establish clear management and auditing requirements and procedures regarding special education at all levels of government.
- Financially assist the efforts of state and local government through the use of federal funds (refer to Section 3 of the Act).

What is Section 504?

Section 504 is a basic civil rights provision with respect to terminating discrimination against America's handicapped citizens. Section 504 was enacted through the legislative vehicle P. L. 93-112, the Vocational Rehabilitation Act Amendments of 1973. Though Section 504 is brief in actual language, its implications are far reaching. The statute reads:

> No otherwise qualified handicapped individual in the United States shall, solely by reason of his handicap, be excluded from the participation in, be denied the benefits of, or be subjected to discrimination under any program or activity receiving Federal financial assistance.

To whom do P. L. 94-142 and Section 504 apply?

P. L. 94-142 applies to all handicapped children who require special education and related services, ages 3 to 21 inclusive. Section 504 applies to all handicapped Americans regardless of age. Section 504 therefore applies to all handicapped children ages 3 to 21 with respect to their public education both from the standpoint of the guarantee of an appropriate special education and from the standpoint of sheer regular program accessibility. Close coordination has thus been maintained between the provisions of P. L.

"Public Law 94-142 and Section 504: What They Say about Rights and Protections," by Joseph Ballard and Jeffrey Zettel, *Exceptional Children*, Vol. 44, No. 3, November 1977. Copyright 1977 The Council for Exceptional Children. Reprinted with permission of The Council for Exceptional Children.

94-142 and those of the Section 504 regulations (refer to Section 611 of P. L. 94-142 and background statement of the Section 504 regulation).

What is the relationship of P. L. 94-142 to the older federal Education of the Handicapped Act (EHA)?

P. L. 94-142 is a complete revision of only Part B of the Education of the Handicapped Act. Part B was formerly that portion of EHA addressing the basic state grant program. The other components of the Act (Parts A-E) remain substantially unchanged and continue in operation. Parenthetically, all programs under the aegis of the EHA, including the P. L. 94-142 revision of Part B, are administered through the Bureau of Education for the Handicapped under the US Office of Education.

Was there a forerunner to P. L. 94-142?

Many of the major provisions of P. L. 94-142, such as the guarantee of due process procedures and the assurance of education in the least restrictive environment, were required in an earlier federal law—P. L. 93-380, the Education Amendments of 1974 (enacted August 21, 1974). P. L. 94-142 was enacted approximately one year and three months later, on November 29, 1975.*

How are handicapped children defined for purposes of this Act?

Handicapped children are defined by the Act as children who are:

> mentally retarded, hard of hearing, deaf, orthopedically impaired, other health impaired, speech impaired, visually handicapped, seriously emotionally disturbed, or children with specific learning disabilities who by reason thereof require special education and related services.

This definition establishes a two pronged criteria for determining child eligibility under the Act. The first is whether the child actually has one or more of the disabilities listed in the above definition. The second is whether the child requires special education and related services. Not all children who have a disability require special education; many are able and should attend school without any program modification (refer to Section 4 of the Act).

If a child has one or more of the disabilities listed in the preceding definition and also requires special education and related services, how does P. L. 94-142 define special education?

Editor's note: See A/E p. 9, article #2 for further discussion.

Special education is defined in P. L. 94-142 as:

> specially designed instruction, at no cost to parents or guardians, to meet the unique needs of a handicapped child, including classroom instruction, instruction in physical education, home instruction, and instruction in hospitals and institutions.

The key phrase in the above definition of special education is "specially designed instruction . . . to meet the unique needs of a handicapped child." Reemphasized, special education, according to statutory definition, is defined as being "special" and involving only instruction that is designed and directed to meet the unique needs of a handicapped child. For many children therefore, special education will not be the totality of their education. Furthermore, this definition clearly implies that special education proceeds from the basic goals and expected outcomes of general education. Thus, intervention with a child does not occur because he or she is mentally retarded but because he or she has a unique educational need that requires specially designed instruction (refer to Section 4(a)(16) of the Act).

How are related services defined in P. L. 94-142?

Equally important to understand is the concept of related services that are defined in the Act as:

> transportation, and such developmental, corrective, and other supportive services (including speech pathology and audiology, psychological services, physical and occupational therapy, recreation, and medical and counseling services, except that such medical services shall be for diagnostic and evaluation purposes only) as may be required to assist a handicapped child to benefit from special education, and includes the early identification and assessment of handicapping conditions in children.

The key phrase here is "as required to assist the handicapped child to benefit from special education." This leads to a clear progression: a child is handicapped because he or she requires special education and related services; special education is the specially designed instruction to meet the child's unique needs; and related services are those additional services necessary in order for the child to benefit from special educational instruction (refer to Section 4(a)(17) of the Act).

Rights and Protections

A Free Appropriate Education

What is the fundamental requirement of P. L. 94-142, from which all other requirements of this Act stem?

P. L. 94-142 requires that every state and its localities, if they are to continue to receive funds under this Act, must make available a free appropriate public education for all handicapped children aged 3 to 18 by the beginning of the school year (September 1) in 1978 and further orders the availability of such education to all children aged 3 to 21 by September 1, 1980 (refer to Section 3(c) of the Act).

What about preschool and young adults under P. L. 94-142?

For children in the 3 to 5 and 18 to 21 age ranges, however, this mandate does not apply if such a requirement is inconsistent with state law or practice or any court decree. Refer to regulations for further expatiation of this provision (refer to Section 612 (2)(B) of the Act).

What does Section 504 say regarding the right to an education?

Section 504 makes essentially the same requirement. However, the 504 regulation says "shall provide." P. L. 94-142 says "a free appropriate public education *will be available*."

The 504 regulation does not refer to specific age groups per se. Instead, it refers to "public elementary and secondary education," and, therefore, the traditional school age population. With respect to that school age population, the 504 regulation accedes to the September 1, 1978, date of P. L. 94-142 as the final and absolute deadline for the provision of a free appropriate public education. However, the Section 504 regulation also precedes that requirement with the phrase "*at the earliest practicable time* but in no event later than September 1, 1978." (Refer to #84.33(d) of the 504 regulation.)

What is required with respect to preschool and young adult programs under Section 504?

The 504 regulation appears simply to say that preschool and adult education programs will not discriminate on the basis of handicap, and further that such program accessibility is to take effect immediately. On the other hand, P. L. 94-142, as previously noted, explicitly states that there shall be available a free appropriate public education for children ages 3 through 5 and youth ages 18 through 21 unless such requirement is inconsistent with state law or practice or the order of any court. Again, P. L. 94-142 does not require such availability until September 1, 1978 (refer to #84.38 of the 504 regulation).

For further information, the reader is referred to the following resources available from The Council for Exceptional Children:

- *Public Policy and the Education of Exceptional Children* edited by Frederick J. Weintraub, Alan R. Abeson, Joseph Ballard, and Martin L. LaVor, 1976, 288 pp., Stock No. 123, $13.95.
- *P. L. 94-142, The Education for All Handicapped Children Act of 1975* by Joseph Ballard, Jean N. Nazzaro, and Frederick J. Weintraub, (multimedia package), 1976, Stock No. 136, $50.00.
- *Special Education Administrative Policy Manual* by Scottie Torres, 1977, 175 pp., Stock No. 164, $27.50.

Since Section 504 and P. L. 94-142 are making, in essence, the same fundamental requirement of a free, appropriate public education, are federal monies authorized under Section 504 as they are under P. L. 94-142?

No. Section 504 is a civil rights statute, like Title VI of the Civil Rights Act of 1965 (race) and Title IX of the Education Amendments of 1972 (sex).

Must there be compliance with the fundamental requirement of P. L. 94-142 (as reiterated in Section 504 regulations) if P. L. 94-142 is not "fully funded"?

It is most important to note that compliance with this baseline guarantee of the availability of a free, appropriate public education is in no way dependent upon whether this Act receives appropriations at the top authorized ceilings, or in other words, is "fully funded." If a state accepts money under this Act, regardless of the amount of actual appropriations, it must comply with the aforementioned stipulation.

What does "free" education, as required in both P. L. 94-142 and Section 504, mean?

"Free" means the provision of education and related services at no cost to the handicapped person or to his or her parents or guardian, except for those largely incidental fees that are imposed on nonhandicapped persons or their parents or guardian (refer to #84.33(c)(1) of the 504 regulation).

What if a public placement is made in a public or private residential program?

If both the school and parents jointly agree that the most appropriate educational placement for the child is in a public or private residential facility, then such a program placement, including nonmedical care as well as room and board, shall be provided at no cost to the person or his or her parents or guardian (refer to #84.33(c)(3) of the 504 regulation).

Does "free" mean that no private funds can be used?

No. Private funds are not prohibited. To reiterate: there must be no cost to the handicapped person or to his or her parents or guardian.

What does "appropriate" education mean?

"Appropriate" is not defined as such, but rather receives its definition for each child through the mechanism of the written individualized education program (IEP) as required by P. L. 94-142. Therefore, what is agreed to by all parties becomes in fact the "appropriate" educational program for the particular child.

Individualized Education Programs

What are the basic concepts of the IEP?

The term *individualized education program* itself conveys important concepts that need to be specified. First, *individualized* means that the IEP must be addressed to the educational needs of a single child rather than a class or group of children. Second, *education* means that the IEP is limited to those elements of the child's education that are more specifically special education and related services as defined by the Act. Third, *program* means that the IEP is a statement of what will actually be provided to the child, as distinct from a plan that provides guidelines from which a program must subsequently be developed.

What are the basic components of an IEP?

The Act contains a specific definition describing the components of an IEP as:

> a written statement for each handicapped child developed in any meeting by a representative of the local education agency or an intermediate educational unit who shall be qualified to provide, or supervise the provision of, specially designed instruction to meet the unique needs of handicapped children, the teacher, the parents or guardian of such child, and whenever appropriate, such child, which statement shall include (A) a statement of the present levels of educational performance of such child, (B) a statement of annual goals, including short-term instructional objectives, (C) a statement of the specific educational anticipated duration of such services, and appropriate objective criteria and evaluation procedures and schedules for determining, on at least an annual basis, whether instructional objectives are being achieved.

(Refer to Section 4(a)(19) of the Act.)

May others be involved in the development of an IEP?

Good practice suggests that others frequently be involved. However, the law only requires four persons be involved (i.e., the parents or guardians, the teacher or teachers of the child, a representative of the local educational agency or intermediate unit who is qualified to provide or supervise the provision of special education, and whenever appropriate, the child). If a related service person will be providing services, then it seems to make sense that they be as involved as the teacher. Also, good practice indicates that parents often want to bring an additional person familiar with the child to the meeting.

Who must be provided an IEP?

Each state and local educational agency shall insure that an IEP is provided for each handicapped child who is receiving or will receive special education, regardless of what institution or agency provides or will provide special education to the child: (a) The state educational agency shall insure that each local educational agency establishes and implements an IEP for each handicapped child; (b) The state educational agency shall require each public agency which provides special education or related services to a handicapped child to establish policies and procedures for developing, implementing, reviewing, maintaining, and evaluating an IEP for that child.

What must local and intermediate education agencies do regarding IEP's?

- Each local educational agency shall develop or revise, whichever is appropriate, an IEP for every handicapped child at the beginning of the school year and review and if appropriate revise its provisions periodically but not less than annually.
- Each local educational agency is responsible for initiating and conducting meetings for developing, reviewing, and revising a child's IEP.
- For a handicapped child who is receiving

special education, a meeting must be held early enough so that the IEP is developed (or revised, as appropriate) by the beginning of the next school year.

- For a handicapped child who is not receiving special education, a meeting must be held within 30 days of a determination that the child is handicapped, or that the child will receive special education.

(Refer to Section 614(a)(5) of the Act.)

Do the IEP requirements apply to children in private schools and facilities?

Yes. The state educational agency shall insure that an IEP is developed, maintained, and evaluated for each child placed in a private school by the state educational agency or a local educational agency. The agency that places or refers a child shall insure that provision is made for a representative from the private school (which may be the child's teacher) to participate in each meeting. If the private school representative cannot attend a meeting, the agency shall use other methods to insure participation by the private school, including individual or conference telephone calls (refer to Section 613(a)(4)(B) of the Act).

Is the IEP an instructional plan?

No. The IEP is a management tool that is designed to assure that, when a child requires special education, the special education designed for that child is appropriate to his or her special learning needs and that the special education designed is actually delivered and monitored. An instructional plan reflects good educational practice by outlining the specifics necessary to effectively intervene in instruction. Documenting instructional plans is not mandated as part of the IEP requirements.

What procedures should education agencies follow to involve parents in the development of their child's IEP?

- Each local educational agency shall take steps to insure that one or both of the parents of the handicapped child are present at each meeting or are afforded the opportunity to participate, including scheduling the meeting at a mutually agreed on time and place.
- If neither parent can attend, the local educational agency shall use other methods to insure parent participation, including individual or conference telephone calls.
- A meeting may be conducted without a parent in attendance if the local educational agency is unable to convince the parents that they should attend. In this case the local educational agency must have a record of its attempts to arrange a mutually agreed on time and place such as: (a) Detailed records of telephone calls made or attempted and the results of those calls, (b) copies of correspondence sent to the parents and any responses received, and (c) detailed records of visits made to the parent's home or place of employment and the results of those visits.
- The local educational agency shall take whatever action is necessary to insure that the parent understands the proceedings at a meeting, including arranging for an interpreter for parents who are deaf or whose native language is other than English.

When must handicapped children be guaranteed the IEP?

- For handicapped children counted under the fiscal funding formula of P. L. 94-142, not later than the beginning of school year 1977-1978.
- For all handicapped children in each state, regardless of the delivering agency, not later than the beginning of school year 1978-1979.

What does Section 504 say with respect to the IEP?

As just discussed, P. L. 94-142 requires the development and maintenance of individualized written education programs for all children. The 504 regulation cites the IEP as "one means" of meeting the standard of a free appropriate public education (refer to #84.33(b)(2) of the 504 regulation).

For further information regarding individualized education programs, the reader is referred to the following resources:

- *A Primer on Individualized Education Programs for Handicapped Children* by Scottie Torres, 1977, 60 pp. Available from the Foundation for Exceptional Children, 1920 Association Dr., Reston VA 22091.
- "Teacher Issues Regarding Individualized Education Programs" by Scottie Torres and Josephine Hays (forthcoming in the January 1978 issue of *Exceptional Children*).

Least Restrictive Educational Environment

P. L. 94-142 requires that handicapped children receive a free appropriate public education in the least restrictive educational environment. What does this mean?

It is critical to note what this provision *is not:*

- It is not a provision for mainstreaming. In fact, the word is never used.
- It does not mandate that all handicapped children will be educated in the regular classroom.
- It does not abolish any particular educational environment, for instance, educational programing in a residential setting.

It is equally critical to note what this provision *does* mandate:

- Education with nonhandicapped children will be the governing objective "to the maximum extent appropriate."
- The IEP will be the management tool toward achievement of the maximum least restrictive environment and therefore shall be applied within the framework of meeting the "unique needs" of each child.
- The IEP document(s) must clearly "show cause" if and when one moves from least restrictive to more restrictive. The statute states that the following component must be included in the written statement accompanying the IEP "and the extent to which such child will be able to participate in regular educational programs."

(Refer to Section 612(5)(B) of the Act.)

Correspondingly, what does the Section 504 regulation say with respect to least restrictive educational environment?

The language of the 504 regulation is, in most important respects, nearly identical to the least restrictive statute in P. L. 94-142. There remains one notable distinction, however. The 504 regulation would seem to consider the "nearest placement to home" as an additional determinant of instructional placement in the least restrictive environment (refer to #84.34(a) of the 504 regulation).

Procedural Safeguards

Under P. L. 94-142, what happens if there is a failure to agree with respect to what constitutes an appropriate education for a particular child?

States must guarantee procedural safeguard mechanisms for children and their parents or guardians. Those provisions of previously existing law (P. L. 93-380, the Education Amendments of 1974) toward the guarantee of due process rights are further refined in P. L. 94-142, and their scope is substantially enlarged.

Basically, the state education agency must guarantee the maintenance of full due process procedures for all handicapped children within the state and their parents or guardian with respect to all matters of identification, evaluation, and educational placement whether it be the initiation or change of such placement, or the refusal to initiate or change. Interested individuals are strongly urged to read Section 615 of the Act ("Procedural Safeguards") in its entirety.

It should be observed that the P. L. 94-142 refinements take effect in the first year under the new formula, that is, fiscal 1978 (school year 1977-1978). In the meantime, those basic features of due process as authorized in the prior Act (P. L. 93-380) must be maintained by the states.

It should be further noted that, when the parents or guardian of a child are not known, are unavailable, or when the child is a legal ward of the state, the state education agency, local education agency, or intermediate education agency (as appropriate) must assign an individual to act as a *surrogate* for the child in all due process proceedings. Moreover, such assigned individual may not be an employee of the state educational agency, local educational agency, or intermediate educational unit *involved in* the education or care of the particular child (refer to Section 615 of the Act).

Does the Section 504 regulation also require the maintenance of a procedural safeguards mechanism?

Yes. However, though most of the major principles of due process embodied in P. L. 94-142 are clearly present in the 504 regulation, *all* of the stipulations of P. L. 94-142 are treated only as "one means" of due process compliance under Section 504 (refer to #84.36 of the 504 regulation).

What does P. L. 94-142 say with respect to assessment of children?

P. L. 94-142 carries a provision that seeks to guarantee against assessment with respect to the question of a handicapping condition when such assessment procedures are racially or culturally discriminatory. The statute does not provide a comprehensive procedure of remedy with respect to potential discrimination but does make two clear and important stipulations in the direction of remedy:

- "Such materials and procedures shall be

provided in the child's native language or mode of communication."

- "No single procedure shall be the sole criterion for determining an appropriate educational program for a child."

The provision, in effect, orders that assessment procedures be multi-factored, multi-sourced, and carried out by qualified personnel. The regulations governing this provision should therefore be carefully reviewed (refer to Section 612 (5)(C) of the Act).

What does the Section 504 regulation say with respect to the assessment of children?

The objectives of Section 504 and P. L. 94-142 are identical on this matter, and the regulatory language for both statutes are also identical (refer to #84.35 of the 504 regulation).

What does P. L. 94-142 say with respect to the confidentiality of data and information?

P. L. 94-142 contains a provision that addresses the question of abuses and potential abuses in school system record keeping with respect to handicapped children and their parents. P. L. 94-142, as did the prior P. L. 93-380, simply orders a remedy and does not go beyond. The governing statutes for this provision are contained in the larger "Family Educational Rights and Privacy Act" (often referred to as the "Buckley Amendments" after the author, US Senator James Buckley of New York). That measure sets forth both the access rights and privacy rights with respect to personal school records for all of the nation's children and youth, and their parents.

Thus, readers should study the Act itself (contained in P. L. 93-380), the accompanying regulations for the "Buckley Amendments," and the modest addendums to those provisions contained in the regulations for P. L. 94-142 (refer to Section 617 (c) and Section 612 (2) (D) of the Act).

What then, in summary, are the rights and protections of P. L. 94-142 (which, for the most part, are also affirmed in Section 504) that must be guaranteed?

P. L. 94-142 makes a number of critical stipulations that must be adhered to by *both* the state and its local and intermediate educational agencies:

- Assurance of the availability of a free, appropriate public education for all handicapped children, such guarantee of availability no later than certain specified dates.
- Assurance of the maintenance of an individualized education program for all handicapped children.
- A guarantee of complete due procedural safeguards.
- The assurance of regular parent or guardian consultation.
- Assurance of special education being provided to all handicapped children in the "least restrictive" environment.
- Assurance of nondiscriminatory testing and evaluation.
- A guarantee of policies and procedures to protect the confidentiality of data and information.
- Assurance of an effective policy guaranteeing the right of all handicapped children to a free, appropriate public education *at no cost* to parents or guardian.
- Assurance of a surrogate to act for any child when parents or guardians are either unknown or unavailable or when such child is a legal ward of the state.

It is most important to observe that an official, written document containing all of these assurances is now required (in the form of an application) of *every* school district receiving its federal entitlement under P. L. 94-142. Correspondingly, such a public document also exists at the state level in the form of the annual state plan, which must be submitted to the US Commissioner.

For further information regarding procedural safeguards, the reader is referred to the following resources available from The Council for Exceptional Children:

- *A Primer on Due Process: Education Decision for Handicapped Children* by Alan R. Abeson, Nancy Bolick, and Jayne Hass, 1975, 72 pp., Stock No. 104, $4.95.
- *Procedural Safeguards P. L. 94-142—A Guide for Schools and Parents*, produced by The Council for Exceptional Children in conjunction with the Children's Television Workshop, (multimedia package), 1977, Stock No. 167, $90.00.

10 steps to special ed

happily, a new script has been written for identifying and placing handicapped children thanks to Public Law 94-142

Tom Lovitt

The author is with the Child development and Mental Retardation Center, Experimental Education Unit, University of Washington, Seattle.

It's a typical morning at the beginning of the school year not so very long ago. A third grade teacher is correcting papers while sipping coffee in the teachers' lounge. Enter the resident psychologist. They exchange pleasantries. They talk about the price of groceries, the pennant race, the impending auto workers' strike. Finally, their conversation drifts to school-related topics: the new principal, the AFT position on class size, and the president of the school board.

The psychologist then asks the teacher how she likes her new group of youngsters. She informs him it's one of her finest classes, but she's concerned about one boy who just moved from a neighboring state. She goes on to describe him. He's constantly out of his seat, talks incessantly, and his reading ability is at the first grade level.

The psychologist frowns and shakes his head, thus indicating a mutual concern. He asks the teacher if she would like him to test the child. She eagerly accepts the offer and they agree that the boy will be interviewed at 10:00 the next morning.

On schedule, the psychologist comes for the boy and ushers him into his chamber. After he talks with the child enough to establish rapport, he proceeds with the assessment. First, he administers the Wide Range Achievement Test (WRAT) and then gives the Wechsler Intelligence Scale for Children (WISC). Following the testing, which takes about 60 minutes, he thanks the boy and escorts him back to his classroom.

The Results. That afternoon he scores the tests and learns that the boy's subtest scores on the WRAT are as follows: 2.2 in spelling, 1.2 in reading, and 2.4 in arithmetic. As for the WISC, his performance and verbal scores are 95 and 89. Although the psychologist didn't observe any out-of-seat behavior or excessive talking during the testing situation, he confirms the teacher's observation that the pupil reads at a first grade level.

The following day he speaks with the teacher of the learning disabilities class and finds out there's room for three more youngsters. After he describes the boy's characteristics—that he's restless, noisy and unable to read—she agrees to work with him. Immediately following that conversation the psychologist informs the third grade teacher that the child will be moved.

That evening he phones the boy's parents and tells them their son is having problems in his regular grade, and that he has been tested. He then asks if they would agree to the child being placed in a special class, one that's smaller and more suited to his needs. The parents

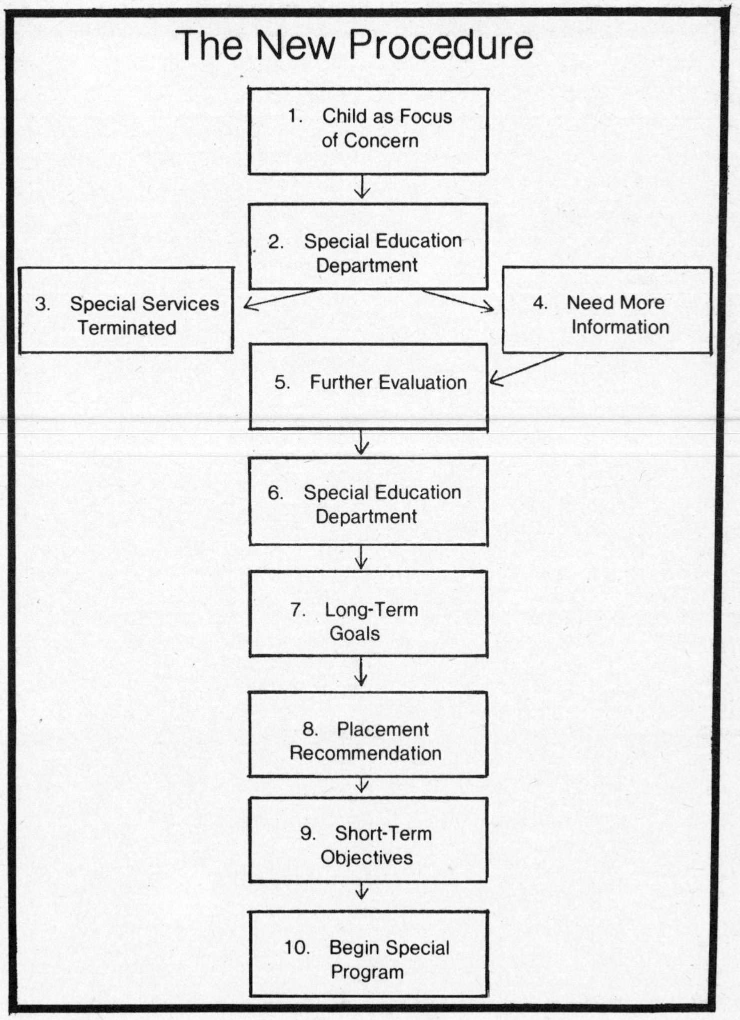

Reprinted with permission of the publisher Allen Raymond, Inc., Darien, Conn. 06820. From the October 1977 issue of *Early Years.*

consent and the boy is transferred to the special room the next day.

Things Are Different. That was the scenario just a few years ago. That informal process landed scores of children in special education. Indeed, many were sent from regular to special education classes on the basis of far less information and consultation. Hundreds of youngsters were transferred to special classes because of a single test score and a few casual observations. Furthermore, the parents of those children were often ill-informed about which tests and observational procedures were used.

Not so today. The process is now very sophisticated from the time a child is defined as potentially handicapped, throughout the many steps which follow before special assistance is either recommended or not. In order to comply with the many features of 94-142—writing IEP's, placing children in least restrictive environments—most states have written detailed flow charts which must be followed from identification to placement.

Although these procedural steps vary from one state to another and from one district to another, there are many similarities. In an effort to explain the process from identification to placement, I'll describe a typical flow chart:

Ten Steps. First of all, a child may become a focus of concern (suspected of being handicapped) when he or she is brought to the attention of the school district by a teacher, parent, or other interested person *(step 1)*. Following, the special education department is informed of this concern *(step 2)*. A representative of the school district records the date of the referral, the reason, and who initiated the referral. The representative then notifies the child's parents in writing.

Next, school personnel collect and review existing information on the referred child and decide whether or not to assess him further. If they conclude that additional assessment and special education placement are not warranted, the parents are notified of those decisions *(step 3)*. They are also given the reason for not recommending special assistance for their youngster, they are told who made that decision, and informed they might appeal the decision.

In the event that the school personnel decided to obtain more information, permission to do so is requested of the parents *(step 4)*. They are told the reasons for requesting further data and whose decision it was to gather that information. They are also told about the steps which will be followed to acquire the information and when the assessment should be completed.

If the parents refuse permission for assessing their youngster, that decision is forwarded to a representative of the superintendent of schools. If they grant permission to continue the process, the school personnel collect additional data *(step 5)*.

According to 94-142, no single test or evaluative procedure may be used as the sole criterion for determining special services. Furthermore, the law states that the assessment materials and procedures must not discriminate children on the basis of culture or race. Youngsters may be assessed in several areas, such as scholastic, physical, adjustment, etc. Depending upon the nature and extent of the handicapping condition, consultants such as physicians, physical therapists, and occupational therapists might be engaged to conduct certain evaluations.

When all the assessment data have been accumulated, a summary is written and signed by a representative of the school. It is then sent to the special education department *(step 6)*. That information is available for review by authorized individuals, including the child's parents.

Following the writing of a summary, long-term educational goals must be written *(step 7)*. As indicated in last month's issue, the goals should cover a one-year period and should clearly specify the desired behaviors.

Once the goals are written, a type of placement must be recommended. That location must be in accord with the educational goals and must be, for the particular child, the least restrictive alternative *(step 8)*. Those placement options were discussed in the September issue. Once again, the parents may accept or reject the decision.

If the parents disagree with the decision, further meetings are held. If they consent, short-term objectives are written *(step 9)*, the features of which were outlined in last month's issue. After the objectives are developed, a school representative must indicate, in writing, which special services will be provided, by whom, and where the instructions will take place. The anticipated time these special services will be offered is also specified. Finally, the child may receive special assistance *(step 10)*.

A New Script. The process just described for identifying and placing handicapped children is quite different from the procedures used earlier. But because of the demands of 94-142, among them the organization of procedural steps such as those I presented, the likelihood is increased that more children will be appropriately placed. Furthermore, this process is certainly more democratic than previous systems in that several individuals are involved in most procedural steps. And it is certainly more considerate, since parents are consulted before each major programming decision is made.

Gone is the casual, often haphazard, process that whisked many children out of their regular classrooms and deposited them in special education classes. Happily, the script has been rewritten.

the who, where and what of IEP's

Tom Lovitt

The author is with the Child Development and Mental Retardation Center, Experimental Education Unit, University of Washington, Seattle.

The enactment of Public Law 94-142 has stimulated considerable activity. Books have been written, and workshops organized, in attempts to explain this legislation. The activity is not without cause, for the new law—also known as The Education for All Handicapped Children Act—is indeed complex.

As welcome as the legislation may be, many teachers and school administrators are deeply concerned about implementing the act. They are, for example, uneasy about setting up procedures which guarantee the many rights of parents and anxious about locating tests which are nondiscriminatory. However, the provision which has probably caused the most apprehension is the one which calls for the maintenance of an Individualized Education Program (IEP) for each handicapped child.

But why be apprehensive? Haven't we all known for years that individualized teaching was the way to go? Haven't we been told that children are unique and that, therefore, programs should be "fitted to their needs" so they can perform "at their own pace"? Such bromides about individualized education have been the bases for countless books and workshops, and have been bandied about the colleges of education for generations. So what's the problem?

Well, part of the problem is that although there's been a lot of talk about individualized instruction, few teachers have been able to bring it off. Because of the numbers of children in their classes, or the lack of varied materials, or whatever reason, most teachers have not programmed individually for their youngsters.

To complicate matters, individualization IEP-style goes far beyond what most teachers think of as constituting individualized instruction. It's not simply assigning children to one group or another for reading or math instruction. Nor is it just anticipating that certain children will accomplish a great deal; others, not as much; and still others, nothing at all.

Under the IEP concept of individualized instruction teachers (and others who design programs for children) must explain in writing the many details of their educational plans. Among other things, they must describe what will be taught and by whom, where instruction will take place and for how long. Furthermore, those plans must be measurable and they must be designed by a group of individuals, many of whom are specialists.

Little wonder then that so much anxiety and confusion exits over IEP's. Not only have most of us managed to avoid specifying individual objectives, but when we did state goals, they defied measurement. What's more, when we wrote down those few nebulous aims, they were invariably our own creations; rarely did we seek the assistance of other professionals or parents.

The intent of this series of workshop articles is to explain the features of IEP's to the extent that teachers and others can develop and implement them in their classrooms. In this first article we'll take a look at some of the who's, where's and what's of IEP's. In subsequent articles, we'll outline the referral process and develop a sample IEP.

Who and Where. In an effort to guarantee that various approaches will be used to assess handicapped youngsters, one of the provisions of 94-142 is that children will be evaluated by a Child Study Team (CST). Depending on the type and extent of the handicap, a CST would include some of the following professionals: regular and special ed teachers, vision and hearing specialists, school psychologist, communication disorder specialist, physician and social worker.

Following an evaluation, the CST holds a planning conference. The purposes of this meeting are to develop an appropriate IEP and determine where the child should be educated. Each school must insure that the following participants are included in the planning conference: a representative of the local educational agency, other than the child's teacher; the child's teacher, or teachers, who have a direct responsibility for implementing the program; the child's parent(s); the child, when appropriate; and other individuals at the discretion of the parent or the school district.

Based on the evaluation of the CST and the recommendation of the planning committee, a placement for the child is sug-

Reprinted with permission of the publisher Allen Raymond, Inc. Darien, Conn. 06820. From the September 1977-1978 issue of *Early Years*.

gested. According to 94-142, the child must be assigned to a facility that is "least restrictive" and the rationale for such a placement must be explained. The following are some of the placement options, ranging from least to most restrictive:

- Regular class with supportive services. The child is assigned to a regular classroom. Special ed and/or other personnel assist the teacher with advice about methods or materials. The child does not receive direct instruction from the support personnel.
- Regular class with support instruction. The child is assigned to a regular classroom and receives some direct instruction in the classroom from a special ed teacher or other specialist.
- Regular class with resource-room instruction. The child is assigned to a regular classroom, but receives some instruction in another location from a specialist.
- Separate class, part-time, regular school. The child is assigned primarily to a special ed classroom, but receives some instruction in a regular classroom. This particular placement is possible only when the school has both kinds of classroom.
- Separate class, full-time, regular school. The child is not integrated in a regular class, but spends full-time in a special ed classroom. Here, too, the school must have both regular and special ed classrooms.
- Special class, part-time, separate facility. The child is assigned to a special class in a separate school on a part-time basis. All of the children in this facility are handicapped. The child receives some instruction, however, in a facility which has classes for regular and special students.
- Special class, full-time, separate facility. The child receives all of his education in a school for special children.
- Homebound. The child receives an educational program in the home from special ed teachers or other specialists.

The wide range of placement options provided by P.L. 94-142 should be reassuring to regular teachers. As you can see, handicapped children are not going to be arbitrarily assigned to regular classrooms, regardless of the nature or extent of their handicaps. However, there's another reason for listing the various placement options here: The conditions of the child's placement figure prominently in the writing of the IEP.

What Is an IEP? In order to develop an appropriate IEP, the CST and others who participated in the planning conference must respond in writing to the following nine components which relate to the handicapped child's program:

1. Statement of current educational level. A report must be written which describes present levels of educational performance. This includes information on the child's academic achievement, social adaptation, prevocational and vocational skills, psychomotor skills and self-help skills.

2. Statement of goals. Written descriptions must be included of the goals to be achieved by the end of the school year under the child's IEP. These goals should be written in terms of the student and should specify clearly the desired behavior. For example, an appropriate goal would be: "The student will increase his reading comprehension skills."

3. Statement of objectives. Written statements must be provided of the short term instructional objectives; in other words, the measurable intermediate steps between the present level of educational performance and the annual goals. The objectives should include the following conditions: descriptive, conditional, evaluative and temporal. An example of an objective might be: "The student will be able to answer, in writing, the comprehension questions which follow stories in *Reading for Concepts*, Book B, with at least an 80 percent accuracy by the end of the quarter."

4. Statement of services. This statement describes specifically the educational services needed by the child. These must be determined without regard to the availability of those services. The statement must include a description of: (a) all special education and related services that are needed to meet the unique needs of the child, including the type of physical education program in which the child will participate; (b) any special instructional media and materials that are needed.

5. Dates of services. Statements must be included about the dates special services will begin and the length of time they'll be in effect. Beginning and ending dates will be entered for each service the child will receive. If he is to be provided assistance from a special ed teacher, a regular teacher and a communication disorders specialist, three sets of dates must be entered in the IEP.

6. Time in regular programs. Information must be furnished which details the extent to which a child will participate in regular education programs. Some children will be integrated in regular classes for only a few activities; for example, music, art and physical education.

7. Justification of placement. A written statement must accompany the IEP which supports the type of educational placement recommended for the child. School personnel, of course, must make every effort to educate handicapped youngsters with children who are not handicapped. Handicapped children should be placed in special classes, separate schools, or otherwise removed from their normal peers only when the nature or severity of the handicap is such that education in regular classes with the use of special aids and services cannot be achieved satisfactorily.

8. Responsible individuals. A list must be furnished of the names of individuals who are responsible for implementing the IEP. For some children, this list will contain only one or two names. For other children, several professionals will be included: special and regular teachers, communication disorders specialist, vision specialist and so on.

9. Evaluation plan. The IEP must include statements about the objective criteria, evaluation procedures and schedules for determining whether the short term instructional objectives are being achieved. The objectives must be evaluated at least once a year. For example, if the objective was to increase a child's ability to comprehend, he might be required to answer in writing, each day, the questions following a story from a specific book. His answers would then be checked against a key. This information, along with other facts provided earlier in our example of an objective, would inform the reader about the criteria, procedures and schedule for evaluating the attainment of objectives.

Hopefully, this brief description of the who, where and what of IEP's will help ease your apprehensions over this provision of P.L. 94-142. Writing an acceptable IEP isn't the easiest thing you've ever done, of course, but at the same time there's nothing in an IEP that need scare any teacher.

In a subsequent issue, we will detail the steps which are followed before a child receives special instruction—from the time he becomes a focus of concern to the implementation of an IEP. We'll also show how an IEP might be developed by providing pertinent data on a special child and using that information to design a plan.

The Educational Least Restrictive Alternative

Alan Abeson

Alan Abeson is associate director of state and local governmental relations with the Council for Exceptional Children.

Handicapped American Children and adults view the 1970's as a decade of appropriate decision making. Recognition of the human and civil rights of this minority group has occurred through official policy declaration by all branches and at all levels of government. And at least as important has been the beginning of an awareness, understanding and activism by the general public in translating these rights into reality.

The breadth of life activities in which progress has been made, at least in policy, is extensive. Among these are education, marriage, voting, transportation, employment, housing, and, in situations where the handicapped necessarily reside in public residential facilities, the right to treatment. Governing the participation of handicapped persons in these and other activities are two well established legal principles—due process of law and the least restrictive alternative.

It is the purpose of due process to insure that decisions about the provision, restriction or deprivation of publicly sponsored participatory opportunities for handicapped persons are made in a fair and rational manner. Adherence to due process procedures means essentially that individuals will be advised in advance about proposed decisions and the accompanying justifications, will be informed as to steps required for accepting or rejecting such decisions, will be provided an opportunity for review of decisions at a due process hearing, and if necessary judical review.

The second principle and the subject of this paper is the least restrictive alternative. While due process governs the manner in which decisions will be made, the least restrictive principle mandates the placement progression that must be considered in the provision of programs to individual handicapped persons. While recognition of this principle as generally applied to the handicapped is rather recent, it is also rather specific when considered in relation to the right of all handicapped children to a free appropriate public education.

The Policy Mandates

Initially, offical recognition of the principle of least restrictive alternative in education occurred in the consent decree in *PARC v. Commonwealth of Pennsylvania*[1] and the order in *Mills v. District of Columbia.*[2] Many subsequent judicial actions, as well as state law and regulation, contained the same requirement.

Perhaps the capstone in official articulation of the principle in education came from the United States Congress as a major requirement of Public Law 94-142, the Education for All Handicapped Children Act of 1975.[3] Section 612(5)(B) mandates that in order for states to be eligible for participation in the benefits of the Act, they must establish "procedures to assure that to the maximum extent appropriate, handicapped children, including children in public or private institutions or other care facilities, are educated with children who are not handicapped, and that special classes, separate schooling, or other removal of handicapped children from the regular educational environment occurs only when the nature or severity of the handicap is such that education in regular classes with the use of supplementary aids and services cannot be achieved satisfactorily. . . ."

Further official support for this requirement came on April 28, 1977, when Secretary Joseph Califano of the United States Department of Health, Education, and Welfare, signed regulations into force for implementation of Section 504 of the Vocational Rehabilitation Act of 1973,[4] which prohibits discrimination against the handicapped ". . . in any program or activity receiving Federal financial assistance." Contained within the portion of the regulation dealing with preschool, elementary and secondary education is the requirement that recipients of Federal funds". . .shall educate, or shall provide for the education of, each qualified handicapped person in its jurisdiction with persons who are not handicapped to the maximum extent appropriate to the needs of the handicapped person. A recipient shall place a handicapped person in the regular educational environment operated by the recipient that the education of the person in the regular environment with the use of supplementary aids and services cannot be achieved satisfactorily."[5]

Least Restictive Alternative and Mainstreaming

Application of these policy directives to public education systems has often been misinterpreted. Frequently, the least restrictive alternative has been described as mainstreaming, which has further been described to mean a multitude of program principles. While the least restrictive alternative principle applies to *all* handicapped children, mainstreaming is usually limited to the mildly handicapped—the educable mentally retarded, the mildly emotionally disturbed and the learning disabled. Thus, children possessing other handicaps but who could participate in some activities with non-handicapped children are denied such opportunities because of this limiting definition of mainstreaming. Least restrictive alternative extends the mainstreaming concept to all handicapped children, regardless of their label and presumed severity.

Another misinterpretation of mainstreaming is that all handicapped children will be placed in programs with non-handicapped children for their entire school career. At the same time, it is wrongly alleged that special education programs as they exist today will be totally eliminated, and that in the past all handicapped children have been inappropriately placed in special education programs. The final inappropriate concept applied to this line of thinking is to exaggerate the severity of the handicaps of the children who will be entering the "regular program." For example, Albert Shanker, President of the American Federation of Teachers, in a column about PL 94-142 in the *New York Times,*[6] included in a list of "the handicaps we are talking about. . .hydrocephalic children who were born with holes in their hearts who turn blue periodically and have water on the brain and tubes in their heads which drain off the excess water."

This form of misinterpretation begins with the erroneous assumption/belief that all handicapped children are the same and possess the same educational needs; therefore, all children should be in either special or regular education. It assumes a sameness which is not common to any group of humans for any purpose. For instance, it suggests that if there are two children who are described as, for example, emotionally disturbed, then the educational program that both need would be precisely the same.

First and foremost in correcting this set of misassumptions is the understanding that each handicapped child, like every other child is unique. This uniqueness, again, as with all children, exists in school ability, personality, physical prowess and motivation. Consequently, to assume that common decisions can be made about the educational placement of all handicapped children in any educational setting is simply incorrect. What must be recognized and is at the heart of applying the least restrictive alternative to education, is that different children have different educational strengths and weaknesses which dictate the need for different education programs. Ultimately, these differences must for educational purposes be determined individually, child by child. It is from such evaluations that individual programs can be designed that are appropriate for each child.

A key element in the program design sequence is the determination of the educational placement in which the appropriate program for each child can be provided. Thus, some handicapped children will, in order to receive an appropriate education, need a program in a special class setting. Others will need a combination of a part time special class/regular class program. And still others will require other settings.

Providing more or less intensity in special education programming for handicapped children through the use of various special education placement alternatives is not new. Many years ago "integration" as an educational objective was applied to the mentally retarded in terms of reducing the time spent in special classes by integration into selected elements of the regular education program. An early and significant description of the range of program placements available for handicapped children was called the "cascade system."[7] The "cascade" contained nine educational placement alternatives beginning with a regular classroom in a regular school, which, as the least restrictive alternative, is the desired setting for the majority of children. Progression through the remaining more restrictive settings, where gradually smaller numbers of children are placed, is determined by the increasing severity of children's handicaps and the consequent need for greater amounts of instructional and support resources. The most extreme setting and most restrictive in the cascade, where the fewest number of children will be served, is the hospital.

As an example of the relationship between the child's learning needs and placement progression, a child who possesses a mild visual handicap may need corrective glasses which, when provided, enables him/her to participate as a non-handicapped child in a regular education program. Another child with a visual handicap of such severity that reading cannot occur without instruction in braille, requires the services of an itinerant teacher who periodically takes the child from the regular classroom to provide instruction in the use of braille. Finally, a child with a congenital visual problem may require surgery and long term hospitalization, in which case his total education must be brought to his bedside and tailored to his unique educational needs.

Any child, handicapped or not who is placed in a regular classroom for public education is by definition located in the least restrictive alternative. Chambers (1976)[8] says this reflects "the apple pie premise that people should in general be free to live as they please." He further says that if the "apple pie premise is accepted then the principle of the least restrictive alternative easily follows; that is, when government does have a legitimate communal interest to serve by regulating human conduct [in this case education] it should use methods that curtail individual freedom to no greater extent than is essential for securing that interest." Consequently, as the educational placement of children progresses away from the regular class, the amount of restrictiveness—the deprivation of individual freedom—increases.

It is the intent of the least restrictive principle that no child be removed any farther from the least restrictive setting than is necessary for educational purposes. In a lawsuit specifically dealing with this issue,[9] Judge K.K. Hall ruled on the basis of Section 504 that "to deny to a handicapped child access to a regular public school classroom in receipt of Federal financial assistance without compelling educational justification constitutes discrimination and a denial of the benefits of such program in violation of the statute."

One final misassumption about the educational placement of handicapped children must be recognized. Placement determinations about handicapped children are not intractable. Critics often allege that once a handicapped child is placed in a program with non-handicapped children, the placement is permanent and forever. Such a belief is not only incorrect with regard to providing handicapped children regular education, but also in providing these children with special education. All children change and as they change may need the benefits of both special and/or regular education. Consequently, educators must understand that appropriate implementation of the least restrictive alternative requires continuous evaluation of handicapped children to assure that as their educational needs change, the children will be provided with programs that may be at a point in time, more or less restrictive.

While the "cascade" represents the usual mode of thinking about the least restrictive alternative, it is itself restrictive. What must be emphasized is that while nine program options are presented, there is in reality an unlimited number of programs needed, if the presumption is that each child who is handicapped possesses unique educational needs and will receive an appropriate education in the least restrictive setting. To assume that all handicapped children will "fit" into those nine options is as faulty as assuming any two children are the same. Educators must conceptualize providing or arranging for the provision of programs that recognize and deal with individual children's needs on the basis of those needs rather than on the basis of rigidly determined program settings.

Congress specifically recognized all of the principles described above in Public Law 94-142. Specifically, the Act requires the provision of a free, appropriate public education for every American handicapped child. Each child must be provided with non-discriminatory evaluation and full rights of due process of law in all placement decisions. Additionally, the Act requires that each child be educated in conformity with an individualized education program which is the basis for determining if the standard of appropriateness is met. Among the requirements of the individualized education program is that it contain "a statement of the specific educational services to be provided to such child, and the extent to which such child will be able to participate in regular educational programs."[10] This provision is coupled with the additional significant requirement that the individualized education program contain "appropriate objective criteria and evaluation procedures and schedules for determining, on at least an annual basis, whether instructional objectives are being achieved."[11]

That individual handicapped children can learn in the least restrictive educational setting in which their individually determined program is provided is clear. That these children who are placed in alternative settings on the basis of educational need and capability can effectively be taught by their teachers is also apparent. Of key importance, however, is that to prematurely place handicapped children in less restrictive programs prior to their readiness is a disservice to the child and the teacher. Finally, implementation of the least restrictive principle in education means not only that handicapped children will receive learning oportunities consistent with their need, but that all students and adults involved in schools will have as the result of relationships with these children an opportunity to enrich their educational experiences.

Footnotes

1. *Pennsylvania Association for Retarded Children v. Pennsylvania,* 343 F. Supp. 279 (E.D. Pa. 1972).

2. *Mills v. Board of Education of the District of Columbia,* 348 F. Supp. 866 (D. D.C. 1972).

3. The Education for All Handicapped Children Act, Public Law No. 94-142, 20 U.S.C. 1401, et. seq.

4. The Rehabilitation Act of 1973, 29 U.S.C. 794.

5. *Id.* at Section 84.34(a).

6. Shanker, Albert. "Where We Stand," *New York Times,* March 20, 1977.

7. Reynolds, Maynard, "A Framework for Considering Some Issues in Special Education," *28 Exceptional Children,* 1962.

8. Chambers, David. "The Principle of the Least Restrictive Alternative: The Constitutional Issues," *The Mentally Retarded Citizen and the Law,* NY: The Free Press, 1976, p. 486.

9. *Hairston v. Drosick,* No. 75-0691 CN (S.D.W. Va.)

10. PL 94-142, Section 4 (19) (C).

11. *Id.* at Section 4 (19)(E).

The Past and Future Impact of Court Decisions in Special Education

Recent court decisions have had a profound effect on legislation for special education. But the central issues today have to do with finance and teacher training. Will there be money to make the new laws and court rulings meaningful? Will we be able to prepare teachers to act positively on the new rights of the handicapped?

H. Rutherford Turnbull III

H. RUTHERFORD TURNBULL III is Assistant Director, Institute of Government, University of North Carolina, Chapel Hill.

The impact of court decisions on special education has been and will continue to be massive. Simply consider five principles of special education law that those decisions have established:

1. *Zero reject* – no handicapped child may be excluded from a free appropriate public education.
2. *Nondiscriminatory evaluation* – every handicapped child must be fairly assessed so that he may be properly placed and served in the public schools.
3. *Appropriate education* – every handicapped child must be given an education that is meaningful to him, taking his handicaps into account.
4. *Least restrictive placement* – a handicapped child may not be segregated inappropriately from his nonhandicapped schoolmates.
5. *Procedural due process* – each handicapped child has the right to protest a school's decisions about his education.

In the following discussion I will review briefly the decisions that have established these principles, demonstrate how they have affected federal legislation, and suggest some of the future litigation the courts will face in the advancement of each principle.

Zero Reject

Case law: Relying on the U.S. Supreme Court's decision in *Brown* v. *Board of Education* that when a state has undertaken to provide public education it must make education available to all students on equal terms, representatives of handicapped children have asserted that they have been denied equal protection when 1) some handicapped children have been excluded from school while others have been included and 2) some handicapped children have been excluded while all *non*handicapped children have been included. They have claimed that the remedy in both situations is to include all handicapped children in a system of public education.

Not surprisingly, the courts have been highly responsive. In the frontier-breaking cases, *Pennsylvania Association for Retarded Children* v. *Commonwealth* and *Mills* v. *D.C. Board of Education*, federal district courts ordered that the public schools of those jurisdictions must furnish a free appropriate education to all handicapped children. With only a few exceptions,[1] federal and state courts have continued to order the public schools to follow the principle of zero reject.

That principle means more, however, than simply that handicapped children have a right to be admitted to the schoolhouse. One of its logical extensions is that handicapped children have a right to an appropriate education, one suited to their conditions and needs.[2] Other logical extensions result in decisions that an appropriate education consists of timely and sufficient evaluations of handicapped children, individual programs, and review of those programs[3] and in court orders that programs must be intended and likely to benefit a child.[4] Still another extension of the zero-reject rule comes from cases holding that the education given to handicapped children must be free to them, since education is provided free to nonhandicapped children.[5] And a final extension of the principle grants the right of handicapped children to be transported to appropriate public school programs.[6]

Claims have been made (but not yet adjudicated) that tuition subsidies are required for private school or technical institute education when appropriate public programs are not available,[7] and issues have been raised (but also not yet adjudicated) whether programs for handicapped children must be equal in quality to those for nonhandicapped children.[8]

Federal legislation: Both P.L. 94-142, the Education for All Handicapped Children Act, and Section 504 of the Rehabilitation Act of 1973 assure handicapped children that they may not be excluded from federally funded school programs. Among other things, these statutes 1) require schools to plan to serve all handicapped children, adopt policies that serve all handicapped children, and conduct searches to locate all handicapped children; 2) apply not only to public schools but also to other public agencies that provide education to handicapped children (e.g., mental health, human resources, corrections, and youth training agencies) and to private schools into whose programs handicapped children are placed by public schools; 3) require schools to give handicapped children an appropriate education; 4) require schools to hire handicapped persons to help operate federally funded programs of special education; 5) place responsibility on a single state agency for assuring that all state and local agencies comply with these acts; and 6) forbid architectural barriers in school facilities.

Looking to the future: Predictably, the zero-reject principle will involve courts in deciding issues surrounding 1) claims of handicapped children to have early intervention or compensatory

"The Past and Future Impact of Court Decisions in Special Education," by H. Rutherford Turnbull, III, *Phi Delta Kappan*, April 1978. Copyright © 1978 by Phi Delta Kappan, Inc.

or extended-school programs; to participate in vocational education programs and extracurricular or other nonclassroom activities; and to be granted access to school health, counseling, and job- and college-placement programs; 2) the effect on handicapped children of laws requiring competency testing and prohibiting a student from being graduated unless he has satisfied certain minimum standards; 3) claims of handicapped persons to barrier-free facilities; 4) issues surrounding the schools' duties to furnish handicapped children with special equipment, translators, or other related services;[9] 5) the extent to which handicapped students in private schools must be given a "genuine opportunity" to participate in public school programs or to receive tuition or other assistance (e.g., loan of equipment) from public schools; and 6) ultimately, the extent to which the interests of handicapped children to a free appropriate public education require nonhandicapped students and "regular" school programs to be inconvenienced or burdened so that handicapped students' claims may be satisfied – a "competing equities" issue.

Nondiscriminatory Evaluation

Case law: The Fifth and Fourteenth Amendments are the bulwarks that safeguard children against certain types of educational evaluations and resulting classifications. These amendments provide that a person may not be denied liberty or property except by due process of law. Denying an appropriate education, it is argued, is tantamount to denying a person an opportunity to acquire property. Thus, if children are classified as handicapped when in fact they are not, or if they are inaccurately classified, they are denied an opportunity to an appropriate education.[10] It follows, it is argued, that a due process violation occurs when pupils are misclassified, because invalid criteria have been used to determine which "track" they will follow in school. Moreover, when evaluation or test results are the primary basis for assigning a disproportionate number of minority students to special education programs, there is a risk of perpetuating or reestablishing dual systems of education based on race. Nor are these the only criticisms of evaluations.[11]

In responding to claims that children have been unconstitutionally misclassified and segregated as a result of evaluation procedures, courts have ordered an almost wholesale change in school psychology practices. They have accepted the argument that intelligence tests bear a scant relationship to intelligence if they are administered in a language that is not the child's native language or in a culture with which he is unfamiliar. In one case a court ordered that IQ tests may no longer be used for placement purposes.[12] Other courts have forbidden schools to use tests that do not properly account for the cultural background of the children tested[13] and from placing minority students in classes for the educable mentally retarded on the basis of tests that rely primarily on intelligence testing if the result of the placement is to create racial imbalance in those classes. They have ordered testing and retesting in the children's native language[14] and placement decisions that take into account children's socioeconomic backgrounds, social adaptation, and adaptive abilities.[15] And they have required schools to justify their reliance on tests that cause disproportionate racial imbalance in special education classes.[16]

Federal legislation: Like the courts, Congress has taken into account the fact that a school's failure to detect a child's handicaps or to assess him adequately can result in his being denied an appropriate education. Accordingly, it has required that procedures for classifying children be selected and administered so as not to discriminate on the basis of race or culture, that no single procedure may be the sole criterion for placement decisions, and that tests generally must be administered in the child's native language or method of communication.[17]

Regulations add requirements that tests be validated for the specific purpose for which they are used; be administered by trained personnel in conformance with the producer's instructions; be designed to assess specific areas of educational need (not just general intelligence quotients); be administered so as not to discriminate on account of a child's impaired sensory, manual, or speaking skills; be administered by a multidisciplinary evaluation team; and take into account all areas related to the child's disability, including health, vision, hearing, social and emotional status, general intelligence, academic performance, communicative status, and motor abilities, where appropriate. Schools also must draw on information from aptitude and achievement tests and teacher recommendations and take into account the child's social and cultural background and adaptive behavior;[18] document the sources of this information and carefully consider it;[19] reevaluate a child every three years or more often if conditions warrant;[20] and not count as handicapped (for purposes of receiving money under P.L. 94-142) more than 12% of all the children in a district, of whom only one-sixth (or 2%) may be counted as "specific learning disabilities" children.[21]

Looking to the future. Laws aimed at eliminating bias in evaluation and placement procedures are particularly fertile grounds for future litigation. Given the relative paucity of evaluation procedures that are validated so as not to discriminate against all the racial and cultural minorities that comprise the nation's school districts and the almost total absence of tests that have been validated for the specific purpose for which they are used, it is safe to assume that the tests themselves will come under attack in court and that collateral battles will be fought over how they are administered and interpreted. The norming of some adaptive behavior tests on institutional populations makes those tests, too, amenable to challenge. If the producer of a test represents that it has been validated for a specific purpose and the validation later is shown to be wanting, attempts will be made to hold the producer liable along with any user of the test. Finally, placement decisions that continue to depend heavily on "soft" data (such as teacher recommendations and assessments that take into account cultural background and adaptive behavior) seem likely to be challenged.

Appropriate Education

Case law: The handicapped child's right to an appropriate education led the courts to hold that alternatives to "regular" education placement (placement in special self-contained classes, homebound instruction, instruction of children who are residents of institutions, and placement in private programs at public expense) must be furnished to handicapped children.[22]

A new line of appropriate education cases is heralded by one alleging that handicapped children are not given an appropriate education where the separate programs in which they are enrolled experience a decrease in the number of teachers and other staff and where an exception to mandatory class size rules is made.[23] This case proceeds on at least these theories: An appropriate education depends on a minimum staff-to-student ratio, and handicapped children are denied an appropriate education when they, but not nonhandicapped children, suffer from decreased staff and increased class size.

Another route for attacking inappropriate placement may be the so-called education "malpractice" cases, typified by the decision of the Illinois Court of Appeals that a local school board could be sued where a student with learning disabilities alleged that his placement in a regular education program forced him to compete with students who were not learning disabled, as a result of which he sustained severe and permanent emotional and psychic injury requiring hospitalization and treatment for his injuries.[24]

Federal legislation: The principal method under P.L. 94-142 for furnishing an appropriate education to a handicapped child is the Individualized Education Program (IEP). The IEP is a statement developed by a group of persons, including the child's parents and the child himself when appropriate, to identify the child's present levels of educational performance, short- and long-term objectives for him, and the special and regular educational services he is to receive, when he should receive them, and for how long.

Preliminary regulations implementing P.L. 94-142 required the IEP to state the child's need for specific educational services, determined without regard to the availability of those services. The final regulations do not require the need for services to be determined "without regard to [their] availability." The Department of Health, Education, and Welfare, acting through the Bureau for the Education and Training of Handicapped Children, cautions, however, that the omission of those key words does not mean that a school must provide only the available services. Instead, the department construes the IEP requirement, the intent of P.L. 94-142 (a free appropriate public education), and the effect of Section 504 and its regulations to mean that the school must provide each handicapped child with all the services he needs, not just available ones.[25]

The IEP is not the only method for determining what constitutes an appropriate education. A second looks to the process for dealing with a handicapped child. Is he provided with a free (publicly paid for) education? Has he been fairly evaluated? Is he in the restrictive placement appropriate to him? Has he been assured of due process safeguards? Have his parents been given full opportunities to participate in decisions affecting his education?

A third method is suggested by the Section 504 regulations. They require a school to provide the child with special education and related aids and services designed to meet his educational needs as adequately as the needs of nonhandicapped children are met. This special education must be based on the least restrictive placement principle, it must consist of preplacement evaluation and nondiscriminatory testing, it must provide for annual reevaluation of the student's special education placement, and it must assure him of procedural safeguards.

Looking forward: Although the regulations under P.L. 94-142 make it clear that no school employee is to be held liable for the child's failure to achieve the progress that his IEP projects for him, it is certain that liability will be at issue if school personnel 1) fail to furnish a handicapped child with an IEP, do not require the IEP to be developed by the required group of persons, or make no good faith efforts to involve the child's parents; 2) exclude a handicapped child from the IEP conference when he could contribute to the development of his IEP; 3) write IEPs that assure only minimum projections of short-term goals and long-term objectives; or 4) fail to furnish or do not make good faith efforts to secure all the services necessary for the child to receive an appropriate education.

The equivalency standards under Section 504 regulations make it likely that litigation will center on placement of handicapped children in special education programs that are understaffed in comparison to regular education programs, instruction by uncertified or otherwise unqualified teachers, and the absence of appropriate materials and equipment (e.g., Braille books or hearing aids).

Least Restrictive Placement

Case law: Just as misclassification and denial of appropriate education have resulted in a form of exclusion of handicapped children from an education, so too did unnecessary placement in self-contained or segregated special education programs. In each of these three circumstances handicapped children were denied opportunity to receive an education – they were functionally excluded.

In *PARC*, *LeBanks* v. *Spears*, and *Maryland Association for Retarded Children* v. *Maryland* there was ample evidence of misclassification with resulting inappropriate placement, denial of meaningful educational opportunities, and general inadequacy of special education programs (inadequate financing, programs, personnel, and facilities). To overcome these deficits, one of the more effective remedies – effective because it could be implemented almost immediately and was supported by sound educational research and theory – was for a court to require that, as a rule, whenever a handicapped student is to be placed, he is to be included in a regular program in preference to a special program and that he is to be educated in the regular school environment rather than in the special school. The principle of "least restrictive placement" does not necessarily apply, however, if a state statute authorizes a state school superintendent to place children in private or out-of-state programs if appropriate public local programs do not exist.[26] On the other hand, a pending case challenges practices of placing socially maladjusted and emotionally disturbed children in programs that segregate by sex and race; the challenge relies on equal protection grounds and raises issues of least restrictive placement.[27]

Federal legislation: Having found that handicapped children have been inappropriately educated, denied the opportunity to be educated with their peers, and not given adequate services in the school, Congress followed the courts' preference for least restrictive placement by requiring schools to develop procedures to assure that, to the maximum extent appropriate, a handicapped child will be educated with nonhandicapped children and will not be removed from regular education programs and placed in special classes, separate schools, or other separate activities unless the nature or severity of the child's handicap is such that his education in regular classes with the use of supplementary aids and services cannot be achieved satisfactorily.

The least restrictive placement regulations make it clear that "appropriate" is determined by the child's needs and IEP; that placement usually should be in the same school the child would attend if he were not handicapped; that, if his placement with nonhandicapped children in the regular classroom significantly impairs their education, the placement is not appropriate for the handicapped child; that a handicapped child should be given a chance to participate in nonacademic and extracurricular services and activities; that a child placed in a private school retains his rights to placement in the least restrictive setting; that the burden is on the school to justify the child's placement outside regular programs, including nonacademic programs and services; that schools that are identifiable as being for handicapped students must be comparable to the school district's other facilities, services, and activities; that a handicapped child ordinarily should be placed as close to his home as possible; and that an orthopedically handicapped child may not be placed in a classroom or school that is "primarily" for other handicapped children (such a placement violates not only the least restrictive placement rules but is unnecessary if the school district complies with the requirements to remove architectural barriers).

Looking to the future: One case already has successfully challenged the nonmainstream placement of handicapped children on the ground that placement in self-contained classes isolates the children from nonhandicapped pupils and fails to meet their educational needs.[28] Another raises the same claims of deprivation of appropriate education because of nonmainstream placement.[29] Both rely not only on the constitutional claims of functional exclusion but also on P.L. 94-142, Section 504, and the respective regulations.

It seems clear that the broad-based challenges to self-contained special education (i.e., programs that are not in the mainstream or do not meet every aspect of least restrictive placement) inevitably will have to answer those parents and educators who remain unconvinced of the educational value of the principle, who can adduce research and expert testimony to indicate that placement in the least restrictive program is not an automatic assurance of an appropriate education, and who assert that the least restrictive placement principle hinges on what is most enhancing or most habilitating for the handicapped person, not what is closest to "normal."

The risk is great that judicial and administrative interpretations of the principle will not depend on two indispensable factors: 1) The principle has its recent history in the massive denial of an adequate education for the many handicapped children who were placed in self-contained and separate programs (a history that is not necessarily doomed to be repeated, given the other rights and access to resources that handicapped children have under case and statutory law); and 2) the principle is best understood and applied in terms of what is appropriate for the child himself where "appropriate" is defined not only by the IEP content but also by concepts of enhancement: What is enhancing is sometimes necessarily more restrictive than "normal" (e.g., a classroom for seriously emotionally disturbed children or severely retarded children may be highly "restrictive" and separated from "regular" programs but also highly enhancing of their abilities to learn). The future issue, then, is whether courts and agencies will apply the least restrictive principle by taking into account the relative "richness" or "poverty" of educational services in separate programs and the likelihood that such programs will be more enhancing for the handicapped child than not.

Procedural Due Process

Case law: The handicapped child's claims to zero-reject, nondiscriminatory evaluation, appropriate education, and least restrictive/most enhancing placement have only a hollow ring unless he has a right to challenge school decisions that affect these claims. Procedural due process – the right to protest and challenge school decisions – is a necessary prerequisite to putting his other claims into effect. That is the ultimate lesson to be learned from *PARC, Mills, LeBanks*, and *MARC*: A handicapped child and his parents have the right to be notified in advance before the school takes or refuses to take action with respect to his other educational claims: a right to be heard by an impartial tribunal, a right to have his case presented by counsel and expert witnesses, a right to confront and cross-examine witnesses, a right of access to school records that are the basis for the school decision that he challenges, a right to have the tribunal's decision based on the evidence presented, and a right to appeal. He also is entitled to challenge the contents of school records so that incorrect decisions will not be based on incorrect, outdated, or irrelevant information in them.

Federal legislation: The procedural (due process) safeguards of P.L. 94-142 and Section 504 mirror almost exactly the right-to-education cases. These safeguards include access to school records; independent evaluations; surrogate parents or other means of representation if a child's parents are unknown or unavailable or he is a ward of the state; prior notice before a school proposes or refuses to initiate or change the child's identification, evaluation, placement, or provision of a free appropriate public education; an opportunity for a hearing before an impartial hearing officer; and the right to be assisted by counsel and expert witnesses, present evidence, cross-examine witnesses, subpoena witnesses, make oral or written argument, receive a copy of the officer's decision, and appeal.

Looking to the future: It is important that the schools themselves may call for a due process hearing when the child's representatives object to or decline to give necessary consent for proposed school action (such as initial evaluation). Educators thus are given a technique that will enable them to do what they believe they should do and what the laws require them to do: provide a handicapped child with a free appropriate public education. The history of school-parent confrontations in special education has been written by reason of parent initiative; it is not at all likely, however, that this history will repeat itself. School-initiated due process hearings could become the order of the future.

Conclusion

Court decisions have had a profound effect on special education practices and special education legislation. That they will continue to do so is beyond cavil. The central issues in special education, however, are not able to be resolved by litigation alone. This is because those issues are 1) the willingness of federal, state, and local funding sources to put money into special education so that constitutional and statutory rights can be made meaningful, and 2) the ability of institutions of higher education to prepare future generations of regular and special educators to know, appreciate, and be able to act positively on the rights of handicapped children. Law reform through the courts and legislatures can only partially satisfy the claims of handicapped children to a free, appropriate public education; political action, appropriations, and adequate preservice training are necessary companions. The extent to which those companions will be forthcoming will determine to a large measure the need and probability of success of future law reform, whether in court or in legislatures.

---

1. *Cuyahoga County Association for Retarded Children and Adults* v. *Essex*, 411 F.Supp. 46 (N.D. Ohio 1976), and *Taylor* v. *Maryland School for the Blind*, 409 F.Supp. 148 (D. Md. 1976).

2. *LeBanks* v. *Spears* 60 F.R.D. 135 (E.D. La. 1973), and 417 F.Supp. 169 (E.D. La. 1976); *Fialkowski* v. *Shapp*, 406 F. Supp. 946 (E.D. Pa. 1975); and *Wilson* v. *Redmond*, No. 75-C-383 (N.D. Ill., August 19, 1975).

3. *Allen* v. *McDonough*, No. 14, 948, Mass. Super. Ct., Suffolk County, consent decree, June 23, 1976, supplemental decree, September 17, 1976.

4. *Frederick L.* v. *Thomas*, 557 F.2d 373 (3d. Cir. 1977).

5. See *Mills* v. *D.C. Bd. of Education*, 348 F. Supp. 866 (D.D.C. 1972) and *LeBanks*, fn. 2, on right to compensatory education for time excluded unlawfully, and *Maryland Association for Retarded Children* v. *Maryland*, Equity No. 100/182/77676 (Cir. Ct., Baltimore County, April 9, 1974) on right to homebound and other out-of-school education.

6. *In re Young*, 377 N.Y.S.2d. 429 (Family Ct., St. Lawrence County, 1975).

7. *Crowder* v. *Riles*, No. CA000384 (Cal. Super. Ct., Los Angeles County, filed December 20, 1976), and *Davis* v. *Wynne*, No. CV-176-44 (S.D. Ga., filed May 21, 1976).

8. *Rockafellow* v. *Brouillet*, No. 787938 (Wash. Super. Ct., King County, stipulations signed September, 1976), and *McWilliams* v. *New York City Board of Education*, No. 21350-75 (N.Y. Sup. Ct., App. Div., filed January 21, 1976).

9. Sec. 121a. 13 of the P.L. 94-142 regulations defines "related services" as transportation and such developmental, corrective, and other supportive services as are necessary to assist a handicapped child to benefit from special education. They include speech pathology and audiology, psychological services, physical and occupational therapy, recreation, early identification and assessment of disabilities, counseling services, medical services for evaluation purposes, school health services, social work services in schools, and parent counseling and training. See *Barners* v. *Converse College*, ____ F. Supp. ____, 46 U.S.L.W. 2045 (August 2, 1977) and *Crawford* v. *Western Carolina University*, ____ F.Supp. ____ (W.D.N.C., 1977), for cases holding colleges responsible for providing interpreters to otherwise qualified deaf students under 504 regulations comparable to the "related services" regulations under P.L. 94-142.

10. *Larry P.* v. *Riles*, 343 F.Supp. 1306, *aff'd.* 502 F.2d 963 (9th Cir. 1974); now in trial on merits.

11. H. R. Turnbull and A. P. Turnbull, *Free Appropriate Public Education: Law and Implementation* (Denver: Love Publishing Co., forthcoming), Chapter 2.

12. *Hobson* v. *Hanson*, 369 F.Supp. 401, 514 (D.D.C. 1967), *aff'd. sub nom. Smuck* v. *Hobson*, 408 F.2d 1975 (D.C. Cir. 1969).

13. *Larry P.* v. *Riles*, fn. 10; *Diana* v. *State Board of Education*, Cir. No. C-70-37, R.F.P. (N.D. Cal., January 7, 1970, and June 18, 1973); and *Mattie T.* v. *Holladay*, Civ. No. DC-75-31-5 (N.D. Miss., filed April 25, 1975).

14. *Diana* v. *Bd.*, fn. 13; *Guadalupe Org.* v. *Tempe*, Civ. Act. No. 71-435 (D. Ariz. 1972); and *Serna* v. *Portales*, 449 F.2d 1147 (10th Cir. 1974).

15. *LeBanks* v. *Spears*, fn. 2.

16. *Larry P.* v. *Riles*, fn. 13.

17. Sec. 612 (5) (C) and Sec. 614 (a) (7), P.L. 94-142, and Reg. Sec. 121a.530.

18. Reg. Sec. 121a.533.

19. Ibid.

20. Reg. Sec. 121a.534.

21. Sec. 611 (a) (5) and Sec. 602 (15).

22. *PARC* v. *Commonwealth*, 334 F. Supp. 1257 (E.D.Pa. 1971) and 343 F. Supp. 279 (E.D.Pa. 1972); *Mills*, fn. 5; and *MARC* v. *Maryland*, fn. 5.

23. *McWilliams* v. *New York City Board of Education*, No. 21350-75 (N.Y. Sup. Ct., App. Div., filed January 21, 1976).

24. *Pierce* v. *Board of Education of City of Chicago*, 358 N.E.2d 67 (Ill. Ct. App. 1976).

25. Letter from Deputy Commissioner Edwin W. Martin, Nov. 17, 1977, cited in *Insight*, December 19, 1977.

26. State ex rel. *Warren* v. *Nussbaum*, 64 Wisc. 2d 314, 219 N.W. 2d 577 (1974).

27. *McWilliams*, fn. 23.

28. *Mattie T.* v. *Holladay*, fn. 13.

29. *California Association for Retarded Children* v. *Riles*, No. 77-0341-ACW (N.D. Cal., filed February 15, 1977).

Mainstreaming: One Step Forward, Two Steps Back

JOYCE G. ASHLEY

Joyce Ashley is a Learning Disabilities Specialist with the Nassau County Board of Cooperative Educational Services, Cerebral Palsy School; Roosevelt, New York. She is also a second-term member of the New York State United Teachers Standing Committee for Special Education.

Passage of the Education for All Handicapped Children Act has added a new word to the teacher's lexicon: mainstreaming. The regulations for the new law require that the handicapped student be placed in a program that provides the least restrictive environment "harmonious with the child's needs and free of stigma." Implicit in this requirement is the notion that the handicapped child will be accepted once he is placed into the regular classroom.

In a book entitled, *Public Law: Implications for Mainstreaming*, Robert Herman said:

> . . . an active policy of mainstreaming means helping handicapped children participate as much as possible in our society. Not only do handicapped children benefit from exposure and involvement with their non-handicapped colleagues, but many educators believe that *all* children benefit from mainstreaming. The non-handicapped child who goes to school with handicapped children has an opportunity to show you his acceptance of individuals who have differences. This acceptance requires a cooperative and compassionate attitude.

But how is acceptance to be legislated? Where is the preparation for the non-handicapped population's compassionate attitude? The closest many of us have come to handicapped children is seeing them on telethons. Now, faced with a handicapped child in our classrooms, we experience fear and anxiety. What can we expect from this unknown person? What does he have to offer other than his handicap? And the most pressing question: Can the handicapped child be assured more than tolerance and pity, or will he face isolation and rejection?

Nearly everything written on the new education for the handicapped act refers to it as the civil rights bill for the handicapped. Like other civil rights legislation, it creates new problems as well as solving old ones. Its merits will be determined only by the test of time. However, it is not too soon to voice some concerns about shortcomings in the law.

Three areas of the act present special problems: (1) the difficulties inherent in developing individualized education programs for each handicapped child; (2) the mechanics entailed in providing due process to the handicapped child and his parents; and (3) the increased costs to the state of complying with the federal regulations.

Individualized Education Program

The term individualized education program (IEP), as required by the new law, means a written statement for each handicapped child which includes: (a) a statement of the present educational levels; (b) a statement of annual goals, including short-term instructional objectives; (c) a statement of specific educational services to be provided, and the extent to which the child will be able to participate in regular educational programs; and (d) the projected date for initiation and anticipated duration of the services, and appropriate objective criteria and evaluation procedures and schedules for determining, on at least an annual basis, whether the instructional objectives are being achieved.

Nowhere in the federal regulations is there a safeguard for teachers against performance contracting. Nor is the teacher protected against malpractice litigation.

The teacher who executes the IEP may not know the handicapped child and may have had no part in writing the statement, yet that teacher may be responsible for the objectives in that statement. Parents of non-handicapped children in regular classes may begin to demand individualized education programs for their children as well.

Due Process

Parents of a handicapped child are afforded certain safeguards including due process in the evaluation, placement, and programming of their child. When the parents or guardians are unknown or unavailable, or when the child is a ward of the state, an individual must be assigned to act as a surrogate for the child in all proceedings. The individual assigned may not be an employee involved in the education of the child, however.

The question of whether or not children are being appropriately served by due process guarantees has yet to be resolved. Local school districts too frequently attempt to avoid due process as time consuming and costly. They adhere to the wishes of the parents in the hopes of avoiding demands for due process as

"Mainstreaming: One Step Forward, Two Steps Back," by Joyce G. Ashley, *American Educator*, October 1977.

soon as any conflict arises, regardless of the best needs of the child.

In an attempt to address himself to this issue, the New York State Commissioner of Education has amended the state's regulations to read:

Unless a surrogate parent shall have been previously assigned, the impartial hearing officer shall (prior to the hearing) determine whether the interests of the parent are opposed to or inconsistent with those of the child, or whether for any other reason, the interests of the child would best be protected by assignment of a surrogate parent, and where he so determines, the impartial hearing officer shall designate a surrogate parent to protect the interests of such child.

Increased Costs

Thomas Hobart, president of the New York State United Teachers, recently recommended that New York elect not to participate in federal funding of the Education for All Handicapped Children Act (P.L. 94-142). In testimony before the State Assembly, Hobart said:

New money required to meet the newly mandated costs has been conservatively estimated by the New York State Education Department to be at least $1,000 per handicapped child in New York State. This means it will cost our state . . . an estimated $310,000,000.

In Florida, an appropriations committee of the Florida state legislature voted unanimously to refuse federal money under the act. In a policy statement following the decision, the committee said:

Although P.L. 94-142 is a laudable attempt to address the unmet educational needs of our nation's handicapped children, the current legislative and regulatory language forces those states with established on-going quality programs to either compromise state laws and existing programs or to refuse money which is badly needed.

The Goals of Mainstreaming

Robert Herman listed eight goals to be achieved through mainstreaming. Those goals provide a useful framework in which to examine whether the Education for All Handicapped Children Act as it is presently written will insure full educational opportunity for the handicapped.

1. *Remove the stigma associated with special class placement.*

It should be obvious that when a handicapped child is placed in a regular class, he comes with a label. Will his teacher be able to understand that disability? Does the teacher feel trapped, threatened, and inadequate? Will there be opportunities for in-service training? Does the teacher have a liaison person, someone who can be consulted regarding the child? Is this a flexible teacher excited by new challenges, or will this child become an enemy in the classroom?

2. *Enhance the social status of handicapped children with their non-handicapped peers.*

In an article in the *New York Times Magazine,* David Milofsky described what took place in Massachusetts when mainstreaming was introduced. A high school student with cerebral palsy had a scholarship endowed in her name by her peers. In an art class, peers wiped drool from the mouth of a handicapped classmate and they cut his paper straight for him. In a local community in New York, a high school student's fallen books were kicked down the hall. A junior high student had his very own graduation. The audience applauded as he crossed the stage. That ceremony was followed by the virtually anonymous graduation for his non-handicapped peers. Peers, if they are friends, do not endow you. They find ways to share their lives with you. They push wheelchairs, they talk to you during free play, they join you for lunch, they accept crooked cutting, and they let you wipe your own drool.

3. *Provide a better learning environment.*

The implication is that the handicapped have been educationally short-changed in the special school. Yet special classes were intended to provide opportunities for personal independence to the fullest extent possible. They have helped students develop good self-images and self-acceptance, and special classes have provided a basis for dealing with reality. These accomplishments should not be minimized so readily.

4. *Provide a real world environment.*

Mainstreaming in education, however, will be meaningless unless it leads to full opportunity to jobs, to transportation, and to buildings without barriers. Only then can mainstreaming truly mean freedom from what Herman calls "restriction of fundamental liberties."

5. *Provide a flexible service delivery mechanism more adaptable to individual children.*

Federal regulations outline numerous supportive services not generally available in regular schools. These include transportation, speech pathology and audiology, psychological services, physical and occupational therapy, recreation, early identification and assessment of disabilities, counseling services, school social work services, parent counseling, and training in child development. The regulations further stipulate that the cost of mainstreaming must come from new money and may not stem from a reallocation of funds from old programs. Furthermore, the money must follow the child. All of these services require funds that school districts do not presently have.

6. *Enable more children to be served.*

Many school administrators regard mainstreaming as a money saving device. A teacher from Ohio related to me that her class size had doubled since mainstreaming was introduced. In addition to her normal caseload of fifteen, she was given an equal number of handicapped children. When I asked what she had done about it, she replied, "I prayed a lot." The handicapped child and his peers are penalized by so callous an attitude. The result of this kind of administrative conduct could be chaos in the classroom or an end to mainstreaming. Nowhere in the federal regulations have reasonable class sizes and teacher caseloads been safeguarded. This translates at the state and local levels into more children to be served by fewer teachers. Everywhere special education teachers, who should be providing additional services to districts, find themselves instead in growing numbers on the unemployment lines.

7. *Provide decentralized services, avoiding costly transportation charges.*

Youngsters who are moderately to severely physically handicapped are transported to physical therapies, occupational and speech therapies, special medical services, and occupational education programs. In some instances, however, decentralized services translate into an increased caseload for the districts' school psychologists. Savings in transportation costs furthermore cannot be used to supplement the cost of appropriate services in the mainstream.

8. *Avoid legal services involved in segregated classes.*

From Public Policy to the Classroom

The Education for All Handicapped Children Act (P.L. 94-142) became law on November 29, 1975. Final regulations implementing the law were issued on August 23, 1977. Both the law and the federal regulations have implications for teachers and other professionals in the school system. The following analysis is an attempt to translate federal policy on the education of the handicapped into the requirements that the law will place on schools and teachers.

Whom is the law intended to serve?
All handicapped children ages three to twenty-one years are the intended beneficiaries of P.L. 94-142. The law stipulates that children ages three to eighteen must be served by September 1, 1978, and children three to twenty-one by September 1, 1980.

Are there priorities among the intended beneficiaries?
Yes, children who are not receiving an education are the first priority. Children who are receiving an inadequate education and are severely handicapped are the second priority.

What proportion of the costs of implementing P.L. 94-142 will the federal government pay?
The federal government will share an increasing proportion of the costs of P.L. 94-142. In fiscal year 1978, the federal share will be 5 percent of the national average expenditure per public school child times the number of handicapped children being served in the school districts of each state; in fiscal year 1979, 10 percent; in fiscal year 1980, 20 percent; in fiscal year 1981, 30 percent; and in fiscal year 1982 and each year thereafter, 40 percent.

Where will handicapped children receive educational services?
The new law is intended to provide services to handicapped children in the "least restrictive environment" consistent with their needs. Placing children in the least restrictive environment will often mean mainstreaming.

What is mainstreaming?
Mainstreaming is the term used to describe the placement of handicapped children into regular classrooms, with supplementary aids and services provided when needed, or into self-contained special education classes within a regular school. Only those children whose severity of handicap mitigates against such placement will be placed into special classes or schools.

How will individual placement of a handicapped child be determined?
Federal regulations outline an elaborate due process mechanism for placing handicapped children into the proper educational environment. The due process requirements give certain rights to the parents of handicapped children and to the children as well. In most instances, parents will have the final word in the placement of their youngster. Local education agencies, however, may contest parents' views through administrative hearings or court action.

Are there due process guarantees in the regulations which protect the teachers of handicapped children?
No, the regulations published on August 23 do not guarantee that teachers have direct access to procedural safeguards when they disagree with the placement of a particular child in their classroom, when they feel their workload has been burdensomely increased because of such placement, or when their class size has been enlarged. If a local education agency decides to support a teacher, it may initiate due process procedures on the teacher's behalf.

How will the educational needs of handicapped children be met in the classroom?
The regulations require that an Individualized Education Program (IEP) be developed for each handicapped child. On October 1, 1977, an IEP must be developed for each child already receiving special education or related services at the beginning of the school year or within thirty days of determination of a child's eligibility for special education.

What is the Individualized Education Program?
The IEP is a written statement for each handicapped child developed in a meeting between a representative of the school, a teacher, the child's parents or guardian, and the child if appropriate. The IEP includes: (1) a statement of the present levels of education performance of the child; (2) a statement of annual goals, including short-term instructional objectives; (3) a statement of

---

On the contrary, two aspects of the new law which are sure to instigate numerous time consuming and costly court cases are the individualized education programs and the due process mechanisms.

* * *

The Education for All Handicapped Children Act is a mammoth undertaking. Some argue that the law goes too far by usurping the policy making function of state education departments. Others claim that it doesn't go far enough by excluding the most severely handicapped children from the benefits of mainstreaming. One thing is clear, however. Educators have had too little time to prepare to meet the requirements of the law.

As the deadline for states and local districts seeking to comply with the federal regulations approaches, let us hope that the handicapped child with his unique individual needs is not swept away and drowned in good intentions. Let us hope, in the words of Robert Herman, that mainstreaming will:

> . . . enrich the lives of all our children and society. It can be the cutting edge of a more realistic educational experience for all children, handicapped and non-handicapped alike. If we look at the school settings as a place where humane and compassionate values are transferred to each child, if we prepare ourselves for the mainstreamed classroom, if we understand the reason behind the trend to mainstreamings, and if we can deal with the broad spectrum of variations that make up the delivery of equal educational services to all handicapped children, then we shall enter a new era.

If not, mainstreaming may have taken us one step forward and two steps back in our efforts to achieve equal educational opportunity for the handicapped.

the specific educational services to be provided and the extent to which the child will be able to participate in regular programs; and (4) the projected date for initiation and the anticipated duration of such services; appropriate objective criteria and evaluation procedures; and schedules for determining, on at least an annual basis, whether instructional objectives are being met.

Does the IEP bind teachers to a contract concerning the achievement of handicapped children?

Although the proposed federal regulations did not clearly absolve teachers of a contractual obligation in achieving the goals outlined in the IEP, the final regulations issued August 23 state:

> the Act [P.L. 94-142] does not require that any agency, teacher, or other person be held accountable if a child does not achieve the growth projected in the annual goals and objectives.

What provision is there in P.L. 94-142 for in-service training for teachers to assist them in dealing with the needs of handicapped children?

Provisions for both preservice and in-service training are part of the act. While the regulations call for a state plan which includes incentives to teachers to participate in in-service training, there is no specific requirement that teachers be involved in developing preservice programs. The incentives which a state educational agency may provide include released time, payment for participation, option for academic credit, salary step credit, certification renewal, or updating professional skills. A state must include some incentives to teachers to participate in in-service training, but the selection of the particular incentives are at the discretion of the state. Although the law requires that there be programs of preservice and in-service training, no new federal funds have been authorized specifically for this purpose by P.L. 94-142

What other provisions of federal law relate to education for the handicapped?

Section 504 of the Rehabilitation Act of 1973 is a nondiscrimination provision which requires that recipients of federal funds provide equal opportunities to handicapped persons. Federal regulations have been interpreted to require that all educational services provided to non-handicapped persons by institutions receiving federal funds be provided to handicapped persons as well. Included would be the right to interpretors for the deaf and mechanical seeing aids to the blind who wished to take regular classes. Some colleges which are receiving federal funds are challenging the 504 regulations in court.

Does the American Federation of Teachers support the Education for All Handicapped Children Act?

The AFT supported the intent of P.L. 94-142 and worked for passage of the legislation. However, certain aspects of the legislation and the regulations are in need of modification. The AFT has, therefore, urged a number of changes in the law.

The AFT has recommended that the federal government move immediately to provide the full 40 percent of the national per pupil average share of the costs of implementing the law. Many states are concerned that funds may have to be shifted from other programs in order to accommodate the needs of serving handicapped children unless the federal government agrees to assume its full share now. In addition, the AFT has also urged that the basis of funding should be changed from a percentage of the per pupil costs to a percentage of the per service costs. Unless such a change is made, states that provide services to multiply-handicapped students will be shortchanged.

The AFT has also made a number of recommendations to correct deficiencies in the law's protection for teachers. The AFT urged that changes be made in the regulations to remove liability from teachers regarding the IEP. Those changes were adopted when the final regulations were issued.

The AFT has also urged that teachers be allowed to initiate due process proceedings on their own and that teachers be given the right to be represented by counsel at due process hearings.

The AFT fully supports improved and expanded federal assistance for education of the handicapped. However, the AFT is concerned that mainstreaming be achieved in a manner consistent with providing quality education to all children.

Are additional materials available on P.L. 94-142?

Yes, the AFT national office will soon have a detailed analysis of the law and regulations.

2 Professional Concerns: Development, Classification, and Parental Involvement

The articles in this section of *Educating Exceptional Children* address fundamental issues in special education. The first article deals with how the teacher or caretaker is to recognize developmental lags and disabilities. In a complex and varied field, there is widespread agreement on at least one point being that the identification and treatment of handicapping conditions is best done as early in the child's life as possible.

Preschool teachers must know how to identify children who might need special education, and they must also know how to integrate special students into early childhood education programs. Consultations with a psychologist, one of many specialists a child may have to see, can be less frightening for all concerned, and is detailed in "How to Prepare the Child for the Psychologist."

Integration of special students into public education programs is a subject of controversy. "Handicapism" is another controversial topic, as the article on this stereotyping of handicapped people indicates. The authors argue that social attitudes toward the handicapped can be as limiting as the primary handicap itself.

Of particular concern to special educators is how to classify students properly so that appropriate education programs or other treatment can be designed for them. It's a necessary starting point, and yet the whys and hows of classifying and labeling are hotly disputed among specialists.

The special education community does not stop at students and their professional educators. As the final articles in this section clearly point out, the parents of handicapped children form an integral and vital part of that community. These articles are addressed in the main to educators who must learn to communicate as fully and effectively as they possibly can with these parents in order to marshal all available resources for the handicapped child. "A Place for Noah," the last article, is written by the parent of a child labeled autistic. It is a personal story, one of several in this volume, and it tells the human, and especially difficult, side of the tale.

Looking Ahead: Challenge Questions

What responses to perceived developmental lags and disabilities should professionals make? At what stage?

What conflicts are likeliest to arise between concerned professionals and concerned parents? Are these conflicts valid? Are they resolvable?

What are the special educator's classification options? Are there better systems? What are they?

What are the most serious limiting factors that society imposes on the handicapped?

Watching for Developmental Lags and Disabilities

Alice Young and Isabel Schleicher

Before her recent retirement, Alice Young was an early childhood special education teacher for the Madison Public Schools and for the Mendota Mental Health Institute's PrePrimary Project in Madison, Wisconsin. Isabel Schleicher is a registered nurse and public health educator currently employed by Mendota Mental Institute, 301 Troy Drive, Madison, Wisconsin. She is working on a parent-education program for the prevention of emotional problems in children.

Interest in the early detection of developmental difficulties has increased sharply as the importance of beginning remediation at the youngest possible age has become better understood. Federal and state right-to-education laws now require public schools to provide programs for children with exceptional educational needs. In some states the public schools are mandated to begin special programs at age three. In other states the special programs must begin at age three and there is the option of starting them at birth.

Nursery school teachers, day care personnel and social workers, realizing their opportunity and responsibility as observers of young children, are requesting more information about determining which children may be in need of specialized help. The following outline was prepared in response to these requests.

The outline consists of a partial listing of behaviors which should alert care givers to the possible need of a child for clinical evaluation. Some items point to possible vision or hearing impairment; others to motor or neurological development problems; and still others to language learning and speech disorders, or social/emotional adjustment disturbances. The outline is a reference for observers and should not be considered an assessment or test from which diagnostic inferences or labels can be drawn.

Many children exhibit some of these behaviors at one time or another. It is the *persistence of the behavior* that may indicate problems.

Consider consultation and referral for the child:

At three months who does not react to sudden noises;
- who does not appear to listen to a speaker's voice;
- who does not try to find the speaker's face with the eyes;
- who has not begun to vocalize sounds;
- who has been left to lie in a crib for hours without visual or auditory stimulation;
- who does not raise the head when lying on his stomach;

At six months who does not turn to the speaking person;
- who does not respond to being played with;
- who is not visually alert;
- who never laughs or smiles;
- who is not babbling;
- who does not reach for or try to pick up a toy;
- who is not learning to sit up;
- who looks drawn and does not appear to be gaining weight;
- who does not arch the back when lying on the stomach and raising the head;

At one year who has not been responding to "Pat-a-Cake," "Peek-a-Boo," or other baby games;
- who has not begun to put syllables together such as da da, or ma ma;
- who is not pulling self up to standing position;

At eighteen months who has not yet begun to feed self with a spoon if a spoon has been available;
- who does not try to imitate speech or vocalize in jargon;
- who is not moving about to explore;
- who does not seek eye contact;
- who has not or does not spontaneously squat when picking up objects;

At two years who is not naming a few familiar objects and using a few two or three word phrases;
- who is not noticing cars, trucks, trains;
- who is not beginning to play with housekeeping toys in imitation of adults' activities;
- who is not moving about vigorously, running, climbing, exploring;
- who does not seem to focus eyes on a large, colored picture;
- who engages in body rocking or head banging for extensive periods of time;
- who is not walking upstairs;

At three years who, much of the time, does not seem aware of other children, of adults, of the weather, of traffic, etc.;
- who uses little or no speech;
- who does not engage in imaginative play symbolic of adult activities;
- who avoids looking at pictures or pointing to pictures of familiar objects;

"Watching for Developmental Lags and Disabilities," by Alice Young and Isabel Schleicher, *Day Care & Early Education*, May/June 1977. Copyright 1977 by Human Sciences Press.

who does not follow simple directions;
who engages for long periods of time in repetitive activity such as flipping the pages of a magazine, spinning the wheel of a toy truck, head banding, tapping;
who cannot ride a tricycle if given plenty of opportunity to do so;
who walks on tiptoes most of the time, or frequently stumbles and bumps into things;
who avoids eye contact (more than ordinary shyness);

At four years who does not have at least partially understandable speech with sentences;
who substitutes the pronoun "you" for "I" (may say "You want to go." Child means, "I want to go.");
who uses echolalic speech (caregiver says, "Billy, tell your mama goodbye." Child says, "Billy, tell your mama goodbye." What the child hears does not seem to get processed through the meaning system);
whose eyes do not track together;
who holds objects very close to the eyes, or who looks at things from the sides of the eyes;
who seems unable to listen to a brief children's story;
who repeatedly tests all limits;
who is so quiet and conforming that he/she never tests or tries anything new;
who has phobias or is preoccupied with exaggerated fears;
who frequently engages in flapping of the arms or flipping of the hands to discharge excitement;
who runs about from one thing to another every minute or so, pulling out materials but never becoming fully involved or goal directed in any activity;
who is still untrained in toileting (relapses do occur occasionally for reasons of illness, a new baby in the family, or unusual excitement);
who does not draw some sort of representation of human beings (at least a head and a few features) if crayons or pencils have been available to the child;
who stays on the periphery of the playroom, paying little attention to other children long after the other children have overcome shyness and begun to play with or beside their friends;
who engages in body rocking or watching spinning objects rather than playing symbolically with toys or equipment;
who cannot tolerate small changes in routine or minor frustrations without great agitation or noisy tantrums.

How does a caregiver go about obtaining the needed professional help for a child?

First, the center director, the staff nurse, and the social worker should be notified of the caregiver's concerns for the child. After further observation the staff members involved with the case should assemble as complete an assessment as possible of the developmental level of the child and take a careful look at the suitability of the activity program and the group placement for the child.

If not already started, a chart should be set up for recording the behavior, the dates, what happens before the behavior, what happens after the behavior, the frequency and the duration of the episodes. This record will be very important as the basis for talks with the parents and conferences with the consultants. It will be needed as the baseline for continuing evaluations to determine the effectiveness of treatment and activity programs. It will be useful in reporting to therapists and clinicians who are working with the child.

As early as possible the concerns of the staff should be shared with the parents of the child. A staff which has always freely confided to the parents its pleasure in the child's small developmental steps as well as its concern over adjustment difficulties will have started a foundation of trust that will help to make a conference on serious problems better accepted and understood. If the staff does not insinuate blame, the parents may confide their own worries over what they have seen at home. In the event that the center director wishes to bring in an outside observer or consultant, permission to do so must be obtained from the parents.

The parents, at this point, usually want to consult their physician to ask for further assessment or a referral to a specialist. Action on a referral usually comes more quickly if the referral is made by a physician than if sought by a non-medical person. Medical ethics protecting the privacy of patients require that the physician may not confer with the staff until he receives a release-of-information statement signed by the parents giving their permission for the physician to discuss the case with the center staff.

Agencies that may be possible sources of services to the child are:

1. The local public schools, many of which are now adding early childhood programs for a wide variety of needs;
2. Local mental health clinics with testing, guidance, and counseling services;
3. Diagnostic/treatment units in state university medical centers;
4. Speech and hearing clinics in a university department of communicative disorders;
5. Outpatient clinics at children's hospitals;
6. Organizations of parents such as the area Association for Retarded Children, the area Society for Autistic Children, Association for the Education of the Deaf, Parents of the Visually Handicapped, United Cerebral Palsy, Learning Disabilities Association, and others.

Integrating Children With Handicaps into Early Childhood Education Programs

Shirley Cohen

Shirley Cohen, Ph.D., is director of the Special Education Development Center, Hunter College, City University of New York.

A mandate contained in the 1972 Amendments to the Economic Opportunity Act requires that at least 10 percent of the participants in Head Start be children with handicaps.* This is one of several victories the handicapped have won recently in recognition of their rights as human beings and citizens. While applauding this mandate and its direction, however, we cannot overlook the probability that its implementation in many early childhood education programs during the next few years may be uneven.

Those of us who have been involved in working with handicapped children, and in training teachers to do so, know that it takes something special to work successfully with many handicapped children, special in the sense of how you feel and special in the sense of what you know how to do.

While there may be no specific mandate to integrate the handicapped into day care centers and nursery school programs, these facilities are increasingly doing so. Local public education agencies are also preparing to recognize their responsibilities toward handicapped children by integrating them into regular classrooms. Early childhood educators must be prepared to receive these children. We in the special education community may be able to help by sharing some experiences and ideas about matters which are basic to any effort to bring handicapped children into the mainstream of child care and education.

First, the feelings that the other children and their teachers and parents will have about the handicapped children who may join the classrooms must be recognized and addressed. Similarly, we should explore the feelings the handicapped children and their parents will have. Some of the questions, then, that we should explore when we plan to integrate handicapped children into Head Start and other programs are:

☐ How do the handicapped children feel about themselves and others?

☐ How do their parents feel about their children and themselves?

☐ How do, or will, the children currently in the group feel about having obviously handicapped children for group mates?

☐ How will their parents react to their children having these new group mates?

☐ And, probably most important of all: How does the teacher or director of the preschool program feel about the admission of handicapped children?

It is almost impossible to discuss the task of integration by drawing parallels between "normal" and "handicapped" children without using extremely broad, almost meaningless generalizations because handicapped children are so many things. They may be competent, gifted children who cannot walk, or bright children who want to explore their world but who cannot see. Some handicapped children may be slow to learn but are friendly and a joy to have in any group. Sometimes children with handicaps are puzzling and hard-to-understand. They may hurt themselves or, because they cannot express themselves in words, they may hit out in anger and frustration. They may also be frightened, withdrawn children who perceive the world and the people in it as dangerous.

Perhaps the best way to approach the task of integration is to consider: What have we been doing for our children that would be right for handicapped children? What can we do better without any radical change in approach? What may we have to work on?

We must also look at what we probably cannot do now or in the near future.

Most young handicapped children need a maximum of acceptance and support and a minimum of competition, unless by competition we mean competition

Reprinted by permission from *Children Today*, January/February 1975.

with themselves toward goals that are appropriate for them and not competition against other children. But handicapped children do need those who will expect them to be able to learn and to do, not those who will feel so sorry for them that they will do nearly everything for them and expect little of them in return. We tend to forget that some handicapped children are very competent except in a limited functional area.

Many who work in early childhood education programs recognize the critical importance of parents to the development of young children and, therefore, the value of working with parents. Parents play an even more central role in the development of handicapped children. What is needed, then, is a partnership between the program staff and the parents of the handicapped children in each program.

The individualization of a program is also an important factor to consider. Head Start is one example of a program that has always been primarily individualized. This means at least two things: that children do not spend most of their day in mandated group activities, and that there has always been room for individual differences among children in Head Start, whether these differences be in interests, style or ability. Essentially, dealing with handicapped children means *extending* this concept of an individualized program. Working with handicapped children is not a totally different experience. The same principles that have been guiding teachers' work up to now still apply. However, the application of these principles will have to be extended in new ways—like changing seeing tasks to feeling tasks for children with severe visual impairments.

When referring to individualization I would also like to point out that Head Start has always recognized the need for at least two adults in each group, so that someone could always be available to relate to individual children. Special education has been behind Head Start in this respect. In the early 1960s when I was a teacher of severely disturbed children in a treatment and research center, I was the only adult in the room. If one child was screaming, crying, attacking others or hurting herself, there was only one person to attend to her and to the rest of the children, too. This situation was the rule, except for a small number of model programs. I suspect that in a majority of special education classes this is still true.

Teachers already know the children in their classrooms who need clearer, more specific directions about what to do. Some children, for example, must be provided with only a few choices at any one time. They must be helped to learn how to make choices by being asked specifically, "Do you want to work with clay or with paints?" With some handicapped children, teachers' directions and suggestions should also be very specific.

Some children already in the group need the teacher to do things *with* them, rather than to just direct them, when they are learning something new. Teachers will have to *do with* some handicapped children in order to help them learn.

Most teachers have worked with children for whom learning tasks must be simplified—broken down into smaller parts to help children master each part. More of this may be required with some handicapped children.

Some children may seem to be confused and overstimulated by the richness of the center environment. Ways will have to be devised to provide areas within the classroom that are quieter, less open and less confusing.

Teachers have probably encountered some children who don't know how to play with the other children in the group. These children need to be taught how to relate to and play with their peers. Some handicapped children, who have had few opportunities to play with other children, may need this kind of help more than other children.

What does the teacher have to work on? I learned a valuable lesson when I was working with a severely disturbed boy in the first grade. Fred had been suspended from first grade the previous fall, and the principal made it clear that she was ready and willing to suspend him again as soon as I could collect evidence of his disruptive behavior. I didn't really know what she meant until Fred had been in the classroom for about two hours. We were absorbed in work when he shouted out, "There's a green cloud in the sky." After that, he really got going! We had trouble in that classroom until I could honestly communicate to Fred and the other children that I was not thrown by Fred's behavior, that I was going to try to help him meet his needs, and that I would not let him interfere with what the other children were doing. After this we did all right, and Fred was a member of that class all year.

Yes, sometimes Fred did "get on my nerves," but so did other children who were not handicapped. What I learned in this situation is that the nature and terms of the relationship between the teacher and the handicapped child will shape the reactions of the other children to him or her and will, in the long run, strongly affect the outcome of the experience.

The next thing that teachers may have to work on is the belief that there is very little which a young handicapped child cannot do in some way. This point would not have to be made in relation to older handicapped children. Unfortunately, when one works with older handicapped children one often has to think in terms of remedial training and a limitation in goals. Happily, we are talking about 3-, 4- and 5-year-olds. We may find a child with mental retardation, but we do not know what his limitations will be in later life. We do not know this because young children are marvelously plastic. We have seen strange things happen when young children were introduced to new environments—both increases in I.Q. scores and the blossoming of asocial creatures into full human beings.

I want to illustrate this point in another way. In one

classroom I observed a 4-year-old child with cerebral palsy. He was bright as can be, a mischievous delight, but he was in wheelchair and could walk only with great support from an adult. He wanted to build with blocks like other little boys. What could the teacher do? She might have set him up at a table with smaller blocks but instead she put him on his stomach on the floor in the block corner, so that he was able to play like the other boys.

Only a small proportion of handicapped children need to be physically handled with caution. For the others, there are some basic safety rules. Once these are satisfied, the teacher will be interfering with the child's growth if she tries too hard to shield him. Teachers have to be unafraid to try methods which are different but which will help the handicapped child to participate more fully.

One reason for reluctance on the part of some teachers and directors to integrate handicapped children into "normal" preschool programs is the fear that these children may "set the other children off," or "show them bad behavior." This is a fear that both teachers and parents may have. However, the handicapped child is probably less likely to engender behavioral contagion than is his active, normal classmate. What the handicapped child may well stimulate is interest which can provide rich learning experiences for all the children.

A former early childhood education teacher described an incident which occurred when a blind boy was being integrated into her kindergarten class. On his first day the child entered the classroom and began shouting. The teacher, thinking that the other children would imitate his behavior, expected them to begin shouting, too. However, the children did not shout—they began to ask questions about the boy's behavior. The boy's mother explained that her son wanted to find out how large the classroom was. Since he couldn't use his eyes to get this information, as the other children did, he used his voice. From the way his voice sounded, from the echoes it made, he could tell whether the room was big or small. What began then for this group of children was a whole new kind of awareness about how people learn, an awareness which grew out of their relationship to their new classmate.

What most teachers can't do at present and probably won't be able to do in the near future is to work with *all* handicapped children, for there are some children whose needs are so extensive that they are best met in a specialized setting. There are also some specialized experiences which are crucial to the optimal development of other young handicapped children. Physical therapy for children with cerebral palsy and a language development program for deaf chidlren, for instance, are obviously among these. It is conceivable that some centers will add these specialized services. In those centers which do not, the regular program can still serve as an extremely valuable, possibly part-time adjunct to specialized treatment programs.

A colleague once asked me to help him find a regular preschool program which his child, who has cerebral palsy, could attend two days a week. Since I knew that his daughter was in an excellent special education program, I asked him why he was looking for another one. He explained that his daughter would go to a hospital one day a week for physical and speech therapy and continue to attend the special educational program two days a week. But for two days a week he wanted her to be just a child, to play and to learn to live in a non-handicapped world. This is the essence of what Head Start or another preschool program can offer to handicapped children.

---

*See "Placing Handicapped Children in Head Start Programs" by Jenny W. Klein and Linda A. Randolph, CHILDREN TODAY, Nov.–Dec. 1974.

How to prepare the child for the psychologist

That first encounter needn't be a startling and confusing experience that leads to negative feelings about the whole procedure

Edward M. Adams

If there was one rule that Jerome learned from his mother, it was not to go anywhere with strangers. In spite of this rule, Jerome's teacher told him to go with Mrs. Johnson to play some games. Afraid, yet powerless to defy his teacher, Jerome clutched Mrs. Johnson's hand and began walking to some obscure part of the elementary school building. Was this a police officer? Was he going to be punished for some evil deed? Were the "games" Mrs. Johnson played similar to those played with the Christians in early Rome? No, Jerome was going to spend some time with the school psychologist.

Let's face it, in most schools, referral to the psychologist tends to be an "adult-centered" activity. Ironically, the child is a forgotten entity lost in the maze of parent conferences, principal-teacher parleys, and teacher-psychologist consultations.

Not so for the adults involved in the referral process. Congress has passed into law "due process" procedures designed to safeguard the rights of parents and educators in relation to school psychological referral, and in the placement of children into special education classes. Due process implies that the parent and school understand and give consent for an individual psychological evaluation of the child. Due process also assures the right of the parent or school to request an impartial hearing to resolve conflicts that may arise out of such an evaluation.

Unfortunately, the most powerless figure within this whole procedure is the child. Children are the least prepared and most inadequately informed persons in the process of psychological referral.

Confused. In the case of Jerome, here is a startled and confused child. The possibility of his associating the school psychologist with his feelings of anxiety may result in the formation of a negative attitude toward the psychologist. This negative attitude may, in turn, diminish rapport and affect psychological test results or observations obtained throughout the child-study phase of the evaluation.

However, with careful planning and honest caring, children in Jerome's situation can be prepared, physically and emotionally, to meet the school psychologist and cheerfully accept this pre-planned encounter.

If it were me, I would be utterly incensed if some stranger suddenly began asking me personal questions, or peremptorily requested that I reproduce drawings of circles, squares, or diamonds. I would demand an explanation until I was satisfied that what I was doing was useful, harmless, and important. Does not a child, unskilled in assertive questioning, deserve the same explanation?

If you agree with the assumption that the child has a right to know what the school psychologist does, what the procedure is, and who will be involved, then consider the following recommendations.

Become Acquainted. If you are not acquainted with the school psychologist working in your school, request an informal conference. At this conference, find out his attitudes toward children. Ask him when his services should be requested. In short, do not be afraid of asking questions. A good school psychologist would be pleased to respond to your questions about his training, experience, and procedures.

Break the Ice. Sometime during the year (the earlier the better) invite the school psychologist into the classroom. Introduce him and ask that he explain his job to the children. Provide the time for questions and answers. This is a good chance to eliminate the many myths that surround psychologists and mental health.

Reprinted with permission of the publisher Allen Raymond, Inc. Darien, Conn. 06820. From the October 1977-1978 issue of *Early Years.*

File all this information away in your head and keep the services of the psychologist always in mind. Within the school year, a child may tell you of a personal problem and seek your advice. This may be an opportunity for you to collaborate with the psychologist in an attempt to meet the child's needs. You may also suggest to the child that he may wish to consider the school psychologist as another person in whom to confide.

Prepare the Child. When the time comes to refer a child to the school psychologist, consider what you will say and thus begin the process of preparation. First of all, have a private conference with the child you are referring. At this conference you may cover the following points:

- Tell the child that the school psychologist sees many children every year. This assures him that he is not being punished, or singled out. Mention also that *you* need more information about him in order to do a better job teaching.
- Describe the school psychologist as a person who helps kids in school. Without mentioning names, give an example of how the school psychologist helped some other child.
- Let the child know that his mom or dad will talk with the psychologist. Also, inform the child that you will be talking to the psychologist about his school work and classroom behavior.
- Describe what the psychologist does. Don't hesitate to mention the word "tests." But explain that these "tests" are different than the kind he is accustomed to in the classroom.
- Make the child aware that the tests are important, that the results will be used to make important decisions.
- Identify the people who will know the results of the evaluation.
- Answer questions and clarify any misunderstandings during your private conversation. Make sure you feel good about your talk. If you feel good, then so does the child.
- When the child returns to the classroom, don't make a fuss. Some children may want to talk about their experience, while others may remain silent.
- If the other children begin teasing the child for seeing the school psychologist, listen to their comments and make an attempt at correcting faulty logic or facts.

The purpose of this preparation is to inform and reassure the child. It has been my experience that children become more cooperative and less anxious about the psychological evaluation once they know what to expect. Best of all, children learn to trust open, honest adults.

It is estimated that there are 8,500 to 9,000 school psychologists in the United States. If each of them receives 50 referrals within the schools they serve, then approximately 450,000 children undergo this procedure each school year.

I point this out to dramatize the need for making this a painless, even pleasant, encounter, so that the hundreds of thousands of children involved get the full benefit of this vital service.

Handicapism

Robert Bogdan and Douglas Biklen

ROBERT BOGDAN is acting assistant dean of graduate studies in the School of Education, Syracuse University, and associate professor of education and sociology at the University's Center on Human Policy. DOUGLAS BIKLEN, associate professor of education and planning, Syracuse University, is director of the Center on Human Policy.

Thomas Szasz (1961), Erving Goffman (1963), Thomas Scheff (1966), Robert Scott (1969) and Dorothea and Benjamin Braginsky (1971) taught us to understand "handicap" categories as well as the term "handicap" itself as metaphors. They laid the groundwork for thinking about so-called handicapped people as societally created rather than as a natural or objective condition. These same authors and their associates in the interactionist or labeling school pointed to the importance of the quality and nature of how labelers interact with the labeled as a prerequisite for understanding handicap (see Lemert, 1967; Goffman, 1961; Davis, 1963; Wiseman, 1970). The interface of human service agencies and clients became an area in which social researchers could develop theoretical perspectives on how labels and definitions were applied (also see Gubrium, 1975; Bogdan, 1974).

While these researchers worked, parallel events occurred in the social action and political arenas. It is not clear who borrowed from whom, but the social construct/labeling school approach to handicap was manifested in a concern for issues of legal and human rights of those labeled handicapped (Kittrie, 1973; Gilhool, 1973). Now a strong "total institution" abolition movement is afoot and various peoples have formed handicap liberation groups. These include Disabled In Action, Mental Patients' Liberation, National Federation of the Blind, The Center On Human Policy, The Mental Health Law Project, and the National Center for Law and the Handicapped (Biklen, 1974; Mental Health Law Project, 1973; National Committee for Citizens in Education, 1976).

In the field of human services, consumer activism and a new professional consciousness have spawned moral and legal imperatives such as due process, "least restrictive environments," the right to treatment, delabeling, and normalization (Wolfensberger, 1972; Wolfensberger and Zauha, 1973; Abeson, 1974). At present, however, neither the social researchers/theorists nor the social activists have developed an adequate conceptual scheme by which to examine collectively labeling, the moral and legal developments, and the structural and cultural aspects of differential treatment of people defined as handicapped.

Our purpose is to introduce the concept of *handicapism* as a paradigm through which to understand the social experience of those who have previously been known as mentally ill, mentally retarded, deaf, crippled, alcoholic, addict, elderly, deformed, deviant, abnormal, disabled, and handicapped. Handicapism has many parallels to racism and sexism. We define it as a set of assumptions and practices that promote the differential and unequal treatment of people because of apparent or assumed physical, mental, or behavioral differences.[1] Three terms—*prejudice, stereotype,* and *discrimination*—are inherent in our analysis.[2]

Prejudice is any oversimplified and overgeneralized belief about the characteristics of a group or category of people. Prejudice toward the so-called handicapped is indicated by such indicting assumptions as: they are innately incapable; they are naturally inferior (the mind set is "Thank God, I'm not you"); they have unique personalities, different senses, and different tolerances than the run-of-the-mill citizen; they have more in common with each other than with nonhandicapped persons and, therefore, they like to be with their own kind (see Goffman, 1963; Wright, 1960). These beliefs provide the background assumptions for our action toward people labeled handicapped; they are the essence of handicapism.

Whereas "prejudice" is the general disposition, *stereotype* refers to the specific content of the prejudice directed toward specific groups. The mentally retarded, for example, are believed to be childlike, to enjoy boring routine work, and to be oversexed (Wolfensberger, 1975). The elderly are said to have deteriorated intelligence and are presumed to be unhappy and undersexed. The mentally ill are expected to be erratic in their behavior, are considered dangerous and bizarre, especially during the full moon (see Scheff, 1966; Biklen, 1976). The deaf are considered terrific painters; the blind are supposed to be melancholy (see Scott, 1969; Jernigan, 1975); and supposedly, once an alcoholic always an alcoholic. While sets of stereotypes are often contradictory, they are nevertheless seriously regarded by a number of people and are used to justify particular modes of treatment. Thus the retarded can be treated like children, the elderly ignored, and the mentally ill locked up.

Although inaccurate, a stereotype is often steadfastly maintained. The maintaining processes are themselves part of handicapism. First peers and culture support the transmission of stereotypes and therefore constantly reinforce them. Second, groups like the handicapped are isolated, have few opportunities for intimate relations to develop between themselves and the so-called normal people, and consequently have little chance of disproving the stereotypes. Last, and perhaps most

[1] Authors who have discussed handicapped categories as minority groups include: Dexter, 1964; Wright, 1960; Yuker, 1965; and Gellman, 1959.

[2] See Yinger, 1965 and Allport, 1954 for a discussion of the use of these terms in the study of ethnic relations.

From *Social Policy,* March/April 1977. SOCIAL POLICY published by Social Policy Corporation, New York, New York 10036. Copyright 1971 by Social Policy Corporation.

important, handicapped people are treated in ways that correspond to their stereotypes and are rewarded for living up to others' image of them (see Lemert, 1951). Thus they learn the role of the handicapped and fall victim to the self-fulfilling prophecies (Merton, 1957).

"Prejudice" and "stereotype" point to the cognitive and ideological substance of handicapism. The concept of *discrimination* provides the structural and behavioral aspect. Unfair and unequal treatment of individuals or groups on the basis of prejudice and stereotypes translates into discrimination. Standards of fairness and unfairness vary from society to society and from time to time as the social criteria for equality or discrimination change in accordance with social values. At one time it was considered the natural state of slaves to labor in the fields for the economic benefit of others, and for married women to serve their husbands; the treatment they received was not thought to be unfair. Similarly, handicapped people are generally thought to experience relative equality in this society especially since the advent of various categorical social service programs. They are considered to occupy their rightful place and to receive deserved treatment. For example, few people question the practice of rescinding drivers' licenses, fingerprinting, and taking mug shots of people admitted to state mental institutions despite the fact that there is no evidence that former patients of state mental hospitals are involved in any more accidents or commit more crimes than typical citizens (Scheff, 1966; Ramadas, 1975). It is equally common for public school districts to segregate handicapped children into special classes and even separate "special" schools although there is no empirical evidence to support any benefit, either educational or social, that results from segregated services. These kinds of policies and practices discriminate against people with disabilities. They are part of handicapism.

In the remaining pages we will demonstrate how handicapism manifests itself in personal interaction, in the organizational structure of the larger society, and in human service policy and practices. Our purpose is to identify and illustrate handicapism in these spheres, and to demonstrate the usefulness of the concept as a paradigm for social scientists. We have based our discussion largely on current lawsuits, studies reported in the professional literature, and our own research and experiences in the area of social policy and disability.

HANDICAPISM IN INTERPERSONAL RELATIONS

Handicapism arises in the contacts between handicapped and so-called typical people as well as in the private conversations of typical people when the handicapped are not present. In face-to-face contacts, labeled and nonlabeled persons characteristically display anxiety and strain about how each will be perceived by the other (see Davis, 1961; Goffman, 1963; Wright, 1960). "The stigmatized individual may find that he feels unsure of how we normals will identify him and receive him" (Goffman, 1963). And the so-called normals feel that the stigmatized individual is too ready to read unintended meaning into our action. This self-conscious uneasiness results in a number of handicapist practices. For example, nonhandicapped persons avoid contact with "nonnormals." When they are forced into contact they tend to seek the earliest possible conclusion. When there is contact there is also the tendency for the disability (the alleged difference) to take on tremendous significance in the nonhandicapped person's mind: it becomes the master status (Davis, 1961). This often results in the nonhandicapped person either being overly gracious and overly sympathetic ("It must be hell to go through what you go through") or patronizing ("What a lovely belt, did you make that all by yourself?") or in some other ways be insensitive or ignore people with disabilities. One such behavior is to treat them like what Goffman (1960, 1963) calls "nonpersons."

In casual contacts with the handicapped, normals tend to measure them against the stereotype and such contacts reinforce common stereotypes. An example may help to demonstrate this process. Recently a number of typical skiers observed a blind skier coming down the slope. They spoke about him and his "amazing feat." They commented on how "truly remarkable" that he could have the courage and fortitude to do what must be exceptionally difficult for a person with no eyesight. From the tone of their comments it was clear that they did not perceive this person as any *ordinary* blind person. The sighted skiers did not question their stereotypes of the blind as physically inept. Instead, they confirmed the stereotype by classifying this skier as an exception to the rule—as "amazing." If he were not skiing but sitting in the lodge next to the fire, one might expect to hear passers-by whispering to each other something to this effect: "It's a shame that blind people have to miss out on so much fun."

Handicapism is also manifested and perpetuated between normals when not in the presence of disabled people. Stereotypes and prejudice abound in daily conversation: "*Poor* Aunt Jane is going blind." "I'd kill myself if I were as disabled as Luke." Our casual interpersonal conversation is heavy with handicapist phrases: "Did you hear the one about the *moron* who threw the clock out the window?" "It's like the *blind* leading the *blind*." "You must think I'm *crazy*." "You babbling *idiot*." "What are you, *deaf*?" "Some of the students are real *retards*."

HANDICAPISM AT THE SOCIETAL LEVEL

To understand handicapism at the societal level one must analyze the culture and structure of basic institutions for manifestations of prejudice, stereotypes, and discrimination. Further, one must examine the legally sanctioned and illegal systematic mistreatment of people because of alleged physical, mental, and behavioral differences. And, as in personal interaction, one must study how major societal institutions routinely reinforce and perpetuate prejudice and stereotypes. Since this brief article can only introduce the handicapism paradigm and not exhaustively elaborate it, societal level handicapism is portrayed in only four of the many possible areas: (1) images of the handicapped in the media; (2) physical and literacy barriers to participation; (3) discriminatory laws, rules, and regulations; and (4) exclusion from basic organizations.

Media Images

To what extent does the mass media

present prejudicial and stereotypic images of the handicapped? What is the specific content of that imagery? What effect does it have on those who look at it? Impression and data suggest as starting hypotheses that mass media present prejudicial and stereotypic images of the handicapped. After reviewing images of mental illness in the media, Scheff (1966) concludes that mental patients appear stereotypically as bizarre and dangerous. Needleman and Weiner, two researchers who examined the relationship between physical attractiveness and crime in various media, found (1974) that physical ugliness and physical differences are often associated with violence and other forms of crime, as shown in the media. Our own study of horror movies, which are experiencing renewed popularity on the American scene, reveals a clear association of physical and mental handicap with acts of violence and hate. In children's stories there are inevitably hunchbacks, trolls, and other deformed and therefore supposedly frightening people hiding under bridges and in forests to grab pretty children who might be passing by. Disney, for example, frequently promoted handicapist imagery. The wicked witch who gives the beautiful Snow White the poison apple has to change from a beautiful woman to a hunchbacked, wart-nosed old lady to accomplish her terror. Dopey has Down's syndrome-like features and lives with the other childlike dwarfs in the forest. Then there is evil Captain Hook with the patched-eyed pirates of *Peter Pan* fame.

In addition to movies and children's stories, cartoons appear to be important carriers of handicapist images. "Stupid idiot," "moron," "dumb," and "crazy" dot the landscape of comic strip captions. Key offenders include prestigious syndicated strips such as "Beetle Bailey" and "Archie." These comics not only confirm prejudicial and stereotypic attitudes toward people with disabilities, they also reveal that everyday words that refer to specific groups have become general curse words.

Handicapism takes more direct forms in the media as well. Often newspaper articles link crimes with various disabilities as if the disability was the cause of the crime. For example, in an Associated Press release published across the country a murderer who was scheduled for execution was referred to as "an alcoholic and mentally incompetent psychotic who was mentally retarded." Further, the media promote images of the handicapped as helpless by selectively covering certain events and refusing to cover others. For example, when Kenneth Jernigan, president of the National Federation of the Blind, called a press conference for one of his group's highly political conferences, newspaper and television reporters ignored the political organizational content, for they wanted, instead, to view corporate exhibits of walking aids, lead dogs, and other stereotyping symbols of blindness (Jernigan, 1975). The media promote images of the helpless handicapped by reporting regularly on charity drives that feature posters of crippled children. Telethons promote the same imagery. Their human interest features more often than not proclaim that the handicapped can be helped by charity, thus really reinforcing an image of dependence. One public service advertisement on mental retardation that appeared nationally in newspapers and magazines carried the headline: "He'll be eight years old the rest of his life." The picture was of a child in front of a birthday cake with eight candles. The message was direct and stereotyped; it portrayed the retarded as childlike.

The effect of images of the handicapped in media on audiences has not been studied, perhaps because of the difficulty in isolating such influences. One can hypothesize, however, that it is an important part of handicapism.

Physical and Literacy Barriers

If you were told that because of your race or sex you were not allowed to enter buildings and to use public toilets, sidewalks, and mass transit, you would claim discrimination. People in wheelchairs are denied such access. The degree to which society's constructions and accessways unnecessarily impede participation for a significant segment of our population can be regarded as a primary indicator of handicapism. Recently cities have begun to establish access ordinances, but that did not save the New York City police from an embarrassing handicapist situation. There was a demonstration launched by Disabled In Action in which many of the protestors, who incidentally were in wheelchairs, blocked a road and refused to move. The demonstrators were about to be arrested when the police realized that the jails were not accessible to wheelchairs—a clear violation of state law.

In much the same debilitating fashion that architectural barriers deny access to the physically disabled, written directions (i.e., for tests, applications, forms, and signs) can provide untold obstacles for the person who cannot read and write. Some people leaving state schools for the mentally retarded, for example, report that their inability to read and write creates obvious barriers for their mobility in a society that relies so heavily on written communication. Most bus signs, maps, and street signs require the ability to read. People who cannot learn or simply were never taught to read and write have an extremely difficult time with the many forms such as income tax, employment applications, credit applications, and registration for school (see Dexter, 1964, for a complete discussion). Because it is generally assumed that everyone can and should read, it is terribly embarrassing as well as difficult for people who don't have such abilities to live independently.

Discriminatory and Exclusionary Laws, Rules, Etc.

For many years it has been common practice for business employers, insurance companies, colleges and universities, and similar organizations to require applicants to identify their disability. The result was discrimination, so much so that the 1973 Vocational Rehabilitation Act mandated no discrimination against disabled workers by agencies that are federally funded. Similarly, some states have passed legislation to end discrimination by all employers and educational institutions (e.g., The 1974 Flynn Act, otherwise known as the Disability Amendments to the Human Rights Law in New York State). Also, the 1973 Vocational Rehabilitation Act established affirmative action requirements for federally funded employers. All of these developments do not suggest that discrimination has ended, merely that widespread discrimination is now acknowledged. Jobs often require physical examinations which automatically exclude disabled people from passing; however, the courts have ruled that all special requirements must reflect the actual nature of the job. Barriers may not be perpetuated simply for the purpose of arbitrarily excluding people with disabilities.

Education, another basic institution in most people's lives, also practices exclusion. Until the 1971 *PARC v. Commonwealth of Pennsylvania* case (Lippman and Goldberg, 1973), the various states freely excluded many handicapped children from public education. While federal legislation has since mandated the right to public education for all children with disabilities (P.L. 94-142, the Education for All Handicapped Children Act), a private research/action group (The Children's Defense Fund, 1974) reported that over one million disabled children still remain out of school altogether, ostensibly because of their disability or, more accurately, because of exclusionary policies.

Still another area rife with exclusionary policies is transportation. Clearly physical barriers create the greatest impediment to disabled people's use of mass transport, but certain modes of transportation have excluded disabled people unless accompanied by an aide. This was the case for several air carriers until a recent challenge by Judy Heumann, a member of the Senate Labor and Welfare Committee and, incidentally, a person whose physical disability requires that she use a wheelchair.

Service Delivery

Ironically, handicapism manifests itself even in the organizations and institutions which have as their official duty the rehabilitation, care, and processing of people who are allegedly handicapped. It seems that most systems that are operating today for the handicapped are based on handicapist principles. Even those that serve clients' specific clinical needs often perpetuate handicapism. First, although the Supreme Court has ruled that separate is inherently unequal, most programs for the handicapped are segregated from the mainstream of society. Not only has society provided state institutions for the retarded, deaf, blind, and emotionally disturbed, governments have financed segregated schools, recreation programs, and sheltered workshops. The large residential institutions and smaller day-service facilities bring together large numbers of labeled people. Alternative integrated placements are usually unavailable. While this separation of the handicapped from the typical population has been recommended by some professionals to facilitate the delivery of services and thus improve the quality of life, research observations contradict this handicapist assertion. Research on the efficacy of separate classes for handicapped children, for example, does not show that children in separate classes achieve any better than children in regular classes (Blatt, 1956; Bennett, 1932; Cain and Levine, 1963; Cassidy and Stanton, 1959; Goldstein et al., 1965; Hottel, 1958; Pertsch, 1936; and Wrightstone et al., 1959). On the other extreme, testimony in recent court cases involving state schools for the mentally retarded [e.g., Willowbrook (N.Y.), Partlow (Ala.), Pennhurst (Penn.), Belchertown, Fernald (Mass.)] gives vivid and definitive evidence of the dramatic regression of skills among people who have been institutionalized.

The culture and structure of service systems for the disabled often work to support handicapism. People are herded, kept waiting, and regimented in barren surroundings designed and maintained to facilitate custodial concerns of cleanliness and efficiency of plant operation (Blatt, 1973; Wolfensberger, 1975; Goffman, 1961; Bogdan et al., 1974; Biklen, 1976; Gubrium, 1975). The handicapped are forced to take endless numbers of examinations. The residential treatment centers including nursing homes, state mental hospitals, and state schools exaggerate handicapist patterns in that residents are often denied personal possessions, have few rights, few opportunities for sexual and other expression, are dressed in ill-fitting clothing, and are often addressed by their diagnosis (i.e., mongoloid, senile, schizoid, low grade).

A cornerstone to the handicapism of professional systems is that services to the disabled people are considered a gift or privilege rather than a right. The American public gives billions of dollars each year to charity, much of which is solicited in the name of helping the handicapped. This system of collecting funds demeans its recipients by supporting the prejudice that the handicapped are inferior people. Moreover, professionals who require charitable contributions to support their programs tend to distort the image of the handicapped in order to play on the public's pity. Thus, the crippled child becomes a poor soul whose disability evokes pity and guilt and the spirit of giving, but also lessens the possibility that disabled people can be regarded as people with personalities, with individual aspirations, and with an interest in being perceived as ordinary people.

The other major funding source for special services is the federal and state governments. But here too the money system promotes handicapism. In order to be eligible for state and federal funds, schools and other human services personnel must label children according to clinical disability categories for which there is reimbursement. They must list the name and diagnosis of the handicap and thereby begin people in their careers of being labeled mentally retarded, learning disabled, autistic, etc. (see Bogdan, 1976; Schrag and Divoky, 1975). In that kind of system the disabled become commodities and agencies become headhunters. In every instance where funds become available for a particular disability group, the number of people so labeled soars geometrically (see Schrag and Divoky). People whose disability might not ordinarily be thought of as a handicap suddenly find themselves labeled; they are pawns in the struggle for agency survival and growth, for they are the essential requisite by which agencies receive government funds. Not too long ago side shows were popular. Deviants were sought out and paraded for a price. While the system we have evolved does not parade its clients, except perhaps during telethons, it does promote labeling and it does thrive on the segregation and exaggeration of the nature and extent of the problem.

NEW STARTING POINTS FOR DISABILITY RESEARCH AND POLICY

Civilizations have always created such categories as "handicapped" and "race" and, along with them, fostered prejudices, stereotypes, and discrimination. Some theorists have suggested that these serve real functions such as allowing us to find targets for our hostility, to find excuses for what goes wrong, to pinpoint people's fear, and to enjoy self-approval in the knowledge that we do not belong to the disapproved of groups (see Erikson, 1966; Barzun, 1965). Barzun suggests that the urge to classify and categorize people is reinforced in modern societies by the belief that scientific theories and systems of facts can account for and explain distinctions between people, differences in temperament and ability, and variation in bodily features and mental habits. By conducting research and formulating theory on commonsense notions of differences between preconceived categories, and by emphasizing statistically significant differences rather than the range within populations and overlapping of characteristics between categories, social science has done much to reify categories and therefore to entrench prejudice, stereotypes, and discrimination (see Bogdan and Taylor, 1976). Professionals and disability-related fields have followed a research tradition which has hindered the questioning of basic concepts in disability research. A disturbing number of handicapist assumptions have been taken as givens, as starting points for research.

We hope that the handicapism paradigm will enable researchers and practitioners to begin to reassess their assumptions concerning segregated service, differential treatment, the real source of the disability problem, labeling and language patterns, and funding mechanisms tied to labeling. Moreover, the concept of handicapism can facilitate research that will result in policy-related data. While we have not yet explored the full ramifications of handicapism, we have attempted to provide the foundation for conceptualizing the experience of handicaps in a way that will not perpetuate prejudicial notions, but rather will help reveal and erradicate injustice

REFERENCES

Abeson, Alan. 1974. "Movement and Momentum: Government and the Education of Handicapped Children—II." *Exceptional Children* 41: 109–115.

Allport, Gordon W. 1954. *The Nature of Prejudice*. Boston: Beacon Press.

Barzun, Jacques. 1965. *Race: A Study in Superstition*. New York: Harper & Row.

Bennett, A. 1932. *A Comparative Study of Sub-Normal Children in the Elementary Grades*. New York: Teachers College Press.

Biklen, Douglas. 1974. *Let Our Children Go*. Syracuse: Human Policy Press.

———. 1976. "Behavior Modification in a State Mental Hospital: A Participant Observer's Critique." *American Journal of Orthopsychiatry*. 46, no. 1.

Blatt, Burton. 1956. *The Physical, Personality, and Academic Status of Children Who Are Mentally Retarded Attending Special Classes as Compared with Children Who Are Mentally Retarded Attending Regular Classes*. Unpublished Ph.D. thesis, The Pennsylvania State University.

———. 1973. *Souls in Extremis*. Boston: Allyn and Bacon.

Bogdan, Robert. 1974. *Being Different: The Autobiography of Jane Fry*. New York: John Wiley.

———. 1976. "National Policy and Situated Meaning." *American Journal of Orthopsychiatry* 46, no. 2: 229–235.

Bogdan, Robert and Taylor, Steven. 1976. "The Judged Not Judges: An Insider's View of Retardation." *The American Psychologist* 31, no. 1.

Bogdan, Robert et al. 1974. "Let Them Eat Programs: Attendants' Perspectives and Programming in State Schools for the Mentally Retarded." *Journal of Health and Social Behavior* 15, no. 2.

Braginsky, D. and Braginsky, B. 1971. *Hansels and Gretels*. New York: Holt, Rinehart and Winston.

Cain, L. and Levine S. 1963. *Effects of Community and Institution Programs on Trainable Mentally Retarded Children*. Washington, D.C.: Council for Exceptional Children.

Cassidy, V.M. and Stanton, J.E. 1959. *An Investigation of Factors Involved in the Education of Mentally Retarded Children*. Columbus: Ohio University Press.

Children's Defense Fund. 1974. *Children Out of School in America*. Cambridge, Mass.: Children's Defense Fund.

Davis, Fred. 1961. "Deviance Disavowal: The Management of Strained Interaction by the Visibly Handicapped." *Social Problems* 9.

———. 1963. *Passage Through Crisis*. Indianapolis: Bobbs Merrill.

Dexter, Lewis. 1964. *The Tyranny of Schooling*. New York: Basic Books.

Erikson, Kai. 1966. *The Wayward Puritans*. New York: John Wiley.

Gellman, W. 1959. "Roots of Prejudice Against the Handicapped." *Journal of Rehabilitation* 25: 4–6.

Gilhool, Thomas K. 1973. "Education: An Inalienable Right." *Exceptional Children* 39: 597–609.

Goffman, Erving. 1961. *Asylums: Essays on the Social Situation of Mental Patients and Other Inmates*. Garden City: Doubleday & Co., Anchor Books.

———. 1963. *Stigma*. Englewood Cliffs N.J.: Prentice-Hall.

Goldstein, H. Moss, J.W., and Jordan, L.J. 1965. *The Efficacy of Special Class Training on the Development of Mentally Retarded Children*. Cooperative Research Project No. 619. New York: Yeshiva University.

Gordon, Gerald. 1966. *Role Theory and Illness*. New Haven: College and University Press.

Gubrium, Jaber. 1975. *Living and Dying at Murray Manor*. New York: St. Martin's Press.

Hottel, J.V. 1958. *An evaluation of Tennessee's day class program for severely mentally retarded children*. Nashville: George Peabody College for Teachers.

Jernigan, Kenneth. 1975. "Blindness: Is the Public Against Us?" An address at the Annual Banquet of the National Federation of the Blind, July 3.

Kittrie, Nicholas. 1973. *The Right to Be Different*. Baltimore: Penguin Books.

Lemert, Edwin. 1951. *Social Pathology*. New York: McGraw-Hill.

———. 1967. *Human Deviance, Social Problems, and Social Control*. Englewood Cliffs, N.J.: Prentice-Hall.

Lippman, Leopold and Goldberg, Ignacy I. 1973. *Right for Education*. New York: Teachers College Press.

Mental Health Law Project (MHLP). 1973. *Basic Rights of the Mentally Handicapped*. Washington, D.C.

Merton, Robert. 1957. *Social Theory and Social Structure*. New York: Free Press.

National Committee for Citizens in Education (NCCE). 1976. *Network* (periodical). Maryland: Columbia.

Needleman, Burt and Weiner, Norman. 1974. "Faces of Evil: The Good, The Bad and The Ugly." Mimeographed. Dept. of Sociology, Oswego State College, New York. Presented at the Conference on Sociology and the Arts, Oswego, New York.

Pertsch, C.F. 1936. *A Comparative Study of the Progress of Subnormal Pupils in the Wards and in Special Classes*. New York: Teachers College, Columbia University Contributions to Education.

Ramadas, K.L. 1975. "Traffic Violation Frequencies of State Hospital Psychiatric Patients." *American Journal of Orthopsychiatry* 45, no. 5.

Scheff, Thomas J. 1966. *Being Mentally Ill: A Sociological Theory*. Chicago: Aldine Publishing Co.

Schrag, Peter and Diane Divoky. 1975. *The Myth of the Hyperactive Child*. New York: Pantheon.

Scott, Robert. 1969. *The Making of Blind Men*. New York: Russell Sage Foundation.

Szasz, T.S. 1961. *The Myth of Mental Illness*. New York: Hoeber-Harper.

Wiseman, Jacqueline. 1970. *Stations of the Lost*. Englewood Cliffs, N.J.: Prentice-Hall.

Wolfensberger, Wolf. 1972. *Normalization*. National Institute on Mental Retardation, Toronto, Canada.

———. 1975. *The Origin and Nature of Our Institutional Models*. Syracuse: Human Policy Press.

Wolfensberger, Wolf and Zauha, Helen. 1973. *Citizen Advocacy*. National Institute on Mental Retardation, Toronto, Canada.

Wright, B. 1960. *Physical Disability: A Psychological Approach*. New York: Harper.

Wrightstone, J.W.; Forlano, G.; Lepkowski, J.R.; Santag, M.; and Edelstein, J.D. 1959. *A Comparison of Educational Outcomes Under Single-Track and Two-Track Plans for Educable Mentally Retarded Children*. Cooperative Research Project No. 144. Brooklyn, N.Y.: New York City Board of Education.

Yinger, Milton. 1965. *A Minority Group in American Society*. New York: McGraw-Hill.

Yuker, H. 1965. "Attitudes as Determinants of Behavior." *Journal of Rehabilitation* 31: 15–16.

Classification Options

Editor's Note: Nicholas Hobbs is Professor of Psychology and of Preventive Medicine and Director of the Center for the Study of Families and Children at the Vanderbilt Institute for Public Policy Studies, Vanderbilt University, Nashville, Tennessee. He has published widely and has contributed to the field in other capacities that include serving as President of the American Psychological Association and as a member of the Institute of Medicine of the National Academy of Sciences, National Advisory Mental Health Council, The National Advisory Child Health and Human Development Council, and the Research Committee of the American Council on Education. He was Director of the Project on Classification of Exceptional Children and is the author of The Futures of Children, *the final report of the project.*

Dr. Hobbs, from your experience, what would you view as the most significant development that has occurred in the issue of classifying children during the last five years?

Dr. Hobbs: I would mention two events. One was the Project on Classification of Exceptional Children. That was important because it involved some 300 scholars in the country who are concerned with the issue of classification, and it produced a summary of that problem along with some recommendations as to what to do about it. Second, the passage of Public Law 94-142, with its extremely important provision of developing individualized education programs, was a significant move away from traditional classical categories.

How has lessening the use of classical categories affected the delivery of services to exceptional children?

Dr. Hobbs: I think it is probably too early to judge. The law requires categories to be used for reporting purposes. As a basis for reimbursement to the states, I think they will remain in use until there is some kind of system available that will permit different ways of conceptualizing the problem of how best to deliver services to children. The existing classification systems serve important functions in schools. It is hard to abandon what we have until there is something to take its place.

Are there any new comprehensive systems for assessment, placement, and programing that have proved successful in the education of individuals with special needs?

Dr. Hobbs: I think so. Again, it is probably premature to make a judgment on their success or effectiveness, but let me tell you about one way of looking at the problem. The term *ecology* or *ecosystem* considers the total life circumstance of the child. Often, a handicapped child, or any child for that matter, needs assistance from many important people in that child's life—parents, teachers, people in the neighborhood, in community centers, in churches, and so on. A classification system is needed that can in some way mobilize the people who are important in the life of the child. Current classification categories are drawn largely from clinical practice, from medicine and psychology, from education, law, and social work. An ecologically oriented system is a classification system that is based on the service needs of children and their immediate worlds. In thinking about classification, one must always ask what the purpose of it is. Traditional classification categories serve clinical purposes reasonably well but are very poor as a basis for a service delivery system. If we say we want a classification system for the purpose of improving the delivery of services, we come out with quite a different scheme. A system based on the service needs of children and their ecosystems has been worked out. Different models of it have been in use in several places: in Massachusetts, for example, in the special education program; in Connecticut, in the juvenile corrections program; and in Greenville County in Tennessee. In Nashville, Peabody and Vanderbilt have been working with service based, ecologically oriented classification systems for a number of years.

What is the single greatest strength of the ecological model?

Dr. Hobbs: It emphasizes the interconnectedness of the lives of children and of other people, the people on whom children are so dependent, and it focuses on the mobilization of normal helping resources instead of turning the problem over to professional specialists who are expensive, hard to find, and hard to keep involved over a long period of time. This way of thinking about the classification prob-

"Classification Option," *Exceptional Children,* Vol. 44, No. 7, April 1978. Copyright 1977 The Council for Exceptional Children. Reprinted with permission of The Council for Exceptional Children.

lem mobilizes needed professionals as well as the natural helpers of children—parents, most importantly, and members of the community, agencies, churches, neighborhoods, teachers, school principals—the people who are readily available to help the child.

What role do parents play in this ecologically oriented system?

Dr. Hobbs: They have a very important role. We have to reconceptualize the role of parents if we take this viewpoint seriously. Professional specialists and public school people have deplorably neglected parents in the past. Schools often treat parents as nuisances, but actually they have to be central in any kind of intelligent programing for children. One of the great things about Public Law 94-142 is that it recognizes the importance of parents and brings them into the planning and programing every step of the way. Parents have to be recognized as special educators, the true experts on their children, and professional people—teachers, pediatricians, psychologists, and others—have to learn how to be consultants to parents.

How compatible is the ecological model with other regulations of Public Law 94-142?

Dr. Hobbs: It is not incompatible, but Public Law 94-142 is primarily an educational law, although it recognizes that a child will have needs other than educational needs. There are nutritional, housing, transportation, and recreational needs as well as educational needs. Somehow these must be embraced in a comprehensive plan that would begin at age zero and continue until the child reaches maturity.

If an intervention strategy takes into account that children vary in their environmental responsiveness, how can mainstreaming be accomplished with this approach that you described?

Dr. Hobbs: It seems to me that we have to think of mainstreaming as many streams. I don't think there is any problem in accomplishing mainstreaming with this perspective, except that we do have to think of the child's total ecological system and not just of the child as an isolated human being without any connections with other important people.

Can minority group handicapped children minimize their double jeopardy in this type of needs based system?

Dr. Hobbs: I think so. There is no problem there, especially if school personnel have some appreciation of the strengths of minority group families and minority group neighborhoods.

In what ways will the teacher preparation programs need to be revised in order to train personnel in an ecological systems approach?

Dr. Hobbs: An ecological orientation will require a radically new perspective on the role of the teacher. Teacher education cannot proceed out of teachers colleges alone or out of field placement in the classroom. Field placement would have to be large enough to embrace the entire community setting where the child is growing up.

I remember one time writing a sentence I was very proud of. It said something like, "We make parents full partners in our efforts to help their children." I thought that was rather advanced because at that time people didn't think much about parents. But then a young teacher spoke up and said, "Oh, don't you think that is rather arrogant?" Indeed it was. How can teachers or psychologists or pediatricians or psychiatrists make parents *their* partners? It seems to me that you simply have to very humbly ask parents if there is some way that you as a professional person can be of assistance to them. They are ultimately responsible for their child. We must abandon the professional role of expert in recognition of the fact that the parents themselves are the experts and the rest of us must fit into that scheme and contribute to it.

Does this model hold promise for enriching the lives of learning and behavior problem youngsters who are incarcerated in juvenile correctional institutions?

Dr. Hobbs: I believe so. These youngsters really are no different from other children. They end up incarcerated in institutions because they are already the dispossessed youngsters in society. They have no effective advocates; they are usually minority group children; and, often, they don't have the resources to get into some other system that middle class children have. Assuming that the children get into difficulties in the first place because of an inadequate support system in the family, neighborhood, and community, mobilization of resources in this ecosystem will support the child and provide an opportunity to develop in directions that would lead away from future involvement in activities that would send the child back to the correctional institution. Such an approach has really worked quite well here in Nashville.

What immediate next steps do you recommend be taken in order to move forward the

coordination of services to exceptional children?

Dr. Hobbs: I see no way of getting an effective coordination of services or ensuring continuity of care as long as we continue to think about children in the classical categorical terms. Thinking of children as mentally retarded or emotionally disturbed or visually impaired precludes an integration of services. I feel that the most attractive feature of the plan I have described is that it does permit one to think about the service delivery problem in different terms, for example, in specifying precisely what a child requires. Examples of those requirements might be dental work, remedial instruction, transportation, or a hearing aid. Once the child's needs are determined, obtain an agreement on that on the part of everyone, including the parents, the child if possible, the teachers, and others. Then ask who will see to it that it is done, and get someone to sign to see to it that it is done. Decide by what date it will be done, and specify a time for accomplishing the delivery of the service. Name specifically the agency or the person and the cost entailed. Have a statement of the criterion the service was designed to achieve in the first place.

This kind of approach involves careful planning. It pinpoints responsibility for seeing to it that specific things get accomplished. It avoids the problem of children falling between the cracks: the mentally retarded, emotionally disturbed child who gets turned down by both program areas, for example. And it provides a good plan for increasing accountability and for getting the kinds of records that are needed for effective management all the way from the classroom to Washington.

It is of concern to many of us that time is wasting and lives are waiting. What new knowledge is needed by the field in order to better the futures of children?

Dr. Hobbs: There is so much that needs to be known. But I am always in favor of going ahead on the basis of what we know, and we do know more than we make use of. A crucial issue is finding out how handicapped children learn. The teaching process remains a very complicated problem. I think we have made quite remarkable advances, but we still have a long way to go before we can help children learn with some certainty of the outcome. I would put a good bit of emphasis on a new area of exploration, how ecological systems work. Most of the research in child development has been focused on individual children in isolation, in laboratories. I think we sorely need a decade of research on children in natural settings as members of ecological systems. We need to conceptualize the interactions of children and families in the larger settings in which they live and die and have their being. Finally, with respect to handicapped children in particular, we need to begin to do research through the life span. We have made progress on understanding problems of handicapped young people, but now we need to take a life span perspective. This means thinking about what will happen to the seriously handicapped child or chronically ill child throughout life, what the implications are for the family, and how society can continue to provide necessary support systems for the handicapped person as long as they are needed.

Labeling

Kate Long

Kate Long's discussion of labeling and its consequences in the preface to "Johnny's Such a Bright Boy, What a Shame He's Retarded:" In Support of Mainstreaming in Public Schools *should be read by everyone interested in the education of children with disabilities. The quality of the preface is typical of the entire book.* "Johnny's Such a Bright Boy, What a Shame He's Retarded" *is available from* THE EXCEPTIONAL PARENT *Bookstore, (S-100).*

The first time I heard the word "labeling" in a teacher-training class, it brought up a mental picture for me of rows of jars with stickers on them telling what's inside. I told a classmate that the idea of labeling people rather than objects seemed odd. She called me one of her favorite names, after making the point that people label each other every day. If somebody calls you a turkey, a genius, or a creep, you've been labeled for a minute, sure enough. But even though a name can hurt as well as feel good, it's just an opinion and usually doesn't permanently affect your idea of who you are and what you can do. When a child in public school is officially labeled retarded, emotionally disturbed, brain damaged, or learning disabled, however, the label is regarded as a factual statement about the child. Because the weight of the school system's judgment is behind the label, it is hard for the child and those who know the child to disregard the label, particularly if it is used to segregate him or her from unlabeled classmates. Such labels often adhere to a person throughout life.

Labeling usually occurs within the context of what is known as special education. Special education was created to provide programs for those children the general school systems weren't willing or able to deal with, for whatever reasons. Originally, the children were very clearly mentally or physically handicapped and the programs were quite specialized. Over the years, however (especially since the late 1960s), more and more children have been labeled handicapped. A child who is misbehaving or having trouble learning to read can now be put into special education, as much as a blind child or a child with cerebral palsy. This diversity creates a very odd and difficult situation. On one hand, special programs make it possible for genuinely handicapped children to receive much-needed programs they would never otherwise have. On the other hand, loose definitions of categories like "behavior disorders" and "learning disabilities" have made it possible to label and segregate almost any child with any difficulty whatsoever. The extent to which this happens depends on an individual school system.

I started working on *"Johnny's Such a Bright Boy, What a Shame He's Retarded"* almost four years ago, when labeled segregation of all special education children was still a fairly automatic practice in most school systems . . . At that time, my work had brought me into daily contact with dozens of children who had been labeled retarded and segregated on a very small amount of evidence. There was much room for error in the labeling process, and the consequences for the children were serious. Published materials and contact with people working in the schools in other parts of the country told me that this near-arbitrary labeling (and all the negative consequences that go with it) had become commonplace in all regions of the United States. In programs for the "retarded" and "emotionally disturbed," for instance, the question "Why is this child here?" had by all reports almost become a cliche.

Labeling and segregation of children is a subject that arouses much strong feeling. When I first began writing, my sympathies were almost totally with the children, and my frustrations were for the most part pointed toward the usual target — other adults in school systems. In the course of researching the book, however, I participated in a variety of programs and talked with a number of people, adults and children, who were involved in special education from many different perspectives. The more I learned about the regulations, politics, and economics that govern special education programs, the more clearly I understood that the complexity of the system itself often traps adults into procedures and situations they themselves would not have chosen.

As one Maryland grade school principal put it, "Don't forget that the intentions for these labels and separate classes were very good in the beginning. But many assorted pressures enter in, and what can actually happen to a child, in my school system anyhow, often doesn't much resemble the original intentions." For years, he explained, the segregated classification system in the schools has been supported by a complicated web of economic, political, legal, and social considerations that are often irrelevant to the

From *The Exceptional Parent,* February 1978. Reprinted with permission of THE EXCEPTIONAL PARENT magazine.
Copyright Psy-Ed Corporation 1978, Room 700 Statler Office Building, Boston, Massachusetts 02116.

educational needs of the child or the natural inclinations of teachers. "There isn't any point in taking out frustrations on each other if we don't like what's happening," he emphasized. "Better to get together and try to do something about it. But then again, you know how hard *that* is." It isn't easy to work together for change, but in many states during the past four years, people have been trying to alter the way children are labeled and segregated.

A few of the major objections to the labeling and segregation approach are worth noting here. Those who look at the nature and future of entire school systems, for instance, have argued that schools that can send children with problems "somewhere else" can also say, in effect, that those children aren't learning because *they* are defective, not because the system itself has faults. There is no doubt that large numbers of children in schools are having day-to-day problems, but the question becomes: Should the system reexamine its programs or should the child be blamed for his lack of progress? Under the labeling/segregation system, it has been too easy to shift responsibility onto the children themselves, without actually doing anything substantial to help them.

The labeling process has also been heavily criticized because it is weighted against low-income and minority children.* Pressure for change from parents and legal advocates has been strongest where labels were used as a justification for segregating the children of groups that were already subjected to discrimination in their communities. The children who had been labeled retarded in this book, for instance, came primarily from white, low-income families. In other parts of the country, they might have been Chicano, black, Oriental, Indian, or other minority-group children.

Many people have agreed that the nature and self-esteem of any group could be negatively affected if the practice of labeling and segregating significant numbers of children in the group was to continue indefinitely. People have also wondered what it will mean to our entire society to have a generation of children — those who are not labeled, as well as those who are — learning that anyone who is different or who has problems will be "evaluated," categorized, and possibly segregated. For me, this often-overlooked argument is particularly powerful. Increased pressure to conform and acceptance of negative attitudes toward those who are different is, I think, one of the most significant impacts of the classification system as it has been put into effect in the past.

If logical solutions were possible, schools would be hiring more elementary-school teachers to reduce the student-teacher ratio, raising teachers' salaries, and improving teacher-training. But the most reasonable solutions aren't going to be possible until some of our basic social priorities are reversed, and school systems are as well funded as, say, the military.

For now the only large available funds for school "reforms" are in special education and other "compensatory education" programs. As long as the funding remains this way, any attempts to deal with children's problems are likely to come through those channels. The extent to which this is true can be seen in the fact that, as early as 1975, at least four states reported to the Bureau of Education for the Handicapped that 25 to 30 percent of their school population was handicapped. Though the government did not accept that figure for funding, the size of those percentages amazed many people. Others who were not so surprised pointed to the fact that, in a time when it is extremely difficult for school systems to get adequate funds, schools can get extra money for labeled children.

It follows then that, partly because of the economic situation, most of the present attempts to find alternatives to labeled separate classes come under the heading of special education "mainstreaming" (also known as "normalization," "least restrictive alternative," and "least restrictive environment"). Mainstreaming means, first of all, that every child has a right to be educated in as normal a situation as possible and appropriate for that child, and, second, that all children will benefit from learning to appreciate differences among people on a daily basis.

Mainstreaming is practiced differently in different school systems. In many schools, a child who is having trouble learning to read might have been labeled and segregated. Under mainstreaming, she could spend most of her day in the general education classroom and visit a special education resource teacher in her school for an hour every day or every other day for intensive help with her reading problem. The resource teacher would work with the general teacher to help adjust the child's total program. In another school, a special education teacher might teach on a team with several general education teachers. However mainsteaming is practiced, it does not mean that every child can or should be put in a general education classroom, but that each child should be placed in as near-to-normal a situation as constructively possible.

*Since the early seventies, lawsuits have been filed in all parts of the United States on behalf of minority and low-income children who have been labeled and segregated through shaky procedures based on white middle-class standards. The Office for Civil Rights has documented widespread excessive labeling of children from minority families.

The Donnellan-Walsh Syndrome

Donnellan-Walsh Syndrome affects those who come in contact with the child. Those most often afflicted are professionals.

Anne Donnellan-Walsh

Anne Donnellan-Walsh is Coordinator of Autism Programs for Santa Barbara County Schools as well as Project Director for the Santa Barbara County Autism Dissemination Project, which trains teachers of autistic children in California. She has authored two manuals on teaching autistic children. Ms. Donnellan-Walsh is enrolled in a Ph.D. program in education at the University of California at Santa Barbara. In her spare time she enjoys writing, reading, theater, opera and playing with her two-year-old son, John.

This article has been adapted from a speech Anne Donnellan-Walsh delivered to the National Society for Autistic Children (NSAC) and was printed in the "Proceedings" of that meeting. While Ms. Donnellan-Walsh concentrates on autism, we believe her remarks are relevant to the concerns of all our readers.*

People have long tried to describe autism accurately so that it may be more effectively diagnosed and treated. In all the research, however, a number of symptoms have been overlooked. These symptoms, which correlate highly with autism and other disabilities as well, are dangerous and debilitating and have been almost totally ignored in the literature. Forsaking attempts at false modesty, I will refer to this disorder or cluster of symptoms as Donnellan-Walsh Syndrome.

This particular syndrome is unique in that it does not directly afflict autistic children at all but, nonetheless, can have a devastating effect on their development. Donnellan-Walsh Syndrome affects those who come in contact with the child. Those most often afflicted are professionals.

As with all good syndromes, Donnellan-Walsh Syndrome contains a number of clusters of symptoms which are more or less serious individually, catastrophic in combination and, unfortunately, not mutually exclusive.

For simplicity's sake, I will deal with just three of these clusters—those that primarily afflict professionals. I am sure each of you can then recognize the syndrome and, I hope, begin to institute preventative measures to halt its spread.

Guruitis

The first symptom is *Guruitis.* It has its roots in the desperation of parents who will go to any lengths to seek help for their children. The professional is usually doing very fine and needed work in schools or laboratories and, fortunately, has some measure of success. Kids begin to get a little better. Not all, but some, get a whole lot better. Wonderful! We are all a little richer when that happens.

Unfortunately, this professional thinks that the improvement is due solely to his talents and encourages the parents to think likewise. The parents buy the notion and reinforce it, because they hope for a cure. Our Guru's head grows and with it his need to control everyone and everything, particularly the parents, in proportion to the adoration paid. When Guru says jump, they ask, "How high?"

The Guru refuses to let anyone challenge or question his methods and becomes particularly prone to tantrums if a parent dares to suggest that another school or professional or drug or whatever might be looked into. For fear of incurring the wrath of the Master, the parent relents and the child continues in the one treatment condition long beyond the point at which common sense would dictate that the parent stop and reconsider. In most cases of Guruitis, as with all of Donnellan-Walsh Syndrome, the child loses.

Let me give two examples with names and details sufficiently obscured to protect my lawyer and myself. Laura had been in therapy with one agency for almost five years. It is a reputable program with a fine success record. However, it has a very rigid protocol and the director makes sure that this protocol is adhered to one hundred percent. Laura had been on step one of the protocol for all five of those years. Her parents frequently suggested that the program be evaluated but were received with stony silence for their efforts. Because they thought

*Reprinted with the permission of The National Society for Autistic Children, 169 Tampa Avenue, Albany, New York 12208.

From *The Exceptional Parent,* December 1976. Reprinted with permission of THE EXCEPTIONAL PARENT magazine.
Copyright Psy-Ed Corporation 1976, Room 700 Statler Office Building, Boston, Massachusetts 02116.

there were few alternatives available, they hung in there for five years.

Fortunately, there are other alternatives these days, and therein lies the ultimate cure for Guruitis. There are many good people in the field who are willing to talk to you and tell you what they think they can offer and what is available elsewhere. Laura will never be cured. The program she is in now — which, by the way, is in a public school — is doing a very nice job of teaching her to be a better functioning human being. She is never going to be a superstar, but she is learning.

I am not suggesting that parents must be shoppers. Any program that has a rational basis must be given a chance. But if it is not helping, at least seek advice elsewhere. And if your local Guru dares to suggest that he is the only one who can help your child or, Lord forbid, if someone in your child's program begins to talk about curing your autistic child, run, don't walk, to the nearest telephone and contact the National Society for Autistic Children.

My second example is probably the epitome of Guruitis. Some years ago a professional began to use a rather unusual approach with autistic children. Although it was not based on any research, it had a rationale. Since nothing else that was in common use at that time seemed to work, many parents flocked to him. One little girl did particularly well at first, and our would-be Guru saw in her a chance for fame — perhaps even the title of *Guru of the Year*. After a while it became apparent that the initial success was just a quirk, and she began to regress. (Bear in mind that this can happen in the best of programs.) When the parents finally decided that this was not the best approach for their child and might, in fact, cause her some problems, they confronted the director with their decision to remove her from the program. His response, in very adamant terms, was, "You can't do that! She is mine."

Needless to say, the parents were wise enough to realize that things were close enough to being out of control and removed her from this program. Nevertheless, it is a good indication of the problems inherent in Guruitis.

Pioneeritis

The second set of symptoms is very much like Guruitis but has an extra little twist. This one is Pioneeritis. The people who are particularly vulnerable are those who did much of the spade work in developing educational programs for our children at a time when information was scarce and resources even scarcer. But in a field as new as this one, anyone can catch this disease, because almost anyone can have the "first" program in a state, city or even district and, therefore, be vulnerable. About this and the first symptom, I can speak from painful personal experience. Having been in this field for over five years, I have found my hats getting tight occasionally.

Pioneeritis works like the Guruitis. But, in addition, Pioneeritis causes the afflicted to make strange pronouncements that give the distinct impression that if their school or program has not already said, done or thought of an idea, it's not worth considering. Therefore, either give up your silly notions and come follow the pioneer, never deviating for an instant, or there is a good chance that you will self-destruct. The obvious danger in this disorder is that newcomers to the field will be afraid to try anything new or innovative unless the Pioneer gives his blessing. This kind of narrowmindedness is hardly conducive to progress for any of us, least of all the children.

Not very long ago I visited a program — a pioneer — and a very good school. I was astounded to learn that most of the parents and some of the staff really did not know that there was any other program in the world using the same techniques. The procedure was "operant conditioning." Anyway, I am happy to say that every time a new school or public school class opens, the chances of Pioneeritis spreading grow dimmer. I only hope that those of us who have the symptoms will open our eyes and see that every teacher and every program that is based on reasonable techniques deserves a chance to share the spotlight.

I was astounded to learn that most of the parents and some of the staff really did not know that there was any other program in the world using the same techniques.

The Chamberlen Symptoms

The final cluster of symptoms in Donnellan-Walsh Syndrome is the Chamberlen Symptoms, named after a British family who were Royal Surgeons from 1596 to 1728. Sometime about 1600, the family began to gain a reputation for managing difficult labor where everyone else was powerless. Usually in cases in which delivery was extremely difficult, if not anatomically impossible, the child died and, as often as not, the mother died as well. However, when called upon, the Chamberlens would come in, chase everyone out of the room, cover the mother's face, have bells ring and lots of noise-makers, and several hours later present an intact baby — who frequently lived.

The methods of the Chamberlens were a closely guarded family secret for over 120 years — until one of the grandsons, apparently in need of money, sold the secret to a Dutch physician. In a very short time the word was out, and by 1733 the first report was published about the use of forceps. I am sure there is no need to comment on their behavior further than to say that in the age before anesthetics were in common use, the amount of human misery which could have been avoided if there had been no secrecy is incalculable. Despite their contributions, few people point with pride to the Chamberlens in the annals of medical history.

I am sorry to say that over the past several years I have seen an analogous situation developing in the field of autism. It saddens me greatly to hear educators say that they have developed beautiful materials, or great systems for behavior management, or well-organized curricula or new and better assessment tools. We get to see the before and after movies, and we are told that this program is super (which it may be); but we never get the nitty-gritty of how it is done. The reasons are varied; you have heard them all, I am sure. "The tapes are not perfect enough yet." Or, "You can't see the material because we are putting it into a book" (which never materializes). Or, worst of all, "If you want to see the material or our program or the assessment guide, you must take the course that comes with it — it costs thousands of dollars and there is a waiting list."

I hoped that kind of cultism went out with bleeding people, but apparently it has not because a lot of people are still bleeding. Don't get me wrong, I do not believe there is malicious intent in any of this. Often the reason is the need for money, grants or other support for a good program which is in financial difficulty. All I ask is that we re-examine our priorities.

The Cure

The cure for all these symptoms is communication. To keep our perspective we must remember that there are many good people doing good work all over the country. To keep information, valuable information, inaccessible for whatever reason hurts everyone. The fact is that public and private programs are popping up all over the place, and their greatest need is for information. Educators have a tremendous contribution to make in terms of developing the potential of the children now among us who will not be cured, but who can be helped. The only way that is going to happen is if everyone begins to share any and all techniques, materials, ideas, innovations or whatever they have found successful. The teacher in a small classroom in Alabama has to know what is happening in Detroit, in New York and in East Overshoe. Time spent re-inventing the wheel is time lost.

I submit that no autistic child now alive can afford to lose any time at all. I am asking that if you have something to contribute, contribute it. Write it up. Sell it. Publish it. Distribute it. This is the only way the dread Donnellan-Walsh Syndrome of Guruitis, Pioneeritis and the Chamberlen Symptoms will be cured once and for all.

LET US ALL STOP BLAMING THE PARENTS

Editor's note: When this article was written in 1971, the passage of P.L. 94-142 was four years in the future. While some of its examples and concerns may seem less applicable now, its basic message remains important.

"I'm sick and tired of being blamed for my child's problems! You guys are all alike. You ask us a lot of questions, make the child go through a lot of tests and then tell us that you can do nothing. If we complain, you say that if we cannot accept the limitations of the child, we'll only increase his problems. Why don't *you* do something, anything?"

How often have you felt like saying this, but stifled the wish because you were afraid you would be labeled a "trouble-maker"; and then, no one would help you?

Occasionally, the professional encourages you to express all of your feelings. He explains that it is really not your fault that there is so little knowledge or so few resources available to help children that have such a disability. He tells you that it is quite common to feel angry when you are in a situation where so little can be done and when you feel that you are at the mercy of professionals. His words can be comforting, but this message is more complicated than it first appears. On the one hand, he is telling you that it is all right to be angry. At the same time, he is making it clear that the professional agency should not be the target.

It is also true that merely expressing feelings is not always helpful. What can you do with these feelings if you cannot attach them to something and/or do something constructive? When people can do nothing to participate actively in the solution of their problems, they usually attach these feelings to themselves. If others can justify their inability to work with you, who else can you attack but yourself when nothing seems to help? Ultimately, you are left with the feeling that because you produced the child, you are to blame for the problems. After all, there would be no problems if there was no child.

This process, by which parents and experts mutually conclude that the major responsibility for failure of programs resides within the parents, is carefully examined by William Ryan in his recent book, *Blaming The Victim* (New York: Pantheon, 1971).

He illustrates how, unaware of society's role, the client and professional scrutinize and attack each other when programs fail. He makes it clear that any problem and its solution is shaped by what takes place in society. For example, in the society that prizes and rewards youth and energy, "old" people become a problem. In this society, resources are expended on helping people remain young. Unless society's attitudes toward aging are changed, problems of adequate health care, appropriate housing, and full opportunities for older people to feel useful may never be addressed. He points out that society, in limiting resources that are available, victimizes both client and professional. This part of their mutual problem can only be solved if they join together in their demands for a reallocation of priorities.

An examination of the typical situations that families with a disabled child encounter will illustrate how Dr. Ryan's thesis can be applied to "exceptional parents."

Let us look at the family when they first decide they need a professional judgment about the child's difficulty. It is customary for the expert to take a family history. He usually asks when the family first observed the child having problems, what life with the child was like before they recognized the problem, about their current activities with the youngster, and what finally made them seek help.

Implicitly, the very act of history gathering, so vital to any diagnostic assessment, contributes to locating the blame in the parent. Both professional and parent assume that the family's current program is inadequate. If this was not so, they would not need help. They further assume that if the family had been able to come sooner, their inadequate program would have begun to be altered. These two assumptions lead both to focus on the family's life and attitudes, thereby reinforcing the feeling that the parent is at fault.

Let us take a broader view of this situation. With many disabilities, it is clear at birth that life for both family and infant will be difficult. Often the hospital staff does not clearly explain to the family what they are likely to encounter. Nor do they make it clear why it will be necessary for them to initiate and maintain contact with a variety of specialists. They seldom take the

From *The Exceptional Parent,* August/September 1971. Reprinted with permission of THE EXCEPTIONAL PARENT magazine. Copyright Psy-Ed Corporation 1971, Room 700 Statler Office Building, Boston, Massachusetts 02116.

responsibility for calling these families after they leave the hospital to find out what has happened or how the child is doing. Until society makes sure that there are adequate assessments and services for all babies and their parents, the problems of early diagnosis and appropriate intervention will persist.

Let us now consider the disabled child when he reaches school age. There may be many problems in providing an adequate education. The family discusses this with their elementary school principal. The principal carefully describes his lengthy efforts to include disabled children in school, either in regular or special class programs. He then points out that all these efforts have failed for children with your child's disability; and that, in fact, many of these children have suffered so much from the school experience, it would have been better for them if they had not attended at all.

Here, the parents are encouraged to accept, not only the assumption that the reason for a lack of educational opportunities lies in the child's disability, but also that their desire to have the child included in public school is part of the child's problem. Once again, they are asked to assume blame for their own activities.

Another possibility is that the school dilemma exists because schools do not have enough experience with children with disabilities. Further, they will never gain this experience unless the school system provides either the resources or money necessary to develop programs for all children with disabilities. In addition, society is not living up to its own mandate that all children have equal rights to educational opportunities.

Failing to find an appropriate public school placement, the family finds a special program for their child. The child has just finished his third year. The family has been called in by the school director to discuss their child's progress. The director tells the family that the child cannot return in the fall. There has been so little progress during the course of the past year that it is not worth the family's money or the school's time to continue the child in this program. The parent is asked to accept the twofold assumption that continuous progress is necessary every year and the lack of it is part of their child's disability.

An alternate view is that the school's expectation of progress may be unrealistic. So little is known about the natural progress of children with disabilities through the course of their development, an adequate judgment about appropriate school progress may not be possible. Further, until society provides a reasonable alternative, this school may still be the most profitable place for the child to be.

Another familiar problem for parents is finding constructive recreational activities for the disabled child. Parents, concerned about the lack of activity in the child's life, go to the special class teacher. They ask her to increase the child's time at school and/or suggest what they can do for him at home or in the community. She reminds them that the child had attended school for full days previously. Supposedly, this was too much for him. Three days a week was found to be more appropriate. She also reminds them that a year ago when they increased his activities at home this had not worked. Again, the parents are asked to locate the reason for the restricted program in the child and themselves.

An alternative is that the school does not have sufficient flexibility to create a better program. In addition, although the family has difficulties with the child, they also have broad experience and understanding of him. This understanding must be utilized if anyone wants to enrich the child's life either at home or in school. Further, the problem also exists because society has not ensured that all of its programs be available to disabled children.

More successful programs of treatment for the disabled child are being developed. Because they usually have limited space, they carefully scrutinize all new applicants. The family of a disabled child, hearing reports of success in a new treatment program, apply in behalf of their child. They tell the director that they are not happy with the child's current treatment agency because it does not seem to be an appropriate place for their youngster.

The family's and child's experience with this program is carefully reviewed. Then the director tells them that his agency has a long waiting list and is unlikely to have space for their child. The director often assumes that these are critical parents and are unlikely to cooperate with any program. The family is encouraged to remain with their own treatment agency. He tells them that their challenge is to learn how they might help the child make better use of the current program.

Here, the parent cannot even confront the assumption that their inability to come to peace with their own treatment agency is an index of their ability to work with any other agency. The family is also expected to accept the premise that no program can truly meet the needs of their disabled child.

A broader view is that their current treatment program has very special weaknesses. Further, parents can adequately assess what contributes to their child's progress. It might be more constructive if society asked why it expends so much energy encouraging parents to accept less than the best for their children.

Families with children with disabilities and specialists who serve them will always have special problems in constructing adequate programs. They must continuously evaluate their mutual activities in order to improve their ability to provide a better life for the child. However, parents and professionals also must have available financial resources and community support if they are to fully expand opportunities for all disabled children. Otherwise, both parents and professionals will travel in a continuous circle; neither having enough experience to plan new programs—and without new programs they can never have the necessary experience.

In the current situation, with limited facilities, the professional selects those families and children most likely to benefit from existing programs. This means that the majority of children with disabilities have minimal support. The family must then examine what they or the child must have or must be able to do to make themselves acceptable for agency service. They often find themselves trying new things, whether they are suitable or not in order to cross the agency threshold. Trapped in this fruitless and, often painful, mutual encounter, family and agency unnecessarily expend a great deal of energy criticizing each other. Until they join forces and also demand that society make more available, they will be limited in providing new and better opportunities for the disabled.

In considering who changes society, some have divided the world into three groups of people. There are those who can tolerate the everyday stresses and strains of life; they say little, and these are the average people. There are those who cannot tolerate the everyday stresses and strains of life; and they shout, and these are our leaders. Then, there are those who cannot tolerate the stresses and strains of life; and they whisper, and these are our victims. Society has generally demanded that families of disabled children whisper. Society has implicitly blamed and punished those parents and professionals who have attempted to shout about their pain and anguish. And finally, professionals and families have often, unwittingly, accepted society's limited investment in them.

We do not believe that the parents or the professionals should stop their search for better ways of helping the disabled child within the current context. We do believe that without dreams of the ideal, they may wander aimlessly, searching for new directions.

We are reminded of one of Robert Kennedy's favorite quotations: "Some men see things as they are and say, why. I dream of things that never were and say, why not."

Communicating with Parents: It Begins with Listening

Paul Lichter

Paul Lichter is Program Manager for Moderately Retarded, Issaquah School District, Issaquah, Washington.

It has been observed in both research studies and autobiographical accounts by parents that one effect of raising a handicapped child is isolation. Parents may feel isolated from members of the extended family, neighbors, and old friends who fear, resent, or feel uncomfortable and embarrassed by the handicapping condition. Many parents either anticipate or actually experience social rejection, pity, ridicule, and the related loss of self esteem and social prestige.

It is not uncommon to find parents of handicapped children withdrawing from social participation and altering plans which might expose them or their child to social rebuff. This withdrawal or rejection may further frustrate the parents and thereby increase their hostility, resentment, or anger toward those around them. This, in turn, makes it more likely that their family, friends, and neighbors will want to have even fewer associations with them. Parents may find themselves in the grip of a vicious cycle of rejection and isolation.

This becomes an even more significant problem for parents of young handicapped children who have only just begun the painful and lengthy "coming out" process in which they publicly acknowledge their child's handicapping condition. Part of this process involves the replacement of unhelpful or negative family members and friends with a new constellation which might include other parents of handicapped children, community agencies or associations, and special educators as their primary source of emotional support and understanding. But, prior to the development of these new relationships, it may be the special teacher who best comes to know and care for the child. The special teacher can be a powerful therapeutic helper as the family struggles with problems of isolation.

NEED FOR UNDERSTANDING

The thrust of recent legislation and judicial decrees has been to bring an increasing number of children with a variety of handicapping conditions into the schools, at earlier ages than ever before. This situation implies an increasing number of contacts with parents who are new to the task of raising a handicapped child and who will need considerable understanding and support as they learn to accommodate and adapt to their child's special needs. This need for understanding, made even more crucial by the possible isolation from traditional sources of family or neighborhood support, places an additional obligation upon the special educator to form a helping relationship, not only with the children in the classroom, but with their parents as well. In addition, these relationships provide the teacher with an opportunity to be a source of positive growth for the entire family, as well as the opportunity for personal growth.

LISTENING TO OTHERS

The process of helping another person begins by accepting the total person in a nonjudgmental manner, and communicating an attitude of acceptance as clearly as possible. One very direct way to communicate acceptance of others, particularly to those in stress, is to *listen* to their feelings and to the ways in which those feelings are "coded" in language.

Listening may be either passive—where one simply listens in relative silence and where silence is an expression of openness and acceptance—or it may take a more active form in which the listener puts his understanding of what was said (and the feeling behind the verbal statement) into his own words and feeds it back to the speaker for verification and clarification.

This technique, described as "active listening," is a profound way to communicate a willingness to hear, to understand, and to have empathy with someone who is isolated and struggling to be heard. Active listening has its roots in the client centered therapy of Carl Rogers (1951). The continuing success of Thomas Gordon's *Parent Effectiveness Training* book (1970) and courses attests to its real value for parents, teachers, and others in the helping professions.

ROADBLOCKS TO COMMUNICATION

Typically, it is assumed that being an effective helper means giving advice. When friends or family members come to us with a problem, they will often ask, "What shall I do?" or "What would you do if you were I?" Rather than actively listening to the content and feelings implied by these kinds of questions, we all too willingly respond with advice; i.e., "If I were you, I would . . . ."

"Communicating with Parents: It Begins with Listening," by Paul Lichter, *Teaching Exceptional Children*, Vol. 8, No. 2, 1976.
Copyright 1976 The Council for Exceptional Children. Reprinted with permission of The Council for Exceptional Children.

FIGURE 1

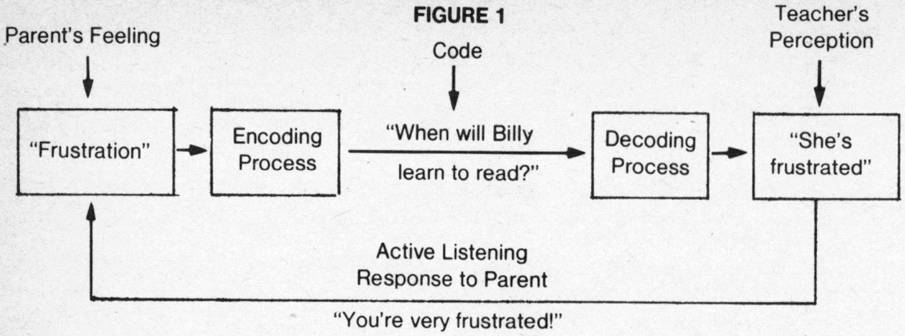

Let's face it, being asked for advice and giving it quickly is a powerful reinforcer and can be interpreted as an affirmation of our wisdom, vision, and mental well-being. Relinquishing this power is difficult and threatening, particularly if the advice giver has occasional second thoughts about his own wisdom, vision, or mental well-being.

Teachers often have the mistaken notion that it is their duty to help parents accept or adjust to their handicapped child by giving advice or direction. This attitude may reflect the possibility that the teacher has already made a judgment of the parents and has evaluated them as maladjusted, unrealistic, or disturbed. Given this predisposition, it is possible that the teacher may turn to any number or combination of generally unhelpful strategies such as ordering, admonishing, exhorting, moralizing, preaching, advising, blaming, psychoanalyzing, ridiculing, lecturing, questioning, humoring, or criticizing the parents.

Take, for example, a hypothetical situation in which a mother has enrolled her young handicapped child in a preschool or infant stimulation program, but fails to bring the child to school on a regular basis. The teacher decides to discuss these repeated absences and reverts to one of the above mentioned strategies. (See box below.)

LISTENING TO PARENTS

Listening is a skill which involves decoding the speaker's message to more fully understand the emotion or feeling behind the message. The listener is *active* in the process in that he reflects or provides verbal feedback to the speaker to test his own understanding of what has been said (see Figure 1). Another reason for listening actively is to communicate to the speaker that you are trying to understand the basic message and, if successful, that you have shared his verbal exploration. Brammer (1973) stated that a reflection accurately executed to the speaker's satisfaction is an objective definition of understanding.

The active listener translates his raw perceptions of what the parent is saying into more simple, precise, and culturally relevant language. The listener feeds back only what was said and carefully avoids adding his own ideas. To help in this process, the listener should constantly be asking internally, "What is this parent saying to me?" At the time of a natural break in the flow of ideas and feelings, the listener gives a concise summary of what he has heard. The feedback may include both cognitive content and feelings, if these are an important part of the speaker's message. The novice active listener would do well to focus initially on the content side and approach the reflection of emotion with some caution until more comfortable and practiced with the technique. Of course, an emotionally loaded message cannot and should not be "diverted" or left unrecognized.

The teacher should look for some cue that his reflection has been helpful and adequately reflected. The box below shows two examples of active listening.

There are some cautions in the use of active listening. If the listener is not careful, he may develop a highly stylized way of responding which may become annoying to the speaker.

Worse, the speaker may interpret the stylized response as artificial, phony, or indicative of the listener's lack of genuine concern. Phrases such as "I hear you saying . . . ." or "What I think you're saying is . . . .", should not be repeated too often. Using a reflection may seem a bit unnatural at first until the active listener begins to experience some rewards in the form of encouraging responses from the speaker. After a while it will feel more like a natural form of communication than the gaggle of questions, opinions, veiled threats, or bland conversation fillers that we too often employ in our everyday communication.

Ordering:	"You must bring Cindy to class on a more regular basis."
Admonishing:	"If you don't bring her to school you'll be sorry later on."
Exhorting:	"You shouldn't act like this."
Moralizing:	"It's your responsibility as a parent to see that Cindy gets all the help she needs."
Preaching:	"You should show more respect for education."
Advising:	"Let me suggest that you bring the child more often."
Blaming:	"You're doing Cindy a lot of harm."
Psychoanalyzing:	"You're just afraid to face the truth about Cindy's handicap."
Ridiculing:	"You're acting like a little child yourself."
Lecturing:	"Handicapped children need this kind of early intervention."
Questioning:	"Why don't you come more often?"
Humoring:	"Maybe you'll be lucky and break your leg so you won't have to come more often."
Criticizing:	"You're not behaving very rationally."
Persuading with logic:	"Don't you realize that early intervention can minimize the effects of the handicapping condition?"

ACTIVE LISTENING EXERCISE

The following is an example of an active listening exercise that can be used by teachers. Find a card or a piece of paper. Place it so that it covers up the first response of the teacher. First read the parent's message, then formulate your own active listening response. Then slide the card down so that you can read the response of the teacher and compare this with your own response. Continue this procedure throughout.

Parent: I wish Jennifer was making as much progress as some of the other kids in her class.

Teacher: You're feeling a little envious of the others.

Parent: Yes. They all seem to be moving so much more quickly than Jennifer.

Teacher: You wish she would make faster progress.

Parent: Yes, I do. It's so frustrating to see everybody—you, me, and Jennifer—work so hard and yet make such slow progress.

Teacher: You really get frustrated when you do so much and don't see results.

Parent: Sometimes I begin to think, "What's the use?"

Teacher: It's more than being frustrated; sometimes you think all our work is useless.

Parent: Yes. Somedays I think she'll never learn anything.

Teacher: You feel that she can't learn.

Parent: Well, not that she *can't* learn—but that it's so much harder for her than the others.

Teacher: Learning for her is very difficult.

Parent: Yes it is. And I guess I feel sorry for her because she has to work so hard. But I also know it's not good to pity her.

Teacher: It sounds like you're really struggling with two conflicting emotions.

Parent: I guess I am. But just talking about this with you makes me feel better.

Ultimately, parents should experience a feeling of being understood as a consequence of active listening; for many parents of a handicapped child, this may be the first step out of isolation. Parents may also experience more specific outcomes in the form of developing a sense of connection and direction to a string of otherwise seemingly rambling statements.

Active listening fosters a kind of catharsis and helps parents initially to identify and subsequently to accept their own feelings. In addition, people tend to feel comfortable with the listener who reflects skillfully. In the school setting this may influence the parent to be more open to a cooperative home-school relationship. Active listening is a technique which encourages parents to think independently and to discover their own solutions; it

Example 1

Parent:	I'm really pleased with the progress Loretta has been making with the new speech therapist; he's so thoughtful and kind to always keep us informed about her progress.
Teacher:	You like him very much, then.
Parent:	I do, very much.

Example 2

Parent:	I just don't understand. One day I feel that Gregory really likes his school, and the next day he says he hates it.
Teacher:	He really confuses you.
Parent:	Yes, he sure does, and besides . . . .

communicates the teacher's belief and respect in the parents' potential for self discovery.

Active listening is a skill which requires considerable practice in a laboratory or clinical setting. Many colleges and universities offer basic counseling or guidance courses which introduce and allow for the guided practice of active listening skills. Inservice programs or some of the commercially available courses such as Parent Effectiveness Training (PET) provide excellent training opportunities for those who desire more experience with this technique.

A summary of guidelines for active listening includes:

1. Listen for the basic message of the speaker.
2. Restate to the speaker a simple and concise summary of the basic content and/or feeling of the message.
3. Observe a cue or ask for a response from the speaker to confirm the accuracy and helpfulness of the reflection.
4. Allow the speaker to correct your perception if it was inaccurate.

ATTITUDES REQUIRED AND RISKS INVOLVED

Gordon (1970) stressed that active listening is not simply an external technique "pulled out of the tool kit" whenever someone has a problem. Rather, it is a method for putting to work a basic set of attitudes about human relationships. Without these attitudes, the teacher who attempts to listen to a parent will appear to be false, empty, mechanical, or insincere. Whenever these attitudes are absent, a teacher cannot be an effective active listener. Gordon listed basic attitudes which must be present during conversation:

1. You must want to hear, and have the time to hear, what the parent has to say. If you don't, say so.
2. You must want to be helpful with the parent's problem at that time. Otherwise, wait until you do.
3. You must be able to accept the parent's feelings, whatever they may be or however different they are from yours. To accept his feelings does not mean that you must accept them as your own, but simply that you allow him the right to feel as he does. It is a way of saying, "I can be me, and you can be you."
4. You must believe in the parent's ability to find solutions to his own problems. This requires the teacher to give up decision making power over the parent's life.

The risks involved in active listening stem from the process itself which requires the listener to suspend his own thoughts and feelings. Active listening is not easy; it is physically and mentally demanding. It requires that we attend fully to another person, that we cease to focus on our own concerns or problems, that we suspend our moralistic and ethnocentric biases and judgments. In short, it compels the listener to see the world as another sees it.

The teacher who willingly listens to parents risks having his opinions and attitudes changed and invites the possibility of having to reinterpret his own experiences. For some teachers this will be seen as an intensely threatening experience and for this reason they should refrain from its use. Others will choose to actively listen to parents as part of their personal and professional commitment to families of handicapped children, as well as in the interest of expanding their own human potential.

REFERENCES

Brammer, L. M. *The helping relationship: Process and skills.* Englewood Cliffs, NJ: Prentice Hall, 1973.

Gordon, T. *Parent effectiveness training.* New York: Peter H. Wyden, 1970.

Rogers, C. *Client centered counseling.* Boston: Houghton Mifflin, 1951.

Perspective on Parental Involvement in the Diagnosis and Treatment of Learning Disabled Children

The provisions of the Education for All Handicapped Children Act can have a profound impact on parent-teacher relationships. The potential exists for a cooperative effort, as well as for an antagonistic one. This paper argues for the importance of parent-professional cooperation. Recognizing that new relationships often have to be consciously developed, the authors suggest a number of roles which can foster cooperation in educational settings. — G.M.S.

James A. McLoughlin, PhD
Denzil Edge, PhD
Bernard Strenecky, EdD

James A. McLoughlin *received his degree in special education from the University of Arizona. At present he is an assistant professor in the Department of Special Education at the University of Kentucky.* **Denzil Edge**, *an assistant professor of special education and coordinator of the graduate program in learning disabilities at the University of Louisville, was trained at Ohio State University.* **Bernard Strenecky** *graduated from the University of Rochester. At present he is an assistant professor of education at the University of Louisville. Requests for reprints should be sent to Dr. McLoughlin at the Department of Special Education, University of Kentucky, Lexington, 40506.*

Parents should be involved in services for their learning disabled children. In clinics, schools, homes, and communities there are many ways parents and professionals can cooperate more fully. Each phase of the intervention process, from identification through evaluation, offers ample opportunities for parent involvement.

Parents are beginning to play an essential role in providing services to children with learning disabilities (Wallace & McLoughlin 1975). Until fairly recently parents have participated in learning disabilities programs basically as advocates and lobbyists for legislative, financial, and other means of support. However, increased parental involvement in the actual diagnosis and treatment of learning disabilities has accompanied the rapid increase of professional services in schools and clinics. The role of parents has been enhanced by the increased recognition of the significance of the home and community as settings in the total learning disability program. PL 94-142 has also had many implications for active involvement by parents of children with learning disabilities.

When parents are actively involved with professionals, three processes occur: (1) the parents and professionals exchange information, (2) the parents are encouraged to grow in their role, and (3) a trusting, productive relationship between parents and teachers is built (Northcott & Fowler 1976). Professionals and parents must recognize their relationship is mutually beneficial; it must be based on respect and cooperation. There is a demand for due recognition of the feelings and emotions of parents. When parents are involved, parents and professionals establish a partnership in assessing and remediating the child's learning disability. Furthermore, a commitment of time and effort has been made by everyone involved.

Parents can become involved in many ways and in many settings. Recent changes in procedures for assessment and remediation suggest concrete activities for parents in coordination with professional efforts. The role played by parents in learning disability services will be considered in clinics, schools, and the home and community. Each of the five major stages of learning disability intervention (identification, assessment, programming, implementation, and evaluation) will also be examined for possible parental involvement. Particular attention will be given the strategies which professionals can use to encourage this participation.

DIFFERENT SETTINGS

Parents of children with learning disabilities are involved in the process of intervention at various settings where their children are being served. Professionals in each of these settings should

"Perspective on Parental Involvement in the Diagnosis and Treatment of Learning Disabled Children," by James McLoughlin, D. Edge, B. Strenecky, JOURNAL OF LEARNING DISABILITIES, Vol. 11, No. 5, 1978, pages 291-296.
Copyright 1978 by the Professional Press, Inc. Reprinted by special permission of Professional Press, Inc.

assume the major responsibility to encourage the participation of parents. These efforts may take the form of arranging procedures with the needs of parents in mind, of establishing a role for parents to play in various aspects of the assessment and treatment program, and of directly training parents.

Clinics

Parents often are directed to a clinic for diagnostic and perhaps tutorial help for their children. The clinical setting is apt to stereotype parental behavior because of its aloofness from the actual situation troubling the parent and its other intrinsic characteristics (McLoughlin 1977). Parents are prone to be passive when faced with the protocol, complexity, and status of the clinic. Further, they travel from clinic to clinic, agency to agency, in order to obtain additional information and a fuller perspective of the child's learning problem. The clinical setting frequently represents the last chance for obtaining substantive help for their child. Parents approach the clinical setting with all the frustrations and disappointments of the past and with fervent hope for the future.

Realizing that the traits of a clinic and the perceptions of parents can work against productive parental involvement, a clinic staff can do much to create an atmosphere in which parents feel secure and contributive. Procedures can be designed with consideration given the affective needs of parents. This consideration may require the clinic staff to: (1) streamline procedures, (2) make requests for a reasonable amount of information, (3) respect the privacy and wishes of the parents, and (4) make a concerted effort to clarify and answer the concerned questions of the parent.

Clinics can also do much to dispel the criticism of producing esoteric and limited information by de-emphasizing the traditional labels of handicaps, i.e., mental retardation, emotional disturbance, etc. (Reynolds & Balow 1972). The alternative to relying solely upon labels is to present a profile of a child's strengths and weaknesses. Thus a parent is not given an excuse for the child's learning problem, but rather a graphic profile of the whole child (Kirk 1972). The parents have an explanation, not merely an answer to the question, "Does my child have a learning disability?" This approach is particularly appropriate in the case of learning disabilities since it provides the parent with a detailed analysis of the child's strengths as well as his concomitant weaknesses, the unique feature of a specific learning disability (Gallagher 1966).

Furthermore, parents realize a greater sense of direction if given educationally relevant information and strategies. A diagnosis that is vague and does not help parents to understand their child's specific learning disability is frustrating; the lack of attention to information that helps in designing educational strategies is lamentable. As parents take a larger role in learning disability programs, they will adopt concrete objectives to accomplish with their children.

Decisions about placement must also be made cooperatively with parents (Abeson, Bolick, & Hass 1975). Such participation is mandatory, not merely advisable. The questionable efficacy of special education services can be attributed in part to the passive or nonexistent involvement of parents (Gorham 1975). If parents recognize the goals of the learning disability program and have a vested interest in their attainment, the results are certainly bound to be better than they have been (Gallagher 1972).

Schools

Public school educators are keenly aware of the trend of more and more school contacts by parents who suspect that their child may have a learning disability. A recent survey in a western New York state suburb indicates that close to 50% of the guidance referrals received in one elementary school were initiated by parents who were concerned about their child's learning difficulties. Such information points to growing awareness and concern of today's parents.

Where parental concerns are involved, it is very important that the school personnel create a feeling of mutual trust and cooperation between school and home. One way of building this bond is to invite parents to discuss their concerns when they have requested a referral for assessment. Those present at this initial conference should include the child's classroom teacher and the member of the school staff who is processing the referral. This conference should provide the parents with an opportunity to discuss the problem and explain the reasons for their concerns. The classroom teacher's presence is essential since he can report firsthand the current academic and behavioral performance of the child.

After the problem has been discussed and all pertinent information has been shared, the group should decide whether an evaluation of the child's problem is appropriate. Whether the referral is initiated by the teacher or another school professional, it is important that a conference be held with the parents before the child is tested to explain the purpose and types of tests to be administered and to alleviate any of their anxiety about the evaluation. This procedure offers an opportunity to establish rapport with the parents and to obtain additional information about the child. Parents can help the school by providing a developmental history or acquiring any information about private evaluations of the child.

After the diagnostic testing has been completed by the school staff, the parents should be invited to the school for a second conference to interpret the results of the evaluation. The test results should be reviewed in light of how they relate to the child's class placement. If the school personnel recommend a special placement for the child, the rationale for the recommendation should be shared with the parents so that they and the school personnel can make a mutual decision of whether or not the child should be placed. The parents should participate in the development of the individualized educational program. They should also be given a copy of the educational objectives for skill areas which will be worked on. It is particularly important that the school provide the parents with frequent written and oral reports about their child's progress (Dembiniski & Mauser 1977).

Schools are also wise to organize parents' groups or, even better, to encourage the development of such groups by parents themselves (Cain 1976). The organization of local ACLD chapters enhances parental involvement. These parents' groups can supply a forum for sharing information on new legislation, school policies and procedures, and problems in the programs, for discussing common problems and experiences, organizing useful activities, and actually training parents (Kroth 1975).

Finally, as aides parents can contribute much to efforts of teachers and other school personnel to offer greater individualized attention to the children (Poper 1976). In some schools parents have served as academic tutors, generally of children other than their own, and as advisors on committees concerned with grading, curriculum, and materials.

Home and Community

Parental involvement ideally should encompass the home and community. Parents can learn skills to help the social and academic progress of their children. They can gather information about a problematic situation at home and subsequently institute a plan to change it. Knowledge of behavior modification, its possible applications, and the reasons for its use have given many parents a vehicle for home involvement (Hall, Axelrod, Tyler, Grief, Jones, & Robertson 1972, Patterson & Gullion 1968). Often parents are offered the opportunity to acquire skills in assisting the child academically or socially in the home through educational assessment clinics, local school districts, and universities (cf. Kroth 1975).

Political and legislative activism is another avenue through which parents can be incorporated into the effort to develop programs for children with learning disabilities. Through political involvement parents can help obtain the necessary support to assure the proper education of their children. Getting the proper education is a long process since the regulations and funding for services must be made available before services can be implemented. Membership in community-action groups concerned with the needs of children is also profitable, since learning disabilities can be associated with other child-related problems such as juvenile delinquency, child abuse, and emotional disturbance.

DIFFERENT SERVICE FUNCTIONS

Across these arenas of parental activity, there are five major service stages in which parents can play a role: (1) identification, (2) assessment, (3) programming, (4) implementation, and (5) evaluation. Professionals can facilitate parental involvement in each of these stages. In Table I there are listed some activities by which parents can become meaningfully involved in various phases of learning disability services and some activities by which professionals can encourage and support their participation.

Identification

Parents perform an indispensible service by being alert to early signs of learning disabilities. It is essential to be aware of the services available and to refer the child if necessary. Professionals must ensure that the information and the services are available and duly publicized.

Assessment

With recent changes in legislation concerning placement procedures and due process, parents

TABLE I. Parental involvement.

Stages	Parental activities	Professional facilitation
Identification	Be alert to early warning signs Be aware of etiology Be aware of services Refer child to proper service Talk to other parents	Be aware of community resources Use public service media Make information available Offer parent education groups Assure adequate funding Make services available
Assessment	Maintain a developmental log Respond to interview questions and written questionnaires Cooperate with teachers and other professionals Be a team member Agree to assessment Attend committee conferences Supply relevant information from previous evaluations	Avoid jargon Be interdisciplinary Conduct conferences slowly and clearly Be realistic Be positive Supply samples of a child's work Write understandable reports Supply assessment reports
Programming	Consider appropriate placement options and program goals Choose a placement site and program goals cooperatively Identify and choose goals for own use Attend committee conferences Visit classrooms Read parents' literature Review materials	Encourage classroom observation Explain educational curriculum Demonstrate strategies and materials Design and supply parent activities Explain placement alternatives Point out goals for parents (if advisable)
Implementation	Be a classroom aide Join parent organizations (PTA, ACLD, etc.) Support efforts of professionals Model good attitude toward program Be a tutor Reinforce child's skills at home	Supply parent education groups Support parents' organizations Supply discussion groups Maintain home programs Design materials and activities for parent use Design formal parent intervention programs in school and home
Evaluation	Hold professionals accountable Be accountable Supply feedback to professionals Help evaluate educational plans Serve on parent advisory boards Support parent activism (ACLD)	Supply parent training programs Establish parent advisory boards Support parents' organizations Include parents' contributions in evaluation procedures Facilitate communication with parents

have a definite role in the diagnostic process. However, without professional encouragement, a more formalized position will not necessarily mean a more active role for parents. For example, beyond granting the necessary permission and accepting the decisions made by the professional, parents should be serving more fully as team members by gathering observational data at home, by supplying relevant information from previous assessments, and by actively participating in the placement decisions. Professionals encourage parents by explaining assessment procedures for learning disabilities, by requesting and using information supplied by parents, and by conducting conferences clearly.

Programming

Perhaps the most sensitive phase of services for learning disabled children is the development of a remedial program. Now, with the signing of PL 94-142, parents must approve of and participate in the deliberations about placement and remedial goals. Rather than contributing mere presence and acquiescence, parents will assist in writing the individualized educational program. Thus parents can reinforce and support the efforts of the teachers. The parents can also accomplish some goals of their own. However, professionals must explain the options in programs and goals. They can help parents identify activities to assist their children, such as reinforcing academic skills, participating in the management of social skills, and providing enriching experiences.

Implementation

Parents can take an active role in implementing the individualized program. As aides and tutors, they can assist teachers in the classroom. Home-based activities can also be performed by parents. Frequently parents find themselves in the position of encouraging and supporting the child in practicing a new skill and participating in a remedial program. Professionals must be prepared to supply parental training and discussion groups and to encourage parental activity in the actual program.

Evaluation

No program is perfect; feedback is essential for improvement. Parents can supply essential information about the generalization of academic skills. They also are in an excellent position to judge significant changes in a child's attitude and social behavior. Professionals would be well advised to include parents' contributions in their evaluation design.

CONCLUSIONS

Parental involvement is a key component for success in serving learning disabled children. The philosophy of including parents in all facets of the diagnostic and treatment procedures requires a great deal of commitment and effort. However, there are countless ways in which professionals can encourage parental activity in the clinic, the school, the home and community. Each and every phase of intervention affords possible, if not mandatory, opportunities for meaningful parental involvement.

REFERENCES

Abeson, A., Bolick, N., Hass, J.: A Primer on Due Process. Reston, Va.: Council for Exceptional Children, 1975.

Cain, L.: Parent groups: Their role in a better life for the handicapped. Exceptional Children, 1976, 42, 434–437.

Dembiniski, R.J., Mauser, A.J.: What parents of the learning disabled really want from professionals. Journal of Learning Disabilities, 1977, 9, 578–584.

Gallagher, J.: Children with developmental imbalances: A psychoeducational definition. In W. Cruickshank (Ed.): The Teacher of Brain Injured Children: A Discussion of Bases of Competency. Syracuse: Syracuse University Press, 1966.

Gallagher, J.: The special education contract for mildly handicapped children. Exceptional Children, 38, 1972, 527–536.

Gorham, Kathryn: A lost generation of parents. Exceptional Children, 41, 1975, 521-525.

Hall, R.V., Axelrod, S., Tyler, L., Grief, E., Jones, F.C., Robertson, R.: Modification of behavior problems in the home with a parent as an observer and experimenter. Journal of Applied Behavior Analysis, 1972, 5, 53-64.

Kirk, S.A.: Educating Exceptional Children, 2nd ed. New York: Houghton Mifflin, 1972.

Kroth, R.: Communicating with Parents of Exceptional Children. Denver: Love Publishing, 1975.

McLoughlin, J.: New Perspectives on the Involvement of Parents in the Diagnosis and Treatment of Learning Disabled Children: Parents and the Assessment Clinic. Paper presented at the International Conference of ACLD, Washington, D.C., March 1977.

Northcott, W.H., Fowler, S.A.: Developing Parent Participation. In D. Lillie and P. Trohanis (Eds.): Teaching Parents to Teach. New York: Walker and Company, 1976.

Patterson, G.R., Gullion, M.E.: Living with Children: New Methods for Parents and Teachers. Champaign, Ill.: Research Press, 1968.

Poper, L.: A Handbook for Tutorial Programs. Brooklyn: Lab Inc., 1976.

Reynolds, M.C., Balow, B.: Categories and variables in special education. Exceptional Children, 1972, 38, 357–366.

Wallace, G., McLoughlin, J.: Learning Disabilities: Concepts and Characteristics. Columbus: Charles E. Merrill, 1975.

ACKNOWLEDGMENT

The basic research for the development of this article was supported by the Education Assessment Clinic at the University of Kentucky and by the Learning Improvement Center at the University of Louisville. Those interested in further information may contact Dr. McLoughlin.

A PLACE FOR NOAH

He is a tyranny you will never quite learn to live with, an obsession you will never learn to live without. He is a brain-damaged child. He belongs to you. And you are angry.

Josh Greenfeld

Josh Greenfeld is a veteran contributor to numerous magazines. He now lives in Los Angeles, where he writes screenplays for movies and television. The Greenfelds' search there for a suitable school for Noah finally led them to launch their own day-care center for developmentally disabled children. This article has been adapted from *A Place for Noah*, to be published in April by Holt, Rinehart and Winston.

MANY PEOPLE WONDER what to name their baby. I still don't know what to call my 11-year-old son, Noah. Perhaps the most definite thing we can say about his condition is the label most frequently assigned to it: "autistic." But I no longer consider or call Noah autistic. The term implies meaning, but defies definition. Though it oozes with scientific promise, it neither specifies a cause nor locates a source. It means self-involved—and who isn't?

My son Noah is brain-damaged. He suffers from severe developmental disabilities and acute deprivation in his fine motor processes. He is definitely mentally retarded, and naturally has behavioral problems. We have yet to discover the exact nature of Noah's trouble—which area of the brain and what perceptional faculties are not functioning properly. But encircling him with an Orwellian word such as "autism"—one that cosmeticizes rather than communicates—is no help.

Of little help, too, have been both the vast number of psychologists and psychiatrists—from Freudian to Skinnerian—we have had to consult, and most of the special-education programs we have had to encounter. Indeed, like most parents of a child like Noah, I have become completely disappointed or disenchanted with both orthodox medicine and public education. I have discovered that those areas which are of life-and-death concern to me are too often treated by their practitioners as merely self-promoting hypes and hustles. I suppose I have had to learn the hard way that most of the people whom our society delegates to know and care about children like Noah neither really know nor genuinely care.

It is six years since I wrote about my son in *A Child Called Noah*. Noah was then five years old and had finally seemed to achieve that great pinnacle, toilet-training. He was capable of a few words of reward-induced imitative speech, but generally behaved pretty much like a one-year-old, with poor sleeping habits and bizarre wakeful activities. We wondered about his hearing and his sight, but these faculties seemed untestable. His intelligence, far below par for his age, was both uneven and untestable.

Since then we have moved from Croton-on-Hudson in New York to Los Angeles. Noah is now 11. He is doing better than he has done, but not as well as I would have hoped. If I had once seen his malady as transient, I now know it to be permanent. But I still must deal with it on a transient basis. I still both enjoy Noah and endure him, which is, after all, the way most of us fundamentally treat one another.

As for Noah's future, I prefer not to think about it, which puts me very much in step with the rest of society. For anyone with stomach enough to visit the kind of state hospital to which Noah will eventually be consigned knows he has no future at all.

In writing *A Place for Noah*, on which this article is based, I have gone back through time, thumbing through the pages of my daily journal. I have transcribed my day-to-day hopes and fears and confusions, to best indicate the experience we as a family have lived through. I am sometimes asked if Noah's presence has changed the nature of our family life. Obviously it has. But since I cannot imagine the way our life might have been without him, I don't know in what way. But I do know it would have been easier. And I have to think it might have been better.

December 10, 1972. We've been in Los Angeles for two and a half weeks. We have rented a house out in the Pacific Palisades. I hope we'll be able to move in by Christmas.

Noah, now age six, remains progress in slow motion. He hears everything, but is slow on the uptake to anything, and I'm still looking for a place that knows how to test his hearing. He does not talk, plays with his blanket endlessly, and still has little interest in his environment.

December 12, 1972. Welcome to California. This morning the L.A. *Times* had a piece telling how terrible a state hospital for the mentally retarded was: Flies all over the place. Inadequate ventilation. Not enough help. I had to come 3,000 miles to read such things at breakfast.

December 19, 1972. Noah is quick to scream, to clutch, to demand, to be unreasonable. He is a tyranny I will never quite learn to live with. He is an obsession I will never learn to live without.

December 30, 1972. Noah urinated in his pants again. It was the third time he's done that in this house. So I took him to his bathroom and placed him under the shower roughly. Just because I can't understand his behavior doesn't mean I have to condone it either. I just can't afford to let him regress so quickly.

"A Place for Noah," Josh Greenfeld, *Psychology Today*, March 1978. From A PLACE FOR NOAH, published by Holt, Rinehart & Winston © 1978 Josh Greenfeld. Reprinted with permission.

January 4, 1973. Alys Harris, Noah's teacher at his special school, advises me that "Noah will reply to the way you come on. So you must come on lightly, low-voiced but firm." Alys, too, has noticed that I have a short fuse.

January 10, 1973. At his school they're trying to teach Noah some basic academics. Meanwhile he's forgetting how to brush his teeth, something he was learning in self-care in his school back East. So it's win one, lose one.

January 15, 1973. Noah cannot understand the concept of "wait." Which is something that most household pets can do.

January 29, 1973. When I am down—and I am down these days—Noah depresses me even further. He seems worse off to me today than a year ago. Nor do I think any longer that operant conditioning is the answer. I don't think there is any answer—unless it's belated infanticide. And it will come. Eventually there will be euthanasia for children like Noah. After abortions, the killing of the very sick, and the very old, it's the next logical step.

February 24, 1973. Foumi, my wife, is really upset: "Noah doesn't let me sleep even on weekends." "He's nothing but a waste of time." "In the end we'll have to institutionalize him anyway." "He's dragging us all down." "We're wasting our lives." And last night she said to me, "I'm waiting for nothing."

February 26, 1973. The simple truth: Noah can't take care of himself, and we can no longer take care of him. We have to find a place for him soon. I don't want him around anymore. In July it will be seven years that we've put up with him. If Job had seven years of afflictions, then seven years of Noah is enough. He has even ceased to be lovely to me. I look into his face and I only see trouble, and more trouble—an endless childhood without a statute of limitations.

February 27, 1973. The other night I told Noah's eight-year-old brother, Karl, we might have to find a place for Noah soon. "I like Noah," Karl said. "He can always stay in my room."

March 13, 1973. Friends ask me about Noah: "How's he doing?" And I don't know what to say. It's not as if he has the kind of illness that goes away, each day showing marked improvement in his condition until finally he is better. All I can truly say is that he has fewer toilet accidents than he used to. But in all honesty, I have less hope in the long run as the long run gets shorter. After all, even Noah's infinite childhood is finite. We keep thinking of finding a place for him. We know we have to start the long weaning process. But how hard it is to wean oneself from a six-and-a-half-year test of love.

May 11, 1973. I drive Noah to school every morning. I buckle him into the seat beside me. I try to talk to him. I say, "Hello, Noah." "We're going to school, Noah." "It's a nice day, Noah." The rest of the ride is in silence.

June 7, 1973. In quick succession I've learned of two fathers of autistic children who have come down with cancer. The stress of an autistic child can do any big daddy in. I should get rid of Noah before he gets rid of me.

June 18, 1973. The Los Angeles County Autism Project has been funded, and I've been informed they have a place for Noah for next year. And that's how it is. A year at a time. Even a month at a time. So we push on with Noah, beating endlessly against the waves.

July 5, 1973. The L.A. County Autism Project is running into a snag. They can only hire teachers who have "credentials." The best people I've run across in the field of special education don't have credentials. They're just too commonsensical to put up with all the classroom nonsense required to get credentials, having learned all the hard lessons in the field.

July 20, 1973. Noah is making some progress at school. He can now place different-size Styrofoam balls into the appropriate buckets. He can put objects upon the words they symbolize. He can also chew his sleeves and cry for no apparent reason.

July 29, 1973. The brain is there, I've decided about Noah, but there is no will, no concentration, as if the chemical that induces the active effort to live and function is missing. It's still hard for me to accept that he's seven—going on nowhere.

August 7, 1973. The Neuropsychiatric Institute of UCLA accepts autistic children in residence for a year or two for extensive observation and study. Naturally they have a long waiting list.

August 14, 1973. Last night I had a long talk with Karl, sympathizing with his problem of having a brother like Noah. But Karl said he was better off than one of his friends who had two older brothers "who treated him rotten, and were so mean to him." "Noah is never mean to me," Karl said, "even if sometimes he can't help himself."

September 14, 1973. Noah has been accepted in the L.A. County Autism Project. But already the project seems to be one in which bureaucratic and professional considerations will override parental needs. It won't be until the end of November that there'll be a nine-to-two program. As for the after-hours day-care program once promised, there is still no funding for it. I looked at the scheduled calendar. It seemed one of constant vacations. Public-school systems just aren't geared for full-day programs, to do full-time jobs.

September 17, 1973. This morning was Noah's first day in the L.A. County Autism Project. We woke him at 7:15, but he wouldn't get up until 8:15. He needed his usual hour to ease himself up from slumber. Otherwise, he gets the behavioral bends; he starts tantrumming and crying and flailing out.

September 22, 1973. I think we can have Noah with us for three more years—until he is 10. It is as if I had a kid with a mental form of leukemia. By the time he is 10, I have little doubt that his seizures will increase, that I will be searching out drugs to contain them. His brain waves, the electrical connections, the chemical processes, the electronic fields of activity, are all uncontrollable and unchartable.

When the human brain works it is marvelous; when it fails to work it is chaos. We do not understand it, neither in performance nor in breakdown. It is the door to everything, but we have been unable to open it more than a crack. All the modish theories of behavior that tend to simplify, to verbalize, to view emotion as the stuff of literature rather than of chemistry and physics are just so much game-playing.

October 2, 1973. Once more the professionals have taken me down a long corridor of promise, only to show me the back-alley door. I've discovered the L.A. County Autism Project will have no after-school day care, no Saturday, holiday, or summer program, as first promised. And the school day itself will be only four and a half hours plus a lunch period. When I called the director to tell her how disappointed I was, she informed me that kids up until the third grade were not *mandated* to get a school day longer than that. As for day-care and summer programs, they were not *mandated* either. I wonder: Was I *mandated* to have a kid like Noah?

October 14, 1973. We don't know what's happening with Noah at the county project. I do know his speech is nil now. He is generally more tractable, but still extremely inscrutable. He can assemble puzzles, group similar objects, broadly mimic certain actions. He can nod yes or shake his head no, but his only sound is "ah."

October 15, 1973. Some of our friends really disappoint me sometimes. They know us, and they know Noah, but after all these years they can still spout Freudian pap at us. We visited some friends in Santa Monica Sunday, and it was disconcerting to discover they still didn't understand that Noah was not suffering from an emotional disorder, but rather from a brain dysfunction.

November 19, 1973. Not one of our better mornings—or nights. Noah tantrummed before going to sleep. And this morning he defecated all over his room. But it was not his fault. Evidently he was unable to open the door to his bathroom. After cleaning up the mess, I tried to relax with the morning newspaper. But there was a piece by a woman telling how enriched her life was because of having a handicapped child who died. My cup must be running over: I have a handicapped child who lives and breathes—and defecates on the floor.

December 1, 1973. The L.A. County Autism Project has turned out to be bad news. Foumi and I visited it yesterday, and our worst fears were confirmed. There is enough staff, but the teachers simply don't know what they're doing—or even what they're supposed to do. In their insecurity, they salespitched to us rather than taught the kids.

The schedule itself was a scam, ending for all intents and purposes at 11:40. After that was recess, lunch, rest, and good-bye time. A nursery-school program—at a cost to the taxpayer of something like $275,000 per year. A cruel and criminal joke.

What hurt the most was watching the treatment of Noah. They were having him do tasks much simpler than he can do. I mentioned this to the teacher who seemed to be spending the most time with him. She said the reason they were having him do such simple tasks was to build up his confidence for independent activity.

But a moment later I observed the music period. He was supposed to follow the instructions of a record that went at breakneck pace. When I complained to her how impossible it was for him, she said flatly, "Noah has to learn to keep up. He's such a slowpoke anyway." That did it for me. Then she told Foumi she wasn't going to listen to any "lousy parents" when it came to handling these children. That did it for Foumi. We decided to take Noah out of the Autism Project if we can get him back into his old private school.

December 6, 1973. Last night I was utterly depressed. Finally, at one point, I took Noah in my arms, and while he giggled remotely, I asked him, "What am I going to do about you? Nobody gives a damn about you but us, you know." And while he laughed, I cried.

December 27, 1973. I'm beginning to suspect there really isn't much point in worrying about Noah's education beyond the fundamentals. There really isn't any way to take care of him other than to take care of him. That is not throwing in the towel; but simply clinging to it all the more tightly.

January 16, 1974. Noah came home from school wet, having urinated in his pants. That's the first time that's happened in a long time. And the teacher didn't even notice it.

January 27, 1974. I brought Noah to the park and he played in the sandbox. A little boy came over to him and asked, "Do you want to play with me?" Noah ignored him. The little kid persisted: "Do you want to play with me?" Noah left the sandbox and ran to the swings. The little boy was confused. "He doesn't talk," I finally told the child.

February 2, 1974. Karl, though now only nine, has become most professional in describing and explaining Noah to his friends. He does it very matter-of-factly: "Noah is not deaf, and he's not blind, even though he can't see or hear perfectly. He has a behavior problem because his brain does not function properly." And then he answers any questions asked by his friends as if he were conducting a seminar.

February 7, 1974. Noah cried when I delivered him up to his old school this morning. I don't know if we've done the right thing in transferring him again, but I'm just sick of autism and autism people.

February 9, 1974. Noah seems happier than he was—at least he knows where the john is at his old school. And the county school has not yet called to discover why he's been absent.

February 10, 1974. Karl asked us, in all seriousness, if he could bring Noah to school for his class science project. We didn't know whether to laugh or cry.

February 11, 1974. One of my oldest friends was in town for some meetings. He's the head of the psychology department at a Midwestern university. When he was over at our house Saturday night, he offered some smart advice about Noah: "Send him to the school that can do the least harm."

February 16, 1974. Noah seems to be more himself—whatever *self* means. The county school was killing the joy, the fun, the humor, the delight in Noah. And if he loses that, he loses his basic survival tool.

February 20, 1974. I called the L.A. County Autism Project to say we were officially withdrawing Noah. The secretary was sweet: "I don't know if you can do that," she said. "We don't have a withdrawal form yet."

February 21, 1974. Whenever people ask about Noah's schooling, the question usually is: "Is he making progress?" But whenever they ask about Karl's schooling, the question is: "Is he happy in school?" It seems to me now that they may be asking the wrong question about the wrong kid. It's perhaps more important for a child like Noah to be happy—if hence more manageable—than anything else.

March 11, 1974. We were at a brunch in Beverly Hills yesterday. Mostly movie people. The host, an old friend, had told us to bring Noah, saying that he was used to him and that his other guests would not mind. But as Noah pranced about the garden, picking at the grass, squealing to the trees, hooting to the skies through twirling fingers, I overheard a couple at the buffet table on the patio talking. "Whose child is *that*?" a tall, bronzed woman in a tennis outfit asked her shorter and younger male companion.

"I don't know." The man shrugged and picked at his mustache. "A child like that belongs in an institution."

"You can say that again," the woman said.

"Excuse me," I could not help but interject. "That child is my son. And I know of no institution where I'd care to put him right now."

"Oh, pardon me," the man said.

"But there must be a place for a child like that," the woman persisted.

"There is," I said. "In my home. With our family." They quickly picked up their food and hurried away.

April 1, 1974. Am I an April fool, or is Noah beginning to talk? His verbal behavior is more imitative, and his sounds seem to be growing out of situations. His teacher at school told me that the other day she was asking another child to say "potato chip," when all of a sudden from behind her back she heard Noah definitely say "potato chip." Last night when I asked him to eat his roast beef he said something that sounded very much like "I don't want to eat." And this morning, while I was playing with him, I put his arms around my neck and I clearly heard him say, "Hug."

May 2, 1974. The whole autism thing depresses me. The word "autism" invites the presence of psychiatrists and psychologists who are of no use at all. I don't know how much more helpful neurologists would be, but at least theoretically they have some knowledge as to how the human brain functions in physical rather than metaphysical terms.

June 16, 1974. Father's Day, and my annual heartbreak: Noah brought home from school his gift, a folder with a silver top hat pasted on its cover, and inscribed, "Happy Birthday to the greatest dad in the world. My work." Within the folder were some of his better line scrawls.

August 1, 1974. There was a meeting at Noah's school at which the director handed down an executive decree: all parents would *have* to undergo counseling. Foumi and I blew up. The assumption that any family who has a child like Noah must need counseling is abhorrent to us. It places the burden of responsibility—read, the assignation of guilt—back upon the parents. If a child has a crippled leg, one would never dream of demanding that the child's parents consent to mandatory counseling before the leg is treated or the child educated.

As always, there is the temptation to accept such a mandate with a loyalty-oath shrug. Especially when it comes from the only school for Noah with which we've been reasonably comfortable. I would find such an action on my part positively repellent; even more so, since, in a sense, Noah is being held hostage.

August 14, 1974. Noah hasn't been behaving very well these past few days. He refuses to sit down at the dinner table, and he's generally irritable. It's almost as if whenever we're wondering where to send him for the immediate short run, he somehow has to call attention to the imminence of a long-term or final solution.

Karl, somehow sensing it all, wrote a lovely poem yesterday:

Noah Noah everywhere
He goes around just like air.
And when you hear his sacred tune
You know he'll come around the room.
And when he comes to stay
He will stay his way.

August 24, 1974. Karl was complaining to me last night. He wants to be adopted into another family. He wishes he had a *real* brother. And how many times do I wish Noah was a *real* son.

September 11, 1974. Our problems with Noah have reached crisis proportions. He tantrums when he comes home from school each afternoon; he tantrums at bedtime each night; he tantrums whenever we run out of a food he likes. And last night we had another sleepless night, Noah wailing unreasonably, to the point where I felt it was cruel to poor Karl, having to stay awake because of his noisy brother.

The decision has been reached. It is only a matter of carrying it out. The time for us to subject ourselves to Noah's tyrannies is over. I've always said I keep Noah because we can do a better job with him, provide a better place for him, than any other person or institution. But now I don't think he's happy with us; nor is there much more that we can do for him.

September 13, 1974. The only solace I will have in putting Noah in some institutional residence is removing myself from the clutches and the whims of these "special school" and "special program" directors. There is nothing special about them. They expect you to humiliate yourself for the sake of your child, which is much like all schools. It will be satisfying to place Noah beyond their special cruelty.

September 24, 1974. Noah refused to eat last night, was up again at an ungodly hour this morning. I've lost my patience with him; I'm beginning to hate him. He ruins my weekends, spoils my days, ravages my sleep, consumes my freedom.

November 6, 1974. I came home late into a lovely evening. I took Noah walking into the dusk, silhouettes together, looking up at a maroon sky. Other people were walking their dogs; I walked my son.

November 7, 1974. Noah was jolly and happy yesterday as I drove him to school in the morning and walked with him along the bluff in the evening. Each day with him is either a blessing or a curse. But I guess that's the way it is with all kids.

November 30, 1974. Noah is a pain. I cannot take long trips or even go off on short vacations. I have to drive him to school in the morning, I have to return from work early because of him. I have to walk him, I have to bathe him, I have to wipe his ass, I have to attend to so many ridiculous chores because of him. And yet . . . I do not look forward to the day when he leaves our lives.

January 7, 1975. At this point let me be honest with myself: What is my attitude toward Noah? How do I view him? I think, put simply, I view him as a responsibility, someone I have to take care of—almost like a job that has to be done. Because if we don't do the job, who will?

January 12, 1975. This morning at breakfast Noah wouldn't eat his egg. "You eat your egg," I said, and thumped my chest. "You listen to me. I'm the boss around here." And then, in imitative reply, Noah thumped his chest. But he still wouldn't eat his egg.

January 24, 1975. We have had our fill of behaviorism or operant conditioning. It is a starting point, a step, but not the whole journey. We are dealing with physical incapacities. It is no accident that Noah's teeth are oddly spaced, that his body is completely lacking in muscle tone, that his coordination varies from poor to nonexistent.

And no educational approach or psychological technique can have any more effect than a cosmetic once-over.

So why do I concern myself about schools and teachers and treatments for him? Because if I were to say there is no hope for Noah, I would be saying there is no hope for any of us.

January 25, 1975. Foumi visited Noah's school yesterday. She had many complaints. He is still getting no more than a steady nursery-school diet. There is not enough emphasis on self-care; there is little in the way of vocational training. But one thing was obvious. Noah is happy there.

January 26, 1975. I ran into a psychologist in a friend's office this afternoon. He spoke about "rage repression," how such therapy has helped "autistic" children. I had to repress my rage as I tried to make him understand that in "autistic" children we are dealing with organic failings, that "rage repression" could no more affect an autistic child than it could alter the genetic makeup of a Down's syndrome [mongoloid] child.

January 31, 1975. At lunch a friend asked me, "What do you ultimately plan to do with Noah?" I shrugged. "We just play it from day to day, as if we are living with someone who has a terminal illness, enjoying the good days and abiding the bad days as best we can."

But now I feel like crying. With all my acceptance of Noah's fate—theoretically, logically, intellectually, verbally—I still do not like to picture him in a setting unhappier for him than our home. A child should not have to leave home just because his continued presence makes his parents tired and unhappy.

February 15, 1975. The politics of "autism" can get me down as much as the malady itself. For just as "autism" doesn't really exist—as a unique and distinct form of brain damage—the game some people are playing with it is real enough. I mean those who have a vested interest in the continuance of the designation. Those who have the clout that comes through the perpetuation of their organization and their positions in it. Those who have the professional authority to trade on the power inherent in their own esoteric expertise. Those who want to play games.

I just want to be as honest as possible with myself. It seems to me that the moment I become dishonest about Noah's condition, or my estimation of the efficacy of any of the proffered treatments, I'm finished.

March 7, 1975. Noah woke me up around five this morning—he had to urinate. Then he woke me at six—he was hungry. I managed to sleep until 7:50, but thinking constantly of Noah. Almost nine years old, but still a baby. How long could I appear with him in public and not be completely embarrassed by him? The answer, I hope, is forever.

March 17, 1975. My patience with Noah is wearing thin. I no longer derive that much pleasure from him. I don't like having to drive him to school every morning and having to pick him up every afternoon. I don't like his yelping and screeching in the middle of the night. I don't like having to clean up after his toilet accidents. I don't like having to explain his condition to strangers anymore. I'm no longer proud of his good looks. I'm simply sick and tired of the tyranny of his inhuman—or all too human—condition.

I don't expect anyone else to care about him. I know that as a society our compassion is as seasonable as a fashion—this year blacks, last year junkies. Next year alcoholics. But the year for Noahs will never come.

July 1, 1975. This morning, Noah's ninth birthday, he sat draped over the love seat in his Charlie Brown pajamas, listening to us sing "Happy Birthday" to him.

He shyly rose when we reached "Stand up and show us your face," and ran into Foumi's arms. So it was tear time again at the Greenfelds'.

July 3, 1975. Last night was a lie-around-the-den night. And Noah took part in it. He just loves it when the rest of us are also not doing anything. After all, not doing anything is his "thing."

July 5, 1975. Last night we saw a film showing how behavior modification has been applied successfully to some brain-damaged children at a school in Rhode Island. The film was impressive. But, unfortunately, all brain-damaged children are not alike—just as all normal children are not the same—and should not be cast into stereotypes. In this case, the children to whom the behavior-mod techniques were applied were much further advanced than Noah to begin with.

July 22, 1975. I was instructed by the state to bring Noah to a local pediatrician for a medical exam. It was strictly a bureaucratic procedure, a medical check on Noah's handicapped status. The pediatrician made us wait an hour and five minutes past the appointment time. And when the nurse finally ushered us into his office, he had no idea about Noah's background; he had not even looked at the preliminary questionnaire.

Noah took one look at the man and knew he didn't know a damned thing; he began to tantrum in protest. I chastised the son-of-a-bitch for not doing his homework, for trying to rip off some easy taxpayer dollars. Noah, thinking my fury was directed at him, bit my hand. Lucky for the doctor. I was one step away from slugging him.

August 4, 1975. The "autism" tag can be destructive. The volunteer assigned to Noah at the crippled-children's day camp told me, "When I heard he was autistic I was frightened. But now I see you just have to treat him as any brain-damaged kid who is way behind his age in certain ways."

September 1, 1975. Noah's mind may be almost a total blank, but his face is still an aesthetic experience. When he is clinging to me in the pool, his face up close against mine, I perceive him clearly as a loved one. Which he is. No matter what else he isn't, that he is.

September 25, 1975. This morning I heard Karl wailing, "Noah, stop eating up my room!" Noah eats up our room, too. Even the Indian bedspread we thought was "eatproof," because it is of such heavy material, is pretty much chewed away at the frills. "Who else," said Foumi, "has to ask a salesperson about a bedspread, 'Is it edible?'"

December 20, 1975. My neighbor told me that he and his wife keep remarking to each other about how good-looking Noah is. I said, "Noah doesn't have anything else to do but be good-looking."

December 26, 1975. For the first time I have been considering keeping Noah with us until we get old, until the end of our natural lives. But even that might be a cruelty to him. His life, no matter how I look at it, can have no happy ending.

December 27, 1975. During the holiday season I overheard a discussion between Karl and a friend of his. "If God's so great," Karl was saying, "how come he made a Noah?"

"Yeah," the friend acknowledged. "God sure blew it with Noah."

December 29, 1975. Sometimes I think it's my feelings that are grotesque, not Noah's behavior. Here is a nine-and-a-half-year-old boy, physically fully developed, that I constantly want to sweep up in my arms and hug and kiss. I'm the freak. But then I become philosophical and realize that every parent wants to do it with his kid, even with his 20-year-old kid. Being a parent is just as confusing as being a child ever was.

January 1, 1976. I celebrated the new year by taking Noah out to a friend's in Malibu and walking along the beach there, my friend and I talking, Noah trailing behind us. My friend said he noticed I didn't talk so much about putting Noah in an institution anymore.

I said it was still a day-to-day situation. If Foumi or I became ill, for example, he would have to go. But right now we do enjoy Noah, as a love object, as a living presence. I said at this point I couldn't visualize my life without Noah. Just as I once could not visualize my life with a Noah.

My friend said it certainly sounded as if I wasn't ready to part with Noah. I said I wasn't. Any more than he was ready to part with his home, which the state beach commission was requisitioning to make way for a parking lot for the public beach. That will probably happen someday, but meanwhile he enjoys his house, and we enjoy our kid.

I think everyone has a Noah, something dear and treasured that will be foreclosed too soon. Only ours is of our flesh and blood.

We want your advice.

Any anthology can be improved. This one will be—annually. But we need your help.

Annual Editions revisions depend on two major opinion sources: one is the academic advisers who work with us in scanning the thousands of articles published in the public press each year; the other is you—the person actually using the book.

Please help us and the users of the next edition by completing the prepaid reader response form on the last page of this book and returning it to us. Thank you.

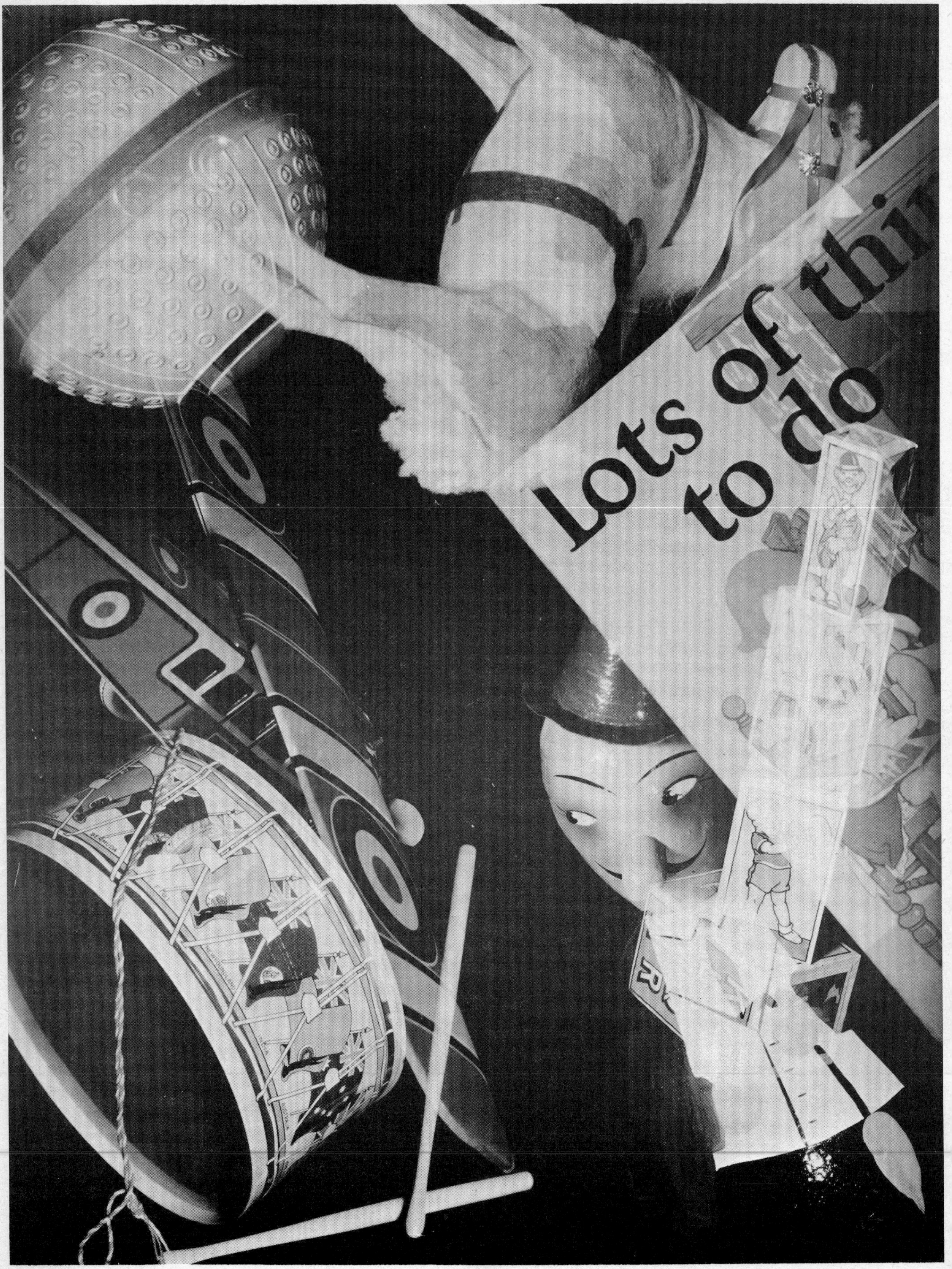
Lots of thin
to do

3 The Gifted Child

There are about two and a half million gifted children in America. They have abilities that place them far above their peers in academic, artistic, or social areas. As a group, their skills may vary widely, from precocity at painting to precocity at mathematics, and a child gifted in one area is not necessarily gifted or even exceptional in another. Identifying and educating gifted children has posed peculiar problems for Americans. An educational psychologist, author of "The Gifted Child," the lead article of this section of *Educating Exceptional Children,* says, "Americans have always had trouble on the question of how to handle people who are different-*better,* rather than different-*poorer.*" And yet not to identify and properly fill the very real needs of gifted children handicaps them severely. They may lose interest in school and develop social and emotional problems.

Several of the articles in this section on gifted children address the problems of how to nurture the gifted child not only intellectually but emotionally and socially as well. Many educators find, in fact, that problems in one of these areas engender problems in others. Priscilla Vail's "The Gifted Child: Common Sense and Uncommon Children" argues that we must remember that gifted children, for all their achievements and apparent maturity, are children nonetheless and must be helped to achieve emotional maturity. How to identify the intellectually gifted child and the special importance of identifying the gifted minority child are the topics of Julian Stanley's "Identifying and Nurturing the Intellectually Gifted."

The articles in this section also represent a range of viewpoints on the benefits or drawbacks of accelerating the gifted child. Joanne Yatvin's "Let's Go Slow on Acceleration" argues that academic acceleration is not always the way to provide the gifted student with "quality education." And finally, in the last article of this section, the reports of gifted students followed over a long period in a longitudinal study reveals what they're like, what they've achieved, and how their lives have been affected by their giftedness.

Looking Ahead: Challenge Questions

What are the differences between enrichment and acceleration?

What are the pros and cons of acceleration for gifted students?

Does a section on gifted children belong in a volume on exceptional children? Why or why not?

How have American schools traditionally dealt with gifted students?

The Gifted Child

No ordinary handbook on child care could possibly have prepared Richard and Sally Hunter for their first baby. When he was just six months old, Kam Hunter began speaking in complete sentences. By the time he was 3, he had taught himself to read. As a first grader, he was allowed to enroll in Spanish courses at a high school near his elementary classroom in Ionia, Mich.; within a year, at the age of 7, he was a full-time high-school student. Today, Kam is a sophomore in the Honors College of Michigan State University. He is only 12 years old. "I just want to be treated like any other college student," says the handsome, blond youngster. "But I know that's probably not possible."

Kam Hunter is one of the gifted children—roughly 2.5 million young Americans who are endowed with academic, artistic or social talents far beyond those of their peers. They are not just the diagnosed geniuses, but comprise a widely varied group whose gifts range from prodigious prowess in chess or music to extraordinary facility in language, mathematics or the visual arts: a toddler in Seattle who amassed (and read) a library of more than 100 books before she was 2 years old; an 8-year-old chess champion from New York City who is well on his way to becoming a grand master; an inner-city 12-year-old from Baltimore whose paintings already hang in public galleries.

"They come from all levels of society, all races and both sexes," says Dr. Harold Lyon, former director of the Federal Office for the Gifted and Talented. "These are the future Beethovens, the Newtons, the Jeffersons, the Picassos, Baldwins and Martin Luther Kings. And like other minorities, they need help."

BEST AND BRIGHTEST

Until recently, gifted children got very little help unless they had parents wealthy enough to send them to good private schools. Most U.S. educators balked at the idea of lavishing public time and money on students whose special talents gave them a head start. The poor and the handicapped desperately needed the extra attention; besides, to single out the best and brightest in public schools struck many as uncomfortably elitist. "Americans have always had trouble on the question of how to handle people who are different-*better,* rather than different-*poorer,*" explains Sheila Vaughan, an educational psychologist at UCLA. With the exception of the post-sputnik period, when American educators mobilized a frenzied effort to develop superior scientific talent, the public schools have generally ignored gifted students. The assumption was that they would make it on their own.

But no one knows how many gifted children don't make it. Some, it turns out, are so discouraged by everyday schooling that they simply tune out education, and never have a chance to fulfill their promise. Others develop crippling emotional disturbances after years of pressure from parents and teachers and resentment from their peers. And many attend schools where their talents are never recognized—or, even worse, where precocity is viewed as a troublesome trait to be quashed in the name of order and "normality."

During the past six years, however, the fortunes of gifted children have been on the rise. In 1972, Congress established the Federal Office for the Gifted and Talented with the mandate to identify and help develop the nation's most promising youngsters. Since 1976, the office has received $2.5 million a year; about $6 million more is channeled toward exceptional students through other Federal education programs. Thirty states now have full-time consultants on education for the gifted, and all 50 offer special programs—ranging from one hour a week to full-time curriculums—in their public schools. And there may be more help on the way. Provisions in the Education Amendments of 1978, which have been accepted by a House-Senate conference, would increase the authorization for Federal spending on the gifted to $50 million a year by 1983.

Despite the recent resurgence of interest, the problems of dealing with gifted youngsters are far from solved. For one thing, modern research has shown that the old measure of exceptional talent—a score of more than 130 on an IQ test—fails to pick up the extraordinary faculties of many students. Educational psychologists are broadening the yardsticks of giftedness to include creativity, advanced social skills and even exceptional physical aptitude—the kind of finesse that marks the finest surgeons, for example—but the process of developing adequate tests is painfully slow.

A WHITE ELITE?

Clever students from poor school districts face obvious handicaps. Last year, the U.S. Office for Civil Rights challenged New York City's three public high schools for high achievers on the ground that their student bodies were disproportionately white. OCR eventually withdrew its complaint; city school officials explained that many black and Hispanic junior high schools simply fail to inform students about the entrance exams for the elite high schools, while parochial and private institutions make sure that their own—mostly white—pupils apply on time.

According to Dorothy Sisk, current director of the Federal Office for the Gifted and Talented, many inner-city schools are so fearful of low scores on IQ tests that they hesitate to test children in the first place. "Or if they do," she adds, "they may be reluctant to give up their star students to a special program."

Many experts trace the new interest in the subject to parental pressure. "Parents have seen money spent on the disadvantaged, the handicapped, the children who don't speak English," says Isabelle Rucker, director of Virginia's Office for Exceptional Students. "They haven't seen it spent on the gifted, and they're beginning to ask why."

Even more important is the increasing recognition by education experts that gifted children do not necessarily thrive without special attention. "We hadn't realized until recently that giftedness is a kind of handicap," says Ted Rifkin, chairman of the English department at New York City's Bronx High School of Science. "Bright kids need a structured and challenging environment just as much as deaf kids need an atmosphere sensitive to their special needs."

As a group, gifted and talented children tend to learn faster and retain more than their peers. Almost all, say the experts, show a high tolerance for complexity and ambiguity at a remarkably young age. Some are individualistic and nonconforming, while others are inquisitive, flexible and open-minded. "A gifted child is a divergent thinker," remarks George Roeper, co-founder of the Roeper School for the gifted in suburban Detroit. "He sees many answers to one question." Gifted kids are also likely to be much more highly motivated than others, competitive, even contentious.

UNTAPPED POTENTIAL

All of these characteristics can be unsettling in an ordinary class. "If a child is always talking out of turn, if he always

From *Newsweek,* October 23, 1978. Copyright 1978 by Newsweek, Inc. All Rights reserved. Reprinted by permission.

thinks things are funny, if he's always trying to teach the class, it is not necessarily a sign that he's a troublemaker," explains Robert Rinaldi, Baltimore's assistant superintendent for exceptional students. "It can also mean he has potential that isn't being tapped."

Inexperienced teachers often misinterpret the gifted child's eccentricities as indications that he is mentally handicapped. One Baltimore fourth grader stuttered so severely and did so badly in all his courses that school officials considered him close to retarded. It turned out that the youngster was actually an outstanding artist. Encouraged to develop his talents in a public-school project called G.A.T.E. (Gifted and Talented Education), he began to do well at academic work, too. Last year, he won a statewide contest with a videotape on blacks in Maryland punctuated with a Scott Joplin score and a flawless narration by the erstwhile stammerer.

Insensitive classmates can also make gifted children miserable, by labeling them "freaks," "creeps" and "egg-heads." Jack Cahill, a 10-year-old from Brockton, Mass., was overweight, precocious and the butt of classroom jokes. "They'd demand that he spell difficult words for them, and he innocently obliged," recalls his mother. "They were taunting him, and he'd make himself ill rather than go to school." Frequently, gifted children's troubles are compounded at home. Their parents, more likely than not gifted themselves, have often forgotten the loneliness that can plague a youngster who is "different," and they are inclined to expect their talented kids to have social maturity equal to their intellectual development.

Recent research indicates that many gifted children become so alienated by these experiences—and so bored with ordinary schoolwork—that they simply turn off at an early age. Psychiatrists working with ghetto youngsters speculate that many a youthful gang leader may be a talented child who, uninspired by school, has simply turned his skills in an antisocial direction. In Boston, child psychiatrist Shepard Ginandes tells the story of a gifted teen-ager who became a "genius drug-dealer." He was enormously successful at his work, and used his huge profits to restore a colonial house. "If society doesn't give kids like these a channel for their energies," says Ginandes, who works closely with troubled adolescents, "they'll find one—often turning into dragons within the system."

Most experts agree that exceptionally talented students should spend at least part of their time with similarly gifted peers. "They need to know that there are other kids like them," explains Jack Mosier, California's state consultant on gifted children. "Can you imagine what it's like to be playing in a sandbox and thinking about a spacecraft, and the kid next to you has no idea what a spacecraft is? These kids need to be around others who are interested in the same things."

LEARNING FOR FUN

Educators are trying to answer that need in a variety of ways. Virginia and Maryland both maintain summer programs for gifted children. Pupils for Virginia's "Governor's School," four-week sessions at three Virginia colleges, are selected from schools across the state for extraordinary academic or artistic talent. They take courses ranging from Asian studies and dance to physics and drama. Maryland youngsters work in a similar program at nine sites around the state. At Frostburg State College, for example, last summer's crop learned about forestry and fishery sciences, while at St. Joseph's College, their peers concentrated on madrigal singing, painting, drawing and drama. The idea is to give the children a chance to do things that are simply not available in their hometown schools. "It's an experience in learning for the fun of it," says Virginia's Isabelle Rucker. "The kids applaud it, they're eager to get in there and dig, and they pick your brain until it's sore."

Some districts prefer to enrich schoolwork for gifted children by providing special education during the school year. In Decatur, Ga., for example, 60 talented students spend two hours a week in such classes. Next spring, they will undertake a remarkable project: a simulated archeological dig. Four teams, made up of fifth and sixth graders from rival schools, will create civilizations, complete with their own languages, technologies and religions. Each team will construct appropriate artifacts, including a Rosetta stone that provides the key to the language. They'll then bury the artifacts, and each group will set out to dig up and analyze another's culture. "We are trying to develop a curiosity about the social system, language and art of their own world," explains teacher Jeannette McClure. "The more concepts they understand, the better they are at making decisions. And these are the kids who are going to be making the decisions that affect history."

'WHAT A NICE ORANGE'

Parents who can afford to do so often enroll their talented youngsters in private schools especially designed for them. The 37-year-old Roeper School outside Detroit is a model example. The 500 students on Roeper's 12-acre campus range in age from nursery-school tykes to seniors in high school. For an annual tuition of about $2,500, they are offered informal—but demanding—courses in everything from dance to computer technology. One group of Roeper students has become so proficient at using the school's private computer that they have formed their own company, providing programing services for outside clients.

The teachers at Roeper are acutely aware that gifted children aren't necessarily wizards in all subjects, and they strive to nurture each student's special talents. Ten-year-old Sarah Nishiura, for instance, cares little about math or science, but loves to play with language. She writes short stories, plays, poems and puns with a precocious mix of cleverness, warmth and imagery. And she does it purely for fun, scribbling the lines on scrap paper, then hurling them away; it is up to her teacher to retrieve Sarah's efforts and save them. One tale Sarah wrote last year involves two birds who fly off to forage for food, and return to find that an orange has fallen into their nest. The papa bird's punch line: "What a nice orange mama laid."

The Avery Coonley School in suburban Chicago offers a much stricter atmosphere. "We are very traditionally minded," says headmaster William L. Kindler. "Ultimately, our concern isn't so much academic orientation as it is to help them build support and self-control. They will get the first in spite of us, but the second is harder—the mind wants to do things that the little body cannot."

All of Avery Coonley's 250 students have IQ's of at least 120, and all perform well above national norms on tests of reading and math achievement. And although all are encouraged to pursue their special interests, they remain in orderly, disciplined grades; the school does not believe in accelerated promotion. "They are children first and gifted second," explains Kindler. Adds teacher Edward Hartig, who has enrolled two of his own children at the school: "What's different here is the attitude. The atmosphere is not down on being able—all the kids know they can do it, and ultimately, no one has anything special to brag about."

Although many experts on gifted children do not approve of accelerating their education, there are a number who encourage it, rather than have talented youngsters languish in classrooms far below their potential. One champion of letting kids progress at whatever rates they can manage is Julian Stanley, a psychology professor at Johns Hopkins University, who seven years ago launched a "Study of Mathematically Precocious Youth." Essentially, SMPY is a talent search for seventh-grade youngsters who rank in the 97th percentile and up on standardized achievement tests given by their schools.

THE BIGGEST DILEMMA

"The idea is to find the extremely talented youths and make them visible to their schools so that the schools feel obligated to do something special to help them develop," says Stanley. "One of the biggest dilemmas has been that the schools oftentimes have either not known kids had talent or have been very reluctant to admit it when confronted by a parent who says he has a brilliant child." Stanley's program certifies the youngsters' genius. In five contests held since 1972, his team has tested about 9,500 children, of whom 6,500 have shown above-average talent. About 100 of his finds are now studying at Johns Hopkins, many more at other colleges and universities.

Many gifted students seem to thrive on acceleration, and show no sign of serious maladjustment. Michigan State's 12-year-old Kam Hunter, for example, loves mystery stories, plays rock guitar and piano and is an avid sports fan who is one of the managers of the Spartan football team. Bill Sebring, 18, one of Julian Stanley's protégés who graduated from Johns Hopkins last spring, is a modest, easygoing youth who says that he is "really glad" he skipped through school. "I think it would have been a lot worse if I had stayed behind," he says. "You sort of lose interest, and you don't get stimulated enough." Sebring made most of his college friends through extracurricular activities like backpacking and spelunking. "They may not all have skipped grades," he notes, "but they're as bright or brighter than I am."

EMOTIONAL TERROR

Most experts, however, think that the ability to handle rapid acceleration depends entirely on the individual student, and that many—perhaps most—cannot take it. "I've known children who had the intellectual ability to skip a lot of grades, but emotionally it would have terrified them," says Jack Nolan, a former elementary-school teacher in Baltimore. "I'd hate to be the teacher who moved a kid up who could handle everything academically, but who had no friends."

And it is clear that many gifted kids—given the right school atmosphere—flourish without acceleration. Andrew Lee, a 15-year-old junior at St. Ann's School in Brooklyn, N.Y., is an excellent example. Andy is an "omnibus" prodigy—a child whose every effort yields superlative results. He likes to shoot pool. He plays the flute (and composes his own music), does magic tricks and drafts anagrammatic crossword puzzles. He polished off advanced calculus at the age of 12, and last year, as a sophomore, scored a perfect 800 on the college-board biology exam. Andy is exceedingly popular. Indeed, he seems to be his only critic. "When I say something stupid, it's *really* stupid," he frowns. "Other people can just shrug it off, but not me."

Many gifted children who are now grownups believe that as long as kids are allowed to do extra work on their own, they can be perfectly happy in ordinary schools. Saul Kripke, now a 37-year-old philosophy professor at Princeton, remembers that his schools in Nebraska did not approve of acceleration. So while his classmates were learning to add and subtract, Kripke, with the help of his parents, taught himself to multiply. When he had mastered that, he bought himself an algebra book, then moved on to calculus. At the age of 5, he taught himself Hebrew. And by seventh grade, he was reading Descartes and Hume—for fun. "I was always being told that things would be over my head," he recalls, "and the principal would try to trip me up. I found it annoying, but I kept saying to myself 'this is not at all incomprehensible'."

Talented youngsters seem to appreciate almost any change from ordinary schooling that gives them more to do. Marvin Long is an eighth grader in Chicago's black ghetto who has shown an extraordinary talent for writing. In elementary school, with his mother's approval, Marvin skipped two grades. Now, at 11, he's one of the smallest boys in his class, and sometimes he finds the public-school atmosphere uncomfortable. "The other kids call me 'Brain' and 'Professor'," he complains. But one half-day a week, Marvin is freed from class for work at one of Chicago's twelve centers for the gifted. There, he concentrates on writing—mostly short stories. "I love it," says Marvin. "I feel more free to express myself there."

NATIONAL RECOGNITION

But Marvin is lucky. This year, the experts estimate, only about 12 per cent of the ablest American schoolchildren will get the extra attention and academic encouragement that they need. Although those concerned with the education of the gifted are pleased by the current surge of interest in their cause, many of them warn that it is not enough. And they worry that it is just a cyclical phenomenon, one that will soon be eclipsed by another period of egalitarian neglect.

"The issue before us is that we don't honor or nurture intelligence in this country," argues Stanley Bosworth, founder and headmaster of St. Ann's. "For years, we've neglected brains and excellence, while spending billions of dollars on the handicapped and the mediocre." Bosworth and his colleagues do not advocate less attention to disadvantaged youngsters. Instead, they urge national recognition of gifted children as another minority group that needs special help. Unless such help is forthcoming, they warn, the U.S. is in danger of squandering its finest minds, talents and leaders—the most precious natural resources of all.

—MERRILL SHEILS with LUCY HOWARD in Washington, SYLVESTER MONROE in Chicago, JON LOWELL in Detroit and FREDERICK V. BOYD in New York

The Gifted Child

Common Sense and Uncommon Children

Priscilla L. Vail

Priscilla Vail is the reading specialist at Rippowam-Cisqua School, Bedford, New York.

The first thing we have to remember about gifted children is that they are children. Like other children, they grow, get measles, cry, laugh, and suffer the glories and pains of growing up. Because they are smart, people are sometimes intimidated by them and think that just because they have giant vocabularies or understand quadratic equations they have the world by the tail. Not so.

Our gifted child introduced us to the wonders and problems of her life. As we and her schools tried to provide the best possible environment for her, we learned a lot about all gifted children from our good choices, and especially from our mistakes. As a parent who is also a teacher, I came to see why some theories about educating the gifted don't have much to do with live children.

Lucia was the third of three daughters born to us at two-year intervals. She was an impatient baby, eager to be rid of the trappings of infancy. She hated being in a buggy or a basket. While her disposition improved when she could sit up and see more, she was frustrated until she could walk. Then, she had both vistas and independence, and she began to laugh.

She played with all of the usual household toys, and her early talking didn't seem unusual, given the constant companionship of her very verbal sisters. In spite of this facility, she kept many of her thoughts and accomplishments to herself in a kind of emotional and intellectual privacy. She was a passionate small person with what seemed like quirkily adult ways of seeing the world.

She did ordinary nursery school things in nursery school and appeared to be doing the same in kindergarten. No one knew she could read until one spring morning when she announced to the class at playground that everyone would be having cupcakes and chocolate milk the next day. Queried on her source of information, she was stopped short. Having blown her cover, she had to admit that she had read it on the teacher's desk.

After recess, the teacher sat down with her to give her some other things to read, ranging from first-grade books through *The Wizard of Oz*. She could read them all with ease and comprehension. No one had taught her. She said she just knew how, and indeed she did.

The school found this extraordinary. We tried to play it down because, although our fourth-grade daughter was whizzing along academically, our second-grade daughter was having a devilish time with the printed word. Had today's knowledge been available then, she could have been spared many needless tears.

Summer came, with its puppets, costumes, bathing suits, picnics, and library cards. Lucia enjoyed them all and made the September journey to the shoe store with enthusiasm and excitement about first grade.

No more than two weeks had gone by before the school called to schedule an appointment. They came right to the point. There was no way they could keep Lucia in first grade.

She already knew all the work planned for the rest of the year, not only in reading, but in math and in general information and concepts. Her being so far ahead was demoralizing to the other children, and some parents had also complained. (In 1961, competition was rampant in rigorous schools. It involved class standing as well as marks, and it began as early as first grade.) Some parents argued that it wasn't fair for their children to have to compete with someone who already knew the material.

The teacher didn't feel she could keep Lucia. No, she wasn't making any trouble. She was cooperative and seemed glad to be there, but surely she would soon be bored, and discipline problems would follow.

We agreed that boredom is a threat to curiosity and that curiosity deserves protection. However, we wondered whether Lucia couldn't be given some projects to do while the group was working on skills she already had. We were told that this wasn't possible. It would be poor for classroom morale and discipline and would single her out and separate her from the group. (How strange this sounds, given today's flexibility in the classroom.)

What was to be done, then, with our cheery little misfit? The school suggested moving her forthwith into second grade. This raised many questions in our minds. Would she be accepted as a member of the class, joining them late, younger, and with some sort of favored status? Surely the kiss of death. Would second-grade work be right for her? She was already reading comfortably at third-grade level and above.

How much of a handicap would a full year's deficit be to Lucia in sports? Her athletic ability was average for her own age, and sports are important for establishing a place in the group. What about always being a year younger than your classmates in terms of psychological development, activities, and boy-girl relationships?

We could see from our fifth grader that these concerns would be upon us in no time. The decision we made now would have to carry us over more than just the next year. It would be foolish and harmful to sidestep a present problem if we were putting up obstacles for the future.

The school acknowledged all these potential difficulties but recommended, or insisted, that Lucia be moved on Monday. They felt they were dealing with an exceptional intellect that was in a period of vigorous growth. If they didn't stimulate her mind at such a moment, Lucia, with her passionate and purposeful nature, could be turned away from learning for life—something the school was unwilling to risk.

Reprinted from *Independent School,* May 1978. From THE WORLD OF THE GIFTED CHILD by Priscilla Vail. Copyright © 1979 by Priscilla Vail. Used with permission of the publisher, Walker and Company.

We were all thinking and trying hard up to this point. Then we all made a wrong assumption. "Because she is so smart," they said, "she will be able to figure out the social problems." We agreed.

Lucia went into second grade and, after some preliminary skirmishing, was fairly well accepted. Her classmates enjoyed her sense of humor and the stories and plays she made up. She was known in the group for being musical as well as smart. That seemed to take away some of the sting. She did well enough in sports, and the work was all right, even though it presented very little challenge. We didn't mind that because we were glad that she had enough physical and mental energy left at the end of the day for extracurricular and creative pursuits.

Lucia had smooth sailing through second, third, fourth, and part of fifth grade. Then the trouble began.

At first, it just seemed to be an energetic wave of showing off. Hoping it was a phase, we decided to ride it out. The school thought she had gotten too big for her britches and decided to crack down.

Now, we and Lucia realized that all of a sudden she saw her classmates moving away from her to some new level. She used her tried and true humor and song and dance routines to call them back to where she was. They, having reached a new level, saw her antics as a pain in the neck and drew even farther away. The problem got worse.

Sixth grade was really bad. Although she was doing excellent academic work, Lucia was friendless, rude, and seemingly uncaring. Moodiness, sarcasm, and antagonism were the order of the day. Her humorous tongue developed a deadly edge honed by practice. She was no joy to others and no joy to herself. Everyone was concerned.

That spring, I went to hear the fifth and sixth grades sing. Music had remained a constant joy for Lucia. I looked at the sixth grade lined up on the stage—tall, faces growing in that bone-expanding way that heralds adolescence. Boys were getting thicker through the chest, and girls had bosoms. Then there was Lucia, flat of chest, delicate of face like—yes—like all the fifth graders.

I wondered whether she should be back with her contemporaries and shared my thoughts with the school. They said that even though she was having a very bad time socially and emotionally her academic work was excellent. The dangers of boredom were mentioned again, and I got the familiar "A kid as smart as she is will figure all this social stuff out." I wasn't convinced, and I got their blessing to talk the idea over with Lucia.

We did talk to her about it, and her initial reaction (as it was to everything) was negative. We said that she might feel better being with people her own age, even though she was so good at her work. We told her honestly that the school was afraid she might get bored repeating a year, but that we didn't feel she was enjoying her work, or life, very much. She didn't really seem to be getting much out of it except good marks.

Memorial Day weekend brought the imminence of final exams. Lucia's sisters did diligent things with Latin verbs and history dates. Lucia played with her hamster, stayed up late, and played the radio—loud. She failed four out of six exams and greeted the news with a matter-of-fact, rather cheerful "Well, I guess I'll have to stay back."

Her own age group accepted her more kindly than one might have expected. They all grew bosoms together. And, though she read the same stories and studied the same history as she had the year before, she brought such different perceptions to them that they were like new.

New, also, was the experience of feeling a certain way about a character or event and finding that other people did, too. That had never happened to her in school before.

No matter how smart you are, you can't be twelve when you're eleven. You don't feel like a twelve-year-old when you're eleven. If you try, you're a fake twelve, and you miss being eleven. You have to go back later and pick up what you've missed, like a dropped stitch. The more rows you knit beyond the dropped stitch, the harder it is to weave it back up. That was Lucia's next task.

Lucia's high scores, high marks, and highest possible percentiles in standardized testing all gave the appearance of a brilliant child working at full capacity. Her great facility with words continued to help her learn quickly and easily from books.

Verbal expression—written, oral, and thespian—was a happy outlet for her creative energies. It was tempting to encourage her to go on in these fields by fostering vertical growth in her strong area. But concentration on vertical growth is not what the gifted child needs.

Lucia moved from elementary school to an extremely demanding intellectually elite high school that gave a surface appearance of individuality and creativity.

In showing us around, the headmaster said, "We have nothing here to force standardized behavior on our students—no uniforms, no one set of academic requirements. We have a community of individuals—all very different. Children this bright and this creative are free thinkers and enjoy being different from one another."

What he didn't say, and what we forgot, is that children of this age seek out kinds of conformity because they need the safety of a group code. It may appear in shared tastes for styles of dress, slang, or antagonisms, but it is part of every adolescent group.

When so much is shifting inside, the child needs visible, external confirmation that others are like him. He already feels different and perhaps frighteningly alone. The world of adult support should provide ways for him to feel more connected, not more isolated.

When the adult world denies the existence and value of such conformity, it doesn't disappear. Instead, it goes underground, and the more subtle it is, the more rigid and binding its requirements, and thus the harder it is to discard or outgrow.

In Lucia's school, once again, adult expectations, based on assessment of intellectual capacity, worked to deny rather than enhance normal progression through developmental stages.

The head said, "Young people with this kind of intellect have different emotional needs from other young people. They are so quick to see and to understand that they are really much older than their chronological age. They don't need as much emotional support or time. They need more intellectual challenge."

Wrong. These children who are so quick to see patterns and grasp implications need even more chances to grow emotionally. Enhanced perception means enhanced perception of both pain and joy, not just joy, and of e discrepancy between how you see yourself and how the orld sees you.

Bringing these two images into focus is one of the major sks of growing up, as it is one of the definitions of auton-ny. Any time the trusted adult world reinforces the discrep-cy in the two images by ignoring or denying its existence, it akes pain for the child. Any time the trusted adult world can y, by implication or words, that "growing up is just as hard r you as it is for anyone else," it brings acceptance and nderstanding from which the child can draw real support.

In this respect, dealing with the gifted is very like dealing ith the learning-disabled. The learning-disabled child's bluffs d camouflages seem to say, "If they find out how bad I am that, they won't like (or accept) me any more." The gifted ild may be worrying, "If they find out that inside of me I'm ot made of magic and excellence they won't like (or accept) e any more." The underlying question for both is, "If I'm ot what they think I am, do I exist?"

One of the first tasks for a teacher who deals with a learn-g-disabled child is to acknowledge his disability while show-g him, at the same time, that you like (or accept) him. We ust treat our gifted students with the same understanding d acceptance.

Socially, the gifted child starts with an extra handicap. The orld is apt to view success with a mistrust born of jealousy nd to withhold. Many people find it hard to be kind and atural with someone rich, famous, or smart. By withholding r remaining somewhat aloof, they can say, "You're not any etter than I am." Wealth and intelligence are two of the ings that make people defensive.

Intellectually, the gifted child should not march in lock step ith everyone else. His mind must not be shackled. His curios-y must be protected and his growth encouraged. Some ways f doing this promote equilibrium; others do not. We should ever diminish the child's gifted area in order to create a bal-nce. Neither should we encourage growth in only one area, ereby creating a monolith.

Look at the child as a mobile. The center of balance is the ore of the child. The long wire or thread holding a large, eavy object can be seen as the child's astonishing facility in ath, science, art, or language. In a mobile, that is balanced y two shorter wires or threads holding smaller, lighter ob-ects. It is to these that people working with the gifted must rn their attention.

The child instinctively turns to the primary weight. It is his ature, or his calling, and he must be precisely taught in what-ver field this happens to be. Unaided, he may turn solely in nis direction, preventing balance. How much better to ncourage him to explore and find the areas that will provide ne secondary counterweights, bringing synergy to his mobile.

Here, the teacher has the task of introducing the child to knowledge or ways of thinking that he might not find on his own. Do teachers and parents need to be trained in this technique, or do they simply need to enlarge their point of view?

One mark of the gifted mind is its ability to see patterns and relationships that less nimble minds might miss. The child whose genius lies in music may find fascination in mathematics or molecular structure. Rhythm in sports or design may provide complementary enjoyment.

Perhaps literature, pantomime, or hieroglyphics would intrigue him as a different kind of symbolic representation. The child with a gift for history might be fascinated by geology or astronomy as a way of comprehending the enormous. Perhaps painting and sculpture as a way of knowing about people, or electronics and communications as sources of information, would bring a complement.

The whole world can be a game of attribute blocks. The gifted mind makes a lifelong search for combinations, which are endless.

Something to do as well as something to think about should be on the smorgasbord, whether it be cooking, painting, carving, weaving, playing an instrument, athletics, or carpentry. Gifted children have an enormous faculty for taking in information. We have to remember to give them widely varied opportunities for giving it out, too.

Caretaking, also vital, can involve smaller children, other people, community projects, or a pet. Responsibility, affection, and being needed as a giver of care and nurture contribute powerfully to a positive emotional base. Caretaking forges a bond between the child and the world, which the gifted child needs badly.

What we have learned over the years seems so obvious now, yet sorting it out has taken time and tears. If you can profit from our experience and the wisdom we have gathered from others over the years, here it is.

First, try to see the gifted child primarily as a developing child. His special learning pattern is an extra, not the main thing.

Second, provide extra opportunities for emotional growth. With a strong base inside, the child will be able to use his extraordinary mind even more effectively. Without it, he is just a circus performer who does breathtaking stunts, but not a whole person.

And third, introduce the child to many different kinds of thinking and doing so that he can develop the counterweights to keep his mobile balanced.

Lucia is nearly through college. She is doing exceptional work there, and she has rewoven her stitch.

IDENTIFYING AND NURTURING THE INTELLECTUALLY GIFTED

Mr. Stanley describes his Johns Hopkins program of radical acceleration for gifted math students. It is clear, he says, that acceleration is more desirable than most forms of enrichment.

Julian C. Stanley

JULIAN C. STANLEY (Harvard University Chapter) is director of the Study of Mathematically Precocious Youth at Johns Hopkins University. This article is an updated version of a speech he originally presented at the Pacific Northwest Research and Evaluation Conference, Seattle, in May, 1975. Another version appeared in the Gifted Child Quarterly *(Spring, 1976).*

The main point of this article is that most of the supplemental educational procedures called "enrichment" and given overly glamorous titles are, even at best, potentially dangerous if not accompanied or followed by acceleration of placement in subject matter and/or grade. To state it more simply, for highly precocious youngsters acceleration seems to me vastly preferable to most types of enrichment. This appears to be especially true where mathematics and mathematics-related subjects are concerned.

But what do I mean by "enrichment" and "acceleration"? Unless we agree on the differences between such processes, my points may be obscured in the minds of those who consider enrichment to be a form of acceleration and acceleration as being enriching. To me, enrichment is any educational procedure beyond the usual ones for the subject or grade or age that does not accelerate or retard the student's placement in the subject or grade. Admittedly, some ambiguity remains after this definition, because it does not tell what is usual for the subject, grade, or age. Illustrations of four types of enrichment may produce better agreement.

One of these forms of enrichment – unfortunately, it is quite commonly used – is what might be termed busy-work. It consists of more of the same, greater in quantity than is required of the average student in the class but no different in level. One of our most mathematically precocious boys, an eighth-grader with an IQ of 187 who had already skipped a grade, was required by his Algebra I teacher to work every problem in each chapter rather than just the odd-numbered ones. He could have completed the whole course with distinction in a very few hours without needing to work many problems, but his teacher was trying to hold him for 180 50-minute periods. It is a pity that at the beginning of the school year he was not allowed to take a standardized algebra test, learn the few points he did not already know, and move on to Algebra II within a few days. At the end of the seventh grade, a boy less able than he scored above the 99.8th percentile on a standardized algebra test (missing only two items out of 40) without ever having had th course called "algebra." Another boy more brilliant than either, scored 40 ou of 40 when still a seventh-grader. Thes are not typical youngsters, of cours but in three years of math talent search ing in Maryland we have found mor than 200 others rather like them.

There is a happy ending to the stor of the boy oppressed by busy-work i his beginning algebra course. After th eighth grade he studied all of h mathematics part time at the colleg level, for credit. This took him throug college algebra and trigonometry, ca culus, advanced calculus, and linear a gebra with an initial B and subsequen As. He also completed an introductio to computer science in the Johns Hop kins day school with a grade of A at ag 12. Furthermore, he completed colleg chemistry through two semesters c organic chemistry with As. At age 1 years and two months he became full-time student at Johns Hopkin having sophomore status because of 3 credits already earned and living happil in a dormitory. As an electric engineering major he completed the fir college year with eight As and only on B and finished the junior year at age 16

Though this boy did manage to tur the usually stultifying effects of busy work into great motivation to detou further such obstacles and forge ahead it would be difficult to make a gener case for this type of enrichment.

"Identifying and Nurturing the Intellectually Gifted," by Julian C. Stanley, *Phi Delta Kappan,* November 1976. First appeared in *Gifted Child Quarterly,* Spring 1976. Reprinted by permission.

A second type often used is what I ıall term "irrelevant academic enrich- ıent." It consists of setting up a special ıbject or activity meant to enrich the ducational lives of some group of ıtellectually talented students. It pays o attention to the specific nature of ıeir talents. If the activity is, for xample, a special class in social studies, may be meant for all high-IQ youths. 'he math whiz may enjoy it as a ɛmporary relief from the general bore- om of school, but it will not ameli- rate his situation in the slow-paced ıath class. It may be essentially ir- ɛlevant to his main academic interests.

My third type of enrichment, "cul- ural," might also be considered ir- ɛlevant to the direct academic needs of ıtellectually gifted students, but it eems much more worthwhile. The pecial social studies class already used s an illustration of irrelevant academic nrichment merely introduces earlier what should, in a good school, be vailable at a later grade level. Cultural nrichment means supplying aspects of he performing arts such as music, art, rama, dance, and creative writing or ffering systematic instruction in oreign languages before it is usually nade available. This can serve the un- net needs of many students, however, ot just those with high IQs or special ntellectual talents such as great mathe- natical reasoning ability or superb nechanical comprehension. Neverthe- ess, if supplied specifically for those tudents talented in one or more of the erforming arts or in languages, cultural nrichment becomes merely a type of 'relevant enrichment," which I describe ext.

If a student is given advanced materi- al or higher-level treatment of in-grade topics in areas of his or her special aptitudes, the enrichment might be said to be "relevant" to those abilities. For example, mathematically able youths might have a unified, integrated modern mathematics curriculum from kinder- garten through, say, grade 7, in lieu of the usual mathematics sequence for those eight grades. This could be splendid, but imagine the boredom that would surely result if as eighth-graders such students were dumped into a regu- lar Algebra I class.

If the special mathematics curricu- lum extended from kindergarten through the twelfth grade, it would be crucial that students completing it well should not begin in college with the standard introductory mathematics courses there. The same considerations apply in English, science, or social sci- ence curricula. The more relevant and excellent the enrichment, the more it calls for acceleration of subject-matter or grade placement later. Otherwise, it just puts off the boredom awhile and virtually guarantees that eventually it will be more severe.

Thus in my taxonomy there are four main types of enrichment: busy-work, irrelevant academic enrichment, cultural enrichment, and relevant academic en- richment. All of these except cultural enrichment may be viewed as hori- zontal, because they are usually tied closely to a particular grade or narrow age range and are not meant to affect the age-in-grade status of the participat- ing students.

"The more relevant and excel- lent the enrichment, the more it calls for acceleration of subject- matter or grade placement later. Otherwise, it just puts off the boredom awhile and virtually guarantees that eventually it will be more severe."

By contrast, academic acceleration is vertical, because it means moving the student up into the higher school level of a subject in which he or she excels, or into a higher grade than the chrono- logical age of the student would ordi- narily warrant. If a seventh-grader is allowed to take algebra, usually at least an eighth-grade subject, that is subject- matter acceleration. If a student is allowed to skip a grade, that is grade acceleration.

Often these two types of acceleration should go together. For example, if a high school student scores well enough on the calculus test of the national Advanced Placement Program, he (or she) will earn quite a few credits that would be accepted by many colleges. At Johns Hopkins he would be ready to take advanced calculus upon entry; he would also have 27% of the credits needed to complete the freshman year. Passing three or four Advanced Place- ment courses will give sophomore status at a number of colleges such as Harvard.

Entering college before completing high school is another example of grade skipping. We helped a boy who was only 11½ years old to become a full-time college student, quite successfully, at the end of the sixth grade. He skipped grades 7 through 12. Two 13-year- old boys entered Johns Hopkins right out of the eighth grade. A 14-year-old enrolled at the end of the ninth grade. Another 14-year-old enrolled as a col- lege sophomore after skipping four grades. He is scheduled to complete the B.A. degree a few days after his seven- teenth birthday. It will be illuminating to see in some detail how he ac- complished this remarkable speed-up.

We first heard of this boy, whom I shall call Sean, in the fall of 1971. As a sixth-grader whose twelfth birthday came that December 4, he was rather old in grade. According to local rules, he could have been a seventh-grader, but his parents had moved to Baltimore from another section of the country that had more restrictive entering regu- lations. Sean had greatly impressed the teachers in the elementary school he attended, so during the summer follow- ing the fifth grade he participated in a special computer science project con- ducted by the Maryland Academy of Science. Through local newspaper pub- licity the academy heard of our new programs for mathematically precocious youths. It recommended Sean to us, thereby making him the first participant in a five-year study funded by the Spencer Foundation, although before the study began we had enrolled two 13-year-olds as regular freshmen at Johns Hopkins.

Sean proved to be exceptionally able both quantitatively and verbally, but especially with respect to mathematical reasoning ability. He had not yet learned much mathematics, however. For example, he did not know the rule for dividing one common fraction by another (that is, invert the second frac- tion and then multiply), but learned the rule and its proof quickly – as Professor Higgins said in *My Fair Lady*, "with the speed of summer lightning."

Sean was not in a high enough grade that year to enter our first mathematics competition, which was restricted to seventh- and eighth- and underage ninth-graders. It was not until we formed our first fast-mathematics class in June, 1972, that he, then 12½ years old, began to get special educational facilitation from us. The story of that class is told in Chapter 6 of our *Mathematical Talent* book, which appeared in 1974 and covered the background and first year of the study. The class continued until August, 1973, and Sean was one of its two stars. He completed 4½ years of precalculus mathematics well in 60 two-hour Saturday mornings, compared with the 810 45- or 50-minute periods usually required for Algebra I through III, plane geometry, trigonometry, and analytic geometry.

Sean skipped the seventh grade, which in Baltimore County is the first year of junior high school, and in the eighth grade took no mathematics other than the Saturday morning class. Also, during the second semester of the eighth grade he was given released time to take the introduction to computer science course at Johns Hopkins. He found this fascinating and at age 13 readily made a final grade of A.

While still 13 years old, Sean skipped the ninth and tenth grades and became an eleventh-grader at a large suburban public high school. There he took calculus with twelfth-graders, won a letter on the wrestling team, was the science and math whiz on the school's television academic quiz team, tutored a brilliant seventh-grader through 2½ years of algebra and a year of plane geometry in eight months, played a good game of golf, and took some college courses on the side (set theory, economics, and political science). He even successfully managed the campaign of a 14-year-old friend for the presidency of the student council. This left time to prepare for the Advanced Placement Program in calculus and, entirely by studying on his own, also in physics. He won 14 college credits via those two exams.

During the summer after completing the eleventh grade, Sean took a year of college chemistry at Johns Hopkins – as usual, earning good grades. That enabled him to enter Johns Hopkins in the fall of 1974 with 34 credits and therefore sophomore status. He lived at home and commuted to the campus with his mother, who took a position at Johns Hopkins in order to make this easier (14-year-olds aren't permitted to drive automobiles, no matter how far along in college they may be). During the first semester he took *advanced* calculus, number theory, *sophomore* physics, and American government, making As on the two math courses and Bs on the other two courses. Also, he began to get involved in campus politics. He got along well socially and emotionally. As he told an Associated Press reporter who asked about this, "Either social considerations take a poor second to intellectual ones, or there are no negative social effects. . . . The most significant aspect of my life is having skipped grades."

Let us recapitulate here. Sean began by being "enriched" in the Academy of Science summer program for brilliant elementary school pupils. That served as a good background for the college course in computer science, which was intended to be both enriching and accelerative. The fast-mathematics class provided radical acceleration, because it telescoped into one year of Saturday mornings 4½ years of precalculus mathematics. Skipping four grades was also highly accelerative, as were the college courses taken and the Advanced Placement exams passed.

Sean is unusually bright, of course, and extremely well motivated, but he is by no means the ablest youth we have found. He has done the most different accelerative things, however. By contrast, another mathematically and verbally brilliant boy simply took a college course each semester or summer term from age 12 to age 15. Besides that, he skipped the second, eleventh, and twelfth grades. This combination of college courses and grade skipping enabled him to enter Johns Hopkins at age 15 years 2 months with 39 college credits – that is, 30% of the way through the sophomore year. Another boy skipped grades 8, 11, and 12, took 17 credits of college courses, and earned eight college credits in calculus via the Advanced Placement exam. In the fall of 1974 he entered Johns Hopkins at barely 15 years of age with 83% of the freshman year completed.

Many students in the study, including some girls, are *eager* to move ahead faster than the usual age-in-grade lockstep. They do so with ease and pleasure. We find that the combination of great ability and personal eagerness to accelerate educationally virtually guarantees success. Nearly all of our 44 early entrants to college thus far have done very well in their studies and social and emotional development. Only one performed poorly initially, and even he improved rather soon. This brilliant but headstrong 14-year-old had signed up for a heavy load of difficult courses and then would not study enough during his first year of college. Compared with the academic and personal record of the typical Johns Hopkins student, the early entrants have been truly outstanding.

Perhaps our most interestingly different course has been college calculus for two hours on Saturday mornings to supplement high school calculus, so that students can do well on the higher level of the Advanced Placement calculus exam. With a class composed mainly of well-above-average tenth-graders, but with one student only 11 years old, this went along so well from September, 1974, until February that by then everyone in the group knew more calculus than most college students learn in two semesters. By early May only nine college students in 1,000 score higher than the lowest-scoring one of the 13 students in this class – and that wasn't the 11-year-old! All of these special students scored excellently on the higher level (BC) of the national Advanced Placement Program examination in calculus in May, 1975, and earned a year of college calculus credit. Nine of them earned the highest score reported – that is, five on a five-point scale, meaning "extremely well qualified to enter college Calculus III." Three earned fours, and one earned a three. A new class with 23 students began in the fall of 1975. All of them were eleventh or twelfth-graders, some as young as 15 years old.

Recently we had an extreme example of what powerful predictors of achievement their scores on difficult tests can be for intellectually gifted youths. The mathematics department at Johns Hopkins conducted a test competition for eleventh-graders. We heard about it only a week before the test date and got permission to tell some of our participants. We hastily located the names and addresses of 19 persons who as eighth graders three years earlier had scored high on the SAT-M in our first talent search. These were not our very best, because most of those had moved along beyond the eleventh grade; several of them were already in college. Of these

19, 10 came for the test. Seven of them had not been identified by their high school mathematics teachers, and one of the three so identified was a member of our calculus class whose father teaches mathematics at Johns Hopkins.

Fifty-one students entered the contest, and their scores ranged from 140 down to 2. One of our group, not nominated by his teachers, was far ahead of anyone else with 140 points. The math professor's son ranked second with 112 points. Another of our group ranked third with 91 points. The highest scorer not in our group ranked fourth with 82 points. The other seven nominated by us ranked down only to 23.5 out of the 51. Isn't it a bit frightening that a single score from a test administered three years earlier identified high math achievers much better than did teachers who have known their students for at least seven months?*

This finding is congruent, however, with Lewis Terman's discovery of many years ago that teachers are not good at identifying students with extremely high IQs. Apparently the math classes simply do not tap the best abilities of mathematically brilliant students, whereas the difficult test does. There's a moral in this for those who lean too heavily on teachers' recommendations where intellectually gifted children are concerned. In selecting early entrants in our study, we pay far more attention to scores on advanced tests and other evidence of marked precocity than we do to school grades or recommendations, because most of the high school courses are not pitched at an appropriate level of difficulty and challenge for such students.

It should be no surprise that educational acceleration works well when highly able, splendidly motivated students are given a variety of ways to accomplish it. From Terman's monumental *Genetic Studies of Genius* and Sidney Pressey's definitive 1949 monograph on *Educational Acceleration* through the experiences of the University of Chicago, Shimer College, the Ford Foundation's large early-entrance study of the 1950s, Worcester's and Hobson's work, and Simon's Rock College, up to the radical accelerative techniques we are developing, it is clear that acceleration can work much better than so-called academic enrichment for those students who really want it. Counter-examples are rare and likely to be atypical. For every William Sidis who renounces intellectual pursuits because of extreme – and apparently quite unwise – parental pressures, there are many persons such as Norbert Wiener and Sean who benefit greatly from the time saved, frustration avoided, and stimulation gained.

We believe that concentrating efforts on preparing "teachers of the gifted" to enrich curricula is, while far better than nothing, a relatively ineffective and costly way to help the ablest student. At least, such teachers should help provide the smorgasbord of accelerative opportunities and counseling in their use that many such students need.*

"It is our responsibility and opportunity to help prevent the potential Miltons, Einsteins, and Wieners from coming to the 'mute inglorious' ends that Gray viewed in that country churchyard long ago. The problem has changed little, but the prospects are much better now. Surely we can greatly extend both the reach and the grasp of our brilliant youths, or what's an educational system for?"

The procedures that we propose are not expensive. Most of them actually save the school system time and money. One does not need a large appropriation in order to encourage grade skipping, identify students ready to move through mathematics courses at a faster-than-usual rate, encourage early graduation from high school, help certain students enroll for courses in nearby colleges or by correspondence study, promote Advanced Placement exams, or even set up special fast-math courses. More than money, they take zeal and a distinctive point of view.

Persons who hear about our study usually ask, "But what about the social and emotional development of the students who become accelerated?" We often counter with, "What about the intellectual and emotional development and future success of students who yearn for acceleration but are denied it?" For more than six years we have been studying the social and emotional development of youths accelerated in a variety of ways. If the acceleration is by their own choice, they look good indeed. Part of the problem is in the minds of those skeptics who automatically assume that one's social and emotional peers are one's age-mates. Performance of gifted youngsters, including ours, on such personality measures as the California Psychological Inventory shows that emotionally they are more like bright persons several years older than themselves than they are like their own age-mates. There is considerable variability, of course, but on the average they are better matched socially and emotionally with able students who are older. Thus, just as their intellectual peers are not their age-mates, their social and emotional peers aren't either. For clarity of discourse, it would seem wise not to use the word "peer" in this type of argument without prefacing it with one or more modifiers.

Another question often asked us is, "Why do you start with 12- and 13-year-olds who reason superbly mathematically? That is awfully narrow. Why not be broader?" Well, neither mathematics as a field nor our various procedures is "narrow." Mathematics undergirds many of man's highest endeavors. In a sense, it is probably the most generally useful subject (although, of course, some philosophers would argue about that statement). We try to approach talent in mathematics comprehensively, but we deliberately chose to specialize in this area where great precocity often occurs because one can be brilliant in mathematics without yet having had many of the usual life

*For details, see my article, "Test Better Finder of Great Math Talent Than Teachers Are," in *American Psychologist*, April, 1976, pp. 313, 314.

*For more about this, see Daniel P. Keating, ed., *Intellectual Talent: Research and Development* (Baltimore, Md.: Johns Hopkins University Press, 1976).

experiences of an adolescent or adult. Also, because of this precocity, many students in school are horribly bored. Imagine having to serve time in first-year algebra for 180 50-minute periods when one knows the subject well the first day of class! That is by no means an uncommon occurrence, and it may partially explain the lack of interest in mathematics among many bright persons.

My own motivation to help accelerate the mathematical progress of fine mathematical reasoners grew out of my early background. It seems sensible to specialize in what one knows and likes best. Many educational researchers dislike mathematics. Of course, they should concentrate elsewhere.

With more than 2,000 mathematically able boys and girls already identified, we do not have time and facilities to look for latent talent or potential achievers, worthy though that pursuit surely is. We leave that to the many persons who prefer to specialize in identification and facilitation of underachievers, "late bloomers," and the "disadvantaged gifted." Aside from some concern about sex differences in mathematical precocity, we have not tried to screen in a set percent of any group. From socioeconomic and ethnic standpoints, however, the high scorers have been a varied lot.

A well-known quotation from Thomas Gray's famous elegy sums up the case for seeking talent and nurturing it:

Full many a gem of purest ray serene
The dark unfathomed caves of ocea[n]
bear;
Full many a flower is born to blus[h]
unseen,
And waste its sweetness on the dese[rt]
air.

Another poet tells us that ". . . man's reach should exceed his grasp, [o]r what's a heaven for?"

It is our responsibility and oppo[r]tunity to help prevent the potenti[al] Miltons, Einsteins, and Wieners fro[m] coming to the "mute inglorious" end that Gray viewed in that countr[y] churchyard long ago. The problem ha[s] changed little, but the prospects ar[e] much better now. Surely we can greatl[y] extend both the reach and the grasp o[f] our brilliant youths, or what's an educa[]tional system for?

Let's Go Slow on Acceleration

Joanne Yatvin

As an elementary school principal, the most frequent requests I get concern academic acceleration. Typically, such requests come from parents of our youngest children, who feel that formal reading and math instruction should begin in kindergarten or that a child who can read should skip kindergarten or that something is wrong when their first grader can't read a book of fairy tales by midyear.

Parents are not the only ones who want acceleration, however. Many teachers and principals, harassed by anxious parents and wanting to look good to the public, have succumbed to the pressure and are now pushing children into advanced work and esoteric subject matter. Their strategies range from trying to cover as many textbooks in a year as possible to directing a group of eight-year-olds in a Shakespearean play.

Upon reflection, it is not difficult to discover the causes of this most recent trend toward academic acceleration. One is our American obsession with competition; we are not satisfied unless our own children excel everyone else's in sports, creativity, and academics.

Another is the current economic recession, which has produced a deep and pervasive fear for our children's future. If our children are not among the best academically, we wonder, how can they get into prestigious colleges or have a chance at the dwindling number of good jobs? Still another is the well-publicized results of various standardized tests, which imply that many children are not learning as much as they should in school.

These three factors have aroused in parents a fierce determination to secure a quality education for their children, which, in turn, has given rise to acceleration programs in many schools.

Meeting the fears and desires that spring from the first two factors is clearly beyond the capability of any school. But providing the quality education parents want is and always has been the primary goal of educators and educational institutions. I certainly have no quarrel with it—only with the mistaken notion that pushing children through subject matter at a rapid rate makes for quality education. Experience has convinced me that this kind of acceleration does not benefit either bright or average students and that it can, in fact, harm them.

Let's begin with the harm. What critics of acceleration have stressed in the past is the possible social maladjustment that can result from skipping children or making them into academic grinds. Although this sometimes occurs, I have not found it a common or lasting problem, since most healthy kids learn to cope.

More serious and widespread, in my opinion—though less obvious—are the attitudes, fears, and self-images that can develop in children who are pushed. They may come to doubt their own worth or their parents' love. They may learn to value only success and successful people. They may feel guilty about wanting to play, to make noise, to act silly—guilty about being children.

Added to the possibility of psychological damage, moreover, is the danger of intellectual damage. Before academic skills can be learned, all children need a strong background of foundation skills. Unless they have (and continue to have throughout their school careers) considerable experience in moving within their environment, manipulating objects, observing phenomena, communicating with people, and formulating concepts about the world, they cannot learn to read, write, or perform various mathematical functions.

They may be able to perform some of the mechanical operations required, but they will have no true understanding and no base of intellectual power upon which to develop further competence. For this reason, children who are pushed into a concentrated program of book and pencil-and-paper tasks before they have a preacademic skill foundation are prone to develop learning disabilities in one or more academic areas.

Even if great care were taken to protect children from psychological and mental damage, however, the lack of any real benefits from acceleration makes it hardly worthwhile. Ample evidence exists to indicate that children who have been accelerated do not do any better in the long run than those who have not.

Several reading studies, for example, show that children who are given formal instruction early are frequently surpassed later on by children who start at a later age. In another vein, my impression is that most of the FLES (Foreign Language in the Elementary School) programs, so popular in this country a few years ago, have been terminated. Apparently, students who participated did not do any

Reprinted with permission from the April 1976 issue of *Today's Education,* Journal of the National Education Association and Joanne Yatvin, Principal, Crestwood School, Madison, Wisconsin.

better in high school than those who began a foreign language in the ninth grade.

Children fail to benefit from typical classroom acceleration because it violates basic learning principles.

In the first place, acceleration focuses on information, not skills, although we know that information quickly becomes obsolete, that it has only limited usefulness in subsequent learning, and that most of it is soon forgotten.

Secondly, increasing the rate of instruction to cover more material each year forces children beyond the point of effective learning. Several research studies have shown that when new material is introduced too rapidly, lumped together for quick teaching, or inadequately practiced, both assimilation and retention decrease. When the emphasis in a classroom is on covering material rather than really learning it, as it is when acceleration is the goal, little attention is given to finding a rate of instruction that suits children.

A too rapid rate increases the likelihood of superficiality. If material is to be covered quickly, the easiest approach is to give everything a once-over-lightly. Letting children explore ideas takes more time than can be spared and does not produce results that will raise scores on achievement tests.

Also tied to increased rate is decreased opportunity for practice. This is unfortunate because skills deteriorate if they are not used regularly, and much of what may superficially appear to be time wasting in some classrooms or on a playground is really necessary maintenance and new applications of learned skills. Such practice activities are indeed more time-consuming than the introduce-drill-test-move-on procedure typical of acceleration programs, but they are a vital part of learning that cannot be eliminated without adverse consequences.

In addition, an acceleration program often introduces skills without regard to whether children are physically and emotionally ready for them. Certainly, five-year-olds can be taught to play chess, but, given a choice, wouldn't most of them prefer more social and physically active games? Skills that are not in tune with a child's development at a particular age are not likely to be practiced in free time and, thus, will fall into disuse.

The concept of readiness is a key issue in a more complicated way also. As Piaget's learning studies have shown, children move through stages of intellectual development, dependent on physiological growth, experience, social interaction, and previously developed mental structures.

Of course, there are individual differences, but by and large all children in a society go through the same stages in the same order at approximately the same age. Teaching that ignores these stages results only in superficial and temporary learning. For example, you can tell kindergarten children to color the sky down to the ground in their pictures, and they will do it if they remember to, but it is not until much later that they come to understand that the blue sky above them and the invisible air around them are one and the same.

Another of Piaget's conclusions sheds further light on the weaknesses of the acceleration concept. Piaget believes that children must be actively involved in order to learn: They assimilate new data through physical and logical operations on phenomena and then reorganize their own mental structures to accommodate them. Because, again, this learning process is time-consuming, it has not found favor with advocates of acceleration. It is far quicker and easier to emphasize rote memorization of facts and acceptance of authoritative opinions than it is to encourage children to think.

From a condemnation of acceleration, I return now to a consideration of our original goal: All children should receive a quality education. And on that basis, I must also condemn much of what might be termed "standard educational practice" along with the various manifestations of the "back to the basics" movement.

The perceptive reader has no doubt realized early in the foregoing discussion that much of what is wrong with acceleration is also wrong with education in general and that the ordinary classroom can wreak its own forms of psychological and mental havoc on children.

It is not necessary, I think, to belabor the often-made points about boredom and destruction of motivation in classrooms where all children must learn the same thing at the same time or to demonstrate that accumulation of information, superficiality, and passive reception of material are fairly typical characteristics of regular and "basics" educational programs.

It should be emphasized, however, that in such programs Piaget's theories of intellectual development are as often ignored as they are in acceleration programs because teaching proceeds in a pattern and at a rate that takes no account of needs or readiness. Moreover, while there may be lots of practice of the busywork variety, insistence on quiet and order in the classroom precludes children's active involvement with learning tasks.

Despite the distressing pictures I have painted, many classrooms exist that foster real learning. For average children, they provide a foundation of skills and understandings sufficient to meet the demands of future schooling and the outside world. For bright and creative children, they provide in addition, a chance to explore new fields and to move ahead at a rate compatible with their development.

Those parents and educators who are seriously determined to improve education should learn to identify such classrooms and exert their influence to help them proliferate.

How does one identify "learning classrooms"? Because they come in all shapes and sizes with widely varying amounts of equipment, noise, and clutter, it takes some time to perceive what is really going on. Essentially, a "learning classroom" is not a "teaching classroom." What children need are not instructions, explanations, lectures, and demonstrations, but opportunities to learn. Learning flourishes when classrooms have the following characteristics:

1. Foundation skills. For considerable time before the 3 R's are introduced, classroom activities focus on physical movement and control, auditory and visual reception and memory, oral expression of ideas, logical reasoning, and social interactions. Though less central in the curriculum in later school years, these kinds of activities continue throughout the education process.

2. Active involvement. Children are continually expected to manipulate, observe, experiment, make guesses, discuss, argue, explain, change their minds, and produce their own creations. Workbooks and drill materials that encourage children to fill in blanks and repeat what they've read without thinking are conspicuously absent.

3. Skills more than knowledge. Most lessons are aimed at enabling children to do things. Information is valued primarily as an aid to doing. Reinforcement activities allow children to practice, extend, and apply skills to new situations.

4. Flexible tasks and time periods. Children frequently have choices of what to do and when to do it. When there is group work, tasks are differentiated to suit individuals, and when a single assignment is given to the whole class, there is considerable latitude in the way it can be done. Although there are deadlines for some assignments, others may go on indefinitely. At times, a child may decide not to finish a task that he or she has started.

5. New experiences, opportunities, and challenges. Remembering that a classroom is a closed and somewhat static environment, the teacher tries to keep it stimulating by introducing new materials, areas of interest, decorations, groupings of children, and types of tasks. He or she also takes children out of the classroom often. The changes are not random—though they are partly dictated by the children's and teacher's feelings—but are organized to broaden experience and increase challenge.

6. Hard work (not to be confused with a large quantity of dull work). Most of the assignments demand thought and sustained effort. Careful workmanship and thoroughness are valued; so is a noble failure. Because drills, exercises, and tests do not provide any real reason for children to work hard, most assignments ask children to produce things that are real, important, and useful to them.

7. Teacher guidance. The teacher knows what each child has done and can do and is sensitive to the child's learning rate and feelings about learning and about himself or herself. The teacher suggests, guides, encourages, criticizes, and allows children to make mistakes. He or she is tolerant of occasional failures, false starts, and time wasting, but in the long run expects excellence from every child.

When a classroom has all these things—or even most of them—children can accelerate their own learning in a natural way. Guided by a wise and perceptive teacher, they can start down the road to the quality education we have, until now, only dreamed of.

REFLECTIONS OF GIFTED LEARNERS

Louise M. Bachtold

Department of Applied Behavioral Sciences
University of California, Davis

Even before the funding of programs for gifted students in California (1962), there were districts where renewed interest in their most able learners was immediately activated by Sputnik's streak through space. Children who participated in these early programs for the gifted would now have reached adulthood; their educational and vocational aspirations should be not only assessable but demonstrable. To what extend has this group pursued academic interests? Have they fulfilled their earlier promise of achievement.?

Answers to these questions were sought through the cooperation of a school district which had inaugurated a special class program for fourth, fifth, and sixth graders in 1958. Students in the program were strong achievers as qualifications for admission required not only ability test scores in the top two percent, but achievement test scores in the top one percent as well. The first students in this program graduated from high school in 1965. With the assistance of school counselors the names and current addresses were obtained of 69 students who had been enrolled in the special classes, and graduated from high school from 1965-1970. A questionnaire was mailed requesting (anonymous) information on their age, marital status, children, health, early school experiences, educational and vocational situations, interests, and talents. The survey concluded with, "Please add comments which you would consider helpful in educational planning for children today."

DESCRIPTION OF RESPONDENTS

Thirty-six of the former gifted students responded: 18 men and 18 women. Ages ranged from 23-30 years (Mean: 25.6) for the men, and 22-30 years (Mean: 26.7) for the women. Five of the men and seven of the women were married: one of the men had one child; two of the women had one child; and two women had three children. All of the women and all but two men rated their health as good.

Occupations. Vocational areas varied widely, and only two men wished to be in a different field: assistant professor; gardener; manager of a rock band and a radio programmer; mobile home assembler; musician (2); real estate salesman; research aide; researcher/teacher; teacher; and teaching assistant (college). Five were still in college or graduate school, and two were unemployed.

No woman expressed dissatisfaction with her chosen field of work, which included: administrative assistant, budget administrator; customer relations manager; college counselor; editor; employment counselor; IBM engineer: housewife (3); preschool teacher; and secretary. Five were in college or graduate school, and one (with a master's degree) was unemployed but searching for a position in a governmental resource agency—a long-term goal.

Of those for whom salary compensated full-time employment, six men and four women were in the $5,000-9,000 range; two men and six women were in the $10,000-14,000 range; and two men and two women were in the $15,000-19,000 range.

Interests. Liking sports was characteristic of 85% of the respondents, and women as well as men presented a spectrum of favorites ranging from auto racing and basketball, to tennis and water-skiing. Most people listed two or more sports they enjoyed.

Half of the respondents named fiction as a favorite reading material, but magazines averaged 3.08 per person, which, almost without exception included *Time* or *Newsweek.*

Hobbies averaged 2.70 per person (excluding a law student who plead "no time"), and varied from auto mechanics and astronomy to jewelry making, ornithology and raising guinea pigs.

All had traveled beyond their state of residence, and only two men and one woman had not traveled beyond continental United States. Many had been in Asia as well as in Europe, and for more than one visit.

Talents. Although there was no response from five men, 13 listed talents such as, diplomacy, "good in my field;" insight into others; "jack of all trades," languages; mechanical ability; music (3); ombudsman; plant taxonomy; poetry and sculpture. Women named 24 talents with only two giving no response: ability to learn almost anything; high adaptability, art (2); cooking; creative textile work; eye-hand coordination; good with animals; good memory (2) graphic design; guitar; insight; intelligence; mechanical ability; organizational ability; music (2) piano; scientific; writing (3).

"Reflections of Gifted Learners," by Louise M. Bachtold, *The Gifted Child Quarterly,* Vol. XXII, No. 1, Spring 1978. Reprinted by permission.

EDUCATIONAL BACKGROUND AND ATTITUDES

Men and women were in fairly close agreement in their evaluations of the "best" and the "worst" times in school. Their delight in challenge, value for freedom and independence in learning, as well as need for intellectual peers are clearly evident in their statements.

The best of school. Half of the men and half of the women checked college or graduate school as the years of their most gratifying experiences. Men gave as their reasons: "I was really involved in learning, in being a student for the first time in my life," "a chance to expand, go beyond conventional wisdom;" "freedom to explore my own interests," "close association with a few teachers." Women's responses were similar, for example, "enjoyed subject matter immensely," "constantly stimulating atmosphere;" "personal freedom in learning;" "People were more at my level of maturity."

The next most frequent response was in the category K-6. Men commented, "We were encouraged (grades 5-6) to do nonstandard nontraditional things;" "The feeling came across much more often that learning is fun;" "I didn't feel as oppressed." Women noted, "stable social position;" "little or no peer pressure;" "fewest personal problems;" "usually interesting."

The worst of school. In view of the periods described as the most favorable, it is not surprising to find that the majority indicated junior and senior high were their worst experiences in school. Men gave boredom and alienation as their major reasons for disliking junior high, and further commented, "Social adjustment was awkward, uncomfortable;" "my first disillusionment with the system." Women recalled that junior high was "a total waste of time," and that "interpersonal relationships were most trying:" "too much emphasis on popularity," and poor self image were problems noted by others.

Senior high received comparable indictment. Men complained, "boring mostly, had no relevance to what I feel is important to know;" "identity crisis—self doubts;" "dull, required courses, too many cliques." Women pointed to "snobbery from peers;" "I was intellectually bored and emotionally distressed."

Acceleration. Eighty percent reported having acceleration in subject matter, but only 20 percent were advanced by grade skipping. Comments regarding acceleration were favorable. Those who graduated early from high school perceived it as an advantage; and one who did not graduate early stated, "I could have; I should have!" As one woman wrote,

> Had I not skipped a grade and several classes, I would have gone nuts from boredom. Academically and intellectually the acceleration was essential to me. On the other hand, I did not mix very well—but who's to say that as the only child of very intellectual parents I would not have been a loner in any circumstance.

Most respondents, rather than generalizing an opinion on early graduation, expressed that it varied in value according to individual situations.

Several persons remarked that good and bad memories could not be categorized by years or grades, as one young woman eloquently explained.

> Best experiences? Any time an idea inspired me—or I made a new friend—or mastered a new skill. It had nothing to do with grade level. Nor did worst experiences: boredom, unnecessary pressure, bad teachers. Overall worst experience: PE teachers, any grade, who made exercise competitive and forgot the importance of enjoying your own body . . . who made fun of the less sports competent.

After high school. All of the gifted students entered college, but 16 "stopped out" at some point before the baccalaureate—more than half (10) of the men, and one-third (6) of the women. Although both men and women gave as reasons their vagueness about goals and loss of interest, less stress was indicated by the women, who referred casually to time out for travel or other interests. Men, on the other hand, were troubled by such difficulties as inability to concentrate because of the military draft, disillusionment with the system, lack of relevance, emotional problems, and simply getting "fed up."

Almost all of those who interrupted their four year college program either returned to complete a degree program, or intended to do so. Most students attended more than one university. Twelve women and five men had earned a baccalaureate as their highest degree: one woman and four men held a master's degree; and one man had a PhD. There were five women and eight men who had no degree at the time of the survey, and of these, two men did not intend to complete an academic program. One man (in the highest salary bracket) affirmed, "I am doing what I want to do." The other whose field also does not require an academic degree said, "I intend to pursue education informally as far as I can." All of the women without degrees, however, planned to complete, or were already enrolled in a college level or graduate program. There were four baccalaureate objectives, one master's degree, two law degrees, and four doctorates planned by the women. Additional degrees were also included by the men in future plans; four baccalaureates, one master's and four doctorates.

Many of the total group were national merit finalists, had been awarded scholarships and fellowships, and were graduated from college with honors. Among honors won by women were four memberships in Phi Beta Kappa, and an Eisner Award for sculpture. One of the men was valedictorian for his university graduation ceremony.

Nearly all of the respondents perceived a change in their expectations about themselves as compared with their self concept in high school. Increased maturity, for most of the men, appeared to bring a more relaxed attitude, for example, "I still want to be a success, but now I define 'success' differently than before. Money is not enough if you lose your freedom;" "I feel more in tune with my capabilities;" "I used to be interested in success in the field of music; now my interest is in *playing* music."

In contrast, change in self-expectations for the women was depicted generally as growth in awareness of abilities and increased motivation to achieve, as, "I had not considered going to graduate school;" "I can do more than I expected;" "I had few expectations at all then—now I expect to advance in a professional career;" "I have more desire to accomplish things."

It is interesting to note that despite these women's confident aspirations, both the men and the women agreed that although women and men have equal access to education, women still do not have equal access to job opportunities.

RECOMMENDATIONS FOR EDUCATIONAL PLANNING FOR CHILDREN

The frustration, tension, and negativism reflected in so many of the men's responses emerged again in most of their suggestions for improving education, as, "Make choices available to individuals rather than to the most;" "Teach children to respect life—especially their own;" "Teach survival and self-reliance;" "De-emphasize competition and develop intrinsic motivation." One man had no specific suggestion, but implied need for a major modification of educational goals.

> Intentionally or not, the whole thrust of schooling from kindergarten to grad school seems to be to produce children who will be "good citizens" without questioning too deeply, and to alter children to fit the niches of society rather than to actively seek and question how to form a society which is better.

Another man urged,

> Most important is to provide more self awareness development so people can know their true capabilities, or at least *begin* to understand, and have some of the skills to continue life planning throughout life.

Similar advice was addressed to the young learner, "Educate yourself—get out in the real world, into your own individual world . . ." and for the older, "Most kids should take a year to work before going to college."

Many referred to the need for more and better counseling at all grade levels.

The(verbal) women offered over 40 suggestions which, in addition to the men's concerns, called for such improvements as greater opportunity for creativity; more individual attention and encouragement; sex education; career education; the teaching of decision making; the teaching about marriage and child development; less time on repetition; more intellectual discipline; and more varied educational experiences.

As one woman wrote,

> Aside from literacy, what kids need to know, particularly in urban environments, is how to deal with people, how to find and use necessary resources, and how to make their lives rich and satisfying.

Another woman valued relaxation, and suggested,

> Best suggestion I can offer . . . for children like myself, find some way to teach them the importance of real relaxation. I learned to work hard, study hard, play hard—but it took me until several years out of school to learn to appreciate leisure—to value a slower pace (not less achievement, just a more relaxed way of getting places) . . . In a world of increasing leisure time and increasing stress-related illnesses this is of vital importance in the educational process.

And another woman cautioned,

> Also I would discourage students from trying to plan their careers (and lives) years in advance. College means much more than learning a discipline or a particular area of thought . . . There are plays, lectures and concerts that I never attended because I felt I had to concentrate on the work immediately at hand . . . Education is as much evolution of the spirit as it is classroom hours.

In Summary

The composite profile that emerges from the modal responses to the questionnaire pictures a confident, healthy, young adult, aged 26, who is still single. Talented, and keenly interested in many kinds of activities, this person likes sports both as a participant and a spectator, has at least three hobbies, of which one is a handcraft; particularly enjoys reading fiction, which is supplemented by three magazines, including one on current events; and has traveled abroad.

The best years spent in school were in college because of the intellectual challenge and sense of freedom, while the worse experiences occurred during junior high school because of poor personal adjustment and peer problems. Acceleration in learning occurred through advancement in subject matter rather than by grade level, but early graduation from high school would have been welcomed.

Highest academic degree was the baccalaureate, which was conferred after a period of "time out" from college, and after attending more than one university.

Employment is in the field of vocational *choice,* with a salary above $10,000 but less than $19,000. Future plans include post-graduate study leading toward an additional degree, although, somewhat paradoxically, this person's advice for improvement of *children's* educational planning emphasized humanistic rather than intellectual dimensions.

While this androgynous silhouette may seem to contradict the oft-quoted statement that "the gifted differ more among themselves than normal persons grouped on any other basis," it does portray the well-being and attainment of this particular group of young adults. And assuredly their differences were evident as well. The men seemed to have come through that particularly traumatic period for adolescents—the late 1960's—with somewhat less ease and more pain than the women. Yet, as a group they showed a realistic perception of who they are and where they are going, and they came across as more committed than contented. As Gilmore (1974) observed, "The common quality shared by productive individuals is a clear sense of identity" (p. 227), and certainly creativity and contentment have not been found to be congenial.

The reasons given for liking or disliking school experiences strongly support Torrance's (1973) continuing plea for differentiation in learning environments, the need for opportunities to learn in ways which are best matched to abilities and motivations. Indeed, a number of studies (e.g. Bachtold, 1974) have well demonstrated the relationship between different classroom stimuli and variation in modes of cognitive response of gifted children. But perhaps the most insistently presented message, implicit in many of the responses and explicitly given as a recommendation, is the need for increased guidance services for the gifted learner. Demos (1972) charged that at all levels of school, including college, the assumption is too prevalent that able students are not in need of the counseling considered necessary for average or lower ability students. In fact, Demos argued the greater need of bright persons for help so they can "handle without disabling stress, and keep in tension longer the problems which they alone can cope with (p. 58)."

Finally, if self-actualization is basic to the development of the creative individual (Gowan, 1972) then perhaps the most critical communication—the essence—in the reflections of gifted learners was that which spoke of the imperative for self-awareness, to "get into your own individual world" and "to learn how to make life rich and satisfying."

References

Bachtold, L.M. Effects of learning environment on verbal creativity of gifted students. *Psychology in the Schools,* 1974, 11(2), 226-228.

Demos, G.D. Issues in the guidance of gifted and creative children. In J.C. Gowan, G.D. Demos, and C.J. Kokaska (Eds.), *The guidance of exceptional children.* NewYork: McKay, 1972.

Gilmore J.V. *The productive personality,* San Francisco: Albion, 1974.

Gowan, J.C. *Development of the creative individual,* San Diego: Knapp, 1972.

Torrance, E.P. Different ways of learning for different kinds of children. In R.D. Strom and E.P. Torrance (Eds.) *Education for affective achievement.* New York: Rand McNally, 1973.

4 The Mentally Retarded Child

The title of the lead article of this section asks "What is Mental Retardation?" It goes on to answer this question, common among educators as well as the general public, by defining mental retardation as: "significantly subaverage general intellectual functioning existing concurrently with deficits in adaptive behavior, and manifested during the developmental period." This formal definition, published by the American Association of Mental Deficiency in 1973, is widely accepted today. It is important to note the two criteria it mentions, subaverage intellectual function as well as deficits in adaptive behavior. This lead article, from The President's Committee on Mental Retardation, also raises some important issues, which are taken up in following articles in this section of *Educating Exceptional Children.* For instance, when is mental retardation accompanied by physical pathology? Do poor living conditions produce mental retardation, or vice versa?

"We Can Do More to Prevent the Tragedy of Retarded Children" argues that mental retardation is not a disease but a symptom of a number of disorders and that society has an obligation to prevent its occurrence during pregnancy, birth, childhood illness, and the general childhood period. The following articles, "The Dignity of Risk" and "First Steps for the Retarded," both argue that we must not hamper the retarded child by our low and restricting expectations of his or her abilities. The more we can expect from them, the more we can help them to become productive members of the community.

"The Child with Down's Syndrome" by Merril Harris provides basic information about this syndrome, a chromosomal abnormality that occurs once in every 700 births. It details not only physical characteristics and intellectual problems of children with Down's syndrome but addresses the issue of mainstreaming these children into early childhood education programs. Mainstreaming the mentally retarded at the secondary school level is the topic of an article by Gary M. Clark, who argues that this population, in fact, is not an appropriate target for mainstreaming. And finally, two special educators bring together information from several sources to help public school educators include the profoundly retarded in their schools.

Looking Ahead: Challenge Questions

How have the definitions of mental retardation varied within the last hundred years or so? Have the variations been significant?

Should profoundly retarded students receive public education? Why or why not?

Who among the retarded population of young people should be mainstreamed? Why? Who should not? Why?

What's the proper role of parents in the education of their retarded children?

What Is Mental Retardation?

Mental retardation presents itself in so many forms, degrees, and conditions, from so many known and unknown causes, with so many questions unanswered, that it is difficult to say clearly: these are the people who are retarded and this is what they can do, and this what we can do for them, and this is how we can eliminate the problem.

To reach into the problem we have to know what it is.

To reach the people who have the problem we have to know who they are, how to understand them and how to help them.

Who Are They?

> Mental retardation refers to significantly subaverage general intellectual functioning existing concurrently with deficits in adaptive behavior, and manifested during the developmental period.

This is the formal definition published by the American Association on Mental Deficiency in 1973 and widely accepted today. It identifies mental retardation with subnormality in two behavioral dimensions—intelligence and social adaptation—occurring before age 18. The definition is a culmination of long debate and revision, and may well be modified in the future.

The severely retarded person has an obvious incapacity to exercise the expected controls of reason and of personal management necessary for normal living in any human culture. Left to himself, anyone so impaired cannot easily survive. The great majority of severely retarded individuals also have physicial characteristics which suggest a central nervous system defect as the basis of the developmentally retarded behavior.

In many cases no detectable physical pathology accompanies the deficiency of intelligence and adaptation. The limited ability to learn, to reason and to use "common sense" is often unexplainable. Can undetected physical pathology be assumed?

Further questions arise when we discover that milder degrees of intellectual and adaptive deficit are commonly associated with particular families who have serious social and economic problems. Do poor living conditions produce mental retardation, or is it the reverse? Or does each condition compound the other? Still further, members of certain minority groups tend to be highly represented among those identified as having intellectual and adaptive problems, especially in the school-age years. Is such overrepresentation of certain groups a product of racial inferiority or of racial and ethnic discrimination and disadvantage?

For a long time, mental retardation (or its earlier terms idiocy, feeblemindedness and the like), was thought to have much in common with insanity, epilepsy, pauperism and social depravity, all of which were lumped together. And so, a concept of mental deficiency in terms of social deviance developed.

Then, as knowledge advanced, retardation was identified with congenital brain defect or damage, and assigned to heredity. This approach led to redefining mental deficiency in medical terms as an organic defect producing inadequate behavior. Mild forms of intellectual "weakness" became associated with forms of immoral behavior and social disturbance (the "moral imbecile"), and ascribed to more subtle defects of inherited character. Legal definitions in terms of social behavior began to appear.

During the 19th and early 20th century what we now call "mild" retardation was not recognized except as associated with disturbed or delinquent behavior. There was no simple way of diagnosing the more

"What Is Mental Retardation?" *Mental Retardation Past and Present,* President's Committee on Mental Retardation, January 1977.

ild or incipient forms of mental retardaon until the development of psychoetrics around 1910. Then the "IQ" rapid- became a universal means, not only of entifying mental deficiency, but also of easuring its severity.

Goddard, in 1910, in applying the new chniques of Binet and Simon in the pub- schools, discovered there were ten mes as many feebleminded as anyone had spected, and promptly coined the term noron" to cover them! Thus a psychoetric definition of retardation came into ing.

The intelligence test actually measured ehavioral performance on tasks assumed be characteristic of the growth of chilren's ability at successive ages, but it was terpreted as a measure of capacity for inllectual growth and therefore as a preictor of future mental status. It was sumed to represent an inherent and usully inherited condition of the brain with a xed developmental potential.

Persistent debate over the nature and omposition of intelligence finally led to n operational definition that it is "whatver an intelligence test measures." Since telligence measurements are scalar, and egrees on the scale were found to correte rather well with other clinical and soial evidences of mental proficiency, low Q became virtually the sole basis for a dignosis of mental retardation and for its lassification at levels of severity from borderline" to "idiot."

This measurement was especially important in schools for which, in fact, the first ests were devised by Binet and Simon. IQ ests became the standard means of deternining school eligibility and classification. ntelligence tests also were used extensivey as sole evidence for determining legal ompetency and institutional commitment, s well as the subclassifications of institutional populations. The leading authorities, Tredgold, Goddard, Porteus, Penrose, Doll, Clarke and Clarke, all rejected a strictly psychometric definition, but it nevertheless became standard practice in diagnosis and classification.

In the meantime, research in twins, siblings and unrelated children had shown that general intelligence (i.e., measured IQ) is strongly inherited as a polygenic characteristic, following a normal Gaussian curve of frequency distribution in the general population. A slight negative skew was attributable to brain damage or genetic mutation. This deviation led to a theory of mental retardation which divided it into two major groups on the basis of presumed causation. One group consisted of the more severely deficient type with brain damage or gross genetic anomaly characterized by various physical abnormalities and IQ generally of 55 or less. The other group consisted of the lower portion of the negative tail on the normal curve of distribution of polygenic intelligence with IQ between 50 or 55 and 70 or 80 and not otherwise abnormal (Kanner, 1957, Zigler, 1967). This theory could explain the association of milder forms of low intelligence with low socio-economic status and its concomitants. In other words, the less competent tend to sink to the bottom of the social scale in a competitive society. The issue of cultural bias was raised immediately, however, with respect to racial and ethnic groups who scored consistently lower on the standard tests.

Evidence began to accumulate which generated a variety of additional controversial issues. The "constancy of the IQ" was questioned on both statistical and experimental grounds. The pioneering work of Skeels, Skodak, Wellman, and others, in the 1930's (e.g., Skeels, et al., 1938) had indicated that measured intelligence as well as other observable behavior could be substantially modified by drastic changes in the social environment of young children. The quality of the infant's nurture was found to have enduring effects of intellectual functioning, especially in the absence of detectable brain pathology.

Follow-up studies of persons released from institutional care and of those who had been identified in school as retarded showed high rates of social adaptation, upward mobility and even substantial increases in measured intelligence in adult years (Cobb, 1972). Epidemiological studies have consistently shown a "disappearance" of mildly retarded persons in the adult years.

Explanations for these findings could be

offered without abandoning previous assumptions: Improvement in low IQ scores over several repetitions simply exemplifies the statistical regression toward the mean, inherent in errors of measurement: those who improve with stimulation and environmental change were never "really" retarded, but exhibit "pseudo-retardation" which masks true capacity.

Eventually, evidence converged to show that measured intelligence is modifiable within limits, that it is not in any case a measure of fixed capacity, but of the continuity of a developing intellectual and social competence in which "nature" and "nurture" are inseparable components and individual "growth curves" may take a variety of forms and may be influenced by many factors.

A gradual trend developed toward the definition of mental retardation in functional rather than in structural terms and not tied either to specific cause or to unchangeable status. There were those, however, who continued to find a dual view of retardation more credible than a single continuum.

The Stanford-Binet and similar measures of intelligence came to be recognized as primarily predictive of school performance of an academic or abstract nature requiring language skills, and less predictive of other non-verbal types of behavior. Consequently, the need developed to measure other dimensions of behavior. The Army "Beta" test of World War I anticipated this development. New tests, such as the Wechsler series, combined linguistic with non-linguistic performance or quantitative elements and yielded a "profile" of distinguishable mental traits. Factor analysis of measures of intellectual behavior had demonstrated that "intelligence" is not a single trait but a composite of many distinguishable functions.

The measurement of adaptive behavior presented even greater difficulty. Such measures as the Vineland Social Maturity Scale were extensively used but had only a limited validity. The Gesell Infant Development Scale, the Gunzburg Progress Assessment Chart, and subsequently, the AAMD Adaptive Behavior Scale all attempted to measure the non-intellectual dimensions of developmental adaptation but they lacked the precision and reliability of the intelligence measures. Consequently, there has been a continuing reliance, especially in the schools, on measures of IQ alone as the criterion for mental retardation. This practice is defended by some authorities as legitimate in the absence of better measures of adaptive behavior (Conley, 1973.)

In the meantime the issue of cultural bias became an increasingly serious problem. All measures of either intelligence or of adaptive behavior reflect social learning, hence tend to be culture-bound. Their validity, therefore, is dependent on the cultural population on which the norms have been standardized. No one has succeeded in developing a universally applicable "culture-free" test of behavior. Attempts to devise "culture-fair" tests which employ comparable but culturally different elements have as yet failed to yield valid bases of comparison.

Recent studies by Mercer (1973 and 1974) and others have shown the extent to which cultural bias affects the frequency with which members of minority cultures are labeled "retarded" and assigned to special education classes. This is especially true when only measures of IQ are used; representatives of lower socio-economic and of Black, Mexican-American, Puerto Rican, Indian and other ethnic groups are identified as retarded far out of proportion to their numbers in comparison with middle-class Anglo children. Social evaluations of such children show that a high proportion are not significantly impaired in their adaptation in non-school environments.

This discovery has led to a coining of the term "Six-Hour Retarded Child," meaning a child who is "retarded" during the hours in school, but otherwise functions adequately (PCMR: *The Six-Hour Retarded Child,* 1970).

Mercer has called such persons who are identified in one or two contexts but not in others the "situationally retarded," in contrast to the "comprehensively retarded," who are identified as such in all the contexts in which they are evaluated. "Situational retardation" occurs by far most frequently in school settings, and next most frequently in medical settings, and much less frequently in ratings by families or neighbors or in settings officially responsible for the comprehensively retarded. "We conclude," Mercer says, ". . . that the situational retardate is primarily the product of the labeling process in formal organizations in the community, especially the Public Schools" (Mercer, 1973).

The work of Mercer and others has led to litigation and legislative action, especially in California, limiting the use of IQ tests as the sole criterion for labeling and special class placement, on the ground that such practices systematically penalize minority groups and violate their rights to equal educational opportunity (Mercer, 1974).

The present tendency is to accept the 1973 AAMD formulation by Grossman which requires *both* an IQ of less than 70 *and* substantial failure on a measure of adaptive behavior. The requirement of age of onset prior to 18 is more open to question and not always regarded as critical. The Grossman formulation differed from the AAMD definition of Heber (1961) principally in requiring a criterion of more than two standard deviations below the mean, rather than more than one s.d., as Heber had proposed. This was an extremely important difference because it excluded the "borderline" category which accounted for about 13% of the school age population!

Mental retardation, by any of the proposed criteria, occurs with varying degrees of severity. Many attempts were made in the past to classify differences of severity, usually on the basis of social adaptation or academic learning criteria. Social adaptation criteria distinguished borderline feebleminded, moron, imbecile and idiot. Academic Criteria distinguished slow learner, educable, trainable (with no term suggesting learning capability for the still lower category). Heber (1958) proposed using neutral terms to indicate standard deviation units on the continuum of the IQ and any other scales employed.

This is continued in the Grossman (1973) AAMD system to categorize levels of intellectual functioning, thus:

Level of Function	Upper S.D. Limit	Stanford Binet IQ/ (S.D. = 16)	Wechsler IQ (S.D. = 15)
Mild	−2.0	67–52	69–55
Moderate	−3.0	51–36	54–40
Severe	−4.0	35–20	39–25 (extrap.)
Profound	−5.0	19 and below	24 and below (extrap.)

Note that the borderline category (−1.0 to −2.0 s.d.) is not included under the definition.

Mercer has identified still another variable of a significant sociological nature. A majority of children who rated low on both IQ and adaptive measures by the Grossman criteria, and therefore technically "retarded," came from homes that did not conform to the prevailing cultural pattern of the community (socio-culturally nonmodal). This group appeared to be identified as retarded more because of cultural difference than because of inadequate developmental adaptation. Further evidence showed that members of this group who were identified as retarded children tended more than the socio-cultural modal group to "disappear" as identifiably retarded on leaving school.

Mental retardation, as an inclusive concept, is currently defined in *behavioral* terms involving these essential components: *intellectual functioning, adaptive behavior* and *age of onset.* The causes of retardation are irrelevant to the definition, whether they be organic, genetic, or environmental. What is indicated is that at a given time a person is unable to conform to the intellectual and adaptive expectations which society sets for an individual in relation to his peers. In this sense, mental retardation is a reflection of social perception aided by a variety of clinical and nonclinical techniques of identification.

Within this broad functional definition, the deficits indicated in a diagnosis of mental retardation may or may not be permanent and irreversible. They may or may not be responsive to intervention. They may persist only so long as the person remains in a culturally ambiguous situation, or at the other extreme, they may be of life-long duration. Or perhaps only their consequences may be ameliorated in greater or lesser degree, not the condition itself.

Consequently, it is difficult to estimate how frequently mental retardation occurs and how many retarded people there are.

How Big Is the Problem?

The *incidence* of a disorder refers to the frequency of occurrence within a given period of time. For example, the incidence of smallpox in the United States might be expressed as the number of cases in a specific year per 100,000 population; the incidence of Down's syndrome might be expressed as the average number of cases per year per 1,000 live births. The purpose of determining incidence is to yield information as to the magnitude of the problem with a view to its prevention and to measure the success of preventive programs.

The *prevalence* of a disorder refers to the number of cases existing at a specified time in a specified population and is usually expressed as a percentage of that population or as a whole number. Thus, the prevalence of *diabetes mellitus* in the United States might be expressed either as the percent or as a whole number of the total population known or estimated to have the disease in a designated year. The prevalence of people crippled from poliomyelitis can be expressed as a gradually decreasing figure as the result of the greatly reduced incidence of the disease following the discovery of the vaccines. This shows that prevalence is derived from incidence, but modified by the extent to which cases disappear by death, recovery or inaccessibility. The value of prevalence rates is in determining the magnitude of the need for care, treatment, protection or other services.

Incidence

By definition mental retardation can be diagnosed only after birth when appropriate behavioral indices have developed sufficiently for measurement. During gestation the identification of certain conditions usually or invariably associated with mental retardation may be detected and *potential* retardation inferred.

From the examination of spontaneously aborted fetuses, it is estimated that probably 30 to 50 percent are developmentally abnormal and that if they had survived many would have been mentally deficient; but this information gives us only an incidence of fetal mortality and morbidity, with an estimate of some types of developmental deviation, not an incidence of mental retardation itself.

The mortality rates of the potentially or actually retarded vary with severity of defect, which means that many developmentally impaired infants die before retardation has been, or even can be, determined. Anencephaly, for example, is complete failure of brain cortex to develop; the infant may be born living and exhibit a few responses typical of the neonate, but survival is brief. Is such a case to be counted as an instance of incipient mental retardation or only of anencephaly in particular or birth defect in general?

Since mental retardation manifests itself at different ages and under different conditions, there is no single time—e.g., at birth or at one year of age—when it can be determined of every child that he is or *ever will be* identified as mentally retarded.

Mildly mentally retarded persons are most frequently identified, if at all, during school years, and frequently disappear as recognizably retarded after leaving school.

The methods of identifying retardation are still highly varied; consequently, surveys of incidence or prevalence are frequently not comparable.

The degree of subnormality employed as criterion for identification as retarded greatly affects the count of incidence. For example, the 1961 AAMD definition used a criterion of standard deviation greater than one (S.B. IQ$<$85). The 1973 version uses a more restricted criterion of more than two standard deviations (S.B. IQ$<$68). This change in criterion reduces the incidence of mild mental retardation automatically by 80%!

A similar problem is created by the use of multiple dimensions rather than a single dimension. If only IQ is employed, say at two standard deviations (IQ$<$68 or 70), a global incidence of about 3% of school-age population will be found (cf. Conley 1973). But if a second dimension of impaired adaptive behavior is also required, then some with IQ below 70 will not be classified mentally retarded, and some with low adaptive scores, but IQ above 70, will not be classified as retarded. This reduces the obtained prevalence rate to more nearly 1%. If, following Mercer, a still further determination is made on the basis of "socio-cultural modality" the rate may be still further reduced in some heterogeneous communities.

Taking many such considerations into account, Tarjan and others (1973) estimate that approximately 3 percent of annual births may be expected to "acquire" mental retardation at some time in their lives, of which 1.5% would be profoundly, 3.5% severely, 6.0% moderately and 89% mildly retarded. Currently, however, in view of the problems of arriving at truly meaningful estimates of the incidence of mental retardation on a global basis, emphasis for purposes of prevention is placed on the incidence from specific known causes. Unfortunately, these comprise only a small proportion of the total identified as retarded (Penrose, 1963; Holmes et al, 1965). The following are examples.

One of the earliest success stories in the reduction of the incidence of mental retardation was in the case of endemic cretinism. This condition occurred rather frequently in certain localities, notably some of the Swiss alpine valleys. The problem was attacked in the second half of the 19th century. The first step was to identify the condition with the occurrence of goiter, an enlargement of the thyroid gland. The next step was to relate this condition to the people's diet, and finally to the absence of trace iodine in the soil and water supply. Iodine was found to be necessary to the functioning of the thyroid gland in its production of the hormone thyroxin, the absence of which can cause cretinism.

The addition of iodine to table salt resulted in reducing mental retardation caused by endemic cretinism to near zero. It also led to the preventive and therapeutic use of extract of thyroxin in the treatment of myxoedema or hypothyroidism from other causes (Kanner, 1957).

The incidence of Down's syndrome is well-documented. It has been identified with a specific chromosomal abnormality which occurs most frequently as an unpredictable non-disjunction of autosome 21, but infrequently also as the Mendelian transmission of a translocated portion of autosome 21. The former type is definitely related to maternal age, occurring at about .33 per thousand live births to mothers under age 29 but rising sharply after age 35 to a rate of about 25 per thousand to women over age 45.

Overall, the incidence of Down's syndrome is 1 in 600 to 700 live births, with over half occurring to women over 35 (Begab, 1974). The overall incidence of gross chromosomal malformation of children born to women over 35 is 1 to 2 percent (Lubs and Ruddle, 1970; Begab, 1974). The existence of the condition is detectable by amniocentesis (analysis of a sample of amniotic fluid) during pregnancy.

This knowledge creates the possibility of reducing the incidence of Down's syndrome substantially by: a) limiting pregnancy after age 35; b) detecting the transmissable karyotype of translocation in either the male or female and limiting reproduction; c) identifying the condition early in gestation and terminating pregnancy.

A third example of incidence is more problematic, but nevertheless significant. From prevalence studies, it is known that mild retardation is more frequently found in families of low socio-economic status, especially in families in which the mother is mildly retarded. Heber and others have determined that the incidence of retardation in such families can be reduced by early intervention in providing stimulation to the child and home assistance to the mother.

These examples are sufficient to illustrate the values of pursuing the study of incidence to identifiable causes or correlative conditions as a means of identifying preventive measures (see Stein and Susser, 1974; Begab, 1974). Further discussion of currently known preventive measures appear in later chapters on prevention.

Prevalence

The principal problems of obtaining reliable prevalence estimates relate to definitions, criteria and administrative procedures on the one hand, and to the absence of uniform and centralized data collection, on the other. The former problems are gradually becoming resolved. The latter requires vigorous and sustained efforts by Federal and State governments to establish an effective data bank.

Prevalence is a product of cumulative incidence modified by loss. Loss may be the result of death or cure or unaccounted disappearance. Whereas measures of incidence are important to the problem of prevention, measures of prevalence are important to the provision of service resources. As prevention requires differential classification by identifiable cause, so service provision requires differential classification by types of need.

Overall estimates of prevalence of mental retardation have been made by two methods: by empirical surveys and by selection of a cut-off point on a Gaussian curve for the distribution of intelligence scores. The latter has led to a widely used estimate of 3%, ambiguously referring to either incidence or prevalence. This would correspond to an IQ level of approximately 70 and is, in fact, an average general prevalence found in some surveys of children (Conley, 1973; Birch et al, 1970).

However, it possible to select a 9% cut-off at about IQ 80 or 16% at IQ 85, the 1961 AAMD criterion. All surveys, however, show that mental retardation does not represent a simple portion of the lower tail on a general Gaussian curve. It is far from being normally distributed, varying widely by age, by socio-economic and ethnic factors. The use of an IQ cut-off alone also assumes a one-dimensional definition of mental retardation, contrary to the AAMD formula and other leading authorities (Tarjan, 1973; Mercer, 1973).

Tarjan (1973, p. 370) points out that the estimate of 3% prevalence, or 6 million persons in the United States, makes four dubious assumptions: "a) the diagnosis of mental retardation is based essentially on an IQ below 70; b) mental retardation is identified in infancy; c) the diagnosis does not change; and d) the mortality of retarded individuals is similar to that of the general population." The first assumption ignores the adaptive behavior component; the second holds only for a small portion, nearly always organically and severely impaired; the third holds only as a generality for those of IQ below 55, and the fourth holds only for the mildly retarded.

As a statement of potential incidence, Tarjan (1973) is probably quite conservative in estimating that 3% of all infants who survive birth will at some time in their lives be identified as mentally retarded in some context—most probably in the public schools.

Epidemiological surveys conducted in various parts of the United States and abroad show comparable prevalence rates for the more seriously retarded—i.e., moderate, severe and profound levels on the AAMD classifications or IQ below 50. Fifteen such studies converge on an average rate of approximately .46% or 4.6 cases per thousand population (Stein and Susser, 1974). These surveys generally covered ages roughly 10 to 20, obscuring the high mortality rate in early childhood. When the surveys are divided between general and rural populations, the three rural studies average at more than double the general rate, or 9.84 per thousand, while the remaining twelve cluster quite closely around 3.6.

Penrose (1963) suggests that prevalence of malformation predictive of profound retardation at birth might be as much as 1 percent, Conley (1973) suggests 1.5 to 1.7 percent, including severe and moderate levels. The rate among prematurely born infants is much higher than among full-term babies. The rate among lower-class nonwhites is higher than among middle-class whites, but the differences are not so striking as is the case in mild retardation levels. Higher rates of prematurity, higher health risk and inferior maternal and child health care could account for the difference at the more severe levels.

In any case, the presumption of actual prevalence of the severe forms of defect predictive of mental retardation would be highest at birth, declining rapidly by mortality to a relatively low rate of .2% in adult life.

Prevalence rates of the severely retarded have been affected by a number of tendencies in the past 20 years. On the one hand, modern medicine has made enormous strides in its ability to preserve life. Infant mortality rates have fallen markedly; survival of prematures at progressively younger ages has become possible, with correspondingly increased risk of developmental damage; recovery from infectious diseases by use of antibiotics has become commonplace. Consequently, along with other infants and young children, severely and profoundly retarded children now have a better chance of prolonged survival.

On the other hand, improved health care, especially for mothers at risk, immunization, protection from radiation exposure, improved obstetrics, control of Rh isoimmunization and other measures have prevented the occurrence of some abnormalities and reduced the complications which formerly added to the incidence and prevalence of retardation. New hazards appear, however, in environmental toxic substances, strains of microorganisms more resistant to antibiotics, new addictive and nonaddictive drugs, new sources of radiation, environmental stress, all of which are potential producers of biological damage and mental retardation (Begab, 1974).

On balance, it is possible that incidence of severe retardation is falling while prevalence is continuing to rise.

The high birth rate of the post World War II period produced a record number of severely retarded children who are surviving longer than ever before. The future, envisioning more control of the causes with a lower birth rate more limited to optimal conditions of reproduction may in time yield lower prevalence rates of the moderate, severely and profound retarded. Currently, a very conservative estimate of their number in the United States is approximately 500,000 (Tarjan, et al, 1973) but may actually be nearer a .3% level or 660,000 surviving beyond the first year of life.

The prevalence of mild retardation is quite a different matter. Where the severely retarded show a declining prevalence by age, based wholly on mortality, the mildly retarded show a sharply peaked prevalence in the school years (6–19) and a rapid falling off in the adult years. This phenomenon cannot be a product of mortality, because the mildly retarded have shown longevity very nearly that of the general population. There are two possible alternatives, both of which may be the case. Large numbers remain retarded but cease to be the objects of attention; or they in fact cease to be retarded. In any case, no survey has yet found prevalence rates of mild retardation remotely approaching a constant across ages, such as would be expected on the assumption of unchanged relative mental status. Tarjan suggests that the rate of 3% traditionally projected as a constant across all ages, actually holds only for the school-age, with rated prevalence in selected age groups of .25% in the 0–5 group, 3.0% from 9–16, .4% from 20 to 24, sinking to .2% in the population over 25; the overall prevalence being approximately 1% (Tarjan, et al, 1973, p. 370). This would yield a total of approximately 2.2 million retarded persons in the United States, as against 6.6 million if an overall 3% is assumed.

In studies of the Riverside, California, population, Mercer (1974) showed that the prevalence and social distribution of mild mental retardation differed markedly according to the definition and methods of identification employed. She compared the application of a "social system" definition ("mental retardate" is an achieved status, and mental retardation is the role associated with the status) with a "clinical" definition (mental retardation is an individual pathology with characteristic symptoms which can be identified by standard diagnostic procedures).

It was found that the use of a one-dimensional clinical definition (IQ less than 69) yielded an overall rate of 2.14% retarded, with Blacks showing a rate 10 times and Mexican-Americans 34 times the rate of Anglos. When a two-dimensional definition is used (IQ less than 69 *plus* deficient adaptive score) the overall rate shrank to .9% which is the "clinical" rate predicted by Tarjan. The distribution now showed Blacks approximately at the same rate as Anglos, but Mexican-Americans still 15 times greater. When pluralistic, culturally adjusted norms were used for both IQ and adaptive behavior, the overall rate reduced still further to .54% but the total shrinkage in this case was accounted for in the Mexican-American group where sociocultural nonmodality (a cultural pattern distinctly different from the predominant mode) and bilingual background were most prominent. Furthermore, when higher criteria for IQ and adaptive behavior were used, the disadvantage to both Blacks and Mexican-Americans, as compared with Anglos, was markedly increased.

The social distribution of mild mental retardation has been found by all investigators to be inversely related to socioeconomic status. It is, according to Conley (1973) 13 times more prevalent among poor than among middle and upper income groups and found most frequently among rural, isolated or ghetto populations. Controversy persists concerning the contribution of constitutional and social learning factors to this distribution, but it is a question of the relative wieght rather than an exclusive alternative. No one doubts the multiple effects of environmental deprivation on both physical and psychological development. Nor is there much doubt that social learning enables the great majority of those with mild intellectual limitations to assume normal social roles in adult life. It is evident that what might appear to be a manifestation of the normal distribution of polygenic general intelligence is really a complex product in which the genetic component is only one among many factors yielding varying degrees and rates of retarded behavior, among varying populations at varying ages.

There is little point, then, in arguing who is "really" retarded. There is great point in determining who is in need of developmental and supportive assistance in achieving a reasonably adequate adult life, in determining the relationships between identifiable characteristics and the kinds of services that will be profitable, and in employing terminology that will aid rather than obscure these relationships. A critical issue is the degree to which cultural pluralism is reflected in the educational process.

The classification suggested by Mercer (1973) involves a four-dimensional matrix in which potentially handicapping conditions, including mental retardation defined in either "clinical" or "social system" terms, may be identified:

a) The dimension of *intellectual functioning,* measurable on a continuous scale represented by IQ. On this scale, following the 1973 AAMD standard, an IQ of 69 or less is regarded as potentially handicapping and is one clinically defining characteristic of mental retardation. Mercer terms the person with *only* this dimension of disability as *quasi-retarded.* Ordinarily this will be reflected in learning difficulties in the school setting and justifies individually prescriptive educational assistance.

b) The dimension of *adaptive behavior,* measurable on a developmental scale of behavioral controls accommodating the person to his environment. On this dimension a person falling substantially below age norms (perhaps in the lowest 3% of a normative distribution) is regarded as potentially handicapped. This constitutes a second clinically defining characteristic of mental retardation of the 1973 AAMD standard. Mercer terms the person who has *only* this dimension of disability as *behaviorally maladjusted,* but she identifies the person with disability in both a) and b) as *clinically mentally retarded,* requiring services in both school and non-school settings.

c) The dimension of *physical constitution,* describable in terms of the health or pathology of the various organ systems of the body. While not a defining characteristic of mental retardation, physical impairment may be in itself potentially handicapping and may be the cause of or magnify the handicapping limitations of a) and b). The probability of organic impairments being present increases with the severity of mental retardation, from 3% at mild retardation levels to 78% at moderate levels and 95% at severe and profound levels (Conley, 1973, pp. 46–7). Individuals characterized by only c) may be termed generically as *physically impaired,* and in combination with a) and b) as *organic mentally retarded.* The term "multiply handicapped" is commonly used, but this would apply equally to persons with more than one substantial physical impairment.

d) *Sociocultural modality* is a fourth dimension which is distinguishable from the other three. It refers to the extent to which sociocultural variables of family background conform or do not conform to the modal culture in which the individual is assessed. When the family background is substantially non-modal, in this sense, the individual may be potentially handicapped in relation to the prevailing cultural expectations because of lack of opportunity for the appropriate learning. Such a person may be termed *culturally disadvantaged.* Mercer found that non-modality yielded effects which, to the dominant culture, appeared as low IQ, low adaptive behavior, or both when measured by the norms of the dominant culture. Utilizing a pluralistic model of mental retardation, sensitive to socio-cultural differences, Mercer found a substantial reduction in the prevalence of mental retardation in the Mexican-American as compared to the Anglo population of Riverside. Throughout the investigation, the Anglo sample yielded a constant rate of 4.4 per thousand identified as mentally retarded (i.e. no Anglos in this sample were judged either quasi-retarded or non-modal culturally). The Mexican-American population yielded the following succession of rates per 1,000:

a) One dimensional—only standard IQ norms, 149.0

b) Two dimensional—standard IQ + standard adaptive behavior norms, 60.0

c) Partial pluralistic two dimensional—standard IQ, pluralistic adaptive behavior norms, 30.4

d) Pluralistic two dimensional—pluralistic norms for both IQ and adaptive behavior, 15.3

(Mercer, 1973, pp. 235–254)

The residual differences between the rate of 4.4 for Anglos and the 15.3 rate for culturally adapted assessment of Mexican-Americans may be attributable to the pervasive effects of their bilingual status.

Granted that Mercer's research is based on a single local population sampling and is a first approach to a "social systems" definition of mental retardation, it suggests the need for much more highly refined procedures in the definition and epidemiology of mental retardation as a basis for the adequate and appropriate delivery of developmental and supportive services where they are needed.

There is complete agreement that it is impossible, at our present state of knowledge, to determine accurately either the incidence or the prevalence of mental retardation. There is far less agreement on what we can do to remedy this situation. Among the most urgent issues in classification:

1. **Definition.** The formulation adopted by the American Association on Mental Deficiency involving two-dimensional deficit in the level of behavioral performance unquestionably is responsive to many problems arising from older definitions. But a number of issues remain:

a) The two dimensions are not independent, but are, in fact, highly correlated, the degree of correlation being related to severity of deficit, suggesting the distinction of intellectual and adaptive measures has not been sufficiently refined. In practice, more reliance is frequently placed on IQ measures than on measures of adaptation or other bases of clinical judgment.

b) The cultural contamination of standardized tests as currently used makes their findings suspect. Mercer and others require a corrective for cultural insensitivity of the instruments employed.

c) The use of a global IQ measure which may be adequate for epidemiological purposes obscures the complexity of intellectual functioning and the variability of individual profiles which is the basis of service provision. Global IQ measures are rapidly losing favor among professional providers of service but are maintained for administrative convenience and ease of determination.

d) Differences in the conditions associated with mild retardation as compared to the more severe forms in terms of organicity, comprehensiveness of impairment, resistance to modification, relatedness to cultural norms, etc., suggest to some that the two types are sufficiently different as to require separate classification, probably based on organic (or presumed organic) versus psychosocial etiology.

2. **Services.** Since the instruments for the measurement of intelligence and adaptive behavior are scalar, with continuous variation on both sides of central norms, the relationship between a specific level of deficit and the need for specific types of service and treatment may be highly artificial. This appears to be the central question underlying the controversy over the criterion level in the AAMD definition which now excludes persons with IQs from 70 to 85 who formerly were included. The fact that relatively few scoring above 69 IQ manifest significant deficits in adaptive behavior may miss the point. Adaptive behavior may be quite specific and situational, especially where culture modality may also be in question. The real issue is to determine individual

need, which cannot be derived from the IQ or adaptive behavior. This issue has been exacerbated by legislation which requires categorical classification as a condition of eligibility for service.

3. **Labeling.** Titles are necessary for any scientific system of classification, and may be useful for certain administrative purposes; but their use in human service systems is a different matter. The attachment of a label to a species of plant or a type of rock makes no difference to the plant or the rock. The label assigned to classify a human being does make a difference. To label a person mentally retarded has consequences of a psychological nature if the person is cognizant of it and can assign a meaning to it; it has consequences of a social nature insofar as other persons assign meaning and respond in terms of that meaning. This is especially the case with the label of "mentally retarded" because all terms associated with deficiency of intelligence are, in our culture, highly charged with negative values.

There have been many attempts to use systems of intellect classification as a means of adapting school and other programs to individual differences without making those differences appear invidious. These have not been entirely successful because value systems, even for children, tend to filter through the most subtle of euphemistic terminology.

This is a difficult issue to resolve. Success is possible only if: a) classification for epidemiological purposes is entirely separated from need-evaluation for purposes of social grouping and prescriptive treatment, b) all treatment is person-centered rather than system-centered, c) cultural value systems are recognized and respected, and d) eligibility for categorical assistance is based, not on global statistical criteria, but on the individual's need.

4. **Recording, Registering and Information Control** (corollary to labeling). Obviously, the best data base for the epidemiologist would be a computerized data bank including all information on every case. This has, in effect, been advocated since Samuel Howe's first attempt to catalogue the "idiotic" population of Massachusetts in 1848, long before modern systems of information storage and retrieval were dreamed of. However, rights of privacy and confidentiality have become a critical issue. The problem is one of reconciling the needs of the service delivery system and the individual recipient, so that he will neither be "lost" as an anonymous number nor stigmatized for having his needs recognized.

5. **"Negativism."** The nature of retardation lends itself to definition and assessment in the negative terms of deficit from desirable norms. The individual person, however, is not made up of deficits but of asset characteristics, however meager or distorted some of them may be. All treatment rests on the positive capacity of the person to respond, whether physiologically or psychologically. The issue of negatively versus positively defined traits and classifications is a basic one between the purposes of epidemiology and the purposes of service assistance.

Who are the people who are mentally retarded? They are individuals whose assets for effective living in their cultural and physical environments are insufficient without assistance. The screen by which they are brought into view to be identified and counted is composed of a mesh of intellectual and adaptive behavior norms. But the screen is a somewhat crude and abrasive instrument and requires to be refined and softened by concern for the individuals it exposes.

How many mentally retarded people are there? The loss of potential for normal development and even survival affects a high proportion of those who are conceived, and probably 3% of those who survive birth. In addition to those hundreds of thousands who are not well-born, there are millions who are not well-nurtured by the world in which they live. How we sort out these millions, how many will be called "mentally retarded" will depend on our definitions and our perceptions of need. The roots of these needs are not yet under control, nor have we sufficiently provided for their assuagement.

REFERENCES

Begab, M.J.: "The Major Dilemma of Mental Retardation: Shall We Prevent It? (Some Social Implications of Research in Mental Retardation)," *American Journal of Mental Deficiency,* 1974, 78:5, 519–529.

Birch H., Richardson, S., Baird, Sir Dugald, Harobin, G., Illsley, R.: *Mental Subnormality in the Community,* Baltimore: The Williams and Wilkins Co., 1970.

Cobb, H.V.: *The Forecast of Fulfillment: A Review of Research on Predictive Assessment of the Adult Retarded for Social and Vocational Adjustment,* Teachers College, Columbia University, N.Y. and London: Teachers College Press, 1972.

Conley, R.W.: *The Economics of Mental Retardation,* Baltimore and London: The Johns Hopkins University Press, 1973.

Heber, R.: *A Manual on Terminology and Classification in Mental Retardation,* A Monograph Supplement to the American Journal of Mental Deficiency, Second Edition, 1961.

Heber, R., Garber, H., Harrington, S., Hoffman, D., Falender, C.: *Rehabilitation of Families at Risk for Mental Retardation,* Rehabilitation Research and Training Center in Mental Retardation, Progress Report, University of Wisconsin, Madison, December 1972.

Holmes, L., Moser, H., Halldorson, S., Mack, C., Pant, F., Matzilevich B. (Eds.): *Mental Retardation: An Atlas of Diseases with Associated Physical Abnormalities,* N.Y.: MacMillan, 1972.

Kanner, Leo: *The History of the Care and Study of the Mentally Retarded,* Springfield Ill,: Charles C. Thomas, 1964.

Lubs, H.A., and Ruddle, F.H.: "Chromosomal Abnormalities in the Human Population: Estimated Rates Based on New Haven Newborns Study," *Science* 1970, 169, 495.

Mercer, J.: *Labeling the Mentally Retarded,* Berkeley: The University of California Press, 1973.

Mercer, J.: "Psychological Assessment and the Rights of Children," *Harvard Educational Review,* February 1974, 44:1, 328 ff.

Penrose, L.: *Biology of Mental Deficiency,* N,Y.: Grune and Stratton, 1963, P. 197.

President's Committee on Mental Retardation: *The Six-Hour Retarded Child, A Report on the Problems of Education of Children in the Inner City,* Washington, D.C.: U.S. Government Printing Office, 1970.

President's Committee on Mental Retardation: *Mental Retardation: The Known and the Unknown, Century of Decision Series,* DHEW Publication No. (OHD) 75-21008, Washington, D.C.: U.S. Government Printing Office, 1975.

Skeels, H.M., Updegraff, R., Wellman, B.L.: "A Study of Environmental Stimulation, An Orphanage Preschool Project," *Studies in Child Welfare,* Iowa University, Published by the University, Iowa City, Iowa: 1938, 15:4.

Stein, Z., and Susser, M.: "The Epidemiology of Mental Retardation," Chapter 31 in *American Handbook of Psychiatry,* Second Edition, Volume Two, N.Y.: Basic Books, 1974.

Tarjan, G., Wright, S.W., Eyman, R.K., and Keernan, C.V.: "Natural History of Mental Retardation: Some Aspects of Epidemiology," *American Journal of Mental Deficiency,* 1973, 77:4, 369-379.

Zigler, E.: "Familial Mental Retardation: A Continuing Dilemma," *Science,* 1967, 155, 292-298.

From *Pictorial Completion Test II,* reprinted from the *Journal of Applied Psychology,* September 1921.

PLATE I

Sketch from the colored illustration of the simplest picture in the series, the demonstration picture, with the inserts which particularly relate to this picture. Of course only one is quite correct, but the others can be inserted with some show of reasonableness.

We Can Do More to Prevent the Tragedy of Retarded Children

Richard Koch and Jean Holt Koch

Richard Koch received his M.D. from the University of Rochester School of Medicine. He is a professor of pediatrics at the University of Southern California School of Medicine and Senior Attending Physician, Childrens Hospital, Los Angeles. The author of over 100 articles, Koch was formerly President of the California Council for Retarded Children and the American Association for Mental Deficiency.

Jean Holt Koch graduated from San Jose State College. She was Chairperson of the Westchester Human Relations Council and is now Secretary of the Mineral King Task Force of the Sierra Club. With Richard Koch, she wrote Understanding the Mentally Retarded Child.

MORE THAN 60,000 mentally retarded babies will be born in the United States this year. One-fourth will be moderately or severely handicapped. Each of these infants brings untold heartbreak, financial hardship, and anguish to his family, and each one who ends up in a state mental institution will cost taxpayers, on the average, more than a quarter of a million dollars to support. Each one who is so retarded that he cannot work will cost society another $650,000—the money he might have earned during an average lifetime. This need not be, for we now have the knowledge and technology to cut the incidence of mental retardation in half.

Mental retardation is not a disease, but a symptom of any of a number of disorders. Defective genes, abnormalities that develop accidentally during pregnancy, birth injuries, childhood illnesses, even a deprived environment can damage the brain. Once the damage is done, it is irreversible.

Society's obligation to the retarded rests in several areas, one of the most important being an enlightened understanding attitude. Most people realize that the retarded are people with the same feelings, rights, and responsibilities as all people. True, they are people with handicaps, just as a person born with a clubfoot or impaired eyesight is handicapped. We do not send the person with a physical handicap off to an institution behind locked gates where he can be hidden away, as we have done with the retarded for many years. Instead, we use all the latest medical knowledge to correct his handicap so that he may live a normal life. The retarded deserve to have their physical handicaps corrected. They deserve an education so that they can develop to their highest potential. And they deserve respect so that they can live with dignity and self-confidence. The other area in which society must be involved is in the prevention of mental retardation. It is inexcusable that in the United States, more than 30,000 needlessly retarded children are born each year.

Prenatal care. First, we must insure that all pregnant women and their babies receive good prenatal and neonatal (newborn) medical care. One out of every four women who gives birth in public hospitals has never seen a physician during her pregnancy. In rural and poor areas, the proportion is even higher. We estimate that approximately 350,000 American women give birth each year without prenatal care, and a like number of newborns receive no medical attention.

Every woman needs medical guidance through pregnancy. Many conditions can arise that may cause retardation in the child of a normal expectant mother, and prenatal care can detect and treat some of them before they damage the fetus. Women who plan to give birth at home should have medical supervision during pregnancy and a physician on call in case problems develop during labor.

We have known for years that a woman with Rh-negative blood who marries a man with Rh-positive blood runs a risk of having a mentally retarded child. Although both parents have normal blood types, the mixture causes trouble. In most cases, the fetus inherits the father's dominant Rh-positive blood. This causes no problems during a first pregnancy because the circulatory systems of mother and baby are separate and their blood usually does not mix. But at delivery, if some of the fetal blood in the placenta inadvertently mixes with the mother's blood, her system will begin forming antibodies to this foreign substance. During her next pregnancy, these antibodies may cross the placenta, enter her baby's circulatory system, and systematically destroy the developing red blood cells. This causes the release of bilirubin, one of the pigments in the red blood cells. This substance interferes with the ability of some brain cells to utilize the oxygen carried by the blood. As a result, the affected brain cells are literally starved for oxygen and die.

When such a baby is born, its tiny liver cannot cope with the continued destruction of blood cells. As the bilirubin level rises, the infant's skin becomes jaundiced. Such an infant may become mentally retarded or have cerebral palsy or convulsions.

Prompt exchange transfusions, in which a newborn is given an entirely new supply of blood, can usually prevent brain damage. But the problem need never develop. A new vaccine, given to the Rh-negative mother immediately after the birth of each child, can keep her system from developing antibodies and ends the possibility of an infant incurring brain damage due to Rh incompatibility.

Some women are more likely than others to bear a defective child, but proper prenatal care can lessen the danger. High-risk women include diabetics and those suffering from chronic diseases of the heart, lungs, liver, kidneys, or from metabolic disorders. Women younger than 17 or older than 37 and

 From *Psychology Today,* December 1976. Copyright © 1976 Ziff-Davis Publishing Company. Reprinted by permission.

women who are carrying more than one fetus also are considered high-risk cases. Women who have deficient diets may contract viral diseases that can damage an unborn child.

When a physician monitors a pregnancy, he is alert to signals that warn of possible complications. For example, the baby may lie in a transverse or breech position, indicating labor will be difficult. In such cases, the doctor can plan to do a Caesarean section, averting the possibility of brain damage that sometimes results from lack of oxygen due to a difficult delivery. If every pregnant woman had good prenatal care, the incidence of mental retardation would probably drop by 10 percent.

Problems of prematurity. Each year 330,000 premature babies are born in the U.S. As birth weight decreases, mental retardation goes up. Ninety percent of newborns weighing less than a pound will be mentally defective, 40 percent of the three-pounders, and 10 percent of the four-pounders. Among babies who weigh six or seven pounds, only from one to three percent will be retarded.

Poverty-stricken women and those who lack prenatal care bear most of the premature babies. Among the poor, there are up to five times as many premature births as among middle-class suburban women; among the medically unsupervised, up to three times as many. Universal prenatal care, coupled with nutritional supplements for women in poverty areas, could drastically reduce the number of premature births. How incongruous it is for society to pay for, say, 30 years of care in an institution at $18,000 a year for each retarded person, but to be unwilling to pay the comparatively small cost of good prenatal care that would prevent mental retardation in the first place. Not all undersized babies are born to poor, malnourished mothers. Heavy smokers also are in danger of bearing babies who weigh less than five pounds, either because the babies are born early or because excessive smoking has retarded the growth of the fetus. And one of the most recent studies indicates maternal alcoholism is a significant cause of mental retardation.

Expert care for these tiny infants can prevent most brain damage. In first-rate hospitals, premature babies are put in intensive-care units, under the supervision of neonatologists and specially trained nurses. Blood is drawn from the babies every few hours to measure their metabolic balance, and their oxygen level, heartbeat, temperature, and respiration are regularly monitored. The incubators have radiant heat and are equipped with mattresses that cause an alarm to ring if the infant stops breathing. Hospitals in many large cities now have such facilities. This care costs about $1,000 a day, but the price is small when compared with the enormous amount of money society pays when a child is severely brain damaged. And this does not even consider the grief and sorrow of the parents involved.

Recent studies show that excellent neonatal care could prevent 90 to 95 percent of all brain damage now suffered by premature babies, even among the tiny one-pounders. It would reduce the annual toll of retarded babies significantly. Similar procedures can minimize or prevent brain damage due to lack of oxygen or to hyaline membrane disease.

One family's experience shows what good medical care can do. Just before Mrs. J. went into the delivery room, her nurse detected a slowed, irregular fetal heartbeat. She summoned the obstetrician, who found that the umbilical cord had descended into the vagina, and was squeezed between the mother's pelvis and the baby's head. While preparations were being made for a Caesarean section, the physician pushed the baby's head back up the birth canal to relieve pressure on the cord and restore the flow of blood to the baby's brain.

At birth, the infant's skin was blue and he was not breathing. The obstetrician suctioned mucus from the baby's air passages, placed him in an incubator, placed a tube in his windpipe to facilitate breathing, and massaged his chest to inflate his lungs. Within three minutes the baby breathed on his own, his pulse became regular and strong. He did well and was discharged from the hospital four days later.

As her son grew older, Mrs. J. noticed that he developed more slowly than her other babies had. He was slightly retarded, but able to attend a regular kindergarten and special classes in public schools. It is likely that, with the special educational opportunities now available, this child will be able to learn a trade, marry, and become a productive member of society. With less skilled care, this child would have suffered severe brain damage and, instead of being able to lead a relatively normal life, he would have been hopelessly retarded and probably institutionalized.

The newborn. Many metabolic disorders and diseases that may cause mental retardation are not obvious at birth. But

The Degrees of Retardation

When a doctor says that a child is mentally retarded, he is saying that the child will probably have an IQ score of less than 70, compared to the average score, among normal children, of 100. The extent of a child's handicap and its effect on his behavior and development will depend upon the severity of the retardation. All retarded children develop more slowly than normal children.

Mild Retardation: Mild cases of mental retardation often are not detected for several months or even years. Such children make IQ scores of 50 to 70. They are considered educable and can learn simple academic skills. With proper education, many can fit into the normal population, marrying and holding simple jobs. Seventy-five percent of the retarded fall into this category.

Moderate Retardation: Such children make IQ scores of 30 to 49. They can learn simple speech and are considered trainable. Although they need supervision all their lives, they can be toilet trained, taught to dress and feed themselves and keep themselves clean. They can often take jobs in sheltered workshops. They generally do not have to be institutionalized. Twenty-one percent of the retarded fall into this category.

Severe Retardation: Such children make IQ scores of 0 to 29. Most cannot be toilet trained. Few will ever walk or talk. They need constant, lifelong care, which families can rarely provide. Most of these children enter institutions before adolescence; many are placed soon after birth. These children frequently die in early adulthood from physical ailments that accompany their severe mental disorders. Only four percent of the retarded fall into this catagory.

—Richard Koch and Jean Holt Koch

simple, effective, inexpensive tests can now uncover these ailments.

One of the best-known metabolic disorders that damages brain tissue is phenylketonuria (PKU). It is an enzyme disorder in which the baby cannot use the amino acid phenylalanine, found in all foods that contain protein. Robert Guthrie, a physician in Buffalo, New York, has developed a blood test that identifies these babies within three days after birth, too soon for accumulated phenylalanine to cause brain damage. Once the disorder is detected, physicians can put the baby on a special diet that is low in this amino acid. The child will nearly always have normal intelligence. Without the diet, severe mental retardation is almost a certainty.

Since the newborn PKU blood test is now mandatory in 44 states, it saves almost 250 infants each year. Similar tests can detect galactosemia, maple-syrup urine disease, histidinemia, homocystinuria, and hypothyroidism. Unfortunately, very few states mandate newborn screening for all these diseases, although, on a mass basis, the cost would be only about $2.00 for the additional procedures, and the testing could be done on the same blood sample used for the PKU test. All these diseases can cause mental retardation, and all can be treated. Universal screening of newborns would reduce the incidence of mental retardation by at least another five percent.

Advances have also been made in the treatment of other conditions that invariably lead to mental retardation. Craniosynostosis is a condition in which the sutures of the skull are fused together at birth so that there is no "soft spot" at the top of the baby's head. Such a child may become mentally defective because the brain has no room to grow. Today, neurosurgeons can create sutures across the top of the head, enabling the skull to expand.

Operations can also correct hydrocephalus, a condition in which cerebrospinal fluid is trapped in the skull, eventually filling the space the brain should occupy. Without treatment, these babies suffer an early death or develop enormous skulls, have severe mental retardation, and generally spend their lives in an institutional bed.

Sometimes during an especially difficult delivery, or as a result of an accident, there may be bleeding into the lining of the brain of the newborn child. This is called a subdural hematoma. Surgeons can remove these potentially dangerous blood clots before the damage occurs. Accidental poisoning is another cause of brain damage in children. The worst offender as far as mental retardation is concerned is lead poisoning. Parents should be aware of the nearest poison center in case of emergency, as most heavy metals, such as mercury and thallium (an ingredient in roach poison) can cause mental retardation.

Another cause of brain damage in newborns is the exposure of the fetus to radiation. This was demonstrated by the sharp rise in mental retardation among offspring of Japanese women exposed to the atomic bomb blasts of World War II. As a result, doctors are careful not to X-ray the abdomens of women during the first three months of pregnancy. With this knowledge of the effects of radiation on future generations, many scientists feel we should use extreme caution in any expansion of nuclear facilities.

The public has become lax about immunizing children. In some states, as many as one in four children is not inoculated for German measles.

Menace of measles. Controlling the spread of contagious diseases would further reduce mental retardation. Of the contagious diseases, regular measles and German measles (rubella) are the heaviest contributors to brain damage.

The complications of regular measles at one time left 2,000 children each year with neurological handicaps, seizures, cerebral palsy, mental retardation, and speech handicaps. When a mother contracts three-day (German) measles during the first three months of pregnancy, her baby may have multiple handicaps, including blindness, deafness, and heart defects as well as seizures, cerebral palsy, and mental retardation.

Inexpensive vaccines ($1.50 per dose when purchased in volume) can prevent both diseases, yet children are still being damaged by measles. Recent data suggest that the public has become lax about immunizing children. In some states as many as one in every four children is not inoculated for German measles. At present, some states require each woman's premarital blood specimen to be tested for German measles. If no evidence is found indicating the person has had the disease, she is encouraged to have this immunization.

If the public were properly educated regarding the serious damage that can be caused by common childhood diseases, not only to the present generation, but to those as yet unborn, it is hard to imagine that this relaxed attitude toward immunization would persist. A possible solution would be for health departments to provide free vaccine to any child. Also, insurance rates could be reduced for families practicing good preventive health measures. If we immunize every well child completely, it has been estimated the savings would approach $1 billion annually.

The newest advance in the prevention of retardation is in the area of genetic counseling. A variety of genetic and chromosomal anomalies such as Down's syndrome (mongolism), Tay-Sachs disease, Turner's syndrome, and Klinefelter's syndrome usually result in subnormal intelligence. In the past we knew little about what causes them, how to treat or prevent them, or what to tell parents about the future of their afflicted child.

The situation is brighter today. We know, for example, that Down's syndrome, characterized by Oriental-looking eyes, flattened nasal bridges, short stature, and mental retardation, is a chromosome disorder. Persons with Down's syndrome have an extra chromosome in each of their body cells.

Down's syndrome occurs among all races, and the risk of bearing such a child increases with the age of the mother. Few are born to young women, and those under 35 have only one chance in 1,000 of having such a child. When a woman is between 35 and 39, she has one chance in 300 of having a baby with Down's syndrome. For mothers who are between 40 and 44, the odds go up to one in 100, and between 45 and 49, up to one in 50.

Most of these persons will be moderately retarded and will need special care. Obviously those who are severely retarded may need institutional care. At present, one in every 10 institutionalized patients in the U.S. has Down's syndrome.

Physicians once thought Down's syndrome was inherited and counseled the parents of an affected child not to have more children. We now know that only about one in 20 cases is inherited. The other 19 come from a simple error in cell division. Today, a laboratory blood test can single out hereditary disorders, and parents of a baby with Down's syndrome can safely have additional children.

The tell-tale needle. Amniocentesis, a technological advance, is now helping many parents who carry genetic defects to have healthy children. During the 13th to 16th week of a pregnancy, a physician inserts a sterile needle through the woman's abdominal wall into the uterus, from which he withdraws a small amount of amniotic fluid. Because the fluid always contains a few free-floating cells from the fetus, the cells can be studied for genetic defects such as chromosomal abnormalities, Tay-Sachs disease, and a number of other disorders. Should any serious defect turn up, the parents then have the option of requesting that the pregnancy be terminated.

All high-risk mothers should be aware of this technique and consult their doctors about it. Although abortion should never be forced on anyone, neither should a woman be forced to bear a defective child against her will. This decision is one that must be made by the couple involved with the advice and counseling of their doctor. In the past, high-risk families were usually discouraged from having another child, but with the advent of this new technique, the couple can be reassured that each pregnancy can be monitored by amniocentesis and they need not fear the birth of a retarded baby.

In September Congress voted to prohibit federal funding of abortions for low-income women except when "the life of the mother would be endangered if the fetus were carried to term." This is a step backward in the prevention of mental retardation, as it completely negates the role of amniocentesis and therapeutic abortion for high-risk women who have committed the sin of being poor. Low-income women are those least able to pay for the abortion or the care of a retarded child.

Because Tay-Sachs disease is an inherited recessive genetic defect, screening, counseling, and amniocentesis can wipe it out. The disease occurs predominantly among Ashkenazi Jews. One in every 30 is a carrier of Tay-Sachs, and on the average one in every 3,600 Ashkenazi infants has the disease. When two carriers marry, chances are one in four that their child will inherit the disease and one in two that the child will be a carrier.

We can detect carriers with a simple blood test. If every Jew knew whether he was a carrier, then couples where both are carriers could have amniocentesis performed during each pregnancy, and a defective pregnancy could be terminated so that a normal child could later be born. A Tay-Sachs baby degenerates rapidly, both physically and mentally, becoming blind, helpless, and mentally retarded, and usually dies before it is three years old. Each case costs society $30,000 to $50,000, and causes untold anguish to the family involved.

Dollars and sense. Americans have never made preventive health care a national priority. Our neglect shows in U.S. maternal and infant death rates, which are among the highest in the Western world. Despite our wealth and advanced technology, we do a poorer job than 14 other countries.

The quality and quantity of prenatal and neonatal care vary widely across the country. One way to improve our medical system might be to liberalize federal and state subsidies and private insurance benefits for maternal and neonatal care. Government agencies and insurance companies could simply refuse to pay benefits to hospitals with inferior standards of care.

Because medical services are poorly distributed, with cities having a surplus of physicians and rural areas desperately in need of doctors, we might do well to follow the example of Mexico and several other countries, where every medical-school graduate must serve a specified length of time in a rural area. The problem is aggravated because the U.S. has a glut of medical specialists and a scarcity of general practitioners.

If we made universal preventive health care a reality, we could save thousands of lives each year and halve the rate of mental retardation. When one considers that in California alone, taxpayers spend about $900 million annually to care for the mentally retarded, it becomes obvious that prevention is not only humane but that it makes good economic sense as well.

For more information, read:

Conley, Ronald. The Economics of Mental Retardation; Johns Hopkins, 1972, $17.50.

Koch, Richard and Kathryn J. Koch. Understanding the Mentally Retarded Child; Random, 1975, $8.95.

Prevention Handbook, The National Association for Retarded Citizens, P. O. Box 6109, Arlington, Texas 76011.

THE DIGNITY OF RISK

Evelyn Lusthaus, Ph.D.
and Charles Lusthaus, Ph.D.

Charles and Evelyn Lusthaus are both professors in the Faculty of Education at McGill University in Montreal, Quebec. Charles is Director of the Division of Educational Leadership, a university-based organization that coordinates professional development opportunities for parents, administrators and professionals in the province of Quebec. Evelyn has worked in the field of special education for more than 10 years, as a teacher, administrator, consultant and professor.

They have two children, Rebecca aged two, and Hannah aged eight months.

When we brought our newborn baby home from the hospital we began to feel a protectiveness that was different from anything we had ever experienced before. At her birth three weeks earlier we learned that the baby had a condition known as Down's syndrome (mongolism), which results in mental retardation. We also learned that she had been deprived of food during her time "in utero" and thus had suffered fetal malnutrition. Poor Hannah! She was helpless, sentenced to her first few weeks of life in an incubator under bright lights to alleviate her jaundice and given "timeouts" primarily for feedings, which (because she could not suck) initially consisted of forcing formula through a tube inserted down her throat. No wonder feelings of protectiveness and pity welled up in us!

Furthermore, once we brought Hannah home, our desire to protect her grew. We were aware that we had not experienced these feelings with our other daughter, who was then one and a half years old. Although there was always the need to protect Rebecca from physical danger, there were few instances when these dangers were apparent, and thus we seldom felt the desire to protect her.

Yet, with Hannah, a nagging urge to embrace her and remove her from harm was often present. Was it increased by some of the reactions of well-meaning relatives, friends and acquaintances? Our desire to steal her away from the world could only have been strengthened by:

—family members who insisted that she was perfectly normal, despite our careful explanations of the baby's condition. (Did they feel her mental retardation was such a stigma that it had to be denied?)

—friends who decided on the day she was born to have no more children, despite the fact that they had been trying very hard to have another child for more than two years. (Did they fear she was such a menace that their yet unconceived child might be affected?)

—friends who sent us a sympathy note saying that "their thoughts were with us in our time of grief." (Did they think she was as good as dead?)

—family members who said they "just could not finish knitting the clothes for the new baby—could not even touch them, in fact." (Did they feel that the expected baby was dead; that Hannah was an impostor?)

—a pediatrician who exclaimed that he just did not like talking about "these kinds of things." (Did he find her repulsive to think about?)

And on and on.

How do we overcome the desire to protect our daughter from the rejection and pain she will inevitably face?

Courage to Risk

Having worked in the field of mental retardation, we were familiar with the concepts of "normalization" and the "dignity of risk" so important in improving life conditions for retarded

From *The Exceptional Parent*, June 1978. Reprinted with permission of THE EXCEPTIONAL PARENT magazine. Copyright Psy-Ed Corporation 1978, Room 700 Statler Office Building, Boston, Massachusetts 02116.

people. Bengt Nirje defined normalization as "making available to the mentally retarded, patterns and conditions of everyday life which are as close as possible to the norms and patterns of the mainstream of society." In *New Directions for Parents of Persons Who Are Retarded,* Robert Perske provided another definition of the term: "Let a retarded citizen live as normal a life as he possibly can in as normal a setting as possible." Nirje explained that living as normal a life as possible involved many dimensions, such as following a normal rhythm of the day and year, living a normal routine of life, deciding and choosing matters for oneself, living and experiencing in a bi-sexual world, living within normal economic standards and so on, to as great an extent as possible.

It is clear that this kind of living requires courage and risk on the parts of both retarded people and their parents. Wolf Wolfensberger and Perske have poignantly described the indignity of smothering children in overprotective environments and the dignity of providing them with situations involving healthy, growth-oriented risk. Perske reminded us that "...the world in which we live is not always safe, secure, and predictable. It does not always say 'please' or 'excuse me.' Every day there is a possibility of being thrown against a situation where we may have to risk everything, even our lives. This is the *real* world you parents have to face. But it is the same world your retarded child must learn to face as well."

As new parents of a retarded baby, however, we were faced with the question of how these concepts, so logical and sensible for others, fit into our lives, into our experiences and into the experiences of our baby as she grows. The responses of others to our baby (such as those cited above) only confirmed our dread of the negative and debilitating attitudes toward mental retardation (and differentness) that continue to predominate in our society. In his book for parents, Perske suggests preparing our children to face these attitudes by programming "prudent risk" into their daily lives. Although we could accept such ideas intellectually, our emotions of protectiveness warred with that acceptance. Thus we were left with the question: *How do we overcome the desire to protect our daughter from the rejection and pain she will inevitably face?*

A Survey of 25 Adults

Recent discussions with adults who are mentally retarded have given us great insight into this question. In the "professional" side of our lives, we have been studying the quality of life of 25 retarded adults who completed a training program designed to help them live independently, and who, in fact, are now living independently in the community.

The results of this study show that these adults live in varied circumstances; for example, some are unemployed with no money saved, while others have interesting, well-paying jobs and substantial savings accounts. However, despite the great range of circumstances involving employment, living comforts, financial status, friendship patterns, leisure time activities, etc., one finding is constant in almost all the persons we have interviewed. When asked the question, "What is the best thing that has happened to you since living independently?" all but four of the 21 people answering this question said that the best part was just being on their own, making their own decisions. These are their answers:

"More freedom."

"I'm happy to make my own decisions."

"I like living on my own—I can do what I want."

"I can take responsibilities—I like that."

"Just moving in here—there is peace and quiet away from my parents."

"I have more freedom."

"Just moving out—I can do anything I want—there is no nagging."

"I like being free—no one tells me what to do—no one bothers me, especially like where I was before."

"Freedom is the best part of the lot. Before everyone was nagging you—it makes you nervous, always having someone there."

"I've been able to leave my parents. You do not have to cling to your parents all your life. Then if you need them, you have them in case something comes up."

"I don't have supervision 24 hours of the day."

"I have more freedom."

"Just like living on my own."

"Just being in my own apartment."

"Like living with my buddy."

"Living here—it's my own home—I do not want to live with my parents."

"I can do things for myself—not dependent on my parents for everything."

We were impressed by the critical importance all these individuals placed on their own independence, their ability to make their own decisions about their own lives. Clearly, the specific characteristics of their living situations were secondary to the opportunity to decide matters for themselves.

Perhaps in our society we take for granted our freedom to make our own decisions, and focus our attention for improving our lives on improving our material and social living conditions: better jobs, nicer homes, more leisure time, more personal growth, increased acceptance by others, more meaningful social relationships, etc. And perhaps as parents of retarded children we tend to place primary importance on the quality of their living conditions when we think of what is best for our children. Perhaps we hesitate to have our young adults live on their own for *fear* that their standards of living would be lowered, that they would be lonelier, have a harder time travelling from one spot to another, or face more rejection by people in their new neighborhoods.

And the fascinating point of this study is that these fears have in fact been realized. The people we interviewed, for the most part, *did* appear to have a lower standard of living, be lonelier, have more difficulty travelling, and face more rejection in their independent settings than they did in their previous, more protected environments. Yet it was clear from our discussions with them that such factors were secondary to their desire for self-determination. It was apparent that none of the 25 people would have wanted to return to their previous living situations, even to more comfortable, accepting situations, because they did not want to give up their primary desire, the desire to make their own decisions.

These retarded individuals are willing to risk the difficulties of independent living circumstances for the dignity of making their own decisions. Can this information help us, as parents, to prepare our retarded youngsters for the "world out there" rather than *protecting* them from it? When they are ready to take the risks, will we be?

First Steps for the Retarded

MICHAEL THACHER

The limitations of the severely retarded may have a lot to do with our expectations. Thanks to innovative new approaches, they're now learning to lead fuller, more productive lives in the community.

Michael Thacher is a contributing editor to HUMAN BEHAVIOR.

Day after day, five-year-old John sat cross-legged on the floor, sucking his thumb. And so John might have sat for years, had he remained in a traditional institution for the severely retarded. Instead, he went home with Edwarda Okkonen, a foster parent employed by the Macomb-Oakland Regional Center (MORC) in Mt. Clemens, Michigan. Okkonen gave John intensive training beyond the means of any institution. "It took a year just to break him of thumb sucking," Okkonen recalls. "First we put his hands in mittens. Later, we tied a brass bell to his middle finger so he would play with that, not his thumbs." After six more months in Okkonen's care, John learned to feed himself and could dress and walk with assistance. He then "graduated" into a normal home.

John benefited from a revolutionary change in outlook concerning the capabilities of severely disabled people who are placed in challenging and unrestricted environments.

Just 10 years ago, the severe and profoundly retarded either lived at home, exhausting their devoted but overwhelmed parents, or vegetated in crowded institutions, virtual prisoners of a society that wanted them tucked safely out of sight. By 1971, however, ambitious community-based programs such as MORC and ENCOR (Eastern Nebraska Community Office of Mental Retardation) in Omaha had begun easing the seriously disabled into the real world.

Now only a handful of the estimated six million mentally handicapped people in the United States still live in institutions. In fact, institutional populations have been dropping about 4 percent each year, from 181,000 in 1971 to 153,000 in 1976. Most of the residents are moving into group homes, foster homes or back with their natural families. Roughly 70 percent of current institutional residents are profoundly or severely retarded. "The capable ones who 20 years ago helped run the institutions have been pretty well placed out. And we're seeing fewer severe and profoundly retarded children admitted unless they have terrific medical complications," notes Richard Scheerenberger, director of the Central Wisconsin Center for the Developmentally Disabled in Madison.

Momentum has picked up recently as landmark state court cases spelled out the rights of the retarded, opening the doors of many more public schools to the severely handicapped. Hundreds of programs coast to coast now teach the "unteachable" to build shelving, dial the telephone and assemble electronic components. Many state agencies operate group and foster homes for the severely retarded and offer extensive support to natural parents who prefer to keep their handicapped child.

"The interesting thing is that the basic research is not new for a good bit of this," says Gunnar Dybwad, professor of human development at Brandeis University and former executive director of the National Association for Retarded Children. The initial breakthroughs were made over 20 years ago in Great Britain by Ann and Alan Clarke, H.C. Gunzburg and others, Dybwad notes. They showed that even the severely retarded could learn a variety of manipulative tasks and hold productive jobs in society. In fact, a few far-sighted professionals consistently urged greater opportunities and community involvement for the severely retarded, Dybwad adds.

Nonetheless, until recent years, most researchers remained blind to the implications of these seminal studies. The severely retarded were usually branded "ineducable" and forgotten. "We lacked the power of conviction," admits Dybwad. "We assumed the children couldn't learn. What we found out is we didn't know how to teach."

In the late '60s, psychologist Marc Gold of the University of Illinois at Urbana-Champaign startled colleagues by demonstrating that even the seriously disabled could learn to assemble a 15-piece bicycle brake and perform other complex tasks.

Gold had found no cure for mental retardation. Rather, he demonstrated that despite intellectual limitations, the severely retarded can function at much higher levels than had been thought possible. Professionals were in part misled, Dybwad suggests, because they judged capabilities too often by such intellectual yardsticks as IQ tests. But the guiding principles of many complex tasks, including bicycle brake assembly, are not adequately measured by such tests. In fact, most of our routines of daily life are quite simple. "You spend the vast majority of your waking hours doing what any four-year-old can do," Gold points out. These activities are within the reach of many retarded people.

To prove his point, Gold visited institutions and took supposedly "ineducable" adults through a few trials at putting together a bicycle brake. Subjects showed rapid progress, and skeptical professionals were impressed.

"It began as a total accident," Gold says. He was describing his research to an agency staff when someone protested that "you don't work with the people we do."

"Okay," Gold replied, "bring me your toughest case." The critic turned to a staffer and said: "Go get Martha." The audience buzzed expectantly. "My stomach was in a knot waiting for her," Gold admits, "but it went great." Martha, absorbed in building a brake, made rapid progress after a few attempts. Such demonstrations, now routine, have always come off. "I could bomb," Gold concedes. "We really haven't had a failure yet, but I'm waiting."

From *Human Behavior,* April 1978. Copyright © 1978 *Human Behavior* Magazine. Reprinted by Permission.

Gold has been criticized for putting retarded people on a stage. He strongly disagrees. "It's no different from asking a normal person to display his or her competence in front of people," Gold insists. The performance is dignified and the subjects enjoy it, he adds.

Gold assumes that with the proper instruction any handicapped person can acquire skills. Ninety-five percent of the time, the disabled don't learn because the teacher failed, he maintains. Organization, analysis and flexibility are emphasized. Tasks such as tying a shoe or packing a first-aid kit must be broken down into as many as 40 teachable parts, then taught step by step.

"Everything we do is consistent with behavior-modification principles, but the applications are often different," Gold explains. "For instance, one of our biggest reinforcers is silence." Often, talk just confuses the severely retarded. Don't explain everything, he suggests, but demonstrate the task or gently guide the student's hands. So Gold's lessons are largely silent. Students bathed in verbal praise tend to focus on the sweet sounds and lose track of the task at hand. In fact, all artificial reinforcers, which Gold calls "those awful smiles, the squeaky voice and all-day-long bits of food," are discouraged. Instead, competence becomes its own reward.

Gold's principles have been picked up by training programs nationwide. California's Department of Rehabilitation, for example, has contracted for Marc Gold & Associates to teach Gold's technology to participating staffers at 28 institutions, schools and workshops. They, in turn, will teach other professionals, and a self-perpetuating training program will be established.

"The exciting new trails were blazed by people who worked with adult retarded," Dybwad of the National Association for Retarded Children points out. That's because vanguard efforts such as Gold's usually focused on vocational training beyond the reach of children. But the lesson was not lost on other researchers. "We said, if they can do this with adults, then we must be more demanding in children's school education," Dybwad says.

Building on Gold's early work, current programs emphasize teaching the seriously disabled useful skills in social settings. If we can teach children with Down's syndrome to throw and catch a ball, they can play with other children, Dybwad explains. Then they learn how human beings get along together. They listen to other children shout, scream, express joy, and thus they receive an education in communication.

So long as the severely retarded could not care for themselves, they ended up in institutions. While they did live at home, beleaguered parents usually isolated them from family life because they were messy and hard to manage. "Mom's really burned out if she's got an eight-year-old who's not toilet-trained," says Barry Lamont, residential director for ENCOR. Eventually, she decides to give her child up.

"We now recognize that the home, the family, is the strongest factor in the education of handicapped children," Dybwad says. Since the early '70s, many state agencies have tried to make sure that parents with severely disabled children no longer must go it alone. They are strongly encouraged to keep their handicapped child for as long as possible. Babysitters and temporary homes are available so parents can enjoy a weekend's respite.

"Our staff is devoted to keeping kids at home or finding other alternatives to institutionalization," says Scheerenberger. The thinking is that children learn and develop best in homelike environments. Once disabled youngsters learn to feed themselves, for instance, they can eat dinner with the rest of the family. Parents and siblings begin to talk and play with them. "Now we have severely retarded young people who are at least social human beings," Dybwad comments. And full-time members of the family.

> ***"We now recognize that the home, the family, is the big factor in the education of handicapped children."***

"What we are saying is not a secret, not a new discovery," Dybwad remarks. "Rather, we have learned to apply obvious methods to severely handicapped people. We have found that they are by no means as handicapped as we made them out to be."

Until the '70s, programs to provide homelike environments for the severely retarded were sporadic and small-scale. One vanguard effort, however, was MORC in Michigan. Created in 1971 as a state agency, it now boasts over 175 homes for 800 people, many with severe disabilities.

Central to MORC's program are over 100 "community training homes," private residences in which up to three disabled children or adults live as family members. Foster parents are trained by MORC staffers in behavior management, speech therapy and other techniques. MORC homefinders actively recruit foster parents through classified ads, talk-show appearances and newspaper articles. Last year, 981 inquiries netted almost 50 foster parents.

"I've always had a feeling for the underdog," admits Edwarda Okkonen, MORC foster parent and retired practical nurse who cares for three seriously disabled youngsters in her Pontiac, Michigan, home.

When he first arrived, three-year-old Nicholas, blind and brain-damaged since birth, just lay on his back, motionless, Okkonen recalls. "But whenever he showed me an indication he was going to smile, I dropped everything to encourage it by blowing in his ear, saying nice things or just barely touching him." Recently, Nicholas rewarded her efforts with a smile. He has also learned to hold his head up and turn his eyes on Okkonen when she talks to him. After three years of life, Nicholas is paying attention to the outside world.

Eating, dressing and toilet-training are the ABCs for the severely retarded. "If they can do those things, they fit into a normal home very well and my work is complete," Okkonen says. So far, 10 severely retarded children have "graduated" from her tutelage.

Teaching the seriously disabled to eat can take months of hard work. "Nicholas came from the hospital with a tube down his throat for nourishment," Okkonen explains. To wean him from the tube, Okkonen began feeding Nicholas with an eyedropper. Eventually, she could dribble small amounts out of a medicine cup into his mouth. Okkonen persuaded him to swallow by closing his lips with two fingers and gently stroking him under the chin. Today, Nicholas eats junior foods and drinks from a cup. Now Okkonen is coaxing him to chew food by putting a soft morsel deep in his mouth between teeth and cheek. When he starts to grind his jaws, she avidly praises him.

Not all foster parents have Okkonen's touch. "The majority

of our foster parents are not whiz-bang behavior modifiers," concedes Gerald Provencal, director of programs for MORC, "but they understand enough not to make a fundamental error such as reinforcing inappropriate behavior." Basically, parents must place the right demands on children and not baby them, he stresses. Retarded kids should eat meals, go to school and take vacations with everyone else, Provencal emphasizes.

Through MORC, foster parent Gloria Fauer received Shannon, a severely retarded five-year-old with cerebral palsy. Fauer and her 12-year-old son have lived with Shannon for five years. "Wherever we go, she goes; whatever we do, she's part of," Fauer says.

When Shannon first arrived, she could not walk, talk or feed herself. "We were excited even when she cried or recognized the fact that it was dinnertime," Fauer confides. After many trials, she found the right combination of bottle and nipple Shannon could hold and suck. Now she feeds herself at the dinner table.

Every afternoon, Shannon receives an hour of exercise to strengthen her legs and hands. During "tracking drills," Fauer puts Shannon in a dark room and shines a flashlight in her face so she learns to follow it with her eyes. These lengthen the child's attention span, which is a crucial factor in learning many basic skills. Three days each week in the summer, a bus takes Shannon to a public school specializing in mentally impaired children. There she further exercises her legs and neck and practices self-care skills.

Besides foster homes, MORC runs group residences in which seven or eight retarded adults live while they develop their self-care and social skills. During the day, they attend sheltered workshops and other community-based training programs where they learn how to hold a job. Well over 100 adults now live in such facilities throughout the local communities.

At MORC, 12 duplexes called "developmental training homes" house adults and children with special problems that prevent them from living in less restrictive places. The duplexes mimic suburban developments.

"There's nothing miraculous about the homes we have here that could not be duplicated within the community," contends David Rosen, MORC director. In fact, the program is designed to prepare the disabled to live in society. Most take prevocational training, which includes speech, sign language, self-care skills and work orientation. Gold's technology is used extensively in training individuals. Recently, it all started to pay off as 10 seriously disabled adults began cutting and drilling aluminum components of solar-heating panels—real work subcontracted by an independent company. "These are the severe and profound who normally would not even be allowed in a workshop," Rosen notes.

In 1969, three years before MORC got rolling, ENCOR was groping to free the severely retarded from institutional constraints. First tried were group homes serving six to eight retarded children or adults. "They were a major improvement over the traditional institution, but we were still running into a problem," admits Barry Lamont. "A lot of negative behavior sharing went on between the retarded residents," ENCOR's residential director further explains. And costs of developing the facilities were high. So ENCOR converted them into administrative centers from which clients were placed in carefully selected community residences. Now ENCOR will rent houses or apartments for just two or three retarded people to live in, closely supervised by professional staffers.

"Ideally, we're looking for retarded people to be as independent within the community as possible," Lamont explains. ENCOR tries to arrange for disabled adults with complementary skills to share a home. "We've got mentally retarded men living together where one doesn't know how to cook but can read, write and develop a menu," Lamont reports. "His roommate does the cooking, because he has those skills."

Another pair of roomies, Mitch and Frank, share a basement apartment in a small town outside Omaha. An ENCOR staffer works with them 20 hours per week; otherwise, the pair are largely self-sufficient. A neighborhood store keeps track of their food bill, and every two weeks the ENCOR staffer helps them settle the tab. Mitch, who is severely retarded, works for ENCOR putting phone jacks together. Frank works full-time as a town trash collector.

Although less disabled than Mitch, Frank has a mental block about numbers and never learned to dial a phone. To solve the problem, the phone company installed an automatic dialing box with 10 picture-coded buttons. By pushing the button next to the picture of a firefighter, for example, the caller is directly connected to the fire department. Buttons are also coded for the police, ENCOR staff and the young men's girlfriends.

The mentally handicapped have the right to live and learn in the freest possible settings, insists MORC director Rosen. Many of the severely retarded can flourish in the community, if they have adequate professional support and receive the services typically available in institutions. "That doesn't mean every group house must have a psychologist, nurse and educator," Rosen explains, "but they must be available."

Parents often worry when their severely disabled children leave the security of the institution for the uncertainty of society. "There are unquestionable risks in encouraging the mentally retarded to be as inquisitive and independent as the rest of us," concedes Rosen. But, he adds, "it is also a certainty that the development of confidence, maturity and discretion . . . must necessarily involve sampling the unfamiliar and the taking of risks."

The Child with Down's Syndrome

MERRIL HARRIS

In cooperation with the effort toward mainstreaming children who have physical and mental handicapping conditions, a large percentage of Head Start and other early education programs are taking mentally retarded children. Many of these are children with Down's syndrome, since this is one of the most common causes of mental retardation.

Down's syndrome is commonly called "mongolism," because one of the distinguishing characteristics of the condition is an oriental-looking slant of the eyes. However, referring to a person with Down's syndrome as a "mongoloid" is offensive, and such usage is discouraged. Down's syndrome has nothing to do with the mongoloid race except that the syndrome appears among orientals as well as blacks and caucasians. It afflicts people of all classes in all parts of the world. The condition is named after the doctor—Langdon Down—who first described this syndrome about a century ago.

Down's syndrome is caused by a chromosome abnormality. Normally, each cell in our body has 46 chromosomes which are arranged in 23 matching pairs. A person with Down's syndrome has an extra chromosome on the 21st pair making it a trio and giving each cell a total of 47 chromosomes. The extra chromosome material somehow causes the characteristics of Down's syndrome. The reasons for the abnormality are not known, but chromosome damage can be caused by such things as radiations, virus infections, and certain drugs.

Down's syndrome occurs once in every 700 births. It occurs most often in births among women over 35 years of age—half of all "Downs" babies are born to women over 35—but younger women can also bear a child with Down's syndrome. Women under the age of 30 have one chance in 1500 of having a child with Down's syndrome, while women over the age of 45 have one chance in 40.

Physical Characteristics

People with Down's syndrome are usually small in stature and have short arms, legs, fingers and toes. Their eyes have the characteristic exotic slant, while the back of the head and the bridge of the nose are slightly flattened. The inside of the mouth may be very small. This can cause the tongue to protrude and can also cause problems with speech. There is usually a single crease across the palm of the hand. The only positive means of diagnosing Down's syndrome is a chromosome study which will clearly show the presence (or absence) or the extra chromosome. (This can also be done through amniocentesis to determine whether or not a pregnant woman is carrying a fetus with a chromosome abnormality.)

Health

One-fifth of Downs babies have low birth weight, and sometimes they do not feed well as infants. They may cut teeth relatively late. Their physiological systems are generally quite immature and growth in all areas—physical, motor, cognitive, language, etc.—will probably be slower than that of other babies. Leukemia is 20 times as frequent in Downs children as in other children, about half of them have congenital heart defects, and many are subject to bronchitis, pneumonia, and other respiratory problems. They may also have neurobiological abnormalities which can result in perceptual disorders, and they often have visual or hearing disabilities severe enough to affect learning.

Mental Retardation

This term is arrived at on the basis of an individual's performance on standardized tests. What it actually means is that a child will be at a level of development significantly below the norm for her or his chronological age, particularly in areas of cognitive and intellectual functioning and possibly also in motor, language and social functionings. "Retarded" means slowed or obstructed, *not* stopped. Children who are mentally retarded go through the same developmental stages as do other children, but the duration of each stage may be prolonged, and the acquisition of basic skills will probably take longer.

The greatest area of delay in Downs children is that of speech and language. Physiological differences give their voices a gutteral quality and can cause problems with articulation, while the entire condition of retardation, especially when combined with perceptual disturbances, can cause delays in language development.

"The Child with Down's Syndrome," by Merril Harris, *Day Care & Early Education*, May/June 1977. Copyright 1977 by Human Sciences Press.

There is a great deal of erroneous stereotyping and fallacious opinion regarding children with Down's syndrome. In fact, Downs children CAN learn to walk, talk, toilet train, feed and dress themselves, read, write, count, and socialize. They can NOT be classified as "stubborn" or "friendly." They CAN understand verbal communication, and they ARE capable of responding appropriately. There are rarely problems with violence or sexual activity—children with Down's syndrome CAN be taught socially acceptable deportment as well as any other child can.

Young children with Down's syndrome can be stimulated into following a normal pattern of development at a rate that is not too severely retarded and can progress much faster than one might expect. Many Downs people, even without the benefit of early stimulation, are capable of formal learning up to or beyond high school level, enjoy socializing as young adults, and have the potential to live independently as contributing members of society.

Mainstreaming

Children with Down's syndrome can function quite well in an early childhood program with all types of other children. If they have been stimulated since infancy, they will probably not be much behind other toddlers or preschoolers. Teachers can rest assured that a Downs child who is profoundly retarded will not be placed in the program to begin with. A retarded child who is recommended for mainstreaming will be a child who can function successfully in a normal program on all levels, although she or he will require some extra care in being educated.

As will any child, children with Down's syndrome will become bored if they are not stimulated, and this can be extremely harmful. Boredom and lack of suitable stimulation will result in further developmental retardation and the acquisition of self-stimulating behaviors. Normal children will, even when left to their own devices, seek out stimulation which will contribute to their growth in learning. Downs children must be taught how to do this; they will not do it spontaneously. Because their physiology is in every way conducive to developmental lags (i.e. immaturity, poor motor coordination, perceptual problems), these children must have more than the usual amount of sensory stimulation as well as deliberate structure for learning experiences in order to provide them with enough input and momemtum to progress in all areas of development. If a child with Down's syndrome is not actively stimulated and taught, especially when very young, she or he will probably fulfill all archaic predictions by vegetating.

Because of their general immaturity, Downs children will probably be slower than the average child in motor development. The shortness of their limbs may require more practice in using them to become proficient. They can benefit greatly from gross motor activities with emphasis on balance, coordination, and movement.

Downs children may take longer to process and respond to verbal communications, and because of this, teachers sometimes feel that the child does not understand. These children will respond more readily to instructions that are simple, well-structured, and clearly spoken. It is helpful to the child for the teacher to combine gestures with speech whenever possible, even to the point of pantomiming an activity. If the child appears to be uncertain of what is expected, she or he can be gently manipulated by the teacher through the proper motions or actions. The teacher should be prepared to break down all skills and activities whenever necessary, finding the level where the child is able to perform successfully independently and then, through practice, to build up abilities from that point.

Except for the fact that Downs children will need more active stimulation and more detailed and simplistic direction when involved in learning activities, they should not be treated differently from other children in the program. They are clever enough to quickly realize when they can get away with being a "poor mentally retarded child" and will not hesitate to take advantage where and when they can. They will test the adult in charge the same as any other child will, and they will develop their relationships on the basis of the responses they receive.

Just like other children, Downs children do not all look alike, act alike, learn in the same manner, or have the same temperaments or personalities. Just like other children, they are curious and enjoy exploring and learning. They can participate in all activities offered by an early childhood program—music, art, blocks, water play, trips, etc—and they can be subjected to the same expectations that the teacher has for the other children with regard to behavior and social adjustment.

Children with Down's syndrome are well aware that they are not like other children. Their inclusion in a normal school program will help them to develop a well-balanced self image through involvement in natural situations with other children. It is also healthy for other children to have contact with children who have handicapping conditions; with familiarity comes an end to the disgust that rises out of fear and ignorance, and these children will hopefully grow to be adults who have a greater tolerance for each other and acceptance of individual differences.

MAINSTREAMING FOR THE SECONDARY EDUCABLE MENTALLY RETARDED: IS IT DEFENSIBLE?

Gary M. Clark

Dr. Clark is a Professor of Special Education, University of Kansas, Lawrence.

Mainstreaming—defined as an educational programming option for handicapped youth which provides support to the handicapped student and his teacher(s) while he pursues all or a majority of his education within a regular school program with nonhandicapped students—is a challenging and viable option of educational service delivery for some handicapped children and youth. It is challenging because of significant shifts in emphasis which must be made to provide support services rather than direct services to children. Although as of yet there are no reports of national prominence which provide empirical data supporting the movement, the logical and legal bases for such a thrust make it an important option for *some* handicapped students. However, if it is not necessarily appropriate for *all* handicapped students, some consideration must be given to the populations for which it may not be appropriate. Smith and Arkans (1974) have done this for the severely and profoundly retarded. This article will suggest yet another population—the secondary level educable mentally retarded.

When Dunn (1968) drew the issues of special class placement for the mildly retarded into focus for the field and gave impetus to a new era of professional self-analysis, he tried to document his position carefully concerning what types of changes should occur, the nature of the population about whom he was concerned, and the environments in which change should take place. One particular point made was a deliberate exclusion of secondary level educable mentally retarded from his population of concern (p. 6). This exclusion has been overlooked amid the sweeping changes in administrative structures and educational programming which has resulted from a rapid wake of court cases and strong advocacies of mainstreaming. There needs to be a re-examination at this time of some of the basic issues involved as they relate to adolescent educable mentally retarded in secondary school programs. The issues which follow are presented with some support for a particular point of view. They are also meant to be a means by which other viewpoints can surface and be considered.

Issue 1

Given the logical and legal bases for the movement toward alternatives to special classes for elementary level mildly retarded children, *are regular secondary programs as well suited for absorbing and serving educable mentally retarded students as elementary level programs?*

One of Dunn's specific justifications for moving the mildly retarded back into the mainstream of elementary education was the capabilities of regular education to handle individual differences more readily than had been possible in the past. These capabilities were described in terms of trends and practices involving organizational changes, curricular changes, multimedia instructional resources, etc. One could add to this more facilitating environment the wider acceptance of the career education concept.

With the exception of some of the nation's more progressive secondary schools, the same claims for capabilities in dealing with individual differences at the secondary level, particularly high schools, cannot be made. Secondary schools are, in comparison to elementary schools, much more inflexible in administrative and programmatic change. For example, high school resistance to the career education concept is witnessed by the paucity of significant changes in programming since the movement began. Size, diversity, complexity, and the sacredness of the Carnegie unit are some of the obvious barriers to change, but there are other more subtle factors operating, including subject matter area "empires," greater activism in teacher negotiating units, academic competitiveness with other schools, and reduced responsibility for each student's total development.

Issue 2

Given the logical and legal bases for providing for the needs of all students, *is the regular class the most advantageous current alternative in providing for the educable mentally retarded at the secondary level?*

To discuss this issue and present a point of view, one must make certain assumptions that become basic to arguments supporting that point of view. The following assumptions have been accepted by the writer:

1. The higher one goes up the grade-level hierarchy, the greater the discrepancies among students in intellectual functioning, academic achievement, social experience, and personal maturity.

"Mainstreaming for the Secondary Educable Mentally Retarded: Is It Defensible?" by Gary M. Clark, *Focus on Exceptional Children*, Vol. 7, No. 2, 1975. Reprinted with permission of the publisher, Love Publishing Company.

2. The higher one goes up the grade-level hierarchy, the greater the desire and/or demand by students for school to be related to immediate and near-future needs.
3. The higher one goes up the grade-level hierarchy, the greater the need by students to have greater identification and personal interaction with one or two significant adults who by proximity and commitment are readily available for guidance and counseling.
4. A democratic philosophy of education and a realistic philosophy of normalization do not dictate that all persons have the same educational experiences.

Based on an acceptance of these assumptions, the arguments which have been used against the special class in general can be challenged in relation to the secondary level class in particular.

Argument: Educable mentally retarded students make as much or more progress in regular classrooms as they do in special classrooms.

Response: This argument is based on data from elementary, not secondary, level populations. On the contrary, there is some evidence to indicate that secondary special class programs are contributed to adult adjustment in the community for their participants (Porter & Milazzo, 1958; Stephens & Peck, 1968).

Argument: Special class placement isolates the handicapped from normal peers.

Response: Secondary classes are not typically as self-contained as elementary special classes and are not as vulnerable on this point. Integration (not mainstreaming) in regular classes of music, art, physical education, homemaking, and industrial arts has been, and continues to be, a common practice in junior and senior high school special education classes. In addition, participation in extracurricular activities as well as both on-campus and off-campus work experiences have added to special students' exposure to and interaction with nonhandicapped peers. Only in the most restricted cases could this argument be justified against secondary special education classes. Certainly, it does not isolate students any more than some vocational education programs or other academic track options.

Argument: Special class placement stigmatizes the handicapped, resulting in loss of self-esteem and lowered acceptance by normal peers.

Response: Negative perceptions of a group or of individuals result primarily as a consequence of socially unacceptable or inappropriate behaviors, regardless of an educational grouping (Baldwin, 1958; Johnson, 1950). Inappropriate behaviors within a regular class will just as likely result in greater individual stigma, with accompanying loss of self-esteem and lowered acceptance by normal peers. It is interesting that the field has come full circle in this problem. The frustrations and pressures experienced by the educable mentally retarded in regular classes resulted in behaviors which were unacceptable and interpreted as indicative of poor mental health. The solution was seen to be their removal from that frustrating environment to one which would foster success, reduce frustration, relieve anxiety, and build positive self-concept. What was once seen as the source of the problem is now seen as the source of the solution.

The issue is not whether stigma exists, however, but rather whether the programming itself can demonstrate effectiveness in reducing or eliminating that stigma, raising self-esteem, and increasing the degree of acceptance by the nonhandicapped. We do not as yet have adequate data on this for adolescents.

Argument: The very existence of special classes encourages the misplacement of many handicapped persons, particularly children and youth from minority groups.

Response: As long as there are options for placement, there are opportunities for misplacement. With fewer options, misplacement is more likely to occur. If the options include only regular class placement or special class placement, minority group youth will be more likely to be misplaced in special classes. However, misplacement can be just as possible in regular classes as in special classes, if misplacement is interpreted similarly in both situations, i.e., inappropriate content and/or level of instruction.

If the special class is kept as one of several options, including learning centers, vocational education programs for handicapped or special-needs students, and mainstreaming with an effective career education component, misplacement is less likely to occur. Hopefully, recent court cases have made us sufficiently aware of the dangers of capricious placement and that placement based on lack of appropriate alternatives for minority group youths, or any youths for that matter, is an issue schools must face.

Issue 3

Given the logical and legal bases for meeting the needs of all children, *are the decision makers who are extending the mainstreaming philosophy from elementary to secondary level giving appropriate attention to the consequences of curriculum focus as a result of their decisions?*

Meyen (1974) has stated the problem this way:

> From a curriculum perspective, mainstreaming for handicapped children is presenting new curriculum problems for special educators. Unless we cope with these problems better and quicker than we did those encountered during the special class movement of the 1950s and 1960s, handicapped children will suffer and the field of special education may very well experience a major setback. . . . (p. 3)

> Except for preventive measures–and in some cases, corrective measures–special education for most children involves curriculum. With most groups of exceptional children the focus is on providing an educational program which maximizes the child's performance and not on remediating his handicap. (p. 4)

The point of view being presented in this paper supports Meyen's statement and suggests that it is an even more crucial problem at the secondary level than at the elementary level. There can be no question that the curriculum focus of high school work-study programs for educable mentally retarded youth has been considered more relevant by that population than in previous years when the curriculum was a "watered-down" academic program. The holding power of the more relevant prevocational program has been demonstrated in report after report in not only reduced dropout statistics but in drawing former students back when they became aware of the new program.

The current curriculum focus in prevocational development and preparation for adult living is based on formal and informal follow-up studies of those who have been in special classes for the educable mentally retarded. This current focus is by no means adequate in terms of scope and sequence, but it is more on target than what is available in general education.

Vocational education, as a component of the regular school program, is appropriate in vocational content but deficient in adult living instruction and is generally inappropriate in terms of level of instruction. Vocational education and special education are on a collision course in the mainstreaming movement, and the resistance by vocational educators is still high. One of their defenses, and one which is undeniable at this point, is that mainstreaming explicitly involves support services for the handicapped, while few special educators are trained or qualified by experience to give technical assistance as one might in an academic subject.

If vocational education is not presently an available option, is the general education curriculum or track any more appropriate? Former U.S. Commissioner of Education S.P. Marland, Jr. has decried the ineffectiveness of general education and has referred to it as an "abomination" (Marland, 1971). The career education concept was conceived and developed with general education clearly in mind. However, until career education programs are operative and demonstrated to be effective, general education has little to offer but removal of group stigma and the appearance of normalization. If educators are more concerned about normalization and the avoidance of group stigma here and now than they are for normalization as adults and avoidance of individual stigma in the future, their concerns and priorities are questionable. Support for this interpretation of the principle of normalization is found in a publication by the National Association of Retarded Children (1972).

> Although the normalization principle is useful in many situations, the fact that a technique is normative does not guarantee that it is the most effective. The developmental model suggests that program effectiveness should be gauged by the degree to which goals are reached rather than by the degree to which procedures are culturally normative. In some cases, normative procedures may fail to foster desirable behavior, whereas specialized procedures may accomplish desired goals. (p. 7)

A side issue to the problem of curriculum relevance for those secondary special education programs involved in a cooperative agreement with state vocational rehabilitation agencies is the basis for third party funding. This concerns the practice of obtaining additional federal funds for rehabilitation from state matching funds—in this case, teachers' and work-study coordinators' salaries. To use these salaries for matching purposes, the agencies must certify that the persons whose salaries are being used for matching are indeed performing a rehabilitation function. The criteria for certification are flexible but generally rest on the requirement that the content and instructional approach are prevocational in nature. Since early federal audits of this practice disallowed "watered-down" academics in special classes, there is no reason to believe that instruction focusing on support of students in an academic mainstream program would be allowable.

Summary

Mainstreaming as the only program option at the secondary level for educable mentally retarded adolescents is presently highly questionable for the following reasons:

1. We have no empirical evidence on adolescent retardates to indicate that movement from a partially developed approach (but demonstrably more effective than previous programs) to a new, untried approach is appropriate.
2. The curriculum focus of mainstreaming at the secondary level is not congruous with what has been identified as the needs of adolescent retarded.
3. The basic assumptions posed for secondary special education programming do not indicate that regular secondary programs or tracks are appropriate.
4. Career education concept programs are not yet adequately established in junior and senior high schools.
5. Support personnel for vocational education teachers, the group most obviously needed for an appropriate mainstreaming approach, are not available.
6. The inflexibility of junior and senior high school policies and goals are not predictive of success for this population.

Implications

Some implications of this position can and should be drawn.

1. Questioning of the appropriateness of mainstreaming at the secondary level for educable retarded adolescents in no way defends the inadequacies of the present special class model. There are tremendous gaps in existing special class programs in terms of curriculum development (scope and sequence), effective instructional approaches, adequate social training and opportunities, prevocational assessment, guidance and counseling, work adjustment training, and placement at appropriate levels of employment. Neither does it deny the probable benefits mainstreaming can provide for a larger number of educationally handicapped youths who have not

been eligible for special class placement and have not been adequately served in the regular program.

2. Any school that has the capabilities of flexible school organization, adequate resource personnel, and a strong career education commitment should assume responsibility for empirically evaluating alternatives to special classes. Chaffin's (1974) suggested guidelines for administrators who are considering the initiation or expansion of a mainstreaming program should be followed. In addition, the evaluation should focus on the following questions[1]:

   a. What benefits will be gained from this alternative over present alternatives?
   b. What curriculum restrictions will be placed on teachers?
   c. What instructional support services are needed for each student and his/her teacher(s)?
   d. What instructional materials are needed to support the student?
   e. What curriculum resources are needed for complete programming?
   f. What curriculum skills are needed by the special education staff?
   g. What instructional skills are needed by the special education staff?

3. The reality of secondary schools rapidly moving into alternatives for special class placement for educable mentally retarded must not be overlooked by teacher education institutions, state departments, and school administrators. The responsibility for training, retraining, certification, and program development must be shared by all in a cooperative effort.

1 Adapted from a list of questions presented in Meyen (1974).

Conclusion

This point of view serves to raise questions, cautions, and issues which must be dealt with immediately. The bandwagon effect of mainstreaming should be avoided at all instructional levels, especially if conditions are not adequate. Moreover, the secondary level is particularly vulnerable to a "spirit of the times" program movement and may stand to lose gains which have been made in the last 15 years. It is hoped that the spirit of the times can be more broadly interpreted to suggested self-evaluation, appropriate goal setting, and innovative delivery rather than acceptance of one delivery model for educational services.

REFERENCES

Baldwin, W. D. The social position of the educable mentally retarded in the regular grades in the public schools. *Exceptional Children*, 1958, *25*, 106-108.

Chaffin, J. D. Will the real "mainstreaming" program please stand up! (or . . . should Dunn have done it?). *Focus on Exceptional Children*, 1974, *6*, 1-18.

Dunn, L. M. Special education for the mildly retarded–Is much of it justifiable? *Exceptional Children*, 1968, *35*, 5-22.

Johnson, G. O. A study of the social position of mentally handicapped children in the regular grades. *American Journal of Mental Deficiency*, 1950, *55*, 60-89.

Marland, S. P., Jr. *Career education now.* Paper presented at the National Association of Secondary School Principals Convention, Houston, Texas, January 23, 1971.

Meyen, E. L. *Mainstreaming: Some curriculum concerns.* Paper presented at Kansas Federation of Council for Exceptional Children, Topeka, Kansas, March 1974.

National Association for Retarded Children. *Residential programming for mentally retarded persons: A developmental model for residential services.* Arlington, Texas: National Association for Retarded Children, 1972.

Porter, R. B. & Milazzo, T. C. A comparison of mentally retarded adults who attended a special class with those who attended regular school classes. *Exceptional Children*, 1958, *24*, 410-412, 420.

Smith, J. O. & Arkans, J. R. Now more than ever: A case for the special class. *Exceptional Children*, 1974, *40*, 497-502.

Stephens, W. B. & Peck, J. R. *Success of young adult male retardates.* Washington, DC: Council for Exceptional Children, 1968.

The Profoundly Retarded: A New Challenge for Public Education

Abstract: This article is intended to acquaint teachers and educators with the training methodology used over the last decade in residential and other non-school settings with profoundly retarded persons. Problems unique to the profoundly retarded and suggested areas are for program emphasis presented to provide a frame of reference for future curriculum development.

ROBERT E. LUCKEY
MAX R. ADDISON

ROBERT E. LUCKEY *is a Consultant, Program Services, and Max R. Addison is Project Coordinator, National Child Advocacy Project, National Association for Retarded Citizens, Arlington, Texas.*

Educational administrators and professionals are increasingly faced with the problem of reconciling the numerous programmatic, economic, architectural and legal factors which are impacting upon the public schools as a result of recent court decisions which expand public school services to include profoundly retarded students (Gilhool, 1973; Lippman & Goldberg, 1973; Sontag, Burke & York, 1973; Weintraub, 1972; Ross, DeYoung & Cohen, 1971). A number of states have also recently passed new special education legislation or modified existing laws to establish full and equal educational opportunities for all handicapped persons (e.g., Education Commission of the States, 1972; Trudeau, 1971). Although the educational systems of many states are still not subject to these new judicial or legislative mandates, there are strong indications that the trend toward "zero reject" in the public schools will eventually spread nationwide.

The influx of markedly retarded students will necessitate new educational resources and provisions which do not commonly exist within the typical public school. In regard to training technology, isolated examples of exemplary or model non-school programs are available at the present time, as is a growing body of professional literature concerning specific methodology for use with markedly retarded students (e.g. Lake, 1974; Watson, 1973 & 1972; Ball, 1971; Gardner, 1971; Bialac, 1970; Girardeau *et al*, 1970; Gardner & Watson, 1969; Barnard & Orlando, 1967; Hollis & Gorton, 1967). However, much pertinent literature is not published or disseminated by the usual communication sources used by public school personnel, particularly the work that was done in residential institutions during the mid and late 1960's.

There is further reason to believe that the educators involved in teacher preparation are not overly familiar with training programs for profoundly retarded persons, since the traditional emphasis in teacher training has been upon techniques and curricula appropriate for mildly and moderately retarded students. As has been pointed out by Sontag *et al* (1973), new classes for markedly handicapped students will likely be staffed by teachers with little or no preparation in this area. To overcome such deficits, teacher training programs will require major reorientation, with an infusion of needed technology from research in related or allied disciplines.

The present article represents an attempt to bring together information from a variety of sources in order to acquaint educators and teachers with existing methodology for training profoundly retarded persons, and to provide a frame of reference for incorporating these training techniques within a longitudinal educational plan.

Where to Begin

The movement toward the inclusion of profoundly retarded students in the public schools will necessitate a revision in traditional definitions of education. In this regard, Roos (1971) has stated that:

> "Education is the process whereby an individual is helped to develop new behavior or to apply existing behavior, so as to equip him to cope more effectively with his total environment. It should be clear, therefore, that when we speak of education we do not limit ourselves to the so-called academics. We certainly include the development of basic self-help skills. Indeed, we include those very complex bits of behavior which help to define an individual as human. We include such skills as toilet training, dressing, grooming, communicating and so on [p. 2]."

In line with Roos' statement, Table 1 presents suggested areas of program emphasis for profoundly retarded students which include skill areas that, in the past, have not been considered to be within the province of public school education. This table is based on generalizations about age and ability groups and does not take into account intra-group dif-

"The Profoundly Retarded: A New Challenge for Public Education," by Robert E. Luckey and Max R. Addison, *Educating and Training of the Mentally Retarded,* Vol. 9, No. 3, October 1974. Copyright 1974 by the Division on Mental Retardation, The Council for Exceptional Children. Reprinted with permission.

ferences. Obviously, the degree of individual variation within a group may be marked. Therefore, the tabular information should be considered only as a general guide when establishing individual training goals and ob jectives.

As suggested in Table 1, systematic training should begin early in the lives of profoundly retarded children. Because these children are growing physically, there is a particular need to ensure that physical problems do not result from abnormal postures assumed during prolonged periods in bed. Such conditions can be minimized by providing opportunities for weight bearing each day, and by placing shoes on the children's feet while they are in bed. Problems such as scissoring of the legs can be prevented by proper positioning exercises and the appropriate use of splints or leg restraints. Other common deformities of the head, rib cage and spine may also be prevented by correct body positioning and physical therapy (Robinault, 1973; Pearson & Williams, 1972; Finnie, 1970).

Improved head balance and trunk control have been accomplished in a number of ways including systematic mat play or exercise (Pearson & Williams, 1972), and through the use of sitting position supports such as automobile tires, sand bags, and pillows (Robinault, 1973). It is important to realize that the position of the child's hips and back greatly influence his ability to develop proper functional balance. Positioning restraints may be used in this regard in conjunction with other approaches (Robinault, 1973).

Physical Development Accelerates

By the time profoundly retarded children reach traditional school age, they should be able to pull erect, stand partially supported or alone, and make their first attempts to walk independently. Obviously, the design of the school environment must not be prohibitive to independent ambulation and other forms of locomotion (Gangnes, 1970; Gunsburg, 1968; Helsel, 1967). To develop optimally, profoundly retarded students should also be involved in a variety of sensory-motor activities (Auxter, 1971; Webb, 1969). Indoor obstacle courses can be constructed in the classroom to supplement outdoor recreational and physical fitness experiences such as walks, waterplay, swinging and the use of standard playground equipment (AAHPER, 1971; Hillman, 1968; Hillman, 1966).

Normal risk taking is also essential to the development of all children, including the profoundly retarded (Perske, 1972). Such children must not be protected to the extent that they are prevented from exercising their gross skeletal muscles and practicing new motor skills. In addition, no child can learn about the relationship of his body to other objects in his surrounding or acquire basic self-protective skills without receiving a few minor bumps or bruises.

Establishing Functional Independence

Experience with mentally retarded persons in a variety of program settings over the last decade has demonstrated that the systematic use of positive reinforcement can facilitate the development of a variety of functional skills including *self-feeding* (Berkowitz, *et al*, 1971; Groves & Carroccio, 1971; Whitney & Barnard, 1966; Bensberg *et al*, 1965; Spradlin, 1964; Blackwood, 1962); *dressing* (Martin *et al*, 1971; Kimbrell *et al*, 1967b; Minge & Ball, 1967; Karen & Maxwell, 1967); *toilet use* (Foxx & Azrin, 1973; Watson, 1967; Giles & Wolf, 1966; Baumeister & Klosowski, 1965, Hundziak *et al*, 1965); *grooming* (Treffry *et al*, 1970; Bensberg *et al*, 1965; Girardeau & Spradlin, 1964); *motor skills* (Auxter, 1971; Smith, 1972; Rice *et al*, 1967; Ball & Porter, 1967; Johnson *et al*, 1966); *language development* (Jeffrey, 1972; Stremel, 1972; Bricker & Bricker, 1970; Peine *et al*, 1970; Risley & Wolf, 1968; Sloane, 1966); and *socialization* (Roos, 1968; Wiesen & Watson, 1967; Bensberg *et al*, 1965; Girardeau & Spradlin, 1964).

The recent work of other researchers with severely and moderately retarded students has definite implications for the development of educational programs for profoundly retarded students. For example, Lake (1974) has presented a summary of current programs which represent educational alternatives for the severely and multiply handicapped. These programs included early intervention, instructional programs for low performance children, work-skill development, and programmed environments for the developmentally disabled. Considerable attention is being given also to the language area (e.g., Tawny, 1974; Bricker, 1972; Lynch & Bricker, 1972; Tawny & Hipsher, 1972; Guess *et al*, 1971; and Mann & Baer, 1971), the analysis and modification of classroom behavior (Haring & Phillips, 1972) and vocational performance (Gold, 1973; Crosson *et al*, 1970).

Although positive reinforcement has been used most generally in the programs cited thus far, negative or aversive reinforcement has also proved useful to decelerate undesirable behaviors. In this regard, the use of punishment procedures has been reviewed by Gardner (1969) and others (MacMillan *et al*, 1973; Smolov, 1971). The deceleration of disruptive behavior has been accomplished using *aversive shock* (Buscher & Lovaas, 1968; Tate & Baroff, 1966; Luckey *et al*, 1968; Hamilton & Standahl, 1969; White & Taylor, 1967; Birnbrauer, 1968); *physical restraint* (Henriksen &

TABLE 1

Suggested Areas of Program Emphasis for Profoundly Retarded Persons

PRE-SCHOOL AGED	*SCHOOL AGED*	*ADULTS*
Sensori-Motor Stimulation a. stimulating sight, hearing, touch, smell, and muscular response b. enriching environment and encouraging exploration of interesting and attractive surroundings	Sensori-Motor Development a. identifying shapes, colors, sizes, locations, and distances b. identifying sound patterns, locations, tonal qualities, rhythms c. identifying textures, weights, shapes, sizes, temperatures d. identifying familiar, aversive and pleasant odors	Sensori-Motor Integration a. sorting, transferring, inserting, pulling, folding b. responding to music activities, signals, warnings c. making personal choices and selections d. discriminating sizes, weights, colors, distances, locations, odors, temperatures, etc.
Physical Development a. body positioning b. passive exercising c. rolling, creeping and crawling d. balancing head and trunk e. using hands purposefully f. standing practice g. training for mobility	Physical Mobility and Coordination a. practicing ambulation b. overcoming obstacles; walking on ramps and stairs, running, skipping, jumping, balancing, climbing c. using playground equipment d. participating in track and field events	Physical Dexterity and Recreation a. riding vehicles; participating in gymnastic-like activities and track and field events b. marking with pencil; cutting with scissors; stringing beads; pasting; and assembling c. swimming and water play d. using community parks, playgrounds, and other recreational resources
Pre-Self Care a. taking nourishment from bottle and spoon; drinking from cup and finger feeding b. passive dressing; accommodating body to dressing; partially removing clothing c. passive bathing; handling soap and washcloth; participating in drying d. passive placement on toilet; toilet regulating	Self-Care Development a. self-feeding with spoon and cup; eating varied diet; behaving appropriately while dining b. removing garments; dressing and undressing with supervision; buttoning, zipping, and snapping c. drying hands and face; partially bathing d. toilet scheduling; indicating need to eliminate; using toilet with supervision	Self-Care a. eating varied diet in family dining situation; using eating utensils; selecting foods b. dressing with partial assistance or supervision c. bathing with partial assistance or supervision d. using toilet independently with occasional supervision
Language Stimulation a. increasing attention to sounds b. encouraging vocalization c. responding to verbal and non-verbal requests d. identifying objects	Language Development a. recognizing name, names of familiar objects, and body parts b. responding to simple commands c. imitating speech and gestures d. using gestures, words or phrases	Language and Speech Development a. listening to speaker b. using gestures, words, or phrases c. following uncomplicated directions
Interpersonal Response a. recognizing familar persons b. requesting attention from others c. occupying self for brief periods d. manipulating toys or other objects	Social Behavior a. requesting personal attention b. playing individually alongside other residents c. using basic self-protective skills d. playing cooperatively with other residents	Self-Direction and Work a. using protective skills b. sharing, taking turns, waiting for instructions c. traveling with supervision d. completing assigned tasks e. participating in work activity center program

Doughty, 1967; Hamilton, Stephens & Allen, 1967); *conditioned aversive presentation* (Whitney & Barnard, 1966); *time-out* (Baker *et al*, 1972; Hamilton *et al*, 1967; Peterson & Peterson, 1968; Wolf *et al*, 1964); *incompatible response* (Patterson *et al*, 1965; Whitman *et al*, 1971; Allen & Harris, 1966); and *extinction* (Wolf *et al*, 1965).

One specific problem associated with the establishment of functional independence, which warrants special mention, involves self-feeding. Among a relatively small group of profoundly retarded children, neuro-muscular difficulties may result in severe feeding problems. There has been a tendency in the past to compensate for severe feeding problems by using gavage techniques (i.e., inserting a tube through the nose and into the stomach). Although this is a valid emergency measure to ensure adequate nutritional intake on a temporary basis, it has too often become a permanent approach to children with feeding problems. Gastric fistula (i.e., tubes inserted directly through the abdomen wall) are also used in some cases. This latter approach is justified in an even smaller number of cases involving rare physiological anomalies.

Educators should be aware that there are a number of facilitation techniques which involve step-by-step stimulation of the lips and tongue to improve muscle control; techniques also exist in teaching proper breath control to permit swallowing and, ultimately, chewing behavior (Pearson & Williams, 1972; Finnie, 1970; Smith, 1970). Such techniques should be incorporated in a systematic program to wean children from feeding tubes as soon as possible. Although there are rare exceptions to the rule, it has been adequately demonstrated that profoundly involved children can be helped to develop sufficient tongue, lip and breath control to allow them to accept food in a normal manner. Before resorting to tube feeding, it should be clearly determined that the child's medical condition truly indicates his inability to obtain nourishment through other means.

Continuing Training Needs

The design of training programs must take into consideration the long-term training needs of the profoundly retarded throughout the life cycle. During the young adult and adult years, programming emphasis should focus upon the maintenance and refinement of self-care, grooming, communication and other social adaptive skills. Although their intellectual development may still be significantly limited, the profoundly retarded should not be considered as "child-like." They are physically developed persons, with years of experience practicing various skills — characteristics which make them markedly different from young children. Therefore, much more should be expected from these persons in terms of independence and self-direction. Unfortunately many parents and professionals alike, guided by the expectation that the profoundly retarded will remain child-like, tend to infantilize these persons and perpetuate their helplessness and dependence.

In the not too distant past, profoundly and severely retarded persons were thought to be incapable of learning, and developmental programming for these individuals was considered futile. In contrast to this pessimistic view, the markedly retarded are now being taught to participate in work activity and sheltered workshop programs (Gold, 1973; Cortazzo, 1972). The types of skills being acquired in these work centers range from self-care and grooming to work skills including such tasks as sorting, transferring, inserting, pulling, wrapping, sealing and folding. In this latter regard, Zaetz (1969) has devised numerous work activities which would be appropriate for markedly retarded persons, and Crosson *et al* (1970) have described systematic training procedures. Even the operation of industrial machinery has been accomplished by profoundly retarded workers when the task consisted of pulling levers or otherwise activating machinery at scheduled intervals. Such innovative ways of utilizing profoundly retarded workers strongly suggest that their alleged paucity of skills may be only valid in a world designed exclusively for non-retarded workers (Screven *et al*, 1971). Although the current training goal is not necessarily to produce competitive workers in the traditional sense, profoundly retarded persons can be engaged on a daily basis in meaningful activities that help prevent unnecessary physical and psychological deterioration, and enhance their acceptability in the non-retarded world.

References

Allen, K.E. & Harris, F.R. Elimination of a child's excessive scratching by training the mother in reinforcement procedures. *Behavior Research and Therapy*, 1966, **4**, 79-84.

American Association for Health, Physical Education and Recreation. *The Best of Challenge.* Washington, D.C.:AAHPER, 1971.

Auxter, D. Motor skill development in the profoundly retarded. *Training School Bulletin*, 1971, **68**, 5-9.

Baker, J.G., Stanish, B. & Fraser, B. Comparative effects of a token economy in nursery school. *Mental Retardation*, 1972, **10**, 16-19.

Ball, T. (Ed.) *A Guide for the Instruction and Training of Profoundly Retarded and Severely Multi-Handicapped Child.* Santa Cruz, California: Santa Cruz County Board of Education, 1971.

Ball, T.S. & Porter, W. An exploration of the uses of the orienting response. Paper presented at the 91st annual meeting of the American Association of Mental Deficiency, Denver, Colorado, 1967.

Barnard, J.W. & Orlando, R. Behavior modification: A bibliography. *IMRID Papers and Reports*, George Peabody College, 1967.

Baumeister, A. & Klosowski, R. An attempt to group toilet train severely retarded patients. *Mental Retardation*, 1965, **3**, 24-26.

Bensberg, G.J., Colwell, C.N. & Cassel, R.H. Teaching the profoundly retarded self-help activities by behavior shaping techniques. *American Journal of Mental Deficiency*, 1965, **69**, 674-679.

Berkowitz, S., Sherry, P.J., & Davis, B.A. Teaching self-feeding to profound retardates using reinforcement and fading procedures. *Behavior Therapy*, 1971, **2**, 62-67.

Bialac, V. *The Severely and Profoundly Retarded.* Olympia, Washington: Washington State Library, 1970.

Birnbrauer, J.S. Generalization of punishment effect—A case study. *Journal of Applied Behavior Analysis*, 1968, **1**, 201-211.

Blackwood, R.O. Operant conditioning as a method of training the mentally retarded. Unpublished Ph.D. dissertation, Ohio State University, 1962.

Bricker, W.A. A systematic approach to language training. In: R.L. Schiefelbusch (Ed.), *Language of the Mentally Retarded.* Baltimore, Maryland: University Park Press, 1972.

Bricker, W.A. & Bricker, D.D. Development of receptive vocabulary in severely retarded children *American Journal of Mental Deficiency*, 1970, **74**, 599-607.

Bucher, B. & Lovaas, O.I. Uses of aversive stimulation in behavior modification. In:M.R. Jones, (Ed.), *Miami Symposium of the Prediction of Behavior, 1967: Aversive Stimulation.* Coral Gables, Florida: University of Miami Press, 1968.

Cortazzo, A. *Activity Centers for Retarded Adults.* Washington, D.C.:President's Committee on Mental Retardation, DHEW Publication No. (OS) 73-43, 1972.

Crosson, J.E., Youngberg, C.D. & White, O.R. Transenvironmental programming: An experimental approach to the rehabilitation of the retarded. In:H.J. Prehm (Ed.), *Rehabilitation Research in Mental Retardation.* Eugene, Oregon: Rehabilitation Research and Training Center in Mental Retardation, 1970.

Education Commission of the States. *Handicapped Children's Education Program Newsletter*, 1972, **1**, 3.

Finnie, N.R. *Handling the Young Cerebral Palsied Child at Home.* New York: E.P. Dutton & Co., 1970.

Foxx, R.M. & Azrin, N.H. *Toilet Training the Retarded.* Champaign, Illinois: Research Press, 1973.

Ganges, A.G. Architecture. In J. Wortis (Ed.),

Mental Retardation, New York: Grune & Stratton, 1970.

Gardner, J.M. & Watson, L.S. Behavior modification in mental retardation: An annotated bibliography. *Mental Retardation Abstracts*, 1969, **6**, 181-193.

Gardner, W.I. *Behavior Modification in Mental Retardation*. Chicago, Illinois: Aldine-Atherton, 1971.

Gardner, W.I. Use of punishment with the severely retarded: A review. *American Journal of Mental Deficiency*, 1969, **74**, 86-103.

Giles, D.K. & Wolf, M.M. Toilet training institutionalized severe retardates: An application of operant behavior modification techniques. *American Journal of Mental Deficiency*, 1966, **70**, 766-780.

Gilhool, T.K. Education: An inalienable right. *Exceptional Children*, 1973, **39**, 8.

Girardeau, F.L., Albright, J.D., Saunders, L.J. & Calia, P.H. *Operant Conditioning and Mental Retardation: A List of Research Studies, Application Reports and General Articles.* Kansas City, Kansas: Bureau of Child Research Laboratory, University of Kansas Medical Center, 1970.

Girardeau, F.L. & Spradlin, J.E. Token rewards in a cottage program. *Mental Retardation*, 1964, **2**, 345-351.

Gold, M.W. Research on the vocational habilitation of the retarded: The present, the future. In N.R. Ellis (Ed.), *International Review of Research in Mental Retardation.* New York: Academic Press, 1973.

Groves, I.D. & Carroccio, D.F. A self-feeding program for the severely and profoundly retarded. *Mental Retardation*, 1971, **9**, 10-12.

Guess, D., Smith, J.O. & Ensminger, E.E. The role of nonprofessional persons in teaching language skills to mentally retarded children. *Exceptional Children*, 1971, **37**, 447-453.

Gunzburg, A.L. Architecture and mental subnormality: Sensory experiences in the architecture for the mentally subnormal child. *Mental Subnormality*, 1968, **14**, 57-61.

Hamilton, J. & Standahl, J. Suppression of stereotyped screaming behavior in a profoundly retarded institutionalized female. *Journal of Experimental Child Psychology*, 1969, **7**, 114-121.

Hamilton, J., Stephens, L. & Allen, P. Controlling aggressive and destructive behavior in severely retarded institutionalized residents. *American Journal of Mental Deficiency*, 1967, **71**, 852-856.

Haring, N. & Phillips, E.L. *Analysis and Modification of Classroom Behavior*. Englewood Cliffs, New Jersey: Prentice-Hall, 1972.

Helsel, E.D. Removing architectural barriers is not enough. In *Architectural Workshop, Conference Report of the Architectural Institute, Portland, Oregon*. Arlington, Texas: National Association for Retarded Citizens, 1967.

Henriksen, K. & Doughty, R. Decelerating undesired mealtime behavior in a group of profoundly retarded boys. *American Journal of Mental Deficiency*, 1967, **72**, 42-44.

Hillman, W.A. Jr. Therapeutic recreation with the profoundly retarded. *Recreation for the Ill and Handicapped*. April, 1966.

Hillman, W.A. Jr. Recreation for the severely and profoundly retarded. In *Programming for the Mentally Retarded.* Washington, D.C.: American Association for Health, Physical Education and Recreation, 1968.

Hollis, J.H. & Gorton, C.E. Training severely and profoundly developmentally retarded children. *Mental Retardation*, 1967, **5**, 20-24.

Hundziak, M., Maurer, R.A. & Watson, L.S. Operant conditioning in toilet training of severely mentally retarded boys. *American Journal of Mental Deficiency*, 1965, **70**, 120-125.

Jeffrey, D.B. Increasing and maintenance of verbal behavior. *Mental Retardation*, 1972, **10**, 35-41.

Johnson, M.K., Kelly, C.S., Harris, F.R. & Wolf, M. M. Application of reinforcement principles to development of motor skills of a young child. *Child Development*, 1966, **37**, 379-387.

Smith, M.A.H. *Feeding the Handicapped Child.* Memphis, Tennessee: Child Development Center, Department of Nutrition, University of Tennessee, 1970.

Smith, P.B. Acquisition of motor performance of the young TMR. *Mental Retardation*, 1972, **10**, 46-49.

Smoley, S.R. Use of operant techniques for the modification of self-injurious behavior. *American Journal of Mental Deficiency*, 1971, **76**, 295-305.

Sontag, E., Burke, P.J. & York, R. Considerations for serving the severely handicapped in the public schools. *Education and Training of the Mentally Retarded*, 1973, **8**, 20-26.

Spradlin, J.E. The Premack hypothesis and self-feeding by profoundly retarded children. A case report. Parsons, Kansas, Parsons State Hospital and Training Center, Paper #79, 1964.

Stremel, K. Language training:A program for retarded children. *Mental Retardation*, 1972, **10**, 47-49.

Tate, B.G. & Baroff, G.S. Aversive control of self-injurious behavior in a psychotic boy. *Behavior Research and Therapy*, 1966, **4**, 281-287.

Tawny, J.W. Acceleration of vocal behavior in developmentally retarded children. *Education and Training of the Mentally Retarded*, 1974, **9**, 22-27.

Tawny, J.W. & Hipsher, L.W. *Systematic Instruction for Retarded Children: The Illinois Program—Experimental Edition, Part II: Systematic Language Instruction*. Danville, Illinois: Interstate Printers & Publishers, Inc., 1972.

Treffry, D., Martin, G.L., Samels, J.L. & Watson, C. Operant conditioning of grooming behavior of severely retarded girls. *Mental Retardation*, 1970, **8**, 29-33.

Trudeau, E. (Ed.), *Digest of State and Federal Laws: Education of Handicapped Children.* Arlington, Virginia:The Council for Exceptional Children, 1971.

Valett, R.E. *Modifying Children's Behavior: A Guide for Parents and Professionals.* Belmont, California:Fearon Publishers, 1969.

Watson, L.S. *Child Behavior Modification: A Manual for Teachers, Nurses, and Parents.* New York: Pergamon Press, 1973.

Watson, L.S. *How to Use Behavior Modification with Mentally Retarded and Autistic Children: Programs for Administrators, Teachers, Parents and Nurses.* Columbus, Ohio:Behavior Modification Technology, 1972.

Watson, L.S. Application of operant conditioning techniques to institutionalized severely and profoundly retarded children. *Mental Retardation Abstracts*, 1967, **4**, 1-8.

Webb, R.C. Sensory-motor training of the profoundly retarded. *American Journal of Mental Deficiency*, 1969, **74**, 283-295.

Weintraub, F.J. Recent influences of law regarding the identification and educational placement of children. *Focus on Exceptional Children*, 1972, **4**, 1-11.

White, J.C. & Taylor, D.J. Noxious conditioning as a treatment for rumination. *Mental Retardation*, 1967, **5**, 30-33.

Whitman, T.L., Caponigri, V. & Mercurio, J. Reducing hyperactive behavior in a severely retarded child. *Mental Retardation*, 1971, **9**, 17-19.

Whitney, L.R. & Barnard, K.E. Implication of operant learning theory for nursing care of the retarded child. *Mental Retardation*, 1966, **4**, 26-29.

Wiesen, A.E. & Watson, E. Elimination of attention seeking behavior in a retarded child. *American Journal of Mental Deficiency*, 1967, **72**, 50-52.

Wolf, J.M. & Anderson, R.M. *The Multiply Handicapped Child*. Springfield, Illinois:Charles C. Thomas, 1969.

Wolf, M.M., Birnbrauer, J.S., Williams, T. & Lawler, J. A note on apparent extinction of the vomiting behavior of a retarded child. In L.P. Ullman & L. Krasner (Eds.), *Case Studies in Behavior Modification*. New York:Holt, Rinehart & Winston, 1965.

Wolf, M.M., Risley, T. & Mees, H. Application of operant conditioning procedures to the behavior problems of an autistic child. *Behavior Research and Therapy*, 1964, **1**, 305-312.

Zaetz, J.L. *Occupational Activities Training Manual for Severely Retarded Adults*. Springfield, Illinois:Charles C. Thomas, 1969.

Karen, R.L. & Maxwell, S.J. Strengthening self-help behavior in the retardate. *American Journal of Mental Deficiency*, 1967. **71**, 546-550.

Kimbrell, D.L., Kidwell, F. & Hallum, G. Institutional environment developed for training severely and profoundly retarded. *Mental Retardation*, 1967(a), **5**, 34-37.

Kimbrell, D.L., Luckey, R.E., Barbuto, P. & Love, J.G. Operation dry pants: An intensive habit-training program for severely and profoundly retarded. *Mental Retardation*, 1967(b), **5**, 32-36.

Lake, T.P. Programs providing alternatives: Educating the severely and multiply handicapped. *Education and Training of the Mentally Retarded*, 1974, **9**, 29-47.

Lippman, L. & Goldberg, I.I. *Right to Education*. New York: Teachers College Press, 1973.

Luckey, R.E., Watson, C.M. & Musick, J.K. Aversive conditioning as a means of inhibiting vomiting and rumination. *American Journal of Mental Deficiency*, 1968, **73**, 139-142.

Lynch, J. & Bricker, W.A. Linguistic theory and operant procedures: Toward an integrated approach to language training for the mentally retarded. *Mental Retardation*, 1972, **10**, 12-16.

MacMillan, D.L., Forness, S.R. & Trumbull, B.M. The role of punishment in the classroom. *Exceptional Children*, 1973, **40**, 85-96.

Mann, R.A. & Baer, D.M. The effects of receptive language training on articulation. *Journal of Applied Behavior Analysis*, 1971, **4**, 291-298.

Martin, G.L., Kehoe, B., Bird, E., Jensen, V. & Darbyshire, M. Operant conditioning in the dressing behavior of severely retarded girls. *Mental Retardation*, 1971, **9**, 27-30.

Minge, M.R. & Ball, T.S. Teaching of self-help skills to profoundly retarded patients. *American Journal of Mental Deficiency*, 1967, **71**, 864-868.

Patterson, G.R. An application of conditioning techniques to the control of a hyperactive child. In: L.P. Ullman & L. Krasner (Eds.), *Case Studies in Behavior Modification*. New York: Holt, Rinehart and Winston, 1965.

Patterson, G.R. *Families*. Champaign, Illinois: Research Press, 1971.

Pearson, P.H. & Williams, C.E. (Eds.), *Physical Therapy Services in the Developmental Disabilities*. Springfield, Illinois: Charles C. Thomas, 1972.

Peine, H.A., Gregerson, G.F. & Sloane, H.N. Jr. A program to increase vocabulary and spontaneous verbal behavior. *Mental Retardation*, 1970, **8**, 38-44.

Perske, R. The dignity of risk and the mentally retarded. *Mental Retardation*, 1972, **10**, 24-27.

Peterson, R.F. & Peterson, L.R. The use of positive reinforcement in the control of self-destructive behavior in a retarded boy. *Journal of Experimental Child Psychology*, 1968, **6**, 351-360.

Rice, H.K., McDaniel, M.W., Stallings, V.D. & Gatz, M.J. Operant behavior in vegetative patients II. *Psychological Record*, 1967, **17**, 449-460.

Risley, T. & Wolf, M.M. Establishing functional speech in echolalic children. In: H. Sloan & B. MacAulay (Eds.), *Operant Procedures in Remedial Speech and Language Training*. Boston: Houghton Mifflin, 1968.

Robinault, I.P. (Ed.), *Functional Aids for the Multiply Handicapped*. New York:Harper & Row, 1973.

Roos, P. Initiating socialization programs for socially inept adolescents. *Mental Retardation*, 1968, **6**, 13-17.

Roos, P. Current issues in the education of mentally retarded persons. In W.J. Cegelka (Ed.), *Proceedings: Conference on the Education of Mentally Retarded Persons*. Arlington, Texas: National Association for Retarded Citizens, 1971.

Ross, S.L., DeYoung, H.G. & Cohen, J.S. Confrontation:Special education placement and the law. *Exceptional Children*, 1971, **38**, 5-12.

Screven, C.G., Straka, J.A. & LaFond, R. Applied behavioral technology in a vocational rehabilitation setting. In W.I. Gardner (Ed.), *Behavior Modification in Mental Retardation*. Chicago, Illinois: Aldine-Atherton, 1971.

Sloan, H. Some procedures for developing verbal behavior in a remedial setting. Paper presented at the Midwestern Psychological Association. Chicago, Illinois, 1966.

5 The Learning Disabled Child

Many people are confused about exactly what learning disabilities are. In this section of *Educating Exceptional Children,* Dr. Kinsbourne, a pediatric neurologist and child psychologist, distinguishes between learning disabilities and mental retardation and states that learning disability "implies a selective weakness that impinges on academic performance." In the second of two articles from a series in *The Exceptional Parent,* Dr. Kinsbourne discusses how educators can best help learning disabled children. He details two general types of approach, the process-oriented and the goal-oriented and presents his reasons for believing why the latter is more likely to produce successful teaching strategies.

Corinne Bloomer's "The LD Tightrope" furthers the discussion of what learning disabilities are, the problems in defining the condition, and what teachers can do to diagnose and teach these special children in their classrooms. A learning disabilities resource teacher, Martha Summers, advances the discussion of learning disabilities, the impact of PL 94-142, and how teachers can recognize children with learning disabilities in "Learning Disabilites . . . A Puzzlement." Stephen Larsen's "Learning Disabilities and the Professional Educator" is addressed to educators who will, as he says, shape the future directions of the field of learning disabilities.

Learning disabilities that pertain to language and reading and word-processing is the topic of "The Silent Crippler: Receptive Language Disability." This article examines the problems of children with specific language disabilities that must be treated and correctly dealt with as early as possible. The section concludes with Margaret Jo Shepherd's " 'Learning Disabled' or 'Slow Learner' ?" which examines the differences between these two terms and the diagnostic implications for parents and children.

Looking Ahead: Challenge Questions

What is a learning disability? What are the problems in defining what a learning disability is?

How is mental retardation different from learning disability? Are they always different?

What learning disabilities have emotional components?

In what directions do you think the field of learning disabilities is headed? Why do you think so?

Myths and Realities in Learning Disabilities

William M. Cruickshank, PhD

The concept of learning disabilities in childhood and youth is based on a confusion of ideas and understandings, and for the newcomer to the problem, it is often difficult to identify myths and unfounded concepts from the realities. The author has attempted to identify a number of misconceptions and to counterbalance these with statements based on historical, research, or theoretical facts. He deals with such matters as the issue of definition of the field, focus of child population included in the concept of learning disability, personnel preparation, and integration of these children into regular grades.

The issue of learning disabilities in childhood and youth is one of the more interesting phenomena that have occurred in education. Its history has been well documented on more than one occasion so that no further reference will be made to it here (Hallahan & Cruickshank 1973, Wiederholt 1974). The field is fraught with misconceptions. It is ill-defined in the minds of most educators and psychologists; certainly it is not understood by physicians, who have only recently become interested in the problem. Its implications are neither understood nor adequately conceptualized by the majority of school administrators. The hopes of parents are not being realized because of these facts. It is essential that serious thought be given to this matter and that more appropriate directions be initiated.

A recent volume indicates that the field of learning disabilities emerged coincident to the development by Kirk of the Illinois Test of Psycholinguistic Abilities (Haring 1974). This is the first myth which should be considered. Kirk's work, uniquely important, nonetheless had antecedents which he recognizes. The ITPA itself is based on the earlier conceptual framework of Osgood, but the additional and perhaps still earlier stimulus for whatever Kirk did in the ITPA came, he says, from personal contact with Ruth Monroe in Chicago and later from Strauss, particularly when he and Kirk were both working in Wisconsin. A still earlier stimulation of Kirk's direction undoubtedly came from his direct association with, and exposure to, both Strauss and Werner in Michigan. There is no effort here to minimize the work of Kirk. The fact of the matter is that he and several others in various institutional and university settings were working simultaneously along somewhat similar lines. With the exception of Monroe and Grace Fernald, to whom Kirk also gives credit for the stimulation of his thinking, most of these investigators were, directly or indirectly, his colleagues at an institutional setting in Michigan: Newell Kephart, Sidney Bijou, Bluma Weiner, William Cruickshank, Ruth Melcher Patterson, Charlotte Phileo, and others who followed.

The reality of this situation is that Kirk was one among several who moved to understand the complexities of children who were *later* to be called learning disabled. Kirk took the route of Osgood and the ITPA; Kephart, the conceptualization of perceptual-motor matching and training; this writer, the concept of the psychoeducational match and structure. Bijou branched off into behavior modification, others into other areas of child growth and development.

But then there are others who have made significant contributions to the field presently known as learning disability, and these were not related to the original Michigan group. Their thinking added much to the understanding of this problem, and is represented by the work and writing of Marianne Frostig, Belle Dubnoff, Sheldon Rappaport, and others whose orientation comes essentially from concepts of ego psychology and introspective clinical orientations. There were still others. All of the initial contributions of these individuals antedated the publication of the ITPA and the term *learning disabilities.* No single person is responsible for this field. The thinking and conceptualization of the individuals to whom reference has here been made are, however, astonishingly similar. There are few points of disagreement among them. There is a difference, from time to time, in the vocabulary employed; but, if careful

---

This paper was the keynote address at the Adams School Annual Conference on Learning Disabilities, New York City, April, 1976.

"Myths and Realities in Learning Disabilities," by William M. Cruickshank, Ph.D., JOURNAL OF LEARNING DISABILITIES, Vol. 10, No. 1, January 1977. Copyright 1977 by the Professional Press, Inc. Reprinted by special permission of Professional Press, Inc.

analysis is made regarding the meanings of words used, it will be observed that underlying concepts are basically similar.

A NEW FIELD

During the 1974 annual conference of the Association for Children with Learning Disabilities, I chanced to hear a speaker state, "The field of learning disabilities is an old one, one with a long history and many precedents." Let us consider Myth No. 2. The field of learning disabilities is perhaps the most recent development of any aspect of exceptionality in childhood. It has few precedents. It possesses an inadequate research base. It is characterized by an inadequate professional corps in colleges and universities and, therefore, by an inadequate supply of appropriately prepared teachers to serve the complex needs of these children.

What is the reality of this field? Wiederholt (1974) has traced the beginnings of this field of interest to Gall as early as 1808, but with discrimination, he points out that the phenomenon of learning disability per se is a contemporary issue. The Michigan group, to which earlier reference was made, had its origin and did its greatest work, however inadequate from present day research standards, in the late 1930s and 1940s. The first extension of this original work (which was done on high grade, mentally handicapped boys) was initiated and completed in 1948-53 with a population of intellectually normal, cerebral-palsied children. The first investigation into structured educational programming for these children started in 1957 and was reported in 1961(Cruickshank, Bentzen, Ratzeberg, & Tannhauser 1961). Kephart's initial publication appeared in 1960 (Kephart 1960). The first publication dealing with the competencies needed by teachers of these children appeared in 1966 (Cruickshank 1966) and the first report of a coordinated program of teacher education in 1969. The ITPA first appeared in 1968. With the exception of Gall, every person and date mentioned in these few paragraphs falls within the life span of the conference speaker referred to above, and is contemporary with him.

This is a new field insofar as its *formalization* is concerned. As a credit to Kirk, he certainly tried to give impetus to its noncategorical implications, an effort which others at the same time, and earlier, had also attempted. It has become categorized as an aspect of child deviance in ways that most of us hoped never would happen and, in effect, have worked hard to prevent. However, it is easier to speak in terms of groups than it is to speak in terms of concepts. It is easier to classify than it is to attempt to meet the peculiar needs of individual children with learning and teaching materials and techniques germane to the problems directly at hand. It is easier to conceptualize groups than it is to envision the variety of developmental needs of children within a group, and to address each appropriately.

The newness of the field in part accounts for the ill-prepared professional and teaching corps which are to be encountered at every turn in professional education. The conference speaker to whom I have referred simply did not know his facts, but his position is frequently shared by school officials who are likewise uninformed. This produces frustration in teachers and disappointment in parents as they see children continuing to flounder without adequate understanding or appropriate educational efforts on the part of school service personnel.

WHAT IS LEARNING DISABILITY?

What is learning disability? There are those who would view this term as a synonym to "remedial reading," or to educational remediation in general. This is completely fallacious. Remedial reading teachers, consultants, or specialists, by these or any other names, are not overnight appropriately converted into specialists capable of working with the problems of the learning disabled. This is Myth No. 3 to which I wish to address myself.

It is important to trace the concept of learning disability back to its neurological origin. Learning disability, specifically defined, is a manifestation of a perceptual processing deficit. It is important to differentiate between the concept of sensory perception leading to normal vision or hearing and processing of a perceptual nature, which not only involves the appropriate recognition of form or sound, but also includes the attachment of learned meaning, or appropriate motor responses, to whatever stimulus is received. This is the essence of the ITPA; it is likewise the basis of the concept of task analysis which Junkala (1972, 1973) discusses in terms of input and output concepts. However, there are numerous means other than the ITPA, equally effective, to qualitatively assess the capacity of the child to process that which he perceives. Regardless of the tools used, it is an absolute in considering the concept of the psychoeducational match that such evaluation and assessment be done, in order that teaching materials and the learning environment can be matched with the specific processing needs of the child under consideration. If the child's disability involves perception or perceptual processing, it logically follows that one is dealing with a neurological dysfunction of some sort. Thus learning disability would, from a practitioner's point of view, be conceptualized more accurately as a *perceptual processing deficit* resulting in a specific learning problem of some sort, involving one or another or all of the sensory modalities. Definitions of learning disabilities which ignore the concepts of either perceptual processing or the neurological base are misleading. Such is not to state that the specific neurological dysfunction can always be identified. From the psychoeducational point of view, the specificity of the neurological deficit (if it could be determined) would be helpful, but it is not a requisite to good programming.

A DEVELOPMENTAL PROBLEM

While those concerned with remedial reading, or other forms of remediation, frequently may need to employ techniques utilized with children who have perceptual processing deficits, remediation is in no way the solution for all the problems of the so-called learning disabled. One must differentiate between problems of learning and perceptual processing deficits resulting in specific learning disabilities. In the former – i.e., problems of learning due to initial poor teaching, problems of mother-child separation in early childhood, or other similar types of problems, remediation undoubtedly has a significant role. One does not, however, remediate a vacuum, and this is essentially the case in the child with perceptual processing deficits. In this child, appropriate learning has not taken place because of neuroperceptual processing problems. A technique of education has to be developed which will provide the child with the necessary initial skills, regardless of chronological age, and which will give him a sound base for the acquisition of more complex learnings later. This is not remediation; it is new learning.

What is an adequate definition of this problem? In 1975, there appeared an appropriate and a logical definition (Hobbs 1975) which merits thorough consideration and adoption. It is a thoughtfully prepared document, the result of the combined thinking of several people with long experience in this field, plus the critique of a much larger field of experts who know the problem well. It is a definition stated in appropriate perceptual terms. The authors define the problem in terms of its "psychoeducational reality." It is stated that this problem refers

> ... to those children of any age who demonstrate a substantial deficiency in a particular aspect of academic achievement because of perceptual or perceptual-motor handicaps, regardless of etiology or other contributing factors. The term *perceptual* as is used here relates to those mental (neurological) processes through which the child acquired his basic alphabets of sounds and forms. The term *perceptual handicap* refers to inadequate ability in such areas as the following: recognizing fine differences between auditory and visual discriminating features underlying the sounds used in speech and the orthographic forms used in reading; retaining and recalling those discriminated sounds and forms sequentially, both in short- and long-term memory; ordering the sounds and forms sequentially, both in sensory and motor acts . . .; distinguishing figure-ground relationships . . .; recognizing spatial and temporal orientations; obtaining closure . . .; integrating intersensory information . . .; relating what is perceived to specific motor functions. [p.306]

The definition ends here, but to this could be added such things as an inadequate ability to conceptualize parts into meaningful wholes; the sometime presence of perseveration; the inability to refrain from reacting to unessential environmental stimuli; and the resulting immature or faulty self-concept or body image. Actually contained within this definition is a total program of teacher preparation as well as a total concept of service to children with such problems in the public schools of the nation.

It is immediately obvious that one is dealing with a complex developmental problem, not a problem of remediation. It is also obvious that students in colleges and universities are not being given the appropriate preservice experiences to meet the challenges of this definition nor of the children who present these characteristics.

LD AND IQ

A continued reading of the definition provides a further concern and Myth No. 4. The committee which prepared this definition, of which this writer was a member, does not go far enough, although there is an important allusion to the relationship of intelligence to processing deficit resulting in learning disability as we are defining the problem. *The reality of the situation is that learning disability is a matter relating to children of any intellectual level.*

Numerous definitions of this problem define learning disabilities by exclusion, i.e., what it is not. It is stated that this is not a problem of primary mental retardation or sensory defect. I would agree. The crucial word is *primary*. This, however, is often overlooked by the nondiscriminating professional person. Indeed, many definitions of learning disability to be found in state and local regulations speak of children with learning disabilities as having IQs above

80. The implication is that the problem is a different one below the 80 level. This is an arbitrary statement, absolutely without a basis in fact. There are reports by parents of mentally retarded children that they have not been welcomed to membership in the local association of parents of learning disabled children. The reality of this myth is that learning disability is a respecter of no intellectual level. Perceptual processing deficits are to be found in children of every intellectual level and are respecters of no given intelligence range.

As a matter of fact and history, practically everything which is known about the nature of perceptual processing deficits was discovered initially from studies completed with exogenous mentally retarded children of educable levels. Certainly this was the orientation of the basic initial studies which were undertaken by Werner, Strauss, and their associates. Recently the author was informed by a representative of a state department of education that the problem could be defined by the state in any manner desired. This may be technically correct, but it is professionally irresponsible. It indicates a lack of knowledge or appreciation of what the problem actually is.

The adherence to a concept of IQ 80, itself an illogical, arbitrary cutoff point, serves to deprive thousands of mentally handicapped children of appropriate understanding and programming and, indeed, in many instances it results in the worst type of discrimination. One does not have to travel far in any direction to find classes for the mentally retarded being essentially black and classes for children with learning disabilities essentially white. The IQ concept does not have an appropriate relationship to this problem, although it may take class action suits to bring the matter into reality for many state and local educators. Under the present myth, thousands of retarded children with perceptual processing deficits resulting in learning disabilities are being misclassified and are, in effect, being denied an educational birthright.

HOW MANY NEED HELP?

One does not have to look far to find Myth No. 5. This has to do with incidence and prevalence. From time to time it is stated that the problem of severe learning disability accounts for 1% of the elementary school population. From still another source it is stated that learning disability is a matter of 12% of the same population. More frequently, in lay groups, the figure of 20% is used. An outstanding elementary school principal stated to this writer that 83% of her center-city elementary school pupils functioned as if they were perceptually handicapped. Somewhere between these extremes lies the truth.

The reality of the situation is that we do not know how many such children there are in the schools of this nation. There are absolutely no adequate data of either an epidemiological or demographic nature to provide a base for adequate programming. At the present time, there is an interdisciplinary group of scientists at the University of Michigan working to put together a valid epidemiological study of this problem, and they hope to be able to study the issue in sufficient breadth to present demographic data as well. These data, however, are still a matter of the future. At the present time, adequate data do not exist, and this results in the horrendous guesses to which I have just referred. The absence of data constitutes the basis for confusion in state and federal legislative houses and, as well, means that local school administrators must respond to parental and community pressures with inadequate information. The collection of this information is an absolute requisite for national planning of all types.

In what I have thus far said, it appears that there is a reason for the crazy-quilt manner in which this field has developed. Originally I pointed out that the underlying processing deficits and an obvious matching of them with teaching materials and environment could provide an outstanding clinical teaching program for the children who needed it. We, at Syracuse University in the 1950s and 1960s, learned that what the investigators of a decade earlier had discovered regarding the learning problems of exogenous mentally retarded children also applied in full force to cerebral palsied children of all intellectual levels. Others of my students and colleagues learned that this was also the case with deaf children whose deafness was of an organic nature; with aphasic children, an observation of Mildred McGinnis of long standing; of some epileptic children, of some blind children, and of many, if not almost all, of the so-called hyperactive, emotionally disturbed children. This last group has been studied more carefully by Haring, a student of mine, and by Phillips. The essence of the matter, however, is one of clinical diagnosis of a penetrating nature. The medical, psychological, or educational category or terminology is meaningless and completely unnecessary. What is essential is the penetrating evaluation of the child in terms of the psychological processing problems mentioned earlier that are inherent in the definition. As these are identified, they must be matched by equally as carefully considered learning and teaching techniques so that new learning will result, and the child will be started appropriately along his developmental route. Although Kirk, and many before and after him, urged that a new category of special education *not* be created, that very thing has happened. Once again we see children being assigned to classes rather than educators being concerned for the child's uniqueness and educated in such terms.

EDUCATION'S ROLE

Myth No. 6 lies in the nature of the professional relationships to the problem of perceptual processing in children leading to specific learning disabilities. This is basically a psychoeducational problem, not a medical problem. It is only recently that pediatricians, for example, have become actively aware of this problem of childhood. Nowhere in the preparation of the physician is there provided training which would permit his discipline to assume major direction of the life management plan for these children. True, medicine has a place in the interdisciplinary attack on the problems of these children. I reiterate once again, however, that the long-term issue is not one of medicine, be it pediatrics or neurology, but is of education. This writer takes no issue with the medical professional, except when that profession enters into arenas for which it is not prepared or is ill-prepared. There are a few medical personnel who are performing outstanding services for these children, but they are doing so generally in conjunction with educators and psychologists who are skilled and experienced with the problem.

I hasten to point out that in instances of research, it is important to have neurological colleagues join the interdisciplinary research team. Neurology is first to state that it does not have all of the refined skills needed to isolate the neurophysiological problem basic to processing deficits. However, the skills of this discipline can go far to refine the diagnostic effort, and this will result in a somewhat more homogeneous population for study. Here, however, I am discussing the learning situation. In this arena, the educator is and must be predominant. Learning disabilities are not a medical problem; this is the problem of numerous disciplines bringing their skills and expertise to the educator, who in the long run must be the implementer. Experience over many years has demonstrated the wisdom and validity of this approach.

TO MEDICATE OR NOT TO MEDICATE?

Myth No. 7 deals with the efficacy of medications in the management of children with specific learning disabilities. There is an appalling lack of adequate research pertaining to the utilization of medications for the control of behavior in elementary school children, other than minimal research stated as having been done by commercial drug companies. This, in my mind and in the minds of others, is not sufficient to warrant the widespread utilization of medications with these children by physicians. There is evidence to the effect that in some classes of children with learning disabilities, medication is a part of the daily intake of 40% of the children. In at least one institution known to this writer, 90% of the total population was on some sort of medication.

The reality of the situation is that if there is an adequately structured educational program with adequate matching of teaching materials to the problem and with built-in success experiences for the child, medication will often not be required at all. Medications are poor substitutes for good educational programs, are often a resort which parents must seek when good programming is unavailable and when teachers are ill-prepared to deal with the unique features of the child with specific learning disabilities.

ILL-PREPARED TEACHERS

There is a myth which is no myth at all to parents whose children are being served by ill-prepared teachers. Myth No. 8 deals with the reality of the instant specialist in colleges, universities, and public schools who presents an aura of quality, but in reality has only the veneer of the specialist. The newness of the field accounts for the lack of a well-prepared corps of university professors in this field. As such, it differs from some of the other areas of special education — mental retardation, for example. That field had been visible since about 1918, when Charles Scott Berry started summer teacher education courses at what is now Eastern Michigan University. In the interval between then and the late 1940s when the parent groups began to organize, quite a large number of persons experienced with mentally retarded children began to write, and later to teach, in colleges and universities. A body of knowledge, although limited, was available. Professors with an orientation both to retardation and teacher preparation were available in small numbers, but sufficient to prepare others adequately when the 1963 so-called Kennedy legislation became a fact. The field of specific learning disability was not a reality until after 1963. Before that, it was a matter of exploration, theory, and clinical research done by a very small number of persons. There was no precedent of teacher education in this field, except for small programs at the University of Illinois and at Syracuse University, whose program began about 1963 with the support of the National Institute of Mental Health.

When the parent group was organized in 1963, there was a general assumption that all was known that needed to be known in order to provide quality programs and that sufficient dollars would provide the treatment services their children needed. Indeed, less was known than was needed to be known about the problem — a situation which continues today in large measure. There were no formalized teacher education programs, nor were there college faculty members with experience to staff them. In contrast to the response which universities were able to make to the Kennedy legislation (which resulted in a splendid new group of university faculty members in the field of retardation), practically no personnel were available in the field of learning disabilities to be able to turn out young faculty members for teacher education institutions. The few who were available often resorted to the mechanism of summer seminars, which were a far cry from what was needed. There has never been a national policy espoused by the US Office of Education or by state departments of education focused on the production of a qualified corps of university professors in this area of child development.

As a result, in this area there is what Kirk long ago called a "cafeteria" approach to teacher education. A little of this and a little of that does not produce good professors or good teachers. Athough university faculties in a certain state were given more than two years of notice to submit programs of teacher education in this area, most universities did nothing about the matter until a few weeks or months before the deadline. As the deadline neared, there were frantic efforts on the part of faculties in special education in the universities and colleges to put together programs. These consisted essentially of utilizing old course titles, since time no longer permitted the development of new courses appropriate to the problem. To these old titles were appended new course descriptions. Since few, if any, of the universities possessed faculty members expert in this field, the nature of the conglomerates that were developed was a far cry from what in reality was needed. To my knowledge, every one of the patchwork programs was approved by the board of higher education in that state, and teachers today are being prepared through them. The response of the mature students in terms of critique is sad to hear. They realize that what they are being given is not appropriate to the need which they face in the classrooms of the public school systems.

Where did the professors come from to staff these several programs? In one instance, a good professor of the education of the emotionally disturbed overnight became the faculty leader in the area of learning disabilities. In another instance, a faculty member in the field of school psychology became the more-or-less self-appointed expert in the field of learning disabilities. In other instances, similarly sad situations prevail. A parent-turned-educator heads the program in one of the facilities. This is no way to guarantee a solid teacher group in the state under consideration. But this state is not unique. Until the national leadership provides a program for the preparation of college professors, and until the program which they experience is one of depth, as has been described and suggested elsewhere, there can be no quality in this field. In my considered opinion, the situation is one of the worst in the total field of professional education. The myth that colleges and universities can presently produce a solid teacher group is being negatively demonstrated on almost every side throughout the nation.

THE PROBLEM OF MAINSTREAMING

The final myth I wish to highlight here, Myth No. 9, pertains to the current unfounded belief that children with specific learning disabilities can, and ought to be, educated in the regular grades of the community. Parents supported this position for many years because they were disturbed with what they oftentimes saw their children receiving in the special classes. General educators, teachers, and administrators for years declared that the better place for handicapped children was in the regular grades. Often there was almost an inquisitional program launched by general educators against special educators, and at best, special educators frequently were granted what amounted to second-class citizenship in the public school system. Special education was placed, and often still is, within the administration of departments of pupil personnel. Special educators did not need more personnel approaches; they needed instructional assistance, something their supervisors were unqualified to give and general instructional personnel did not provide because of their own lack of background with atypical children. Against this poor situation, parents saw integration, mainstreaming if you must, as a way out. The general educators supported this, and some of the special education leadership also advocated it on the basis of a few case studies, not on the basis of any adequate research. Today we see a backlash developing. We had better be prepared to meet that backlash with some powerful educational tools.

Children with perceptual processing deficits resulting in specific learning disabilities have needs which the general elementary or secondary educator cannot meet in the normal classroom setting. Probably some integration for short periods each day might be valuable, but until genuine success experiences are integrated into the child's self-perception, either through the medium of well-prepared teachers working in resource rooms or in special clinical teaching stations, the capacity of the child with anything short of a very mild learning disability is going to be less than that needed to function in a normal or ordinary classroom situation. Unless general elementary educators understand the nature and needs of the problems of processing deficits and know how to adapt the learning situation and teaching materials to the child's needs, the potential for continued failure on the part of the child is present. It is unlikely that preparation of elementary general educators will include this emphasis in the foreseeable future. In the meantime, what of the children who are physically, but neither educationally or psychologically, integrated?

EDUCATIONAL CATASTROPHE

In my considered opinion, the status of learning disabilities in the public schools of this nation is one of educational catastrophe. We have too many instant specialists in positions of leadership, positions which, because of their lack of preparation or knowledge, they must defend with the pretense of expertise. This can be rectified if a hard line is assumed. There is sufficient knowledge available to put together overnight a splendid program of university professor preparation. Within two years, a corps of well qualified professors could be ready which, with some national support to universities, could result in the beginning of a steady stream of qualified teachers being released to function in the public schools. We do not have all the research needed in this area, as I have stated, but we have enough to turn around the field of education for children with specific learning disabilities from a position of chaos to one of logic and satisfaction to the professional educator and parent-consumer alike. It will take intestinal fortitude to do this, but unless strong stands are immediately taken, the chaotic situation throughout the country, as evidenced in the mediocre local school programs, will continue unabated. — *Institute for the Study of Mental Retardation and Related Disabilities, University of Michigan, 130 S. First St., Ann Arbor, Mich. 48103.*

REFERENCES

Cruickshank, W.M. (Ed.): The Teacher of Brain-Injured Children. Syracuse, N.Y.: Syracuse Univ. Press, 1966.

Cruickshank, W.M., Bentzen, F., Ratzeberg, F., and Tannhauser, M.: Teaching Method for Brain Injured and Hyperactive Children. Syracuse, N.Y.: Syracuse Univ. Press, 1961.

Hallahan, D.W., and Cruickshank, W.M.: Psychoeducational Foundations of Learning Disabilities. Englewood Cliffs, N.J.: Prentice-Hall, 1973.

Haring, N.G. (Ed.): Behavior of Exceptional Children. Columbus, O.: Chas. E. Merrill, 1974.

Hobbs, N. (Ed.): Issues in the Classification of Children, Vol. 1. San Francisco: Jossey-Bass, 1975.

Junkala, J.B.: Task analysis and instructional alternatives. Academic Ther., 1972, 8, 33-40.

Junkala, J.B.: Task analysis: The processing dimension. Academic Ther., 1973, 8, 401-409.

Kephart, N.C.: The Slow Learner in the Classroom. Columbus, O.: Chas. E. Merrill, 1960.

Wiederholt, J.L.: Historical perspectives on the education of the learning disabled. In L. Mann and D. Sabatino (Eds.): The Second Review of Special Education. Philadelphia: JSE Press, 1974.

The Tenth Myth: A Rejoinder to Cruickshank's Myths

Dear Editor: In a recent article, Cruickshank (January 1977) identified nine myths related to the learning disabilities movement. In this article, Cruickshank points out the reality, as he believes it to be, covering each of the nine myths. While there is ample room for disagreement with several of his positions, we wish to discuss his position with respect to Myth No. 3: the term *learning disabilities* is synonymous with educational remediation.

Basically, Cruickshank defines learning disabilities as "a manifestation of a perceptual processing deficit" (p. 59)*. He believes the dysfunction is rooted in the child's neurological system, thereby producing or causing learning difficulties. Thus to him the problem is not one of remediation but rather one of initial learning. In his words, "It is immediately obvious that one is dealing with a complex developmental problem, not a problem of remediation."

The value of this definition depends on the development of scientific propositions based on the definition. If the propositions are properly formulated, they may be stated in such a way as to be falsifiable. A field of knowledge is advanced when propositions derived from definitions can be tested in an empirical fashion. If propositions cannot be derived from a definition in testable form, we find ourselves engaged in tautological reasoning, which makes any proposition derived from a definition "true" by definition and not by empirical testing. In this situation, the definition of a learning disability would be accepted on the basis of "authority" or the one definition most frequently presented. Investigators could be indicted without sufficient empirical grounds because they have not accepted the definition as "true."

To avoid such tautological consequences, we have logically deduced certain propositions from Cruickshank's definition as testable:

(1) A direct relationship between learning problems and perceptual processing exists.

(2) Once identified, such deficits are reduced through instruction, which claims to improve perceptual learning.

(3) Effective teaching of learning disabled children is markedly different from that advocated by authorities of remedial and corrective instruction.

Support for the Perceptual Processing Theory

Since "minimal brain dysfunction" is rarely inferred in medical examination, advocates of the first proposition have had to rely on psychological tests. Such instruments as the Illinois Test of Psycholinguistic Abilities (ITPA) have been justifiably criticized because of their low validity and reliability (Ysseldyke & Salvia 1974, Ysseldyke 1974, Salvia & Clark 1973, Carroll 1972). At present we have no psychological measures that clearly distinguish children with learning problems due to perceptual disorders from those who display similar problems due to other reasons.

When one considers the validity and reliability of subtests on the perceptual processing measures, it is doubtful that these can be used with any degree of confidence as prescriptive measures. Ysseldyke and Salvia (1974), Salvia and Clark (1973), Waugh (1973), and Stephens (1977) have all pointed to the low reliability and validity correlations often reported for the ITPA's various subtests. When Guilford's (1956) coefficient of determination and his index for forecasting efficiency are applied, some of the ITPA subtest may account for as little as 4% of the aptitude purported to be measured (Ysseldyke & Salvia 1974, Stephens 1977). Predictions on some subtests have been shown to be as low as 2% better than chance (Stephens 1977).

Results of Perceptual Training

The second and third propositions fare no better. Results of research studies using one or more comparison groups with control of appropriate variables do not support Cruickshank's enthusiasm for testing perceptual difficulties. Nor has perceptual training proved to be an effective means to improve academic achievement among normally functioning students.

Jacobs (1968) and his associates (Jacobs, Wirthlin, & Miller 1968) found that the Frostig Program for the Development of Visual Perception (Frostig & Horne 1964) resulted in higher scores on the Frostig test but not on reading scores for regular class students. Wiederholt and Hammill (1971) have similar findings. Nonperceptually handicapped pupils scored higher on the Frostig test following training but not higher on academic achievement tests and readiness tests. Perceptually handicapped pupils, however, failed to score higher on posttests after the Frostig training program. Similar findings have been reported by Falik (1969) and by Elkind and Debbinger (1968).

Editor's note: See A/E page 150.

"The Tenth Myth: A Rejoinder to Cruickshank's Myths," by T.M. Stephens and L.A. Magliocca, JOURNAL OF LEARNING DISABILITIES, Vol 1, No. 7, August 1978. Copyright 1978 by the Professional Press, Inc. Reprinted by special permission of Professional Press, Inc.

The ITPA has not demonstrated any better results than the Frostig program. Although Kirk and Kirk (1971) report studies of individual students who improved as a result of following their guidelines for remediation, Waugh (1973) has emphasized the fallacy of generalizing individual reports to groups of students. After an extensive review of the ITPA, he concluded, "Remediation directed toward strengths and weaknesses in sensory or perceptual processing has not been effective" (p. 468).

Wilson, Harris, and Harris (1976) studied ways to improve auditory perceptual problems and reading and spelling performances. They reported that auditory perceptual training resulted in higher scores on measures of auditory perception. They consistently found that increased competence in auditory perception had no significant influence on reading and spelling performance. They concluded that a reading program is more effective than an auditory perceptual training program.

It is reasonable to conclude from the evidence currently available that perceptual training at its best may only improve performance on perceptual training tests. Also, this result tends only to be true when the tests and the training are keyed to each other. Further, if we wish to help learning disabled students to achieve better in schools, we should teach those skills directly to them.

In summary, the perceptual processing deficit notion, as espoused by Cruickshank and other early authorities, has not been verified by research evidence. For that reason, its proponents have been on the decline. Chastising those researchers who have found serious flaws in this notion concerning learning disabilities through extensive empirical testing is to elevate Cruickshank's definition to a myth.—**Thomas M. Stephens and Larry A. Magliocca, Faculty for Exceptional Children, College of Education, Ohio State University, 356 Arps Hall, 1945 N. High St., Columbus, Ohio 43210.**

REFERENCES

Carroll, J.: Illinois Test of Psycholinguistic Abilities, revised edition. In O. Buros (Ed.): The Seventh Mental Measurements Yearbook, Vol. I. Highland Park, N.J.: The Gryphon Press, 1972, 815-823.

Cruickshank, W.: Myths and realities in learning disabilities. Journal of Learning Disabilities, 1977, 10, 51-58.

Elkind, D., Debbinger, J.: Reading achievement in disadvantaged children as a consequence of non-verbal perceptual training. ERIC Document Reproduction Service No. ED 021704, 1968.

Falik, L.: The effects of special perceptual-motor training in kindergarten on second grade reading. Journal of Learning Disabilities, 1969, 2, 325-329.

Frostig, M., Horne, D.: The Frostig Program for the Development of Visual Perception: Teacher's Guide, Chicago: Follett, 1964.

Guilford, J.: Fundamental Statistics in Psychology and Education, 3rd ed. New York: McGraw-Hill Book Company, Inc., 1956.

Jacobs, J.: A follow-up evaluation of the Frostig Visual-Perceptual Training Program. Journal of Program Research and Development, 1968, 4, 8-18.

Jacobs, J., Wirthlin, L., Miller, C.: A follow-up evaluation of the Frostig Visual-Perceptual Training Program. Educational Leadership Research Supplement, 1968, 4, 169-175.

Kirk, S., Kirk, W.: Psycholinguistic Learning Disabilities: Diagnosis and Remediation. Urbana, Ill.: University of Illinois Press, 1971.

Salvia, J., Clark, J.: Use of deficits to identify the learning disabled. Exceptional Children, 1973, 40, 305-308.

Stephens, T.: Teaching Skills to Children with Learning and Behavior Disorders. Columbus, Ohio: Charles E. Merrill Publishing Co., 1977.

Waugh, R.: Relationship between modality preference and performance. Exceptional Children, 1973, 39, 465-469.

Wiederholt, J., Hammill, D.: Use of the Frostig-Horne Perception Program in the urban school. Psychology in the Schools, 1971, 8, 268-274.

Wilson, S., Harris, C., Harris, M.: Effects of an auditory perceptual remediation program on reading performance, Journal of Learning Disabilities, 1976, 9, 670-678.

Ysseldyke, J.: Accountability of Diagnostic-prescriptive Teaching. Washington, D.C.: American Psychological Association, 1974.

Ysseldyke, J., Salvia, J.: Diagnostic-prescriptive teaching: Two models. Exceptional Children, 1974, 41, 181-185.

LD and the Problem of Scientific Definitions

Ronald P. Grossman, PhD

Editor's Note: *Ronald P. Grossman studied architecture with Mies van der Rohe, and took his BA and PhD (1965) at the University of Chicago, where he held the Catherine Cleveland Fellowship. He has taught at the University of Nebraska, St. Olaf College, Michigan State University, and Lake Forest College, where he is currently associate professor. He also has been a visiting fellow of the Newberry Library. During 1974 he was a consultant to a study of special education facilities in Illinois made for the Office of the Superintendent of Public Instruction, and the coauthor of its final report. He also is a consultant on interethnic affairs to the Institute On Pluralism and Group Identity of the American Jewish Committee, a member of the steering committee of the Illinois Consultancy on Ethnicity and Education, and a frequent contributor to the popular press on a variety of social and educational issues. His articles have appeared in newspapers and magazines such as the Chicago* Tribune *and* Chicago Magazine, *as well as scholarly journals such as* Contemporary Psychology, Canadian-American Slavic Studies, *and* Balkan Studies. *His article, "State Initiative in Learning Disabilities," appeared in the November 1975 issue of this* Journal. *Among his current research interests is psychohistory — the application of the concepts of psychoanalysis to the study of historical problems. This invited article derives from Dr. Grossman's continued interest in the validity and lawfulness of the extension of the methods of the scientist to other scholarly fields — in this case the concept of learning disabilities. He is currently working on a book comparing the failures of the criminal justice system and the high schools to provide for the needs of contemporary young people at both ends of the social ladder. Dr. Grossman is the author of a book,* The Italians in America *(Lerner, 1975).*

A few years back I met a teacher in a small, rural community who had a problem. At the time, I was traveling across Illinois studying special education facilities for the office of the Superintendent of Education. During the course of my research I visited some very sophisticated learning disability programs, shared ideas with leading investigators in LD remediation, and also met with parents to see the problem from their perspective. But in many ways, my interview with that one teacher made the greatest impression upon me.

In smaller places like my friend's home town, neither the experience nor the money is available to meet state and federal mandates. So in the end, one of the veteran staff members is called into the principal's office. "Listen," he says, "we're getting static again about this LD thing. Do me a favor," he adds, throwing a bunch of files across the desk, "see what you can do with these kids." Trained in mainstream education, and that many years before, my friend was assigned the responsibility of working with two LD students. This process has been repeated many times over the years in small, out-of-the-way school districts.

In my friend's case, these files contained the histories of two students who just could not seem to learn to write. Until seventh grade they had resisted the efforts of previous teachers to turn their childlike scrawls into something like adult handwriting. But down in the basement my friend found an old typewriter. So she sat her new students in front of it, and taught them to type. When I visited, the two were just about at grade level, and one had become the editor of the school paper. As the next order of business, my friend was about to get back to the problem of the students' handwriting, and while I never had a chance to get back there and see how that worked out, I have a pretty good hunch.

PONDERING THE QUESTION OF DEFINITIONS

When asked to discuss definitions in LD, I recalled that teacher because, as we shall see, the question of definitions involves both scientific and political issues. As such, any change will affect a host of individual investigators and the

"LD and the Problems of Scientific Definitions," Ronald P. Grossman, Ph.D. JOURNAL OF LEARNING DISABILITIES, Vol. 11, No. 3, March 1978. Copyright 1978 by the Professional Press, Inc. Reprinted by special permission of Professional Press, Inc.

institutions through which they do their work. But it is also important to remember that learning disabilities has a dual mandate — to dispense services to its clientele, like the two students in an out-of-the-way school district, and at the same time await the increased scope of LD scientific knowledge.

The complexity of the question of definitions can be better appreciated by looking at the history of the physical sciences, to which all other disciplines are indebted for their most fundamental conceptions. Thomas Kuhn, the historian of science, studying the most significant revolutions in each of several sciences, reports in every case a discernible pattern. As a body of new scientific data develops, concepts are formulated, and these in turn are assembled into the basic, classic definitions of the field. All new data must then be measured against these "normative definitions." Once established, these definitions serve to keep crackpots, and their theories, out of the field. They shield astronomy from its onetime handmaiden, astrology, and chemistry from the speculations of the alchemists.

But there comes a time in the history of most sciences when a breakthrough occurs, and the burgeoning data cannot be absorbed into the normative definitions. In retrospect, such events seem to mark a turning point in the field's development, and in time this newer data will be the basis for constructing a new set of normative definitions. Indeed, it often happens that the older definitions become a special, or limited subset of the newer ones — just as Einstein's theories did not so much invalidate Newton's as they absorbed them into a more general set of basic, physical laws.

During such change, a field seems chaotic and factious. To the established scientists, proponents of the new data must inevitably seem to be charlatans, somewhat like astrologists and alchemists. Conversely, the old guard must seem to be self-interested hacks trying desperately to hold on to their positions and conspiring against the acceptance of any new information.

HISTORICAL LESSON

Now what has this to teach those of us interested in the field of LD and its future? I think it is this — scientific definitions created to further communication, to enable one investigator to compare his results with those of another, often distant colleague, can also prevent communication. Often too this potential can have positive results as when it prevents pseudoscientists from distracting serious researchers. But at the critical points in the growth of a science this potential to limit the range of discourse can also keep legitimate, and even pioneering, investigators from getting a hearing for their findings.

The history of the physical sciences also teaches that quantum leaps in knowledge often do not come through periods of slow, orderly growth, but rather in the midst of bitter internal strife, in which the conceptions of one set of investigators seem to their opponents to be utterly without worth. This does not mean that the champions of unorthodox conceptions are always the creative thinkers. But this perspective does offer us the following caution as a lesson of history. When new scientific definitions challenge an older orthodoxy, it is difficult to know in advance which side will ultimately be vindicated. There is an ethical corollary to this historical law, to which we will return in a moment. But first let me briefly outline the history of LD and its normative definitions, at least as I read the record.

THE PATTERN OF LD

We can identify three basic periods, the first of which began in the early 1960s and ran until the middle of the decade. During this period, the problem was discussed chiefly in medical circles, and as a result the normative definitions of the phenomenon were expressed in anatomical language. Thus "minimal brain dysfunction" came to describe those children whose functioning is not quite that of their peers, but is still clearly above that of the retarded.

In the second half of the decade, leadership began to pass to a group who saw the problem from another perspective. This group includes those who joined together in 1963 to form the ACLD, and those who shared a common perspective — be they parents or teachers — of looking at the disabled child in a classroom setting. Correspondingly, their normative definitions, and the very concept of learning disability, were drawn from the lexicon of the educator. This group proposed to measure the disability, now defined as the difference between a child's potential and actual performance, by the educator's standard.

Towards the end of the 1960s the field of LD moved into a third phase. This phase dates to

1969 when legislation was passed laying upon the federal government the responsibility to see that no student is deprived of an educational opportunity because of a handicap. By itself, the government's entry into the field was bound to alter its character. For now the earlier speculations into the question of what percentage of the school-aged population might be learning disabled became translated into a budgetary problem for school administrators. For how many children, they immediately wanted to know, do they have to make funds available? Also by this point the earlier certainties about the cause and the remediation of LD had dissipated. Neither the medical nor the educational model, or any one of a dozen rival schools within each camp, had been able to demonstrate the clear superiority of its position, and thus of its definition of the problem.

Faced with this competition between rival schools of thought, the new bureaucracy called into being to discharge the government's responsibility could not avoid the temptation to translate the field's normative definitions still one more time. Thus the definition of LD has been subtly reworked until for all practical purposes it is "that disability which is manifest among X percentage of the population." Defined this way, the only remaining question becomes: where should the line be set which separates the normal from the LD child, the percentage for whom the government must make special financial provision and those for whom it is freed of that responsibility? Inevitably, the bureaucrat's answer must be closer, rather than farther from zero.

The bureaucrat might also decide that the disputes of the scholars mean that all of their theories may be considered equally lacking in significance, the thinking which apparently underlies the recently announced federal regulations governing LD programs. For in returning to a definition with limitations now patent to virtually all workers in the field, the Bureau of Education for the Handicapped seems to say that it will henceforth fund whatever categories of students the several states certify to be in need of special services. All the while, of course, these federal officials know that the financial responsibility the states must share for those certified students will act as a natural brake upon any new, large drain on the federal treasury.

These actions are taken irrespective of what these regulations might or might not do to the scientific advancement of the field, for federal officials must serve two masters — the recipients of the program and their superiors. From the latter they are under constant pressure to trim budgets, or at the least to hold any increases to a minimum — especially as the compass of human needs for which government accepts responsibility increases each year, and the competition for governmental dollars rises proportionally. Moreover, the rancor and the sharp divisions within the field of LD only increase governmental responsibility as the officials become convinced that nobody has now, or ever will have, the answer to the puzzle of what causes the learning disabled student.

ETHICAL COROLLARY

Here, then, after a long detour we come back to that ethical corollary I promised. Precisely because of sharp divisions of opinion in the field, we must be careful lest we close the doors to any theory which, whatever its present status, might prove a fruitful one. We must exercise such care for three reasons: (1) because the history of science tells us that we must; (2) because the more energy we use in party squabbles, the more the normative definitions will pass into the hands of the bureaucracy, to be established on fiscal rather than scientific or humanitarian grounds; and (3) because in a field which is both healing art as well as theoretical science, we have an obligation to see that every student in need — such as the two my friend sat down in front of that abandoned typewriter — get just as much service as is humanly possible, until a final remedy might be available.

Learning Disabilities:

Diagnosis and Management, Part One

Marcel Kinsbourne, M.D., Ph.D.

Dr. Kinsbourne is a pediatric neurologist and child psychologist. He is currently Professor of Pediatrics at the University of Toronto Medical School and Professor of Psychology at the University of Toronto. He heads the hospital's Learning Clinic and Neuropsychology Research Unit. Dr. Kinsbourne's research deals with brain-behavior relationships in adults and children, with heavy emphasis on learning disability and hyperactivity both from the point of view of the basic mechanisms involved in these disorders and common sense ways of helping the children overcome them.

In Part One of this article, Dr. Kinsbourne discusses and defines learning disability.

It is important for both parents and teachers to understand the differences between "learning disabilities" and other more general labels. If distinctions are blurred between learning-disabled children and the larger group of children who have various other kinds of trouble in school, then programs cannot be planned for an individual child. Using a term in too general a way is confusing for people who wish to fit the remedy to the child, because children differ with respect to their learning requirements.

In order to learn anything an individual needs both ability and motivation. Motivational problems are not learning disabilities, strictly speaking. The majority of illiterate people, who are not motivated to learn because of their family background, social circumstances or emotional state, are not considered to be learning disabled.

If a child is not motivated, then the logical remedy is to find something that does motivate him. This course is invaluable for individuals who have the ability necessary for learning, but it is of no use for those people who lack that ability — who, in other words, have a learning disability. Of course a young child whose ability is inadequate and who consequently fails for several years will acquire a low self-image and expect to continue to fail. Later, even though the child's abilities may have matured enough for him to learn successfully, he may lack the motivation to use them. In that special circumstance particular rewards are initially useful, but the most consistent motivator is success in the learning situation.

Two types of ability are important for learning. One is attention, or concentration — what one might call "task orientation." The other is processing or mental capacity — the ability to solve the problem once the individual is trying to do so and is concentrating on it.

If a person has the necessary mental power but does not focus it on the task, his processing power is not being used. It might as well not be there. That is the case with "hyperactive" children, who have a deficit of attention. Conversely even a person who concentrates very hard may fail if he lacks the mental processes needed to perform tasks. Such people have a deficit of processing, such as selective reading unreadiness. So on the one hand some people cannot focus their attention; on the other hand some are unready for a particular level of instruction. Some unfortunate children have both problems, which must be sorted out because the steps to take toward solving them are quite different. Terms such as "dyslexia" should not be used to include both problems of attention and problems of processing. Labeling both with a single word implies that two quite different entities are either the same or always linked. This confusion obstructs the helper's own mental processes as he tries to figure out how to help the child. Of the misleading general terms, only one — "minimal brain dysfunction" — is even less productive than "dyslexia," but others, like "selective language disorder," "selective reading disorder" and so forth are also harmful. It is important to keep in mind that children who have trouble learning differ from one another. Even two children who have reading problems differ in the exact nature of the disability.

Definition of Learning Disabilities

Children with learning problems are not those

From *The Exceptional Parent*, October 1977. Reprinted with permission of THE EXCEPTIONAL PARENT magazine.
Copyright Psy-Ed Corporation 1977, Room 700 Statler Office Building, Boston, Massachusetts 02116.

who score low on tests of most cognitive abilities. Rather, children who are slow in all mental processes and in their ability to focus on a task are more appropriately considered mentally retarded. Sometimes they are called "slow learners." Mental retardation is very different from learning disability.

Children with learning disabilities have selective difficulties. They are neither bright nor dull; in fact they are both bright and dull, in different respects. But not all learning difficulties qualify as learning disabilities.

"Learning disability" implies a selective weakness that impinges on academic performance. The inability to carry a tune is a clear-cut selective deficit. It does not differ in principle from a selective deficit in reading or arithmetic. The only differences are practical ones; no one cares greatly about humming tunes, there are meager social and financial rewards for the ability, and one cannot be admitted to college on that basis. So adult anxiety does not focus on that particular selective deficit.

But the learning-disabled child is unfortunate enough to do a poor job at school, one of the few areas where society insists that children do well. One cannot overestimate the impact of societal expectations on the child or the ways that they distort our efforts and theories. One disturbing consequence of social pressure is that children with school-related learning difficulties are constantly stuck with labels like "brain damage" or "minimal cerebral dysfunction," whereas tone-deaf children are not. Although the reading-disabled probably have a dysfunction in one brain area, the "amusicals" certainly have a similar dysfunction in another. Learning-disabled children, as I have said, are only those whose deficits obstruct traditional school learning.

Reading is the topic most often discussed under the heading of "learning disabilities." Some children are selectively immature in abilities relevant to reading. In order to understand them it is useful to think first about how individuals differ from one another and then about the ingredients of reading readiness.

Individual Differences

Adults differ from each other with respect to many physical and mental attributes, but children differ from each other much more, because they differ in an additional way. Adults are static at the level of full development; their differences will probably be about the same five years from now.

Children also vary in their patterns of development. At any given time normal children have different patterns of ability. These patterns themselves change within a child over time. Mental development is not linear; children do not grow at a steady rate but rather in fits and starts, just as their physical height increases unevenly. A child's current abilities do not reliably predict future abilities, particularly in the first three years of life.

The age at which a child first learns to walk, for instance, is a topic of great concern. Parents whose children walk at nine months are proud, and parents whose children walk at 18 months are ashamed. But at five years all these children are walking, and it makes no difference at what age they first learned. Nor does it predict anything else. The early walker is not necessarily going to be the person who walks through examinations with no trouble in high school. This pattern is almost equally true for language development. Among thousands of children, some of whom develop language early and some late, there will be group differences 20 years later, but for the individual child the timing of language development predicts very little. This is something to keep in mind when one talks about early identification and early action.

The typical feeling reported by parents of a learning-disabled child is surprise: their child seemed normal during the first five years of life, so why isn't he learning now? This reaction distinguishes learning disability from mental retardation, where it is usually clear from the beginning that the child is slow. That feeling of surprise (if he has been so smart all along, why is he dumb now?) is really based on an unjustified expectation — that human beings will be uniform in their development. They are not.

Many children who, on entering first grade, have unexpected difficulty in mastering the material, are experiencing a temporary lag in mental development. That initial difficulty does not necessarily predict an enduring disability, but it can be made permanent if the child becomes so discouraged that an ongoing problem develops. This crystallization of problems occurs increasingly because parents and other helpers are excessively anxious.

What Is Involved in Reading Readiness?

When we ask children to learn to read, we are asking them to do quite new things, which are not required in the everyday preschool environment. So the way they handle mental challenges in preschool situations may not indicate how they will do when they have to perform the tasks required to learn to read. One word describes what it takes to read, though there are many subsidiary tasks: in order to learn to read, the child has to be analytic. Language learning involves learning both spoken language and written language. Superficially, the only difference is that the first is based only on sound and the second also involves sight. The difference is an important one. An infant learning a spoken language is surrounded by it, almost cannot stop hearing it. The sentences at first sound to him like gobbledygook; but because no one has told him that he has to study those sentences, the baby is not anxious about it. Then he begins to notice recurrent words or phrases, and they begin to make sense. Not much selective attention is needed to pick up individual words when the child keeps hearing them. So in a natural environment the beginnings of oral language come easily.

But with vision an incredible amount of richness competes for notice; moreover, letters and words are not as eye-catching as colors, bold shapes and movement. The ability to focus selective attention on one or two letter shapes, or even one or two attributes of these shapes, does not come naturally to the young child. It is something that he has to develop over the years.

Selective looking, looking at the important attributes of the written code, is hard for young children. They are not necessarily very efficient lookers. They see normally, their eyes are perfectly in order and the world looks to them as it looks to us. But they are not good at looking actively. They do not know, for instance, how to scan a page efficiently in order to pick up the information they need and reject the rest. They generally stop too soon, before they have seen all that is relevant. They look redundantly, going over one part twice rather than proceeding efficiently over the whole page. They look unsystematically, scanning in one direction one time and another direction the next. Without systematic strategy it is hard to pick up the distinctive features of letters, which have to be noticed in order to learn what goes with what.

Quite a few children entering first grade are still not very analytical either in listening or in looking. It is much easier to hear and reproduce a total word than to identify the sounds that make it up. The ability to say "hat" comes very early, but saying "h-a-t" is hard and unnatural. Children need specific teaching to learn to do that; they will not do it spontaneously. They will learn whole words spontaneously, but to break words up they need an analytical listening attitude.

Thus reading readiness necessitates selective and analytical looking and listening. Teaching strategies should be based on knowing what the child is looking at and listening to and then on adapting the child's style of paying attention to the specific task at hand. This statement generally applies to the slow reading learners in the early grades. If they use better looking and listening strategies, they learn to read more easily. It is less true of older children who are behind in reading but are still achieving above second- or third-grade level in other subjects. Children like this need different teaching strategies, which parents should understand in order to make sense of what is going on with their child.

Problems in Reading

In order to achieve at a third-grade level, for instance, a child needs to be a reasonably good looker and listener. To read beyond that level he needs additional language skills. Even a child who has learned to break words down and put them together again can have very poor paragraph comprehension. Such a child may not understand the paragraph's content, even though he can decode each individual word.

We have developed listening comprehension paragraphs, comparable to reading comprehension paragraphs. Each child reads such paragraphs and also listens to them read aloud. Then the comprehension level for those paragraphs the children read and those they heard are compared. We find that some older children comprehend no better when listening to text than when reading it. In a natural environment this problem is easily overlooked. It is less obvious when a child is not listening well to complex material than when he is not reading it well; we have more control over determining what a child is getting out of a paragraph he reads than one he hears.

This evidence suggests that the remedial work children need for reading falls into one or both of two separate categories. One is decoding work, which is focused on calling the words, saying them right and spelling them right; it requires practice in looking, listening and remembering and is highly structured. The other category, language performance, is less well understood. It has something to do with flexibility in combining phrases and grammatical forms.

Verbal memory is built on an implicit knowledge of language structure. For example, the more a child knows about how a language is structured, the more easily and efficiently he can remember the material, because some of the groupings are so familiar that they can be coded as a unit rather than element by element. I also suspect that an older, selectively backward reader who managed to get beyond the decoding stage usually has a language performance problem that interferes with his remembering material.

Learning Disabilities:

Diagnosis and Management, Part Two

In the conclusion of his article, Dr. Kinsbourne discusses methods used to help children with learning disabilities.

Children with learning problems are children who particularly need really good teaching, as opposed to average, everyday teaching.

Marcel Kinsbourne, M.D., Ph.D.

The Process-Oriented Approach

There are two different general approaches to learning disabilities: (1) the brain-based or process-oriented approach and (2) the behavior-based or goal-oriented approach. As I will explain, I believe that the second has turned out to be more useful in helping children overcome learning disabilities than the first.

The process-oriented approach assumes that part of the reason the child is achieving less than expected is that his brain is not working as well as it should. Its aim is to find out the cause of this and then to correct the defect, so that the brain works with the desired efficiency. Educational gains are presumed to follow from change in brain function. This medical model is a sort of Procrustean bed for brains: if a child's brain is out of shape, squeeze it into shape.

Subtypes of the process-oriented approach postulate a deficit, delay or difference about the structure and development of the brain in question. The deficit model is based on the view that the cognitive difficulty reflects a brain deficit. An area of brain is not working properly, although the rest is. Whereas the rest of the brain continues to develop, the damaged part does not, so that the selective deficit is aggravated over time. The deficit model generates conversational gambits — "I can't do a thing with my child. You see, he's brain-damaged" — often heard around the bridge table and at other social functions. It is the cop-out model.

The second is the delay model. It proposes that a child with early brain damage will develop the usual abilities but will do so more slowly. This is the notorious pediatrician's promise, "He'll grow out of it."

The third model stresses that people's brains differ. People have different strengths and weaknesses; they express themselves in varying ways. It is not just reading or nothing. Instead there are a variety of intellectual ways in which human beings of any age can express themselves (and for which they deserve praise). It is unjust to focus narrowly on one, to the exclusion of the others. This model is realistic and opens the way to a goal-oriented approach.

Theories and Treatments

Now, with respect to these supposed brain deficits, delays or differences, some theories about treatment are called "optimistic" (as opposed to the "pessimistic" view that they are inaccessible to therapy). One method of treatment is to flood the brain with stimulation, to try to make it grow. It is based on the enrichment theories. Parents may ask, "Does this approach work?" Undoubtedly if any individual, human or animal, is deprived of a minimally normal environment, he will not acquire skills in the usual way. Of course if his environment is enriched, he can be helped to acquire skills in the normal way. But these are cases of clear deprivation, and the same does not apply to learning-disabled children, who generally come from normal homes where other children have been reared in he same way and have flourished. The

From *The Exceptional Parent*, December 1977. Reprinted with permission of THE EXCEPTIONAL PARENT magazine.
Copyright Psy-Ed Corporation 1977, Room 700 Statler Office Building, Boston, Massachusetts 02116.

theory that if some stimulation is good, more is better, is unfounded. The notion that brute stimulation of the brain can help children think differently is unsupported by evidence from experiments with humans or animals.

One variant of this theory is the multimodality approach, the notion that if you somehow bang in stimuli from various channels, "blocks to learning" will be circumvented. In fact the opposite is the case. To perform better children need to focus more selectively and think more analytically and discriminatingly. This ability is not fostered by a torrent of multimodal stimuli.

Another distraction from clear thinking about learning disabilities is the notion that children's brains are barred from normal function by poisons. With all the food fads current within the organic food movement we are inevitably told that various disorders are caused by too much or too little of something or other. We hear that learning-disabled children are vitamin-deficient, that they need megavitamins, that they are being poisoned by additives, preservatives, flavorings, salicylates. Researchers cannot disprove all these claims; there are too many and they come too fast. It is up to their proponents to produce evidence instead of assertions. So far they have not conducted scientific, straightforward research to test their claims.

Pending the evidence, what do we lose by trying this and that? If a treatment is not going to work, we lose a lot. Resources are limited at the individual level, the family level and the societal level. If you are not doing A, you could be doing B. It is as dangerous to do the wrong thing and waste time as it is desirable to do the right thing and save time. Children should be protected from senseless measures.

Why are people so readily attracted to magical cures? The answer lies in the bewildering failure of the instructional system. In a situation in which other children learn, one child is not learning. Teachers are just as frustrated by this failure as parents. They can take one of two basically different views of the situation. They can say, catastrophically, "Teaching does not work, therefore let's try something completely different, like putting the child on a balance beam." Or they can say, "My teaching, so far, has not been good enough; perhaps I could teach the child better. If he were taught in the usual ways but more slowly, more clearly, in an individualized setting, he might be teachable in unsensational but sensible ways."

To seek out a totally different program, quite prematurely, is really an abdication of responsibility on the part of the teacher. If a child is not learning, his problem should be seen initially as an educational one. Every case of learning disability is, in part, a case of teaching disability. An alternative to average teaching that has not succeeded is extraordinarily good teaching, which may well succeed. Only when we can prove that even extraordinarily good teaching cannot succeed should we go to a different approach.

The Goal-Oriented Approach

The goal-oriented approach to learning disability says, "Here is a human being with certain characteristics at a particular time. This is what the child is good at, is not good at, likes, dislikes, and so on. Given those facts, and given certain desirable goals in the child's particular social setting, can we get the child and society together? Can the child bend a little? Can society bend a little? Can the child try a little harder? Can the environment demand a little less? Can the two somehow meet?" This is a sensible approach and it is the most likely to produce teaching strategies that will work.

By the very nature of learning disability, any uniform educational program must fail. Children are so diverse that no approach could possibly succeed with more than a small number of them. So rather than a rigid program, teachers need guidelines. These are really none other than the guidelines for good teaching of anything to anybody. Children with learning problems are children who particularly need really good teaching, as opposed to average, everyday teaching. We can be sure of this need because, by definition, the child does not learn in the casual, everyday situation.

Good teaching of a learning-disabled child must be individualized. A learning-disabled child does not conform to any large group setting; he is neither average nor slow but is some of one and some of the other. Indeed, it is for this very reason that he is in a predicament. Also, such a child has to be taught at his achievement level. If the child is reading at a second-grade level, it does not matter that chronologically he is in the sixth grade. That child has to be taught second-grade material. It is no good having him repeat the sixth grade either, although this is a customary device. The child has to be taught where he is.

Nor should children be too blatantly classified or evaluated. It is not humane to throw a person's deficits into continual sharp relief with tests, gradings and talk of being in this stream or that class. A certain ambiguity and flexibility between grades can blur some of that unnecessarily harsh focus on how well a child is doing right now. In any case the child has to be taught at his level, because at that level there is something he does not understand. If he had understood it, he would not be stuck at this level. On this first item he has not understood, he has built further and further noncomprehensions.

Now, if the child did not understand something when it was explained in the customary fashion, there must have been a teacher failure. The explanation was not right for that particular child.

If any explanation does not work, it has to be because some step in the argument was left out. In any interchange between people points are not always fully spelled out; a lot is considered common ground. If an explanation does not work, it is necessary to dissect that information into its logical components, make the reasoning manifest and deal with each element separately. Tell the child first one thing, then the next thing and then the next; check for comprehension of each point before putting in the next point.

This sounds like common sense, but it is often neglected. If people adjusted their information to a rate tolerable for each child, with continual checking to make sure the child is following, the great majority of learning problems would be soluble without other special methods. All but the most extreme cases would be remedied.

Teaching Strategies

No rigid structure should be allowed to curtail learning time. What should determine when the teacher stops is the child's need, not the ring of a bell or some preconceived notion. The teacher should not stop before the child has understood. He or she must give the child just the right amount of material, enough time to work it out but not so much time that the child is worn out. Obviously, individualized instruction is required to meet this goal.

When the teacher has given a child a difficult task, he or she must punctuate it with success experiences, giving the child something to do that he will enjoy and can do well. In that way the child can improve his self-concept, experience some satisfaction and a raised morale, and then return to the difficult chore. The motivating factor for the child should not be material rewards or winning a competition. Instead it should be based initially on a warm relationship with a teacher and ultimately on internalized standards.

The way for a teacher to discuss the child's progress with him is not to compare his progress with some arbitrary standard (the norm or some other child's progress) but rather to contrast the child's knowledge today with his knowledge yesterday. The only valid way to praise a child is to say, "You know these three things today that you did not know yesterday. Good for you."

A learning situation that fulfills these specifications is right. A problem-solving approach and a personal approach are needed, not any higher structured material-based methodology. Two mistakes are easy to make in remedial education. Teachers can either challenge the child too little and not use his potential, or challenge him too much and put him under such stress that his potential is lowered even further. The challenge that is appropriate for a child cannot be predetermined. The appropriate challenge should emerge from the teacher's knowlege of the child.

What the Parents Can Do

What the parents have expected and thought, what the other children have done, what anyone has hoped for the child and family — all these considerations take second place to setting up an educational environment in which the child can function optimally. The clinical team is a task force. Its goal is to set up an optimal environment for each child to help him learn as well as he can, so that the child is sufficiently but not excessively challenged. It is the task of the psychologist and others to define the level of challenge a child can meet at any time.

This information is presented to the parents, who have a responsibility to see that the teaching team is proceeding responsibly and with attention to the individual child's needs and abilities. If the child is overchallenged, you — and the child — will pay doubly for it later. If he must be kept back for a year, the earlier the better. Furthermore, because children clearly develop in fits and starts, the appropriate level of challenge may change. Nothing is lost if the child is held back for a year, as long as we are also vigilant. When his maturation accelerates, the program for the child must change with corresponding sensitivity and speed. It is important for parents to understand this for your child's sake and for your own.

THE LD TIGHTROPE

A variety of teaching techniques, carefully balanced, will keep the learning disabled child from falling and failing

CORINNE BLOOMER

Ms. Bloomer is Coordinator of Learning Centers for the public schools of Tarrytown, N.Y. She teaches in the Education Department of Marymount College, and in the Child Study Center, Special Education Department, Teachers College, Columbia University. She is a former classroom teacher.

IN ALMOST every classroom there are children who have to struggle to learn. Some of these youngsters have an invisible handicap: They have a learning disability or a combination of disabilities.

Learning disabilities (LD) is the newest and fastest growing subspecialty in special education. It is the "baby" in education and like every baby, it has had its growing pains. Defining the term, identifying children who have learning disabilities, planning appropriate educational programs for these children and determining who is responsible for identifying and teaching LD children are continuing sources of concern and confusion.

Despite still unanswered questions and shifting definitions, learning disabled children can and are being recognized earlier, specific disabilities can and are being identified and successful classroom procedures can and are being implemented. The purpose of this article is twofold: to help the classroom teacher recognize the child with learning disabilities and to present a teaching philosophy conducive to optimum learning for most children and the LD child in particular.

DEFINING LEARNING DISABILITIES

A brief history of the field of learning disabilities may be helpful in trying to reach a working definition of the term. The field got its official start in 1963. Prior to this date, terms such as "brain injured," "perceptually handicapped" and "neurologically impaired" were used to describe the child with normal intelligence who had difficulty learning. Parents and educators dissatisfied with these labels met in April, 1963, to explore terminology and to form a national organization devoted to the education of this group of "special" youngsters.

At this meeting Dr. Samuel Kirk, an eminent leader in the field of special education, suggested the term "learning disabilities." Thus, the term and the Association for Children with Learning Disabilities were born. The stated purpose of the organization is "to advance the education and general welfare of children of normal intelligence who have learning disabilities of a perceptual, conceptual or coordinative nature."

One parent of the learning disabilities "baby" is the medical or neuropsychological field; the other, the educational or psychoeducational. The neuropsychological field dates back to the 1920s, when investigators sought a physical cause for poor reading. The psychoeducational "parent" goes back to that conference of 1963 and reflects an attempt to focus instead on education and training.

Defining the term learning disabilities is analogous to family members deciding who the new baby looks like. The description depends on which side of the family is talking. Some definitions are medically oriented; some are more educationally focused. Thus, there are many definitions of LD currently in use, and these differ from discipline to discipline and locality to locality. They run the gamut from conservative definitions that include one to seven percent of all children in school to general definitions that take in 15 to 20 percent.

Controversy continues to rage over mislabeling slow learners and other children who don't seem to fit into any category as learning disabled. Looking at the other side of the coin, some severely impaired LD children may be mislabeled mentally retarded because they are functioning academically at a retarded level. Regardless of definition, a class of 25 children is likely to have one to five members who are learning disabled.

An educator's definition of learning disabilities might be based on the definition worked out in 1968 by the National Advisory Committee on Handicapped Children, which is sponsored by the Bureau of Education for the Handicapped in the Office of Education: "Learning disability refers to one or more significant deficits in essential learning processes requiring special education techniques for remediation. Children with learning disabilities generally demonstrate a discrepancy between expected and actual achievement in one or more areas, such as spoken, read or written language, mathematics and spatial orientation.

"The learning disability referred to is not primarily the result of sensory, motor, intellectual or emotional handicap, or the lack of opportunity to learn."

The following points can be made in interpreting this definition:

1. The LD child is considered to be average or above average in intelligence. That is why there is a "discrepancy between expected and actual achievement." A gifted

Reprinted from the March 1975 issue of *TEACHER* Magazine with permission of the publisher. This article is copyrighted © 1975 by Macmillan Professional Magazines, Inc. All rights reserved.

underachiever could be learning disabled.

2. Other handicapped children such as the emotionally disturbed, the blind (a sensory impairment), culturally disadvantaged, etc., are excluded by this definition. The term refers to a specific type of handicapped child.

3. "Significant deficits" are uncovered and identified by diagnostic procedures generally used in education and psychology. These "diagnostic procedures" include formal and informal testing. Some formal diagnostic tools are not as sophisticated or as valid as professionals would like, but they provide valuable information and identify learning deficits.

Of the many commercial tests available, some test IQ, some help determine how children process information and some provide insight into the nature and magnitude of a learning problem. These tests are generally administered by a trained professional.

4. Children receive information in the classroom primarily by looking or by listening. Children express themselves by talking or doing. A weakness or deficit in receiving or expressing information interferes with learning.

The learning skills implied in "essential learning processes" are the receiving/processing/expressing skills. This is a generalization, but will serve as a guide for a teacher dealing with a child who may be learning disabled.

It is generally assumed that such disturbances in the LD child are caused by a neurological dysfunction. However, proof of this is not always possible or necessary in order to get help for a child or to help him or her yourself.

5. The term "special education techniques" for remediation refers to educational planning based on diagnostic procedures and results. Educational planning means that materials and activities are presented to the child when he or she is ready and presented in such a way that he or she can learn. Many of these "special" strategies and materials are in the repertoire of the classroom teacher. What makes them special is that they are called into use prescriptively.

EDUCATIONAL ALTERNATIVES

Educational planning also involves the use of educational alternatives for LD children. Two major types are special class placement, which provides full-time educational therapy, or regular classroom placement with support services such as resource rooms, learning centers, itinerant teachers and consultive services. The educational alternative implemented depends on the severity of the problem and the availability of a program.

Generally, children with severe learning disabilities are in a self-contained, special class in a regular school. But the preferable alternative for most LD children with milder disabilities is to provide as near to normal a school setting as possible. Regular classroom placement with supportive services is the prevailing approach.

This approach places emphasis on labeling the learning problem and identifying the appropriate teaching strategies rather than on labeling and categorizing the child. However, the LD label is sometimes necessary to make a school district eligible for state and federal funds allocated for extra educational services for handicapped children.

CHARACTERISTICS OF LD CHILDREN

Although learning disabilities can be identified before a child reaches school age, it is usually the classroom teacher who first recognizes a problem. The teacher realizes that the child is not learning as well as expected or recognizes a behavior that may indicate a learning problem. Renowned special educator Samuel Clements, as part of a project sponsored by the U.S. Department of Education, surveyed the available literature and compiled a list of about 100 specific behavioral characteristics displayed by LD children.

These characteristics, some of which are not readily discernible or seemingly "invisible," tend to fall into six areas. They include disorders of *motor activity* (hyperactivity, hypoactivity, incoordination, etc.), *emotionality* (aggressiveness, withdrawal, frustration, anxiety, etc.), *perception* (auditory, visual, visual-motor, tactual, etc.), *symbolization* (inability to understand spoken or written words), *attention* (distractibility, perseveration, etc.) and *memory* (visual, motor, auditory, short-term, long-term, etc.). Specific definitions of these terms can be found in books on learning disabilities and on the psychology of learning.

Each LD child is different, and each exhibits a different combination and severity of problems. However, all LD children have in common the lack of adequate achievement in school.

LD CHILDREN IN THE CLASSROOM

Although the LD child's handicaps may be hidden, they can be extremely debilitating. The child doesn't learn many things by chance the way other children do. He or she needs to be specifically taught, and the regular classroom teacher is likely to have the major responsibility for the instruction.

Let's assume you have identified a child whom you feel is not learning as well as she or he should and who exhibits some of the characteristics mentioned above. If possible, refer the child to the appropriate professional for an evaluation. This may be the psychologist and/or learning disability specialist. If "expert" help is not available or will be long in coming, don't wait. You can do a great deal to help the child learn.

It isn't always easy to isolate problem areas, but careful classroom observation can help you learn where the breakdown in the learning situation is occurring. If you *can* determine specific strengths and weaknesses, you will be better able to plan appropriate educational tasks. The following questions will serve as a guide:

1. Is the student able to concentrate *and* look *and* listen to gain information?

2. Does the student have difficulty or avoid responding orally or in writing?

3. Can he or she integrate, organize and remember information for use at a later time (process)?

4. Does noise, movement or visual stimuli distract the student?

5. Does the student learn best by doing, seeing or listening, or through a combination of the three?

6. Does the student fidget a great deal during certain learning situations? This might indicate anxiety about doing some tasks. Squinting or tilting of the head may indicate an eye problem.

Student attitudes also provide clues. The learner who is reluctant or refuses to try a task is really telling you that he or she can't cope with it or feels insecure about succeeding at it. Some students set expectations that are too high and become anxious about their performance in school. These may or may not be LD children. *(One symptom does not mean a child is learning disabled.)*

Attention to these questions and students' attitudes can provide an informal diagnosis. Let me illustrate with a specific example.

Situation: Eight-year-old Johnny took longer than his classmates to get ready for the weekly spelling test. Grading of his test indicated that seven out of 10 words were misspelled. Beginning letters were correct, but many words were unfinished. Johnny's performance has been similar on most other weekly spelling tests.

Analysis of task: Receiving–the

orally given spelling test requires that John pay attention and listen. Processing—memory of the sequence of letters and/or a sound/symbol match—is required to spell depending on whether or not the word is phonetic. Expressing—a written response—is needed. This response requires the translation of auditory stimuli into a visual symbol, which in turn requires following a visual/motor pattern.

Possible diagnoses:

1. Johnny is trying to avoid taking the test by delaying tactics, indicating that he finds the task unpleasant, difficult or threatening.

2. Johnny may not be able to recall the visual sequence of letters in words, indicating a possible visual memory weakness.

3. Johnny may not have learned phonics skills well enough to apply them in spelling. He might be unable to adequately process visual or auditory information, depending on the teacher's method of presentation of phonic generalizations.

4. Johnny may not be able to translate sounds into their written form because of slow auditory processing or inadequate auditory discrimination.

Any or all of the above diagnoses could be further investigated through formal and informal testing and observation. However, if the situation came up in your classroom, and any of the above were consistent with previously noted behavior, you could probably reach a fairly valid conclusion and plan some strategy. Let's say you determine that Johnny has trouble responding in writing to things he has heard. Or technically speaking, he may have an auditory processing dysfunction because of inadequate speed when a visual/motor translation is required. What can you do?

Possible classroom adjustments:

1. Cut down on the number of words Johnny studies each week.

2. Have him write his spelling practice to provide integration of letter sounds with its visual/motor equivalent. Ask him to say the word slowly to himself so he can hear the letter sounds in phonetically regular words. He should be given all the time he needs to finish his assignment.

3. Allow Johnny to take his test orally until he feels he can take the test successfully in written form.

4. Pronounce the words slowly, repeating as necessary.

There are many professional resources available to help the classroom teacher plan a prescriptive educational plan once a child's weaknesses and strengths have been determined. (See the bibliography following this article.) Trying out various materials and methods to find out if they meet the child's needs is often the only way to find out what really works.

CLASSROOM AID

Once a classroom teacher has recognized a child's problems, with or without professional assistance, there is much that can be done. Some suggestions are:

1. Teach the child through his or her strengths to provide successful learning experiences. If Johnny learns best by looking, include a visual component.

2. Bypass activities that require the child to use his or her deficit area in order to eliminate repeated failures. If Johnny can't write his work well, let him do it orally.

3. Work with deficit areas only after a pattern of success has been established.

4. Define and specify the concepts to be learned to eliminate possible confusion. Teaching a concept is different from teaching a skill. Relate new concepts to previous material whenever possible. For example, when you teach the silent "e" rule, relate it to the other rules concerning silent vowels. Often the LD child cannot draw general conclusions.

5. Make the child aware of goals *and* their achievement. Point out what was achieved yesterday, what is achieved today and what can be achieved tomorrow. This gives a sense of success.

6. Establish clearly defined short-term goals that can be reached and that will foster progress and build self-confidence.

7. Provide immediate feedback on performance. Nothing is more defeating for a child than to have to redo papers from the previous day.

8. Use a positive approach to correction. Suggest the child find another or better answer rather than simply calling a response wrong.

9. If the child fails to make progress with a new approach or activity, drop it for the time being.

10. Do not try to teach something that the child can't or won't learn.

11. Select materials and techniques that have not been used before. Try starting one year below the child's present level.

12. Use concrete materials as much as possible.

13. Make learning fun by involving the child in games that allow him or her to move, feel, hear and see. A child who gets actively involved in the learning situation learns faster than a spectator to it.

14. Provide for seemingly overlearning of skills. The LD child usually needs more exposure to an experience than other children.

We know that a significant number of tomorrow's adults are now so-called LD children. We also know that without help, children grow up taking their problems with them. Classroom teachers have been providing successful individualized instruction for years. They have made and are continuing to make dynamic and crucial contributions in educating LD children. There isn't time to wait for more research or clearer definitions. We can help them now.

LEARNING DISABILITIES RESOURCES

☐ *Best Wishes Doc* by Martin E. Cohen, (Arthur Fields Books, 1974). Many stories of LD children depicting their struggles with learning.

☐ *A Diagnostic and Prescriptive Technique* by Robert R. Farrald and Richard Schamber (Adapt Press, 808 West Ave. N., Sioux Falls, S. Dak., 1973). A wide variety of helpful techniques to help the classroom teacher diagnose and teach the LD child.

☐ *Handbook in Diagnostic Teaching* by Philip Mann and Patricia Suiter (Allyn and Bacon, 1974). Informal methods of diagnosis to help the teacher identify the LD child and his/her deficits, along with teaching suggestions.

☐ *Informal Reading Diagnosis: A Practical Guide for the Classroom Teacher* by Thomas C. Potter and Gwenneth R. Rae (Prentice-Hall, 1973). Methods for determining the reading needs of students through informal test materials and suggestions for working with individuals and groups within the classroom.

☐ *Learning Disabilities: Selected ACLD Papers*, ed. Dr. Samuel Kirk and Jeanne McRae Macarthy (Houghton Mifflin, 1975). Includes major articles of the past decade and some never before published articles.

☐ *Prescriptions for Children With Learning and Adjustment Problems* by Ralph F. Blanco (Charles C. Thomas, 1972). Provides the teacher with specific help in formulating psychological and educational activities after diagnostic assessment.

☐ *The Remediation of Learning Disabilities* by R. Valett (Fearon, 1967). The author provides a definition, illustration, educational rationale and activities for remediation of each of 53 learning skills.

☐ *Something's Wrong With My Child: A Parents' Book About Learning Disabilities* by Sylvia Richardson, Milton Brutter and Charles Mangel (Harcourt, 1973). A handbook designed for parents and helpful for teachers, too.

☐ The Association for Children with Learning Disabilities welcomes requests for help with questions about LD. The address is: 5225 Grace Street, Pittsburgh, Penn. 15326. The phone number is 412-881-1191.—*C.B.*

Learning Disabilities ....a Puzzlement

MARTHA SUMMERS

The field of learning disabilities is a puzzlement. One reason is that children with learning disabilities usually have strengths that can obscure their weaknesses. They may not be able to write but be able to tell wonderful stories; they may not be able to follow simple directions but be able to put together complicated model cars. They may not be able to find their way around the school but be able to rebuild an automobile engine.

Children who are able to perform well on some tasks but perform poorly on other tasks are said to have discrepancies in their learning capabilities. Such discrepancies may also be observed when comparing their current performance, e.g., being unable to read at grade level, with their intelligence, average or above average. Specialists refer to this predicament as a discrepancy between performance and potential ability.

Since learning disabled students are so capable in some areas, teachers sometimes incorrectly attribute their learning difficulties to lack of motivation, emotional problems, or a myriad of other causes. Unlike physical handicaps, which are relatively easy to diagnose, a learning disability is a hidden handicap, not easily seen and often complicated by adjustment problems.

The new federal law on education of the handicapped, PL 94-142, gives the following definition of learning disabilities:

> Children with specific learning disabilities are those children who have a disorder in one or more of the basic psychological processes involved in understanding or in using language, spoken or written, which disorder may manifest itself in imperfect ability to listen, think, speak, read, write, spell, or do mathematical calculations. Such disorders include such conditions as perceptual handicaps, brain injury, minimal brain dysfunction, dyslexia, and developmental aphasia. Such term does not include children who have learning problems which are primarily the result of visual, hearing, or motor handicaps, of mental retardation, of emotional disturbance, or environmental, cultural, or economic disadvantage.

Perhaps the most significant aspect of this definition is the last sentence, which indicates what a learning disability is *not*. Moreover, although some LD children appear hyperactive, not all hyperactive children are learning disabled.

Although the concept of learning disabilities has only recently been defined, the disabilities themselves are not new. King Karl XI (1655-97) was judged one of Sweden's wisest kings but had difficulty with reading and spelling all his life. Thomas Edison could not seem to learn arithmetic by rote, yet he made immeasurable contributions to science. General George Patton never learned to read well, though he could memorize whole lectures and texts. Albert Einstein was described as "mentally slow, unsociable, and adrift forever in foolish dreams," yet his "dreams" were of the highest mental caliber. Though not all persons with learning problems become so distinguished, they all can compensate to some degree for their deficiency.

A number of theories have been advanced about the cause of learning disabilities. Among these are cerebral interference, inherent neurological tendencies, and mixed dominance. However, many authorities today are suggesting that this last condition, left/right confusion in the brain (which might be manifested by a boy who writes with his left hand but kicks a ball with his right foot), does not appear to cause learning disabilities.

While no definite conclusions have been drawn about the major cause of learning disabilities, it is felt that people are not "cured" of their handicap. They can learn to cope and to compensate to various degrees, but the learning weakness will always remain. It is for these reasons, the lack of knowledge about the cause and the absence of a known cure, that educators emphasize symptoms and remediation rather than etiology.

But basic research is searching for the causes of such disabilities, and when the causes are determined, some think prevention or "cure" may be possible.

For many years, children with learning problems were considered brain-injured. Thirty years ago, A. A. Strauss and L. Lehtinen, early pioneers in special education, described the brain-injured child as one

Reprinted with permission from the November/December 1977 issue of *Today's Education,* Journal of the National Education Association and the author.

Glossary of Common LD Terms

Auditory blending—the ability to recognize individual letter sounds and to put those sounds together to form a word.

Auditory perception—the ability to interpret what is heard.

* *Auditory discrimination*—the ability to distinguish among words and sounds that are nearly alike. [Children who have difficulty with auditory discrimination can't "hear" letters and may confuse *map* and *nap* or *lip* and *dip*, for example. Therefore, they may have trouble with spelling.]

Closure—the ability to recognize a whole, especially when parts are missing, and to fill in the missing parts automatically [for example, knowing what is said even if a word or two is not heard; reading a word when one letter is missing].

Cognition—thinking and processing skills. [See definition for *processing* below.]

Dyslexia—a disorder of children who fail to attain the skills of reading when taught with conventional techniques. [It includes much more than the tendency to reverse letters and numbers, though that is one symptom.]

Etiology—the cause of a condition.

Expressive language skills—the ability to communicate using speech, gestures, or written language.

Figure-ground perception—the ability to focus on the part of a visual stimulus that is important, such as one math problem on a page of problems.

Hyperactivity—a state of constant and excessive motion.

* *Individualized education program* (often called Individual Educational Plan or IEP)—a written statement composed for each handicapped child that includes present level of educational performance, annual goals, short-term instructional objectives, specific educational services to be provided, and evaluation procedures, including a time schedule for remediation. [Based on PL 94-142.]

* *Least restrictive environment*—educational placement that ensures that, to the maximum extent appropriate, handicapped children are educated with children who are not handicapped. [Based on PL 94-142.]

Memory—the ability to store and retrieve previous perceptions. [People with auditory memory deficits quickly forget what they have just been told; people with visual memory deficits forget what they have seen, including how letters look and what order they are in.]

Mixed laterality or *lateral confusion*—the tendency to perform some actions with the right hand or foot and others with the left, i.e., the shifting from right to left for certain activities.

Modality—the pathways through which an individual receives information and thereby learns. The primary learning modalities are auditory, visual, tactile/kinesthetic. Some individuals learn better through one modality than through another.

Perception—the process of organizing and interpreting information obtained through the senses. [The modalities of perception include visual, auditory, and tactile/kinesthetic.]

Perceptual disorder—inadequate awareness of objects, relations, and qualities because of difficulty in interpreting information obtained through the senses.

Perceptually handicapped—a term applied to a person who has difficulty in learning caused by perceptual disorders.

* *Processing*—internal thinking skills such as generalizing, abstracting, classifying, and integrating.

Receptive language skills—listening and reading, the skills of receiving language that is spoken or written by others.

Social perception—the ability to interpret the social environment [for example, being aware of people's moods and realizing the causes and effects of one's own behavior].

* *Visual discrimination*—the ability to distinguish among shapes, colors, numbers, and other visual stimuli that look similar. Someone with a difficulty in this area may confuse "b" and "d" or "6" and "9."

Visual-motor coordination—the ability to coordinate vision with the movement of the body or its parts. [This is a necessary skill for many academic activities, such as handwriting, mathematics, and physical education.]

Visual perception—the ability to interpret what is seen.

Except for those marked with an asterisk *, the above definitions are paraphrased from *Children with Learning Disabilities* by Janet W. Lerner, 2nd ed. © 1976. Houghton Mifflin Co.

who "may show disturbances in perception, thinking, and emotional behavior . . . disturbances [that] prevent or impede a normal learning process."

In the early 1960's, the term *brain-injured* was replaced by the term *learning disabilities*, emphasizing the behavior, not the unknown cause, of learning problems. All brain-injured children do not have learning problems, and all children with learning problems do not show clear evidence of brain damage. One of the leaders in the field, Samuel A. Kirk, defined a learning disability as "a retardation, disorder, or delayed development . . . of speech, language, reading, writing, arithmetic, or other school subjects. . . . It is not the result of mental retardation, sensory deprivation, or cultural or instructional factors." This definition closely parallels the definition later used in PL 94-142 (stated above).

Most estimates indicate that perhaps between 2 and 10 percent of schoolchildren have a learning disability requiring special teaching techniques. In recent years, the federal government has recognized learning disabilities as a handicapping condition deserving financial support. Consequently, Congress passed the Education of the Handicapped Act in 1970 and included funds for professional training, research, and demonstration activities for children with learning disabilities.

More recently, in 1975, Congress passed the Education for All Handicapped Children Act, PL 94-142 mentioned earlier, which revises previous legislation on education of the handicapped, including the learning disabled.

A learning disability is difficult to diagnose in a young child. To date, there are no foolproof neurological tests that diagnose a learning disability. Therefore, the burden for early identification often falls on classroom teachers. It is generally agreed that the earlier the diagnosis, the better the prognosis.

Because of the current interest in learning disabilities, there has been an increase of specialists in the field, and the potential for helping a disabled child is greater than it was in the past. Today in many school systems, specialists are available to help the regular classroom teacher diagnose a child's problem, devise an educational program, and then remediate the problem within the regular classroom. However, the new emphasis on educating handicapped children in the "least restrictive environment" places the responsibility of teaching LD children on the classroom teacher to a greater extent than ever before. Only massive in-service education for *all* teachers can make the new law into reality.

As PL 94-142 goes into effect, procedures for identifying and placing handicapped children will become more comprehensive and explicit than they have been in many school systems.

Ways To Recognize an LD Child

Children with learning disabilities may exhibit any combination of characteristics in the classroom that inhibit "learning efficiency." Such characteristics usually reflect some discrepancy between the child's age and the way he or she acts and include the following:

Classroom Behavior
- Moves constantly
- Has difficulty beginning or completing tasks
- Is often tardy or absent
- Is generally quiet or withdrawn
- Has difficulty with peer relationships
- Is disorganized
- Is easily distracted
- Displays inconsistencies in behavior
- Seems to misunderstand oral directions

Academic Symptoms

• Reading
- Loses place, repeats words
- Does not read fluently
- Confuses similar words and letters
- Uses fingers to follow along
- Does not read willingly

• Arithmetic
- Has difficulty associating number with symbol
- Cannot remember math facts
- Confuses columns and spacing
- Has difficulty with story problems
- Fails to comprehend math concepts

• Spelling
- Uses incorrect order of letters in words
- Has difficulty associating correct sound with appropriate letter
- Reverses letters and words (mirror image)

• Writing
- Cannot stay on line
- Has difficulty copying from board or other source
- Uses poor written expression for age
- Is slow in completing written work
- Uses cursive writing and printing in same assignment

Verbal
- Hesitates often when speaking
- Has poor verbal expression for age

Motor
- Displays poor coordination
- Has problems of balance
- Confuses right and left
- Lacks rhythm in movements, loses sequence
- Has poor muscle strength for age

5. THE LEARNING DISABLED CHILD

The classroom teacher still has the major responsibility of recognizing students with learning problems and then referring them for appropriate support. Most teachers have taught children with learning disabilities, though they may not have been categorized as such.

When a teacher suspects that a child may have a learning disability, he or she usually refers the child to the learning disabilities specialist. In many systems, the specialist will then meet with the teacher, observe the child informally, and confer with the parents and get their permission to test the child. Then, the specialist will work with the child, using formal testing procedures and informal learning tasks to determine the child's strengths and weaknesses. The specialist will be looking for the preferred modality for learning, such as the visual or the auditory mode. The specialist will also note weak areas, such as deficiencies in visual discrimination, auditory perception, or visual-motor skills (see glossary). For example, a child who gets letters mixed up when spelling (*was* for *saw*) or reads *god* for *dog* may have visual-processing difficulties. Although the eyes are seeing correctly, the brain is not receiving the information properly. Likewise, a child who hears but can't remember what he or she hears may have an auditory memory problem. This child may turn to the wrong page in the book or attempt the wrong assignment when he or she has to rely solely on oral directions.

After diagnosis, all persons concerned with the child, including the parents, develop an individualized education program, or IEP (PL 94-142 requires such a plan), which will specify the goals of the child's instructional program and the methods for achieving them. Special adaptive techniques can be designed to help the student compensate for his or her weaknesses. Just as you would not expect a person on crutches to run a 50-yard dash, an LD child with an auditory deficiency cannot routinely be expected to learn to read primarily via phonics. Some regular classroom teachers are helped in their planning for these children by thinking of students with auditory-processing difficulties as deaf and those with visual-processing problems as blind. Although LD students with these problems can see and hear, teaching methods that are helpful with deaf and blind students often work with these LD students.

Most LD children can remain in the regular classroom and learn there through adaptive techniques (PL 94-142 requires that to the extent appropriate all the handicapped be educated in the "least restrictive environment"); others require additional support by the resource teacher or specialist, who either acts as a consultant to the regular teacher or actually teaches the child for short periods of time. A number of LD children can remain in the regular classroom most of the time but require a special resource program. Still another group needs a self-contained situation in which all subjects are taught by the specialist, not by the regular classroom teacher. Another group needs a special school in which their entire education is in the hands of educational specialists. Finally, some students will need a private school or institution that can provide services not available through the public schools.

A California high school teacher of the learning disabled estimates that 75 percent of the students with learning problems leave high school unemployed, unemployable, and with no plans for job or job training. A recent General Accounting Office study found that 26 percent of the incarcerated delinquents tested in two states had primary learning problems (learning disabilities). It is not known whether such problems helped cause the children to turn to delinquency, but the hypothesis seems worth investigating.

Most students with learning disabilities do not become criminals. Rather, their frustrations and low self-esteem force them into passive behavior; they sit in class and quietly struggle. They may even graduate and enter into jobs much less rewarding and demanding than those they might have been able to attain if they had had the appropriate education. An able math student may not be able to enter college because he cannot read well. Thus, skills and knowledge are often wasted.

A learning disability is a lifelong problem. Persons with a learning disability, however, can compensate and can become contributing citizens. Perhaps PL 94-142 holds the key to the door that has locked LD students in frustrating, unproductive lives for generations.

LEARNING DISABILITIES AND THE PROFESSIONAL EDUCATOR

Dr. Stephen Larsen, President of D.C.L.D., has identified four central issues in the learning disability field as they relate to the educator: 1) determining the true parameters of the learning disabilities field; 2) monitoring the proliferation of tests and materials presumed relevant to educational practice; 3) insuring that learning disabled students are provided instructional opportunities in accordance with their educational needs and civil rights; and 4) determining professional standards that are necessary for competent and ethical practice. The professional educator is seen as the central person in the resolution of these issues as well as the central professional in planning, conducting, and/or coordinating the overall diagnostic and remedial efforts used with the learning disabled individual. *—D.D.D.*

Stephen Larsen, D.C.L.D. President

STEPHEN LARSEN, Ed.D is Associate Professor of Special Education at the University of Texas, Austin, Texas. He became the tenth president of D.C.L.D. on July 1, 1977.

Throughout its relatively brief history, the field of learning disabilities has experienced a rate of growth that has not been equaled by that of any other handicapping condition. As would be expected from an educational endeavor that attained wide popularity in a short period of time, learning disabilities quickly became innunadated with numerous theories about how the learning disabled student may best be served in the home, clinic, and school. In the early stages the physician was the primary professional consulted in the diagnosis and treatment of suspected learning disabilities and subsequently, optometrists, social workers, and occupational therapists also developed programs designed to mitigate the effects of learning disabilities. In most instances, the professional educator was considered to be the person who carried out the prescriptions of these other professionals within the context of school. In other words, the extremely crucial and pervasive role of the educator was largely diminished and underplayed when compared to other, supposedly more expert, professional disciplines.

As the field of learning disabilities progressed, it became increasingly obvious that the idiosyncratic and frequently self-protected stance taken by various professions was not adequate to meet the multitude of needs exhibited by learning disabled pupils. Equally apparent was the fact that learning disabilities is largely an educational phenomenon whose primary characteristic is academic underachievement and/or language disorders. On the basis of training and experience the professional educator is now being placed more and more in the predominate position regarding the management of learning disabled students. This task is by no means an easy one, and how well it is addressed still remains to be seen.

The traditional lack of attention given to the roles and responsibilities of the professional educator in the treatment of learning disabilities is symptomatic of general confusion in the field itself and has made effective programming for the learning disabled a most difficult and arduous undertaking. Unlike some other handicapping conditions, learning disabilities is epitomized by a wide spectrum of educational characteristics that are resistent to convenient classification and categorization and consequently, a common frame of reference for understanding and intervening with the learning disabled pupil has not been developed. Until 1975 and the passage of Public Law 94-142, learning disabilities was not recognized as a legally designated handicapping condition, in fact some states actually denied the existence of learning disabilities and thus did not serve their learning disabled students or placed "severely underachieving" pupils in classes for the emotionally disturbed, mentally

"Learning Disabilities and the Professional Educator," Stephen Larsen, *Learning Disability Quarterly,* Vol. I, Winter 1978.
Reprinted by permission.

retarded, or brain injured. In addition, educators specializing in learning disabilities did not possess the strong professional voice necessary to promote their interests both from within and without educational circles. As a result, learning disabilities specialists were, and to a certain extent continue to be, a loosely organized group of individuals who lack professional identity and a sense of common purpose. These factors, along with others too numerous to mention, account for the somewhat minimized and confused status within the field of learning disabilities of professional educators and their specific role and responsibilities.

Regardless of the reasons why educators have experienced difficulties in defining their appropiate place in the management of the learning disabled, it is important that this trend not be allowed to continue. That is to say, professional educators must come to realize that they are in a singular position to affect the untimate development and future lives of their learning disabled pupils. Next to parents and siblings, teachers spend the most time with learning disabled students and are intimately familiar with their unique characteristics and learning problems. This fact, along with the knowledge that learning disabilities is basically an applied, programmatically oriented discipline, attests to the central role of the educator. Since learning disabilities is largely recognized to be an educational phenomenon, teachers frequently find themselves with the sole responsibility for intervening in those language and/or academic areas in which the student is experiencing significant difficulty. If learning disabled pupils are not assisted in overcoming their school related problems, continued failure will in all likelihood plague them throughout their scholastic career and into adult life. Obviously, if educators are unsuccessful in effective programming for the learning disabled pupils in their care, the students will most surely be deprived of the opportunity to achieve at a level that is commensurate with their ability. In order for the professional educator to better meet his/her unique charge and at the same time develop a viable sense of identity, purpose, and destiny, several key issues must be directly confronted. The remainder of this paper will delineate some of the major issues that need to be addressed by educators as a prelude to establishing a base from which continually improved instructional opportunities will be offered the learning disabled person.

ISSUES CONFRONTING THE PROFESSIONAL EDUCATOR

Currently, many issues are extant in the field of learning disabilities. some of those reported in the professional and popular literature revolve around topics pertaining to the role of the physician, social worker, speech pathologist, and occupational therapist, etc. However, it is important to note that while issues such as dietary treatments, "deviant" home environments, articulatory disorders, and neurophysiological retraining may have some relevance to learning disabilities in general, they are largely tangential to the primary characteristics and behaviors that have caused the pupil actually to be labeled as learning disabled. As was mentioned previously in this paper, learning disabilities is basically an educational problem that must be solved by the educator in conjunction with other professionals and the parents. It is no longer feasible to expect other disciplines or governmental agencies to provide leadership in determining the best methods by which learning disabled pupils may be served. Rather, the responsibility for effective amelioration of the learning problem falls squarely upon the shoulders of the professional educator. By not accepting the responsibility for the achievement or non-achievement of students under their care, professional educators are placed in an indefensible position that begs weakness and "second-class" status. It is crucial that *educators define for themselves* the important and very real issues that must be addressed as a prelude to providing the learning disabled with intervention strategies necessary to maximally compensate for their learning problems. Perhaps the most basic issues confronting the professional educators are 1) determining the true paramenters of the learning disabilities field; 2) monitoring the proliferation of tests and materials presumed relevant to viable educational practice; 3) insuring that learning disabled students are provided instructional opportunities in accordance with their educational needs and civil rights; and 4) determining professional standards necessary for competent and ethical practice. These issues are particularly pressing and their resolution will make the appropriate education of the learning disabled a more meaningful and realistic proposition.

LEARNING DISABILITIES AS A HANDICAPPING CONDITION

The question of which students will be included in the category of learning disabilities is basic to many of the problems confronting the educator. In some instances, school systems, and in fact, entire states seem to view the category of learning disabilities as a convenient avenue by which the vast majority of their underachieving students may be provided special assistance. This tendency to label anywhere from 5-10 percent of a given school pupulation as learning disabled (i.e., handicapped) is indeed indicative of gross misconceptions of what actually constitutes learning disabilities and detracts from the provision of service to popils who exhibit severe problems in achievement and/or language usage.

In this connection it is crucial for professional educators carefully to consider the prevailing notions of what constitutes the constructs of "normality" and "handicapping conditions." When as many as 40 percent of all students in a given school district are referred from regular classrooms for suspected learning disabilities and 5-10 percent are actually labeled, it is apparent that a significant breakdown in the educational system has occurred. Is it conceivable that such a large proportion of a school population can be significantly *handicapped* (i.e., suffering from some indigenous disorder that precludes normal acheivement and adjustment)? It is far more likely that the large numbers of students who are referrred for mild to moderate underachievment are simply unmotivated, poorly taught, come from home environments where scholastic success is not highly valued, or are dull-normal in intelligence. For all intents and purposes, these students should not automatically be considered as learning disabled, since there is little evidence that placement in special education will improve their academic functioning. In addition, the increased emphasis upon providing special services to the non-handicapped pupil will undoubtedly result in a lessening of attention given to the pervasive needs of the student who is truly learning disabled.

To the professional educator specializing in learning disabilities, the widely proliferating numbers of students being labeled as learning disabled is particularly distressing. The willingness of school administrators to use learning disabilities as a "dumping ground" for all students who underachieve or misbehave in the schools destroys the *integrity* of the field and makes the development of viable instructional programming extremely difficult to carry out. In many schools, the learning disabilities specialist is viewed as nothing more than another tutor, reading teacher, or teacher's aide whose main responsibility is to assist all underachieving students to be maintained within the regular classroom. To a profession whose members are trained to intervene with pupils exhibiting severe problems, this capricious use of their talents is regrettable and wasteful.

It is important that learning disabilities specialists be continually aware of the tendency to expand the category of learning disabilities beyond useful limits and thus criteria must be developed to provide guidelines for determining whether a given student is learning disabled. In all probability, labeling of more than 2-3 percent of a given school population as learning disabled results in the inclusion of many non-handicapped children who could best be served by other professionals within the school (e.g., remedial reading and math teachers). By keeping the category of learning disabilities reserved for those students whose severe disorders require intensive intervention by specially trained personnel, learning disabilities specialists will be able to direct their energies upon the development of viable educational strategies that are necessary for effective and ethical instructional programming.

TESTS AND MATERIALS

Since the field of learning disabilities is somewhat fragmented and moving in many directions at the present time, it is not surprising that many tests and materials have been produced that purport to be effective in diagnosing and remediating the academic and behavioral problems exhibited by the learning disabled student. The area of learning disabilities, more than any other handicapping condition, has been besieged by publishing companies who generate tests and materials based upon vague and ill-defined theoretical constructs and with little or no research to support their often extravagant claims. The use of poorly designed and/or instructionally irrelevant materials with the learning disabled (or any other pupil, for that matter) is highly questionable and will undoubtedly waste valuable time for both the student and educator.

Just as professional educators must take responsibility for maintaining the basic integrity of learning disabilities as a viable handicapping condition, they also have the concomitant right to expect and demand instructional media that have been experimentally shown to be useful with the individuals for whom they were designed. Given the existing state of the science, it is apparent that learning disabilities is most realistically and profitably viewed as being exemplified by severe academic underachievement often accompanied by language disorders. Consequently, tests and materials that focus upon variables with no demonstrated relevance to these areas should be considered with great caution.

Perhaps the most obvious example of this phenomenon are the literally hundreds of tests and materials that are being touted to "diagnose" and "remediate" process and/or perceptual disorders. The assumption behind the development of these tests and materials is that if a student is thought to possess process or perceptual disorder, academic underachievement will be the inevitable result. Theoretically, until these disorders are circumvented, it is impractical to expect improved school functioning. Regrettably, many, if not most, tests and materials purported to deal with these psychological constructs offer little in the way of experimental validation or adequate reliabilities. In addition, most educators are aware that recent research findings have repeatedly questioned the viability of these media, i.e., perceptual and/or process tests do not appear to be able to differentiate between learning disabled and "normally learning" students. Furthermore training programs designed to remediate deficits in these areas have been somewhat less than successful. Continued use of these devices should be curtailed until their publishers and authors supply the field with experimental evidence demonstrating that their techinques are of definite educational value.

While perceptual and/or process tests and materials have been soundly criticized for their apparent lack of instructional utility, many devices suggesting that they are academically or language oriented suffer from the same criticisms. Simply because a test or material *appears* to address an educationally relevant curricular area does not mean, that its use will provide instructionally relevant data or will improved scholastic performance. For example, while initially helpful in directing attention to the broad curricular areas in which the student is demonstrating failure, the development of academically oriented, and commercially produced "criterion-referenced" tests has seeingly led to the blind acceptance of potentially unreliable and non-validated assesments of skill attainment. Comparison of pupil's performance with him/herself (i.e., rather than comparing performance with some normative sample) is probably advisable in some instances, however, educators should be constantly on guard to insure that the skills being tapped are, in fact, reliably measured and relate to the problem exhibited by the student. Many reading specialists, for example, have serious reservations regarding the necessity of a student knowing the sound-symbol relationships of individual consonants and vowels when considered in isolation. Yet many tests and materials spend exorbitant amounts of time testing and training isolated sound-symbol relationships. The point is not whether these skills are, in fact, necessary for reading but, rather, that we as professional educators must demand that tests and materials be accompanied by descriptions of research supporting their use with handicapped youngsters and particularly with learning disabled children and youth. The alternative to insisting upon appropriately verified tests and materials is to put blind faith in commercial producers and frequently unnamed authors.

The selection of viable tests and materials is never an easy assignment. However, several indications can be employed for identifying questionable tests and materials. These indications include the 1) promise of quick and easy "cures"; 2) elaborate use of "clinical" descriptions or testimonials attesting to effectiveness; 3) absence of research to demonstrate reliability, validity, or efficacy of the test or material, and 4) claims that the device in question is better than others found on the market. Additional helps are also available to the educator. The Board of Trustees of the Division for Children with Learning Disabilities has recently adopted a code of ethics dealing in part with tests and materials. Interested readers are encouraged to obtain a copy of this document for use as a starting point for evaluating the effectiveness of various tests and materials.

INSTRUCTIONAL PLACEMENTS

It is the responsibility of the professional educator to provide for the many and diverse instructional needs of learning disabled students. While this statement appears straightforward and clearcut on the surface, every experienced educator is aware that to accomplish this task an extensive amount of time, effort, and money must continually be expended. Frequently, a great deal of dedication and expertise is required to even provide minimally for the often severe and pervasive nature of the exhibited learning problem. Alternative instructional placements must be identified or new ones developed geared to the particular needs of individual students. Clearly, the adequate educational programming of the learning disabled remains one of the most arduous assignments of the professional educator.

In an effort to meet the challenge presented by the learning disabled, many state education agencies and individual school systems have adopted a regrettably simplistic and inflexible attitude toward the development of programs for learning disabled children and youth. More specifically, some individuals administering these state education agencies and school systems have come to conceptualize students labeled as learning disabled as exhibiting *universally mild* scholastic problems that can be dealt with most expediently by brief visits to the resource room with the remaining school time spent in the regular classroom without any supportive arrangements. In many instances, the time spent in the resource room will be no more than one and one-half to three hours per week. This absurd trend to consider all learning disabled pupils as having only mild learning problems is probably an outgrowth of other issues discussed earlier in this paper, i.e., learning disabilities is frequently seen by school administrators as being a convenient depository for the majority of cases of underachievement and misbehavior regardless of cause or level of severity. Regardless of the origin of this practice so prevalent in our schools, it is now apparent that many learning disabled students evidencing moderate to severe problems are not now being served in a manner that will optimally meet their unique learning needs. It is patently unrealistic to assume that merely because a pupil is labeled as learning disabled, he/she should automatically be "mainstreamed," placed in a resource room, or assigned to a helping teacher. While these alternative are certainly appropriate for some students, they will in many cases be woefully lacking in the intense and long-term educational programming that is absolutely necessary to assist significantly handicapped pupils in overcoming their pervasive learning disorders.

For many seriously involved learning disabled students, the extent of the observed academic failure (and concomitant emotional overlaps) preclude cursory attempts at "mainstreaming." This is particularly true with adolescents for whom hasty attempts to "correct" a long-standing language, reading or math problem are inadequate for preparing the student ot function in the world of work. Obviously, pupils whose problems are moderate to severe in intensity will require an educational arrangement where their needs can be addressed on a full-day basis until skills and abilities are elevated to a level where successful matriculation into the regular classroom is a definite possibiltiy. To deny moderately to severely involved students the instructional alternative that will *maximally* attenuate their problems is, in fact, to deprive them of their rights under the law. Many school systems are now being innundated by parents and professionals who are demanding that other alternatives than the resource room be made available to the learning disabled. In all probability, legal suits will be filed against school systems and states refusing to the learning disabled their duly mandated educational rights.

The role of the professional educator to provide many instructional alternatives to the learning disabled is apparent; one is better acquainted with the unique needs of this population than the professional who is given responsibiltity for his/her education. Therefore, it should not be the task of the parent out of necessity to seek alternatives to the public school as a means of securing assistance for their moderately to severely handicapped youngsters. On the contrary, the professional educator must insist that they be provided the necessary school resources in order to perform in the manner in which they have been trained and which, at the same time is in the best interest of the student. In other words, the need for continual and persistent *advocacy for both the rights of students as well as teachers* is as necessary in the schools today as it has been at any other time in history. It is untenable to assume that improvement of educational practice will be forthcoming without the concerted and dedicated efforts of its major participants—the professional educators.

PROFESSIONAL STANDARDS

In order for any profession to maintain high levels of ethical practice, it is essential that certain standards be developed to act as touchstones for members of that profession. In most instances, such standards are typified by 1) guidelines for the preparation of the practioner, and 2) a code of ethics serving to govern to some extent the activities of individuals currently functioning in the field. The establishment of a set of standards usually signifies that a profession is moving toward maturity and is willing to take stands regarding what knowledge and skills are necessary for its members to attain as a prelude to at least minimum levels of competent performance. In other words, professional standards are specified hallmarks attsting to the quality of service afforded by a given profession.

The development and utilization of standards for professions responsible for the welfare of large portions of the public have been particularly important throughout history. Professional standards were indeed an inhibiting influence upon snake oil salesmen and leechers in the medical profession and the ambulance chasers in the legal profession. Unlike other disciplines, education has not yet been able effectively to develop professional standards from a broad-based national perspective. The reasons for this are quite apparent. Education is obviously not a "hard" science where a solid core of fundamental data is available as a needed basis for subsequent mastery of more advanced concepts. Furthermore, responsibility for certifying teachers is vested in individual state education agencies which require widely varying numbers and types of college courses and work experiences in order ostensibly to produce "competent" practioners. As a result, no common frame-of-reference is employed when considering the basic skills and abilities necessary for educators to attain prior to proficient performance.

While it is somewhat understandable why the various associations within education have not yet generated professional standards for the preparation of teachers and on-going practices of teaching, the development of guidelines for educators specializing in learning disabilities is rapidly becoming a crucial and pressing issue. In a field where growth hs been unpresidented and basic philosophical positions are many and varied, order and professionalism is urgently called for. Consequently learning disabilities specialists must take it upon themselves to delineate standards that will serve as guideposts for the 1) initiation and modification of learning disabilities teacher training programs; 2) continual up-grading of certification standards for learning disabilities specialists; and 3) establishment of criteria for monitoring on-going professional practices. The degree to which professional standards are developed and utilized throughout the field will directly determine the quality of service provided learning disabled children and youth by protecting them from questionable and possibly detrimental intervention techniques.

At present, the Division for Children with Learning Disabilities (DCLD), the only nationally organized group of professional educators specializing in learning disabilities, has adopted a code of ehtics intended to crystallize the beliefs and policies of that organization. The code of ethics pertains to such topics as ethical standards in the delivery of service, welfare of the individual served, research and publications, and tests and materials. Hopefully, these ethics statements will be used as a basis for conceptualizing what constitutes optimum educational practices when providing services to the learning disabled. Additionally, DCLD is also close to completing a statement of competencies needed by professionals who work with the learning disabled.

These competency statements are geared to the educator who is primarily responsible for assisting the student in overcoming his/her significant academic underachievement and/or language disorder. To accomplish this task the learning disabilities specialist must obviously possess knowledge skills in the areas of mathematics, reading, spelling, oral language, written expression, behavioral management, counseling and consulting, career education, as well as historical/theoretical perspectives. The DCLD standards of competence address each of these areas from the psoition that it is not possible for an individual educator to be equally proficient in each. Rather, the extent to which any professional would be expected to achieve mastery or proficiency in any specific competiency area would depend upon the particular nature of the position held. Most important, these competency statements provide an estimate of what skills and information are required to perform adequately in those areas from the perspective of general knowledge, assessment, instruciton, and implementation. This document promises to be of immeasurable assistance to educators who wish to up-grade their own skills or have responsibility for conducting training programs and/or evaluating ongoing teaching activities with the learning disabled. Apparently, the organization of educators concerned with the learning disabled student have begun the long and tedious process of developing professional standards as a means of insuring ethical and viable practice. This is indeed a healthy sign and should be continued at all costs.

To summarize, the field of learning disabilities finds itself at a point in time where significant and pervasive advancements may be attained if appropriate actions are taken. Basic to any modifications of the current situation is the realization that the educator is the central person in planning, conducting, and/or coordinating the overall diagnostic and remedial efforts employed with the learning disabled individual. In order adequately to meet this challenge, professional educators must take steps not only to define the parameters of the field but also, continually to up-grade the many and varied services necessary to maximally provide for the learning disabled. Educators are encouraged continually to advocate for the rights of their students and themselves as they pertain to ethical and competent practices. The means by which advocacy actions may be most acutely felt is not only by individual efforts but also through active participation in appropriate professional groups at the local, state, and national levels. The professional standards developed by viable professional groups will also be of assistance when attempting to increase skills and evaluate programs. Let there be no doubt that the direction which the field of learning disabilities takes in the future is in the hands of the educator. Let us take steps to assure that we are equal to the task.

The Silent Crippler

Receptive Language Disability

Priscilla L. Vail

Priscilla Vail is the reading specialist at Rippowam-Cisqua School, Bedford, New York. In this capacity, she tries to solve puzzles about children's learning. Working with reading problems that persist beyond initial decoding, Mrs. Vail believes that most are language-based. Supported by current research, this belief has led her on an expedition to see where early recognition and remediation might be possible.

Who is the child with receptive language disability? What is this disability, and what do we need to know about it? What warning signals does the child send us?

We know quite a lot about receptive language ability, the cornerstone of psychosocial development and intellectual growth. It may come as a surprise to learn how many children —more boys than girls—are afflicted by receptive language disability, a sleeper and a devastating handicap when it goes undiagnosed. You may have seen it called aphasia, anomia, central auditory processing difficulty, or receptive language impairment.

So what is it? To begin with, we need to separate receptive language ability from hearing acuity, which is the physical awareness of sounds. We are not talking about the child who has a fluctuating or permanent hearing loss. We are talking about the child who can hear but who is unable to "process" and take meaning from the language he hears around him.

Imagine being suddenly deposited at a foreign airport. Entering the terminal, you can hear plenty of sounds. Because you have already made some sense of the world around you, you use clues to fill in. International signs, with pictures, show you where to go for what. You probably look for someone in a uniform with a handcart to take your bags. Without understanding the language, you can probably get to your hotel by writing the name down on a piece of paper for the taxi driver, whom you identify by other clues.

You'll miss all the jokes, any warnings, and feel strange, but you'll probably get to the hotel, with your bags. You might even manage to get something to eat and pay for it. You can't make any choices, but you're alive and well, existing on a functional level by inference, experience, and luck.

If we make the central character of this story a child with receptive language disability, it's already easier to understand him and his problem. How does he behave, and how does the world react to him?

What are the warning signals? Here are a few.

- Delayed onset of talking, sometimes with distorted pronunciation
- Apparent lack of interest in stories and the adult verbal world
- Great difficulty in retelling plot or describing
- Reliance on gestures, body English, or short labels for communication
- A hands-on approach to activities or problem solving and fascination with concrete and visual things
- Sentence memory incompatible with level expected for chronological age
- Difficulty in carrying out a three-part command
- Spoonerisms or malapropisms in speech and difficulty in understanding idioms and metaphors
- Word-finding difficulty
- Bizarre spelling
- Extra politeness

All of these are found to some degree at some times in all children. Frequency is the tipoff to a problem.

To understand what we may see in a school-age child, let's look first at a very young child whose language is just starting to develop.

The little child hears Daddy's car in the driveway, is startled by loud noises, hears Mommy's footsteps coming closer or going away, and reacts accordingly. No problem hearing sounds. But if he has trouble understanding and using language, he misses the accompanying reassurances and explanations that help him make sense of these sounds and the new ones he encounters.

He has to learn which sounds are important so that he can begin to filter out some and choose others that merit his attention. The child who can be reassured that Mommy's footsteps are indeed retreating but that she will be right back can begin to understand and anticipate what may come next. Think what it must mean for a child not to understand "I'll be right back" or "I have to leave now, but I'll be home after lunch."

The child needs to learn names of people and things—to learn words. He needs them for communicating with the outside world and himself. He needs words for sorting blocks by size or cars by color. He needs words for judging the qualities of things—whether they're soft or hot or sweet or fuzzy. He needs words for directing his body and planning his forays into the world.

The child learns words by taking them from his surroundings. When language is a meaningless external, he tunes it out. If language is threatening because he can't understand it, he blocks it out, literally as a survival technique.

Think of all the things this child misses: fairy stories, admonitions, the gift of new big words to keep and use, jokes, the

Reprinted by permission from *Independent School,* October 1977, copyright 1977 by the National Association of Independent Schools.

feeling of being attached to the adult world through comprehension and conversation. How does the child who misses these things behave?

He may have a hard time establishing rapport with adults, even his parents, because he is missing the reassurances and explanations—the talking—that foster trust. The child who has trouble interpreting language will probably draw away from adults and move toward solitary play or play with other children, where action is more important than words.

The child's earliest experiences with adults, especially in developing trust, have a strong influence on his later relations with other adults, including teachers, and thus on his social and intellectual development. When trust is present, peace is probably there, too, and learning can grow well. Without trust, the child has little energy left for learning because so much is drained off in self-protective activities.

How does the world see the child? Parents, sitters, grandparents, and teachers are human, and they respond in kind. They are not apt to be drawn to a child who seems uninterested in them and what they have to offer. With apparent coolness on the child's side, they are less inclined to seek him out. A sad picture emerges of a lonely, needy child connected to the world around him by a thin string instead of a stout, intertwined line.

How can such a thing exist in our society, where we are all surrounded and bombarded daily by words? Being surrounded by words doesn't help a bit if they don't mean something. (To go back to our foreign airport: after you've been around for a while, you begin to isolate and recognize words and phrases, but it's hard to tell them apart. You're in the same boat as the young man of five who assured me that "elemenopee" is one of the letters of the alphabet.)

It is in the very process of separating language sounds and endowing them with meaning that the child with receptive language disability is hampered. Giving him more words more quickly or more loudly (do you shout at foreigners, too?) only aggravates the problem and solidifies tuning out or withdrawal. For this child, we must lighten the language load, not increase it, by going back as far as we must to reach the level at which language does have meaning for him.

It is easy to spot a severely handicapped child, but how do we spot the child whose handicap is subtler? First, we must become more generally aware of this disability; then, we must remember that it is different from loss of hearing.

In the wake of a teacher's concern, parents may take their child to a pediatrician and then to an otolaryngologist, who checks his hearing acuity and, on finding it normal, reassures them that nothing is wrong. These are important first steps, but we can't stop here.

We then have to find out whether words have meaning for the child, how many he can handle, how long he can remember them, and whether he is doing this at a level appropriate to his chronological age.

Not all pediatricians know much about this area of development or particularly look for it, probably because they don't see most children that often. Most children only see the doctor when they're sick or when they go for their annual checkup. It's safe to say that the doctor is probably looking for signs of health or disease, not language disability.

So the parents and the school may have to look farther for language help. It's not hard to find. Most large hospitals have speech and language clinics, and local hospitals can always refer you to one. If the clinic confirms language disability, or "lag," much can be done. However, the longer the problem goes unrecognized, the harder it is to make up for lacks of the past.

It would be so convenient if there were a visible or audible danger signal, like a rash or a fever or a nonstop cough, but there isn't. Although the child's speech may be very revealing to a trained ear and his use of body English, action, and labels to avoid real talking very telling to the trained eye, the untrained observer needs to have his general level of awareness raised.

Every time we interpret the warning signals and give the child the help he needs, as early as possible, we give him the chance for a rich childhood and the foundation for a rich intellectual and emotional life. Every time we miss, he misses, too.

Here are some of the more charitable comments you'll read or hear about this child: "Bill's the strong, silent type." "Tim's a doer, not a talker." "George is a man of action." "Fred is usually found in the block corner." "Ellen is a gentle, quiet child. She is willing to let others go first." "Barbara is so interested in everything. She just can't wait to get her hands on new things."

But soon the pejorative ones appear: "Mary doesn't pay attention." "Allen doesn't seem interested in stories. When the other children are listening, he travels around the room. It's annoying and distracting." "Why can't Sandy just settle down like everyone else?" "I have to tell Joe everything three or four times." "Larry just doesn't follow directions. He's off in a world of his own." "William needs a firm hand."

And indeed he does—one that will lead him and his family to get some help. When? As soon as possible, for this kind of difficulty can be spotted as early as the age of two.

Teachers must certainly be on the lookout, but precious time has already passed by the time the child is old enough to go to school. We can do better.

Parents are the ones who have the first responsibility, and parents are sensitive diagnosticians. They often know when something isn't quite right, and it makes them feel uneasy. If we teachers can help parents know more about receptive language disability and encourage them to seek advice, we will have done a good deed for future children.

Preschool teachers and those who work in admissions must be aware of this problem. It's a suitable topic for any school that has a community education or parent awareness program.

Some professionals feel more important when they exclude parents. It's sort of a quick ego-trip ticket. "Only I can really help this child." "Of course, given his home situation . . ." "That mother is certainly an alarmist." This kind of thinking throws out a giant national resource.

Most parents care. They care very much. When things aren't going perfectly, they may feel anxious, guilty, apprehensive, tired, or even angry—"Why me?" But once a problem has a name, much of the mystery and fear (and guilt) can go away. Once there is a program for dealing with it that includes both school and parents, a mother and father can move from apprehension to participation, from angst to action. The school, the child, and the parents can invest themselves in helping, thus strengthening an existing natural bond.

Once a diagnosis is made, corrective and compensatory work can begin. Both the adults and the child can understand what is going on, and the child can begin to invest himself in himself and be freed to mine his own assets.

5. THE LEARNING DISABLED CHILD

People used to think that language develops as a result of reading and other intellectual, print-based activities. Current research tells us that language must precede cognitive development. Language has to exist *inside the child* to give incoming information something to stick to. With language inside, the child joins new information to his existing store like the two sides of a zipper.

But what of the child whose problem has slipped past his preschool teachers, his parents, and the pediatrician? How will he do in elementary school?

By the age of five, most children can carry out a three-part command: "Please put your sweater on the chair, get a glass of water from the sink, and sit on the blue chair." Our child either omits one or two of the three commands, or puts his sweater in the sink and pours water on the chair, and then wonders what to do next. He is confused and hurt by displeased reactions to his efforts. If these instructions had been given to him one by one, he'd have had no trouble. His mother or teacher would probably say, "If he'd only listen!"

In first and second grade, reading is mainly a matter of decoding small words that mostly function as labels—"The cat is black." Creative writing is encouraged, but no one worries much about lack of fluency or volume. And math involves simple operations. A pandemic of loose and missing teeth results in aberrations of speech, many of them amusing and most of them temporary.

Many children, especially boys, are still heavily action-oriented at this age, so chances are that our child will slip by again. In gym or group activities, he may be quiet when instructions are given. He may seem to be listening, but when the instructions are finished and it's time for action, he probably has to see what his neighbors are doing so that he can do it, too. He can mimic the marchers but not lead the parade.

Very often he responds to spoken instructions with an anxious smile and even a nod, as if to make up with friendliness for not being able to do what is asked of him. The child's seeming inattentiveness is a source of great annoyance to all—parents, teachers, and the child himself.

People may think he doesn't follow directions because he isn't trying or doesn't want to. But the child with receptive language disability simply cannot follow directions. And just think how much elementary education depends on verbal instructions and explanations—"Take a blue crayon and draw a line under all the horses, and draw a circle around the houses with a red crayon."

By the end of second grade, the child has probably learned 75 sight words and can read at second-grade level. But the clock is ticking.

When he hits third grade, these skills no longer suffice. Our child is in trouble. Reading takes a huge jump into the abstract with such concepts as "unless," "until," and "whenever." And what a sophisticated structure rests on the tiny word "if." By third grade, a child must be able to begin to understand more complicated aspects of language—how prefixes and suffixes change a word, the difference between active and passive, how to divide big new words by rules of structure and syllabification.

Creative writing takes a comparable leap. And third-grade disputes are more likely to be settled by arbitration or bitter argument than by bodily attack. Math, previously safe territory for our child, plays traitor to him with the advent of the word problem. He is in real trouble now.

Childish lisps are no longer considered cute, and the real world becomes impatient with the child who can't express himself accurately, come to the point, and develop his critical intellectual faculties. And he can't, of course, because expressive language depends on receptive language. You can't express what you don't have. Expressive language difficulty is easy to spot because you can hear it. But trying to fix it when the root problem is receptive is starting at the wrong end.

When a child is familiar with the words he reads, they become part of his working language and experience, but unless they are words that meet his existing language level, they do not stick or become a genuine part of him.

From third grade on, children work on such skills as inference, finding the main idea, description versus action, and distinguishing among imaginary, factual, and poetic writing. Using punctuation for emphasis, they bring their reading and writing skills closer to the level of the spoken syntax, cadence, and vocabulary they developed earlier. To be able to do these things, however, they must already *have* that earlier level of reception and expression.

Marginally developed syntax prevents a child from reading with rhythm and fluency, thus greatly impairing his comprehension. Much of our reading is done by anticipating what logically comes next and then letting the eye match the probability. Familiarity smooths the way. If you start reading in a new field that has a new vocabulary, you probably have to read word for word, going back over phrases and sentences before you can really understand. But most reading isn't done this way.

Enter the pun and the riddle. Without language inside, you can't get the joke. Young school-age children are sociable and want to join in the fun. The child who can't get in on the joke that involves language may be forced to withdraw or play the buffoon (if you can't pun, burp, or maybe talk baby talk and roll on the floor). When this kind of activity runs counter to the child's own nature and level of intelligence, he feels ill at ease with himself—an added burden he doesn't need.

Spoonerisms can be an important diagnostic signal. The child who asks you to retell the story of *The Rittle Lead Hen* is telling you something important. What does he think his favorite story is all about? Malapropisms work the same way; he who tries to "take the ball by the horns" has a difficult task indeed.

Idioms and metaphors are very hard for the child with receptive language disability, as I learned from Gwendolyn, a young lady of six. I thought I had done a wonderful job of explaining something to her and asked her what she thought of it. "I don't know," she said, "I'll have to think it over." With that, she tipped her head sharply to one side and shook it.

I saw her do this again later and finally asked her if her ear was bothering her. "Oh, no," she said cheerily, with an added shake of her head. "I'm just thinking it over." I finally understood. She was waiting for the idea to travel by gravity from one side of her head to the other.

What terror must have come to the heart of the boy who told me he was definitely "tone-death." No wonder he looked me straight in the eye at the beginning of a lesson on vowels and consonants and said, "Well, you know, I'm not a very consonant person." I pressed him for more information on this confession, and he said, "I get scared of lots of things."

If you're not really sure of the difference between "consonant" and "confident," how can you tell a reading lesson from a pep talk? And if you can't tell them apart, how do you react appropriately? In reading, your eye must match what your ear hears. If your eye sees "confident" and your ear hears "consonant," you'll score two thirds on accuracy in decoding and zero on comprehension because it just isn't going to make sense.

These inaccuracies can go unnoticed for years. Just as we anticipate what we will see in reading, we anticipate much of what we will hear in conversation. If we like the speaker and are concentrating on content, we will supply what is missing and unconsciously transpose the incorrect to correct. Because teachers as well as parents often make this kind of unconscious correction, our child may continue to slip by.

Compensation, disguise, and good intentions all around may conspire to keep the disability undetected and the child misunderstood. Comments from school may turn critical in a general way, cause alarm, and disguise the root problem: "I know Jack could do good work if only he'd try harder." "Unless there is a major improvement, I think Terry should be seen by a psychiatrist." "Mark isn't living up to his potential." "Martha must learn to open up more. She needs to take more initiative and participate in class discussions." "Charles is too old for this restless behavior." "Tom's spelling is dreadful."

Dreadful spelling gives us yet another chance to spot the real underlying problem. As a child gives out in his expressive language an echo of what he hears coming in, so he writes a reflection of what he hears in his head. Let us give thanks for bizarre spelling when it allows us to look with our eyes at this hidden mystery. We must learn to interpret a child's expressive language as an indication of his receptive language.

Here are two sentences written on the same day by two different children. One I shrug off, the other I take as seriously as I would a temperature of 105.

"It is a byoutophylle day."

"I ate pancakes the smorning."

I worry not a whit about "byoutophylle"; in fact, I admire its sophistication, its advanced use of *y*, its awareness of sounds and rules (though misapplied), and its obvious enjoyment of embellishment.

I find "the smorning" very scary. Is the writer not sure that the day divides into sections, and that one is called "morning?" Is he not sure that Tuesday morning and Thursday morning can be distinguished from each other by using "this," "that," "the other," or "the"? Doesn't he know where one word ends and another begins? If he doesn't, does he know what a word is at all? Are words constant, reliable units for him, or do they slide around and bang into one another without warning?

What is a "smorning"? It turned out to be a word born, in the mind of the writer, of a hazy connecting of early-in-the-day activities and the rumbling sounds of a noisy sleeper. Funny? No, terrifying. The child who wrote it is thirteen. He's a very bright boy who is failing in school, trying hard, plagued by guilt and remorse, and clinging to obedience as a way of appeasing a disappointed family and a threatening world.

"Children are like Ballantine beer," a sedate teacher said to me one day. She's definitely not the alcohol type, so I waited for more. "You know," she continued, "the three rings. You can't separate them. In children, the three are emotional development, cognitive development, and language development. If one of the three is hampered or depressed, the other two will suffer. The whole child cannot grow without all three."

As Harvard child psychiatrist Leon Eisenberg says, "Real children think and feel." They need language for both. They need receptive language to help them order and interpret their thoughts and feelings to themselves. Then they can use their expressive language to give their thoughts and feelings back to the world.

Remember Gwendolyn. Think it over.

'LEARNING DISABLED' OR 'SLOW LEARNER'?

Careful diagnosis avoids false hopes

Margaret Jo Shepherd

Dr. Shepherd is an associate professor at Teachers College, Columbia University, in New York and Coordinator of the Learning Disabilities Program in the Department of Special Education. She is a senior faculty member on the staff of the Child Study Center, the department's diagnostic center for children with learning problems.

"Shouldn't our son be called a child with specific learning disabilities?" ask the worried parents of a nine-year-old boy who has finished a long day of educational testing in the Special Education Child Study Center at Teachers College, Columbia University in New York. I pause before responding no, anticipating and, for a moment, wishing to avoid the certain signs of disappointment and deepening concern the response will bring.

We will go on together to explore the difference between the learning problems affecting their son, a slow learning child, and the learning problems of a child with specific learning disabilities. Like so many others before them, these parents had read and heard about "specific learning disabilities" and had come to the Child Study Center because they wanted to be told that their child's failure in school was caused by learning disabilities.

THE LD LABEL MEANS HOPE

Learning disabled appears to be the one descriptive term that can be applied to children with school learning and adjustment problems without eliciting negative connotations. To most parents and teachers the diagnostic label "learning disabilities" has become an optimistic diagnosis. It implies that the child's educational problems are temporary, that constructive action can be taken and that the outcome will be favorable. Consequently, the identification of a child as learning disabled has a positive influence on attitudes toward that child and particularly on adults' expectations for the child. It is easy to understand why learning disabled is the preferred diagnosis of most informed parents and of many teachers and psychologists.

My intent is not to disparage the attitudes of hope and optimism associated with the term learning disabilities. The search for constructive solutions to children's learning problems, which the current interest in learning disabilities has brought about, is one of the major developments in the field of special education during the past 15 years. Further, the effort to develop effective educational programs for learning disabled children has produced a rapprochement between regular and special education that should delight even the most cynical among us.

There is cause, however, for caution against the misuse of the term and misinterpretation of the diagnostic concept. This article is a plea for caution in the use of the diagnostic term learning disabilities.

CAN WE DEFINE LEARNING DISABILITIES?

The idea that normally intelligent children, who do not have primary sensory or emotional deficits, could still have specific learning problems didn't begin to influence educators' attitudes and school policies in the U.S. until the early 1960s. Unfortunately, it has been unusually difficult to give a precise definition to the condition of specific learning disabilities. There is as much confusion today about the exact meaning of the term and about the nature and causes of learning disabilities as there was in 1968 when an Advisory Committee appointed by the U.S. Office of Education first formulated its official definition of the term.

CAREFUL DIAGNOSIS

Despite the fact that there is no real consensus about the definition of learning disabilities and that learning disabled populations vary widely, there are at least two commonly held views about the condition of specific learning disabilities that should be considered in making a diagnosis.

The first and most important of these considerations is that children with specific learning disabilities *demonstrate* normal intellectual ability. Second, these children manage to develop normally in some respects despite learning disabilities. Thus, their development and skill attainment is markedly uneven. They show learning *abilities* as well as learning *dis*abilities.

It is this combination of normal intelligence and learning strengths with learning disabilities that encourages optimism about the corrective effect of special educational techniques. When these conditions

Reprinted from the March 1975 issue of *Teacher* Magazine with permission of the publisher. Copyright © 1975 Macmillan Professional Magazines, Inc. All rights reserved.

are present in a diagnosis of specific learning disabilities, optimism is warranted. But if they are not, and a diagnosis of specific learning disabilities is made, optimism may soon turn to disillusionment for parents, teachers and children.

MISDIAGNOSIS OF SLOW LEARNERS

The children who stand the greatest chance of suffering as a result of being misdiagnosed as learning disabled are those who, like the nine-year-old boy mentioned earlier, fall into that gray area between mental retardation and average or normal intellectual ability. These children are familiar to all teachers. Their school performance is consistent with their own abilities, but below the expected standard. They have obvious achievement and learning problems, but they do not qualify for special education services in most school districts. Whether it is desirable or not, these children have traditionally been called "slow learners."

Given current attitudes about specific learning disabilities, the dangers in misdiagnosis should be obvious. Resultant expectations may not be consistent with the child's ability and may cause erroneous decisions about the type of instruction a child needs, the rate at which new learning will occur and the standards of performance a child can be expected to maintain.

Perhaps the greatest danger lies in the possibility that inappropriate, long-range academic goals will be established. The slow learning child, incorrectly diagnosed as learning disabled, may be exposed to a highly specialized form of remedial instruction when the real need is for systematic developmental instruction paced at a rate consistent with learning ability.

It is acknowledged that a differential diagnosis between slow development and specific learning disabilities is often difficult to make. It is also true that when there is doubt as to which diagnosis should be made, one would always hope for and want to give the most positive diagnosis—learning disabled. But, recognizing that mislabeling is dangerous, it is important that the distinguishing features between slow development and specific learning disabilities be carefully considered when a diagnosis is made.

LEARNING PATTERNS

Perhaps the most important distinguishing feature is that a slow learner's development is even. The child doesn't demonstrate the erratic pattern in development and skill attainment that is characteristic of the child with learning disabilities.

A slow learner's language and perceptual-motor development may be immature and may reflect behavioral deficits similar to those of a learning disabled child. Both types of behavior in the slow learner, however, will be similarly immature, and developmental levels will be consistent with intellectual ability.

A slow learner's school achievement will be below that expected for the child's age level in the basic academic subjects. There will be remarkable similarities in performance levels and a discernable consistency between academic achievement levels and mental development.

An examination of the child's developmental history should reveal the same consistent pattern. This is the child who was slow to learn both to walk and talk, rather than slow to learn one set of skills but quick to learn another—a learning pattern often true of the learning disabled child.

The slow learner is the child whose performance on intellectual ability tests places him or her at the lowest point within the range designated as average intelligence. And when you examine actual performance, it is apparent that, once again, it is even. The child performed equally well on all types of tasks used to measure intellectual ability. In contrast, the learning disabled child may have attained *exactly the same score* but performed very poorly with some types of tasks and exceedingly well with others.

Observation of a slow learner is likely to reveal that once a skill has been learned and accuracy has been achieved, it is maintained. Long-term observation reveals a steady pattern of academic progress rather than a pattern of progress and subsequent regression. Erratic performance is the sine qua non of the learning disabilities syndrome.

Finally, the slow learner is less inclined to impulsivity. Attention spans may be shorter than desired or expected, and restlessness and distractibility may be present, but the tendency to respond without reflection is less characteristic of these children than of those with specific learning disabilities.

BEHAVIORAL SIMILARITIES

It is important to recognize that slow learners do demonstrate many of the same behavior patterns that are characteristic of children with learning disabilities. This is particularly true with regard to errors in letter and number reproduction—a characteristic symptomatic of perceptual-motor dysfunction. It is also true of the kinds of errors made when the child is learning to read.

Behavioral similarities between the two types of children cause diagnostic confusion. The difference is this: Behavior that appears to represent a specific deficit fits into a pattern of developmental retardation when the child is a slow learner. Behavior that appears to represent a specific deficit is usually just that when the child is learning disabled.

To sum up, a diagnosis of learning disabilities implies the probability of ultimately normal academic progress and the possibility that educational intervention may actually alleviate the learning problem. Consequently, such a diagnosis has a powerful effect on the attitudes of those who set educational goals and determine educational expectations for children. This seems sufficient reason to make that diagnosis with accuracy and caution.

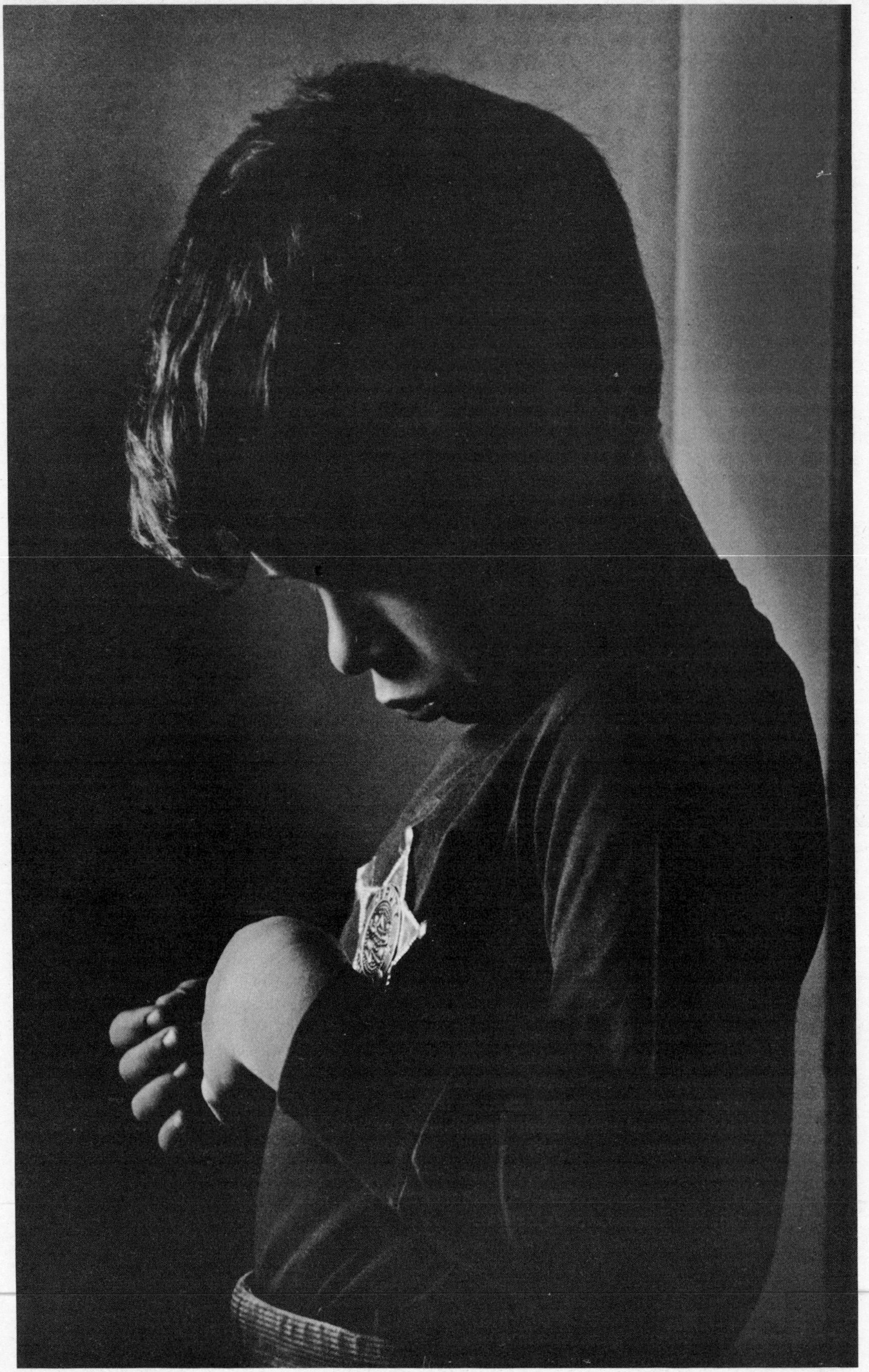

6 The Emotionally Troubled Child

Troubled children are those with urgent or severe emotional problems and disabilities such as autism, schizophrenia, depression, and hyperkinesis. Conservative estimates place at 1.4 million the number of children under 18 who are troubled enough to need immediate attention. In "Troubled Children: The Quest for Help," the president of the American Academy of Child Psychiatry says, "If we used really careful screening devices, we would probably double and maybe treble the official statistics." These statistics tell us that 10 million children need psychiatric help.

The lead article of this section of *Educating Exceptional Children* not only describes autism, hyperkinesis, childhood schizophrenia and depression, but it posits a trio of forces that conspire against the emotional well-being of the American child. These forces are the disappearance of the extended family, the learning of abnormal behavior from television, and the recognition that emotional disturbance runs high among prematurely born children or those subject to other environmental stresses.

Childhood autism, a devastating disorder that occurs in about 1 in 2,500 children, is the topic of several articles in this section. The condition is sometimes difficult to diagnose, and parents may spend painful months taking their child from one specialist to another in search of the correct label and treatment. But today we still do not know the cause of autism, although the presumption of inadequate parenting is recently out of favor among special educators. And there is no cure. Some educational strategies are more helpful than others, and teachers and parents can learn ways of significantly helping autistic children, as these articles point out. But autism remains a mystery.

More readily susceptible to treatment and less hopeless than autism is hyperkinesis, also called hyperactivity, minimal brain dysfunction, and even learning disability. It is a physiological condition, but a condition of which we do not know the cause. Hyperactive children exhibit excessive motor activity, have poor attention spans, and are impulsive and irritable. How to treat these children, especially whether to treat them with psychoactive drugs, is the topic of "Why Can't Bobby Sit Still?", "Battle Lines in the Ritalin War," and "Helping the Hyperkinetic Child." The final article in this section on troubled children addresses the problem of childhood depression, an affliction that may occur in up to 20 percent of children at any one time.

Looking Ahead: Challenge Questions

What does *not* knowing the cause of autism or hyperkinesis mean for special educators? For parents?

How have educators been most successful in helping troubled children?

Do troubled children suffer more from genetic or hereditary factors or from environmental factors?

What are the particular problems in mainstreaming troubled children?

Troubled Children: The Quest for Help

MATT CLARK

The control of the often deadly diseases of childhood is the proudest achievement of medical progress in this century. Thanks to vaccines and antibiotics, the average American child no longer must run a gauntlet of physical threats such as the crippling effects of polio, the heart damage of rheumatic fever or diphtheria's death by slow strangulation. Thanks to better nutrition, today's children grow inches taller and pounds heavier than their forebears did. In short, the American youngster has never had better prospects for a long and healthy life.

But for all that modern medicine has done to protect and nourish the child's body, surprisingly little has been done to assure him of an equally healthy mind. Despite all the talk about America's child-centered society and all the best sellers purporting to tell parents how to raise happy, well-adjusted youngsters, the number of emotionally troubled children is appallingly high.

Robert R. McElroy—Newsweek

A test of patience: Autistic child with mother in North Carolina

By the most conservative estimate, at least 1.4 million children under the age of 18 have emotional problems of sufficient severity to warrant urgent attention. As many as 10 million more require psychiatric help of some kind if they are ever to achieve the potential that medical progress on other fronts has made possible. "If we used really careful screening devices," says Dr. Joseph D. Noshpitz, president of the American Academy of Child Psychiatry, "we would probably double and maybe treble the official statistics."

The hard core of these children are those who are autistic or schizophrenic. They are helplessly withdrawn from reality and exist in an inner world that is seldom penetrated by outsiders. More than 1 million other children are hyperkinetic. They turn both living rooms and classrooms into shambles by their frenetic and uncontrollable physical activity. Millions more troubled children are plagued by neurotic symptoms. They are haunted by monster-ridden nightmares, frightened of going to school, held in the grip of strange compulsive rituals or lost in the loneliness of depression. Harder to pinpoint but just as troubled are those who simply don't function in society. They fail in school, they run away, they fight, they steal. Eventually, they fill reform schools and prisons.

Until recently, childhood emotional disorders have been tragically neglected as a national health problem of dramatic proportions. Because of his bizarre and often repellent behavior, the emotionally disturbed youngster has never made an appealing poster child for mothers' marches and annual fund-raising drives. While most of the nation's 7.6 million physically handicapped children receive educational and medical services through a variety of public and private channels, fewer than 1 million of the emotionally handicapped are receiving the help they need. All too often, the disturbed child has been expelled from public school as unteachable, or shunted into special classes for retarded children with brain damage. "We are in the Year One in care and treatment of these chil-

From *Newsweek* April 8, 1974. Copyright © *Newsweek, Inc.* 1974. Reprinted by permission.

dren," declares Josh Greenfeld, a 46-year-old writer whose 1972 book, "A Child Called Noah," vividly described his own agonizing search to find help for his autistic son. "We are going to have to shock ourselves into the fact that we are killing these children as well as destroying the lives of the families the kids are part of." *

But within the past few years, parents like the Greenfelds have made some important gains in winning better care for their troubled children through the legislators and the courts. In one of the most far-reaching decisions of all, a District of Columbia Federal judge ruled in 1972 that all handicapped youngsters—including the emotionally disturbed—are entitled to public education under the Fourteenth Amendment. Thanks to the relentless lobbying of the National Society for Autistic Children in Albany, N.Y. —composed largely of parents—more than 30 states have passed laws providing special education for autistics in the last four years.

One reason for the increasing recognition of the needs of the troubled child is the strong evidence that his ranks are growing. The number of children receiving treatment for emotional problems in institutions and outpatient facilities has risen nearly 60 per cent in the last seven years—from 486,000 to 770,000. "The drift," says Noshpitz, "is toward seeing more and more very disturbed children, youngsters who need residential treatment." And psychiatrists in private practice note similar trends. "There is now a widening scope of patients with childhood disturbances," says one veteran New York psychoanalyst, "and it is not just because more people are deciding to put their children in therapy."

Freud, who preached that the root causes of emotional disorders were to be found largely in a disturbed relationship between parent and child in early life, is no longer quite so predominant an influence on child-care professionals. The more eclectic psychologists and psychiatrists hold that childhood mental ills seem to arise from three intertwining influences: predisposing physical and hereditary factors, forces within the family —including the Freudian traumas—and stresses imposed by contemporary life. "The fortunate child," says Ner Littner of Chicago's Institute of Psychoanalysis, "is the one with good heredity and adequate care provided by two parents who are able to recognize and meet the child's needs in early life, and a minimum of chronic, overwhelming stress situations as the child grows up."

But now more than ever before, the triad of forces seems to conspire against the emotional well-being of the American child. First, there is a growing recognition that children born prematurely or as a result of difficult labor, those suffering from complications of measles and other viral infections and those raised by parents who are themselves victims of mental disorders run a high risk of emotional disturbance. Boys, for reasons perhaps attributable to hormonal differences, are up to five times more vulnerable than girls.

Editor's note: See A/E article #21 for a recent discussion by Josh Greenfeld.

Robert R. McElroy—Newsweek

Six-year-old girl with doll: Nightmares, compulsions and loneliness

Second, today's mobile society has all but abolished the extended family. Parents can no longer count on grandparents, aunts and uncles to act as authority figures in the raising of their children. "I'm personally convinced that no two parents can rear a child entirely alone," says Dr. Sally Provence of Yale's Child Study Center. "Yet young parents have fewer supports for parenting than ever before—it's either drag the kids along or get a sitter." With the increasing number of young women carving out careers for themselves, some experts see a threat even to the integrity of the nuclear family. "I'd much rather see people not have children at all than leave infants in a day-care center," says Dr. Lee Salk, chief child psychologist at New York Hospital-Cornell Medical Center and author of the best seller "What Every Child Would Like His Parents to Know."

Third, in today's push-button society children tend to learn about the world around them vicariously by television. "Many of our children and young people have been everywhere by eye and ear," notes a recent report of the Joint Commission on Mental Health of Children, "and almost nowhere in the realities of their self-initiated experiences." And much of what the children see is the vivid depiction of war, violence and social upheaval; aggression has become one of the most pervasive childhood experiences of all, says Dr. Ebbe Ebbesen of the University of California at San Diego. "Children learn abnormal behavior from observing other people," the California psychologist contends. "The more aggression a child is exposed to, the more likely that he himself will be aggressive."

Because there is no one cause of childhood emotional problems, many methods of treatment have evolved in recent years. Since a young child can hardly be expected to lie still for long, deep-probing sessions of analysis on the couch, psychiatrists have developed other ways to get at the source of his troubles. One involves watching how he plays with his toys or interpreting the pictures he draws. Other therapists ignore the deep-rooted sources of a child's problem and use reward-and-punishment conditioning techniques to modify the child's abnormal behavior. In many cases, the children with the overactivity syndrome of hyperkinesis can be helped with drugs. Unfortunately, no truly effective treatment has yet been found for the child afflicted with the most devastating of all the disorders—autism.

AUTISM

The term "early infantile autism," from the Greek for "self," was coined 30 years ago by Dr. Leo Kanner of Johns Hopkins to describe a group of disturbed schizophrenic children who showed a uniform pattern of disabilities in responding to their environment. As an infant, the autistic child may go limp or rigid when his mother picks him up. He may seem deaf to some sounds but not to others. He may show no sensitivity to pain, even to the extent that he can blister his fingers on a hot stove without flinching. For long periods, he may rock monotonously back and forth, flap his hands in front of his face, walk on the tips of his toes or whirl about like a dervish.

Autistics show unusual deviations in reaching the milestones of development. They may never sit up by themselves or crawl, but instead suddenly start walking. Some start to talk, but then abruptly stop using language altogether, or only echo words and phrases they have overheard. They reverse personal pronouns, such as saying "you" for "me." They seldom look anyone in the eye. When an autistic child wants something, he may, without looking at his mother, steer her hand toward the object as if manipulating a pair of pliers. Because many autistic children show certain "splinter skills" above and beyond their otherwise poor level of functioning—such as the ability to rattle off strings of numbers—they have traditionally not been classified as retarded or brain-damaged.

After Kanner's description of autism was published, some psychiatrists observed that the parents of such children tended to be intellectual, emotionally detached and with a tendency to think in abstractions. With the prevailing influence of Freud on child psychiatry at the time, it was hardly surprising that the condition should be blamed on these "refrigerator parents." Autism was supposed to result from rejection of the child by the mother at an early stage in infancy. Dr. Bruno Bettelheim, a distinguished psychoanalyst who recently retired after 30 years of dealing with autistic children at the University of Chicago's Orthogenic School, is a forceful exponent of the Freudian view.

The autistic child has an inherited predisposition to emotional trauma, Bettelheim says, but unconscious rejection by the mother is the major traumatizing event. The parents, he says, tend to deal with the child in a mechanistic way, out of a sense of obligation rather than genuine affection. "This is interpreted by the child as a feeling he shouldn't be alive," says Bettelheim. "When animals are threatened, they either play possum or fight back. Some children fight back, but the autistic child plays dead."

But the current trend is away from the Freudian view. Recent studies show that the parents of autistic children display no emotional traits that set them apart. "The only differences these parents show from other parents," notes Dr. Eric Schopler of the University of North Carolina School of Medicine, "is that they are all under stress themselves because they have a difficult child."

Moreover, researchers have made a number of observations that suggest that autism is more of a neurologic problem than an emotional one. A number of autistics, for example, show so-called "soft signs" of neurologic impairment, such as poor muscle tone, uncoordination and exaggerated knee-jerk responses. Drs. Edward Ornitz and Edward Ritvo of the UCLA School of Medicine have studied the eye reactions of normal and autistic children placed in a spinning chair. If the chair spins to the left, a normal person's eyes will move to the right, snap back and wander right again; when the chair stops, the eyes will reverse their movement. Autistic children show the same pattern of eye movement, but for a much shorter period. This suggests that the disorder involves a maturational lag in neural development. "The overwhelming evidence," says Ornitz, "is that this is an organic condition."

Because of the evidence suggesting that a physical abnormality is involved, there is a tendency among experts today to regard autism as a form of mental retardation rather than an emotional illness. "Autistic children both will not and cannot perform many tasks," says Ornitz. About 75 per cent of autistics remain retarded through life, he notes, and more than half eventually are institutionalized.

It is the parents of an autistic child who suffer the most. Many of them spend years going from specialist to specialist in a fruitless search for cures. At first, a pediatrician may tell them their child is deaf or simply "spoiled." Psychoanalysts may suggest that they, the parents, need treatment as much as their child does, only adding to an already unbearable burden of guilt. Psychiatrists may give the child tranquilizers, stimulants or even electroshock therapy. But the child remains his autistic self. Recently, some physicians have prescribed massive doses of such B vitamins as niacinamide, pyridoxine and pantothenic acid for both autistic and schizophrenic children. But most experts insist that the so-called megavitamin therapy has no scientific basis. "This is the false-hopes business," says one researcher, "and it causes a lot of anguish." "Every time you go to someone you're desperate," says Connie Lapin, a Los Angeles mother of an autistic son (box). "They say they'll treat him. But then they can't reach him and they give up."

But while there is no specific treatment for autism, a number of centers now offer special training that has produced promising results in some children. One of them is TEACCH (Treatment and Education of Autistic and related Communications handicapped Children), begun by Drs. Eric Schopler and Robert J. Reichler eight years ago and now funded by the State of North Carolina. One of the outstanding features of the program, according to Schopler, is the participation of parents as co-therapists in training their own children.

Basically, the parents are instructed how to use reward-and-punishment behavior modification to train their children during daily half-hour sessions in their

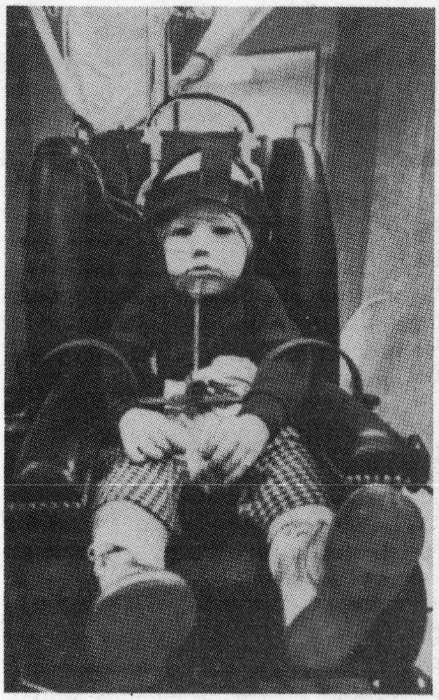

Lester Sloan—Newsweek

Normal child taking eye test for autism

homes. Through a one-way glass, therapists show parents how to reward the child with hugs, or candy, when he performs an expected task. The early exercises focus on such basics as looking the parent in the eye, learning concepts such as "same" and "different" by sorting knives, forks or other objects, and learning to identify objects with words. Parents are taught to distract their children from psychotic movement, such as rocking. When a child fails to respond, the parent is assured that it is correct to show displeasure.

The road to advancement is painfully arduous, but many children *do* improve. Michael, a brown-haired 5-year-old, couldn't talk and was unmanageable when he entered TEACCH a year and a half ago. Now he has a vocabulary of 750 words and behaves well enough to attend a special school. David, who had an IQ of 70 when treatment began nine years ago, now scores 30 points higher and is getting average grades at a regular private school. "By getting to them early," says Schopler, "some children can be salvaged."

SCHIZOPHRENIA

Schizophrenia in children bears some resemblance to autism and many psychiatrists consider them related. The child may be withdrawn and fail to use words. He may also be overactive and aggressive. Unlike schizophrenic adults, children affected by the disorder don't usually hear voices or otherwise hallucinate. But they do fantasize, according to psychiatrists, and they often can't distinguish between the real and the imaginary.

In the past, psychoanalysts tended to ascribe schizophrenia largely to the influence of a castrating "schizophrenogenic" mother. Many psychiatrists today believe the emotional environment of the home may play a greater part in the disorder than is the case with autism. But a growing number of the experts are now persuaded that a genetic defect, coupled with neurologic impairment of some kind, constitutes the underlying cause of the disorder.

The influence of genetics in childhood schizophrenia has been demonstrated by Dr. David Rosenthal of the National Institute of Mental Health. Rosenthal compared children with a schizophrenic mother or father who were raised by normal adoptive parents with adopted children of normal parents. In this way, the possible environmental influence of parenting was equalized. It turned out that the children of psychotic parents in the study had about twice the incidence of schizophrenic disorders as did those of normal parents.

The outlook for the schizophrenic child is considerable brighter than it is for the autistic. Many of these children are educable and never have to be institutionalized. Brooklyn's League School is typical of centers across the country that use a "psycho-educational" approach to treating schizophrenic children while the child lives at home.

Children are usually accepted at the school between the ages of 3 and 5 and most stay several years. Tommy Harper of Brooklyn began when he was in second grade. Throughout his childhood he had displayed a vicious temper. He threw blocks at his teachers when he couldn't get his way, and once pounced on a little girl and broke one of her teeth. Consigned to the cloakroom, he was later found sitting on a shelf, beating himself over the head with a toy gun and crying, "I want to die."

With the structured environment and intensive individual attention he received at the League School, Tommy settled down and learned to read, do math and function in groups. He was bright, a fast learner and in four years he was back in regular school. Today, at 15, Tommy is still a bit of a loner. But he can play sports such as football and not lose his temper in defeat; more important, he is an honor student. Dr. Carl Fenichel, director of the school, estimates that about 80 per cent of the children at the school had been destined for state institutions. Now, the majority go on to satisfactory jobs, regular schools and some even to college.

HYPERKINESIS

Of the more serious childhood behavior disorders, hyperkinesis has become the most widely publicized of late because it is being diagnosed in an increasing number of schoolchildren. The symptoms may be discernible in infancy, when the mother finds that her baby is unusually restless and difficult to soothe. They become more obvious when he reaches school age. Typically, hyperkinetic children are highly excitable, easily distracted and impulsive. They have trouble concentrating and therefore become disruptive in the classroom. Because they are failures in their work, they develop the emotional side effect of low self-esteem and frequently compensate by delinquent acting-out. "These youngsters consider themselves worthless," says Dr. Lawrence Taft of the College of Medicine and Dentistry of New Jersey, "because everyone is telling them they're no good."

Hyperkinesis seems to run in families, but there is also evidence that the disorder may be related to minimal brain damage, possibly occurring at the time of birth or after a viral infection such as measles. There is also evidence that lead intoxication may produce hyperkinesis among ghetto children who habitually put pieces of peeling lead-based paint into their mouths.

At least a third of hyperkinetic children show marked improvement on daily doses of stimulants such as amphetamines and even coffee (NEWSWEEK, Oct. 8, 1973). Just how the stimulants have this paradoxical calming effect isn't known, but they seem to improve the child's ability to concentrate.

Dosing large numbers of schoolchildren with the very drugs that constitute a major abuse problem in the U.S. has stirred controversy among many parents and even some psychiatrists. Some charge that the stimulants are prescribed as "conformity pills" for rebellious children. The drugs may produce side effects, including loss of appetite and sleeping difficulties. As a result, children who take them for several years may not grow as tall as they might have otherwise. But the effect of the drugs can be so dramatic, says Taft, "that you wonder whether an extra bit of height is all that important."

DEPRESSION

Among the childhood emotional disorders in which the relationship with the parents is of unquestioned importance, the outstanding example is depression. Some experts estimate that depression accounts for at least a quarter of the troubled children they see. The so-called "endogenous" form of depression, which seems to arise without any evidence of a traumatic life experience to account for it, is rarely diagnosed in youngsters. In nearly all cases, childhood depression is "reactive," associated with an event in the child's life, usually involving the parents. "The child-psychiatry books of twenty years ago may not have even mentioned it," says Dr. Leon Cytryn of the George Washington University School of Medicine. "But we're beginning to realize that there are many depressed children and we suspect a lot of them become depressed adolescents and depressed adults."

Its most pathetic form is the "anaclitic" (from the Greek, "leaning on") depression that is observed in infants separated from their mothers in the first six months of life and raised in institutions where they get little attention and neural stimulation. These babies, starved for warmth, withdraw and display some of the signs of autism, such as monotonous rocking and, as they grow older, difficulties with language. They will improve with regard to language and motor skills if moved to a favorable environment, but the profound emotional impact of their early experience may be devastating.

Beyond the age of 6, the depressed child may show signs of sadness, social withdrawal and apathy similar to the symptoms of adult depression. But usually it is masked. In young children it may be expressed in psychosomatic headaches or vomiting; in older children it may show up in aggressive behavior, truancy, vandalism and, particularly among girls, sexual promiscuity. The periodic episodes of sadness that are the tip-off, notes Dr. Donald H. McKnew Jr. of the Children's Hospital of the District of Columbia, may be overlooked by the parents for months, but psychological testing may bring out the true extent of the child's depression quite quickly.

Asked to draw a picture and then tell a story about it, an 8-year-old boy brought to McKnew recently drew a picture of a small whale. Then he told how the whale was lost and was trying to get home. He tried to hitch a ride with another whale, but slipped off its back.

Then he joined a school of whales, but they swam too fast for him to keep up. So the whale in the picture was lying with another whale, also lost, waiting to be found. "If an adult told you a story like that," notes McKnew, "you'd immediately give him antidepressants."

Depression in children almost always follows a sense of loss. Acute reactions occur, understandably enough, after the death of a parent or close relative, divorce or a move to a new community. Often, they are more like grief reactions and disappear with time. But many depressions occur because the child senses a withdrawal of interest and affection through frequent separations from, say, a father who travels a lot; or because a parent conveys an attitude of rejection or deprecation. In most instances, one or another of the parents has a depressed personality, McKnew observes.

Antidepressant medication is seldom prescribed for children. Most often, psychiatric counseling, involving both parent and child, is required. Fortunately, psychotherapy usually is effective. Here psychiatrists have devised methods that sidestep the completely verbal methods of communication used in more adult forms of psychotherapy. One of the most widely used is play therapy, in which the child uses a variety of toys to expose, under the therapist's watchful eye, the situations that may be at the bottom of his problem. The play-therapy concept is based on the common-sense notion that play is a more natural mode of expression for a child than verbalizing dreams.

One of the most common problems that call for psychiatric attention in children is school phobia. It may be a symptom of depression, but may also have a far more readily treated cause. Dr. Lee Salk recalls the case of Stephen, age 5, who lived on the twelfth floor of a New York apartment with his parents and grandparents, who continually expressed their fear of burglars. His mother warned him constantly of the evils that could befall him when he went out to play and often warned him not to let the elevator doors close on him. Soon, he had developed a fear of both burglars and elevators, and was afraid to go out alone.

Not surprisingly, his anxieties continued at school; his mother would drop him off at the door but could count on his coming out again minutes later. The problem, as Salk explained, was that the child had become totally helpless outside his mother's purview and dependent on her attention—a common source of school phobias. Salk explained to the overanxious mother that Stephen should hear fewer dire predictions about the world outside and be allowed more independence. In weeks, he was spending full days in school.

The relief of the most serious problems of troubled children—autism, schizophrenia and hyperkinesis—must await much further research into the physical and biochemical mysteries of the brain. What is required is the same sort of commitment on the part of private agencies and the government that has lately been mounted in the war against cancer and heart disease. At the same time, the children who are already victims of these tragic disabilities must be afforded the special training that will give them the best chance of finding a useful life. In view of the fact that 10 per cent of the nation's children are now destined to develop some form of emotional disability, the effort would seem a small price to pay.

Meanwhile, in the view of child experts, there is a good deal that parents can do to protect their children from many kinds of serious emotional damage. First, says Salk, is to recognize the child's dependency during the first year of life and respond unstintingly to his need for warmth and affection. Once the child has learned to trust his parents, it is time to set limits that prepare him for his encounters with the world. To contend with the child's impulse to explore his environment, knocking over countless glasses of milk as he goes, may be a frustrating and seemingly endless task, Salk concedes. "But," he adds, "for the parent who loves his child, has patience and can still see the world through a child's eyes, the rewards are beyond measure."

CHILDHOOD AUTISM

Donald J. Cohen and Barbara Caparulo

Donald J. Cohen, M.D., is associate professor of pediatrics, psychiatry and psychology, Yale University School of Medicine. Barbara Caparulo is a special educator and research associate, Child Study Center, Yale University School of Medicine.

Childhood autism, a puzzling and devastating disorder, was described in 1943 by Dr. Leo Kanner, America's first professor of child psychiatry. He identified a small group of children with a profound inability to establish affectionate and meaningful relationships, even with their parents, and who failed to develop normal language.[1]

Although no one knows exactly, it is now estimated that autism occurs in about 1 in 2,500 children, making it far more common than PKU (1:15,000) and less common than Down's Syndrome (1:700). It appears to affect more boys than girls, and rarely is it found in more than one child in a family. Because of its severity and the uncertainties surrounding its causes, diagnosis and treatment, childhood autism has generated a great deal of scientific research and discussion.

The Early Years

The emotional and behavioral disturbances of childhood autism are sometimes apparent from the child's first weeks of life. A mother may note how a child's attention fades in and out or how uncomfortable he seems in her arms. Later, the child may not prepare himself to be picked up or may look beyond his mother, and never into her eyes when being fed. The infant may be "unusually good" or cry inconsolably. During the first year of life, an autistic child may have difficulties with feeding. He may become preoccupied with one object or toy or spend hours looking at his fingers or repeatedly banging his head against the crib. The parents' vague but persistent feeling that something is wrong becomes more certain as the baby grows older and fails to babble socially or to learn to use language normally. Because of his social inaccessibility, lack of language and apparent unresponsiveness to noises, the child may be thought to be deaf. However, he often responds violently to certain sounds, such as the whirring of a washing machine, although he may appear not to hear others, including a parent's voice or the sound of his own name.

Most autistic children are attractive and physically quite healthy; they usually learn how to sit, crawl and walk at the usual times. The pediatrician or family physician may advise anxious parents to remain calm and take a "wait and see" attitude. By age 2½ to 3 years, however, the child's increasing hyperactivity, social aloofness, difficulties with language and odd mannerisms are in such sharp contrast to the behavior of normal toddlers that everyone who sees the child recognizes that something is wrong.

The preschool autistic child is unable to play imaginatively or to share with other children. He often seems driven in his hyperactivity, or he may be sluggish and underaroused. He may become panicked by even small changes in his routine or physical environment, such as a rearrangement of furniture. His sleeping patterns are often quite abnormal, permitting both the child and his family only three or four uninterrupted hours of sleep a night.

The universal, and for parents the most devastating, symptom of autism is the child's inability to relate to other human beings in a normal way, a lack that becomes more noticeable as the child grows older. Parents may be used as objects for the satisfaction of basic needs, but the child may show no signs of closeness, mutual enjoyment or concern with them.

Many autistic children have very limited vocabularies, or no language at all. A variety of peculiarities are noted in the language of those who do speak, including the repetition of a word or phrase, sometimes long after it was originally heard. Autistic children's speech in general is socially inappropriate or intrusive, and its content tends to be silly or out of context. Often, the odd, mechanical quality of their speech makes it appear that they are repeating memorized sentences.

Although autistic children may have other areas of intellectual competence, their intelligence is often expressed negatively, through mischief. For example, an autistic child may be able to figure out how to remove a lock from a door or disassemble a toy.

Diagnosis

A family of a 3- or 4-year-old autistic child may go from one physician to another in search of a diagnosis, and may, in turn, be given such labels as severe mental retardation, schizophrenia, aphasia, atypical personality development, learning disability or severe emotional disturbance. Each of these diagnoses captures one particular facet of the child's mutiple handicaps.

Reprinted by permission of *Children Today* and the authors, Donald J. Cohen, M.D., Associate Professor of Pediatrics, Psychology and Psychiatry, and Barbara Caparulo, Associate in Research, Yale University School of Medicine and the Child Study Center.

6. THE EMOTIONALLY TROUBLED CHILD

Because there are many organic diseases with symptoms similar to autism, the arrival at a diagnosis requires thorough clinical study. Brain damage from lead poisoning; inborn errors of metabolism, such as PKU (for which all newborns should be screened); congenital rubella; retrolental fibroplasia found in premature infants exposed to high oxygen; and measles encephalitis may all mimic the behavioral symptoms of autism. There are also children with severe brain damage who, on initial examination, may seem autistic, but who have additional problems in coordination, movement and intellectual functioning. Children with one of these organic brain disturbances and secondary childhood autism may require treatment similar to that of children with primary autism. As medical research reveals more biological causes for severe behavioral disturbances in children, some children now diagnosed as having primary childhood autism may be moved to the category of secondary childhood autism.

Diagnosis of childhood autism entails evaluation from several disciplines. Intellectual assessment requires procedures which must be adapted to the child's social and emotional capacities. Many hours of observation may be needed and a careful developmental history should be obtained. The child's medical history and current medical condition must be evaluated, and even the standard pediatric examination may require a great deal of patience. The medical evaluation, aimed at determining if the behavioral characteristics are secondary to any known disease, should include careful examination of vision and hearing, neurological and pediatric physical examination, urine screening for metabolic disease and other laboratory studies. Additional diagnostic procedures could include an electroencephalogram (EEG), X-rays of the skull, blood screening tests and examination of the cerebrospinal fluid.

Detailed medical and social evaluation may indicate that a child is not suffering from primary childhood autism but from some other type of severe developmental disturbance. For example, a child may become anxious, withdraw, fail to make warm attachments or show general developmental lag as a result of disruption or inadequacy in his care or because of traumatic experiences.

Clearly, the evaluation involves careful consideration and collaboration among various medical specialists and the child's parents. Because children with autism are difficult, uncooperative patients, their medical care and evaluation may be too limited. For example, one of the symptoms of autism is pica—eating strange objects, dirt and such items as paint chips. We have found that many autistic children have elevations in their blood lead because of such ingestion over many years.[2]

Remarkably, however, most children with primary autism are physically healthy and multidisciplinary study usually reveals no physical basis for their behavioral disorder.

The Later Years

There have been many descriptions of physically attractive young autistic children. Far less is known about the less appealing autistic adolescent or adult.[3]

The fortunate 10 to 15 percent of older autistic persons who have developed language and improved social relations may still seem odd, immature or eccentric. Their behavior in social situations usually lacks spontaneity and reflects the hard work they, and their parents and teachers, have put into their education. For example, they must be taught the social conventions, to say "Fine, thank you." and "How are you?" instead of honestly responding with a discussion of their daily lives. In school, autistic children may show areas of high intellectual ability and they may learn to read well; yet their comprehension may be relatively limited and the information they acquire of questionable utility, such as memorized dates. The older autistic individual's speech usually remains deliberate and stiff.

In spite of major improvements, older autistic persons remain anxious and perhaps depressed as they recognize their limitations. They may continue to have odd mannerisms or flapping behavior, especially when they are upset or excited, and they may be unable to engage in imaginative activities or to work or play in a mutually meaningful way with others. Nevertheless, pre-vocational and vocational education may offer the possibility of some form of independent living for better functioning autistic young people, although they may still require a half-way house and parents (or parent-substitutes) who can provide constant guidance and emotional support.

For the less fortunate autistic child whose language does not progress, behavior during the school-age and adolescent years remains similar to that of the preschool years. Hyperactivity may decrease with training, but the child's ability to communicate, use symbols, follow commands or relate to peers may be extremely limited. A child may engage in self-destructive biting, head-banging and skin picking, or spend hours rocking, twirling or flapping his hands. He may show little concern about the comings and goings of even his parents and patterns of behavior—such as twirling a string or leaf—may become crystallized, to remain unchanged for years.

Even for such children, however, special education may make a great deal of difference, although the prognosis is much more guarded. These children will require the constant care of thoughtful adults and, most often, lifetime care in a hospital or other institution.

Between the children with the best and the worst natural histories, there are those who show every shade of improvement.

Causes of Autism

The cause of primary childhood autism is not known. In the 1940s and 1950s, psychoanalytic and psychodynamic theories were most prominent and parents were often blamed for their child's condition. Autistic children withdrew, according to this idea, because they were responding to the cold, detached, unloving or even hateful feelings of their parents. Advocates of this theory often prescribed long-term psychotherapy for the child and his parents. Therapeutic results were discouraging and considerable research during the past decade has now rejected the extreme psychodynamic viewpoint.

Today, parents of autistic children are considered to be like the parents of other handicapped children whose care poses tremendous burdens. Naturally, they become unhappy, worried and exhausted, and perhaps angry and discouraged, but they are not, as a group, unconcerned or unloving. On the contrary, improvements in the education and treatment of autistic children during the past years have been in large part the result of the devotion of parents brought together in such groups as the National Society for Autistic Children, which also serves as an information clearinghouse.[4] The remarkable health of an autistic child's siblings is a testament to the concern of parents who struggle to maintain a family life, most often with little professional support.

There have also been theories about the possible organic basis of childhood autism.[5] Recently these theories have gained more support, although no organic basis has yet been demonstrated. In supporting this viewpoint, investigators point to various kinds of evidence, such as pervasive language problems, disturbances in sensory-motor coordination and the sequential ordering of behavior, and disturbances in the part of the brain concerned with balance and coordination. Since in almost every case in which one identical twin has autism the other also has this condition, the disorder may have a congenital basis. Many autistic children have abnormal or borderline abnormal brain wave patterns, and a small proportion develop seizures. Finally, autism is found throughout the world, in every social class, with a uniform clinical picture. All of this evidence suggests that autism is like some of the now well-known inborn disorders of metabolism.

At times, autism has been considered a form of mental retardation. Yet there are ways in which primary childhood autism is different from most other forms of retardation. While most retarded children are more competent socially than intellectually, the opposite is true for autistic children. Also, many profoundly retarded children have other signs of brain damage, such as slow motor development, abnormal reflexes, odd head shape or unusual appearance. Autistic children, on the other hand, may be quite retarded in their social, emotional or intellectual skills but more or less normal in their motor development, appear quite attractive, and show no other evidence of brain damage.

A disturbance in language comprehension and use has been postulated as the basis for autism, and this is a promising area for research.[6] However, autistic children differ from those whose central problem is only a severe language impairment, such as is found in childhood aphasia. Aphasic children tend to have good social relatedness and they invent signs to express themselves. In contrast, autistic children are poor mimics and inventors of symbols, and even those who do show social improvement with the use of language may remain quite handicapped socially and emotionally.

Another promising field of investigation is the possible biochemical basis for severe developmental problems.[7] Recent research on manic-depressive disease and schizophrenia in adults, as well as on neurological diseases such as Parkinson's syndrome, has greatly increased knowledge about the way in which messages are chemically transmitted by nerve cells in the brain. This process involves various chemicals—such as dopamine and norepinephrine—which are stored in nerve endings and then released when needed. There may be abnormalities in the way in which these chemicals are synthesized, released or broken down after performing their function. This knowledge has been the basis for the treatment of Parkinson's disease with DOPA and for explaining the chemical action of medicines used in the treatment of depression and schizophrenia.

There is increasing interest in the possibility that autism may also reflect abnormalities of central nervous system function. Autistic children's stereotypic behavior, hyperactivity, disorganization, lack of pleasure and other symptoms are consistent with some patterns of abnormalities which affect brain metabolism. However, knowledge about possible metabolic problems in autistic children will require considerably more research than is now available.[8]

Treatment

Just as there is no known cause, there is no cure for autism. The mainstays of treatment are parental guidance, special education and vocational training, psychotherapy, drug therapy and institutional treatment.

The major advance in recent years has been the use of behavior modification.[9] Parents may be taught to educate their own child from the preschool years. Procedures involve specifying what behavior is to be modified (such as learning how to establish eye contact or to use the toilet), charting situations in which the behavior occurs or does not occur, and then using rewards such as candy or praise to encourage the desired behavior. The outline of the method is simple, but its effective use requires intuition and perseverance, and collaboration between experienced professionals and parents. In precision education, teachers use behavior modification to teach academic as well as self-help skills. The name of this approach derives from the educator's precise definition of the child's capacities, the objectives for each teacher-child activity, the methods to be used in shaping the child's behavior and the success or failure of each intervention.

Families require emotional support and guidance in relation to both their autistic child and their other children. An autistic child may create extreme tensions between a husband and wife, as Josh Greenfeld describes in his chronicle of his own family's experiences.[10] The anxiety and guilt generated by these tensions may ultimately lead to separation and divorce.

There has probably been no psychoactive medication which has not been tried with autistic children. LSD and various shock therapies have also been attempted. No medical treatment, however, has proven to be very useful. Today, judicious clinicians may suggest a trial of a medication with demonstrated value in the treatment of severe psychiatric disturbances, hoping to reduce a target symptom—such as extreme hyperactivity or anxiety—or to help a child make use of special education or therapy. Children should not be kept on medication for years, however, unless there are very clear reasons for doing so. Close monitoring of the dose and side effects by a responsible physician, parents and teachers is essential.

A lovely autistic 5- or 6-year-old may bring out a clinician's deepest desire to be helpful. Many such children have been worked with in feelings-oriented, expressive psychotherapy for years. These therapeutic efforts aim at helping the child form a personal relationship and then to express and better understand his feelings. Parents are often concommitantly involved in personal psychological treatment. The devotion and intuitive skills of child therapists have probably been of value for some of their patients, and their humanity has been an example for all professionals concerned with handicapped children. Similarly, the support offered to some parents has no doubt allowed them to survive their child's hardest years. However, psychotherapy plays a very limited role for the most severely disturbed autistic children and the abuse of parents by therapists has left many deep scars and general resentment. While we have the sense that psychotherapy is perhaps of value for older, behaviorally modified youngsters, there are no firm data to support this belief.

Desperate parents will turn to any available therapy, even if there is doubt or no proof of efficacy. Some are generally harmless, such as hypo-allergenic diets or the use of megadose vitamins, although long-term side effects may yet appear. Some may carry serious emotional and financial burdens and distract the parents from providing the kind of educational opportunities which are known to be useful. And yet others—such as the use of shocks and physical punishment—have a very limited and controversial application in the hands of well-trained and conscientious professionals but pose real physical and emotional harm to a child when used thoughtlessly.

Unfortunately, there is no single agency or professional to whom most parents can turn for knowledge and guidance throughout the many years of their struggle. The professional care of most autistic children tends to be fragmented, and parents are still forced to learn by bitter experience, experimentation and the advice of other parents.

Education

Speech therapy and instruction in the use of the language of the deaf appear to be of special value for autistic children. Both techniques aim at facilitating a child's communication, the former by working with spoken language and the latter by offering an alternative medium. Another component of special education is systematic training in athletic and other gross motor activities. Swimming, ball play and work on balance beams and trampolines provide a child with a sense of competence, an awareness of his body and the opportunity to work and play with peers.

Autistic children may be taught simple vocational skills, such as those involved in operating a printing press or working in a greenhouse. For some, these provide a channel for partial self-support as well as an acceptable role in society. Yet, in contrast with the detailed understanding of how to teach younger autistic children, there is a great need for systematic research in curricula for vocational education, such as those being developed by Benhaven in New Haven, Connecticut.[11]

Young autistic children usually remain with their families when there are adequate schools available, which can also offer help and guidance to parents. However, some young children and many adolescents cannot be maintained at home. Their behavior may become too disorganized, or they may require 24-hour behavior modification and careful environmental control. Often their parents or siblings are too stressed, or the community may lack an appropriate school. By far the most appropriate placement under these circumstances is a residential school with specially trained staff and a family-like living arrangement. The child requires continuity of care and stability of educational planning. Autistic children should generally not be placed on general wards in institutions for the retarded or emotionally disturbed. When they are, they almost always do badly and lose areas of competence.

Childhood Autism and Other Severe Disturbances

There are many children with severe disturbances who are not precisely "classical autistic" children. They, too, may receive many labels, and what we have said about the lack of knowledge of the cause and treatment of autism applies almost as well to them. Some of these children may be described as "atypical" and suffer from difficulties in the control of their emotions, in forming mature social relations and with hyperactivity. They may have subtle signs of central nervous system problems (such as clumsiness) or other indicators of biological impairment (such as unusual facial appearance or odd gait). Frequently, their behavior reflects stresses and strains in their lives compounded by a biological predisposition. Other children may have vivid symptoms, suggestive of the kind of hallucinations, preoccupations and delusions of adults with schizophrenia.

There has been a great deal of discussion about whether atypical and schizophrenic children should be classified along with autistic children. If so, these might be seen to form a spectrum of handicapping conditions. For many practical purposes, for example, in designing a regional network of services or educational programs, all developmentally disabled children should be included. They all require more or less similar kinds of evaluation and frequently similar types of educational and therapeutic opportunities. However, for many types of scientific research, subtle distinctions between these syndromes are useful.[12]

Future Prospects

In the past decade advances in understanding more about the nature of childhood autism have helped create better educational, therapeutic and diagnostic procedures. But until the cause of autism is understood many children and their families face a long and exhausting course in trying to attain these services. There remain many avenues to be explored by teachers, mental health workers and laboratory researchers.[13] For example, advances in understanding brain chemistry, which have cast new light on the basis and treatment for several forms of adult psychopathology, may now be extended to include research on childhood behavioral disorders.

Researchers and educators are also interested in the ways in which handicaps of autistic children change as they grow up and they are beginning to study children over a long period of time. It is also important to document the strengths and weaknesses, failures and successes of autistic children in the classroom so that teachers can follow a well-defined rationale for working with them.

It is clear that intensive and thoughtful research with autistic children requires close collaboration between families and scientific investigators, as well as collaboration among special educators, parent groups, child development specialists and those working in the fields of psychiatry, pediatrics, psychology and endocrinology. Such an interdisciplinary effort offers the most promising approach to understanding more about these severe childhood disabilities.

---

[1] See Kanner, L., *Childhood Psychosis: Initial Studies and New Insights,* Washington, D.C., Winston & Sons, 1973.

[2] While pica is a well-known symptom of autism, too few autistic children have their blood lead evaluated routinely. We have shown that it is often elevated, and this increased lead burden may interfere with the autistic child's attention and learning. See Cohen, D. J.; Johnston, W. T., and Caparulo, B. K., "Pica and Elevated Blood Lead in Autistic and Atypical Children," *American Journal of Diseases of Children* (In Press).

[3] Wing, L., *Autistic Children,* New York, Brunner/Mazel, 1972.

[4] For more information contact: Mrs. Ruth Sullivan, Director, The National Society for Autistic Children Information and Referral Service, 101 Richmond Street, Huntington, West Virginia 25702.

[5] Rimland, B., *Infantile Autism,* New York, Meredith Publishing, 1964.

[6] Rutter, M. (Ed.), *Infantile Autism: Concepts, Characteristics and Treatment,* London, The Whitefriars Press Ltd., 1971.

[7] Cohen, D.J., "Competence and Biology: Methodology in Studies of Infants, Twins, Psychosomatic Disease, and Psychosis," *The Child in His Family—Children at a Psychiatric Risk,* edited by E. J. Anthony and C. Koupernik, New York, John Wiley & Sons, Inc., 1974.

[8] Cohen, D. J.; Shaywitz, B. A.; Johnson, W. T.; Bowers, M., Jr., "Biogenic Amines in Autistic and Atypical Children: Cerebrospinal Fluid Measures of Homovanillic acid and 5-Hydroxyindoleacetic Acid," *Archives of General Psychiatry,* Vol. 31, 1974.

[9] See various issues of the *Journal of Childhood Autism and Schizophrenia.*

[10] Greenfeld, J., *A Child Called Noah,* New York, Warner Books, Inc., 1973.

[11] Lettick, A., *Benhaven's Way,* a monograph published by Benhaven, New Haven, Conn., 1971.

[12] Hobbs, N. (Ed.), *Issues in the Classification of Children,* (2 volumes), San Francisco, Jossey-Bass, 1975.

[13] Churchill, D., Alpern, G., and DeMeyer, M. (Eds.), *Infantile Autism,* Springfield, Ill., Charles C Thomas, 1971.

We want your advice.

Any anthology can be improved. This one will be—annually. But we need your help.

Annual Editions revisions depend on two major opinion sources: one is the academic advisers who work with us in scanning the thousands of articles published in the public press each year; the other is you—the person actually using the book.

Please help us and the users of the next edition by completing the prepaid reader response form on the last page of this book and returning it to us. Thank you.

THEIR FINGERS DO THE TALKING

Carole Wade Offir

Carole Wade Offir is a West Coast correspondent for *Psychology Today* and a freelance social-science writer. She received her Ph.D. in psychology (specializing in psycholinguistics) from Stanford University and currently teaches psychology at Mesa College in San Diego. Offir's research interest is the study of the linguistic bases of effective communication.

Autistic children strangle on the spoken word. But imaginative teachers are breaking down the walls of silence by teaching sign language. Thus freed, a majority of autistics break through to real communication.

IN A CHICAGO CLASSROOM, as in thousands of other classrooms around the country, children laugh and tease, play games, or work on lessons in reading and arithmetic. But this particular classroom, at the David School, is different. All of its students were once branded with the label "autistic." All were once considered hopelessly psychotic, destined to spend the rest of their lives in worlds inhabited only by themselves. All are now busily knocking down the walls of those worlds with their bare hands.

For many autistic children, language is an insurmountable obstacle. The children at the David School have eased past that obstacle by learning to let their fingers do the talking. Instead of sounds and syllables, they use the hand configurations, movements and positions that are the building blocks of sign language, a type of communication usually reserved for the deaf. As a result, all gain most of the joys of language, and their success gives us a basic new insight into the way normal children learn to communicate.

Contrary to popular belief, sign language is no makeshift system of communicating. One of its forms, American Sign Language, has a unique and complicated grammar of its own; another, signed English, which is used at the David School, closely follows the complex word-order rules of spoken English.

It would have been impressive enough if any of the 30 children in the original program learned this complicated language. In fact all learned to use signs to make requests and express feelings. Seven also learned to speak with ease; after only a couple of years of practice, they were able to articulate words clearly, and more important, to use and understand the sophisticated sentence structures of four- and five-year-olds. Thirteen other children advanced to the point where they could speak single words or could approximate English sentences. So two thirds developed some speech. In a few cases, they spoke with the strained, monotonic intonation typical of deaf people, but speak they did. Twenty-eight of the 30 were able to leave the David School and enroll in other public or private programs.

Ritualistic Stimulation. To appreciate what sign language can mean to autistic children, one must consider what they are like before they learn it. Unlike normal children, autistic children do not try to explore their environment or make contact with other people. Instead, they spend a great deal of the time ritualistically stimulating them selves; for hours on end, they rock bac and forth, flap their arms, wave the fingers in front of their eyes, pace up ar down the room, or twiddle small o jects. Some seem obsessed by a desire injure themselves. An autistic chi may slap and punch his own face, bar his head against the wall until it bloody, pull off fingernails or chew h shoulder to the bone. A few of the mo self-abusive have spent years tied to bed because their caretakers didn know how to cope with them.

To loving parents, the most frustra ing characteristic of an autistic child his unsociability. Autistic children ne ther give love nor care about receivi it. They do not meet your eyes wh you speak to them. Even as infants, th may go rigid when an adult tries to cu dle them. Some sink into a chronic sta of apathy; others throw violent ta trums at the slightest frustration. Ma autistic children are totally mute, wh others merely repeat, parrotlike, wh ever is said to them. Yet autistics do n seem to be intrinsically retarded, ev though they may be unable to lea their own names or dress themselve Many have excellent memory and sp tial skills. They may be able to solve difficult jigsaw puzzle, or to restack bunch of blocks into a pattern seen on once before.

Jolts of Electricity. Until the 1960s, t standard approach with autistic ki was to load them up with unqualifi love and expensive psychotherapy. T results were usually nil. Then a few searchers, notably Ivar Lovaas at UCL discovered that behavior-modific tion techniques could help. By sy tematically rewarding appropriate b havior and punishing or refusing

From PSYCHOLOGY TODAY, June 1976. Copyright © 1976 by Ziff-Davis Publishing Company; reprinted by permission of PSYCHOLOGY TODAY.

reward inappropriate behavior, therapists were able to teach autistic children to behave in a more civilized way, to show and accept affection, and even to speak. To the horror of many professionals, Lovaas even used spanking and jolts of electricity. But his results were persuasive, though some of his patients still had stereotyped speech and could speak only in limited situations. Others remained stubbornly silent.

In the late '60s and early '70s, a handful of research scientists began to think about sign language as an alternative mode of communication for autistics. At the same time, and quite independently, a few practitioners stumbled on the same idea. One of the first actually to use sign language was psychologist Margaret Creedon. She formerly directed the program at the David School, which is part of the Dysfunctioning Child Center at the Michael Reese Medical Center. It was 1969, and Creedon was working with a mute, extremely self-destructive boy who had previously been in a program for children with impaired hearing because of a suspected, but unconfirmed, hearing loss. She was getting nowhere, and in frustration consulted a sign expert, Candy Haight. Soon the child was making good progress.

Like many breakthroughs in psychology, this first success was largely fortuitous. The child was thought to be slightly hard of hearing; sign was a natural technique to try. Creedon next supervised other therapists, who used the approach with five other patients at the center, severely disturbed boys who were spending much of the day twiddling, staring, and filtering the light through their fingers. Perhaps, thought Creedon, teachers could build communication on a foundation of hand movements that already existed, bizarre though they were; perhaps those hand gestures could be turned to advantage. Again, she was rewarded with rapid success, as the boys began to acquire signs.

Soon there was a day-school at the center devoted to a program of simultaneous communication—the use of both signed and spoken English. The school challenged its own philosophy by admitting children who were psychiatrically at the bottom of the barrel, the dropouts and rejects of other programs. The first children in the program all functioned at a severely retarded level; many could not even take the standard psychological tests. All had classical

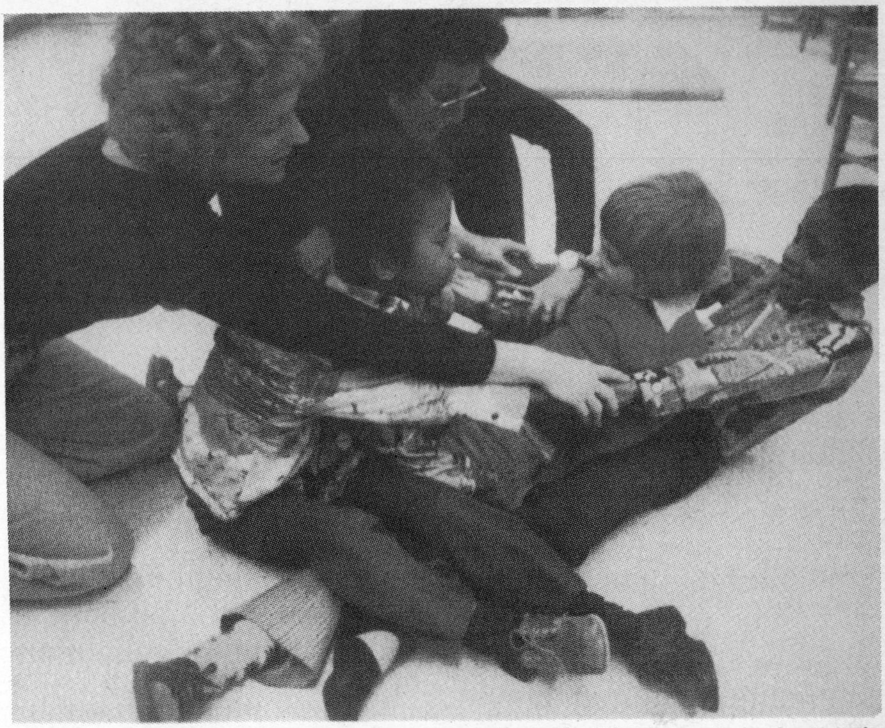

Teachers Virginia Bell and Jessica Bornstein remind the boys to look at each other while playing "Row your Boat." Such games help them become more aware of, and get pleasure from, their bodies.

symptoms of autism; and though they ranged in age from four to nine, they were linguistic infants, with no intelligible speech. The usual prognosis for such children is life in an institution.

One of the stars at the school was a child I'll call Mike, an appealing little boy with a sweet smile and flashing brown eyes. In 1971, when Mike was five, he appeared to be severely retarded. No one knew his IQ because he was considered untestable. Linguistically he was like a 19-month-old toddler. Within three years Mike learned to sign and to speak. On a test of language skill, he scored at the level of a five-year-old, which means that he had mastered the basic features of his language. (Language development after five is largely a matter of adding new words and putting the finishing touches on grammatical competence.) His IQ was in the low-normal range, and he was able to transfer to a learning-disabilities class in a public school.

When Mike entered the program, he was the sort of autistic child who is apathetic, who goes limp as soon as an adult tries to reach him. His friend Robbie, on the other hand, was hyperactive. He threw frequent temper tantrums, and cried constantly. Sometimes he chewed on his hand. At the age of three, Robbie could understand about as much as a 10-month-old infant. Like Mike, Robbie eventually learned both to sign and to speak. Before he left the program, he scored a whopping 105 on a nonverbal IQ test, above the average for a normal child his age.

The first step in treating an autistic child is to get him to pay attention to you. The therapist orders the child to "Look at me." At the same time, she makes the corresponding sign slowly and deliberately. Her manner is intrusive; in effect, she is telling the child, "I'm here, and you'd sure better know it." If the child meets the therapist's eyes, he gets praised, verbally and in sign language. He may also get a tickle, or a tender pat. If the child does not respond, the therapist gently guides his head to the desired position and repeats the order.

Learning the First Label. The first signs the child learns to make himself are related to his personal needs and desires—for food, toys and activities. One child may begin by learning the sign for candy, or potato chip, while another learns the sign for ball, or toy car. If the child is unable to imitate the sign, the therapist puts his hands into the correct configuration, then gradually withdraws this help. She does not insist on perfect ex-

(Above) Parents also learn the sign language, and help teach their children to use it. Here, a mother teaches her son to make the sign for "peanut." Shaping his hand with hers, she says and signs the word. When he succeeds in signing the word without physical prompting, she rewards him with the peanut and a delighted kiss.

ecution of the sign.

It's surprising how quickly some of the children learn their first label. Paul, a child of six, was a dropout from a program that stressed verbal imitation. He could produce some guttural sounds, but no meaningful speech. During his first visit to the school, Paul noticed some cookies and decided he had to have one. An alert therapist seized the opportunity, insisting that he make the sign for cookie. Paul had never seen a sign before: he tried to get around the therapist and steal the cookie. She persisted. Within 10 minutes, this mute, severely disturbed child had mastered his first sign. The next morning he awakened his mother, hauled her over to the cupboard, and made the sign for cookie. Though his sign was not quite right, his mother recognized it and promptly rewarded him with a cookie.

Once they have a few labels, the children are ready to learn to respond to the question, "What do you want?" and to put signs together in short phrases and sentences. Some children respond to the question at the very first session, while others take months. Eventually, all the children are able to put signs together in combinations they have never seen demonstrated before—a sure indication that they are internalizing the rules of the language. After a while, some even start to correct the signs of their classmates and parents. Their signing may be a bit slow, like the speech of an adult learning a foreign tongue, but it is language.

As the children begin to join the rest of humanity, they become more responsive to smiles, hugs and praise. Unlike most autistic children, they also learn to give praise by applauding the accomplishments of their fellow students. This is no accident; at the David School there is constant emphasis on group experience and group approval. The children are encouraged to touch and wrestle with each other (increasing their body awareness, in the process), to play circle games, and to sign among themselves. Creedon is highly critical of behavior-modification programs that rely solely on the one-to-one relationship between child and therapist. If the goal is to get the children to relate to others, then relating is what you must teach. Only then will the children realize that communication is its own reward. "We don't want these kids talking for M&Ms all their lives," says Creedon.

Mindless Imitation. The spontaneous development of speech is always welcomed and rewarded at the school, but communication, not speech, is the goal. It is wrongheaded, Creedon believes, to concentrate on the mindless imitation of sounds, syllables and words, as many therapies do, when success is reachable by another route.

She cites the case of Larry, one of her early students. At the age of four, Larry seemed profoundly retarded. He had the language ability of a four-month-old, and spent most of his time spinning a little nut in front of his eyes. Yet, after a couple of years of treatment, Larry showed one of the largest gains in IQ of any student, and developed one of the most extensive vocabularies in sign. He came out with sentences like, "I want to have help with (the) zipper" and, "It is time to work with Bonnie." As his language improved, his self-stimulating became less frequent, until he was able to behave appropriately in the classroom about 80 percent of the time. Larry still has no speech—the only sounds he makes are unpleasant screeches—but that hardly seems to diminish his victory.

"Jacket Is Sick." Once they have sign language, autistic children find they've got the whole world in their hands. For the first time, they can ask questions when they're confused. They can label their own creations. They can tell their parents when they are hungry or feel under the weather, or need to go to the bathroom. They can say when they are annoyed or amused, and can criticize others, ("George is silly"; "John is a baby"). Like normal children, they can juggle a limited vocabulary to make their needs known. For instance, what do you do when the zipper of your jacket is broken, and you can't sign either "zipper" or "broken?" One child's solution was, "Jacket is sick." They can even use their new language to control their own behavior. Robbie was once caught on videotape ordering himself to "Stop, stop!" after Mike signalled that he had had enough roughhousing for a while. Another boy was observed telling himself to sit down.

In short, sign language allows the child to grow both socially and intellectually. But just why sign is so successful remains a mystery, as does autism itself. The simplest explanation is that autistic children have some sort of language deficit, and need all the language cues they can get. By both talking and signing, you multiply your chances of getting through to them. As Creedon observes, "The children feel, see and hear the language when we use simultaneous communication."

But the opposite may also be true—sign language may work because it allows the child to attend to one mode of communication—the visual—at a time. Many autistic children seem to have trouble processing verbal and visual information all at once. "It is very often the case," says Lovaas, "that if they see

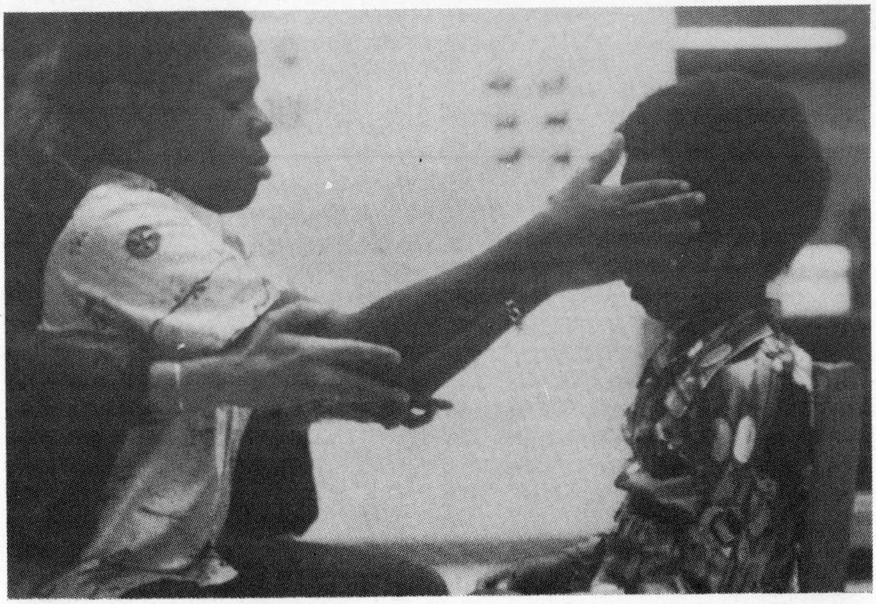

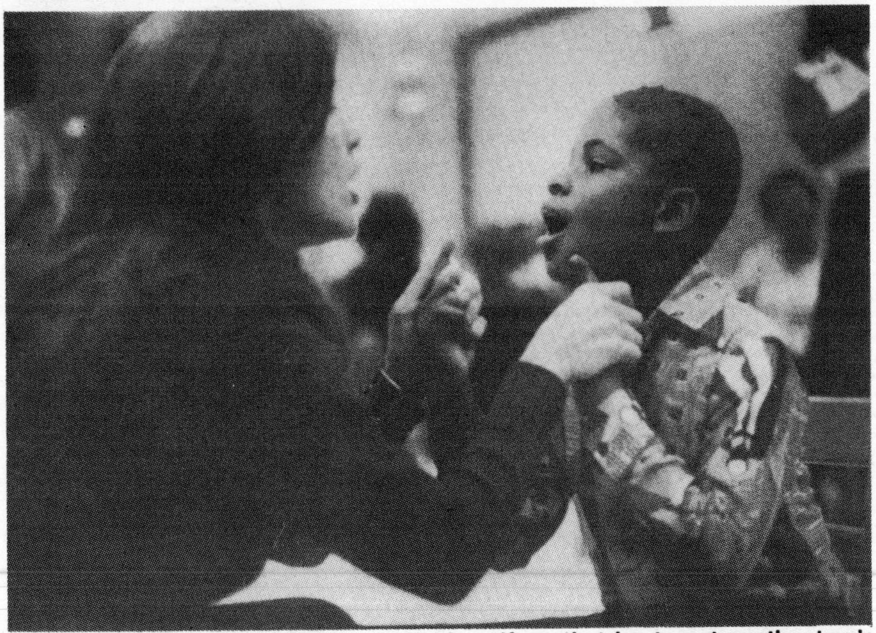

(Above) A child just learning to speak himself gently tries to get another boy's attention. By helping each other learn, the children begin to realize their need for one another. (Below) Recognizing and communicating feelings are essential to further development. Here, teacher Candy Haight shapes the child's hands into the sign that enables him to express his feeling of utter frustration.

you they do not hear you, and if they hear you they do not see you"—a case of overly concentrated concentration [see "A Conversation With Ivar Lovaas," *pt*, January 1974]. Psychologist Bernard Rimland, the founder of the National Society for Autistic Children and a sort of one-man clearing house for data on autism, makes a similar point. Research shows that autistic children tend to have highly intelligent parents. Perhaps, Rimland speculates, they have inherited too much of a good thing—the ability to focus attention selectively. This ability, normally a useful one, becomes a cognitive straitjacket for the autistic child.

The theory of overly selective attention makes a good deal of sense. A child who could not handle all the messages coming at him from a speaker's face, body, hands and voice might very well react by filtering out all sources of stimulation but one. If that source were visual, he literally would not hear the speaker's voice. Because all of his energy was directed toward reducing the amount of information to be processed, the child would become rigid and would insist that the environment stay always the same. Some autistic children are so inflexible that they cannot tolerate a magazine or ash tray out of place. Locked in a silent cage of his own making, such a child might turn to self-stimulation, either out of frustration at his inability to communicate or because there was nothing better to do. Even normal children self-stimulate when they're bored. Constant self-stimulation, however, gets in the way of all other stimulation, and the stage is set for a vicious circle.

Bewildering Reality. If this view is correct, it explains why autistic children in many ways resemble young deaf-blind children. For the deaf-blind, too, reality is at first confused and bewildering. Helen Keller, you may recall, threw terrible temper tantrums and generally made life miserable for her parents before Anne Sullivan introduced her to sign language for the deaf.

Another possibility raised by Rimland is that autistic children are deficient in skills handled by the left hemisphere of the brain, the side responsible for processing sequential auditory input, e.g., speech. They are usually better, he notes, at musical and spatial tasks, which are associated with the right hemisphere. Sign language, then, may work because it capitalizes on the stronger half of the child's brain. Unlike speech, which consists of sounds strung out sequentially like pearls on a string, sign language expresses meanings by the simultaneous combination of hand positions and movements in space. And it is visual instead of auditory. Says Rimland, "Our view of the ultimate capabilities of autistic children may have been unduly pessimistic as a result of our failure to recognize the hidden assets of their heretofore silent hemisphere."

Pointing, Nodding, Shrugging. At the University of Oregon, Benson Schaeffer, George Kollinzas, Arlene Musil and Peter McDowell have taught three autistic boys to use both signs and words. They believe autism is primarily an inability to deal with abstract linguistic symbols, and they suggest that sign language is effective because gesture serves as a natural bridge between a child's intended meaning and language. Normal children seem to rely heavily on pointing, nodding, shrugging, and other gestures before they learn to speak. Though sign language is much more complicated than simple gesturing, it does make use of some basic gestures, and thus may be less overwhelming than speech to a child who has difficulty with language. Once the bridge has been crossed, some children are then ready for the spoken word.

Fortunately, autistic children do not have to wait for the theorists to explain the power of sign. There are now scores of public and private programs that use simultaneous communication with children labeled either autistic or retarded. These programs use different forms of sign language and different techniques, and have varying philosophies. By measuring their degree of success, researchers should be able to identify the features of sign therapy that are critical. For autistic children and their parents, that's a hopeful sign, indeed.

For further information read:

Rimland, Bernard, *Infantile Autism.* Appleton-Century-Croft, 1964. $11.95.
Creedon, Margaret P., ed. *Appropriate Behavior Through Communication: A New Program in Simultaneous Language,* 1975, available through Dysfunctioning Child Center, 2915 Ellis, Chicago, Illinois 60616. $10.00.
Creedon, Margaret P., "Language Development in Non-Verbal Autistic Children Using a Simultaneous Communication System," paper presented to Society for Research in Child Development, Philadelphia. March 31, 1973. Available from EDRS, Leasco Information Products, 4827 Rugby Ave., Bethesda, Md 20014. Reprint No. ED 078624 in microfiche and hard copy.
Rimland, Bernard, "Where Does Research Lead," Proceedings of the 1975 Annual Meeting of the National Society for Autistic Children, San Diego, June 1975. Available through National Society for Autistic Children, 169 Tampa Ave., Albany, N.Y. 11208
Schaeffer, Bernard, George Kollinzas, Arlene Musil and Peter McDowell. "Signed Speech. A New Treatment for Autism." paper presented at the annual meeting of the National Society for Autistic Children, San Diego 1975.

Why Can't Bobby Sit Still?

NANCY C. BAKER

Nancy C. Baker, a freelance writer, specializes in subjects concerning children and the family. She teaches journalism at California State University, Northridge, and is currently writing a book for Vanguard Press.

During naptime at his day care center, Bobby is the child who never sleeps. He spends that time fidgeting on his cot, humming and talking, and annoying the other children.

On center outings, Bobby is the one who disappears the minute the teacher's back is turned. He's the one who's found hanging by his knees from the top of the swing set, who leaps off the jungle gym without thinking. He's the child who impulsively grabs a toy away from another child and then is mystified when his actions make him unpopular.

Though Bobby has at least normal intelligence, he doesn't seem to learn—either academic things such as his alphabet or numbers, or social behavior such as obeying the teacher and making friends with the other children.

Nobody likes Bobby very well, least of all Bobby himself.

Until a few years ago, a youngster like Bobby was usually labelled a troublemaker, a bad boy, a child in need of a good spanking. His teachers and parents were blamed for their lack of control over him, and they carried around a load of guilt as a result.

But today, research has shown that Bobby's problem may not be a lack of parental or school discipline or simply a poor disposition, but a medical syndrome known as hyperactivity. This condition has also been called hyperkinesis, minimal brain dysfunction and learning disability. Unfortunately, there is no one term that correctly describes the complete syndrome.

No one really knows what causes a certain child to be hyperactive, but most theories now state that he is born this way. The condition is physiological in origin, not psychological, and is not caused by either neglect or overindulgence, though they can irritate and magnify the behavior.

Hyperactivity is not an uncommon problem. Dr. James Satterfield, a leading researcher in the field, estimates that it affects five percent of all children under 12. It is from three to nine times more common in boys than in girls.

It is somewhat more difficult to recognize and diagnose hyperactivity in preschoolers than in older children, but not impossible. The reason for this is that "any normal 5-year-old is more active than a normal 6- or 7-year-old," Dr. Satterfield explains. However, level of activity is only one of the symptoms of the disorder.

Dr. Satterfield has spent the last eight years researching hyperactivity at Gateways Hospital Hyperkinetic Clinic in Los Angeles and has diagnosed and treated more than 1,000 children with the syndrome. He says there are four major symptoms of hyperactivity.

The first, as the name suggests, is excessive motor activity. This might include constant fidgeting, bothering other children by poking at them, crawling around the room at inappropriate times, the inability to sit at the table through an entire meal, etc. This is why Bobby can't nap like the other children.

Second is a poor attention span. "This actually is more a core symptom than excessive motor activity," Dr. Satterfield said. "These children are not able to selectively attend in a learning situation. Some are so distractible that they often don't even know what's going on in the classroom."

Included in the problems caused by poor attention span is the inability to finish projects and forgetfulness. Timmy is an example. His teacher has told him a dozen times to put on his snowsuit and boots, that it's time to go home. He repeatedly begins the task, only to be distracted by something else. When the teacher returns to him, Timmy is playing or talking, the snowsuit forgotten on the floor. She loses patience with him and becomes angry. Timmy decides the teacher does not like him. He can't do anything right. He must be a bad boy.

The third symptom is impulsivity. Dr. Satterfield explained, "The normal child would stop and think of consequences before jumping into a deep pool if he can't swim or riding his tricycle into traffic, but these children don't have normal fears. They will also hit another child, not intending to hurt him, but they lack restraint."

They talk impulsively, too, speaking out in the middle of a class or storytime. It is as if there were no

"Why Can't Bobby Sit Still?" by Nancy C. Baker, *Day Care and Early Education,* May/June 1977. Copyright 1977 by Human Sciences Press.

reaction time between when the child thinks of an action and his performance of it.

The fourth symptom is irritability. For example, it seems that some days there is just no pleasing Joey. His class is baking the cookies he loved last month, but today he reacts as though the event were planned solely to make him miserable. Other times he may cry for an hour because a favorite TV show is over and he won't see it until next week. He overreacts.

Other symptoms of hyperactivity include learning and perceptual difficulties and social aggressiveness.

A given child may be hyperactive and not have all these symptoms. Or, he may have some symptoms on one day and others on another. Professional diagnosis is needed.

Most hyperactives are not diagnosed before they reach elementary school. One reason for this is that they may be at home enjoying the full attention of their mothers until that time. For some unknown reason, they do much better on a one-to-one basis than they do in groups. "If they could go through school that way," Dr. Satterfield said, "they'd probably be all right."

Another reason is that they are at their worst in a situation where they are expected to sit quietly and pay attention. This often doesn't occur until elementary school.

But there is one important reason why it is to the child's advantage to be diagnosed and treated earlier. While the hyperactivity itself is a medical problem, it often does not take long for the child to develop an overlaying layer of emotional problems.

Bobby soon realizes that he's different from other children and that this difference makes him unpopular. He is forever being criticized. His mother and father constantly compare him to his siblings, who don't have his problems. Bobby learns early that he is a failure. He then begins tasks expecting to fail at them. Pretty soon he doesn't even try. When he becomes a teenager, he may well become delinquent if he is not helped. He almost surely will be an academic failure. The earlier Bobby and children like him receive help with their problems, the easier it will be either to overcome what emotional damage has been done or to prevent such damage.

Many of the symptoms of hyperactivity are observable in very young children. Among parents surveyed in the Gateways Hospital research, most said they first noticed this child was different by the time he began to walk. More than half said the following traits were observable in their hyperactive youngsters before age 5: "more active than siblings," "fidgety," "into things that don't concern him," "low frustration tolerance," "irritable and quick-tempered," "can't take no for an answer," "can't take correction," "has trouble completing projects," and "doesn't listen."

Almost any child has times when he or she fits one or more of the symptoms of hyperactivity. This is one of the problems in correctly diagnosing the syndrome. But, Dr. Paul H. Wender of the National Institute of Mental Health and Johns Hopkins Hospital says the difference is in the "*intensity,* the *persistence* and the *patterning* of these symptoms" in the hyperactive child. The author of *The Hyperactive Child,* he says that hyperactivity is the single most common behavioral disorder seen by child psychiatrists.

Yet, Dr. Satterfield says that "it's almost criminal that there's this group of children who could be helped, who will become serious risks in their teens if they're not helped, and 80 to 90 percent of them don't get any treatment at all." He cites current research on a group of untreated hyperactives in their mid-teens. Three-quarters of this untreated group were academic failures by this age and one-quarter were seriously delinquent.

Clearly, then, help at the earliest possible age is what is best for the child, his school, his family and society.

What help is available for hyperactives? Here the picture becomes a bit cloudier, for there is some disagreement on what treatment is most effective.

The first step is to have the condition diagnosed correctly. This might be spurred by the day care teacher's talking to the child's parents and relating her observations of his behavior and her suspicions that he might be hyperactive.

Unfortunately, many areas of the country do not have ideal facilities for diagnosing and treating hyperactives, so the parents may have to do some detective work to get the help their child needs.

Dr. Satterfield says that a minimal diagnostic evaluation should include psychiatric, psychometric and psychosocial evaluations.

The psychiatric evaluation is done to rule out serious psychiatric disorders which might cause the behavior or to find any additional disorders which might be present in addition to hyperactivity. "What we find are about 10 percent with serious psychiatric illness in addition to their hyperactivity problems," he said. "Some are borderline psychotics and some are very seriously depressed."

The psychometric evaluation will identify several different learning disabilities the child may have. "The majority have some learning disability," Dr. Satterfield has found. "Some may also be very bright, but could be doing much better than they are." Tests of both intelligence and achievement should be given.

The psychosocial evaluation is to determine the child's home life and background. It could be part of the psychiatric evaluation. "Many of these children are from chaotic homes," Dr. Satterfield said. "The parents say they have tried everything with this child and nothing works. I have encountered mothers who are ready to give up and have the child placed in an institution."

A neurological examination is recommended only for children who have additional evidence of neurological problems. A routine EEG on all children is of little or no value. Dr. Satterfield said, "Twenty to 40 percent of these children have an abnormal EEG in that it is like that of a younger child, but that doesn't help manage the treatment."

Gateways' own evaluation process also includes extensive questionnaires filled out by parents and teachers and a staff psychiatrist's interview of parents and child.

Since most cities do not yet have a clinic specializing in hyperactivity, one way to find help might be to call the nearest major university. Dr. Satterfield recommends talking to both the psychiatric outpatient clinic and the pediatric clinic there and asking to speak to someone familiar with the syndrome. A parent may have to seek his evaluations separately if no one place can do the whole job in his town.

"Many pediatricians find it difficult to manage a hyperactive child due to their busy practices and the many non-medical aspects of this disorder (educational, emotional and psychiatric). Look for a physician who is open-minded and knows all the treatment approaches and is willing to try them all," Dr. Satterfield said.

He recommends a trial with stimulant drugs for most hyperactives and says this helps about 70 percent. But, he warns, "Proper use of medication is not as easy as it seems. The medication has to be carefully monitored for proper amount and possible side effects."

Unfortunately, the idea of medicating children with stimulants has received a great deal of adverse publicity in the past few years. Dr. Satterfield says that one negative side effect uncovered by research is evidence the growth rate of children on stimulants is slowed somewhat. "We don't know yet if this effect occurs only during the first year of treatment or is ongoing," he said.

As for the danger of future drug addiction, Dr. Satterfield says that the risk of a hyperactive child's becoming a drug addict as a teenager if his condition is left untreated is probably greater than if he had been treated properly with stimulants. In the small doses used by informed physicians and when prescribed for truly hyperactive children, the danger of later drug abuse is minimal.

It is not fully known why stimulant medications work in hyperactive children, but Dr. Satterfield has a theory. "We like to use a car analogy. These children are like a car going at full speed with faulty brakes. We think that stimulant medication stimulates the brakes so the child is able to slow down."

The medication by itself does not improve the child's behavior, though. It merely gives him the ability to control himself. He still must want to be good and most hyperactives do. So the correct medication can be a large first step in the right direction for many.

Gateways Hospital sees hyperactives as multi-handicapped children. "For the underlying disorder of the nervous system, medication is the treatment of choice," Dr. Satterfield says, "but no one treatment can solve all his problems. If he is behind in school, he will need special education. And medication won't solve his emotional problems, so he may need help for them, too."

Gateways has had success with a combination of medication, behavioral modification techniques and special education and psychiatry where indicated.

Research has shown that behavioral modification techniques alone have been no more effective than medication alone, Dr. Satterfield said, and psychotherapy alone has been found to be relatively ineffective.

Dr. Ben F. Feingold of the Kaiser Research Institute in San Francisco has developed a unique course of treatment. He theorizes that many hyperactives (perhaps between 40 and 70 percent, he says) have developed the condition because of food additives, specifically artificial colors and flavors and the preservative, BHT. He also includes aspirin and some natural foods on his list of items which must be excluded from the diet of hyperactive children.

He thinks that the tendency to hyperactivity is inborn and that "if infants are given such things as baby vitamin drops and colored, flavored medicines shortly after birth, the hyperactivity will come to the surface early."

Dr. Feingold is the author of *Why Your Child is Hyperactive*, in which he describes his diet. Since the book's publication in 1975, he has added BHT to the list of forbidden additives and foods.

Though he says that the diet is easy to follow, in practice it takes a good deal of effort and dedication. Foods without additives are difficult to find and in many cases manufacturers are not even required to list the food's ingredients on the package. (Dr. Feingold advocates better labelling and hopes to get food manufacturers to adopt a logo he has designed to identify their products as additive-free.) Such items as toothpaste and mouthwash must be homemade or purchased in health food stores and medicines for children pose a special problem as almost all are artificially colored or flavored. Perhaps worst of all, most foods heavily advertised to children are packed with additives.

If, however, Dr. Feingold is right and a special diet can lift the curse of hyperactivity from some children, the effort to give them that special diet would be well made. He says that it would also be worthwhile for a school or day care facility to offer the diet.

Though some physicians say the Feingold diet is a waste of time and that its worth has not yet been proven, none claim that there can be any bad effects from using it. In fact, children on the diet are likely to receive improved nutrition.

An association of parents groups has been formed in support of the theory and may be contacted at the Feingold Association of the United States, 759 National Press Bldg., Washington, D.C. 20045.

Gateways Hospital has not yet tried the Feingold diet on its patients because staff there feel its worth has not yet been proven. Dr. Satterfield expects, however, that responsible research proving whether or not the diet is helpful to hyperactives should be completed within a year.

Hyperactives, like all children but to an even greater degree, respond to a system of rewards better than to punishments. In fact, too much punishment merely spurs on the emotional damage and self-image problems to which these children are prone.

Using a system of rewards for accomplishments of which the child is capable allows him to taste success and improve his self-image. For example, 5-year-old Brian's parents prepared a chart for him. He received a gold star for each night he came to the dinner table with no more than two reminders. At the end of the week, if he had earned at least five stars, he was entitled to a treat—a small toy or inexpensive outing. When he had conquered this problem, a second task was added to the chart. Soon Brian was succeeding in behavior that had caused conflict in his family for years. Similar behavior modification techniques could be adapted for use in a classroom situation or day care center.

The program should be structured so that the child has the freedom to be active. If Billy can't sit still as long as the other children, don't expect him to.

Flexibility is also very important. If Bobby can't take a nap and he bothers the children who can, then perhaps he should be allowed to play by himself in another room during naptime. Trying to force him to do something he cannot will only make everyone miserable.

The bright spot in this picture of children victimized by their faulty nervous systems is that now they can be helped. With proper management of the problem, hyperactives can grow up to be normal, productive adults with strong self-images. But it takes alert teachers and parents and informed physicians to help these children realize their potential. Their alternative is a future of classroom disruption, social ostracism, educational failure and, possibly, delinquency.

Hyperactive children don't want to cause trouble. They want—and desperately need—someone to understand and to help.

Battle Lines in the Ritalin War

;ONNIE BRUCK

For a long time, the schools had labeled hyperactive children nd dosed them with Ritalin. And nost parents, trusting the system, vent along with it. It took a while o see where it was all headed—lown a road paved with such good ntentions.

Connie Bruck is a frequent conributor to HUMAN BEHAVIOR. She recently profiled psychologist 'hilip Zimbardo.

When Interstate 5 drops down from e eagle aeries and dust storms of the ehachapi Mountains into the sudden tillness, the sun-baked flatlands of the an Joaquin Valley, Southern Califoria is left behind. Only 100 miles north f Los Angeles, the freeway heads toard the town of Taft by crossing the Maricopa flats." It is a stark expanse vhere blackened rigs go up and down in reless, hypnotic obeisance to the oilich earth, while migrants work the ows upon rows of wooden crosses vound with gnarled grapevines. And it eems as if the present is rapidly recedng into the past, when geographical arriers such as the Tehachapis really lid mean separate worlds. I have been raveling this route lately because there s an idea whose time has come—the yperkinetic behavior syndrome and ts treatment with stimulant drugs. It ame with such quiet but all-encomassing power in Taft that it finally riggered a civil suit, the first to emerge n what is a growing national controersy. Filed by the Youth Law Center of San Francisco, the class-action suit rought on behalf of 18 schoolchildren gainst the Taft City School District harges that school authorities coerced hildren into taking the psychoactive lrug Ritalin as a condition of attending chool. The suit also charges that chilren were placed in classes for the mentally retarded without the knowledge or consent of their parents.

It is odd in a way to think that the first hard, unified stand against this medical incursion upon individual freedoms should be taken in such a remote oilfield town. Taft hardly has a history of taking such civil liberties seriously. It emerged briefly into the national eye last spring, when 13 black athletes from Taft College had to be escorted by police to safety in Bakersfield—an incident replete with nostalgia for those elderly Taftians who can recall the town's Ku Klux Klan chapter in its hooded heyday; and a billboard warning "Don't Let The Sun Set On You, Nigger" is said to have been taken down just a few years back. The prejudice that rides so easy and high in Taft, however, is not only racist but the expression of an insularity that maintains indifference and distrust towards any outsider. Most of the people in that tightly knit town of 18,000 were born there. Most will tell you how their forefathers arrived in Kern County in covered wagons. Most do not leave even on holiday. Clannish and proud, the children of fourth- and fifth-generation Taftians are still marrying one another in sacramental ceremony and sending their offspring to be taught by the teachers of their youth. The men are drilling the same Midway-Sunset oilfields their fathers drilled before them.

But Taft is not hermetically sealed. Should some fashion of the day find its way in, it could flourish unchecked in such an inbred and self-contained place. So, like the cultured pathogen, one grew and grew until finally, on September 8, 1975, a suit—*Benskin et al. vs. Taft City School District et al.*—was filed. It was not an act that came easily to the plaintiff parents. Most of them are very poor, some can neither read nor write and, in attempted negotiations with the school board in past months, it had been hard for them to even voice their plaint. "We're pretty much a group of people who never stood up for anything in our lives," one would say later—and here they were calling into question the practices of more educated people, an upper class of teachers, principals, a superintendent, a physician. They had had to fight back that universal urge, aroused by merely entering a school building—even after a 20-year absence—to whisper, to tread softly, to show respectful obedience before the authorities of their youth.

But as they had repeatedly reminded one another, these were *their* schools, responsible for teaching *their* children, and better than they had been taught. Above all, these were their children. If they couldn't stand up for them, what would they fight for, ever? As their commitment and solidarity grew, their sense of impotence began to fall away. They would do this, they decided, not only for their own children but for others in Taft, in all of Kern County, in big cities and small towns all across the country. They would do it for children everywhere.

* * *

The classical description in medical literature of a hyperkinetic is that rare individual—one in 2,000, according to a 1970 British study that concluded it is a "decidedly uncommon disorder"—who appears driven by an "inner tornado," with activity completely beyond control. This, however, is not what we are talking about in the vast majority of contemporary cases. The labels are myriad because the entity is unknown; it is referred to alternately as cerebral dysfunction, hyperkinesis, minimal brain dysfunction (MBD), learning disability (LD), hyperactivity, organic behavior disorder. There are no universally accepted symptoms, no anatomical or biochemical characteristics that can be discerned through examination. Yet, according to more conservative estimates, roughly 10 percent of American school-age children are affected; and from 500,000 to 1,000,000 children

From *Human Behavior,* August 1976. Copyright © 1976 *Human Behavior* Magazine. Reprinted by permission.

are taking stimulant medication—not as cure but as treatment—until adolescence, when the malady is generally thought to be overcome.

Probably the most popular current catchall term is MBD, said to cause hyperkinesis that in turn causes learning disability and, if not treated—according to hard-line true believers—leads to juvenile delinquency, divorce, economic failure, criminal deviance. The shift from the medical to the social realm occurs with beguiling ease, because what we are talking about from start to finish is behavior. The groundwork for MBD seems to have been laid in the '20s, when a behavioral syndrome—including hyperkinesis, distractibility, short attention span, impulsivity and poor coordination—was noted in children recovering from encephalitis. Over the years, the circular notion took hold that this syndrome must in itself indicate brain damage, and labels such as "minimal cerebral injury" and "minimal brain damage behavior syndrome" were coined. It was not until the '60s, however, that medical journals and drug companies' advertisements began to reflect and stimulate the growing interest in what was deescalated to the least specific and alarming label yet: minimal brain dysfunction.

By 1966, a national task force headed by Sam D. Clements of the University of Arkansas Medical Center produced a report that is still the disease's key legitimizing document—a kind of patent to be shared. Although the team conceded that "from the purist point of view," MBD was "in most instances an unproven, presumptive diagnosis," they went on to deliver the following definition: children with MBD are those "of near average, average or above average general intelligence with certain learning or behavioral disabilities ranging from mild to severe, which are associated with deviations of function of the central nervous system. These deviations may manifest themselves by various combinations of impairment in perception, conceptualization, language, memory and control of attention, impulse or motor function."

Among its 99 most prevalent "symptoms" were: "hyperkinesis," or its opposite, "hypokinesis"; "general awkwardness"; "low tolerance for frustration"; "reading disabilities"; "spelling disabilities"; "arithmetic disabilities"; "easy fatigability"; "physically immature, or physical development normal or advanced for age"; "possibly negative and aggressive to authority"; "sensitive to others."

The report was a "sophisticated statement of ignorance," wrote Lester Grimspoon and Susan B. Singer in 1974, in their comprehensive study of literature on hyperkinesis and its treatment with amphetamines, published in the *Harvard Educational Review*. They warned that there is still no consensus among experts about the nature of the supposed syndrome, and that the possibility of amphetamines producing adverse or toxic physiological damage over the years is very real. "Before scientists have had a chance to systematically study and refine the issue," conclude Grimspoon and Singer, "the field has become the domain of educators and the drug industry."

And this pseudoscientific abuse is no lone aberration, argue Diane Divoky and Peter Schrag, coauthors of the well-researched *Myth of the Hyperactive Child*. They feel it is just one more component in a growing technology of social control, including the use of drugs, psychological testing, data banks, "predelinquency screening," behavior modification. Gone are most of the corporal punishments and expulsions of yesteryear, as well as the '60s' commitment to change disabled and disabling institutions. In their place in these brave new '70s, they point out, comes an ideology of early intervention and therapy that translates nonconformity into medical illness and makes the *individual* the target of remediation—through chemical management.

* * *

Divoky and Schrag has become a household phrase at the Montoyas' home in Taft where parents first began to gather and consider the source of their common trouble. Theirs is a median neighborhood, neither the homogenized respectability of Taft Heights nor the real squalor of South Taft, with its ramshackle one-room dwellings where many of the families in the suit live. The Montoyas' house is small and spare, as are the others on its dusty street, with no sidewalks but for one proud homeowner who laid his own, and a huge oil storage tank overlooking the dead end. Diane Montoya, a dark-haired, expressive woman in her early 30s, offered me coffee in delicate rose-printed cups and spoke about how she appreciates Divoky and Schrag's book, how it has given a stamp of authenticity to her experience. For even though she and another woman, Juanita Morrison, did all the organizing, and she has lived this conflict day and night for the past year, still it often seems like a dream—and all the small jigsaw pieces she has put together so many times must be examined and touched, then fit into the same oppressive shape once more.

It all began in 1971, when her son Frank's kindergarten teacher began complaining that he was withdrawn, given to staring off into space. The Montoyas were called for a conference at which their family doctor, Agnes Tarr—who was also school physician and the town's only pediatrician—said Frank wasn't keeping up with his peers because he was hyperactive; and unless he took Ritalin, he would not learn. Diane Montoya remembers being reassured there were no adverse side effects to the drug, no long-range hazards; nevertheless, she and her husband were upset at the thought of their son being medicated. But both Diane and Frank Montoya had attended parochial schools—she in Bakersfield, he in Taft—where the nuns, their teachers, were vested with divine authority. They were not given to questioning authority, even in these more secular agents. Looking back, Diane Montoya is angry to think of her sweet submissiveness, her childlike docility that always won her a smile and a pat on the head from her children's teachers, their principal, their doctor. However, she registers this sole defense for her, and the other parents', naiveté: "Who are you to believe in, if not your school and the doctor who's taken care of your kids from the time they were born?"

So Frank took his Ritalin, but he did not learn. Research indicates that Ritalin does not in fact increase learning but does make the child more manageable. Manageable, Frank spent two years in kindergarten, then moved on to a class for the "educationally handicapped" (EH). By this time, his brother Joe had started school. (Now seven, Joe is a bright, eager little boy, who immediately pulled me outside to display and recite the names of a dozen varieties of cacti he found in the Mojave. "He doesn't know a stranger," Diane Montoya says, laughing in her own oblique way.) But Joe's impetuous curiosity was not so appreciated at school. Phone calls from an irate teacher began: Joe had gone out for a drink of water without permission, he had removed a worm from a tree well and had refused to put it back. "The anxiety just mounts and mounts," says Montoya. "You know your kid's bright, but the teacher keeps saying he's a behavior problem, he won't learn."

Finally, in March of his kindergarten

ear, the teacher called with a solution: e should be on Ritalin. The Montoyas ere again called in to conference and ld that Joe could not sit still in class cause he was hyperactive; he needed talin to function in school. They now d two children on the drug. Their el-st, Donna, had somehow escaped—rhaps because hyperactivity is said occur four times more often in boys an girls, so school officials were less gilant with their female pupils. Then, o, by the time most little girls reach hool, their behavior has already been st into a decidedly nondisruptive, ost obliging mold.

Neither boy had any authorized diag-ostic exam, nor any follow-up exam ce they were on the drug. Even the ue believers in hyperkinesis insist the importance of a complete physi-al and neurological examination—if ly to rule out other problems—fol-wed by careful, regular monitoring ong with an individualized school d home program. In Taft, it was all uch less complicated. "That Ritalin as just little magic pills to help them arn, and it wasn't dangerous." Mon-ya paused, hearing herself. "How does happen? We're not *that* stupid—but I uess the days just kind of slid by. . . ."

Frank would sit listlessly for long eriods, cry easily, complain of leg ramps. Joe also had the cramps; so iane Montoya brought the boys to r. Tarr, suspecting they had Valley ever—a dust-borne fungus peculiar to he San Joaquin Valley. On another oc-asion, she told Tarr that Joe was acting trangely, his usual talkativeness sped p into an incessant chatter. Embar-assed by her own temerity, she halt-ngly mentioned that she'd read about a an Francisco allergist, Dr. Ben Fein-old, who has attracted a great deal of ttention with his claim that children laced on a special diet free of artificial olors and flavors showed a marked essening of their hyperactive behavior. Montoya recalls Tarr replying brusque-y that the diet approach was unproven, nd medication was still the safest and best treatment for hyperactivity.

Frank was *still* not learning, and school psychologist Bill Kent now ad-vised that he needed to be in a yet more special and individualized class. Mon-toya agreed, signing a form that author-ized Frank's placement in a "special education class for slow learners." But Frank started coming home from school in tears because kids had called him "retarded." It seemed to Montoya that the only thing special about the class was that nothing happened there; so she finally contacted Juanita Morrison, whose son was also in the class and on Ritalin for his hyperactivity.

That was the start. Having shared their anxieties, the two decided to talk to other parents with kids on the drug, which was easy enough. As Morrison says, "You can't find anyone in this town who doesn't either have a kid on it or know somebody who has." Donna Montoya knew that James Schaffer, with whom she walked to school, suf-fered frequent stomachaches and head-aches; his parents said he'd been on Ritalin for the past three years, ever since they were told it was the only way he could stay in school. His father had had a terrible motorcycle accident, in which he suffered slight brain dam-age and for a time knew no one, and shortly after that James began fighting every day on the playground. That he might have been traumatized by his father's condition was apparently not a consideration, and this child who would work intently for hours at a time building model planes was nonetheless declared hyperactive. His parents say they did not see him when he was on the drug, since he took it only on school mornings, not on weekends or vaca-tions—except for the one time they gave it to him on a trip to Arizona. The usually irrepressible James stared at the back of his father's head for the en-tire nine-hour drive. "He was like a zombie," says his mother. An evalua-tive team at UCLA's Neuropsychiatric Institute has since declared him (first of the children in the suit to be tested) decidedly *not* hyperactive.

Then there was Brian Fairhurst, who'd been on Ritalin for a week and had an epileptic seizure; and Eddie Reed, who'd been taking the drug for eight years, since he was three. One by one, the stories came in, and the reac-tions that had been brushed aside as growing pains or unrelated problems in the daily struggle to keep hard lives going came into focus. There was an-other, more subtle side effect, too; per-haps the most dangerous of all—the sense the children were getting that their behavior could only be directed by an external influence, that they could not develop and rely on their own inner controls. Anthony Morrison was in the habit of saying to his mother, "Give me a pill so I can be good and not fight."

Not every parent contacted was ready to even contemplate protest, however. Some were afraid. Some were just content to have their kids docile and the school happy. They exemplify what appears to be the hyperactivity phenomenon's true target population: middle-class parents who may be cava-lier about living on Librium and Valium themselves, overconcerned about their progeny's success in school as the first rung up the financial ladder, unpre-pared for the mammoth demands of child-raising and, ultimately, quite eager to have the whole burden of guilt lifted from them by the diagnosis of a medical—not emotional—problem.

By January 1975, the revelations be-gan to quicken. Aware of her daughter's distress, Diane Montoya's mother con-tacted attorney Suzanne Martinez in San Francisco at the Youth Law Center, and Martinez soon came down to Taft. She escorted Montoya and Morrison to see their children's records and found that the special class was for the "edu-cable mentally retarded" (EMR). Each child was so labeled in his records, so considered by his teacher, so taunted by other kids. The parents, school offi-cials would later claim, had been "spared the stigmatizing label." And the parents confirmed that Ritalin was indeed no magic pill. The *Physicians' Desk Reference (PDR)* warns, among other possible reactions, of loss of ap-petite, anorexia, nausea, abdominal pain, toxic psychosis, significant growth retardation. Ritalin is also said to lower the threshold for epileptic seizures.

The first confrontation with school officials was scheduled for March 19, which happened to be Frank Montoya's ninth birthday. In the early morning hours, he suffered his first grand mal epileptic seizure. Diane Montoya, at the hospital in Bakersfield, missed the meeting—but Morrison, her voice trembling with rage, declared, "If you don't stop giving Ritalin as a panacea for everything under the sun, you're going to kill a child! We want all these children examined to make sure they're hyperactive, and that Ritalin is the proper drug." The parents also charged that teachers had repeatedly told them their kids needed Ritalin, or higher dosages. Although Superintendent Gordon Cairns later told me that he had scolded teachers for this "time and time again," at the meeting he reportedly replied, "Don't you know a teacher would be fired if one told parents their child should be on Ritalin?" "You wouldn't have a teacher left!" Morrison shot back.

One month later, the parents pre-sented their demands—essentially ask-ing that the most flagrant disregard of their children's rights cease, by grant-ing them full information and choice of alternatives. As the demands were being read in the tense, overpacked auditorium, Juanita Morrison had a severe coronary and was rushed off in an ambulance. "These people don't stop at anything, do they?" a group of teachers was heard to chortle. (Morrison later died from a subsequent coronary.) And at the final meeting, Cairns simply read a legal opinion stating that their policies regarding the hyperactive and the retarded, as related by school authorities, were within the law, and added that there would be workshops on hyperactivity in the fall.

The matter was thus decorously laid to rest. But parents were hurt and raging mad to have been dismissed out of hand. And Suzanne Martinez was shocked. "The parents said that they were at fault, too, and they just wanted help—and the demands were *very* low-key. But the school board took them under submission for six weeks and somehow got frightened and polarized rather than being willing to change the situation. Had they been an urban, sophisticated school district," Martinez added, "I'm sure they would have."

So the 83-page complaint was drawn up. In legal litany, parents allege that they authorized no examinations of their children, that they were told their children needed Ritalin to stay in school, that the children suffered adverse reactions of which they had not been warned, that children unlawfully placed in EMR classes suffered stigma and ridicule and were deprived of their opportunity to learn. "The suit doesn't attack Ritalin per se," Martinez explains, "but the process of not giving parents the right to informed consent, the involvement of the school district in making decisions that ultimately belong only to the parent." They are moving for summary judgment on the EMR issue now, she added; the Ritalin issue will probably not come to trial for at least a year. Although their objective is to tighten up controls on the drug and remove schools from this sphere of influence, Martinez admits some ambivalence about what the suit will actually accomplish. "The fact is I'm afraid it may just teach other districts to be more careful. Still, I don't see how we could have passed up such a blatant situation, where people have been injured and there's a proposal to continue the violation."

She adds that one reason the suit does ask for damages—$250,000 for each wronged child—is that it is a tool to stop future school action. "If you sue the school principal for damages and the district has to pay, it has a remarkably prophylactic effect."

To many of the more well-to-do townspeople, of course, the motivation for the suit appears transparent enough—what could so strongly move these poor but the gilded dream of profit? To all the parents whom I have met, however, the idea of such sums—which would be put in trust for the children—seemed so foreign as to be immaterial. Rather, since they do not yet feel Martinez's doubts about the far-reaching efficacy of the suit, they are still warmed by that first flush of having stood against a common wrong—and of being passive pawns no more. They harbor a dawning belief that they can exert some measure of control in the world; and they feel in this effort "like brothers and sisters," suddenly related.

It brings back for a moment that erstwhile dream of America, fostered in classrooms of innocence with initial-carved wooden desks with inkwells, pencil grooves, a proper place for everything: this is a place where all men and women are equal—not because they are the same but because they are unique—with equal share of justice, and ready recourse for righting any wrongs. Part of that lesson was a lie, and part has been lately and perversely transmitted into an expectation that we all be the *same*—learning at the same rate, in the same way, behaving by the rule. Now if we deviate, we are no longer healthily diverse; we are LD, we have MBD, we are medically malfunctioning in some imperceptible but correctable way. Science must make us right.

On September 11, three days after the suit was filed, the first of the promised workshops on hyperactivity was held. The speaker was Dr. Leon Oettinger, the expert Ciba (manufacturer of Ritalin) brought along to testify before a senate committee of the California legislature in July 1974. Oettinger, who says he has specialized in the hyperkinetic behavior syndrome for 30 years, believes the syndrome may well extend past puberty into adulthood—he has grown-up patients who have been on stimulant drugs since they were children. He also told me that although he would not, 90 percent of the time he *could* diagnose MBD over the phone.

The second workshop was offered by Dr. Arnold Zukow, who is especially enthusiastic about spotting the hyperkinetic syndrome early (so as to avert the failure syndrome) and is confident about putting three-year-olds on Ritalin—despite the fact that even the drug company that makes it warns it is not
indicated for children under six. Abo
that, and possible adverse reactio
listed in *PDR*, Zukow says it is just ba
advertising. He suggests that we mu
rely on people such as Dr. Stanle
Adler, who has worked with so man
thousands of children.

The third speaker was Dr. Stanle
Adler—whose book *Your Overactiv*
Child: Normal or Not opens up a ne
genre of black humor—who empha
sizes that Ritalin may not be enoug
He hypothesizes a child who needs Ri
alin for his hyperactivity, Tofranil f
a bed-wetting problem, Stelazine
improve his self-image, and Dilanti
for seizures. In a list entitled, "Beha
ior That Teachers Should Watch for i
Preschool and Elementary-Level Chi
dren," the last six of 78 "signs" are: "i
ordinate interest in monsters; avoid
or resists physical contact; seeks ex
cessive physical contact; is not affe
tionate; lies, steals, deceives, sneak
habitually sits between back-turne
feet."

* * *

After sending her nurse forth to ob
tain my driver's license as a positive ID
then a sample of my published work
Dr. Agnes Tarr was ready to receiv
me. A diminutive woman, close to 7
with neatly marcelled, blonde-gra
hair and an imperious air, she sat ram
rod straight in her tiny office with va
Gogh's "Sunflowers" on the wall an
began to reminisce in East Coast ac
cents about the route that brought he
to such an unlikely place as Taft. Bor
and bred in Baltimore, Tarr attende
Goucher College and went on to John
Hopkins Medical School, with amb
tion altogether unorthodox for a wom
an in the 1930s. Then she transferred t
Stanford University because she ma
ried a "Stanford man" who in tur
wanted a private practice in a sma
town. She spent one last cosmopolita
year at Los Angeles Children's Hospit
and, in 1938, came to Taft to stay.

Unlike most Taftians, however, Tar
did leave town fairly often, to atten
medical conferences. There, in the earl
'60s, a new idea began to grow. "Ped
atric meetings were devoting whol
afternoons to hyperactivity," Tarr re
called. "And pretty soon, I realized tha
we had the hyperactive child right her
in our own classrooms."

It was an exciting, galvanizing no
tion—particularly for the town's onl
pediatrician, who was also the schoo
physician. School is the perfect labo
atory—a captive population, as it wer
—for the detection of this conditio
said to manifest itself most often i

that group situation. Teachers were requested to fill out forms listing children's behavior problems. "Hyperactive children are impulsive, aggressive, they talk out of turn—things that are normal at times but abnormal at others. We don't expect much in the first half of kindergarten, but toward the second, they have to get ready for a more regulated situation."

Tarr told me that teachers' and parents' input contributed greatly to her diagnosis. She also performed modified neurological exams, but the condition rarely showed up there. Had an examination ever given her the key? "Sometimes," Tarr replied. "Just recently I was examining a little girl of six when I was called out of the room for 15 minutes. When I returned, my nurse said, 'This child hasn't stopped talking the entire time.' "

She admitted that until this year, she never gave follow-up exams to the children on Ritalin. "Nothing in the literature gave me reason to feel that it was anything but a very safe drug," she said crisply. "Dr. Adler says it's safer than aspirin."

But what about the two children who had had seizures? What about the fact that *PDR* says it lowers the threshold for epileptic seizures? What about all the other possible reactions listed? "That is the only place I've ever seen mention of them," she retorted, "and we must go on the evidence of people like Adler and Zukow."

What became quite clear in the course of our interview was that Tarr remains convinced that she only did what was best for the children. The concept of accountability is alien to her. The judgment of such medical people as herself, Adler, Zukow and Oettinger is not to be questioned. Apparently disoriented in a time when doctors have begun to be demystified, and a consumer consciousness about overprescribed drugs is growing, Tarr finds the suit bewildering. "I just don't know what popped them off," she said. For Taft was Agnes Tarr's Africa; she dedicated herself to the children's health with a messianic fervor and maintained the colonialist's attitude toward their, and their parents', right to self-determination. When Diane Montoya asked her recently why she hadn't told her anything about the drug, or about Frank being labeled "mentally retarded," Tarr replied brusquely, "You wouldn't have done anything, anyway."

To the elite minority in Taft, Tarr apparently gave more credit, and more option. One parent she suggested I contact, Frank Hauff—"He s a gracious man, he owns his own business"—told a rather different story. He had a disabling career of school failure due to his own overactivity and constant punishment, and he hated seeing his energetic little boy begin to reenact that painful past. When Tarr said he needed Ritalin in kindergarten, Hauff refused; but the next fall, he acquiesced. The boy is doing better in school, Hauff said. And Tarr did warn them to watch him closely, especially for loss of appetite, and has done repeated follow-up exams. Was he sorry that Ritalin hadn't been available when *he* was a kid? Hauff frowned. He couldn't answer that. And he's not happy about the drug. But schools being what they are—no one's changed them yet—and jobs being hard to come by, he feels the more philosophical stand is a luxury that he, and his son, can't afford.

There are many others, Tarr said proudly, who will speak up for her. Now she was bustling off to a weekend medical conference in Palm Springs, but she wanted to add one last statement: "We thought we were doing something to help these children, and we're unhappy now that many of the teachers and principals are shaky about mentioning an overactive child. But maybe," she brightened, "this will all die down, and we can go on with it."

When I had phoned school psychologist Bill Kent for an interview, his voice shook and he instantly threatened to sue if he were misquoted. The press was sensationalizing the story, he said, and what enraged him most was that the word of these people was being taken over that of *professionals*, such as himself. But when I met him in his office, Kent was calmer, happier. He had just come from a parent conference concerning a six-year-old, extremely distractible little girl. "As I pointed out to them," Kent began, "the extremely distractible person is going to get a driver's license at 16 and then may become distracted and run a red light . . . there are all kinds of very, very tragic outcomes which can be attributed to this—behavior. I don't like to call it behavior but function, because it's a physiological thing."

Kent was, of course, talking about MBD. He is an important figure in this case, instrumental in the labeling of the children. I knew I should encourage him to expound, but my overwhelming desire was to escape. The room was small and close. Kent, a gray-haired man in his 50s, went on musing about the "deadly" possibilities of distractibility. I thought in dazed sequence of the daydreaming little girl, and whether her parents had that day determined to put her on Ritalin . . . of my own characteristic state of reverie, of countless classes I only rejoined when the bell rang . . . of the parents' angrily telling me that it was Kent who needed testing, not their kids.

" 'Distractible' is much more important than 'hyperactive,' " Kent was saying. "I've seen an awful lot of children who were not hyperactive, but very distractible daydreamers. They couldn't maintain their focus of attention, but they didn't jump around or yell or scream or cause any disturbance."

Was he saying, then, that distractibility is the prime sign of MBD? Kent considered. "Poor impulse control is probably the *key* issue. It's commonly associated with hyperactivity, but it's the instant response. . . . The child who gets pushed in line and slugs the kid who pushed him when it really wasn't anybody's fault . . . who sticks his foot out and trips someone coming down the aisle. I think it's the classic example. We all have impulses, but lack of impulse control is something else again. The impulsive child has no constraints. He may have remorse afterwards—but when it occurred to him that if he stuck his foot out this person might fall flat on his face, the foot went out."

I see. And how would you find these children? "They find you," Kent said and sighed. "I've never had any trouble finding them."

Gordon Cairns was more specific. In his spacious superintendent's office, just down the hall from Kent's, Cairns opened the interview with a formal, flat denial of the suit's allegations. Then he relaxed and finally did describe with considerable pride the "m.o." for finding these children, the spore that blew into town and developed into a comprehensive system the parents never knew existed.

"I guess it was back in '66 that the then-superintendent notified us that federal funds were available, through the Elementary and Secondary Education Act of 1965," said Cairns, who—beleaguered though he is these days—still speaks with the measured confidence and authority of a bureaucrat risen well in the ranks. "So we just sat down and thought, what kind of a project can we write? And we came up with this idea of finding out why a child didn't learn."

The three-year Title III Cairns-directed project deployed Tarr, a psychologist, a neurologist and all primary-grade teachers in the search for children who, because of some vague neurologic dysfunction, could not behave or learn as they should. "We had *everybody* studying these children, as early as preschool and kindergarten, to see whether they were going to have learning problems. They were using Ritalin as well as other medications."

According to a continuation application for 1969-70, the estimated cost for that fiscal year was $74,603—said to cover, among other things, medical, dental, social and psychological evaluation. Out of about 500 thus screened, 76 were found to have learning disabilities, said Cairns—and noted, glancing down at a project list, that some of the children there were now in the suit.

He showed me a memo, sent to all kindergarten and first-grade teachers in the early fall, instructing them to submit a series of forms on children "who appear headed for educational problems." Lest the teacher not know exactly what is expected, sample paragraphs follow. States one, about a five-year-old: "Michael's attention span is short and he has trouble sitting still. He plays well on his own during activity time, especially with blocks, but tends to be silly and want his own way when in a group situation."

After this come five more pages of prodding questions. Is the child distractible, does he get along well with others, can he express himself easily, does he have manual dexterity, is his performance consistent, from day to day—from one part of the day to another—from one activity to another? The questions are insistent, relentless, and they dog the mind of the teacher who will now turn her searching gaze upon a roomful of five- or six-year-olds—with which ones will she fulfill her given task? Once the mechanism was set in motion with an ESEA Title III Screening Checklist filled out on a child, what chances did one have of rejoining the ranks of the normal?

Since the project grant ran out in 1970, are they still carrying on with the work? We try to, Cairns replied. He also has a new project in the works—"Values Clarification." It aims to instill in primary-grade children the proper values, so that when they reach the age of temptation by drugs—*illegal* drugs, he said and smiled—they will abstain. "Drug abuse," he allowed, "is a problem in Taft." So Values Clarification becomes the natural sequel to Project Title III—for when someone's been on stimulant drugs all through childhood to control one behavior and produce another, when drugs are that much a part of daily regimen and dependence, how does one differentiate between a "good" and a "bad" pill? As Bruno Bettelheim wrote in 1973, nearly all the middle-class drug addicts with whom he had worked were given drugs as children to modify their troublesome behavior.

* * *

Is Taft a place apart, or is the parents' story more common than we know? Cairns maintains that Taft and its project were simply "ahead of the times." And with preschool testing for learning disabilities now begun in school systems all over the country, he may well be right. But what is most clearly typical about Taft is not the alleged coercion but the unctuous unfolding, the nonconspiratorial coalescing of those in various positions of authority—school administrators, federal government, drug companies, teachers, doctors. With something there for everyone, they ally because their interests are compatible. But there is no conspiracy to sedate the children of America, no overt design to manage them chemically now that corporal punishment is on its way out. "That's the only unfortunate thing about the whole *1984* model," says Peter Schrag. "We'll have *1984 without* Big Brother."

In *Twilight of Authority,* Robert Nisbet argues that the bulk of power in our society has become largely invisible, manipulating us through the vast array of bureaucracy's commissions, agencies, departments and committees with a "soft power." It is their professed humanitarianism that smooths the way, their capacity for entering into the smallest details of human life, their ability to affect not only human actions—as governmental power did in more ingenuous and brutal times—but the human will, that makes them most dangerous. It is indeed difficult to militate against doctors who want to treat your child's ailments, teachers who want your child to do better in school, projects that want to help children learn. The thrust of these stated intentions is to lull us into quiescence while we go on unaware that nothing is what it seems. Nisbet quotes Justice Brandeis, who warned: "Experience should teach us to be most on guard to protect liberty when the Government's purposes are beneficent. Men born to freedom are naturally alert to repel invasion of their liberty by evil-minded rulers. The greatest dangers to liberty lurk in insidious encroachments by men of zeal, well-meaning but without understanding."

Well aware of this gravest of encroachments, Divoky and Schrag have mounted their attack not only against the medical miasma of hyperactivity but, more important, against the ideology of early intervention and treatment that offers social control in a medical mask. If we focus solely upon the potential dangers of Ritalin, Schrag inquires, then what happens when we get the perfect pill—something absolutely safe, that produces perfect models of classroom decorum, gone from autonomous to automaton in a transposition so neat and quick we need hardly know?

Dr. Sidney Walker, director of the Southern California Neuropsychiatric Institute, objects, however, to Divoky and Schrag's emphasis upon the social and political implications of the hyperactivity issue. "They're like the radical psychiatrist Thomas Szasz who says it's all social nonconformity and there's no such thing as mental illness," Walker says. Conceding that many cases are undoubtedly behavior problems, Walker insists that most children who have come to him labeled "hyperactive" have had some other specific and treatable problem. "Hyperactivity is *not* a diagnosis," he states flatly. "MBD is only a descriptive term for a collection of symptoms which should be a signal for stepping back and making a complete evalution—not stepping forward and offering a pill that only masks the symptoms."

Walker, though, is a maverick. Divoky and Schrag's most vehement critics are teachers, doctors and drug company employees, those with the most vested interests in this pandemic syndrome. Their ranks are tightening now, and in a recent issue of *Science Weekly*, educator Robert Havighurst from the University of Chicago is quoted as having discovered that current claims of amphetamine overuse in treatment of hyperactivity are grossly exaggerated, inasmuch as only 1 percent or 300,000 American schoolchildren are receiving medication; and he urged school personnel to cooperate fully with physicians' prescriptions. When I questioned Havighurst about his sources, he replied that they were "scientific." Examination of his paper, delivered at an American Association for the Advancement of Science symposium in Boston, yielded the information that he labeled Divoky and Schrag as "individualist-anarchists," and their book, "sleazy." One of his chief sources was one Dr. Irving Abrams, medical director for the Chicago Public Schools, who delivered his remarks at a conference sponsored in part by Ciba. Havighurst's estimate of 300,000 medicated children came from a three-year-old article in that most scientific and reliable journal of all, *Time Magazine*.

So the public debate continues to be waged. In the Montoyas' small frame house in Taft, however, the issues are intensely personal. It is mostly the women who come—they are the activists in this case—and they sit over coffee and fuel one anothers' righteous indignation in a responsive liturgy. "Why not investigate every alternative—why just maintain a child on drugs?" "It was just an experiment. They shouldn't do our kids that way." They have all taken their children off Ritalin, and so feel relieved that that chapter, at least, is closed. For Diane Montoya, however, this story has a keen edge of continuance to it. Clinic doctors at UCLA have declared Frank to be not hyperactive. But they did find that he is now epileptic—and have put him on Dilantin and Tegretol. What *PDR* has to say about those two drugs is more dire than the warning about Ritalin. So Montoya tries to figure out what to do with the bitter lesson that the responsibility is hers and her husband's alone. She must find whom to trust, now that she's learned whom not to. Sometimes, as it all slips away in a haze of uncertainty, she pulls out her children's records to revive the bare outlines of fact. One memo from Bill Kent to the school nurse is especially noteworthy. He says Frank's teacher thinks he may be EMR, and he wonders whether Frank is taking his Ritalin regularly, and in what dosages. Also, another school employee has described Joe Montoya, in kindergarten, as "a second edition of Frank." "I expect a referral on Joe will come in," Kent concluded (apparently for Ritalin), "and now I wonder what has happened to big sister Donna."

At this writing, Donna is a high-achieving sixth grader who is also sensitive and mature beyond her years. When she was recently asked by her teacher to think of any way that this country in its Bicentennial might be improved, Donna wrote: "I wish certain people would stop drugging children before they have a chance to prove who they are and what they can do. PLEASE! Donna Montoya, Room 13."

Helping the Hyperkinetic Child

ARNOLD H. ZUKOW, M.D.

Pediatrician, Encino, California, and Associate Clinical Professor of Pediatrics, UCLA School of Medicine.

Dr. Zukow spoke at greater length on this topic before the Nevada Academy of Family Physicians earlier this year.

Readers are invited to send in their reactions and comments on the article and/or on the subject of treating hyperkinetic children with drugs, a topic that has aroused considerable controversy in the press, despite the favorable experience of many physicians in using drugs such as Ritalin to treat so-called hyperkinetic disorders.

Dr. Zukow's views are in general agreement with the HEW Report of the Conference on the Use of Stimulant Drugs in the Treatment of Behaviorally Disturbed Young School Children, *prepared by panelists from the fields of education, psychology, special education, pediatrics, adult and child psychiatry, psychoanalysis, basic and clinical pharmacology, internal medicine, drug abuse, and social work.*

For further reading on the topic, see the bibliography at the end of the article.

Hyperkinetic children can have a negative effect on all those who care about them—especially their teachers. They have a short attention span and their actions are without direction, focus, or object. Their restlessness and impulsiveness disrupt discipline in the home and in the classroom. These children are often regarded as spoiled, ill-mannered, strange, or uncoordinated. They are in constant motion; have few friends; and exhibit temper tantrums, persistent sleep problems, learning problems, and aggressiveness.

These children frequently share two problems, both of which are developmental: social and occasionally physical immaturity and the inability to select discriminately from the stimuli in their environment.

They are not brain-damaged or psychotic. They do not possess an overt neurological syndrome, deafness, visual disability, or mental retardation. Their hyperactivity (always present in one degree or another in the hyperkinetic syndrome) should be viewed from a developmental frame of reference, i.e., the toddler is more restless and distractible than the school-age child, and the younger child is more distractible than the adolescent.

Unfortunately, the medical literature and lay press use the terms *hyperactive* and *hyperkinetic* interchangeably. In my opinion, they are not the same.

The problem which arises in using the terms *hyperactive* and *hyperkinetic* interchangeably is more than semantic. For instance, frustrated adults reacting to a child who does not meet their standards can easily exaggerate the significance of the child's occasional inattention or restlessness and label the youngster hyperkinetic.

A January 1971 HEW report on hyperkinesis says "the normal ebullience of childhood, however, should not be confused with the very special problems of the child with hyperkinetic behavior disorders." The report gives the following definition: "There is no known single cause or simple answer for such problems. The major symptoms are an increase of purposeless physical activity and a significantly impaired span of focused attention. The inability to control physical motion and attention may generate other consequences, such as disturbed moods and behavior within the home, at play with peers, and in the schoolroom."

This report further emphasizes the importance of the quality of hyperactivity. Children in whom the diagnosis is obvious are described as acting as if they possess an "inner tornado." The media have gone further, it seems to me, and have created a misleading stereotype of these children. They are depicted as the ones who destroy the supermarket, who set fire to sister's hair, the ones with clenched fists and bared teeth who seem to appear more animal than human.

It is true that some hyperkinetic children have signs of structural damage to their nervous system but most do not, and this point is very important.

I would describe hyperkinesis as a treatable illness characterized by involuntary behavior and/or learning problems in a child whose brain maturation is delayed. The history of the problem and the obvious tendency for a number of children identified as hyperkinetic to improve as they grow older supports this definition. An unknown number of children who have hyperkinesis and go untreated may certainly outgrow the syndrome without apparent sequelae.

The hyperkinetic child's inability to control his or her span of concentration for a period of time long enough to assimilate and utilize incoming data results in uncontrolled emotional outbursts and emotional highs and lows. This leads to poor relationships with parents, teachers, and peers.

Identifying hyperkinetic children presents a perplexing problem. There is no way to identify and separate the children who

Reprinted with permission from the November/December 1975 issue of *Today's Education*, Journal of the National Education Association and the author.

would "naturally" outgrow the disability even if untreated from the ones who would develop serious emotional and learning deficits as a result of being untreated.

However, I would like to make several statements, based on my knowledge of and experience with hyperkinesis.

1. All hyperkinetic children are hyperactive.

2. All hyperactive children are not hyperkinetic.

3. All learning or behavior problems are not the result of hyperkinesis.

4. About 75 percent of hyperkinetic children do have a learning problem as a direct or indirect result of the condition. This is probably related directly to the intensity of either of the two (i.e., the child with a behavior problem can have a learning problem, which can lead to a greater behavior problem, which can similarly lead to a greater learning problem, etc.).

5. Learning disorders probably constitute the single most serious disability of childhood and have the greatest socioeconomic impact in adult life.

6. A youngster does not suddenly, at age six, become hyperkinetic. The signs are present very early in the child's life.

Medication prescribed by a qualified physician is valuable in the overall care of children with hyperkinesis because it reduces their excitability and impulsivity and increases their attention span and concentration. Specific stimulants can help these children improve their self-control and their relationships with those around them.

Many articles that have appeared in the nonprofessional press and even in many professional publications appear to have missed the object of drug treatment. The primary object of medication is not to calm these children. Rather it is to improve the functioning of their brain so that they can select from their environment the stimuli that will allow them to act appropriately in a situation. There are several well-documented studies which point out that the symptoms of hyperkinesis can be markedly improved by the judicious use of medications, especially methylphenidate.

Several researchers have clearly shown that not only are children on such medication less hyperactive, less belligerent, and more able to follow directions, but their attention span is improved and their distractibility is decreased. In addition, their coordination also improves if that was poor. There is, indeed, often a striking and at times almost unbelievable improvement in both the academic performance and the behavior of the children, which results in higher self-esteem and increased acceptance by their teachers and peers.

A case history will illustrate my point. When E. G., a six-and-a-half-year-old boy, became my patient, he was about to be expelled from school for kicking his classmates and the teacher. He was a bright child but was doing poorly in his schoolwork. He was hard to reason with at home, and he wanted to be the center of attention at all times. His peers avoided him whenever possible.

He was the product of a full-term uncomplicated pregnancy and was adopted by his parents at the age of three-and-a-half months. He had no history of serious trauma or serious illness, and his developmental milestones were normal.

I had his parents and teacher fill out evaluation forms about his behavior. On the school evaluation one, the teacher checked the column headed with one of the following, *never, almost never, sometimes, almost always*, or *always*, for statements such as "Finds it hard to play with peers" and "Reacts adversely to changes in routine." (The teacher's evaluation form has proved successful in informing teachers as well as in assessing the child's behavior.) On their form, the parents circled *yes* or *no* for statements such as "Short attention span," "Overly sensitive," "Panics easily," and "Quick-tempered."

After examination of the patient and the forms and after consultation with the parents, I prescribed Ritalin for E. G. The parents reported that after one week on the drug, his behavior had improved. A second teacher evaluation indicated great improvement in E. G.'s behavior.

After several months on Ritalin, he is a changed child—and all for the better, according to parents and teacher. His ability to make and maintain friends appears to be greatly improved and his ability to concentrate on schoolwork has also.

Generally speaking, when I prescribe Ritalin for a child, I begin with a very low dosage for five days of the first week. This enables parents and teachers to see differences in the child's behavior on and off the medication. Then I increase the dosage over the next two weeks.

I have contact with the parents at the end of each of these three weeks and then again at the end of six and 12 weeks. I advise parents that there may be several dosage changes until the most effective one is found.

The suggestion that the administration of this medication can lay the groundwork for future physical drug addiction is unfounded, in my opinion. As a matter of fact, many of these children resent the idea of having to take medication in order to function within their environment in an appropriate manner.

I believe that untreated youngsters who have had years of frustrating humiliation in the classroom and at home are much more likely candidates for addiction than are hyperactive children whose use of a drug has helped their self-control and ability to function in their environment.

Parents and teachers can, and must, be helped to view hyperkinesis as a treatable condition and to recognize that delayed brain maturation is not only an important but a common contributing factor to this syndrome. Then they will be more able to be understanding and patient with the hyperkinetic child.

Teachers and parents should give these children clear instructions and should avoid rigid scheduling of activities of fixed length. Their activities should be brief and should not exceed their capability for sustained attention.

When teachers detect early signs of an impending temper tantrum, they should take immediate steps to remove the child from the situation and offer an alternative distraction which could avoid the tantrum. However, once an explosion has occurred, there is nothing to do but wait it out, making sure that the child does not harm himself or herself or tyrannize others. This is about the same advice I would offer a parent or teacher dealing with a "normal" child who was having this type of behavior problem.

Teachers can be important partners in identifying hyperkinetic children and in carrying out the proper therapy with them—but only if they understand the problem and are willing to cooperate with doctor and parents. Teachers and doctor should focus on the ultimate goal: a child who is capable of functioning at his or her highest potential for learning within the classroom environment.

Teachers must be aware of their own abilities and limitations in dealing with the hyperkinetic child. Recognition of these abilities and limitations can only be helpful to teacher, child, and class.

If the hyperkinetic child gives any indication of having or developing a mental illness, the mental health profession should enter in the treatment. I often find a need for consultation from psychologists and psychiatrists in cases in which children are past the age of seven-and-a-half or eight, because they and their parents have had a greater chance of having suffered moderate to severe emotional sequelae as a result of the primary problem.

The mental health professional who becomes involved in such a case should have proper facilities for testing, evaluating, and treating. The treatment might involve medication, educational therapy, counseling by the child's doctor, family counseling by a mental health professional, or psychiatric counseling—any of these alone or in combinations, as appropriate.

One final point: If we, as teachers and physicians, can accept the fact that hyperkinetic children react to their environment in their own special way—*involuntarily*—we can understand and therefore we can help.

For Further Reading

Adler, S. *Your Overactive Child.* New York: MEDCOM Press, 1972.

Conners, C. K., and Rothschild, G. H. "Drugs and Learning in Children" in *Learning Disorders.* J. Hellmuth (editor). Vol. III. Seattle: Special Child Publications, 1968.

Conners, C. K., and others. "Effects of Methylphenidate (Ritalin) on Paired-Associate Learning and Porteus Maze Performance in Emotionally Disturbed Children." *Journal of Consulting Psychology* 28:14-22; No. 1, 1964.

Laufer, M. W., and Denhoff, E. "Hyperkinetic Behavior Syndrome in Children." *Journal of Pediatrics* 50:463-74; April 1957.

Millichap, J. G. "Drugs in the Management of Hyperkinetic and Perceptually Handicapped Children." *Journal of the American Medical Association* 206: 1527-30; November 11, 1968.

Report of the Conference on the Use of Stimulant Drugs in the Treatment of Behaviorally Disturbed Young School Children, January 11-12, 1971. Washington, DC: Office of Child Development and Office of the Assistant Secretary for Health and Scientific Affairs, Department of Health, Education, and Welfare, 1971.

Safer, D. J. and Allen, R. P. "Factors Influencing the Suppressant Effects of Two Stimulant Drugs on the Growth of Hyperactive Children." *Pediatrics* 51: 660-67; April 1973.

Stewart, M. A., and others. "The Hyperactive Child Syndrome." *American Journal of Orthopsychiatry:* 36 861-67; No. 5, 1966.

Weiss, G., and others. "Comparison of the Effects of Chlorpromazine, Dextroamphetamine and Methylphenidate on the Behaviour and Intellectual Functioning of Hyperactive Children." *Canadian Medical Association Journal* 104: 20-25; January 9, 1971.

Causes, Detection, and Treatment of Childhood Depression

Herbert Yahraes

"I am the biggest troublemaker in my family," said a worried-looking 10-year-old girl. "I cry a lot and feel weird a lot."

Between spells of crying, a 12-year-old boy said, "I think I am the stupidist kid in class. . . . I never really try to kill myself, but sometimes I think to drown myself."

A dejected 8-year-old girl declared: "I feel ugly and like a dumbbell. . . . Sometimes I would like to kill my friends or my own stomach or arm. . . . Friends make fun of me all the time."

These children were talking to child psychiatrists at the National Institute of Mental Health (NIMH). Although none of these children was psychotic, all had high depression scores, as derived from two scales designed to measure depressive symptoms in children. The subjects were among the 30 children or grandchildren of 14 consecutive patients recently admitted to NIMH for observation and treatment of a depressive psychosis. The children were between the ages of 4 and 15.

Of the 30 child subjects, more than half were considered "overtly depressed" at the time of the interview.

A considerably lower rate of childhood depression had been reported in this same sample population by earlier investigators—perhaps, according to the NIMH team, because the earlier workers either did not get to know the children or else did not realize that the symptoms of childhood depression might be less marked than, or even different from, those of adult depression. At any one time, various studies indicate, as many as 20 children in 100 may be suffering from symptoms of depression. Though the incidence of this disorder used to increase steadily with age, as a recent report points out, "the growing rate of depression in the young has brought about a peak period in youth that outstrips middle age and is exceeded only by the elderly."

Masked Depression

Child psychiatrists Leon Cytryn and Donald H. McKnew, Jr., who were two leading members of the NIMH investigatory team, agree with Dr. William E. Bunney, Jr., Chief of the Adult Psychiatry Branch, NIMH, that many children diagnosed as hyperactive may actually be depressed. Certainly, they report, among children with *masked depression,* which is the commonest childhood type in these investigators' experiences, hyperactivity is common. This type of depression may also be masked by school problems, delinquency, and either behavior or psychosomatic disorders. Every once in a while, though, such children are likely to actually look or act depressed. The investigators arrived at their diagnosis when they discovered that many children who were not obviously depressed nevertheless manifested in their dreams and fantasies the same depressive elements—such as frustration, despair, and hopelessness—as those shown by the clearly depressed children.

To gently remove the mask and get at the underlying trouble, these child psychiatrists, who work not only with the NIMH group but also at George Washington University Medical School and at Children's Hospital, Washington, D.C., use several measures. One is a psychiatric

"Causes, Detection, and Treatment of Childhood Depression," by Herbert Yahraes, *U.S. Department of Health, Education and Welfare,* 1978.

interview which notes any background of depressive signs—such as sadness, despair, feelings of hopelessness or helplessness, and thoughts of suicide. The investigators also evaluate what the child thinks of himself; that is, his self-esteem. And they elicit "fantasy material" by having the children make up stories, interpret pictures, and recount their dreams.

As an example of masked depression, these authorities tell about Albert, a 12-year-old boy, who had been sent to them because of his disruptive behavior in school. He was aggressive and hyperactive. His grades were poor and his social adjustment marginal. A look at the home situation suggested two major probable causes: The mother held a full-time job, was usually unavailable to her children, and had once been investigated for child abuse; the father was an alcoholic who assumed no responsibility for the family and who frequently beat Albert. In sum, the child, like many others with a similar condition, had experienced both rejection and depreciation.

Throughout the interview, Albert was apathetic and sad. "He described himself as dumb, as the laughingstock of his schoolmates, and expressed the belief that everyone was picking on him." He saw himself as inadequate and helpless. "On the fantasy level the boy showed a strong preoccupation with themes of annihilation, violence, explosions, and death, invariably with a bad outcome for the main figures. . . ."

Albert did not improve. In fact, 1½ years later he was sent to a residential school for delinquent boys.

The investigators suggest that the boy's delinquency and aggressiveness were attempts to escape from a basic depression. They admit that such a defense is self-destructive, but "it helps ward off the unbearable feeling of despair" and, on the basis of the newest evidence, seems to be far commoner than most of us think. In other words, many children who have a behavior problem may be basically depressed.

If a child is marked by hyperactivity, delinquency or other behavior disorders, school difficulties, or psychosomatic complaints, Cytryn and McKnew believe it would be a good idea to have him or her checked for depression.

The family members of the children with a masked depression, report these investigators, "often presented a picture of disorganization and severe psychopathology, usually in the form of a character defect, but gave no history of a clear-cut depressive illness."

Acute Depressive Illness

In addition to masked depression, Cytryn and McKnew have found two other types of depression among children: *acute* and *chronic*.

In the *acute* type, there always seemed to be a clear cause, usually the loss of a beloved relative or someone else very close. Though the loved one had died in some cases, usually he or she—for any one of a variety of reasons, such as personal problems or a move—had simply reduced or cut off the love and care that the child had been counting upon and the loss of which was seen as rejection. In the case of 6-year-old Beatrice, the precipitating cause was traced to the rape of an older sister, 17, who had been serving as a mother substitute because the mother herself worked full time outside the home. "After the incident the sister became withdrawn, preoccupied, and less attentive," and within 3 months young Beatrice was admitted to a psychiatric ward because she had gradually withdrawn from activities, was failing in school, slept poorly, and lacked appetite. "Her mood," the psychiatrists report, "was markedly depressed, as evidenced by a sad and tearful facial expression, slowness of movement, monotone voice, and verbal expressions indicating hopelessness and despair."

After several days of hospital care and attention, but with no specific treatment for depression, Beatrice "became outgoing and started to eat and sleep regularly, her mood brightened, and she was sociable, active, and alert. . . ." Two years later the mother reported that the girl was still maintaining her gains.

Interestingly, Cytryn and McKnew report that such improvement, "despite the absence of any formal treatment program," has been "almost universal" in cases of acute childhood depression, such as Beatrice's. They suspect that it occurs because the child has been removed from one or more noxious environmental circumstances, "coupled with the rallying of the family around the child who is labelled ill because of the hospitalization." Many such children, whether or not they had availed themselves of followup psychotherapy, were found to have maintained their improvement, initiated during a brief hospital stay, even after 5 years.

Chronic Depressive Illness

Children afflicted with the third type of depression, *chronic*, report Cytryn and McKnew, differ from the others in these major respects: They have a chronically depressed parent, evidence that a genetic element is probably at play; they have been separated several times, from infancy on, from persons they had counted upon, evidence of an environmental force; and no single precipitating incident can be found.

Consider Caroline, who was referred to Cytryn and McKnew as an emergency case at the age of 7. She couldn't sleep, couldn't eat, and for several months had had screaming episodes. She had often threatened suicide because she was "a bad girl" and nobody loved her. Part of the problem was the girl's mother, a helpless woman overwhelmed by family responsibilities, poor self-esteem, and a tendency toward frequent depressions. "Her only marriage was stormy;" Caroline's stepfather had beaten the child severely; then he and his wife had separated, but only for a while.

The trouble may have started many years before Caroline was born. For there is evidence that her mother, as a child, had been neglected by her own mother and been brought up in an atmosphere of violence. Evidence has been found that a condition which might be mildly described as "poor parenting" often is passed on from generation to generation, particularly in the case of child abuse. The abusing parent, investigators often have shown, is frequently the individual who was abused himself, or herself, as a child. Some children who were physically assaulted or otherwise maltreated as youngsters manage as adults nevertheless to become good parents; many others do not.

One of the most important persons in Caroline's life as an infant had been her paternal grandmother, but suddenly, when Caroline was 1 year old, her chief care had been shifted to a maternal aunt. The mother herself, when Caroline was 1½ years old and again when she was 4, had left her for several months.

After Caroline had been discharged from the hospital, she again "became depressed and developed abdominal cramps and diarrhea. When the mother again separated from the stepfather, these symptoms rapidly disappeared."

Two Forces: Heredity and Parental Behavior

In their observation of many children having at least one manic-depressive parent, Cytryn and McKnew found that more than 50 percent of the offspring were at least moderately depressed when interviewed—usually overtly so. Environmental forces were undoubtedly at work, because the shifting moods of the bipolar patient lead to "a sense of uncertainty and bewilderment on the part of the child."

Research by other investigators demonstrates that hereditary forces were probably heavily involved, too. Among the general population, the incidence of manic-depressive psychosis has been estimated at less than 1 percent; among close relatives of manic-depressives, it hovers around 10 percent. Further, studies of identical twins have shown that if one twin has this condition, the likelihood that the other twin also has it ranges from 50 to 100 percent. All of which is to say that the strength of the genetic element has been demonstrated but is not, usually, the whole story.

Obviously, in addition to heredity, the parent-child relationship is of prime importance.

Cytryn and McKnew found that many of their patients had "suffered rejection and depreciation by their parents or loved ones either all during their lives or at least over a period of many years." Such rejection may take many forms: blunt statements stressing the child's inadequacy; attitudes and actions that indicate a lack of respect or caring; a constant barrage of criticism and humiliation. Sometimes there was no frank rejection or depreciation, just "a void in the parent-child relationship." The investigators say that the parents "may or may not be consciously aware of their behavior." They say, too, that "depreciation of the child can be shown through overprotection as well as through rejection; both attitudes convey the same basic message of the child's inadequacy and worthlessness." Conceivably, the child's depressive outlook is caused either "by identification with this negative view of himself" or "by a sense of alienation from important love objects," or by both.

Studies in Denmark strongly suggest that the relative importance of the two factors can be readily assessed. In children who are at risk to psychosis because they may have inherited a predisposition to it, the genetic factor is of primary importance, rather than the quality of the parent-child relationship. When there is no reason to suspect a genetic factor, however, the quality of the child's mental health seems to be strongly influenced by that of the parent-child relationship.

Detecting Childhood Depression Early

Indications of depression in children—particularly when something has gone wrong at home, playground, or school—are quite common, as Cytryn and McKnew point out. Usually, though, they do not last long. The problem is judged to be depressive illness when it continues for at least several months "and is associated with severe impairment of the child's scholastic and social adjustment and with disturbances" in eating and sleeping. "In more serious cases the child's thinking is affected by feelings of despair and hopelessness, general retardation, and, in the severe form, by suicidal thoughts."

In the best position to detect early indications of childhood depression, these investigators say, is the pediatrician or the family physician. Each knows the family's history and the parent-child relationship "and can observe the child directly for any sign of depressive mood and behavior." Also in a strategic position is the school or child guidance clinic.

The doctor's role may be particularly valuable in suspected cases of masked depression, "in which the child is usually regarded by the family [and often by the school] as delinquent or lazy." The doctor may try to investigate the case himself "through the use of simple playroom techniques which will elicit fantasy material in drawings, dreams, or selected projective tests or he may . . . refer the child to a psychiatrist. In either case, if the suspicion of a masked depressive reaction is confirmed, the all-too-frequent mishandling of such cases will have been avoided."

Any person evaluating or treating a depressed parent, Cytryn and McKnew advise, should "inquire about the emotional status of the patient's children. . . . Conversely, all child psychiatrists, when seeing depressed children, "should consider that a similar disorder may exist in the parents and siblings.

Treating Depressed Children

When the child is younger than 8 years old, and when the illness has not been very severe or of long duration, Cytryn and McKnew select parental counseling as "usually the treatment of choice." Through such counseling an attempt is made to change parental or other family practices, including depreciation of the child and preventable losses of loved adults, which are damaging to the child's feeling of self-worth. Otherwise these authorities advise family therapy, which includes the affected child, often coupled with individual psychotherapy for the young patient. Where the child has lost a major loved one, "the family needs help and guidance in providing adequate substitutes either from its own ranks or from outside resources. Where there have been frequent early losses, the family is encouraged to help compensate by increased involvement with the child."

These psychiatrists point out that many families, particularly those in which a child has a masked depression, "respond better to direct guidance and emotional support" than to the traditional interpretive and nondirective form of psychotherapy. "Of course," they add, "there are situations where traditional psychiatric intervention of any kind is not feasible. In such cases, the psychiatrist may have to collaborate with community resources such as juvenile court, halfway houses, foster homes, and even the police."

In adults, a wide variety of antidepressive drugs—including lithium carbonate, which is virtually a specific for treating manic-depressive, or bipolar, illness and then for preventing or markedly reducing the frequency and intensity of future attacks—have been proved efficacious. Bipolar illness is rare in children, so lithium is rarely used with them. The other antidepressives are being more widely used, but no comprehensive evaluation has been made of their effectiveness. However, in laboratory work with Rhesus monkey babies that had reached the stage of despair (retreating to a corner of the cage, ceasing to vocalize, and refusing food and water), antidepressant drugs have been shown to reverse the symptoms.

Another major question for research, in addition to the effectiveness of antidepressant medication in youngsters, is whether or not childhood depression leads, or predisposes, to adult depression.

References

Cytryn, L., and McKnew, D. H., Jr. Proposed classification of childhood depression. *American Journal of Psychiatry*, 129:149-155, 1972.

Dutchess County, N.Y., Society for Mental Health. Depression touches the young, too. *Poughkeepsie, N.Y. Journal*, Nov. 11, 1976.

McKnew, D. H., Jr., and Cytryn, L. "Detection and Treatment of Childhood Depression." Paper presented at the annual meeting of the American Psychiatric Association, May 1975.

McKnew, D. H., Jr., and Cytryn, L. Historical background in children with affective disorders. *American Journal of Psychiatry*, 130:11, 1973.

McKnew, D. H., Jr.; Cytryn, L.; Efron, A. M.; Gershon, E. S.; and Bunney, W. E., Jr. "Offspring of Manic-Depressive Patients." Paper presented at the annual meeting of the American Psychiatric Association, 1976.

On Understanding Depression. A report on the 1975 national conference on depressive disorders. Arlington, Va.: The National Association for Mental Health, 1975.

7 The Physically and Sensorially Handicapped Child

Special educators are faced with the challenge of educating children with a wide variety of physical and sensory handicaps as a result of PL 94-142. The articles in this section of *Educating Exceptional Children* are designed to offer not only an overview of the field but also constructive suggestions on how to incorporate this population into public school classrooms.

"Can Schools Speak the Language of the Deaf?" is the first of several articles on deaf children and it questions whether mainstreaming is the proper solution for these children. "There's a Deaf Child in My Class" is addressed to teachers who may find deaf children in their care, and it offers specific and detailed advice. Similarly, speech pathologist Donald Mowrer's "Speech Problems: What You Should Do and Shouldn't Do" addresses teachers of children with problems such as lisping and stuttering.

Blind children too are the subject of articles on the proper kind of education. As Robert Rottman argues in "Some Thoughts on the Education of Blind Children," blindness is both a physical nuisance and a social handicap. Educational programs for blind children should have as their goal "the graduation of informed, responsible, self-confident, and self-reliant adult citizens who will participate in and contribute to their society."

The last articles in this section discuss directions in educating the severely and multiply handicapped. They are directed especially at special educators and school administrators.

Looking Ahead: Challenge Questions

What facilities are necessary for mainstreaming the severely handicapped? The less severely handicapped?

What seem to be important factors in determining whether a physically handicapped child will succeed in school?

According to what criteria should concerned adults measure success in school for the physically handicapped child?

CAN SCHOOLS SPEAK THE LANGUAGE OF THE DEAF?

Joanne Greenberg and Glenn Doolittle

Joanne Greenberg is the author of "I Never Promised You a Rose Garden" and "In This Sign," a book about deafness. Glenn Doolittle is a junior high school teacher trained in special education. Both live in Colorado.

"I thought of myself as a cold woman, like my mother and her mother before her. We knew when we had children and they were deaf, that when they were 6 or 7 years old we would have to send them away to Colorado Springs, to the state school. You can't invest too much love then—it hurts too much. I know this 'mainstreaming' isolates my kids—denies them many of the important things they need—but I have a need, too, to be a real mother. I kept them home and mainstreamed them."

We had gone to see Mrs. Elaine Beery, a highly vocal deaf mother, because we'd been told she was a teacher's aide who was strongly supportive of the new program called mainstreaming—the integrating of handicapped children of all kinds into the regular public school system. We also knew that her school had one of the finest of all such programs in Colorado. With a handicap of such low incidence (there are about two million deaf Americans), it is exceptional to have 17 deaf children of various ages in one district. Her children's teacher is the hearing child of deaf parents and reads the sloppy sign language of his students exceptionally well. The Beery children are happy to be home and are well pleased with the school and with mainstreamed education, but when I asked Mrs. Beery what she would do if she could have anything she wanted for them, she smiled broadly and answered quickly, backing her speech with a graceful and fluid American Sign: "Oh, of course, a deaf school here in Denver, with lots of deaf teachers. Our community—for us." It was hardly the answer we had expected.

Last October 1, P.L. 94-142, the Federal act passed in 1975 that "guarantees" free and appropriate education for all handicapped children, went into effect. By next September, education in a "least restrictive environment" is to be available to all handicapped children between the ages of 3 and 18. For most children, this will mean attending public school.

The law, which is regarded as a civil-rights bill for the disabled, looks fair, decent, reasonable and humane. But the experience of many deaf children in Colorado and in other states that have recently enacted mainstreaming laws points to something far less than positive. Parents and educators in these states say we may be forcing untrained teachers in overcrowded classrooms to deal with a new group of students who are tragically vulnerable—educationally, psychologically and socially. The dream is equality and social acceptance. The fact is that nine out of 10 deaf children will receive neither. For some, mainstreaming may be catastrophic.

Deaf education has followed, a day late and a dollar short, the changes in philosophy and ideology undergone in the larger culture. In the 1870's, Colorado—like other states—began to think of protecting mental patients and the retarded with a system of hospitals and "asylums"—healthful rural retreats built away from the stress and disease of the city. It created schools for the deaf with the same protection and rural simplicity in mind. Neither the mental hospitals nor the schools for the deaf were meant to isolate. Isolation, however, was the result.

The state schools had a practical and uplifting philosophy: to provide safety from exploitation by the unscrupulous and immoral and to provide an education in some useful trade so the deaf individual would not be a drain on society. As the goals of general education became more progressive, so, at a respectful distance, did those of the state schools. In the 1930's, for example, when the interest was in a protected trade and steady work, deaf students were taught to develop skills in printing, auto body and fender work, power sewing and boiler repair. The students had few choices, but they did have an advantage because they were not affected by the shattering noise of these trades. When college began to be the goal for the larger society in the late 40's and early 50's, academic programs for the deaf were geared up, and in many places trades training lost its edge.

Now the word is "integration" or "mainstreaming," and the schools for the deaf are being called ghettos; their

From *The New York Times Magazine,* December 11, 1977. Copyright © 1977 by The New York Times Company. Reprinted by permission.

programs, institutionalization and segregation. Not that integration is a new idea. The integration of new and special groups into the larger society is part of a strong and consistent thread in the American experience. *E pluribus unum.* And deaf children in urban areas like New York and Chicago, where there have been large numbers of trained people to teach, were integrated into public schools at various times since the 1940's.

What is different this time is the scope and scale of the plan. Each state and each school district must have an integration plan, in conformity with the Federal law, in effect by next September. For the first time, local school districts are being forced to accept the responsibility for the education of the deaf and all other handicapped children, and great numbers of deaf students are being guided into the public schools. This phenomenon is being cheered by some parents and education theorists and deplored by other parents and by psychologists of deafness like Dr. McCay Vernon of Western Maryland College. One of the few authorities considered with equal respect by both the deaf and hearing communities, Dr. Vernon calls mainstreaming "a devastating and destructive experience for huge numbers of deaf children." He stresses that "mainstreaming, when optimal, will work for only 10 percent of these children." As mainstreaming goes into effect, many others are beginning to echo his concerns.

The deaf constitute the only subculture whose members do not speak the same language as their parents. For most, American Sign is the language of social contact. State schools and the Washington, D.C.-based Gallaudet College, the world's only liberal-arts college for the deaf, teach in a combination of sign and speech called "total communication." Mrs. Beery is more fortunate than most deaf parents because she has the vital contact with her deaf children that sign language provides. For the mainstreamed deaf child of hearing parents, there is a double isolation, first from the hearing world at school and then from his own parents. In most cases, he is further separated from people by his inability to read lips, since only 20 to 30 percent of a given message is decipherable on the lips.

It was the hearing parents of deaf children, who usually do not master sign, who created the pressure to effect a radical change in both state and Federal law. They were angry at seeing their children either refused admission to local schools and sent off to the state schools for the deaf or else pushed through a system that gave them busy work but no education. Their demands, codified into the legal jargon of P.L. 94-142, the Education for All Handicapped Children's Act, reflect the following convictions:

Integration serves both deaf and hearing children. Deaf children have been "put away" for years, out of the mainstream of education and social life. This stifles their development and allows normal children to develop hostile attitudes and fears about them. Since the deaf child will have to get along in a hearing world, he should grow up interacting socially and intellectually with his hearing contemporaries. This integration also benefits hearing children, because they learn to appreciate that all people are different, with individual strengths and weaknesses. State institutions, besides isolating their students, foster dependency and promote cloistered behavior and idiosyncratic attitudes. Mainstreaming, while wrong for the profoundly deaf or multiple-handicapped, is an alternative. Each child should be evaluated on a case-by-case basis. To the greatest extent possible, the deaf child should attend regular classes.

Ardith Lehnerz, who has two hearing and three deaf children (one a foster child), and her husband, Don, vice president of the International Association of Parents of the Deaf, were leaders in the fight to pass P.L. 94-142. "In 1968, the word was integrate. They told us: 'Your child must grow up in a hearing world,' " Ardith explains. "It failed miserably [in Colorado] because the teachers were not trained to handle an occasional deaf child in full classes of hearing youngsters. The kids were unprepared for the deaf student and he was isolated if not actually laughed at. There were no backup services, psychological or educational, no special classroom materials for the child. I don't see where it is much different now. With a population of about 7.5 profoundly deaf children in 10,000 hearing, it means one deaf kid here and one deaf kid there, isolated in schools that are really not equipped to handle them. Yes, I know, 'institution' has a bad name. We sent the kids to the state school in Colorado Springs. They are flowering there. Why don't you go down and see?"

Don Lehnerz smiled when his wife said, "Institution." "When it's a fancy private prep school, it's traditional education. When it's a state school for the deaf, it's an institution. Integration tries to be all things to all men. It may wind up being something very little for very few."

Of course, different school districts interpret the word "integration" differently. For some, it seems to mean a sign language teacher in a special room with eight or nine deaf children between the ages of 6 and 13, "integrated" only in music and physical education, but without sign interpreters in these classes, where they are as vital as anywhere else. For some, it means one deaf child in a class with a sign interpreter. For some, it involves integration in a regular class where the teacher "has access" to a resource person who may or may not know anything about deafness. To a school in a rural district, it may mean nothing at all, a teacher grappling with 30 hearing students who does no more than give the simplest standard individualized reading material to her single deaf student.

More alarming was what we heard from parents and teachers in the area of student socialization. No matter which kind of integration was mentioned, both deaf children and their parents contradicted the glowing hopes of theoreticians and the picture presented so compellingly on the recent public-television special "Including Me." Except for the stories about the very few whose handicaps are negligible or correctable with hearing aids and who have good speech and outgoing personalities and were physically attractive, the picture we got from parents was one of consistent loneliness, isolation and social loss:

●"If they can, they find other deaf kids and stay with them."

●"The others don't tease them [the deaf students], they just ignore them."

●"There is only one other deaf boy in the school, a boy who also has cerebral palsy. My child is dying of starvation."

●"The new integration is the same old dumping. The teacher still turns her back and writes on the board, talking as she does. The same old visual aids, shown in the dark where no sign can be seen . . ."

After school, the loneliness of the day only deepens:

●"Oh, yes, on the surface there is communication, a greeting when he comes in—a sign or two that the kids learned or picked up from him. It isn't enough for real social contact; it's strictly a token thing. He's a curiosity."

●"No one understands her speech. She is continually frustrated."

●"The kids have 'friends' from 8 to 4," a teacher says. "After that they sit home alone."

"Watch those kids at lunch," Dr. Vernon, the psychologist of the deaf, told us. "What you see is that the normal and the handicapped eat separately. The low incidence of deafness almost guarantees that in most local schools there won't be any deaf child of his own age that he can be with. Never having heard speech, he may not be able to make intelligible words. Put this together with the fact that the overwhelming number of kids have little or no verbal communication with their parents and what you get is the very opposite of what you want—deaf children feeling self-worth and confidence with accepting, unafraid, normal peers in the classroom."

Special-education courses for teachers are supposed to train teachers to teach any student who comes into an integrated class. Such courses may mention deafness, but unless the teacher knows a great deal about the conceptual world of the deaf and the psychology of deafness, his deaf student will retreat into that handicap's old defenses: silence, a simulacrum of retardation or false acceptance—the nodded head, "Yes, I understand"—and responses based on the body language of the teacher. The child says whatever he thinks the teacher wants to hear.

"My son Donald spent a year in an integrated class," Ardith Lehnerz said. "When he was sick one day and I asked him how he was feeling, he said, 'Fine.' His face showed that he was having a terrible time. He had been taught to say, 'Fine' in response to 'How do you feel?' Who is going to take the time to make sure that these deaf kids really know such concepts—things the hearing kids get automatically?"

We pointed out that some schools will supply sign language interpreters, to which Ardith replied, "In the whole greater Denver area there aren't 15 interpreters competent to interpret and reverse-interpret a classroom situation. Years of training and a huge outlay in time and money will be necessary to give all these scattered children a fighting chance at integration. In places outside of the large cities the situation is even worse, because a deaf child will probably spend years at a school for which no interpreter may be available.

"I have seen some of the interpreters and watched them work," Ardith continued. "They have to be tutor-interpreters. How can you expect a person to teach important concepts taken for granted by hearing kids while she is interpreting the new material being taught? Is she supposed to teach sign while she interprets? And who interprets the john, the playground, the backchat that goes on from one kid to another at lunch, the entire social web of any group?"

"One child, one interpreter," said another parent. "Robinson Crusoe and Friday."

"It was my dream," confessed the mother of a temporarily mainstreamed child who later returned to the Colorado School for the Deaf and Blind in Colorado Springs, "to have my child belong, to see her get on the yellow local school bus, not the red special bus. For years people told me, 'At all costs, keep her out of the state institution, keep her with normal children.' In the end, I had to realize that my dreams were keeping her from her real friends. I sent her to the Springs. It was a defeat for us, a terrible defeat. In six months she was better adjusted, happier and learning more than she had with us in all her years at home. Of course, I miss her."

We spoke to a teacher in an inner city school, the kind of school where most of the integration of all kinds takes place, who told us: "I haven't got the time to give. The plans talk about small classes, no more than 10 in an integrated classroom and with backup services, interpreters, sign classes, psychological and evaluation service people who stay in constant contact with the teacher. It hasn't happened and I don't believe it will. How come we have never been able to have smaller classes before this, although everyone knows the classes for normal kids are too crowded to give individual attention? Where are all these supertrained people going to come from? Who is going to pay for all of it, all that expertise in every district in the county, the way the law says? The Legislature makes the law, but no one seems serious about funding it. I can't even get money for half the stuff I need for my regular kids. Where are the special, individualized aids to come from? There isn't even an individualized reading program for the deaf or the learning disabled. Deafness is a very special problem. I don't understand it, and I haven't the time to become an expert for the possible one or two deaf kids I will have integrated into my class in 30 years."

Legislators had hoped that the cost of mainstreaming deaf children would be less than the cost of maintaining eparate state facilities. In fact, mainstreaming is very xpensive. The legislators may not have realized how nuch it would take to fund the huge administrative ıetwork needed to screen, review, place and keep track of ıll the deaf children, to see that each child who is ntegrated into a school gets the appropriate services, to rain teachers and paraprofessionals to deliver these ervices, to test the progress of the students and make any ıecessary changes. The costs of a 10-student room—one of the main conditions under which the National Federa-ion of Teachers approved the mainstreaming idea—are ery high.

Furthermore, the state and other special schools, will till need money to continue educating those deaf students who are unable to succeed in the mainstream—an es-imated *90 percent.* Educators say that the Federal share ıt present breaks down to about $78 per deaf child a year, ess $25 for proposed administrative costs. How much of he remainder will filter down through the state system is a noot point.

An administrator of the new law admitted that costs to the states will be high, perhaps prohibitive, for a plan which will include necessary services, "but anything is preferable to dumping these deaf kids in a state institution. Only if they fail with us, fail even in the fullest of our programs, will we abandon them to life there." Since most of the successful and productive deaf people we know are graduates of the state schools, or of Gallaudet, the college for the deaf, we asked this administrator if he had discussed these problems with any deaf adults. He said he did not know any deaf people. We asked him how often he had visited the state school. He said he never had.

The Colorado School for the Deaf and Blind is within easy walking distance of downtown Colorado Springs. It is on a low hill and looks like a small Middle Western state college around which a city has grown. We had made an appointment with Robert Dawson, the superintendent of the combined deaf and blind facility.

Dawson is a hearing man whose background is in deafness. He has taught in or directed schools for the deaf in five states and has a good reputation in the deaf community both in Colorado and beyond. This is not easy. Deaf people judge their hearing intermediaries with deep ambivalence.

He was frank with us and worried. "Large numbers of deaf children are being guided by social workers and educators into mainstreaming programs. The brighter kids at this school have the idea that 'least restrictive environment' means freedom to goof off. They are leaving to give integration a whirl. We'll be left with kids who take more staff and more support services, while the money will go with the brighter, easier kids. Of course, there is going to be a huge waste of time and people. When the pendulum begins to swing back—and there are already some signs of it—our money and services will have been cut drastically. I've been bucking the institution stigma for years. With our budget cut, and the upper-level kids being counseled away, the pejorative meaning of the word 'institution' can very quickly become a reality."

We asked him why the state schools have a stigma. "Part of it is cultural, I think." Dawson said. "People remember overcrowded snake pits years after they have been improved and humanized. The state facilities are underfunded and always have been. We can't pay enough to get the top trained people we need as houseparents for the dorms, the supportive help, psychological and other. We need vision screening for the deaf kids here, for example, for Usher's syndrome [a genetic condition beginning in deafness and resulting in deaf-blindness]. I don't know how the Legislature thinks it can afford it for every district. We have deaf people teaching who not only understand deafness as we never could, but who also serve as role models for deaf youngsters who on the outside are seldom permitted to see or interact with a deaf adult. It hurts me that so little of this is appreciated in the larger educational world. They never deal with it."

"Are you afraid of losing your job if mainstreaming really takes over?" we asked.

Dawson smiled. "My job has never been more secure. No one's been watching the statistics on deafness except us, I guess. In the old days—before so many of the childhood diseases were eradicated, most of our students had been deafened post lingually. They were kids of 5 and 6 and already had a good grasp of language—of its metaphoric uses and the thought patterns English imposes. When language is already there, you get an entirely different kind of deaf person, one who is much less handicapped. Now, the overwhelming number of deaf children are born deaf and have no language skills whatsoever to build on. Furthermore, because of advances in surgery, in pediatric care, most of the birth-defect kids are not dying, but living with multiple handicaps, one of which is often deafness. Ever larger numbers are deaf-blind, deaf-blind-retarded, etc. These children can't ever be mainstreamed."

We asked him to comment on the talk we had heard from the integration people that the state school fosters dependency. "We get many kids who are already dependent," Dawson said. "Talk to the teachers here who are deaf and blind. They see much more deeply into the psychological aspects of these things."

We went to the deaf school's teachers' lounge. Deaf and hearing teachers came by between classes and talked to us, curious to learn what we had heard from special-education teachers, parents and kids. Many of them had previously taught in other systems—in special-education classes in integrated schools or in itinerant-tutor programs for homebound deaf children.

"I wasn't getting any cooperation from the regular teachers at the mainstreamed schools," one of the teachers said. "The regular teachers had been forced to take their deaf students. They were at a loss as to how to integrate them into what was going on in the class. Their bitterness was reflected in their treatment of us."

"We put three of our top kids in a math class," another said. "The administration said that the math was supposed to be individualized—learning-program stuff that did not require interpreters. Within six months all of them had gone up the spout in math and were losing what math they did have."

We asked what proportion of the deaf student population could be successfully mainstreamed. They said they thought somewhere between 10 and 15 percent.

We asked about dependence again. "We get little support for these kids, and the parents get even less." one teacher said. "There is no agency, organization or service in most states to train parents for the special problems and needs of deafness. Few mental-health clinics or counseling organizations include people with that kind of expertise. The kids learn little in the public schools and the parents are not capable of teaching them the ordinary life skills—dressing and personal hygiene, shopping, money, sex information, human relations, traveling in the city. Sometimes they do too much for the kids; they're afraid and overly cautious—mostly because they don't know *how* to teach them. And to one extent or another there is guilt, shame, anger, disappointment about having had a deaf child in the first place. With some, the feelings are so bad that they ignore their deaf children, and the kids come here at age 9 or 10 with the social development of a child of 6 or 7, and with no words, no signs, no communication but some idiosyncratic 'family' gestures. Yes, they are dependent."

"Is this true for all deaf kids?" we asked.

"Hell no!" Alonzo Whitt, a deaf teacher, said emphatically. He used "total communication," the polite and attractive combination of sign and speech. His speech was clear. "You're talking about some of the children of hearing parents. My folks are deaf and so are my brothers and sisters. I had a normal family life, without the dependency and isolation of the child deprived of communication."

We asked him about his schooling. "I went to a hearing school from age 6 to 10." Whitt said. "My parents heard the business about 'having to live in a hearing world.' They thought it might be a good idea. I was lost. I am so tired of that old phrase. I am living in a hearing world right now; I've always lived in one. I relate to hearing neighbors, storekeepers, all the rest, the same as you do.

"The paradox is that without the education I got in 'deaf' schools I would be hopelessly lost in the hearing world now," Whitt continued. "Isolation in such schools is a fallacy. Half the people in this school are hearing. The kids interact with them all the time. In the hearing schools I went to, including college, I always had to make the first move, to adjust, to ask for help, to ask others to repeat, to depend on others. It was O.K. in college because I had the verbal skills then, and, luckily, the speech, and it was O.K. in deaf high school because I went with hearing kids on weekends, but it was up to me how much I wanted."

At lunch we listened to the kids. We sat with Donald and Terry Lehnerz. The school's lunchroom was comfortably noisy. The ugliness of deaf voices is not jarring here, possibly because it "belongs" as they do and is unself-conscious. The room roared with sign. We asked the kids what they thought of their experiences in hearing schools. "It was great!" one boy said. "They never make you go back over anything and do it again, like you have to do here. You can turn in anything. I had a great time."

The Lehnerz children were not as enthusiastic about the state school as their parents had been. They liked it but did not admit that they had become less dependent and more mature. Most of the kids admitted that the sports and the social life were much better than they had been in integrated schools. Some students mentioned an improved learning situation. They weren't eager to please us and there were none of the great big smiles common when the deaf are on display in token situations. There was about these children no bizarre or idiosyncratic insitutionalized behavior at all.

Social pressure at a school for the deaf is as strong as it is in any community. Reasonably, some deaf people choose to leave. What impressed us was a feeling of flow here, and that each deaf student was choosing how much of the hearing world he wanted and was ready for. Some deaf kids had lots of hearing friends and it was generally admitted that the hearing world is more exciting, powerful and alluring. But we also got the feeling that some of the kids were using the hearing world as if it were a Disneyland, "passing" into it as a vacation from responsiblity.

We went to the building where the blind children had their section of the state school and into Bambi Marcantonio's room, where a group of first graders were working. It is a pity Bambi's children could not see their teacher. She looks like everyone's dream of a grandmother.

"I asked to see you—I have so much to say about this integration thing, even though I teach only the blind," she said. All the planners of integration schemes talk about the handicapped, but each group's problem is different. When my sightless children come to me, most of them do not know what a room is. How can a teacher with a class of sighted children take the weeks necessary to acquaint her blind student with everything in his environment until it is familiar and comfortable to him? Others get it at a glance.

"Mainstream people will tell you about the little blind child coloring along with the others, using special guides. Why? Does this teach concepts he must have? Colors? Forms? Or is it a kind of puppetry? I have been blind all my life, and I have seen this idea of integration a dozen times in a dozen forms. On the surface, they want you to think, 'We want you blind and deaf people to be part of us. We're accepting you—including you.' But it is non-acceptance, it's really saying, 'We want you to be *like* us. We cannot accept your blindness.' "

There was no bitter edge to Bambi's voice. A child came over and was introduced. After asking a question and receiving a reply, he was not guided back to his work but told to return to it. He went quickly, competently.

"Don't you see?" she asked. "We want to compete at our own level. This is their room. They are not the ones always having to make the adjustments. Here they participate in everything. What blind kid in public school can play the lead in the school play, sing in the choir, be fully integrated into a sports program?"

What blind child, we wondered, was likely to have a blind teacher?

When we left the state school we wondered what other opinions in the deaf community might help us to put what we had seen into a wider perspective. We arranged interviews with Dr. Fred Schreiber, head of the National Association of the Deaf, the most powerful deaf organization in the country and Dr. Edward C. Merrill, president of Gallaudet College in Washington, D.C.

Dr. Schreiber sounded dubious. "People say great things about integration and it certainly has some possibilities—if it will work. I don't think it will work. It is the law now and we'll try it, but I honestly don't hold out much hope for it. Without all the necessary support, you're back to the same dumping I grew up with. I was a fantastic lip reader, one of the few, and I was 'integrated' into a regular schoolroom. Regardless of how good you are, you can't 'get' enough to make sense of things and to keep from making the mistakes that brand you as a clown or a fool. The teacher asks a question. The student behind you or to the side gives an answer. It is wrong. The teacher then calls on you. Not having lipread the other student's wrong answer, you inadvertently make the same mistake. A little of this is all it takes to make you prefer the corner and a school career of the nodded head and the phony acquiescence."

We asked Dr. Schreiber why the kids at the state school had more positive feelings about integration than their parents and teachers. He laughed. "Everyone knows that the hearing world is where it's at. There is a mountain of false expectation in young deaf people. What magic, what power, what glory there is in that other country. The kid knows too that in hearing schools he can get away with murder, can be lazy or aggressive or a clown and be tolerated because there are no other deaf people to call his bluff. Because he is handicapped."

Dr. Merrill expressed his support of the law but wondered about its implementation. "I see very strong positive elements in the handicapped children's act. The mandate that local schools be responsible for programs for all their children, the insistence on personalized education, the concept of least restrictive environment, and last but most important, the natural commitment by the Government to qualify education for all handicapped. In my view, this is the only way that the handicapped are going to get an equal share in the educational possibilities existing in the community. Gallaudet does not see integration as a threat. Of course, the terrific language problems even at the college level do not allow for the usual teaching methods used for the hearing. I view this act as progress because it gives options. Where the worry comes is in the implementation of the law."

Dr. Vernon, the psychologist of deafness and co-author, with Dr. Eugene Mindel, of a landmark book about the dynamics of the early years of deaf children, "They Grow In Silence," was less sanguine. "Admittedly the law has many things to recommend it, and for some marginally handicapped children, it represents a fine statement of the Government's good intentions.

"Unfortunately, the decisions are now and will continue to be in the hands of people who do not understand the severity of deafness's linguistic and social deficits." Vernon continued: "We've been told, for example, that one of the great advantages of integration is its positive effect on the normal children in the classroom. Research done over a long period of time shows that this is true only if certain other conditions are present. It is the quality of the interaction that makes for success or failure. The hearing students will have had to undergo a realistic and careful orientation to the specific nature of deafness. They will have to have teachers and paraprofessionals trained in deafness and with a positive attitude toward it. They will have to see enough deaf children functioning at a high enough level to dispel the formation of stereotypes strongly imbedded in the culture and, last but not least, they will have to have a continuous and active instruction in sign by a competent person.

"This orientation and understanding of deafness does not come in a two-hour workshop," Vernon said. "It takes not only study but close association with deaf people. The administrators who plan and design this program are going to be people who have never seen a deaf child."

A deaf friend who had grown up without sign but who learned it later in life discussed his early education with us: "It was as though I had been told: 'Now you must draw an animal that a teacher will describe to you. You will not be permitted to see the pencil or the paper or a picture of the animal you are to draw. And please, don't keep starting over. You are smudging the paper.' "

The marginally handicapped were never the problem. For them, the choices have usually been there. For the moderately and seriously handicapped, integration may result in loss of money and staff from the places of greatest need, funneled away into programs that serve some parents' capacity for denial and many teachers' and students' capacity for indifference.

THERE'S A DEAF CHILD IN MY CLASS

Whether mainstreaming advocate or opponent, you soon may have a deaf child in your class. Here's how to cope and to enhance the education of all children.

Barry R. Culhane and Richard Curwin

Barry R. Culhane is chairperson of the academic department for general education at the National Technical Institute for the Deaf and a psychology teacher. Richard Curwin, a faculty development specialist at the same institution, has worked with Barry Culhane in presenting workshops about mainstreaming deaf students.

Proponents of mainstreaming make some basic assumptions about the advantages of hearing impaired students being in regular classrooms rather than in special schools. One is that if the hearing impaired student has a chance to interact with the kind of people who will make up the world in which the student will ultimately function, the student's communication skills will be increased, and the basic skills in reading, math and other school subjects will be maintained at a higher level. They further assume that the social skills of hearing impaired students will develop in a way similar to those of hearing students.

There are opponents to mainstreaming, however, who disagree with the assumption that integrating disabled and nondisabled students in the same classroom has these benefits. Although these educators agree that disabled children should receive the best educational experience possible, they believe that mainstreaming is not the solution because disabled students should have special attention geared to their individual needs. Regular classrooms and teachers, the argument goes, are just not equipped to meet these needs. There is, in addition, a great fear that the disabled student will be misunderstood and possibly ridiculed by the other students. Also, hearing impaired students attain different levels of language development depending upon their age at the onset of hearing loss, the degree of the loss, whether or not the child has deaf parents, the child's communication training and how early the deafness was discovered. Severely inhibited language development can create special problems because one of the major criteria for success in most American classrooms is written or oral fluency in English.

Regardless of Your Beliefs, Prepare for the Situation

Regardless of your beliefs about the pros and cons of mainstreaming hearing impaired students, you might eventually find yourself proclaiming, "There's a deaf child in my class!" The Education for All Handicapped Children Act of 1975 (PL 94-142) mandates that all handicapped children have an opportunity to receive free and appropriate educations in the least restrictive environment. The law also provides for due-process safeguards for handicapped individuals and their parents by insisting that states receiving federal aid implement guidelines that guarantee a maximally effective Individual Educational Plan for each handicapped child. We offer the following suggestions for coping with changes that the entry of hearing impaired students will make in your class. In many cases, these suggestions can enhance the education of all students.

1. Do not allow initial awkwardness to develop into lingering, uncomfortable feelings. Acquaint yourself with other hearing impaired individuals before meeting your new students for the first time. Many cities have schools for the deaf that would welcome a visit from an interested teacher. You may meet teachers, many of whom may be hearing impaired themselves, who work with hearing impaired students. Visit their classrooms and interact with their students. A call to your local vocational rehabilitation agency might provide you with another opportunity for meeting hearing impaired individuals. It may even be possible for you to meet with a local deaf club

Reprinted by special permission of LEARNING, The Magazine for Creative Teaching, January 1978. © 1978 by Education Today Company, Inc.

member who may be willing to accompany you for a visit to a local club. These interactions can help you become familiar with deaf students and adults. Occasionally, one or both parents of a hearing impaired child may be deaf, and these experiences will help you develop positive relationships with both students and parents.

2. Understand that all hearing losses are not the same. They can be mild or profound and involve one or both ears. Different kinds of losses produce different effects on students. Find out the nature of each student's problem and learn the best way to deal with the individual rather than attempt to find general ways of dealing with deafness.

3. Do not assume that deaf students are mute. A large majority of deaf people have no physical problem with their sound-producing mechanisms. But because these individuals cannot monitor their voices, they may sound different with respect to loudness, pitch, tone and discrimination of specific sounds. Many hearing impaired people do not like to use their voices because they lack training or fear embarrassment. Differences in speech and communication modes can create the misconception that deaf persons are somehow less intelligent. This, of course, is nonsense—intelligence is distributed normally among deaf students.

Encourage the student to ask questions by developing a non-threatening atmosphere in which the hearing impaired student does not feel embarrassed by what she perceives as inappropriate questions.

4. Do not expect all deaf students to speechread (lipread) well. Not every deaf child learns to be a good speechreader, and even those who are highly skilled cannot depend on speechreading alone. Good speechreaders can comprehend 25 to 30 percent of the spoken message.

5. Be ready to accept a wide variety of communication skills from deaf students. Those students who come to you from "oral" schools, or schools that stress speech and speechreading, have different skills from those who were trained to use sign language.

6. Do not expect all deaf students to be exceptional readers. And don't think that deaf students will understand a concept by merely reading it. Most deaf children do not read as well as their hearing peers, and just giving a deaf child reading material will not guarantee understanding any more than it will with most children. In fact, deaf youngsters might have difficulty with reading comprehension because of poor vocabulary development and problems with English sentence structure.

7. Reject all the other misconceptions, such as deaf people see better, cannot appreciate music or dance, cannot drive. These give false impressions about deaf students and can limit what might be done to meet their needs and educational requirements.

Some Specific Suggestions

Ideally, before a deaf child enters your classroom, your school system will have provided faculty and administrators with in-service training about the impact of deaf pupils on school programs and the communication processes that will be used in teaching the hearing impaired. In addition, resources for communication training and consultation should be readily available. Finally, the school system should have addressed issues of curriculum modification, adaption of the environment to include visual media as supplements to instruction, and provision of support services including note-taking, tutoring, interpreting and counseling.

This fall, some teachers will find themselves with a hearing impaired child in their classrooms and will need practical suggestions for meeting the challenge of teaching that child. Here are ten:

1. Get the student's attention when you speak. Tapping loudly on a desk or lecturn or waving your hand will help. In a group discussion, have the speaker point to the next person to talk. If an interpreter is present, he or she will do this. The main purpose is to ensure that the hearing impaired student knows the visual or auditory source of information. Be aware, however, that continuous visual attention could lead to visual fatigue; allow time for a rest.

2. Using a normal tone of voice, speak clearly at a moderate pace. Exaggerated speech can interfere with lipreading. To facilitate speechreading, look directly at the student as much as possible. Try to maintain eye contact with the student and to avoid moving around the room too quickly. When you use the chalkboard, wait until you are finished before speaking so that words directed to the board are not lost to the hearing impaired child. Try not to block sight of your lips with a book, pencil or other object when you are speaking.

3. Rephrase a thought or question to make it more understandable to the deaf child. Give test directions, homework assignments, discussion notes and any important instructions *in writing*. You may have to clarify questions and repeat them during fast-moving discussions. If an interpreter is involved, translating may cause a slight time lag that can make it difficult for the hearing impaired student to follow a discussion. If aides are not available for note-taking and tutoring, ask a hearing peer to volunteer. Although the hearing impaired student will need assistance to gain information initially, allow the student to demonstrate independence and creative thinking abilities.

4. Use as many visual aids as possible, including overhead projectors, captioned films, slides, newsprint and the chalkboard. Avoid having the source of information (including yourself) in a poorly lighted area or in an area where bright light is behind it. Pacing around the classroom or changing sources of information rapidly can hinder understanding.

5. Obtain feedback from the student so that you know he understands. Be aware of any vocabulary limitations or difficulties with English idioms. Present new vocabulary in advance. If the student does not seem to understand, repeat or rephrase the information and ask the student to demonstrate his understanding. You may need to slow the pace of communication.

6. Encourage development of communication skills including speech, speechreading, finger spelling and manual communication. Encourage the use of any residual hearing the student may possess. Work with your committee for the handicapped to get needed resources. Encourage the student to ask questions by developing a nonthreatening atmosphere in which the hearing impaired student does not feel embarrassed by what she perceives as inappropriate questions.

7. Seat the student where he will have visual access to the instructor, other students and visual media. Allow the student to change seats to gain this access in all situations.

8. When critical information is presented, be sure the hearing impaired student understands. Be sure someone repeats loudspeaker an-

nouncements, such as early or late bus arrivals. If you know there will be a practice fire alarm, share the information with the hearing impaired student so that he is not thrown into a panic. If critical information is announced or a fire alarm sounds, flicking a light off and on can gain the student's attention.

9. Become knowledgeable about hearing aids. You may be able to replace hearing aid batteries, to reduce certain kinds of noise levels and even to make minor repairs. Be aware of changes in hearing caused by colds, chronic ear infections or other illnesses.

10. Work closely with the support personnel available to you. Provide the interpreter with an outline of the classroom presentation and notify her of any materials requiring special lighting arrangements. Reproductions of charts, graphs and diagrams in the form of hard copies and transparencies can help note-takers, tutors and the hearing impaired students. A profile of the course content, resources and methods of evaluation can help give the student realistic expectations for the class.

If you know there will be a practice fire alarm, share the information with the hearing impaired student so that he is not thrown into a panic.

These suggestions are merely a start. Your own creative approaches can add to a basic understanding and awareness of the needs of a deaf student as well as diminish the initial apprehension both you and the student may have.

Resource List

- *A Bicentennial Monograph on Hearing Impairment: Trends in the U.S.A.*, edited by R. Frisina. From Alexander Graham Bell Association for the Deaf, Inc., 3417 Volta Pl., N.W., Washington, DC 20007.
- *The Deaf Experience: An Anthology of Literature by and About the Deaf*, edited by T.W. Batson and E. Bergman. From Merriam-Eddy Co., P.O. Box 25, South Waterford, ME 04081. Cost: $7.50.
- *Educating the Deaf* by D.F. Moores. From Houghton Mifflin Co., 1 Beacon St., Boston, MA 02107. Cost: $13.95.
- "An In-Service Program for Integrating Hearing Impaired Children" by L.W. Nober in *The Volta Review* (1975), vol. III, pp. 173–175. From Alexander Graham Bell Association for the Deaf, Inc., 3417 Volta Pl., N.W., Washington, DC 20007.
- *In This Sign* by Joanne Greenberg. From Avon Books, 959 Eighth Ave., New York, NY 10019. Cost: $1.50.
- "Mainstreaming: Issues and a Model Plan" by M. Vernon and H. Prickett in *Audiology and Hearing Education* (1976), vol. II, pp. 5–11. From Audiology and Hearing Education, Inc., 12849 Magnolia Blvd., North Hollywood, CA 91607.
- "Partial Integration of Deaf With Hearing Students: Residential School Perspectives" by W.M. Craig and J.M. Salem in *American Annals of the Deaf* (1975), vol. 120, pp. 28–36. From Convention of American Instructors of the Deaf, Inc., 5034 Wisconsin Ave., N.W., Washington, DC 20016.
- *Sound and Sign: Childhood Deafness and Mental Health* by H.S. Schlesinger and K.P. Meadow. From University of California Press, Berkeley, CA 94720. Cost: $10.00.
- *They Grow in Silence: The Deaf Child and His Family* by E.D. Mindel and M. Vernon. From National Assoc. of the Deaf, 814 Thayer Ave., Silver Spring, MD 20910. Cost: $5.50.

SPEECH PROBLEMS: What You Should Do And Shouldn't Do

Teachers can assume increased responsibility for meeting the needs of their lisping, stuttering students. Here's some advice from a speech pathologist.

DONALD MOWRER

Donald Mowrer is a professor in the speech department at Arizona State University.

For many years, speech clinicians in schools seemed to be working under a philosophy that said: the more, the better. With school administrators eager to collect state funds that were based on special education head counts, speech clinicians were forced into building enrollments by signing up children from the lower grades—children whose chief speech problem was misarticulated sounds. Back in 1960, when some 750,000 kids were enrolled in speech therapy classes around the country, one national study discovered that 81 percent of the children being seen by the speech clinicians in the survey had problems of articulation and that 75 percent of the clinicians worked mainly with students in the kindergarten, first and second grades.

This entire effort had glaring flaws. Large enrollments meant that speech clinicians were able to see children only in groups and only for short periods of time. These conditions often made the therapy ineffective. What's more, misarticulating children were not the ones who most needed the skilled therapist's help, because the majority of children enrolled in these speech therapy classes had articulation problems that were developmental in nature. In other words, most children would outgrow their speech problems, would acquire adequate speech, *with or without the aid of speech therapy*.

The numbers game, however, may be passing away. With the advent of the accountability movement and with the increased emphasis on educating and mainstreaming handicapped children, the trend now is to give speech therapy primarily to those who are seriously handicapped. The state of Wisconsin has stipulated by law (Chapter 115) that only those children whose deviant speech can be shown to interfere with the child's learning process may be enrolled in speech therapy classes. No longer is a speech clinician permitted to include in her or his schedule children who misarticulate a few sounds such as *s*, *r*, *th* or *l*, because these minor sound problems could hardly interfere with the child's learning process. Speech clinicians in Wisconsin now see only severely impaired handicapped children, such as those with delayed language, with moderate to severe cases of stuttering, children who have developed vocal nodules, the hard of hearing and deaf children, as well as those children who have *severe* articulation problems or multiple handicaps. Other states may follow Wisconsin's lead.

The Role of the Classroom Teacher

What has all this got to do with the classroom teacher? Simply this: You can expect to receive less help with children in your classroom who have mild articulatory problems. If they are going to receive help, *it must come from you*. On the other hand, you should expect more help with the children who have severe communication handicaps. But servicing the severely handicapped will require much of the speech clinician's time. Many speech clinicians in Wisconsin now see only 20 or 30 children annually. Some have established language programs that operate on a half-day basis to serve 10 to 15 language-impaired children. During the other half day, these children return to their regular classrooms. Special language-instruction programs headed by speech clinicians are appearing in all parts of the country. In many cases, speech clinicians are teaming up with special education teachers as well as remedial reading teachers in a joint effort to meet the needs of the severely handicapped child.

Few could argue against such a change in the speech clinician's role. The severely handicapped children must be served. But what about those children who lisp, or who pronounce "rabbit" the way cartoon character Elmer Fudd does?

Fortunately, there are many things the classroom teacher can do that should help children "outgrow" their articulation difficulties more rapidly than if we simply wait for time to pass. Classroom teachers have several distinct advantages over the speech clinician: A teacher is in contact with the child for four to six hours each weekday and therefore has the opportunity to structure daily speaking activities to meet the needs of the child. If the teacher has some knowledge

Reprinted by special permission of LEARNING, The Magazine for Creative Teaching, October 1978. © 1978 by Education Today Company, Inc.

about how sounds are learned, the teacher is in an ideal position to help kids learn correct articulation habits.

What You Need To Know

By the time a child is four years old, he should be talking in sentences with a fair degree of fluency. When he's five, the structure of his sentences will be correct for the most part and he'll have enough words in his vocabulary to describe most of his daily wants. His ability to articulate all of the sounds in our language may not occur until he reaches seven or, at the most, eight years of age. Even at eight years we can expect to find some lingering children who occasionally confuse pronouns, treat irregular verbs as regular ones, repeat some syllables or words in a hesitant fashion and misarticulate *s* and *r* sounds.

Generally, we can expect the bulk of the children to have mastered the mechanics of communication skills by the time they enter second grade, certainly by the time they are third graders. But roughly 10 percent of schoolchildren will not achieve adequate communication skills. Their faulty speech will have an adverse effect upon their social and academic adjustment in direct relation to the severity of their communication handicap.

Articulation habits, however, can be changed—and changed rapidly, *provided certain procedures are followed.* Example: A substantial number of children will be found in the primary grades who misarticulate the *s, r* and *th* sounds. Whenever I speak to groups of classroom teachers, I ask them to tell me the first instruction they would give to a child who misarticulates one of the three sounds just named. Without fail, the majority of teachers reply that they would ask the child to imitate their own production of the sound. But when I asked 400 speech clinicians this question, only about 13 percent made this suggestion. Eight times out of ten, when you ask a lisping child to imitate your production of the *s* sound, you will get *th* in return. What else should you expect from a child who has lisped for five years?

The speech clinicians I have surveyed almost always recommend telling the child where to put his teeth or tongue in order to make a new sound. The simple request, "Close your teeth and say *e*," followed by a second request, "Keep your teeth closed and say *es*" (as in *east*), will almost always result in a correct *s* sound from the child who lisps. After a few more trials saying *es*, the instructor says, "Now keep your teeth closed and say *s*" (the *s* in *sun*, not the alphabet letter pronunciation). After *s* is practiced several times, it is combined with a few vowels such as long *o, e, a* and *i*. Before the child realizes it, he is saying words like *so, see, say* and *sigh*. A consonant is then added, resulting in the words *soap, seat, sail* and *sight*. Phrases are constructed, followed by sentences containing these words, and finally, the child is encouraged to repeat short stories loaded with *s* words. The process is a simple one and has been accomplished, under the supervision of a speech clinician, by third graders acting as tutors for lisping first grade children.

The obvious cue, "close your teeth," appears to be the critical instruction to help children who lisp, and it's a cue teachers could easily employ. But it only works for children who have normal dentition (arrangement of teeth). If teeth are missing, if there is a space between the teeth when they are closed, or if the child has a sizable overbite, then the close-your-teeth cue will not be effective. (It would be best if a speech clinician could quickly check dentition to see if some physical anomaly is causing the lisp.)

Teaching a correct *th* sound is almost as straightforward as teaching *s*. The key cue is, "Stick your tongue out and blow." By using a mirror, the child can easily imitate your tongue position. Once in a while a child will bite on his tongue and blow the air laterally from the sides of his mouth. You can remedy the misdirected air stream by holding a lighted match about four inches from the center of the child's mouth and asking him to blow it out while following the cue. Or a straw can be placed directly in front of the mid-portion of the mouth. Once the air stream blows through the center portion of the mouth between the top of the tongue and the cutting edges of the front teeth, you can advance to step two. While the child is blowing out air as just described, ask him to quickly open his mouth saying, "Uh." This will result in the syllable *thuh*. Practice it a few times until the child can say it quickly. Add an *m* sound to the end and you have the word *thumb*. The child still may not recognize the word until you hold up your thumb and say, "What's this?" Chances are he'll quickly say, "Fumb." That's your cue to tell him to stick out his tongue and slowly say it like this, "Th---------umb," as you prolong the *th* sound. Other words can soon be added—*thing, thick, think* and *thin*.

Words that end with *th* (*both, bath*) can be learned easily by prolonging the word and stressing the *th* sound. It may be a little more difficult for him to pronounce words containing the voiced *th* as in *they, them* or *breathe*.

The third sound commonly misarticulated by children in the primary grades is *r*. It is one of the more difficult sounds to evoke from children because you can't *see* it. But again, tongue position is probably the most important cue you can provide. The most likely reason a child misarticulates *r* is because his tongue rests relatively flat on the bottom of the mouth. The tongue must be in a raised and back position before *r* can be articulated. Actually, the position for *g* and *r* are very similar. The tongue moves very little when the sounds *g* and *r* are produced together (*gr*).

One effective way to evoke the *r* sound is to tell the child to lift his tongue tip up and back while saying, "Ah." The "ah" sound should change to "ahr" (*r*) as the tip curls up and backward. Once "ahr" is established, it is easy to produce words like *car, far, bar* and *tar*. Then the child can practice sentences such as: *I see the car; he is far; lift the bar.*

An alternative method for evoking *r* is to tell the child to use his tongue to draw a circle around the roof of his mouth, making the circle swing as far back as he can on the roof of his mouth. He is to vocalize "ah" while doing this. You will find that as the tongue swings backward, the "ah" sound will change to sound more like an *r* sound. That's when you say, "Good." Encourage the production of more sounds of a similar nature and shortly you can dispense with the circular motion while retaining the *r* sound from the backward tongue position.

Evoking the *r* in the initial position can often be accomplished by starting from an "er" sound and adding the vowel "uh." Once "eruh" is produced, move to words like *run, rough* and *rug*. Other words with different vowels can then be added.

Building articulation skills cannot be done overnight. It may require five to ten minutes of daily practice for a week or two before the child feels comfortable saying sounds in this new way. If the parents provide support at home by helping the child practice saying word lists that you devise, then you can expect to hear rapid progess.

Most speech clinicians would be happy to provide several in-service training workshops for teachers.

During these workshops, procedures for detecting and treating many communication problems commonly found among young children could be learned.

There are, however, some speech problems that can be more serious than misarticulation. Children with these problems should be referred to a speech clinician, who should be able to work with a teacher in setting up a plan for therapy. Following are a few examples of these problems.

Stuttering—How the Teacher Can Help

The person who discovers the cause of stuttering will indeed become famous. The search for the elusive cause of this speech disorder has spanned 2,000 years, and even today, with all of our accumulated knowledge, we still are not sure what causes stuttering. But we have collected many facts about this unusual communication disorder. We know, for example, that stuttering affects approximately 1 percent of the general population and is found in almost every society from African Bushmen to Asian merchants. The prevalence of stuttering appears to be greatest within societies that stress communication skills and least, if not absent, within societies in which there is little, if any, emphasis placed upon the importance of oral communication.

We also know that there are four boy stutterers for every girl who stutters, and that three fourths of those who stutter are labeled as stutterers before the time they reach the age of 3½ years. Some stutterers can sing without stuttering, can read aloud with another person with no problem, can become fluent by changing the pitch of the voice or by speaking rhythmically. In some cases, stutterers can become more fluent simply by slowing down.

One theory is that stuttering is triggered by stimuli that evoke fear or anxiety in the mind of the stutterer. These stimuli may consist of certain sounds or words. They may be situational—speaking on the telephone, or to an important person, or to a group of people. Generally, stutterers have the most difficulty when they are requested to answer a specific question or when they wish to make a request. Simple, automatic statements such as "Hi," "How are you," "Let's see now" or "You know" may not present a problem to a stutterer.

Sooner or later, almost every classroom teacher is certain to encounter a student who stutters. The big problem is what to do about the inevitable speaking situations that occur in the classroom. Should the teacher treat the stutterer like everyone else, or should special compensations be made? Should the teacher call upon the stutterer to answer questions in class or should he be gracefully passed over? And most important, what should the teacher do while the child is stuttering?

What you do about stuttering in your classroom depends upon some assumptions you must make about the cause of stuttering. If you see the problem as a learned behavior resulting from past speech conditioning through which the stutterer learned to fear certain speaking situations (a widely held theory), then your course of action would be to reduce the amount of fear the stutterer may have of such speaking situations. The easiest way to accomplish this is to create speaking situations that produce the least possible fear. From a series of observations, you will probably discover that giving a report while standing in front of the class will create the greatest amount of stuttering, but if you go to a stutterer's seat and ask a question that can be answered with a simple yes or no, he will be much less likely to stutter. By purposefully engaging him in unstressful speaking situations while avoiding anxiety-producing speech situations, it is possible to help build the child's confidence in his ability to speak fluently. Gradually, as he develops confidence in speaking fluently, the child is asked to speak under more stress-producing speech situations, such as giving brief answers while seated at his desk or joining in small group discussions.

During these speaking episodes, the teacher may reward fluency by commenting, "That was a good job of talking" or "You said that very well." Reprimands are unwise.

A different approach, equally defendable, is one that emphasizes personality adjustment and positive self-image rather than fluent speech. Proponents of this view inform children that it is perfectly all right to stutter. It is how you feel about yourself and your speech that is important. Feelings of self-worth and confidence, rather than speech patterns, are targets for change.

Speech clinicians may use widely differing approaches to the treatment of stuttering, depending upon how they were trained and what method they think is best for a specific individual. The teacher should work closely with the speech clinician in devising a treatment model for the stuttering child.

What About Disorders of Voice?

Voice disorders are found among from 1 to 5 percent of schoolchildren, depending upon one's definition of a voice disorder. The most common voice disorder is one resulting from vocal abuse. Persistent yelling, screaming and loud talk may result in a noticeably hoarse or low-pitched and breathy voice quality. Some teachers might assume that some children just naturally have hoarse voice qualities and, therefore, never refer these children to the speech clinician or the school nurse for a checkup. But frequently, prolonged misuse of the voice can result in the formation of small growths, called vocal nodules, on the vocal cords.

Early detection, then, is the best protection against vocal nodules. A laryngologist (throat specialist) is qualified to make the diagnosis, but once it's made and treatment is begun (to reduce vocal abuse), the classroom teacher can be of great aid in the treatment program. By pointing out to the child those occasions on which he uses his voice to imitate cement trucks or machine guns, the teacher can help the child become aware of how he is misusing his voice and thus help him reduce these instances of abuse.

Another disorder the teacher may notice is a nasalized quality some children's voices have. Children who were born with inadequate tissue in the soft palate (a valve which keeps the air from escaping through the nasal passages) or who have a cleft in the roof of the mouth will have nasal speech. Sounds that require a buildup of pressure in the oral cavity (such as the plosive sounds of *p, b, k, g, t* and *k*) will especially be affected. Often, the child will have a visible scar on the upper lip as a result of an early operation to close the cleft lip as well as the roof of the oral cavity. The teacher should, of course, consult with the speech clinician when problems of nasality due to a cleft palate are suspected.

The opposite of nasal speech is a denasal voice quality. In this case, the child sounds as though he has a head cold all the time. The *m, n* and *ing* sounds that normally are released through the nasal cavity are blocked from entering this cavity due either to enlarged tonsils or adenoids or some other nasal obstruction. The teacher's role is one of referring these children to the speech clinician.

When a Language Problem Is Suspected

It is important to distinguish between what are considered problems of English language *usage* and the more deeply rooted deficits of language ability. The child who uses double negatives, improper grammar, or who pronounces some words oddly, probably does so as a result of learning these speech patterns from his parents or peers. Some black dialects may violate many Standard English "rules," but most linguists view these dialects as being appropriate within the language community in which they are used. But the child who is unable to use his speech to communicate his needs or is unable to understand the speech of others has a language problem.

Unfortunately, there are no easy one-two-three step solutions to the problems language-deficient children have. Each child's problem is unique and requires special diagnosis to identify exactly the type of training needed to remedy the problem. Language improvement kits used by many classroom teachers were not designed to cope with serious language deficits. A great deal of individual attention is needed to help those children develop adequate language skills, and frequently the time required and the training needed to deal with these problems is far beyond what the classroom teacher can provide. The best service the teacher can offer is identification of children who have language problems so that they can be referred to the speech clinician. Once the child is enrolled for language therapy, the teacher will be in a much better position to work with the clinician in helping the child gain language skills.

RESOURCE LIST

The following reference materials are recommended by the American Speech and Hearing Association:

- *Helping Children Talk Better* by Charles Van Riper. From Science Research Associates, Inc., Order Dept., 259 E. Erie St., Chicago, IL 60611 (48 pages, $1.05, No. 5-921). Review of speech development with suggestions for encouraging communication skills. Intended for parents and teachers.
- *Rules of Talking*. From Language Development Programs, Bill Wilkerson Hearing and Speech Center, 1114 19th Ave. S., Nashville, TN 37212 (10 pages, $.25). Suggests activities to stimulate language and speech. Intended for parents and nursery school teachers.
- *Stuttering Words*. From Speech Foundation of America, 152 Lombardy Rd., Memphis, TN 38111 (32 pages, $.25, Pub. no. 2). A glossary of terms associated with stuttering and its treatment. Intended for educators and health professionals.
- *Your Cleft Lip and Palate Child: A Basic Guide for Parents*. From Meade Johnson Laboratories, Dept. 822, Evansville, IN 47712 (14 pages, free). Provides information for stimulating speech behavior, decreasing ear-infection problems and encouraging emotional development.

The following three publications are available from The National Easter Seal Society for Crippled Children and Adults, 2023 W. Ogden Ave., Chicago, IL 60612:

- "A Speech Pathologist Talks to the Parents of a Non-verbal Child," a two-page reprint from *Rehabilitation Literature*, 1969, vol. 30, no. 12 (single copy free). General tips for stimulating language development. Intended for parents and teachers working with severely handicapped children.
- *Toward Understanding Stuttering* by Wendell Johnson (36 pages, $.25). Historical overview of the research in and beliefs about stuttering. Practical suggestions for parents, speakers, teachers and students.
- *Bright Promise: For Your Child With Cleft Lip and Palate* by Eugene McDonald (21 pages, $.25). General information in a question-and-answer format.

Single copies of the following three pamphlets are available free from the American Speech and Hearing Association, 9030 Old Georgetown Rd., Washington, DC 20014:

- *Speech and Language Disorders and the Speech and Language Pathologist;*
- *The Speech-Language Pathologist;*
- *Recognizing Communication Disorders.* ■

Some Thoughts on the Education of Blind Children

Robert Rottman

Educators today will scarcely question the proposition that modern education is dedicated to the academic and social development of every student to the fullest extent permitted by his individual capacities; that its goal is the graduation of informed, responsible, self-confident, and self-reliant adult citizens who will participate in and contribute to their society. Educational programs for blind children, which serve a particular segment of that total group comprised by "every student," must, of necessity, be imbued with the same philosophy and committed to the same goals.

Blindness is a physical nuisance and a social handicap. Both of these currently inevitable characteristics begin to affect the life of a blind person from the moment his blindness becomes apparent to himself or to others, even if that moment occurs on the day of his birth. These characteristics of blindness together with their cumulative effect on the developing blind child, are of primary concern to the educator of blind children, for they must constitute the nucleus around which his understanding of the special problems of blind children and his provision for their solution will be formed. Given this understanding and these solutions to supplement a normal school curriculum, a blind child can be expected to achieve, upon graduation, those goals of knowledge, confidence, self-sufficiency, and responsible participation in the work and play of society for which public education today is striving.

The physical nuisance of blindness derives from the fact that most people can see and have organized the physical environment on the basis of the possession and use of vision. Sight is not essential to the performance of the tasks of daily living, but in a world geared to seeing the blind minority must employ "abnormal"—that is, not ordinary—ways of doing many things. Thus a blind infant identifies his mother by footstep, voice, scent, and feel, and his bottle by size, shape, temperature, weight, time of appearance, and—of course—contents. A blind toddler can distinguish the bathroom from the kitchen by size, location, smell, temperature, sound, and—again—contents. A blind child can read and write, in braille, by touch; or with recordings, by hearing.

A blind teen-ager can do geometry, apply make-up, choose clothes, and go out on dates through a variety of non-visual adaptations. A blind housewife can cook, sew, clean house and change diapers; and a blind man can run a lathe, wire a house, manage a business, conduct an experiment, teach a class, or argue and win a legal case.

All of these things can be accomplished without sight; all can be done as well without sight as with it. Sometimes the non-visual methods require equal or even less effort; often they demand extra time, extra concentration, extra exertion, or extra tension. But the important facts are that the methods exist and that they work, that they make of blindness at worst a physical nuisance, but not a physical deterrent.

The implication of these facts for educational programs for blind children is obvious. Such programs, however organized and wherever located, must teach blind children, in addition to the content of the normal school curriculum, the tools and skills which will enable them to fulfill independently, with competence and confidence, the physical demands, not only of school activities, but of normal daily living and competitive employment. This is both necessary and feasible. It is necessary for the simple reason that without such tools and skills, blind students will be extremely limited, if not totally lacking, in the ability to put their education to independent and constructive use. It is feasible because proven tools and skills do exist, and, when competently taught, fit easily and appropriately into the purposeful learning environment of the school; indeed are indispensable—even in school—if this environment includes the expectation of independence, responsibility, and self-direction on the part of students.

The basic physical tools and skills which can make a blind student independent and self-sufficient are not hard to conceive nor difficult to teach. They include such things as the mastery of a system for independent reading, writing, counting, and measuring, which for blind students means braille; the ability to travel independently under all circumstances, which for blind students means the skillful use of a cane plus the employment of other senses and common sense; and the general ability to do things for themselves, which for blind students means primarily the long-established habit of planning and organizing. Whether these tools and skills are learned, and, if learned, whether they are used will depend a great deal on the effect of the second significant characteristic of blindness.

Blindness is not only a physical nuisance, which can be readily overcome, but a social handicap which, in our

"Some Thoughts on the Education of Blind Children," Robert Rottman, *National Federation of the Blind.*

present society, is not so readily removed. The blind as a group are handicapped socially, not because they are essentially inferior, maladjusted, or anti-social, but because people with sight, who constitute a vast majority, grossly over-estimate the physical and mental limitations imposed on the blind by their blindness, and regard the blind as necessarily helpless and dependent, kept alive by the charity of their more fortunate sighted brothers, unable to contribute their share of society's work, and, consequently unentitled to full participation in society's benefits. This feeling is rarely articulated in words, but it speaks for itself in the general actions and attitudes of the sighted toward the blind. The stereotyped concepts of helplessness, loneliness, and utter wretchedness which have been formed about the blind; the pity, wonder, or disgust with which they are regarded; the protective concern which their presence arouses; and the sheltered and limited activities which are organized to occupy their time all bespeak relegation to an inferior status in the eyes of society at large.

The influence of society's attitudes on blind children and blinded adults is strong and pervasive. It extends from infancy to advanced age, and, unless counteracted with a powerful and positive program of education and training, its effect is generally the discouragement of independence and initiative, the limitation of adaptive skills, the development of feelings of inferiority, and, too often, the ultimate acceptance and personification—and thus the perpetuation—of the very stereotype of which the blind are the victims. The over-protection of parents, the pity of friends and relatives, the pessimism of teachers and counselors, and the refusal of employers—all these are at the same time the result and the direct implementation of society's misconceptions about the limitations of blindness; all must be negated, and the strength and desire to resist and surmount them must be instilled in blind students if they are ever to fulfill their potential as self-supporting, fully participating citizens enjoying the same rights and assuming the same responsibilities as their sighted peers.

Tools and skills—while essential—are not enough in themselves to achieve this end, and no educational program for blind children can be considered adequate which confines itself solely to the physical adaptations made necessary by blindness. The major effort of a complete and effective program must rather be directed toward the development in the child—and in the homes, school, and community environment around him—of a full acceptance of blindness without shame and without loss of incentive or aspiration; a firm conviction of the right of the blind to equal status with their sighted peers; an unshakable belief in the ability of the blind to fulfill completely the physical, mental, and social requirements of equal status; a thorough understanding of existing concepts and attitudes about the blind and the barriers to equal status which they present; an unwavering confidence that these barriers to equality can be levelled; and a positive, aggressive determination that these students are going to do the levelling. It cannot be emphasized too strongly that blind students must be equipped with the *confidence* as well as the *competence* to achieve independence and self-sufficiency in a sighted world as yet only too ready to support and "protect" them—at the cost of segregation, dependency, and social and economic inferiority.

All this, then, is to say that the major problems of blindness, at any age, stem from the mistaken attitudes held by the sighted toward that blindness, and from the economic and social impact of those attitudes on the blind. A sound program of education for blind children must first of all free itself from attitudes which limit and discourage; second, help blind students to develop the knowledge, the skills, and the inner strength to meet and overcome these attitudes when they encounter them—as inevitably they must—outside of school; and third, vigorously support and actively assist independent blind persons everywhere, and those who know their true abilities, in a great campaign to educate—and even, where necessary, to legislate—degrading and restrictive public attitudes out of existence.

What does this ringing statement imply for you as an educator of blind children in terms of the program you have organized or are now organizing? What must you do, in addition to meeting the blind child's curricular needs with appropriate special teaching tools and techniques, to instill the confidence and develop the competence so necessary to the survival of his social and economic equality and integrity in an unbelieving sighted world?

The answer lies primarily in the realm of attitudes, specifically in the formulation of a thoughtful, consistent, and vigorous campaign of education designed to accomplish three main objectives: (1) to enable the student to accept his blindness and himself as a blind person; (2) to establish firmly in his mind the conviction that he not only *can* but *should* lead a normal, happy, productive life in full and equal competition with his sighted peers; and (3) to help him to accept and master the tools, skills, and aids that will contribute to his ultimate equality, independence, and self-sufficiency.

With a few possible exceptions, no blind student likes or wants to be blind. Many resist the idea with great determination. Even those who freely call themselves blind may be fighting an inner battle against blindness, a battle that can take the form of hope for a miraculous operation; rejection of anything associated with the special needs of the blind; resentment against parents, school, or the entire sighted population; or the refusal to do anything for oneself. It goes without saying that preparation for life as a successful blind adult cannot begin until the student has come to accept himself as a blind person without loss of self-esteem, and to adopt, confidently and unashamed, the special modes of operating that blindness makes necessary. If the parents have handled their child's blindness well, the chances are that the school will need only to reinforce an accepting attitude already established. Unfortunately such instances will be rare, and on the school—as the second great influence in the life of the child—must devolve in most cases the imperative obligation of counteracting—and sometimes flatly contradicting—the home and other influences which have occasioned resistance to blindness in one or more of its forms.

Acceptance of blindness is not brought about in the school environment by repeated lectures on the acceptance of blindness. Instead, the nature of the school environment itself, and the child's relationship with his teachers, will serve as the primary media for an effective conversion. Resistance to blindness is subtly attacked from two closely related points of view, which might be expressed in simplified form as "blind people are normal" and "blindness is not a limitation." The first requires a sincere conviction on the part of the school as a whole, but of the child's teachers in particular, that blind people *are* normal. The very fact that special education programs are provided for blind children can indicate to a particular blind child that he is not unique, that society expects a certain percentage of its children to be blind and considers these children equally worth educating. If the word blind is used freely by the school staff, and the child's blindness treated with quite evident matter-of-factness, and with no lessening of requirements for him because of it; if his special tools and materials and the instruction in the special skills he needs to function adequately are provided as a matter of course; if his outside activities and interests are discussed without wonder, surprise, and undue admiration as they would be with sighted students; if even in the primary grades his future is spoken of with the expectation of a normal life made obvious in such phrases as "when you're in college . . .," "after you've been on the job awhile . . .," "your wife may have something to say about that . . .," "that will come in handy when you're doing your own cooking," or "wait until you're a parent yourself," then the student cannot help but consider himself a normal person. When it is apparent that the school staff, whose opinion in these matters he respects perhaps even more than that of his parents, is not particularly disturbed by his or anyone else's blindness nor holds toward him an attitude different from that bestowed upon his sighted age-mates, then one main objection to blindness is gone.

The second point of attack is closely allied to the first, and is even more important to the bringing about of a true acceptance of blindness. The unshakable conviction that blindness need not limit anyone from anything which makes life worthwhile is the key that unlocks the door of achievement for blind children and for blind adults. It is the foundation upon which every program for the blind which truly meets the needs of the blind has to be built. Blind students, from the very beginning, must be surrounded with this idea, with demonstrations of tools and methods used by blind persons in accomplishing seemingly difficult or impossible tasks; with accounts of the successes of blind persons in such occupations as those of electrician, chemist, physicist, classroom teacher, lawyer, businessman, salesman, farmer, machinist, and homemaker; with the simple, often-repeated statement itself: "Blindness need not bar anyone from anything important in life. Whatever has to be done, there's a way for a totally blind person to do it." (The idea of a totally blind person is important. The students who have the hardest time accepting blindness and the efficient methods of the blind are those with a slight degree of sight, insufficient for the visual performance of most tasks.)

The most effective avenue to the acceptance of blindness, however, is through actual contact with it. The school program should plan and provide numerous opportunities for blind students at every level to meet and talk with self-sufficient, self-confident blind adults from many occupational areas. In no other way can the absence of permanent barriers to normal life be brought home so effectively; in no more convincing manner can blind students learn the value of the skills they are acquiring in a school; from no more competent authority can they get answers to questions about blindness lying long unspoken in their minds;—and from no better source can they learn of the obstacles to integration imposed by society's misconceptions about blindness and the blind.

For these obstacles, too, are involved in the acceptance of blindness. The world of today, a little more sophisticated than it was twenty-five or a hundred and twenty-five years ago, would still rather build a recreation center to fill idle hours than an orientation center to restore self-esteem, self-confidence, and self-sufficiency; would still rather send a newly-blinded wage-earner or professional to a sheltered shop or a vending stand than return him to his former occupation; would still rather drop a daily quarter in a street corner musician's tin cup than trust a competent blind worker with a machine or a decision. The world of tomorrow, barring a miracle or a miraculously effective campaign of public education, will not be drastically changed ten, twenty, even fifty hears hence, in spite of the considerable progress that has been made so far by the blind as individuals and as a group. It is important that blind students, as they acquire a firm belief in their own capability, be also arming themselves for the fight to maintain this conviction and to convince the world around them in the face of disbelief, disappointments, and the constant temptation to surrender their dignity and independence in exchange for the meager security of permanent state aid or the limited offerings of a sheltered shop. Made aware from the first of the difficulties imposed by public attitudes, and thoroughly convinced of the injustice thereby done, blind graduates can be helped to develop, not bitterness or resentment, but a realistic evaluation of the hurdles ahead, a compelling sense of the need to surmount them and an aggressive determination not to fall victim to them.

One further consideration for educators in guiding blind

students toward their attainment of self-sufficiency remains to be discussed. This is the responsibility of providing for a thorough acquaintance with every available means to the desired end. The importance of a mastery of the physical skills of competence is self-evident. It is taken for granted that no self-respecting educational program would allow a normal blind student to leave without a high degree of proficiency in the reading and writing of standard English braille, considerable skill in the use of a standard typewriter, practice in the use of sighted readers and various types of recorded materials, and, above all, the ability to organize, keep track of, and otherwise assume responsibility for his own material possessions.

Likewise it is assumed that every program will provide for its students training in the skills of independent travel. Sometimes ignored, but of vital necessity in this regard, is the skillful employment of the long white cane, which gives protection and confidence in moving outside the familiar environment of home and school. Independent travel should be associated with the use of a cane in the minds of blind youngsters long before they begin actual instruction in cane travel techniques in the intermediate grades. Here again discussions with a competent blind adult, who carries his cane with pride and employs it with confident skill, can be of invaluable assistance to both student and teacher in gaining acceptance and appreciation of this indispensable tool of independence.

But the physical skills are not the only aids available to blind students in their efforts to achieve personal independence, competitive employment, normal family life, and the satisfying and constructive use of leisure hours. Society, while failing to recognize its own culpability, has long recognized the state of social and economic inequality in which the blind have traditionally lived. Many programs have been instituted by the states and the federal government, and by private organizations, to ameliorate this unequal condition in one way or another. These programs run the gamut from recreation centers to rehabilitation services, from monetary assistance to missionary efforts; from home teaching to sheltered "homes." Educational programs in which blind students are enrolled must assume the responsibility not only of informing them about every service, every aid to which they are legally entitled, but of helping them to develop, as a part of their overall philosophy of self-sufficiency, that fine discrimination which distinguishes between those offerings based on mistaken charity and the desire to relieve lonely, useless hours with time-filling palliatives, and those services which operate to equalize the opportunities for blind persons to take their places as self-reliant, self-respecting, contributing members of society.

Data Concerning the Partially Sighted and the Functionally Blind

Samuel M. Genensky, Ph.D.

Dr. Genensky is director, Partially Sighted Center, Santa Monica Hospital Medical Center, and is on the staff of the Engineering and Applied Sciences Department at the Rand Corporation, Santa Monica.

Abstract: *Examines the relative sizes of the nation's partially sighted, legally blind but not functionally blind, and functionally blind populations as a function of age. It also examines the frequency with which partially sighted people occur in the nation's population for various age ranges. In addition, under a set of stated assumptions applied to the 1969-70 Model Reporting Area data, it has been found that most people who are partially sighted and legally blind will never become functionally blind.*

The following definitions are used throughout this paper:

A person is *functionally blind* if he is either totally blind, or has at most light perception or light projection.

A person is *partially sighted and legally blind* if he is legally blind but not functionally blind.

A person is *partially sighted* if the acuity in his better eye even with ordinary corrective lenses does not exceed 20/70 *or* if the maximum diameter of his visual field does not exceed 20° *and* if he is not functionally blind.

[In the United States, a person is declared to be legally blind if his visual acuity is 20/200 or less in the better eye with best correction or his visual acuity is more than 20/200 but the widest diameter of the visual field extends to an angle no greater than 20°.]

The National Academies of Science and Engineering estimated that in 1970 there were at least 420 thousand legally blind Americans and at least 1.28 million other Americans who could not read newspaper column type even with the help of ordinary corrective lenses (the partially sighted who are *not* legally blind). More than 75 percent *of the legally blind,* with or without the help of optical or electronic optical aids, have enough residual vision to be able to use that vision to read ordinary printed or handwritten materials, to write with a pen or pencil, and to maneuver safely even in an unfamiliar environment without the help of a guide dog, a white cane, or a sighted person. This means that as of 1970 there were more than 315 thousand legally blind Americans who were partially sighted and not functionally blind. In that same year it was estimated that the population of the United States was about 204.8 million. Assuming a growth rate of 1.0 percent per year for that population, and assuming uniform distribution of the partially sighted (both legally blind and non-legally-blind) as well as the functionally blind throughout the nation's population from 1970 to 1977, we may conclude that there are more than 1.7 million partially sighted people in the U.S.

Age Distribution

Reliable data concerning the age distribution within the visually impaired population are not readily available, but we can gain insight into what it may be by analyzing the 1970 prevalence data on a large sample of the nation's legally blind (LB) population published by the National Eye Institute (NEI) in a booklet, *Statistics on Blindness in the Model Reporting Area 1969-1970.* From that report (Table 27b, p. 113) we readily see that the 99,347 legally blind people contained in the sample, breakdown by age as shown in Table 1.

If we assume that the 3,095 unknowns are distributed proportionally among the various age groups, then, on the basis of the sample, the frequency distribution of the legally blind is that given in Table 2.

If we adhere to our decision to define the functionally blind (FB) to be the legally blind (LB) who are either totally blind or who have at best light perception or light projection, then from the same table in the NEI report we find that the functionally blind and the legally blind who are not functionally blind (the partially sighted who are legally blind), are distributed by age as shown in Table 3.

The percent breakdown between the functionally blind and the legally blind who are not functionally blind in the 0-4 age group shown in Table 3 is suspect because:

1. The data in the NEI report indicate that 201 of the 518 entries in this age group are unknowns; hence nearly 40 percent of the data in that row of the table *cannot be assigned to a visual acuity category.*
2. The data pertaining to this age group also indicate that an unusually low percent of the cases reported fall in the visual acuity classes that are included under legal blindness but not functional blindness. This, we believe, is due to the fact that clinicians rarely make accurate visual acuity measurements on children this young. Rather they tend to state that these children are either "blind" or "sighted," and here "blind" is usually taken to mean "functionally blind."

In view of this, it is safe to say that in the 0-4 age range the two categories—the legally blind who are not functionally

"Data Concerning the Partially Sighted and the Functionally Blind," by Samuel M. Genensky, Ph.D., *Visual Impairment and Blindness,* May 1978.

Table 1. Age Distribution of Legally Blind Persons in the 1970 MRA Prevalence Sample

Age	*Number*
0-4	518
5-19	9,153
20-44	16,346
45-64	25,785
65-74	16,518
75-84	16,399
85 and up	11,533
Unknown	3,095
Total	99,347

Table 2. Frequency Distribution of Legally Blind Persons Based on 1970 MRA Prevalence Data*

Age	*Frequency*
0-4	0.005
5-19	0.095
20-44	0.170
45-64	0.268
65-74	0.172
75-84	0.170
85 and up	0.120

*"Unknowns" in Table 1 distributed proportionally among the age categories

Table 3. Percentage Split by Age Group Between the LB-FB and the FB According to 1970 Model Reporting Area Prevalence Data

Age	*Legally Blind but not Functionally Blind*	*Functionally Blind*
0-4	25.2%	74.8%
5-19	65.5	34.5
20-44	72.7	27.3
45-64	75.2	24.8
65-74	76.9	23.1
75-84	79.2	20.8
85 and up	80.2	19.8

blind, and the functionally blind—split up more like 60/40 rather than 25/75.

Now let us assume that the Model Reporting Area (MRA) sample of 99,347 legally blind people is truly representative of the legally blind population as a whole and that that population numbers 450,000. Let us also assume that, with the one exception noted above, that the legally blind population contains the same proportion of functionally blind and legally blind who are not functionally blind as were found in the sample. (It should be noted that there are unknown biases in the MRA data. For a discussion of this point, see Kahn and Moorhead, (1973.)

Let us further assume that the age distribution of the 1.37 million partially sighted people who are not legally blind is the same as that of the partially sighted who are legally blind (the legally blind who are *not* functionally blind). With these assumptions, we can then compute the estimated partially sighted population (both legally blind and non-legally blind) as a function of age. Table 4 lists the estimated size of the legally blind but not functionally blind (LB-FB) and the functionally blind (FB) populations for various age ranges. Table 5 gives similar data regarding the partially sighted and functionally blind.

If the visually impaired population is now defined as the sum of the partially sighted population and the functionally blind population, conclusions under the

Table 4. 1977 Estimated Population Distribution By Age of Legally Blind and Subsets

Age	*Legally Blind*	*Legally Blind but not Functionally Blind*	*Functionally Blind*
0-4*	2,200	1,300	900
5-19	42,800	28,000	14,800
20-44	76,500	55,600	20,900
45-64	120,600	90,700	29,900
65-74	77,400	59,500	17,900
75-84	76,500	60,600	15,900
85 and up	54,000	43,300	10,700
Total	450,000	339,000	111,000

*Estimated proportions of legally blind but not functionally blind to functionally blind within this age group are adjusted to correct for errors as noted.

Table 5. 1977 Estimated Population Distribution of Partially Sighted and Functionally Blind

Age	*Partially Sighted*	*Functionally Blind*
0-4*	6,500	900
5-19	141,200	14,800
20-44	280,300	20,900
45-64	457,200	29,900
65-74	300,000	17,900
75-84	305,500	15,900
85 and up	218,300	10,700
Total	1,709,000	111,000

*Estimates of partially sighted and functionally blind populations within this age group have been adjusted to correct for errors as noted.

Table 6. Distribution of 1975 U.S. Population by Age

Age	*Number*
0-4	15,896,000
5-19	58,781,000
20-44	73,001,000
45-64	43,551,000
65-74	13,874,000
75-84	6,649,000
85 and up	1,878,000
[65 and up	22,401,000]

assumptions made above are that *more than 93 percent of the visually impaired are partially sighted, and hence, less than 7 percent are functionally blind.*

It is of interest to estimate how frequently partially sighted people occur in various age groups of the national population. Using data in the *Information Please Almanac* (1977), on U.S. population by age, sex, and race, we arrive at the population distribution for 1975 in Table 6.

Dividing the entries in the second column of Table 5 by $(1.01)^2$ (to allow for population growth) provides estimates of the partially sighted population by age group in 1975. Dividing these estimates by the corresponding entries in the second column of Table 6 and multiplying the results by 100, yields percentage estimates of the occurrence of partially sighted people in the general population by age. Table 7 gives the results of this important calculation.

Table 7. 1975 Estimate of Frequency of Occurrence of Partially Sighted Persons in the General Population by Age

Age	*Frequency of Occurrence (percentage of general population in age group)*
0-4	0.04%
5-19	0.24
20-44	0.38
45-64	1.03
65-74	2.12
75-84	4.50
85 and up	11.40
[65 and up	3.61]

From Table 7 we see that partially sighted people occur with rather high frequency among the nation's elderly population. For example, 21 of every 1000 who are between 65 and 75 years old are partially sighted, as are 45 of every 1000 who are between 75 and 85 years old, 114 of every 1000 who are 85 or older, and 36 out of every 1000 who are 65 or older. This data indicates the importance of providing services designed to meet the particular needs of these older people.

Partially Sighted Unlikely To Become Functionally Blind

We have frequently heard it argued that nearly all those who become partially sighted and legally blind (the legally blind who are not functionally blind) will eventually become functionally blind, and therefore it makes good sense to give those people services that will prepare them to live successfully as functionally blind people. Dr. Winston Chow, of The Rand Corporation, and I have examined the validity of this argument and found it fallacious even under assumptions that are very pessimistic from the point of view of the partially sighted. These assumptions were made because the 1970 MRA prevalence data that was available to them at the time this paper was prepared would not permit them to make more realistic and, as it will be seen, less pessimistic assumptions. The assumptions that were made are:

1. Every time a functionally blind person dies, he or she is replaced by a partially sighted person who is legally blind;
2. Every partially sighted person who is legally blind is equally at risk to become functionally blind;
3. Every time a partially sighted person who is legally blind dies or replaces a functionally blind person, he or she is replaced by a non-legally-blind person;
4. No one who is functionally blind ever becomes partially sighted and legally blind, or non-legally-blind; and
5. No one who is partially sighted and legally blind ever becomes non-legally-blind.
6. Within the functionally blind population, the number of people who enter an age group from the next younger age group equals the number of people who leave that age group to enter the next older age group.*

Using these assumptions, we were able to show, for example, that if a child becomes partially sighted and legally blind at age 5, he or she has less than 12 chances in 100 of becoming functionally blind by age 65. Thus, even under these pessimistic assumptions, a partially sighted child who is 5 years old has less than 12 chances in 100 of becoming functionally blind *at any time throughout his or her years of education and employment.*

More realistic models of the flow of people into and out of the legally blind population and between subsets of that population may show that the probability of becoming functionally blind at age N_2 after becoming partially sighted and legally blind at age N_1 ($N_2 > N_1$) is less than is predicted by the model referred to above. This is because of several factors:

1. All partially sighted people who are legally blind are *not* at equal risk to become functionally blind, and in

*I have some reservations concerning this assumption and in a future paper plan to develop a model that does not require that this assumption be made.

fact some have an extremely low probability of making this transition, such as those with senile macular degeneration and those with myopia.

2. Not all the people who are functionally blind come from the partially sighted and legally blind population. This is true of most people who become functionally blind because of infectious diseases, injuries, poisonings, or neoplasms.
3. People who are functionally blind sometimes return to the partially sighted and legally blind population or to the non-legally blind population because of corneal transplants or the removal of cataracts.
4. Others who are partially sighted and legally blind later return to the non-legally blind population, again because of such things as corneal transplants or the removal of cataracts.

An analysis of the 1969-1970 MRA incidence data (data concerning legally blind people who were added to the MRA population in 1969 and 1970) reveals that 26.7 percent of the people who were added to the MRA population in those years and who were at least 65 years old had retinal degeneration. Most of them had senile macular degeneration, an ophthalmological pathology that very rarely leads to functional blindness. Thus, most of a rather substantial fraction of persons over 65 who are partially sighted and legally blind are virtually not at risk to become functionally blind. It is very likely that many persons with other ocular pathologies are also virtually not at risk, or have only a small probability, of becoming functionally blind.

From all that has been said above, we believe that it is safe to say that *most people who are partially sighted and legally blind will never become functionally blind.* We also believe that if appropriate data were available concerning the entire visually impaired population, it could then be shown that nearly all partially sighted people have very little chance of ever becoming functionally blind.

Data presented here support the contention that all partially sighted Americans, regardless of age, deserve the opportunity to learn how to use all of their remaining sensory capabilities in order to be as independent and self-sufficient as is humanly possible.

Reference

Kahn, H.A., & Moorhead, H.B. *Statistics on Blindness in the Model Reporting Area 1969-1970.* Washington, D.C.: DHEW Publication No. [NIH] 73-427, 1973.

MAINSTREAMING HANDICAPPED STUDENTS: ARE YOUR FACILITIES SUITABLE?

James R. Russo

A new type of student will be entering public schools more in the years ahead—the handicapped student. Previously, lack of proper facilities and services prevented many handicapped children from attending regular schools. But recent court decisions are changing that. In essence, the courts are saying that handicapped children should not be denied equal educational opportunities, and that proper facilities must be provided. Also, the courts have ruled that inadequate funding is no excuse for inadequate facilities.

Furthermore, the courts are requiring schools to follow policies of "least restrictive" placements of handicapped children. This means that the settings for educational programs must be as close to normal as possible. For example, placement in regular public schools with appropriate support services is preferable to placement in special schools. Always, the concern is to maintain the child in that setting which is most normal and in which he can learn most effectively.

LANDMARK DECISIONS

Two "landmark" U.S. District Court decisions in 1971 started this new era in education for the handicapped. The first decision, in Pennsylvania, held that all mentally retarded children in that state must be provided with an education at public expense. The second, in the District of Columbia, extended that principle to cover all handicapped children. The consequences of these decisions was an explosion of suits in other states seeking—and obtaining—the same end.

When viewed from a statistical perspective, the problem is staggering. Overall, about 7 million youngsters in the U.S. suffer some form of physical and/or mental handicap. That adds up to about 1 out of every 10 children. According to the U.S. Office of Education, less than 50 percent of these 7 million handicapped children receive the education they need (in some states the proportion is less than 15 percent).

Now, however, machinery is in the works for something to be done about the problem. The courts have provided direction and the states, in turn, have enacted legislation to comply with court rulings. Now it is up to the schools to comply with the law.

IMPLICATIONS

What does all this mean to facility planners? In short, facilities must adequately meet the special needs of handicapped students. But what exactly are those needs?

To begin with, different types of handicaps dictate different requirements for school facilities. If, for example, mentally retarded children are being mainstreamed, relatively few changes may be needed in the facilities, per se. With mentally retarded children, the big hurdle for schools to overcome is in developing proper programs and teaching methods.

On the other hand, if students are physically handicapped, extensive changes in facilities may be required. Some of the changes are obvious—ramps, special restroom facilities, elevators, etc. But there's a lot more to it. To find out exactly what's involved from a facilities standpoint, AS&U surveyed schools, colleges, architects, consultants, and organizations for handicapped persons. Here's what we found:

NEW SCHOOL IN CALIFORNIA

Non-handicapped children and those with cerebral palsy, polio, birth defects, and accident-caused limb-losses, are learning and playing together in the Urbain Plavan School, Fountain Valley, Ca. The school, which opened in 1973, was planned and built specifically to integrate orthopedically handicapped and typical children.

Since moving from one activity to another requires considerable effort by handicapped children, the school was designed for maximum circulation efficiency. This was achieved by an irregular oval-shaped building in which 4 distinct elements surround and feed into a fifth element—an 8,100 sq. ft. central learning center. The 4 basic elements are an administration section, classrooms, a special services section for handicapped students, and a music platform and storage facility. The focus of the

Reprinted from *American School and University* magazine Vol. 47, No. 2, 1974.

complex is inward with 11 interior circulation paths leading to, through, and out of the learning center. Carmichael-Kemp Architect, Los Angeles, designed the facility.

Although one section of the school is devoted entirely to handicapped students, no real boundaries exist. Orthopedically handicapped children participate in all regular activities.

Ninety-six handicapped children attend the school along with 330 typical children in pre-school through eighth grades. The teaching staff consists of 10 teachers for typical children, 8 teachers and 8 teacher's aides for orthopedically handicapped children, 2 learning center coordinators and 2 aides, 1 teacher for educable mentally retarded children, and 1 speech therapist.

The normal children attending the school are drawn from a "walk-in" area immediately surrounding the school site. The orthopedically handicapped children come from cooperating school districts.

Some of the special orthopedic equipment in the school includes electric parallel bars, balance beam, rocking beam, rocking boat, walking rails, bicycle exerciser, foot placement ladder, triplex pulleys, punching bag, shoulder wheel, finger ladder, wrist rolls, and a standing tilt table. There is also a training bedroom for daily living skill adaptation, a training bathroom, training kitchen, and hydrotherapy room.

The orthopedically handicapped section of the school also functions as a fulltime clinic. Parents can bring children here for doctor's examinations, consultation, and therapy. A separate reception and waiting room with an outdoor play area serve these parents and children.

PLAYGROUND FOR *ALL* CHILDREN

An innovative school playground has been carefully designed for use by handicapped children as well as regular children at the James Madison School in Sheboygan, Wis.

One highlight of the playground is a 60 × 60 ft. area containing a multi-level play structure which offers therapeutic exercise as well as fun for all. Ramps, platforms, railings, steps, and slides with cargo net, poles, balance beams, and a horizontal tire swing make up the inviting structure. Challenged in a play setting, handicapped children don't think of the structure as a therapeutic unit.

Hard surface approaches allow wheelchair users to pull themselves onto the lower platforms, and the various levels of the structure are connected by *both* steps and ramps. In fact, one ramp simulates the exercise walker therapeutic unit.

Another highlight of the playground is an area called the "Trike Run." Designed to develop motor perception, it encompasses some 13,500 sq. ft. with a maze of hardtop trails complete with an overpass and underpass for wheelchairs and tricycles used by handicapped children. Of course, non-handicapped children enjoy cycling along these trails, too.

Other features included in the playground are a cantilevered play unit of utility poles with tire swings from an earth berm, teeters with impact spring shocks, an arched climber, culvert and standard climber play area with earth berm frames.

An extensive landscape plan complements the entire playground and provides year-round color stimulus. Open field play areas, basketball and bouncing ball areas (special adjusted heights for handicapped), sitting benches conveniently placed, and tether ball poles complete the setting.

For enjoyment on a somewhat quieter scale, a courtyard has been developed in a 4,800 sq. ft. area. One section contains a sand and water-sluice-unit at several wheelchair heights so that sand play can be made convenient. Also, work benches for various crafts are at wheelchair heights, and a raised planter permits children to work with plants above ground level.

A "ball and target" area within the courtyard has been designed so that the ball returns to the person after he has thrown it at the target. Another popular item in the courtyard is a "swing tram" that gives youngsters the chance to move themselves along a beam via a swivel pulley, providing fun as well as therapeutic exercise.

For the most part, the courtyard has a hard surface to facilitate free movement by handicapped children using wheelchairs, crutches, or canes.

Many good ideas often get stalled by lack of money. But community spirit overcame that problem in Sheboygan. The playground and courtyard is financed almost entirely by gifts. The project was initiated by the Sheboygan County Easter Seal Society and it has been enthusiastically supported by the Sheboygan School Administration.

"Many different groups contributed time, money, and equipment to make this playground a reality," explains Walter Lau, Director of Buildings and Grounds for the Sheboygan Public Schools. Lau, along with the Sheboygan County Easter Seal Society, played major roles in coordinating efforts of the different groups.

Early in the planning stage, a detailed list of items required for the playground was prepared and a price was established for each item, no matter how small. That way, money for specific items could be donated. For example, someone could donate $50.00 for sand, or $38.36 for an I-beam, etc. In addition to numerous individual and business donations, community organizations and groups pitched in. They ranged from the PTA to the Naval Reserve, and included Sheboygan's Junior Women's Club, the Lake Shore Garden Club, The Sheboygan Service Club, and dozens of others.

The playground is the latest addition to the James Madison School which is a lively, working example of a successful "mainstreaming" school. All facilities within the school are shared as much as possible by handicapped and non-handicapped students. In addition, a new wing of the school contains special equipment and areas needed for therapy of various types of handicaps.

BEGAN PROGRAM IN 1947

At the University of Illinois, the entire campus has been planned, or modified, to be equally accessible by physically handicapped students. Such efforts were pioneered by the University in 1947.

Handicapped students reside in regular residence halls and attend all regular classes. Also, they participate in all activities, i.e.: student government, fraternities, sororities, newspapers, radio, TV, instrument groups, vocal groups, dramatics, and wheelchair athletics—to name a few.

For visually-handicapped students, the library contains essential texts in Braille, including encyclopedias, logarithmic tables, periodicals, dictionaries in both English and foreign languages, and tapes of recorded text books. The library also has a raised map of the campus so that blind students can become oriented to the campus and travel independently to their classes.

A complete rehabilitation center was added to the University in 1966. It contains medical services, facilities and equipment for occupational and functional therapies, counseling, services for the blind and deaf, an environmental control laboratory, a library, recreation and athletic facilities, a drivers' education simulator laboratory, and many other offices and services for the handicapped.

As a supplement to the formal therapy program offered at the University, a variety of adapted sports and recreational activities abound for physically handicapped students. Swimming, bowling, baseball, football, basketball, archery, tennis, deck tennis, volleyball, track & field, fencing, and square dancing are some of the activities specially organized for disabled students.

Transportation is also an important part of the program at the University. Four buses with specially engineered lifts for wheelchairs run on regular schedules and routes. The buses make it possible for handicapped students to come and go independently, whether it be to class, residence halls, or an activity.

SPECIAL COMMUNICATIONS SYSTEM

At the Brooklyn Center of Long Island University, a special telephone intercom system is available to connect a home or hospital-bound student with the classroom. A student in this program is able to hear classroom presentations and discussions. Also, he can participate in the discussions simply by pressing a button.

The program does not, of course, serve as an adequate substitute for the actual experience of classroom attendance. However, for the mature, well-motivated, but severely disabled student who is unable to be transported to school, it does serve to offer a real classroom situation. For the disabled student who has not had classroom experience, the system also can be used as an introductory phase, prior to actual attendance.

The telephone communications system is only one aspect of Long Island University's commitment to serving handicapped students. All building entrances on the 13-acre campus are accessible at ground level, or by ramp; elevators are large enough to freely accommodate wheelchairs; all restrooms are accessible; and water fountains, telephones, etc., have been lowered.

The University is not equipped to function as a rehabilitation center, but it does make it possible for a disabled student to participate in regular student activities.

BUILT WITHOUT BARRIERS

Right from the inception of Southwest Minnesota State College, the goal was to provide facilities that would not hinder handicapped students from obtaining an education. The college, which is not 10 years old, occupies 216 acres of the flat plains area in southwestern Minnesota.

Enclosed halls interconnect all academic buildings, the student center, and the food service building. All multistory buildings have elevators. Wide halls and electric doors are found in major traffic areas. Movable furniture in the classroom is provided at a height for easy use by wheelchair students. Special typewriters, Braille books, readers, and writers are also available.

Over 175 handicapped students are enrolled at the college and some 65 of these are in wheelchairs.

Handicapped students share the same residence hall facilities with the able-bodied. One significant change in the dormitory facilities (in addition to modified washrooms) is that ground floor rooms are larger to make it more convenient for wheelchair students. In some cases, an able-bodied roommate may function as a paid aide and provide some physical assistance to the handicapped, but the choice of roommates is up to each student.

COOPERATION WITH CITY

The University of Baltimore, with its campus in downtown Baltimore, made a number of "curb cuts" at street intersections to permit convenient travel for handicapped students. The city gave the university free permits to cut the curbs and substitute ramps. In addition to waiving nearly $2,000 in permits, the city removed 10 parking meters and designated the areas as, "Parking for Disabled Persons by Permit Only." The permits are issued each semester by the Dean of Students. Local police have been diligent in their protection of the restricted areas. Many $12 tickets have been issued to nonhandicapped drivers who chose to park without a permit.

The university is also implementing a master plan to remove architectural barriers from the campus. In an effort to help provide funds for this plan, the Student Veterans' Organization started a Rathskeller at the university and all profits are being used to remove architectural barriers.

Another display of the university's concern for the handicapped is the presence of a security officer in his wheelchair in the main lobby. Performing as the "Information Officer" he assists all strangers. Also, the officer is preparing a supplement to the student handbook which will feature particular advice to handicapped students at the University.

CHANGES CAN BE MADE

An amazing transformation has taken place at Portland Community College. A 1970 survey of buildings showed that getting around was a matter of exertion and careful deliberation for someone in a wheelchair. Choice of courses was limited by classroom inaccessibility: using lavatories was a difficult and public affair; and getting a drink of water or making a phone call was often impossible.

Now, ramps have replaced stairs at the entrances to classroom buildings; two restrooms on each floor have been refitted with wide stalls and grab bars; and towel racks, mirrors, and sinks with lever-type faucets have been lowered, along with some telephones. Also, new physical education facilities including a swimming pool have been made accessible.

One noteworthy service provided for handicapped students is the transportation system. With the help of two vans containing a special lift, the college is able to transport students in wheelchairs from home to the campus and back again. For this purpose, two full-time drivers and two part-time drivers are employed. At the present time, 26 students are using this service.

For handicapped students who are not capable of taking notes in class, volunteer note-takers within the class may be used. Special note-taking pads with pressure-sensitive carbons are supplied to the student taking notes.

The deaf student is also integrated into the regular classroom through the services of an interpreter who translates the instructor's remarks into sign language.

For the visually handicapped student, there are reading and taping services available.

WHEELCHAIR REPAIR

Many handicapped students at the University of California, Berkeley, depend upon electrically-powered wheelchairs to move around the large campus. If a chair breaks down, there are provisions on campus to repair it—quickly.

The repair program is a function of the Office of the Physically Disabled Students. Most of the standard daily repairs can be made with auto mechanics' tools.

When a defective part has to be replaced on wheelchairs, the chances are good that the university has the part that's needed. Certain breakdowns are anticipated and parts are bulk-ordered in advance. In addition, as power chairs are "junked," the parts are saved. If parts are not on hand, they can be ordered through a distributor. In any case, if the chair cannot be repaired quickly, there are two loaner chairs (electrically-powered) available to students until their chairs are fixed.

Most of the electrical repairs consist of changing transistors, transistor boards and malfunctioning wiring on chairs and battery chargers. Mechanical repairs consist principally of changing tires, motors, bearings, and other moving parts. When a motor is repaired, the wheelchair repair department boasts that repaired motors last longer than the new factory-built ones. The department also modifies wheelchairs to make them more useful to the particular user.

FINDING THE BARRIERS

While some architectural barriers are readily apparent, many are not. Realizing this, the University of Baltimore engaged the services of a handicapped student who spent days touring the campus in his wheelchair, noting problems. In addition, a safety engineer and an architect were hired to study the facilities with regard to making the campus barrier-free.

A slightly different approach—but just as thorough—was used at the University of Alabama. The University organized an architectural barriers committee to investigate the campus. The committee included representation from the academic divisions, the university engineer, the director of physical planning, members of the student development office, members of the office contracts and grants, members of the rehabilitation counseling program, and handicapped students.

Once all of the barriers were identified on campus, an organized approach was undertaken to eliminate them. Major projects were closely planned and coordinated with the University's maintenance department so that eliminating barriers coincided with maintenance work schedules. This helped lessen the cost considerably.

BETTER TOILET FACILITIES

There is nothing more inconvenient than the way a wheelchair student has to use a conventional toilet, even though a wider stall door is provided and the space around the toilet is enlarged. In order to use the facilities, he must: (1) get into the stall; (2) stand; (3) awkwardly turn around using the special grab bars provided; and (4) sit down. If his wrists or ankles are weak, the situation becomes dangerous.

At the University of New Mexico, the university architect and the physical plant department came up with an obvious solution. They asked a plumbing fixture manufacturer to design a narrow, low fixture that will permit the wheelchair student to lift straight off his chair and onto the toilet, facing the wall. This eliminates the dangerous turning movement described. The question is, "Why didn't someone think of this before?"

GUIDEBOOK FOR HANDICAPPED

The University of Texas has an outstanding publication which includes detailed maps of the campus with symbols noting the location of curb gradings, barrier-free entrances to buildings, modified rest rooms, wheelchair routes, and the degree of angles of incline of sidewalks on these routes.

Detailed questionnaires were used to help obtain organized information for the guidebook. For example—Do doors swing one way or both ways? Do they slide, fold, or revolve? How wide are they? Is there a threshold? How much pressure is required to open doors? How fast do they swing back? Is the door tactilely marked for the visually handicapped? etc.

Similar questionnaires were used for parking areas, horizontal work surfaces, inclines, handrails, stairs, elevators, and toilets.

The survey was funded by a $1,500 grant from the Ex-Students Association and the information was obtained by a University group called MIGHT (Mobility Impaired Grappling Hurdles Together).

WHAT ABOUT DISABLED TEACHERS?

The need for all buildings to be accessible to handicapped students is paramount. In addition to helping students obtain an equal education, barrier-free facilities also benefit physically disabled teachers.

Presently, if a teacher is disabled, his choice of a school or college is severely limited to only those institutions where there are a minimum of physical barriers. Often he is prevented from following the vocation for which he is trained because he cannot find a position at one of the few accessible schools.

As one teacher said, "Since being forced to use a wheelchair, many of the attractions on campus no longer exist for me. Not only for the facilities largely inaccessible, but even if I could get inside, additional frustrations and barriers only add to my discomfort. What value is it to get inside only to find that interior steps, narrow halls and crowded areas will not allow a wheelchair to pass?

"Fixed seats and narrow aisles, telephones that are mounted too high to be reached from a wheelchair and restrooms that have narrow doors, slick floors and no assist-bars further disappoint us who try. Accessibility is important; critical in fact, but very little seems to be getting done about it."

Hopefully that will change.

THE SEVERELY/ PROFOUNDLY HANDICAPPED: WHO ARE THEY? WHERE ARE WE?

Ed Sontag, Ed.D.
Bureau of Education for the Handicapped

Judy Smith, M.S.Ed.
University of New Mexico

Wayne Sailor, Ph.D.
San Francisco State University

The misunderstanding and misuse of the label "severely/profoundly handicapped" may appear to call for the possible creation of yet another special education category. To create a new category would be a serious error, since it would tend to remove these children from the educational and social mainstream; it also would obscure the fact that the severely/profoundly handicapped exist across all of special education. This article examines various approaches to the problems of definition and categorization of the severely/profoundly handicapped, proposing a service-need definition, with emphasis on teacher competencies. Finally, the authors review what must be done within the profession to make it possible to achieve such a classification system.

THE CHILDREN BEHIND THE LABEL

Children with severe or profound handicaps are children who are divergent in degree, not in kind. The very label "severely/profoundly handicapped" may, however, contribute to the notion that such children are somehow different in kind, since it refers to a very low level of intellectual functioning and therefore suggests that those children so labeled have a homogeneous pattern of neurological impairment. On the contrary, they form an extremely heterogeneous group, comprising not only the organically impaired but also those whose serious emotional disturbance, deafness, blindness, or severe orthopedic impairment renders them *functionally* retarded. These seriously disabling conditions occur with a low incidence in the general population. Thus, when we speak of the severely/profoundly handicapped, we are referring not simply to the severely mentally retarded but to a population of multiply handicapped persons, including the severely emotionally disturbed, the severely health-impaired, and so on.

Inasmuch as a severe or profound handicap is a matter of degree of disability, it follows that children with such impairments may start out both in life and in education at relatively the same point, but their individual potentials will vary spectacularly. An excellent example of a child with a profound functional handicap is the young Helen Keller who, without proper education and training, manifested extreme intellectual impairment but, with enlightened help, became quite another person. Although it now appears that few of the severely/profoundly handicapped (or, for that matter, the gifted) will duplicate the achievements of Helen Keller, these students can make very significant educational gains, and the demonstration of this by special educators has provided the impetus for their intensified public education.

The fact remains, however, that the misunderstanding and misuse of the label severely/profoundly handicapped may appear to call for the possible creation of yet another special education category. To create a new category would be a serious error for two reasons. First, it would promote the placement of these children in settings away from the educational and social mainstream. In some states, trainable mentally retarded students are finally being included in the regular schools, while severely/profoundly handicapped children are being excluded. By creating another category of students outside the educational mainstream, we may find ourselves in the near future fighting to place them in regular schools, much as we have sought and are still seeking regular school placement for trainables. In the past, placement of the trainable mentally retarded in special schools was partially a result of low expectations concerning their abilities to develop traditional academic skills. However, such current work as that of the University of Washington's Experimental Education Unit has dramatically shown that the trainable mentally retarded, as well as children with far more severe impairments, can indeed acquire primary level reading skills.

Second, use of the label severely/profoundly handicapped has already prompted universities and state departments to create new divisions of special education for a category that we believe cannot and should not be given categorical status. The most crucial step that professionals can take at this juncture is to focus on a group of children

"The Severely/Profoundly Handicapped: Who Are They? Where Are We?" by Ed Sontag, Ed.D., Judy Smith, M.S. Ed., Wayne Sailor, Ph.D., *The Journal of Special Education,* Vol. 11, No. 1, 1977. Reprinted by permission.

who do not fit existing educational labels and who must not be trapped in still another educational classification. The severely/profoundly handicapped exist across all of special education. To view them otherwise is to deny their individuality, their special needs and, most unfortunate of all, their educational potential.

IDENTIFYING A NONCATEGORY

Perhaps, then, we need to take a totally new stance toward the entire issue of defining the population of severely/profoundly handicapped children. To do so, we shall first critically examine three current propositions which reflect various approaches to the problems of definition and categorization. We shall briefly pose arguments for rejection of each of these propositions and conclude with a fourth proposition which represents our position on the issue of determining who are the severely/profoundly handicapped.

Proposition 1. *There is a new disability category entitled "severely and profoundly handicapped" (SPH), or variants thereof.*

According to the proposition, this disability category has specifiable parameters, and through diagnostic assessment procedures, children who are appropriate to a disability class of this type can be identified. This concept reflects the position taken by the Bureau of Education for the Handicapped and by university special education departments in 1974 when services for the severely handicapped began their rapid expansion. Parameters were spelled out: e.g., disabilities so severe or complex that they restrict ambulation or locomotion by means of typical transportation modes; behavior characteristics that are injurious to self or others; hyperactivity, impulsivity; frequently uncontrolled bowel or bladder functions; epilepsy, grossly inadequate communication skills; mixed or multiple sensori-motor disabilities.

When parameters to define a population are necessarily subjective and when no adequate standardized instruments exist, then parameters must include such qualifiers as "*must* be characterized by" or "*may* be characterized by." The first qualifier necessarily creates the possibility of a false negative: A child who is severely handicapped will be rejected for services because of failure to display one or more of the descriptors. The second qualifier can easily produce a false positive: A child who is not severely handicapped is mistakenly identified because he displays one or more of the parametric descriptors. Thus, Proposition 1, in our opinion, should be rejected as a basis for defining the severely handicapped in the absence of a reliable diagnostic classification system based upon standardized observation and assessment. Moreover, there are already too many rigidly defined disability categories. The addition of still another category compounds an already difficult problem in educational service delivery.

Proposition 2. *The severely handicapped do not represent a new disability category. They represent the lower limits of functioning in the continuum which exists in each established disability area.*

This solution to the definition problem represents a current effort by several state education agencies to handle the problem of certification. It represents, in part, a reaction to the pressure to create a new disability category.

Proposition 2 must be rejected on the basis of the inadequacies that exist in the established system of disability categorization. A child who is *very* orthopedically disabled (who represents the lowest extreme of the continuum of crippled and other health-impaired children) would be considered severely handicapped by this definition and placed with children from the lowest strata of the mentally retarded population, even in the absence of any indication that he was academically retarded. The same would hold true for the emotionally disturbed, the deaf, the blind, and others. The potential for misplacement of children in service settings is probably greatest when this solution to the definition problem is adopted.

Proposition 3. *The severely handicapped belong in one of three global instructional areas, under a reorganization plan which would include early childhood education, general special education, and severely handicapped education. Assignment of children to the new areas would consist of reassignment of the existing disability categories.*

This proposition represents a current thrust in solving the definition problem by many state education agencies. Through this solution, the existing disability categories would be collapsed into a dichotomy of general special education and severely handicapped education, with early childhood education, determined primarily by age, representing a broad new component of special education under Public Law 94-142.

The problem with Proposition 3, and the reason that it too should be rejected, rests again with the inadequacies of the existing disability category system. General special education would encompass, for example, the learning disabled, educable mentally retarded, orthopedically disabled, emotionally disturbed, deaf, speech-impaired, and so on. Severely handicapped education would include the trainable mentally retarded, seriously disturbed, deaf-blind, and others. The potential for misplacement of children in terms of homogeneity of services is great. Trainable mentally retarded children typically do not belong in an educational program designed to benefit the profoundly retarded nonambulatory child; their curriculum requirements are substantially different. Nor does the profoundly retarded deaf child belong in a program designed for disturbed children who can deal with an academic curriculum. New subgroupings within each of the areas would no doubt become necessary at the local education agency level, and these subgroupings might well provide less functional service than the existing system of disability categorization provides.

Proposition 4. *Severely handicapped education represents one of three global instructional areas under a reorganization plan which would include early childhood education and general special education as the other two areas. Assignment of children to the new areas would be according to the nature of the children's service requirements and, indirectly, on the basis of the competencies of teaching personnel.*

This proposition resembles Proposition 3, except that reclassification into either the general special education or severely handicapped education categories (with assignment to early childhood education based on age) would be determined by the type of service required. It assumes a clean slate from the outset, as far as disability categories are concerned. Regardless of his handicapping condition, if a child or young (school-aged) adult requires instruction in basic skills, this proposition specifies that the individual belongs in a program for the severely handicapped. If a child, regardless of handicap, primarily requires academic instruction, then he belongs in a program of general special education. Children in need of both types of service would divide their time between programs. Indeed, a prime goal would be to move students gradually from severely handicapped education to general special education programs and, further, into the mainstream of regular education to the maximum extent. Exceptional children below school age would enter early childhood education programs in which the emphasis would also be divided between services for the severely handicapped (basic skill development) and general special education (preacademic instruction).

In addition, teachers whose training has produced competencies in basic self-help, motor, perceptual, social, cognitive, and communication skill development areas would teach classes for the severely handicapped. Teachers whose competencies lie in preacademic and academic instruction would teach general special education.

With this service-need definition we may cut across disability areas and create a truly programmatic and need-centered model of service delivery. Equally important, this manner of identification, placement, and programming should facilitate a progressive inclusion of the low-incidence population into the mainstream of school and community.

HANDICAPS WITHIN THE PROFESSION

Various teacher training and public education programs focusing on low-incidence children are in operation across the United States, in different stages of development. These programs differ in their degree of emphasis on this population's longitudinal needs and problems and on the competencies needed by teachers to deal with these problems: e.g., training to compensate for severe sensorimotor deficits; beginning verbal and nonverbal communication; home management and living skills; parent involvement; use of prosthetic, orthotic, and adaptive equipment to enhance general development; basic social skill mastery; basic self-help and maintenance (including feeding and toileting); behavior management; community mobility skills.

Although these models are in the process of evolving, there continue to be problems that hamper our professional efforts. We need programs that focus not just on one or two longitudinal areas but on all educational requirements of the severely/profoundly handicapped population. We need the kind of information exchange that would enhance work in all aspects of educational programming. And we need coordination and quality control on a national scale.

High on the list of priorities for dissemination is the creation of a matrix of teacher competencies and a means for measuring the attainment of those competencies. Continued research, as well as the full sharing of information among programs, is a requirement in developing competency-based training programs. Moreover, until a full spectrum of those proficiencies can be developed, we must have a system for refining and updating what is currently known. In the meantime, an exchange program for doctoral students, mutual doctoral training programs, and a national exchange of professionals at all levels may encourage programs to impact on one another.

Evident needs exist for coordination: to create skill sequences; to match existing curricula to assessed skill deficiencies; to evaluate existing curricula through systematic measurement for effectiveness; to create curricula where none exist through task analysis; and to evaluate and control the quality of these curricula. The pressing need for national curriculum and assessment programs can be met if we make a concerted effort in identification, evaluation, development, and dissemination.

From a base of such activities, it may well become possible to develop quality control for our training programs. In view of the requirements of Public Law 94-142, standards of quality and continuity become more than ever a pressing issue. We need continuous evaluation and decision making regarding relevant course content and performance skills, as well as the cost-effectiveness of our personnel preparation programs. Many existing evaluation systems simply do not cover both the courses and the experiences designed to provide competencies. We need to generate statements of standards for preservice training in terms of practicum sites, staff qualifications, student-staff ratios, competency statements, evaluation procedures, and professional standards that are exclusionary in the sense of admitting only the most highly qualified people to the task of educating the low-incidence population. A permanent data-monitoring system must also be established as an aid to planning for the rapidly accelerating demand for service delivery. Such a system should generate up-to-date printouts of all enrollment information from state departments, thereby supplying the nation with standardized needs-assessment figures on a current basis.

As we move toward an objective content evaluation system to measure acquisition and toward a series of skill-assessment systems to be administered by independent evaluation teams, we must ensure that the evaluation system reflects child-change data, as well as teacher acquisition. In directly measuring performance change, the trained teacher must be able to assess his own effectiveness in terms of reliable and demonstrable progress on the part of his class.

Related to the evaluation of our training programs, our graduates, and the educational progress of the children they serve is the matter of certification. Several years are required for teacher trainees to complete the typical university training sequence. Yet there is currently a considerable nation-wide demand for people who can work with the severely/profoundly handicapped in public school settings. To fulfill this demand we cannot continue to provisionally certify surplus teachers from other areas of education. While provisional certification may help alleviate the teacher shortage, we cannot expect that it will promote high-caliber educational programming for children. An additional danger is the certification of too many teachers who have an inappropriate range of competencies to serve severely/profoundly handicapped children, thus glutting the market with a surplus of inadequately trained teachers.

To provide a broader certification program for trainees in preservice programs, consistent with Proposition 4, we might consider the merits of a state plan that calls for two types of special educations: those with competencies for high-incidence populations of exceptional children, and those with competencies for low-incidence populations. With the addition of training for preschool programs, certification would follow the attainment of specifiable competencies in one of three areas: general special education, severely/profoundly handicapped education, and early childhood education.

In order to meet the immediate need for staffing, however, we should consider controlled inservice training, in which universities with preparation programs for teachers of low-incidence populations develop a close link with state departments in a coordinated training effort. Two critical factors are the selection of highly qualified professionals to provide such inservice training and the assurance that programs for severely/profoundly handicapped children and their prospective teachers take place within the mainstream of education.

An additional way to meet the demand for personnel is to elevate the paraprofessional within the educational strata. Educational systems have traditionally resisted financing personnel beyond the teaching staff on a local level, and the paraprofessional has been viewed as an assistant, rather than as a therapist or educator in his own right. However, programming for the severely/profoundly handicapped population engenders a teaching situation in which the ratio of professionals to children is optimally around one to three. To help meet this requirement and fulfill a greatly expanded role, paraprofessionals must be trained or retrained, must have professional status as teaching associates, and must be paid in accordance with their contributions, which are often considerable. We must continue, in addition, to make fuller use of occupationl, physical, and speech therapists (as well as professionals trained in deafness, blindness, and other specialty areas) as resource persons, teacher consultants, and trainers of children.

For all of these personnel, there must be an effective licensing mechnanism, such as peer review or certification by state education agencies, with cooperation from universities. Specialized support personnel (e.g., consultants to programs for the blind) and allied health professionals (e.g., occupational therapists) should be given a coordinated opportunity to enter the competency-based training model. Consortia of training colleges and medical schools, for example, could provide an integrated training program across all the multidisciplinary training components of quality education for the severely/profoundly handicapped. State licensing agencies for specialty educators and support therapists should be encouraged to consider specialized licensing requirements. These would reflect the highly differentiated competencies and expertise acquired by those therapists who complete relevant components of university education preparing them to become effective members of the educational team.

Finally, through the competent people we now have, we must provide technical assistance to localities whose leaders have shown the potential for integrating low-incidence children into the community and into the public schools. That leadership must be reinforced by solid professional support and by the extensive sharing of expertise. Indeed, mutual support and sharing of information are the best and perhaps the only means we have to meet the needs of all professionals who are working to raise the potential of the severely/profoundly handicapped child. Then, perhaps, we will make sure that no Helen Keller goes unrecognized.

Some current directions in education of the severely/multiply handicapped

Wayne Sailor
Norris G. Haring

The current phase in our national education program for handicapped people began in November, 1975, with passage by Congress and signature by President Ford of the National Education for All Handicapped Children Act (P.L. 94-142). Before this legislation was passed, no specific agency assumed responsibility for the education of severely handicapped children and youth. In a few instances, school districts carried out experimental programs. Other programs were conducted by special facilities operated by county and local Association for Retarded Citizens programs. For the most part, "education" fell to large, understaffed, ill-equipped state institutions for retarded children, where most of the children and young adults were maintained. As a result of the often very primitive assessment, diagnosis, and classification systems available, many severely and multiply handicapped children–who are functionally retarded–were diagnosed as mentally retarded and placed in these institutions. So the primary milestone in the impetus for educating the severely/multiply handicapped was a legislative one, sponsored by a relatively small group of professionals.

Milestones in the educational process for this population are coming thick and fast. As a rapidly growing cadre of highly competent professionals gains experience with these children in 6-hour-per-day classes, new and creative developments in their educational strategies become legion.

SOME BASIC CONSIDERATIONS

Referral

A child should be assigned to a program for the severely/multiply handicapped according to whether the primary educational service needs of the child are *basic* or academic, a distinction to be discussed. If the diagnosis and assessment process determines that a child with multiple handicaps needs *academic* instruction, that child should *not* be referred to the severely/multiply handicapped program. If the child's service need is *basic skill development,* the referral to the severely/multiply handicapped program *is* appropriate.

Basic skill development consists of: (1) self-help skills, (2) fine and gross motor skills, (3) beginning communication development, (4) beginning social skill development, (5) beginning cognitive or preacademic skills. For a more detailed discussion of the placement of special education children as a function of educational service needs, see Sontag, Sailor, and Smith (in press).

Obviously, this solution to the problems of program referral and placement is not perfect. Some children may be found who require both *basic* skill training and *academic* instruction. Perhaps these children should divide their school time between two separate programs. The placement decision will continue to pose problems, in many cases, but we hope that the referral *process* has been simplified—that children can be referred to the severely/multiply handicapped program on the basis of service need.

In general, the lower incidence population of children who are most severely impaired are the children for whom this program designation pertains. *Retardation* is the underlying factor—not mental retardation as a primary diagnostic consideration, but *functional* retardation resulting from severity of handicap. Most severely/multiply handicapped children are functionally severely retarded (and, hence, untestable by

"Some Current Directions in Education of the Severely/Multiply Handicapped," Wayne Sailor and Norris G. Haring, *AAESPH Review,* 1977, Vol. 2, No. 2, pp. 67-87. Reprinted by permission.

standardized measures of intelligence). The issue, again, is that *regardless* of handicapping conditions, the factor determining a child's placement in a class for severely/multiply handicapped children is basic skill development needs.

Family–School Cooperation

The severely/multiply handicapped child can benefit from public instruction! To some, that statement may, by now, seem a truism. Among others, it will provoke skepticism. But the data are in. The children benefit, and they benefit immensely. Children who were previously institutionalized and fed pablum while flat on their backs at age 14 are now upright, head on midline, and self-feeding, all because of exemplary instructional programming. The gains are striking *whenever* the program begins, whether the child enters the program at age 18 or age 3. The extent and speed of the gain can depend, in part, on educational carry-over in the home with family members. The closer the ties between the parents and the school, with the family and teacher working together to make the child's education relevant and functional, the greater the educational impact on the child.

A child learning to communicate for the first time, to sign exact English, for example, must have an audience at home to interact with. To the parents we say: learn the signs your child is learning. To teachers: teach the parents whenever and wherever you can, when you want your instruction to *generalize* from the classroom to the home. Dressing skills, feeding skills, toileting—all require home participation to become rapidly successful and durable new behaviors. The child *will learn* even if there is no cooperation and active participation between school and family, but he will have the extra burden of having to learn which setting is appropriate to which behaviors. For instance, the child who is learning toilet regulation will learn to go to the bathroom at school but may continue to soil his clothes at home if the family does not participate in the toilet-regulation curriculum.

Integrating Handicapped Children

The time the severely/multiply handicapped child enters the school is the time to stop feeling sorry for him. What has happened has happened. What will happen next is up to the teaching staff and the family. Children, handicapped or not, *learn by having demands made upon them and by experiencing the positive consequences of succeeding in meeting those demands*. Parents who have cuddled and over-protected their severely/multiply handicapped child must be encouraged to "toughen up" and treat that child as a *learner,* not as an invalid. Handicapped children are human beings, equal under the law.

Many parents of severely/multiply handicapped children fear the placement of their child in a regular school situation. They fear their child will be ridiculed by normal children, or even by the less retarded or handicapped children. These parents should somehow see the public schools of Madison, Wisconsin, where severely/multiply handicapped children have been associated with regular education students for several years now. The results of this association are striking. Regular education children benefit significantly in positive social ways from the close association with severely handicapped children. They learn to assist these children when appropriate, and they learn tolerance for differences. The severely handicapped children learn from the normal peers as role models. It is a *mutually* beneficial integration of programs which should be effected where feasible and where the public school building constitutes the *least restrictive environment* for the child.

Of course, most schools will need some physical adaptation, unless very new and modern in design, before they will accommodate severely/multiply handicapped children. The school room must be large and must contain a toilet and a sink. There must be space for wheelchairs and freedom from architectural barriers.

Historically, the "community" of the severely/multiply handicapped child has been the back ward of the state institution. We now know that the impact of the human community on the severely handicapped child is immense. The community at large is a source of beneficial stimulation in which day-to-day encounters provide opportunities for real learning. To deprive a child of the human community is to deprive him of his right to learn.

The impact of the severely handicapped child on the community at large is nearly equally important. Severely/multiply handicapped children frequently look odd and elicit puzzled—sometimes horrified—looks from strangers, perhaps because society has been sheltered from these deforming conditions for so long that no one knows they exist. It is time for change. Parents and teachers of severely/multiply handicapped children have as much right to hold their heads high and be proud of their children in the public setting as do parents and teachers of nonhandicapped children. There need be no guilt, no shame, because there is no fault. The inevitable consequence of the exposure of multiply handicapped children in public settings is public education. The public must learn to *assimilate* its experience with different kinds of people, if for no other reason than to learn why to vote yes on the next school bond issue to finance the increasing cost of special education.

WHERE ARE WE IN OUR PROGRESS?

What is the national picture for the severely/multiply handicapped child? Legislators are frequently concerned with whether this child will become a future taxpayer, a part of the Gross National Product. The parent and teacher hope at least for substantial measures of increasing independent functioning. Not long ago the future for severely handicapped children was bleak indeed. Today, it is considerably brighter, but still in question. The technology of education for the severely/multiply handicapped child is currently being developed. It will be fully implemented during the next decade. The fruits of these labors will be seen most dramatically with children as yet unborn. The picture is optimistic.

Diagnostic procedures for the detection of multiply handicapping conditions before, during, and shortly after birth are an area of scientific breakthrough. And early detection leads to early intervention and appropriate referral. P.L. 94-142 provides special funding for early education programs for the prevention of later severely handicapping conditions.

Early diagnosis and intervention are national efforts aimed at the *prevention* and *reduction* of severely handicapping conditions. But what about the older multiply handicapped person? Again, national legislation encouraging the development of vocational rehabilitation programs to benefit the severely/multiply handicapped person of high-school age and older is brightening a formerly dull picture.

The outcome of the legislative, judicial, and professional thrust over the past few years in the right-to-education movement has been to guarantee the severely/multiply handicapped student a free, public, 6-hour-per-day education in the environment most suited to his needs and his rights. The impact on the philosophy of education is significant. Educators cannot now provide a program and merely expect students to respond or be failed. *A tremendous responsibility has been placed on the educator.* The timing is unfortunate, since the teaching staff cannot and should not bear the brunt of society's failure to develop an instructional system for these disadvantaged children. Much new information, however, is available or forthcoming, and the responsibility will become easier to bear as time progresses.

Some Management Decisions and Questions

Where Should the Class Be Located? The "cluster" or self-contained school for special education students offers the advantage of high community visibility, concentrating parents, administrators, and resources—which are apt to be scarce in a community—in one central location. Staff and consultant communication and problem sharing are maximized under this model. Ancillary professional personnel spend less time in transportation and thus more time in service. Supervised practice teaching and inservice programs are easier to administer, and specialized support services, e.g., medical personnel, can be concentrated in one place.

On the other hand, the "dispersal" model—or the spreading of classes for the severely handicapped throughout several, or many, schools in a district—offers the possibility of integration into community life and normalization. (Sontag, Burke & York, 1973). The students are apt to be closer to home and there are fewer transportation problems. Finally, a broader range of educational personnel are apt to come into contact with the problems of the severely/multiply handicapped child, and the possibilities for new approaches to remediation are increased.

The Physical Structure of the Facility is an important consideration. Stairs, crash-bar doors, narrow doorways, and so forth may provide barriers to the student's mobility. Often an expensive renovation of an existing facility is the only alternative. Specialized facilities and equipment become a major consideration. A classroom for the multiply handicapped child should, whenever possible: (1) be on the ground floor, near the entrance to the building; (2) be a large space (e.g., 600 square feet) and at least partially covered with indoor-outdoor carpeting; (3) have toilets and sinks *within the classroom,* which are accessible to wheelchairs and contain the necessary specialized features; (4) have specialized adaptive (orthotic and prosthetic) equipment for physical-motor development, including special or modified wheelchairs with trays, standing tables, mats, mirrors, barrels, Bobath positioning and facilitation equipment, etc.; (5) have specialized materials for perceptual, gross, and fine motor activities, and (6) provide accessories such as friction-release door stops and pressure-free faucets.

Transportation of the multiply handicapped child remains a major challenge. Specialized vehicles are often required, equipped with wheelchair locks and hydraulic lifts. An additional consideration is training the bus driver and the driver's aide to deal with students who display seizures, gross hyperactivity, self-destructive behavior, and so on. Conversely, part of the educational curriculum for the student must include "travel skills," proper behavior during transportation to and from school.

The Instructional Method of providing educational service to the severely/multiply handicapped student is a major challenge for research and development. We know only that it requires a *mix* of one-to-one and small group instruction. In no case should the class size exceed 10, and the ratio of students to teaching staff (teacher and teaching associates) should not exceed three-to-one whenever possible.

The prevalent instructional model in the education of the severely/multiply handicapped child is the *behavioral* model. This model focuses on *specific skill building* activities derived from *assessment* techniques and *measured* in progress. For a severely handicapped child to learn a skill, it must be *operationalized*. The instructor must state precisely what is requested and when it should be manifested. This *task analysis* approach to instruction delineates starting points and terminal objectives, thus assuring that essential component skills will not be neglected. The instruction is tailored to individual functioning levels, with each student proceeding within the sequence *at his own pace* under optimal reinforcement control, taking longer on trouble spots and skipping objectives on which he quickly demonstrates mastery.

The Selection of a Particular Skill to Teach must be made on the basis of its inclusion as one *segment* in a developmentally sound and remedially important longitudinal curriculum sequence. The *criterion of ultimate functioning* (Brown, Nietupski, & Hamre-Nietupski, 1976) must be implicit. That is, the skill segment must be part of a curriculum which is designed to insure independent functioning. In other words, you should be able to visualize the independent function which will result when a long sequence is completed, within *each* tiny segmental skill taught. For example, you are teaching your student to "relax fingers." The paradigm is release of a small round object held 3 inches above a flat container. The skill is one of a three part chain: grasp, raise, and release. The ultimate function for this sequence might, for example, be self-feeding. Education of the severely/multiply handicapped child is still awaiting the development of well-defined skill sequences across curricula domains. At this point much is up to the teacher's creative use of task analysis.

Direct Measurement of Skill Acquisition, rather than inference or subjective judgment, is essential to the instructional system. Severely handicapped children have too much to learn in too short a time for teachers to waste time performing "ritualistic" quasieducational activities for which no verifiable student learning is demonstrable. Measurement tells you if the child is learning (acquiring the skill) and, equally important, tells you if he has learned (has "reached criterion.") Sometimes teachers are tempted to repeat already learned activities. The teacher empties a pegboard after the student has filled it, and encourages the student to begin again, because a busy student must be a learning student. But task repetition following completed learning bores the student and creates a pattern of behavior which depresses other learning activities. If you're not skill training according to plan (the Individual Educational Plan required by P.L. 94-142), let the student rest or play. Don't force him to engage in educational ritual.

Selection of Materials should be tailored specifically to the skill being taught. Tasks and task materials are vehicles through which skills are taught. Tasks and materials should be functional, easily discriminated by the student, accessible to repeated trials, of reinforcing value to the student when possible, facilitating later skill development where possible. When selecting materials, the teacher should consider the ultimate function for which the skill is being taught, the durability of the material used (can it be used again to teach the same skill to different students?), and the cost of the materials. Much educational material for the severely/multiply handicapped is, unfortunately, a rip-off. In many cases, creative teachers can design and build adaptive equipment at a fraction of the cost of less functional, less durable materials and equipment from the manufacturers.

The Teaching Environment. Specific skills are best taught in a highly specific teaching environment. Variations in the environment should be programmed when the skill is beginning to be mastered. If the changed environment is *gradually* made different from the initial environment, the student may learn to generalize the taught skill to new situations, different people, etc.

What Skills Must Teachers Have to Educate Severely/Multiply Handicapped Children? Until very recently with the advent of personnel preparation programs for the severely/multiply handicapped, the major prerequisite to teach a class of these students was courage. Few teachers could be located anywhere who had previous exposure to severely handicapped students. Many persons, even today, don't know that these children even exist. How could they know? The children have been kept at home or locked away in institutions. Present teacher training programs have few applicants for the severely handicapped programs. Most college student prefer initially to work with children who have learning disabilities and with groups of higher functioning mentally retarded children. This is really all they can visualize from their own experience. Fortunately, student teachers are often surprised to find that they gravitate toward the severely/multiply handicapped following a few weeks' practicum exposure to them. This is particularly true when the student teachers discover how rapidly the children, who initially looked hopeless, learn new skills. It is also our experience that the brightest and most creative special education student teachers elect to work with the severely/multiply handicapped, perhaps because of the challenge (or perhaps because we are biased).

Higher functioning special education disability areas allow student teachers to transfer much that they know about normal child development and much that they have learned in the college classroom about special education to the instruction process with their handicapped students. This is unfortunately not often the case for teachers of the severely/multiply handicapped child. These teachers must learn teacher-child interactions that may be totally different from anything they've ever done before. These student teachers should have intense and durable experiences with severely handicapped children from their first week of the college training program. A competency-based practicum training program is nearly mandatory. Similarly, inservice training programs for teachers of the severly handicapped child should be practicum-based, with demonstrations and workshops as the primary instructional models.

A Definition of Teaching. Severely handicapped children are severely handicapped *because* they cannot perform skills that other children can perform—*not* because they are severely retarded, quadriplegic, brain-damaged or fixated in some primitive stage of someone's theory of development. This is a difficult concept, or implication for teaching, to fully grasp initially; but when you understand its full significance, it can act as a powerful catalyst. *Teaching the severely/multiply handicapped person is the process of arranging a relationship between the student and his environment which results in positive experiences for the student and small positive changes in skill acquisition.* This definition of teaching requires that the teacher:

1) Delineate *precisely* the responses the child must make to acquire the specified skill;
2) Delineate and precisely specify the teacher's activities to insure those responses; and
3) Verify the existence of changes in the level of responses indicating skill acquisition.

In other words, the teacher must task analyze a skill in terms of discrete responses, specify training techniques for each step of the chain, and measure the progress toward a discrete *criterion*.

When a student teacher has demonstrated that his or her teaching techniques have resulted in new functional skills for his severely handicapped children, then that student has begun to become a teacher. A teacher of the severely/multiply handicapped must be competent to arrange an instructional environment (which includes the teacher's behavior) that results in students' learning new skills leading to independent functioning—and one hopes that they learn these rapidly. If a student is not toilet trained, but is *physically* capable of becoming so, the teacher must have within his instructional repertoire an applicable technology which will result in the student becoming toilet trained.

Teacher Competencies for the Severely/Multiply Handicapped Preparation Program, thus, must include:

1) techniques for managing severe behavior problems;
2) procedures for developing teacher-made instructional materials;
3) engineering physical properties of a classroom;
4) basic principles of the acquisition of operant behavior;
5) basic principles and techniques of measurement;
6) basic principles of imitation training, generalization, discrimination, and maintenance;
7) basic principles of task analysis;
8) development and implementation of instructional programs, and
9) procedures used to develop curriculum sequences (from Horner, Holvolt, & Rieber, 1976).

Basic Skills

Regardless of the severity of the severely handicapping conditions for each child, the service need is for basic skill development aimed at increased independent functioning. Basic skill development does not take place strictly in a group instructional mode. It requires one-to-one instruction for a significant portion of the school day. It also requires instruction within a group context for social skill development. The most successful instructional model to date for severely/multiply handicapped children has been a mixture of one-to-one instruction by some teaching staff and group instructional activity in a semicircle with another teacher.

The classroom should be *engineered* to move the child in and out of various instructional activities in an *engaging* environment appropriate to the skill being developed. An engaging environment is one which (1) requires a response from the student, and (2) supports that response with an encouraging event. The child, through each new response in skill acquisition, comes to have more and more rewarding *impact* on his environment. The educator may engage the child at either end of each response.

Engaging activities occurring prior to the desired response are called *antecedent events*. Engaging activities which occur following the skill-acquisition response are called *consequences*. The skill will be learned *because* of the consequences which follow each response, each step of the way. Antecedent activities do not "cause" learning. But skillfully programmed antecedent activities will *enable* a response to occur, which can then be followed by a pleasurable consequence for that response, which will *cause* learning to occur. In teaching severely/multiply handicapped students, the teaching staff should be skilled at programming *both* antecedent and consequent events in building new skills in their students, but should recognize that success, for the student, lies with the latter. Too many classrooms seem to operate as if the child will learn by being a passive recipient of pleasurable, relaxing stimulation. He will not. He must *respond* before learning can occur, and the environment must be arranged to respond to him in turn.

Persons interested in studying engaging instructional models appropriate to severely/multiply handicapped students should check the following sorces: Cohen and Filipczak, 1971; Doke and Risley, 1972; Hamilton and Allen, 1967; Haring and Whelan, 1966; Hewett, Taylor, and Artuse, 1970; Lelaurin and Risley, 1972; Stabler, et al., 1974; and Vogel, Kun, and Meshover, 1968.

Emotional Needs. What about the emotional needs of the severely/multiply handicapped student? Don't these children need love too? The answer is yes. A nurturing, loving, and pleasurable environment is exactly what the SMH student needs, but he needs one which very intensively programs for and fosters learning. The two are not necessarily incompatible, although in some cases it may seem so. Consider Classroom One, which operates on the theory that severely/multiply handicapped children need warmth, love, relaxation, and stimulation. Children in this classroom are felt to be capable of learning by antecedent stimulation. Responses which are more complex than the ones they presently display are not demanded of the children because "they are not yet at that stage." A glance at Classroom One at nearly any time will show children being held, rocked, and cooed at by members of the teaching staff. Some children may be lying on their backs having their tummies and faces stroked by electric vibrators. A physical or occupational therapist may be "exercising" a child's undeveloped muscles by stimulating the area around the joints (rubbing) or by pulling and pushing on a child's leg. Another child may be physically being guided through the act of playing in wet sand, while another is being helped to clap his hands to a record on the record player. The staff all *feel* that the children are learning, but come and look again in six months and what do you see? The same activities with the same children. Classroom One is full of ritualized quasieducational activities. The students are probably enjoying the activities, but they aren't learning.

Consider Classroom Two. The students are also enjoying the activity, which is also warm, nurturing, and loving. The only difference is that the children in Classroom Two are learning as a function of the consequences for their actions. Action is required. The child is given the benefit of the doubt about whether he is at the correct stage of development to learn what the teacher is trying to teach him. The observed sequence or stages of normal development are not a particularly useful guide to the education of the severely/multiply handicapped. These students have missed the boat and need to catch up. A *remedial* strategy should determine the educational tactics with this population, not a normal-developmental strategy.

In Classroom Two, we might see a teacher supporting a child in a sitting position, listening to music from a radio or record player. However, the difference from Classroom One might be that the radio stops when the child's head slumps from midline and starts when he raises it again to midline. Music to this child is a pleasurable *consequence* of an action he is learning to make in his environment, in this case strengthening neck muscles to achieve midline. Another child may be having his back stroked with the vibrator and obviously enjoying it, just *after* he has produced in the potty as part of his toilet training program. In Classroom Two, when you return in 6 months to observe, you will see the same children engaging in *different* activities—activities which are more complex and more demanding of the child than 6 months before, and which build on those earlier activities. Yet the children will be obviously enjoying these exercises too. Learning to exert increasing control over one's environment is a rewarding experience for all children, including the severely/multiply handicapped. It is also progress toward independent functioning.

High School Students

The educational needs of the high school age severely/multiply handicapped student are either basic, in which case there should be no distinction between this program and the program for elementary and intermediate age students, or prevocational, preparation for sheltered living and employment or sheltered workshop training activity.

A Good Example. One of the most advanced programs of its type for severely/multiply handicapped youths is Project MAZE (Madison, Wisconsin, zero-rejection program), directed by Dr. Tim Crowner of Madison Public Schools in conjunction with Dr. Lou Brown at the University of Wisconsin Department of Behavioral Disabilities. Within this program, the criterion of ultimate functioning is employed. The most probable living environment of the classes' graduates is carefully analyzed to determine the structure of the curriculum which will enable the students to survive (and thrive) in that living environment. Programs are designed and implemented to instruct students in human sexual expression, in using of the local mass transit system to get to and from work, in shopping for food and other personal need items, in handling money, in home living skills such as washing and ironing, cooking, house cleaning, etc. (*both* sexes), and in constructive and enjoyable use of leisure time. Prevocational training experiences include the basics of small-part assembly and production at maximum rate as well as appropriate job behavior. Students are taught to punch in and out *on time,* to be appropriately groomed, to put things in their proper place, and to be polite to coworkers and (particularly) management. In one striking aspect of the program, severely handicapped students are being taught to get to and from, and to operate, the laundry facility in the large state-operated institution for the retarded near the high school from which they start out (theirs is a high school class in every sense of the word). A nice bit of irony: those who graduate successfully from the training program become eligible for classified state positions as laundry workers, positions within the same state institution at which they were *patients* not too many years before.

The severely handicapped student, to succeed in the public sector, must be taught by the criterion of ultimate functioning and must be prepared for the reactions of nonhandicapped persons, many of whom will not have the patience to adapt themselves to the individual's handicap.

Persons interested in the structure of educational programs for the severely/multiply handicapped, high school youth, should read Bellamy, Peterson, and Close, 1975; Brown, et. al., 1972, 1976; Buschard, 1967; Crosson, 1967, 1969; Gold, 1973, 1974; and Silvern, 1963.

ASSESSMENT

For the severely/multiply handicapped child, the *key* member of the assessment team must be the teacher. There are no standardized tests or check lists which will, in a single administration, produce educational objectives and a program plan for these children. Comprehensive *educational* assessment of the SMH child should take a *minimum* of 2 to 4 weeks and should be a joint endeavor, wherever possible, of the teaching staff, support staff, and the student's parents.

The point of educational assessment is the formulation of a set of precise, terminal-performance, instructional objectives with which to begin the child's education. The end product of assessment is the formulation of goals and precise objectives into the Individual Educational Plan mandated by P.L. 94-142 (IEP). Severely/multiply handicapped students require basic skill development activities. Their instructional objectives must develop *components* of complex skills in a meaningful, functional *sequence*.

Picture a pyramid. At the base are the most basic behaviors imaginable—tracing a moving object with the eyes, for example, or grasping an object with the hand. As you move up the pyramid, the skills interlace laterally, so that new, more complex skills may be learned which are partially dependent upon various of the skills just acquired slightly down the pyramid. The process continues toward the point of the pyramid, which represents complex, independent functioning, characteristic of a normal person of the child's age. The assessment should show precisely where the student is on the pyramid and, thus, to show the teacher precisely which skills need to be taught immediately to advance the child's educational development up the pyramid. Obviously, the best system of assessment, then, is one *whose items are prescriptive for instructional objectives.*[1]

Sailor and Horner (1976) have provided a recent detailed analysis of several assessment systems of use in programs for severely/multiply handicapped children. These systems tend to fall into three positions on a continuum of comprehensiveness.

Screening: Position 1 Systems

Position I systems are really screening instruments. They take a relatively short time to complete (e.g., 2 weeks) and provide a thumbnail sketch of the student's

[1]The authors are grateful to Dr. Doug Guess of the Department of Special Education, University of Kansas, for the conceptual pyramid model for remedial-behavioral sequencing.

current skill level across various domains. Examples are the TARC Assessment System (Sailor & Mix, 1975) and the Portage Project Guide to Early Education: Instructions and Checklist (Shearer et al., 1970).

The Pennsylvania Model: Position II System

Position II Assessment Systems fall midway between thumbnail screening instruments and full-scale comprehensive assessment systems. By far the best of these to date is the Pennsylvania Training Model, Individual Assessment Guide (Somerton & Turner, 1975) which appeared in print too late for review in Sailor and Horner (1976). The student's current competency in sensory, motor, self-care, communication, perceptual-cognitive, and social interaction development is assessed. Subdomains sampled include auditory, visual and tactual discrimination, gross and fine motor competencies, feeding, drinking, toileting, dressing, washing, and bathing. Under Fine Motor (Motor Development domain) for example, the teacher scores 0 (no competency) to 3 (complete competency) on each of 32 observable behavioral checklist items. To illustrate the range of the sample, Items 1, 2, and 3 and 30, 31, and 32 are reprinted here.

Item 1 Child will, while lying on back, follow a moving object or a light with his eyes from the center 2 inches to the left and right side of his head.
Item 2 Child will grasp a toy that is placed in his hand and hold it for 3 seconds.
Item 3 Child will bring his hands to face and look at them. . . .

Item 30 Child will be able to copy a square drawn on paper.
Item 31 Child will build a pyramid of 6 blocks in imitation of an adult.
Item 32 Child will copy a diamond-shaped figure made by an adult.

Ideally, a system of this type would *reliably* (two or more persons get the same results scoring independently) communicate to the teaching staff:

1) the child's current baseline skill level;
2) on a wide number and range of basic service need skill areas;
3) which fall into a progressive developmental-remedial sequence, such that;
4) when a child fails an item, that item becomes an instructional objective and teaching continues up the sequences.

Obviously, the Pennsylvania system (and all present systems) is inadequate for this purpose, but it represents a start in that direction.

Position III Systems

Position III systems are fully comprehensive and are therefore quite complex and time consuming. Examples are the Balthazar Scales of Adaptive Behavior (Balthazar, 1971a, 1971b, 1971c, 1971d) and the AAMD Adaptive Behavior Scales (Nihira, et al., 1974). A newer comprehensive system which was received too late for review in Sailor and Horner (1976) but which seems quite promising is the Behavior Progression Checklist (BCP, 1973). The BCP rates the student on up to 59 "strands," each of which may contain up to 50 sequenced items rated on a 3-point scale. The number of strands used in the assessment as well as their content are up to the teacher. Examples of the strands are: feeding/eating, drinking, toileting, grooming, visual motor I and II, writing, spelling, and reasoning. The BCP attempts to encompass all ranges of handicapping condition, not just severely/multiply handicapped.

To compare BCP with the Pennsylvania system, the first and last three items of the visual motor I strand are presented.

1.0 Responds to light when introduced into room (e.g., turns head in direction).
2.0 Follows moving objects with eyes and head. Fixates on object momentarily.
3.0 Follows moving object (with eyes and head) on its horizontal path from side of body to midline (90° arc). . . .

48.0 Matches circles, squares, triangles, diamonds.
49.0 Matches above shapes to proper holes on formboard,.
50.0 Puts together simple puzzles.

Visual motor II then continues with another 50 more complex items. The range and sequencing of the BCP and Pennsylvania systems are, as you can see, quite similar. The difference is primarily in the inclusion of finer components in the larger instrument (BCP).

Sequencing for Assessment and Instruction

The sequencing of items in the BCP, Pennsylvania, or any system, at present, is done largely on the basis of some attention to normal developmental milestones and pure speculation. The *actual* optimal sequence for assessment and instruction, within each skill domain, is an empirical question and must await extensive research on child acquisition of skills under optimal teaching conditions.

As a rule of thumb:

1) Use a Position I instrument for *screening* purposes or *to get started* with a child or class when time is short.
2) Use a Position II instrument to conduct educational assessment and formulate an Individual Educational Plan.
3) Use Position III instruments as guides to formulate instructional objectives following assessment.

Each school district program for the severely/multiply handicapped should have sample assessment systems within each of the three positions of comprehensiveness.

The continuum of sequenced skill development for the severely/multiply handicapped student has yet to be developed, but as demonstrated above, there has been recent hopeful progress.

Basic skill sequences. The basic skill domains which encompass most educational programming efforts for the severely/multiply handicapped student are as follows:

1) Self-Help Development
   (a) Washing
   (b) Eating
   (c) Toileting
   (d) Dressing/undressing
   (e) Appearance/hygiene
2) Sensory-Motor Development
   (a) Fine motor
   (b) Gross motor
   (c) Sensory-motor integration
   (d) Prevocational skill development
   (e) Use of adaptive equipment
3) Communication Development
   (a) Receptive language (speech and/or nonspeech)
   (b) Expressive language (speech and/or nonspeech)
4) Social Skill Development
   (a) Behavior
   (b) Recreation
   (c) Cooperative interaction
   (d) Independent social-sexual functioning
   (e) Independent home-living skill development

Instructional objectives. Within each specified domain, specific instructional objectives can be derived from assessment. The particular items comprising Position III Assessment Systems can be used to specify the terminal objective in each case. Curricula can then be *selected* (c.f., TARC Computerized Curriculum Selection System, Sailor and Mix, 1975),[2] or designed by the method of task analysis. Only one comprehensive curriculum for the severely/multiply handicapped classroom has appeared in print to date, and that is the Teaching Research Curriculum (Fredericks, et al., 1976). This effort, while it represents an excellent beginning for moderately to severely retarded students, is, of course, inadequate as a comprehensive curriculum for severely/multiply handicapped students. The creativity of the teacher in task-analyzing instructional programs to meet instructional objectives will determine curriculum for SMH students over the next few years.

EVALUATING PROGRAM DELIVERY

An adequate *evaluation* system for program delivery to severely/multiply handicapped children has not yet been designed, but is sorely needed. Such a system

[2]A more recent and timely system for curriculum selection is available from NIMIS (Elder, Pellow, & Jipson-Greenstein, 1977).

should, and will, concern itself with the child, the classroom, the teaching staff (including all support services), the total educational ecology (including the school, parents, and home), and the administrative framework overlying the service.

Level I: The Child

(a) Is the service appropriate for the child and vice versa? In California, the method for determination of service relevance to the child is through employment of an *instructional management system*: DASIE (California State Department of Education, 1975). Under this system, a combination of teacher and parents performs a careful evaluation of the child's performance, develops instructional objectives, chooses curricula and teaching methods, and then evaluates progress resulting from educational intervention. The components provided in the DASIE system represent parameters which must apply to every severely handicapped child receiving educational service: assessment, instructional objectives, curriculum selection and design, instructional method applied, outcome evaluated.

(b) Is there an adequate *Individual Educational Plan* for each child in accordance with P.L. 94-142?

(c) Is the child receiving appropriate physical, nutritional, and medical care? For example, are braces needed? a modified wheelchair? a medical regime indicated? seizures controlled?

(d) Are *assessment* data on the child adequate for the specification of precise instructional objectives?

(e) Are the *instructional objectives* appropriate, functional, specific, directly determined from assessment data, and realistic?

(f) Is the identified or designed *curriculum* adequate to fulfill the instructional objectives?

(g) Are data collected to determine by reliable *measurement* if objectives are being fulfilled?

(h) Is the child progressing; and if not, are *remedial measures* being implemented?

(i) Is the child properly provided with needed *equipment and supplies* in accordance with his deficits and program?

(j) Is there a mechanism to determine when equipment such as braces or a wheelchair need *modification or change*?

Level 2: The Classroom

(a) Environmental considerations.

1. Architectural-physical properties.

This should include, for example, barrier freedom and accessibility, room size, lighting, noise level, accessibility to toileting and washing facilities, diaper-changing facilities, etc.

2. Use of adaptive devices.

Special adaptive devices either available or properly used to meet both the motor and sensory impairments of children in the classroom (e.g., modified wheelchairs, walkers, positioning mats, head sticks, communication boards, etc.).

3. Staff-child interactions.

A measure should be taken of the adequacy of particular instructional models (e.g., one-to-one; holding activity plus one-to-one; semicircle-mixed; etc.) to meet the specified instructional objectives for each child.

4. Child-environment interactions.

The extent to which the classroom environment engages the child should be considered. Procedures should be developed to assess the frequency with which students are engaged in appropriate and constructive activities throughout the class period and, conversely, the extent to which they engage in appropriate, nonadaptive, and noninstructional activities.

(b) Instructional considerations.

1. Curriculum selection.

Considering the class as an entity (rather than focusing on the specific child), is the overall curriculum in accordance with realistic and functional educational goals for the class? How much classroom time is devoted, for example, to communication development, motor development, self-help training, discrimination learning, social skill development, and prevocational training or preparation?

2. Curriculum utilization.
Provided that the teacher has scheduled the use of classroom instructional programs which meet the assessed needs of the students, the next analysis would center on the efficiency with which these programs are being implemented. In this domain, the evaluation would likely be concerned with teaching technique. Are, indeed, the instructional programs being carried out in the prescribed manner? Is the instructional model prevalent in the classroom the most efficient in terms of class size, staff-child ratio, and role and competency differentiation of teaching personnel?

3. Data recording systems.
This subdomain refers to the use of measurement procedures to document student progress in the classroom. Initially, the question is whether or not a recording system for charting student progress is present. Secondly, if a measurement system is being used, is this system appropriate to the instructional objectives identified in the classroom curriculum for each student? Finally, is the measurement system used appropriately in making program decisions for the students?

Level 3: Teaching Staff

(a) The teacher.
The system would be concerned primarily with whether or not the teacher displays the competencies to implement a functional and realistic program plan for each severely handicapped child in his or her classroom. Factors such as adequacy of preservice training programs, participation in the progress through inservice training, certification, and experience in classroom education of the severely handicapped child would all be relevant secondary considerations.

(b) Teaching associates (paraprofessionals).
The use and competency level of classroom teaching associates are extremely important. The involvement of classroom associates ranges anywhere from "custodian" to an actively involved "teacher." This particular parameter should be evaluated in terms of the efficiency with which teaching associates are utilized in relation to their training and competency levels. Obviously, in many cases teaching associates should also be evaluated on other parameters (e.g., staff-child interactions, curriculum utilization) in the same manner as the classroom teacher.

(c) Ancillary personnel.
With respect to ancillary personnel such as physical therapists, occupational therapists, speech therapists, psychologists, etc., the evaluation effort would attend to three major questions: (1) Do ancillary services exist? (2) If the services exist, are they adequate and how are they used? (3) If the services require assistance from teachers and teaching associates, does the classroom staff have the necessary competencies to collaborate in the planning and implementation of effective educational services?

The incorporation of severely/multiply handicapped children into the public school systems has clearly made the case for a strong interdisciplinary approach to the education of these children (e.g., Bricker & Bricker, 1974). The need for new roles for occupational and physical therapists in service to the severely handicapped has become a pressing issue (Sailor, 1976). Another important issue is the type of physical and occupational service delivery model. Would services best be rendered through an isolated therapy model (students are taken to the therapist on an individual basis in a "therapy room,") or through an integrated therapy model (therapists supervise and consult with teachers in the child's classroom) (Sternat, et al., 1976).

A third issue concerns the competencies that classroom staff must demonstrate if an integrated model for occupational and physical therapy services is used. Utley, Holvolt, and Barnes (in press) and Bigge and O'Donnell (1977) have specified procedures and techniques for handling the physically handicapped for use by classroom personnel in conjunction with physical and occupational therapists. Utley, Horner, and Rinne have identified specific competencies for both teachers and teaching associates. Evaluation procedures could assess all of these competencies and procedures as well as the amount of help received by the child under the different models.

The three essential questions also apply to the delivery of speech therapy services. Evaluation systems should be developed to determine: (1) the presence or absence of speech therapy services; (2) the model in which the services are delivered (i.e., integrated or isolated); and (3) the extent to which classroom personnel need and demonstrate necessary competencies for teaching language skills to the severely handicapped (Guess, Sailor, & Baer, in press).

With regard to the delivery of psychological services, the evaluation system could be developed to determine: (1) the presence or absence of services from psychologists, (2) the adequacy and relevance of the types of services provided, (3) if the services require the utilization of classroom personnel, whether they demonstrate the necessary competencies, and (4) the effectiveness of the process of relaying transdisciplinary results of evaluative instruments to parents and care persons with the emergent recommendations.

(d) Parents.

The system should evaluate the quantitative and qualitative aspects of parent training efforts in addition to evaluating the supervision of instructional programs for children which are extended into the home.

There have been many demonstrations that parents can be effectively taught to competently use behavioral procedures for teaching new skills, as well as controlling deviant behavior of their own children (e.g., Lovaas, et al., 1973; Cooper, 1973; Berkowitz & Graziano, 1972; Peine & Munro, 1973). However, little has been done to evaluate the effectiveness of parent involvement in the educational process when severely handicapped children are involved.

Three primary areas of concern are (1) the quantity and quality of parent training and/or involvement efforts, (2) procedures used to teach parents, (3) the actual teaching performance of the parents, and (4) the supervision of instructional programs for children which are extended into the home (i.e., maintenance and generalization).

Level 4: Total Educational Ecology

(a) School.

The system should consider whether the child is placed in an environment which meets the "least restrictive" implication of the 94-142 guidelines. If the program is in a church basement, is a more "mainstreamed" environment needed and available for this child or class? Is the facility segregated (restricted to the handicapped)? If so, are the reasons justifiable for the present class and individual programs? Is the school facility for the class on a par with the regular education facilities of the local education agency (LEA)? Are long- or short-range plans in evidence for movement along a desegregated or least restrictive environment continuum for each child? each class?

(b) Transportation.

The system should consider the adequacy, legality, and functionality (for comfort, safety, and education) of the transportation system for each child and class. The analysis should consider the interactivity of components such as distance from home to school and necessity for transport to specialized facility. Special consideration would be given to transportation of children with orthopedic disabilities. For example, a child whose educational program calls for intensive training in positioning and midline maintenance would not be expected to be transported slouched with legs scissored in the back seat of a taxi cab, and so on.

(c) Home and community.

The system should concern itself with the severely handicapped child's *total* educational environment. Evaluation of the residential environment in the promotion of generalized learning of the relationship of the school personnel to the parents in transsituational educational programming (in parents' spoken language, for example), of exposure of the child to the community at large in a "normal" fashion, all would comprise the total educational ecology level.

Level 5: Educational Administrative Considerations

(a) Legal.

The evaluation system should concern itself with at least two primary legal considerations: compliance by the school district with the dictates of 94-142, including the letter of specified relationships among the state education agency (SEA) and LEA; and compliance with the Civil Rights Act and HEW guidelines as they bear on nondiscrimination of handicapped persons (Federal Register, 1976).

(b) Funding.

Are all real and potential funding resources for education of the severely handicapped engaged? If not, are the resources adequate for the program in terms of the other components of the evaluation?

(c) Accountability and reporting.

Are the dictates of 94-142 met? Are parents reporting satisfaction with the program offered and with their relationship to the LEA staff?

(d) Interagency relationships.

Is there, for example, an adequate and well-documented inservice training program in effect for the teaching staff of the severely and profoundly handicapped? Is the relationship between the LEA and the SEA positive and functional for the program's development? Is there a close working relationship between the LEA and the community resources such as family guidance, developmental disabilities agencies, training colleges, public health agencies, etc., which bear on education of the severely handicapped?

REFERENCES

Balthazar, E. E. *Balthazar scales of adaptive behavior, Part one: Handbook for the professional supervisor.* Palo Alto, Cal.: Consulting Psychologists Press, Inc., 1971. (a)

Balthazar, E. E. *Balthazar scales of adaptive behavior, Part two: Handbook for the rater technician.* Palo Alto, Cal.: Consulting Psychologists Press, Inc., 1971. (b)

Balthazar, E. E. *Balthazar scales of adaptive behavior, Part three: The scales of functional independence.* Palo Alto, Cal.: Consulting Psychologists Press, Inc., 1971.(c)

Balthazar, E. E. *Balthazar scales of adaptive behavior, Part four: Workshop and training manual.* Palo Alto, Cal.: Consulting Psychologists Press, Inc., 1971. (d)

Behavior Progression Checklist (BCP). Office of the Santa Cruz County Superintendent of Schools, 1973.

Bellamy, T., Peterson, L., & Close, A. Habilitation of the severely and profoundly retarded:Illustrations of competence. *Education and Training of the Mentally Retarded,* 1975, *10,* 174-186.

Berkowitz, B. P., & Graziano, A. M. Training parents as behavior therapists: A review. *Behavior, Research, & Therapy,* 1972, *10*(42), 297-317.

Bigge, J., & O'Donnell, P. *Teaching the physically and multiply handicapped.* Columbus, Ohio: Charles E. Merrill, 1977.

Bricker, W., & Bricker, D. An early language training strategy. In R. L. Schiefelbusch, & L. L. Lloyd (Eds.), *Language Perspectives–Acquisition, Retardation, and Intervention.* Baltimore: University Park Press, 1974.

Brown, L., Bellamy, T., Perkmutter, L., Sackowitz, P., & Sontag, E. The development of quality and durability in the work performance of retarded students in a public school prevocational workshop. *Training School Bulletin,* 1972, *69,* 58-69.

Brown, L., Nietupski, J., & Hamre-Nietupski, S. The criterion of ultimate functioning and public school services for severely handicapped students. In Brown, L., Certo, N., Belmore, K., & Crowner, T. (Eds.), *Madison Alternative for Zero Exclusion: Papers and Programs Related to Public School Service for Secondary Age Severely Handicapped Students. Volume VI: Part I.* Madison, Wisc.: Dept. of Specialized Educational Services. Madison Public Schools., November 1976.

Burchard, J. Systematic socialization: A programmed environment for the habilitation of antisocial retardates. *The Psychological Record,* 1967, *17,* 461-476.

California State Department of Education *DASIE, Instructional Management System.* Sacramento: Special Education Support Unit, 1975.

Cohen, H. L., & Filipczak, J. *A new learning environment.* San Francisco: Jossey-Bass, Inc., 1971.

Cooper, J. Application of the consultant role to parent-teacher management of school avoidance behavior. *Psychology of School,* 1973, *10*(2), 259-262.

Crosson, J. A technique for programming sheltered workshop environment for training severely retarded workers. *American Journal of Mental Deficiency,* 1969, *73,* 814-818.

Crosson, J. *The experimental analysis of vocational behavior in severely retarded males.* (Final report, Grant N. OEG 32-47-0230-6024), Washington, D.C.: U.S. Department of Health, Education and Welfare, 1967.

Doke, L. A., & Risley, T. R. The organization of day-care environments: Required versus optional activities. *Journal of Applied Behavior Analysis,* 1972, *5,* 405-420.

Elder, J. K., Pellow, M. L., & Jipson-Greenstein, J. A direction for the future: AAESPH's role in S-3 materials accession process. *AAESPH Review,* 1977, *2*(1), 50-59.

Federal Register. DHEW: *Handicapped Persons Nondiscrimination.* Monday, May 17, 1976.

Fredericks, H. D., Riggs, C., Furey, T., Grove, D., Moore, W., McDonnell, J., Jordon, E., Hanson, W., Baldwin, V., & Wadlow, M. *The teaching research curriculum for moderately and severely handicapped.* Springfield, Ill.: Charles C Thomas, 1976.

Gold, M. *The severely retarded in nonsheltered industry.* Paper presented at the Annual Convention of the American Association on Mental Deficiency, Toronto, Canada, 1974.

Gold, M. W. Research on the vocational habilitation of the retarded: The present, the future. In N. R. Ellis (Ed.) *International Review of Research in Mental Retardation.* New York: Academic Press, 1973, *6,* 97-147.

Guess, D., Sailor, W., & Baer, D. M. A behavioral approach to language training for the severely handicapped. *Education and Training of the Mentally Retarded,* in press.

Hamilton, J., & Allen, P. Ward programming for severely retarded institutionalized residents. *Mental Retardation,* 1967, *5.* 22-23.

Haring, N., & Whelan, R. (Eds.). *The learning environment: Relationship to behavior modification and implications for special education.* Lawrence, Ks.: University of Kansas Press, 1966.

Hewett, F. M., Taylor, F. D., & Artuso, A. A. The engineered classroom: An innovative approach to the education of children with learning problems. In R. H. Bradfield (Ed.), *Behavior modification–The human effort.* Sioux Falls, S. D.: Dimensions Publishing Co., 1970. Pp. 77-122.

Horner, R. D., Holvolt, J., & Rinne, T. *Competency specifications for teachers of the severely and profoundly handicapped.* Unpublished ms., University of Kansas, Dept of Special Education, Lawrence, Kansas, 1976.

Lovaas, O. I., Koegel, R., Simmons, J. O., & Long, J. S. Some generalization of follow-up measures on autistic children in behavior therapy. *Journal of Applied Behavior Analysis,* 1973, *6*(1), 131-166.

LeLaurin, K., & Risley, T. R. The organization of day-care environments: "Zone" versus "man to man" staff assignments. *Journal of Applied Behavior Analysis,* 1972, *5* (3), 225-232.

Nihira, K., Foster, R., Shellhaas, M., & Leland, H. *AAMD adaptive behavior scale manual.* Washington, D. C.: American Association on Mental Deficiency, 1974.

Peine, H. A., & Munro, B. C. Behavioral management of parent training programs. *Psychological Record,* 1973, *23,* 459-466.

Sailor, W., & Horner, R. D. Educational and assessment strategies for the severely handicapped. In N. Haring and L. Brown (Eds.), *Teaching the Severely Handicapped: Volume I.* New York: Grune & Stratton, 1976.

Sailor, W., & Mix, B. J., *The TARC Assessment System.* Lawrence, Ks.: H & H Enterprise, 1975.

Sailor, W. UAF and the education of low-incidence children. Keynote address presented to the National UAF Conference of Nurses, Occupational and Physical Therapists, February, 1976.

Shearer, D., Billingsley, J., Frohman, A., et al. *The Portage Guide to Early Education: Instructions and Checklist (Experimental Ed.).* Portage, Wisc.: Cooperative Educational Service Agency, N. 12, 1970.

Silvern, L. Object analysis and action systemic methods in developing a program for the assembly of a television antenna in a sheltered workshop. *Mental Retardation,* 1963, *1,* 140-147.

Somerton, E., & Turner, K. *Pennsylvania Training Model: Individual Assessment Guide.* Pennsylvania Department of Special Education, 1975.

Sontag, E., Burke, P., & York, R. Consideration for serving the severely handicapped in the public schools. *Education and Training of the Mentally Retarded,* 1973, *8,* 20-26.

Sontag, E., Sailor, W., & Smith, J. The severely handicapped: Who are they? Where are we going? *Journal of Special Education,* in press.

Stabler, B., Gibson, E. W., Cutting, D. S., & Lawrence, P. S. Zone planning for accelerating adaptive behavior in the retarded. *Exceptional Children,* 1974, *40* (4), 252-257.

Sternat, J., Nietupski, J., Lyon, S., Messin, R., & Brown, L. Integrated vs. isolated therapy models. In L. Brown, N. Scheiserman, & T. Crowner (Eds.), *Madison's Alternative for Zero Exclusion: Toward an Integrated Therapy Model for Teaching Motor, Tracking and Scanning Skills to Severely Handicapped Students, Volume VI, Part 3.* Madison, Wisc.: Public Schools, Department of Specialized Educational Services, 1976.

Utley, B., Holvolt, J., & Barnes, K. Handling positioning and feeding the physically handicapped. *Education and Training of the Mentally Retarded,* in press.

Vogel, W., Kun, K. J., & Meshorer, E. Changes in adaptive behavior in institutionalized retardates in response to environmental enrichment or deprivation. *Journal of Consulting & Clinical Psychology,* 1968, *32,* 76-82.

Administering Education for the Severely Handicapped After P.L. 94-142

Mr. Orelove discusses administrative problems in six vital areas: identifying the handicapped, placing them, training teacher personnel, individualizing educational plans, adopting procedural safeguards, and avoiding lawsuits.

Fred P. Orelove

FRED P. ORELOVE, is Assistant Professor, Department of Special Education, West Virginia University.

The field of special education has been influenced greatly in the past eight years by legal and political events. Judicial decisions have mandated public education for all handicapped children, regardless of the nature or degree of their handicaps. Right-to-education cases led to the passage of P.L. 94-142, the federal Education for All Handicapped Children Act of 1975. Congress stated its purpose thus:

> . . . to assure that all handicapped children have available to them . . . a free, appropriate public education and related services designed to meet their unique needs, to assure that the rights of handicapped children and their parents or guardian are protected, to assist states and localities to provide for the education of all handicapped children, and to assess and assure the effectiveness of efforts to educate handicapped children.

This comprehensive law has already had a dramatic impact on the operation and administration of public schools, but we are only at the beginning. Let us try, first, to define what the school administrator must do to comply with the legal mandate.

Perhaps P.L. 94-142 will most strongly affect the administrator who is now directed to provide services for the severely and profoundly handicapped. The class includes children

> . . . who are not toilet trained; aggress toward others; do not attend to even the most pronounced social stimuli; self-mutilate; ruminate; self-stimulate; do not walk, speak, hear, or see; manifest durable and intense temper tantrums; are not under the most rudimentary forms of verbal control; do not imitate; manifest minimally controlled seizures; and/or have extremely brittle medical existences.[1]

These are the students who until recently were almost never found in the public schools. They are kept in the home, in private care facilities, or in noneducational institutions. It will take many new resources, including qualified teachers, support personnel and services, facilities, and materials if the schools do the job.

The paradox of the legislation becomes apparent; P.L. 94-142, designed to provide an appropriate education for all children, including the severely handicapped, creates a new set of concerns and dilemmas for the public school administrator. An important first step in helping administrators is to identify those broad areas in which they will in all likelihood have to make significant adjustments in the school program. Administrative problems will be presented for each of six areas, emphasizing the provision of services to the severely handicapped.

Identification

The first step in providing a free, appropriate public education for all handicapped children between the ages of 3 and 18 (3 and 21 by 1980) is to locate them. It is singularly difficult to do so. Many parents, especially in rural areas, keep their physically impaired or retarded child hidden. Have you ever gone door-to-door asking if there is a handicapped child at home who has never been enrolled in school?

The administrator will need to ask the local mass media to issue announcements and notices. He must work with various local agencies in making phone calls, sending letters, etc. In *Exceptional Children* for October, 1975, R. Reid Zehrbach describes a method of locating, screening, and evaluating handicapped children.

After the severely handicapped children are located, the administrator must determine whether they are receiving needed special education and related services. Is it "appropriate," as the law defines that term? This is a very complex problem with respect to the severely handicapped. For some, it may include simply the teaching of eye contact and imitative response; for others, the development of community survival skills or the elimination of self-destructive and self-stimulatory behaviors.

Placement

Traditional placement choices available to administrators have been either serving all severely handicapped in a centralized and self-contained school ("cluster" approach) or operating classes of these students in schools throughout the district ("dispersal" approach). Although placement issues remain, P.L. 94-142 promises to change the question into, How can integration best be accomplished? Specifically, the act requires states to establish "proce-

"Administering Education for the Severely Handicapped After P.L. 94-142," by Fred P. Orelove, *Phi Delta Kappan*, June 1978. Copyright © 1978 by Phi Delta Kappan, Inc. Reprinted by permission.

"... P.L. 94-142, designed to provide an appropriate education for all children, including the severely handicapped, creates a new set of concerns and dilemmas for the public school administrator."

dures to assure that to the maximum extent appropriate handicapped children ... are educated with children who are not handicapped." This requirement has several administrative ramifications.

First, many severely handicapped students are nonambulatory and/or possess sensory deficits which require modifications in school facilities (e.g., ramps, special toilet facilities, and crash bar doors). Building adaptation requires a combination of architectural/administrative/engineering expertise and a sensitivity to a student's abilities and limitations. Even small mistakes, such as one inch too steep a slope on a ramp, could be educationally and fiscally expensive.

Second, the least restrictive placement doctrine necessitates that administrators work closely with directors of private agencies and institutions to develop transitional plans for moving severely handicapped students into the public schools. Educational, legal, economic, and logistical concerns will be confronted as the student is brought into the everyday school environment. The administration will assume a strong child-advocacy role to allay fears of those private school personnel with vested interest (educational and/or financial) in keeping the children.

Third, the administrator must confront angry, upset, and confused parents of both handicapped and nonhandicapped children. The former group, whose children have been served in self-contained public or private schools or in institutional settings, may fear that they will be subject to ridicule by nonhandicapped children or that the demands of an integrated school setting will be too stressful. Some of these parents may already have been rejected by the public schools because "no program exists" or "there is not enough room" or "he has to be toilet trained." They may be fearful, indignant, and/or cautious because of the sudden willingness of that district to assume responsibility for their children.

Similarly, it is likely that parents of nonhandicapped children will express concern that they are being educated with retarded and physically impaired children, or that facilities and resources will be usurped by the handicapped children. They fear that their child may be slowed educationally, that he will "catch" retardation if not a spinal deformity. Administrators can instruct both sets of parents and work closely with parent/teacher organizations to rectify possible misunderstandings.

Fourth, as handicapped children become spread over a larger geographic region and enter neighborhood schools, their visibility increases proportionately. Local storeowners, policemen, and neighbors may have little experience with such children and may find it difficult to accept a child who makes strange noises, laughs at his hands, or has no arms or legs.

Finally, the law requires placement of handicapped with nonhandicapped children to the *maximum extent appropriate*. The administrators must resist those parents, teachers, and school board members who insist that it would be more "appropriate" to educate severely handicapped children in a self-contained school. Integration may actually enhance community acceptance and encourage attempts to remediate and/or resolve medical, instructional, and transportation problems.

Personnel

There are few programs for training teachers for the severely handicapped relative to the number of teachers who will soon be required.[2] Barbara Wilcox notes that "more has been done to date to provide severely handicapped students with appropriate educational programs than has been done to insure appropriate educational programs for their teachers!"[3] Administrators, meanwhile, must actively recruit teachers who can handle the child with severe handicaps.

Partly as a result of the limited teacher pool, administrators may want to provide inservice training for teachers who are in contact with handicapped children. Even teachers who have had excellent preservice training periodically require fresh methods and materials.

Teacher morale is another important concern that must be addressed. Severely handicapped children often display behavioral excesses that are distasteful (e.g., rumination, self-mutilation) and behavioral deficits (e.g., language, social skills, motor behaviors) that are extremely hard and time-consuming to remediate. Furthermore, since skill performance needs to be verified across a number of different settings and personnel, those times that teachers of nonhandicapped children normally have to rest and plan (such as lunch and recess) are spent in teaching leisure-time, dining, and social skills. Thus the administrator must provide a relief system to prevent them from "burning out" and becoming ineffective and dissatisfied.

Fourth, administrators must locate qualified supportive staff, both professional (e.g., physical therapists, occupational therapists, recreational therapists, nurses, psychologists, and social workers) and paraprofessional (e.g., teacher aides and student teachers) and take an active role in coordinating a multidisciplinary service approach. Some problems to avoid in establishing a multidisciplinary program include: 1) misunderstanding or lack of respect for the techniques used by other disciplines, 2) lack of common terminology, and 3) competition for specific times during the day to work with students.[4]

Individualized Educational Plans

P.L. 94-142 requires that an individualized educational plan (IEP) be formulated for each handicapped child. The IEP is a written statement developed in an individualized planning conference by a representative of the local education authority (LEA), the teacher, the parents or guardian, and, when appropriate, the child. The statement includes a description of the present levels of educational performance; annual goals and short-term objectives; a statement of specific educational services to be provided and the extent to which the student will participate in regular educational programs; the projected date of initiation and termination of services; and objective criteria, evaluation procedures, and schedules to determine progress at least annually.

Written IEPs provide accountability in the provision of needed services, help to prevent misclassification of handicapped children, enable the parent or guardian to become better acquainted with the child, and help to foster better cooperation between the home and school.

The administrator, however, faces veral problems in conforming to the :P requirements. First, teachers and ther school personnel must be taught write IEPs in a format acceptable to e state. It is difficult in most cases to npoint the length of a given service or predict at the beginning of the school ear exactly what services a severely andicapped child will need.

Second, the scheduling of individual lanning conferences promises to be ormidable. The law makes it clear that ıch conferences must be at a time and lace mutually agreed upon by the chool and the parents. What about the arent who works or cannot leave other hildren at home, or the teacher whose nion contract does not require him to ttend meetings after school hours?

Third, it will take large investments f time and money simply to involve he parents and to inform them of their ights. Conceivably, a person could be mployed whose major responsibility vould be to send out notices of proposed identification, evaluation, or placement; to make phone calls and ome visits; and to translate notices into he parents' native language.

Fourth, confidentiality could pose ome inconvenience. For the IEP to be seful to a child receiving several different supportive services, it will have to be ather widely available. Since IEPs are ept on file with the LEA, the recordkeeping system will need to be closely scrutinized.

Procedural Safeguards

Due process of law refers to the right to have any law applied reasonably and with sufficient safeguards, such as hearing and notice, to insure that an individual is dealt with fairly. P.L. 94-142 includes such procedural safeguards for the handicapped child and his parents or guardian, including: the requirement of written notice to the parents in their native language or mode of communication prior to the identification, evaluation, or placement of the child; the opportunity to request an impartial due process hearing; and the right to appeal the findings to the state and eventually the courts.

P.L. 94-142 places strict controls on the functions of the administration. There are guidelines that explicitly describe, for example, steps to be taken to insure that parents have received information informing them of their right to appeal. Furthermore, while procedures exist to permit a school district to make an educational placement without parental consent, the school must present extensive documentation of attempts to incorporate parents into the decision-making process.

Due process proceedings can be uncomfortable and emotional for both the parents and the child. Prudent administrators will take all necessary steps when dealing with parents to prevent direct confrontation and litigation. Administrative finesse becomes especially important if there is a sudden influx of severely handicapped children improperly placed in the public schools. This can happen if psychologists and other personnel have used outdated and inappropriate evaluation instruments. An adversary relationship between the professional staff and the family must be avoided. The administrator can help accomplish this by making it clear that his interest is the same as that of all other parties in the transaction: the best possible services for the student.

Professional Rights and Responsibilities

Since P.L. 94-142 requires educators to be accountable for "appropriately educating" handicapped children, administrators become subject to legal action. They may fail to advise parents and professionals of their rights or fail to implement mandated due process procedures correctly and fully.[5] John Melcher speculates in *Exceptional Children* (November, 1976) that over the next 10 years "liability suits against school systems, teachers, support personnel, and administrators will increase markedly as the quality and accountability issues gain momentum. . . . Post hoc damage suits will be brought by adults who feel that the special education they received or failed to receive as children has harmed their development."

The high incidence of medical problems in severely handicapped children presents another administrative concern. However, competent and careful administrators need not fear being sued as a result of a teacher or therapist's mishandling a child's seizure or dislocated hip. As citizens and employees, they are also entitled to due process procedures when confronted with legal action.[6]

The "criterion of ultimate functioning,"[7] – a phrase referring to the cluster of skills that persons must possess to function with maximum productivity and independence in socially, vocationally, and domestically integrated adult community environments – creates additional concerns. Since skills taught to severely handicapped students in school rarely generalize to other environments, skills must be taught in the environment in which they are to be performed. The curriculum and instructional environment will need restructuring to include community-based programming (e.g., grocery shopping, bus riding, and laundromat use). Administrators must therefore support nontraditional educational activities while protecting themselves against the possibility of a student's getting hit by a car or being lost on a bus trip.

The supportive but cautious administrator will insure that his most competent staff people are implementing the programs and that they are appropriately insured.

Additional Considerations

Other problems relating to provision of services to the severely handicapped include:

1. The employment of natural settings and realistic materials and facilities to promote generalization of skills across environments. For example, some teachers will need food and a kitchen in which to prepare it.
2. The need to maintain low student/teacher ratios. Achieving them means involving students, parents, volunteers, and teacher aides.
3. The need to provide service in a regular rather than episodic manner. Thus assessment, intervention, and follow-up are part of an ongoing system.
4. The need to follow an integrative rather than isolative therapy model,[8] whereby assessment and therapy are implemented in the classroom and in the child's natural environment.
5. The problems of transporting students with severe physical, medical, and/or behavioral disorders. Considerations include special buses and routes, training of drivers and aides, special seating arrangements, and help for the physically handicapped in loading and disembarking.
6. The long-range effects of the presence of severely handicapped students on attitudes, service delivery, and evaluation.

7. The necessity to work cooperatively with parents, including involving them in program planning and implementation and providing inservice activities to enable them to handle difficult medical or behavior management problems.

Conclusion

I have detailed some implications of P.L. 94-142 for administrators responsible for educating severely handicapped students. While *problems* were emphasized, no task is insurmountable. Some school districts in the U.S. have been educating severely handicapped and other exceptional children for several years. Having weathered the initial tribulations and the aftershocks, they now handle the daily affairs routinely. Thousands more are conforming to the legal mandate. Administrators are an essential link in putting into action the spirit of the law: that every child, despite his/her physical or mental condition, can benefit from an appropriate program of education and training.

---

1. Ed Sontag, Philip J. Burke, and Robert York, "Considerations for Serving the Severely Handicapped in the Public Schools," *Education and Training of the Mentally Retarded*, April, 1973, pp. 20-26.

2. Susan Stainbach, William Stainbach, and Steven Maurer, "Training Teachers for the Severely and Profoundly Handicapped: A New Frontier," *Exceptional Children*, January, 1976, pp. 203-210; see also Barbara Wilcox, "A Competency-Based Approach to Preparing Teachers of the Severely and Profoundly Handicapped: Perspective I," in E. Sontag, J. Smith, and N. Certo, eds., *Educational Programming for the Severely and Profoundly Handicapped* (Reston, Va.: Council for Exceptional Children, 1977).

3. Ibid., pp. 418, 419.

4. Timothy T. Crowner, "A Public School Program for Severely and Profoundly Handicapped Students: Zero Exclusion," in L. Brown, T. Crowner, W. Williams, and R. York, eds., *Madison's Alternative for Zero Exclusion: A Book of Readings* (Madison, Wis.: Madison Public Schools, 1975).

5. H. Rutherford Turnbull III, "Account bility: An Overview of the Impact of Litig tion on Professionals," *Exceptional Childre* March, 1975, pp. 427-33.

6. Frederick J. Weintraub and Mary A. M Caffrey, "Professional Rights and Respons bilities," in F. J. Weintraub, A. Abeson, Ballard, and M. L. LaVor, eds., *Public Polic and the Education of Exceptional Childre* (Reston, Va.: Council for Exceptional Chi dren, 1976).

7. Lou Brown, John Nietupski, and Susa Hamre-Nietupski, "The Criterion of Ultima Functioning and Public School Services f Severely Handicapped Students," in Brown, N. Certo, K. Belmore, and T Crowner, eds., *Madison's Alternative for Zer Exclusion: Papers and Programs Related t Public School Services for Secondary Ag Severely Handicapped Students* (Madiso Wis.: Madison Public Schools, 1976).

8. Jan Sternat, John Nietupski, Steve Lyon Rosalie Messina, and Lou Brown, "Integrate vs. Isolated Therapy Models," in L. Brown, N Scheuerman, and T. Crowner, eds., *Madison Alternative for Zero Exclusion: Toward a Integrated Therapy Model for Teachin Motor, Tracking, and Scanning Skills t Severely Handicapped Students* (Madison Wis.: Madison Public Schools, 1976).

NDEX

Credits/Acknowledgments

Cover design by Charles Vitelli.
Color insert: CHILD WEARING A RED SCARF (2462), Edouard Vuillard, National Gallery of Art, Washington, Ailsa Mellon Bruce Collection.

1. Legislative Concerns: Special Education and the Law
Facing overview—Freelance Photographer's Guild/Peter Gridley.
2. Professional Concerns: Development, Classification, and Parental Involvement
Facing overview—Freelance Photographer's Guild/Richard Norwitz.
3. The Gifted Child
Facing overview—Freelance Photographer's Guild/Ace Williams.
4. The Mentally Retarded Child
Facing overview—David Attie © 1975.
123—From PICTORIAL COMPLETION TEST II, reprinted from the *Journal of Applied Psychology,* September 1921.
5. The Learning Disabled Child
Facing overview—Jeremy Brenner.
6. The Emotionally Troubled Child
Facing overview—Georgy W. Gardner © 1979.
199-201—Richard Fegley, *Psychology Today,* June 1976. Reprinted by permission.
7. The Physically and Sensorially Handicapped Child
Facing overview—Freelance Photographer's Guild

About you

I am a student ☐ an instructor ☐

Name ______________________ School ______________________

Term Used ______________________ Date ______________________

Address ____

City ______________________ State __________ Zip __________

Telephone ______________________ Office Hours ______________________

To order a copy of Annual Editions

To order a copy, simply check off the volume you want on the list below and send this order form along with your check to us. We will take care of the postage. All orders are automatically filled with the latest edition—should you wish an older edition please indicate which edition you want. We will contact you should that edition be no longer available.

Volumes now available in the Annual Editions series:

____AE Aging	$6.55	____AE Health	$6.55
____AE American Government	$6.95	____AE Human Development	$6.95
____AE American History Pre-Civil War	$6.55	____AE Human Sexuality	$6.55
____AE American History Post-Civil War	$6.55	____AE Macroeconomics	$6.55
____AE Anthropology	$6.95	____AE Management	$6.95
____AE Biology	$6.55	____AE Marketing	$6.95
____AE Business	$6.55	____AE Marriage & Family	$6.55
____AE Criminal Justice	$6.55	____AE Microeconomics	$6.55
____AE Unexplored Deviance	$6.55	____AE Personality & Adjustment	$6.55
____AE Early Childhood Education	$6.95	____AE Psychology	$6.95
____AE Economics	$6.95	____AE Social Problems	$6.95
____AE Education	$6.55	____AE Sociology	$6.95
____AE Environment	$6.95	____AE Urban Society	$6.55
____AE Educating Exceptional Children	$6.95		

Prices higher in Canada

Connecticut Residents: Add 7% Sales Tax

First Class
Permit
No. 84
Guilford, Ct.

BUSINESS REPLY MAIL

No Postage Stamp Necessary if Mailed in the United States

Postage will be paid by:

Attention: Annual Editions Service
The Dushkin Publishing Group, Inc.
Sluice Dock
Guilford, Connecticut 06437

EXC 79/80

We want your advice.

Any anthology can be improved. This one will be—annually. But we need your help. Annual Editions revisions depend on two major opinion sources: one is the academic advisers who work with us in scanning the thousands of articles published in the public press each year; the other is you—the person actually using the book.

Please help us and the users of the next edition by answering the questions below and then returning it to us.

Thank you.

What do you think of this Book?

1. What do you think of the Annual Editions concept?

2. Which article(s) did you like the most? Why?

3. Which article(s) should we drop from the next edition? Why?

4. Have you read any articles lately that you think should be included in the next edition:

What basic text did you use with this Annual Editions reader?

Title ____________________

Author(s) ____________________

If you didn't use a text, what did you use?

Was it a good combination?

(continued on back)

EXC 79/80